VOICE FOR THE MAD

VOICE FOR THE MAD

The Life of Dorothea Dix

DAVID GOLLAHER

THE FREE PRESS

New York   London   Toronto   Sydney   Tokyo   Singapore

The Free Press
A Division of Simon & Schuster Inc.
1230 Avenue of the Americas, New York, N.Y. 10020

Printed in the United States of America

printing number

1 2 3 4 5 6 7 8 9 10

Text design by Carla Bolte

Library of Congress Cataloging-in-Publication Data

Gollaher, David
    Voice for the mad: The life of Dorothea Dix/David Gollaher.
        p.   cm.
    Includes bibliographical references and index.
    ISBN 0–02–912399–2
    1. Dix, Dorothea Lynde, 1802–1887. 2. Social reformers—United States—Biography. 3. Mentally ill—Care—United States—History. I. Title.
    HV28.D6G65   1995
    362.2´1´092—dc20
    [B]   95–4134
                                                              CIP

FOR MOYA

CONTENTS

PREFACE

If deeds more than words are the measure of effectiveness in public life, Dorothea Dix was surely the most productive woman in nineteenth century American politics. While other Victorian women, if they stepped outside the domestic circle at all, circulated petitions and formed benevolent associations to influence a masculine system from which they were excluded, Dix invaded the system itself, grasped the levers of government, and exercised substantial power.

She was no amateur; and this set Dix apart. She sponsored and drafted legislation, built major institutions around the country, directed the Civil War army nurses, and forced her countrymen to confront one of the nation's ugliest and most perplexing social problems. She earned world-wide acclaim not because she invented the asylum, but because she thrust what we have come to call mental disease and homelessness squarely into the center of public policy. In a age of boisterous laissez-faire capitalism, she held that to provide a decent level of care for those so lost to reason that they could not care for themselves was an essential obligation of the modern state. That the solutions she advocated ultimately withered should not obscure what she did. After all, nobody since has solved the problems of poverty and mental illness.

Despite her remarkable record, though, even in an era of feminist scholarship, Dix has floated outside the mainstream of American history. For generations, historians duly noted her among the cavalcade of antebellum reformers, but no one probed deeply into her life and work. She has remained famous, yet unknown.

There is no simple explanation for this. Certainly it has to do in part with the decay of the asylum and the mental hosiptal as progressive institutions. Their failure has clouded her achievement, giving her a dated air of belonging to a generation that was naively optimistic about mental disorder and social welfare. More important, however, history has not been kind to Dorthea Dix because she fails to fit into the main explanatory frameworks historians have used to interpret woman's lives. She was not, as progressive historians characterized her, simply a selfless missionary to the mad. Nor was she a victim of oppression. Above all, she was *not* ahead of her time when it came to women's rights and antislavery—two broad fields of historiographical interst in which contemporary social problems, along with abiding questions about rights and equality, have inspired countlless studies of nine-teenth-century women. Since social equality between the sexes, or dif-ferent races, was inconceivable to her, Dix has received a chilly reception from scholars who focus on such issues. She and her cause were unfashionable in the last century, and remain so today.

Of course there have been biographies. The first was penned shortly after Dix died. The executor of her estate, Horatio Appleton Lamb, commissioned a Unitarian minister, Francis Tiffany, to sort through her papers and write an account of her life. The result was titled *Life of Dorothea Lynde Dix* (1891), a hagiographic book quickly pieced together from her letters and papers, actually more compendium than biogra-phy. Tiffany was hired to commemorate the life of an American saint, and he fulfilled his duty, naturally omitting inferences that might have cast his subject in an unfavorable light.

In the 1930's. stirred by her interest in New Deal liberalism, a young scholar named Helen E. Marshall set out to produce a scholarly biography. To her chagrin, though, the Lamb family, who retained con-trol over the bulk of Dix's papers, refused to grant Marshall access to the archive. In consequence, she had no choice but to rely on Tiffany's book as her primary source. Like Tiffany, she wished to celebrate, not criticize, her subject, so Marshall's *Dorothea Dix: Forgotten Samaritan* (1937) tends to portray lunacy reform as "the triumphant upward march" of progress, which Dix's life, in her view, perfectly exemplified.

Over the years, several writers have reworked the basic material in Tiffany and Marshall. The most readable of these, Dorothy Clarke Wil-son's *Stranger and Traveler: The Story of Dorothea Dix, American Reformer* (1975) is a sentimental blend of fact and fiction, with Dix presented as a longsuffering paragon of Christian charity. In an odd way, this book, written by a minister's wife, distills precisely the interpretation of her life that Dix promoted on those rare occasions when she spoke to the press.

Apart from Tiffany's biography, the most useful published source for understanding Dix is Charles M. Snyder's well-edited book, *The Lady and the President: The Letters of Dorothea Dix and Millard Fillmore* (1976). Unfortunely Fillmore was a dull correspondent. Still, though quite narrowly focussed, these letters convey Dix's voice, provide glimpses of her trying emotional life, and offer insights into how she operated as a lobbyist.

As it turns out, the dearth of reliable biographical information about Dix has presented an opportunity to write the story of her life based on original manuscript sources. The Lamb family donated its collection of her personal papers to the Houghton Library of Harvard University where they are now catalogued and beautifully preserved. This is by any standard a marvelous resource. Among Harvard's ten thousand or more items are journals, diaries, reams of private correspondence, autograph drafts of published works, boxes of newspaper clippings, daguerreotypes of Dix and her circle, and even examples of her fancy needlework and locks of her hair. Like so many Victorians, she had the habit of jotting notes to friends, relatives, and acquaintances on the slightest impulse. In turn, she was a magnetic personality whose life was a constant source of amazement to others. As she climbed into the higher reaches of public life, Dix cultivated an illustrious group of correspondents. Fortunately she saved most of their letters. Thus from her papers, augmented by manuscripts in other collections around the country, it has been possible to figure out a detailed chronicle of where she went, who she saw, what she did.

More important, there is an excellent basis for addressing the questions that intrigued those who knew Dorothea Dix: What inspired her to take up her cause? What hidden aspects of her own experience drew her to the mad? Why would a woman of her standing choose to spend her days among the homeless insane? She never directly answered these questions. She was a perceptive woman—keenly self-aware and, in equal measure, self-controlled—with a genius for self-presentation. Reading her papers, one becomes attuned to her restraint and her intuitive knack for using language to keep up the official and expected image of herself. Biographers live for those moments when their subjects let the mask slip; but Dix, especially once she found her calling, strove to hold it very firmly in place. There is, nevertheless, ample evidence, including rare moments of self-revelation, from her own pen and from those who knew her, to explore her motivation, describe her behavior, and illuminate her personality. Closely read, the manuscript sources reveal glimpses at first, and then, with increasing clarity, the outlines and details of flesh-and-blood character.

Without the collection of Dorothea Dix manuscripts at the Houghton Library of Harvard University, I would never have thought to undertake this study. Accordingly, I must begin my acknowledgements with Richard Wendorf, Director of Houghton, and the Library's staff, who cheerfully fulfilled my thousands of requests. They set the highest standard for facilitating archival work. Following the long and winding trail of Dix's correspondence around the counrty, I was helped by dozens of archivists, antiquarians, librians, and hospital officials. I am especially grateful to staffs of the American Antiquarian Society, Boston Public Library, Countway Library at Harvard Medical School, Huntington Library, Institute of Pennsylvania Hospital, Library of Congress, Maryland Historical Society, Massachusetts Historical Society, Manuscript Division of New York Public Library, National Archives, Pennsylvania Histoical Society, and the Society for the Preservation of New England Antiquities.

During the early stages of my research, I received important financial support from Harvard's History of American Civilization program. More recently, a Houghton Library Fellowship enabled me to revisit the Dix papers and discover much I would otherwise have missed. Subsequently, a fellowship from the National Endowment for the Humanities afforded me an uninterrupted period of research, writing, and revision which, I hope, has made it possible for me to complete a book that constructively connects the humanities to public policy.

Harvard professor William R. Hutchinson, who followed this study from its inception, provided rigorous intellectual criticism, sharp editorial commentary, and fresh infusions of encouragement at every stage. His guidance, his friendship, and his example as an intellectual historian mean more to me than I can say.

Along the way, several teachers, friends and colleagues have been kind enough to read portions of my manuscript, or discuss salient aspects of Dix's career and its context with me, raising the sorts of questions that are all too easy to overlook. Among them are Daniel

Aaron, April Bernard, David Herbert Donald, Donald Fleming, Gerald Grob, Ronald Numbers, Barbara Rosenkrantz, Stephan Thernstrom, and Nancy Tomes. At the Free Press, senior editors Joyce Seltzer (now at Harvard University Press) and Beth Anderson have been, in just the right ways, patient, helpful, and demanding. Also, my literary agents, Glen Hartley and Lynn Chu, offered expert editorial advice, and my book has benefitted greatly from their comments.

Among my academic colleagues, I am indebted to F. Douglass Scutchfield, and, above all to Stephen J. Williams for providing an environment that encouraged my research and stimulated my thinking. Howard Kushner, intelligently challenged my understanding of nineteenth-century psychiatry—and I have benefitted a great deal from his wisdom. I would like finally to thank my friend Andrew Scull, the dean of British lunacy reform historiography, who has been a colleague, a terrific example, and whose work led me to see the subtle and critically important interconnections between the English and American asylum movements.

My Harvard and my Yale of practical experience in medicine and public policy was Scripps Clinic and Research Foundation. My professional association with Dr. Charles Edwards began there, and continues, as does our friendship. Without his support, this biography would never have been completed.

As for the woman to whom the book is dedicated, she has, by her own words and deeds, so profoundly shaped my thinking about women's role in the public sphere that she deserves the fullest thanks I can give.

VOICE FOR THE MAD

"I tell what I have seen."

For New England, January 1843 was a hard month, bitterly cold, with blizzards sweeping off the North Atlantic, dismasting ships in harbors along the seaboard, stalling trains on the Providence line, clogging roads with ice and snow. When the weather finally broke, as Boston was digging out, the city's newspapers carried vivid accounts of the damage wrought by the storms. Among these was one story about how snow shovelers clearing the New Bedford road had stumbled upon a body, evidently that of a pauper lunatic, who, homeless and confused, had wandered about until he froze to death. The reporter treated the incident as a minor tragedy, a bit of local color, an anecdote to fill a column.

Dorothea Dix, however, scanning the *Evening Transcript*, as she did every night in her cherry-paneled sitting room on Beacon Hill, paused, cut out the item, and laid it in her commonplace book. To her way of thinking, the incident was yet another symptom of a disease of the body politic, a problem whose enormity she was just beginning to unveil.[1]

In fact, just a few weeks earlier she had sparked a controversy by publicly urging the Massachusetts legislature to come to the rescue of the state's homeless insane. Over the past two years, she had been working quietly behind the scenes, documenting the condition of the mad. Methodically, she had visited jails, almshouses, and private homes, county by county, town by town. When at last she finished her survey, she set down her findings in a petition to the General Court. The legislature, scandalized by her revelations, voted to reprint her petition as a government pamphlet and distribute five thousand copies throughout the state.

The message and the messenger were equally startling. For up to that time, Dix had been a schoolteacher, with a modest reputation as writer of children's books and devotional verse. A few months shy of her forty-first birthday when her pamphlet *Memorial to the Massachusetts Legislature,* was published, she was to all appearances a daughter of the Puritans. Tall, angular, bone-thin in a way that caused people to call her frail, Dix impressed her fellow Bostonians as a dignified woman. Whenever she went out in public, her dark brown was pulled back tight, accentuating her strong features—especially her prominent nose and firm jaw. Habitually modest, she preferred dark dresses of silk or cotton with starched white collars. She wore no jewelry except for a simple gold necklace and, whenever she traveled, a ring. She had not married and seemed, except to a few friends whose affections she trusted, a remote woman, restrained even by Victorian standards.

Her aloofness, along with her intellectual self-assurance and moral certitude, had become more pronounced with age, all contributing to an air of imperiousness. Every aspect of her bearing—her polished manners, her implacable reserve—added to an impression of solemnity and, equally important, old money. And this impression was confirmed whenever she spoke. Contemporaries remarked on her voice, full, deep for a woman, bearing traces of a cultivated British accent that was all but irresistible to Americans of the period. She seemed to epitomize upper-crust Boston. For this reason, Dix was a most improbable, and thus supremely compelling, guide to the geography of hell.

In the space of thirty-two pages she painted a picture that was almost too graphic, shameful, and grotesque to be believed. "I proceed, Gentlemen," she warned the lawmakers at the outset, "briefly to call your attention to the *present* state of Insane Persons confined within this Commonwealth, in *cages, closets, stalls, pens! Chained, naked, beaten with rods*, and *lashed* into obedience!" These words are from the fiery opening of the *Memorial to the Massachusetts Legislature*, the American asylum movement's call to arms. With its unvarnished sketches of gibbering madmen and madwomen, brutalized, smeared with their own excrement, penned up like animals, the *Memorial* smoldered with a searing moral outrage. Dix's ostensible object was to rouse the General Court into action. But her message was not limited to lawmakers. It was by implication a withering indictment of her fellow citizens, with their callous indifference to suffering and their lofty pretensions of Christian virtue that struck her as hypocritical so long as they tolerated such flagrant brutality in their midst. Public reaction was shock and outrage. Samuel Gridley Howe, then a freshman member of the legislature, admiringly likened the impact of Dix's words to blasts of "red-hot shot into the very hearts of the people."[2]

"*I tell what I have seen*," she insisted, submitting the episodes that followed as literal "extracts from my Note-Book and Journal."[3] Dix herself was the "I" of her first-person account. Throughout she constantly called attention to herself, her thoughts, feelings, and judgments. At every turn, she reminded her audience that they were reading fact— truths wrung from painful personal experience—not fiction. Nevertheless, personal as it was, the story she told was not entirely new. In fact, because the specter of human anguish she uncovered had long lurked in the shadows of popular awareness, her account rang true. Her gruesome portraits were familiar enough to carry the shock of recognition.

At the same time, the New England conscience was primed for her message because traditional attitudes toward madness and its victims were in a state of flux. For generations, since the founding of the Bay Colony, the indigent insane had been lumped in with the broad class of deviants—beggars, vagrants, petty criminals, the infirm and aged— who occupied the lowest rung on the social ladder. During the seventeenth and eighteenth centuries, the institutions of last resort for the mad were jails or almshouses. Better-off lunatics were cared for by their families or, if that failed, lodged in private homes. Insanity, like poverty and disease, was simply accepted as an unwelcome fact of community life. Traditionally, it was assumed that counties and towns, relying on an informal system of family and communal resources, were responsible for coping with the mad in their midst. Before the turn of the nineteenth century, Americans did not consider the deranged a special class of beings who needed special treatment or a special kind of hospital.

By the early 1820s, however, when Dix was a young woman in

Boston, the time-honored approach to madness was being transformed. She had watched Boston's elite clergymen, merchants, and
physicians join forces to found Massachusetts General Hospital, then,
searching for the best way to deal with mentally disordered patients,
build a separate structure in Charlestown for lunatics. This facility,
called the McLean Asylum for the Insane, was thought to be a major
step toward solving the problem of madness.

The trouble was, however, that McLean was a small private hospital
for well-to-do patients. It made scant provision for the indigent insane.
Realizing this, in the early 1830s a group of liberal reformers designed
a large state lunatic hospital for the poor, incorporating all the latest
innovations in treatment. When it opened its doors in the spring 1833,
the Worcester State Lunatic Hospital shone as a model of Christian
charity and civic responsibility for the helpless.[4]

Its moment of glory was brief. Despite its founders' dreams of a
therapeutic hospital, Worcester swiftly deteriorated into a receptacle
for hopeless cases. Within a few years, overcrowded with lunatics and
idiots who had been shipped in from towns all around the state, the
model asylum was cracking under the strain. Worse, it was turning
away new patients.[5]

The state hospital's predicament posed a special problem for
Boston. There a rising tide of transatlantic immigration was turning the
Puritans' city on a hill into a metropolis. A kind of urban poverty hitherto associated with the cities of Europe overwhelmed the local welfare
apparatus. With the severe economic depression that followed the
Panic of 1837, things went from bad to worse, and homelessness
increased visibly. Beggars in rags, many of them recent immigrants,
roamed the brick streets.

This disturbing spectacle prompted the newspapers and community
leaders to demand a remedy. To get the worst cases—people bereft of
relatives or friends and completely unable to fend for themselves—out
of sight (and out of the workhouse, where they were disruptive of good
order), the mayor and city council rushed through measures to build a
special asylum in South Boston. It was designated exclusively for the
incurably mad. The Boston Lunatic Hospital, completed in record time
using prison labor from the nearby House of Correction, commenced
operations in December 1839.[6]

Given the snail's pace of lunacy reform elsewhere, Massachusetts
was making notable progress. In the early 1840s, most informed citi-

zens, reflecting upon the Commonwealth's record, placed it at the leading edge of social welfare. No other state took its obligations to the insane poor more earnestly nor vaunted its civic virtue more confidently. And it was, in part, this prevalent sense of rectitude that explains why Dix's exposé struck so sensitive a nerve. For indigence and insanity were misfortunes that seemingly were being handled in a prudent, humane manner.

Dix violently turned this cherished belief upside down. After her *Memorial*, the comfortable presumption that the Commonwealth had progressed to a point where its most wretched citizens lived above some threshold of decency was discredited and, in most respects, destroyed.

Predictably, a backlash of protest arose from those who had responsibility for the system she rebuked. Stung by her criticisms, a number of local officials—almshouse keepers, overseers, and selectmen, among others—counterattacked. They resented her interfering in their business. So they endeavored to cast doubt on the accuracy of the *Memorial* as well as the competence and motives of its author. They soon learned, however, that anyone who thought she could be brushed off as some meddlesome spinster vastly underestimated Dorothea Dix.

The secret of her power lay not in horrible details. She addressed a reading public that, after all, had cut its teeth on *Foxe's Book of Martyrs*. People responded rather to the angry personal narrative embedded in her text, a narrative that captured the meaning of insanity in human terms. Her interjections, and the way she depicted her own interactions with the insane, implied a mysterious affinity for these beings, as she characterized them, "reduced to the extremest states of degradation and misery." She represented them as people. And this was strikingly unconventional. Not only had she entered the squalid realm of madness; once there she refused to keep her distance.

Before she arrived on the scene, the infrequent reports produced in America about the condition of the mad—even the ones written by asylum doctors—had been written from the outside. Earlier writers naturally had found it easier to discuss ideas and institutions at arm's length than to identify too closely with so repulsive a class of human beings. Faced with the unspeakable ugliness of mental disorder, they shrank into abstraction. Accordingly, their portraits of madmen and madwomen are nervously detached, largely devoid of color and personality. Dix, on the other hand, displayed personal compassion. As she explained it, her willingness to make simple human contact with these outcasts sparked flashes of unanticipated humanity and serenity. She was the first in America to identify with their plight and to invest the insane with the dignity of individual identity. She was the first to give madness a human face.

In January 1843, Dix's volatile mixture of data, compassion, imagination, and anger, with her personal charisma as its catalyst, was ready to explode into American politics.

Already she foresaw the possibilities. Researching her first memorial had taken her well beyond the borders of Massachusetts into Vermont, New Hampshire, Rhode Island, and New York. As her circle widened, she learned that many state legislatures were debating how to cope with the mushrooming population of insane. Meanwhile, leading alienists (as asylum doctors were then called) in Massachusetts and New York were sharing with her their profession's latest discoveries in diagnosing and treating mental disorders. Given sufficient resources, they contended, medical science could cure the living death of insanity. With a wave of political and professional interest in lunacy reform building, the perfect moment had come for a leader to inspire the movement.

It was, unexpectedly, the beginning of an astonishing career. In some ways, Dix's auspicious public debut calls to mind Emerson's comment when an unknown poet named Walt Whitman sent him *Leaves of Grass*, that such an amazing feat "must have had a long foreground somewhere."[7] Dix was in middle age when she took up the cause of the insane. Afterward, the discovery of her vocation transformed her and eclipsed her early years, both in her own memory and in the view of those who knew her as a famous reformer. Yet the long struggle to find her life's great work—beginning with a childhood of rural poverty, entrance into Boston society through her wealthy grandmother's household, frustrating efforts in teaching and writing, and finally a traumatic breakdown—shaped the temperament, intelligence, and moral imagination that drove her public career. Nothing came easy for Dorothea Dix. Indeed, her distinctive vision of madness and human suffering, the relentless moral outrage that inspired her crusade, the personal meaning and sense of achievement she won from struggling with these problems—each of these was rooted in a painful past that, try as she might, she could never put entirely behind her.

CHAPTER ONE

The Making of an Angry Young Woman

In the early years of the nineteenth century there were two New Englands. One, still familiar, was a settled region of small villages, towns, and the Puritan city on a hill, Boston. It was, by and large, an orderly land in which commerce, religion, and the life of the mind thrived, if not in perfect harmony, at least in comfortable equilibrium. Beyond the white picket fences and stone walls, however, lay the obscure reality of another New England: the frontier. There, in the thickly wooded expanses of unsettled land that seemed to run west and north without end, disorder reigned. Dorothea Dix was, to a remarkable degree, the product of both New Englands.

The real frontier was a far cry from the picturesque landscape celebrated in James Fenimore Cooper's Leatherstocking tales. Its savagery was less noble than squalid, for its inhabitants existed on the edge. Poverty was endemic. White pioneers and settlers were mainly men and women who had lost their foothold in civilization. In many cases, they were driven by sheer desperation, not romantic longing, to brave the brutal hardships of the wilderness. If they succeeded in life, ambitious men born on the frontier later usually regarded their struggles to

7

succeed as a test of willpower, hence a source of pride. In women, by contrast, toughness and aggressiveness were viewed as deplorably vulgar and unfeminine. No matter how high she rose, for a lady birth in the proverbial log cabin remained cause for regret.

Accordingly, all her long life Dorothea Dix, a child of the Maine back country who came of age in Boston, was to harbor a deep estrangement from her upbringing. "I never knew childhood," she used to say, flatly dismissing the subject whenever people asked about her early days. And in the end, she tried to ensure that no one else would know it either, burning any letter, any diary, any shred of evidence that threatened to expose what she had seen as a girl.

So thoroughly did she wish to forget, in fact, that she blotted out even the brightest presence in her early life, the memory of her grandfather. This was Elijah Dix—Doctor Dix, as he was known—the family patriarch and a legend in his own right. When Dorothea was a young child, he took it upon himself to catechize her in the gospel of worldly success. Whenever he had the chance, he told his granddaughter his own story, for he was fiercely proud of his climb. Overcoming poverty through aggressiveness, hard work, perseverance, and an obstinate unwillingness to compromise, he had become a professional man—a doctor—then a prominent merchant, a great landowner and, he boasted, a pillar of Boston society.

His was indeed an archetypal tale of Yankee enterprise. Elijah was born in 1748 in Watertown, several miles west of Boston, into a farming family down on its luck. A physically powerful, restless boy, he was dissatisfied with the limited horizon of his parents' home. So at age eleven or twelve he struck out on his own to board with the Reverend Andrew Hutchins of Grafton, Massachusetts, a Congregational minister who tutored him in exchange for chopping firewood and cleaning stables. Bright and ambitious, he applied himself diligently. Over the next six years he acquired a grasp of practical science and literature, not to mention a distaste for theological speculation. Compared to the rich possibilities of the world around him, prospects of the world to come held little appeal.

Medicine, he decided, was to be his calling. With no money for college, at seventeen, in 1765, he apprenticed himself to a doctor by the name of John Green to master "the art of physick and chirurgery." In his master's office, he quickly discerned that the most lucrative end of the medical business was the pharmacopoeia. Before anesthesia, patients naturally preferred a soothing elixir to the scalpel. So the finishing touch to his training was a year spent assisting Doctor William Greenleaf, a successful Boston druggist, brewing potions for the ails of humanity. When he was twenty-two, confident in the basics of his trade, he moved forty miles west to the village of Worcester and hung out his shingle.[1]

The seat of Worcester County, with its soft hills and small lakes, its farms, set off by low stone walls, thick with rye, maize, oats, wheat, and abundant grass for grazing the region's horses and cattle, was a magnet for settlers. The year Elijah moved there, the town had fewer than two thousand inhabitants. They were, by and large, a hardworking lot whose work ethic was renowned throughout New England. Touring the county in the 1790s, Timothy Dwight, Yale's well-traveled president, observed that "in no part of this country is there a more industrious or thrifty collection of farmers." Its solid agricultural prosperity made Worcester a prefect place for a determined young man like Elijah to launch his career.[2]

Every age has its own hierarchy of medical practitioners, and in the eighteenth century medical men who performed surgery and sold drugs were held in low esteem by the premier class of physicians who had earned degrees at colleges like Harvard and Yale. Generally speaking, doctors of medicine regarded their profession as a dignified, intellectual pursuit whose legacy stretched back to Hippocrates and Galen. Elijah, self-taught and ever a pragmatist, had no interest in being a medical philosopher. Capitalizing on his gift for commerce, he approached health care like a competitive business. And he prospered wonderfully. Citizens of Worcester admired the enterprising young doctor with his unlimited appetite for work. They consulted him about their health and about their lives; they brought their old glass vials for him to fill with his proprietary syrups, nostrums, and strange-smelling herbal compounds; and for all this they paid him handsomely. At an age when most young men were just getting started with their careers, Elijah Dix had already saved enough money to build an impressive two-story house under the old elms near the meetinghouse that soon became a local landmark.

Meanwhile, he carried on a courtship with the winsome daughter of an affluent farmer and landowner. Her name was Dorothy Lynde, a tall, slender young woman with fine features and auburn hair, known in her circle as "the belle of Worcester." They were married in the fall of 1771.

True to form, it was strategic matrimony, Elijah's marriage instantly boosting the little-known apothecary-surgeon into the society of the town's first families. Being married to Dorothy Lynde opened the door to new realms of commercial enterprise—above all, land speculation. In Worcester, as elsewhere, the landed class preferred to do business within its own group. Now, as an insider with plenty of cash, Elijah was presented with opportunities to funnel his money into real property. In the wake of the Revolutionary War, land prices in eastern Massachusetts soared, and Worcester experienced a period of lively growth. The value of his investments mushroomed. By his fortieth birthday Doctor Dix, who had started out with nothing but aspirations, had built an estate that surpassed even that of his wealthy father-in-law.[3]

The New England social ethic, rooted in Puritanism, dictated that those who did well should also do good. Elijah was hungry for respect, so he set out to show his watchful neighbors that his devotion to the community was every bit as great as his prosperity. When the county grand jury cited the town for neglecting its grammar school, for example, he championed the cause of school reform. He pointed out that he had a vested interest in education, what with being the father of seven children and one of the town's heaviest taxpayers. Quickly pulling together a group of leading citizens, he formed a joint-stock company to buy land and underwrite the construction of a new grammar and elementary school building. Charitable projects like this, he realized, were investments rich in intangible dividends. Determined to be a moral entrepreneur as well as an entrepreneur of the more traditional kind, the Doctor spearheaded a number of civic ventures, from financing the Worcester-Boston Turnpike to planting rows of elm trees along Worcester's Main Street.[4]

His most distinctive public deed was the construction of a massive new jail in the center of Worcester. The old jail had collapsed during the Revolution and had become an eyesore. Concerned about an apparent rise in vagrancy and rowdyism, and noticing heaps of surplus granite in a nearby quarry, Elijah organized a literally monumental construction project. The imposing structure, across the street from the town's First Unitarian Church, marveled a writer in the *Massachusetts Spy*, was "judged to be at least the second stone building of consequence in the Commonwealth; none being thought superior to it, except the stone chapel in Boston."[5]

In 1795, having exhausted the commercial possibilities of provincial

Worcester, Elijah Dix set his sights on Boston. The city, with its great harbor and well-developed trade channels, was then in the midst of a spectacular business boom. A contemporary observer standing at the end of the city's Long Wharf described swarms of merchant vessels, reckoning "that not less than four hundred and fifty sail of ships, brigs, schooners, sloops, and small craft are now in this port." This fleet combed the eastern seaboard of the United States, the Caribbean, and Europe, and branched out as far as China. In the eyes of Doctor Dix, its presence made Boston an irresistible hub of commerce.[6]

He first invested in a partnership with the John Haskins, Jr., (Ralph Waldo Emerson's maternal uncle), and the two merchants distributed drugs and general merchandise under the banner of Dix and Haskins. Timing the market perfectly, they flourished in the late 1790s, making a name for themselves as importers and commission wholesalers who operated a small fleet of merchantmen in the brisk transatlantic trade with England. With another partner, Elijah opened a new shop on the south side of Faneuil Hall Market to sell drugs and medicinal herbs. It was called Dix and Brinely, and by the end of the decade it grew to become the largest apothecary in the city. Eventually this enterprise expanded into a large plant in South Boston that housed furnaces and ovens for refining sulfur and other pharmaceutical chemicals.[7]

As his prosperity blossomed, the Doctor made two decisions that would leave indelible marks on his granddaughter Dorothea.

First, in 1795 he began building a fine house in the middle of the city. Dorothea would one day live in this house, which would place her well within the orbit of Boston's elite society. Elijah bought his lot at the beginning of a period of commercial and residential development that would, over a period of fifteen years, completely transform the Boston landscape. In the year 1795 a group of investors calling themselves the Mount Vernon Proprietors purchased from John Singleton Copley an expanse of pasture land the eminent artist owned between the new state capitol and the mouth of the Charles River. With an eye to tapping the reservoir of merchant wealth they saw rising around them, the Proprietors proceeded to carve up Copley's pasture into building lots. This was the beginning of Beacon Hill. Architects like Charles Bulfinch, the brilliant designer of the statehouse, eagerly drew plans for city residences for the Proprietors. The wealthiest were persuaded to commission "mansion houses," large, free-standing structures, three or four stories high, built of brick or stone.[8]

Few of these homes were more impressive than Dix Place on Orange Court. Elijah Dix surely had the money, but he lacked the proper social connections to buy a parcel on Mount Vernon Street. So he located a mile or so southwest, off Washington Street near Boston Common. Anything it lacked in location, though, his house made up for in ostentation. He spared no expense, and the result was, according to one nineteenth-century observer, magnificent: "a fine, large, brick, double house, surmounted by a cupola." With its ornate craftsmanship, its formal gardens and hybrid pear trees, its polished mahogany furniture and Persian rugs, the house displayed the Doctor's mercantile success and symbolized his rise from provincial to urban splendor. To young Dorothea, who came occasionally to visit, her grandfather's house was symbolic as well. It represented a world of abundance and material comfort, a world that she took for genteel.[9]

Elijah Dix's second decision that was to shape the contours of Dorothea's life also concerned land, though on a much grander scale. Not incidentally, it was a decision that led to his undoing.

By the turn of the nineteenth century, with money streaming in from his chemical plant and ships, the successful merchant faced the question of how to reinvest his immense profits. Recalling that his investments in Worcester land had paid off splendidly, he began to consider the huge northern land market as the territories of Maine, New Hampshire, and Vermont started opening up. Land speculation was in his blood. And a man with reserves of capital, along with sufficient temerity, could see the opportunity of a lifetime.

In those days the Maine frontier was largely wilderness. Since the mid-eighteenth century, when a royal decree set the New York–Massachusetts border twenty miles east of the Hudson River, the Berkshire regions of Massachusetts and Connecticut had attracted colonists in droves. As the Connecticut River valley filled up, however, New Englanders migrated northward in ever-increasing numbers. Inspired by growing demand for farmland, the promise of political stability, and confidence that battle-hardened militiamen could suppress Indian uprisings, the contagion of land fever swept the region. Individual proprietors and land companies bought townships, cleared small portions, and advertised to recruit settlers. Their strategy was to sell some real estate cheaply to people who would, in turn, agree to move onto their land and improve the property. Later, when the new community reached the right stage of development, the absentee owners of the township could sell off choice parcels (which they had held back) at astronomical profits. At least this was the theory. And sometimes it worked. In any event, prospects of making a killing on his investments, and the cachet attached to becoming a land baron, rekindled the Doctor's appetite for land. And so he set about purchasing tracts of forest in central and southern Maine.

He began opportunistically, around 1800, stepping in to buy three thousand acres of wilderness whose previous owner had defaulted on a loan. It was timberland, densely wooded with cedar, spruce, balsam, and pointed firs, crisscrossed by streams, and thus perfectly situated for sawmills. Bustling shipyards and homebuilders, from Portland to New York, offered ready markets for Maine timber. Elijah Dix's property was within easy reach of the Saco River, where so much lumber was being sawed and shipped that it clogged the wharves and passageways. To his delight, his land was already being cleared by a small community of Methodists who had moved up from Cape Cod. His first township was in Penobscot County, part of the original land grant to Bowdoin College. Soon he bought more land in Orono and Hampden, and in 1803 incorporated the township of Dixfield at the confluence of the Webb and Androscoggin rivers. The Doctor's grandiose plans for his eponymous towns are apparent in the remnants he left behind: designs for streets, public buildings, and parks, and in the instance of Dixmont, a charity school.[10]

But his lofty dreams never materialized. In 1809, without warning, as he was moving to consolidate his entrepreneurial empire, Elijah Dix was killed in cold blood. Although rumor had it that he was ambushed by mysterious cutthroats during one of his periodic visits to Dixmont, the crime was never solved. Relying on hearsay, Worcester's nineteenth-century historians blamed it on a conspiracy of "squatters and fraudulent contractors and debtors." Whether or not the Doctor's notoriously aggressive personality, which some people said had alienated local settlers, triggered the deed is unknown. Rarely a man to suffer fools, he had reputedly grown more acerbic with age, bragging about riding through the backwoods alone with his trusty bulldog, armed to the teeth with his knife and a brace of double-shotted pistols.[11]

His body was interred unceremoniously among the lowly Methodists near the center of the tiny Dixmont burial ground, the grave marked by a plain granite headstone. Whatever its motive, his murder profoundly scarred the Dix family. His widow, Dorothy, was horrified. Her whole world had revolved around him. She had never crossed over the threshold into Boston society. Without her husband, she was stranded in Dix Mansion. Moreover, it soon became evident that she had no idea how to preserve the fortune he had built. To her dismay, his holdings were entwined in an intricate financial web of debt and speculation that only he had understood. Without him, everything began to unravel.

The murder was also catastrophic for his children, most of all for his shiftless son, Joseph. While he lived, Elijah had tried to make sure the young man and his family had some regular means of support. And Joseph, left to his own devices, needed whatever help he could get. Whereas Elijah Dix astounded people by how much he achieved in his career, Joseph Dix, Dorothea's father, dismayed them by how little he accomplished in his.

Family tradition remembered him as a charming, innately talented young man, intelligent and articulate, whose natural gifts seemed to promise distinction of some sort. Sadly, however, his "habits of intemperance again and again mocked his undertakings and shortened his life." Baffled by how a man as shiftless as Joseph Dix could have begotten such an industrious daughter, his relatives decided that Dorothea inherited "something of the parent's ability," subsequently refined by the "wisdom and benevolence" of her grandmother, Dorothy Lynde.[12]

For her own part, when it came to her relationship with her father, Dorothea Dix maintained an adamant silence. Still, of all the images locked in the recesses of her memory, none lingered more wraithlike than the shade of Joseph Dix. A presence conspicuous by his absence, he haunted her; and her work—redeeming lost souls—reflected his imprint throughout her life.

In all her extant letters and papers his name surfaces only once, in a note on his vital statistics in which Dorothea wrote that her father was born in Worcester on 26 March 1778.

He was Elijah Dix's third son, assuming the name of the firstborn Joseph, who had died in infancy. The Doctor was as tyrannically ambitious on the boy's behalf as he was on his own, pushing him to make something of himself and bring honor to the family name. To set him on the high road to success, the year before he moved his family to Boston, Elijah proudly enrolled Joseph at Harvard. If the boy did have native ability, however, it did not come to light in his student days. Faculty records for the years 1794–97 show that he adapted poorly to college life. He was in trouble constantly for infractions and breaches of discipline, and punished by fines: $0.48 "for absence from the public prayers in the Chapel"; $1.54 "for neglect of the Collegiate exercise for the third quarter"; $1.50 "for disobedience to the lawful authority of the College." His academic record was equally disgraceful. He garnered citations for absence "from private lectures and reciting," and was admonished before the faculty "for neglect of College exercises and duties." Finally in June 1797, after a prolonged absence from classes and failure to pay his bills, Joseph was notified that his undergraduate status had been terminated.[13]

So, to the chagrin of his father who, like many other self-made men, dreamed about giving his son the advantages he never had, Joseph moved back home. To save face, Elijah concocted a story about illness forcing his son to withdraw from Harvard. He was indeed a frail specimen, but anyone could have seen through the pretext. Groping for some occupation that would make Joseph self-supporting, the Doctor disgustedly packed him off to Worcester, where he was to learn the apothecary trade. His apprenticeship was a failure from the start. Joseph, distracted and bereft of his father's drive, showed no more interest in being an apprentice than a scholar. He chafed at being expected to follow in the Doctor's footsteps. More than anything else he yearned to do something on his own.

What he finally did to assert his independence came as a rude shock. Out of the blue, Joseph announced his engagement to a penniless young woman named Mary Bigelow. She was a year his junior, born in Shrewsbury 15 July 1779, and she was vastly inferior in social station.[14] As far as Elijah and Dorothy Dix were concerned, the Bigelow family consisted mainly of losers in the all-important competition to secure material advantages in life. And Joseph, with masochistic determination, was deliberately spoiling his future by marrying beneath himself. The Bigelows' long history of decline seemed to mock the very ideal of success that the Dixes exemplified.

Two generations earlier, in 1729, Mary's grandfather, Captain Joseph Bigelow, had moved from Marlboro, Massachusetts, to improve his fortunes in the new town of Shrewsbury. There, following a typical pattern of resettlement, he staked his claim to a large house lot and one hundred acres of undivided land. For a time he and his family prospered. By 1748 townspeople deemed the Captain respectable enough to vote him in for a term as selectman. As it turned out, however, this modest success marked the high point of his family's rank in the community. Except for vital statistics, town records pass over the next two generations. Beneath this simple fact lay a cruel economic reality: namely, that during the era of the American Revolution, the Bigelows became poor enough to drop off local tax lists while, according to birth records, they were producing large families. Their predicament was not at all unusual. For many eighteenth-century New Englanders erosion of economic status over a few generations was a bitter fact of life as population growth outstripped the supply of arable land. In the view of the Dix clan, though, whose fortunes were ascending, an alliance with the likes of the Bigelows was an embarrassing step backward.[15]

The couple's marriage on 28 January 1801, in Mary's hometown of Shrewsbury, was for Joseph an act of defiance, a rebuff of his father's ferocious acquisitiveness and social climbing. At first, Mary Bigelow, flattered that a man of Joseph's station had married her, must have underestimated how the match rankled on the Dixes. She had ample reason to imagine their future in one of Worcester's large houses. This was a life to which her husband seemed destined once his rebelliousness subsided and he discovered his vocation and settled down to his career. But it did not take long in Worcester for her to sense her in-laws' withering contempt. Elijah Dix was no shrinking violet when it came to voicing his opinions. From their wedding day until his death eight years later, the old Doctor seldom missed an opportunity to remind his son and the rest of his kin that he considered Mary Bigelow unworthy.

The newlyweds found this environment stifling. Shortly, when a sympathetic friend offered to let Joseph manage a bookstore he owned in Vermont, they jumped at the chance to flee Worcester. Ironically enough, this move allowed them to elude the patriarch's grasp only temporarily. Two years later, as they were scraping by in the Maine woods, Joseph and Mary Dix found themselves squarely in the path of Elijah Dix's land schemes. They were unable to avoid their gloomy destiny. By that time, unable to make a decent living selling books or farming, Joseph was in no position to refuse his father's offer to sign on as manager of the Dixmont township. Had he possessed an ounce of business sense, Joseph might have thrived. The market was strong, and he was supposed to oversee the sale and settlement of several large tracts of Maine land. Instead, he was a poor excuse for a land agent, embittered and unenthusiastic about taking on responsibility. The Doctor, too, had misgivings about the arrangement, frequently sailing up the Maine coast to check on his son and inspect his properties.[16]

If Joseph's squandering his birthright were not shameful enough, he confirmed his reputation as the family's black sheep by taking up Methodism. This religious denomination, with its origins in the fervent pietism of John and Charles Wesley, was at heart an evangelical offshoot of Anglicanism. In the mid-eighteenth century, brought by missionaries from England to America, it began to take hold in the New World. And by 1800 Methodism was spreading like wildfire along the new nation's frontier.

In hundreds, perhaps thousands of camp meetings from Georgia to Maine, revivalists preached its two cardinal tenets: Arminianism and Perfectionism. (Followers of the Dutch theologian Jacobus Arminus repudiated John Calvin's concept of predestination, especially the notion that God had already assigned each individual to heaven or hell before Creation.) Salvation, the Methodists proclaimed, depended purely on one's personal acceptance of Christ, because Christ had atoned for all humankind, not merely the predestined elect. Those who accepted Christ's sacrifice for their sins were urged, literally, to follow the scriptural injunction "Let us go on to perfection" (Hebrews 6:1).

The call to perfection inevitably made it a religion of storm and stress. Psychologically, the crux of Methodism was a savage struggle between the flesh and the spirit, between one's sinful nature and the redemptive, purifying power of God's grace.

When Elijah Dix, no theological hairsplitter himself, began selling land to Methodist settlers, he probably gave little thought to their faith. But he could not ignore it when he heard that his son Joseph had been caught up in the backwoods revival, had groveled in the straw and wept at the beseeching of some common exhorter, and had undergone a radical conversion. The unwelcome news stung his pride. In Hampden, Methodism was a crude, homespun evangelism, scorned by people of means and the established churches, whose leaders dreaded its successive waves of enthusiasm. Emphatically, it was not a denomination of prosperity. Maine Methodists tended to be the lowest of the low— downtrodden bands who took comfort in the doctrine that the Kingdom of God was not of this world. In polite society, even among the most tolerant, New England Methodists were ridiculed as a laughing-stock. No less a liberal than Emerson derided them as monstrously absurd fanatics, what with their "jumping about on all fours, imitating the barking of dogs and surrounding a tree in which they pretended they had '*treed Jesus*.'"[17]

Joseph never cared a great deal about what others thought, though. In the new light of his conversion, he became convinced that, after years of dabbling at farming and bookselling, he had at last found his purpose in life. Accordingly, acquaintances recalled, "he joined the Methodist denomination and became a very ardent and zealous member, and was a sort of lay preacher."[18] Whether or not his wife underwent a religious rebirth of her own, she was never one to challenge his authority. Henceforth she went along with her husband's new career. In the meantime, the Dixes in Boston and Worcester, as well as the prim Congregationalists among the Lyndes on Dorothy's side of the family, had one more reason to lament the disgrace of Joseph and Mary Dix.

The couple's first child—two brothers would follow—was a daughter, named Dorothea Lynde for her grandmother. She was born in Hampden on 4 April 1802, a little more than a year after her parents were married. In reality, her birthplace bore little resemblance to the tidy rustic cabin later constructed in 1902 on the site by a group of New England ladies in honor of her centennial.[19] The local midwife delivered the baby in a small, sparsely furnished room her father had rented in the house of one Isaac Hopkins to make his wife more comfortable during childbirth than she would have been at home. April in central Maine is more the end of winter than the beginning of spring; it is not unusual to encounter snowstorms and subzero temperatures into early May. As soon as mother and child were able, though, they moved back into their one-room pine shack, there to spend the muddy spring amid the small Methodist colony of cabins.

Theirs was by any standard a poor home. But its material impoverishment mattered far less to Dorothea than its dearth of nurture, of example, and of respect.

Joseph's lay ministry was an enormous strain on his family. It amounted to taking a vow of poverty. As an itinerant preacher, he was expected to move his young family from place to place, eking out a hand-to-mouth existence at the margins of the economy. Some years they moved three or four times, sometimes more, and once they had settled, Joseph frequently struck off on his own to carry the Gospel to obscure outposts. The frontier was a place where people were on the move—citizens restlessly searching for new means of livelihood, cheaper housing, or escape from their debtors. Dorothea was disturbed by her family's rootlessness. Worse still was her feeling that, no matter where they went, they were losing ground. In depressing contrast to her prosperous Worcester cousins, her own family seemed always to be slipping deeper and deeper into social inferiority.

For their labors, Methodists ministers were allowed a stipend of eighty dollars a year, sixteen dollars for each child under the age of seven, and a little money to cover travel expenses. This was scarcely enough for subsistence. Yet most of the time their congregations paid them even less. One of Joseph's colleagues, Elijah Robinson Sabin, said that whenever his own children complained how poor they were, he hushed their discontents "by relating stories of his long and weary journeys, guided by bridle paths, or by spotted or marked trees, mid snow and rain, in patched and thread-bare garments, with coarse and scanty food, and not seldom with the fear of outright starvation." Nor was starvation their only peril. From New Hampshire and Vermont there were reports of "field preachers" being robbed, whipped, tarred and feathered, "surrounded by rabble that blew horns and trumpets, [and] put to silence by drum and fife [and] the shouts and epithets of a mob."[20]

There is no question that this danger and violent derision preyed on Dorothea's mind. Constantly dislodged, thrust into hostile surroundings, unable to feel safe in any special place of her own, she envied those who had permanent homes. She missed the sedate familiarity of routine, the sense of reassurance that comes from assuming a known and recognized position within one's community.

Nonetheless, her lot might have been bearable if she had at least been assured of her parents' love. But Joseph and Mary Dix, absorbed in their own problems, were unpredictable, high-strung, and incapable of giving her the affection she craved. Indeed, what interest they took in Dorothea seems to have sharpened, not soothed, her anxieties. Bent on preparing their daughter for the Kingdom of God, from the cradle onward they set about trying to break her spirit. They were ardent Methodists, and they deemed a brutal discipline to be their solemn religious duty. In their view, repentance and conversion—bending sinful human nature to the dictates of God's will—were life's defining experiences. And they had no intention of pampering their child and delaying her onerous journey toward religious perfection.

Exactly what Methodist discipline meant is reflected in letter that Susanna Wesley, the mother of Methodism's patron saints, wrote to her son John. For generations the faithful revered this letter as a guide to child rearing, second only to the Bible. The main theme is clear-cut: harsh chastisement, with no allowances for sentimentality or parental indulgence of babies' undesirable behavior. Corporal punishment was to begin as early as possible. "When turned a year old (and some before)," Susanna Wesley declared, "they are taught to fear the rod and to cry softly, by which means they escaped abundance of correction which they might otherwise have had: and that most odious noise of the crying of children was rarely heard in the house, but the family usually lived in as much quietness as if there had not been a child among them." God meant for children to be seen and not heard, even if this required a ruthless stifling of childish impulses. Methodist parents, like most Evangelicals, were warned not to spare the rod. As Jonathan Edwards's grandson explained, "until its will was brought into submission to the will of its parents [so that] a child will obey his parents, he can never be brought to obey God."[21]

Dorothea left no written account of the physical punishment visited upon her as a child. Unlike their male contemporaries, Victorian women seldom mentioned this part of their upbringing. Nevertheless, the pattern of Dorothea's life suggests that she experienced a good deal of physical and emotional mistreatment. Typically, as they grow up and reach positions of authority, people who were whipped as children inflict on others the very pain they suffered themselves. Dorothea conformed exactly to this model. More than three-quarters of a century later, for example, children who attended her first nursery school, which she started in her teens, indelibly remembered her as a birch-wielding martinet. "I don't know that she had any special grudge against me," one old man recollected, "but it was her nature to use the whip, and use it she did."[22]

The most deep-seated and important legacy of her painful childhood, though, was Dorothea's anger. Anger, particularly in early childhood, is a complicated emotion. In most cases, very young children cannot focus their outrage directly on their parents. They turn their feelings back on themselves. The result of most abuse, from mild to severe, is lingering guilt and shame. No matter how harshly, or unreasonably, they have been treated, children usually feel responsible for what has befallen them. As they grow up, their suppressed anger takes many forms, beginning with an impulse to distance themselves from their parents. In this respect, Dorothea's bitter disavowal of her child-hood fits the classic paradigm of physical assault.

While there is no way to tell how severely she was castigated, the noteworthy thing is the intensity of her reaction. She not only with-drew from her parents; she wiped them out of her past. From the moment she moved away from home, she began describing herself as an orphan. Letters and diaries written in her twenties make it seem as though she had been abandoned and never knew her parents, and that her early years had been a blank. On many occasions, she spoke of her-self as a person whom Providence had deprived of a family. "I am a being almost alone in this wide world," Dorothea wrote to a friend in the early 1820s. "How mercifully [God has] given me dear friends but not kindred!"[23] She acted as though Joseph and Mary Dix had never existed. Her reasons for erasing disturbing memories are understand-able. Yet the trouble with closing the book on her early family life—her ultimate revenge—was that she replaced the normal emotion of parental love with a void.

Over the years this void was filled by dejection, self-reproach, and loss of the capacity for intimacy. She perpetually kept her distance from others. Melancholy and anxiety were so pervasive in Dorothea Dix's life that it is tempting to interpret these traits as inbred qualities of temperament. But the substratum of rage, deriving from parental mal-treatment and neglect, and long repressed before it finally found an outlet in her public career, places her depressive tendencies in a differ-ent light.

Indeed, it fits into the pattern of early-Victorian New England, where the cycle of abuse, repressed anger, and depression was for Dorothea's generation a common phenomenon. Considering the somber cognitive life of New England in the early national period, it might even be viewed as archetypal. Evidence from hundreds of diaries, journals, and autobi-ographies shows that most Evangelicals, whether Congregationalists, Baptists, or Methodists, whipped their offspring, often to the point of raising welts and drawing blood. The psychological result was an epi-demic of depression, the notorious "iron of melancholy" at the core of the New England religious conscience. Among the children of the twice-born, it has been plausibly argued, this pervasive melancholy "was and is rooted in the consciously forgotten but unconsciously persistent trau-mas of physical abuse from punishments in early childhood."[24]

Growing up, Dorothea expressed a number of virtues that seem to have been formed in direct reaction to her mercurial father. Where he was emotional, she was reserved; where he was a drunkard, she was abstemious; where he was irresponsible and self-centered, she was driven to take on the burdens of others. Most of all, where he was erratic, she was disciplined, obsessed with self-control. Bottling up all her anger and frustration, she manifested what her pupils later called an "iron will," an excruciating exactness in every corner of her life that left no room for impulse or error. At the same time, she also developed a striking capacity for dissociation, that is, the ability to survive in the midst of pain by detaching herself emotionally from those around her. As a child unable to control the outside world, she learned to insulate her innermost self, to create a place within herself that no one could harm because no one could reach it.[25]

The nightmarish aspect of her girlhood was that her father's religion demanded precisely her innermost self, in a word, her soul. The revivalist presumed that conversion required violent confrontation. No daughter of Joseph Dix was going to reach puberty without giving a satisfactory account of her own spiritual health. Beginning when she was five or six, her parents, Joseph's fellow ministers, and the entire community of the faithful goaded Dorothea to bear witness to that faith that alone could prepare her heart for God's saving grace. Along with being switched, Dorothea was exhorted to be contrite, repent of her sins, and desperately throw herself upon the mercy of God. Only at this point, purging her soul of sin and committing it purely to the divine will, could she receive sanctification. From everything she saw around her, though, this message rang false. The unbridled emotionalism and abandonment of self-control she witnessed around the bonfires of camp meetings ran against the grain of Dorothea's personality.[26]

Mistrustful of others, she wished to become the mistress of her own fate. But mastery of any sort was an impossibility in the turbulent home of Joseph Dix. After Doctor Dix's death, when Dorothea was seven, her father began careening between violent extremes of alcoholic dissolution and abject religious frenzy. If anything, alcohol intensified his penchant for physical abuse and fueled his proclivity for self-destruction. As a child, she had no way of escaping the frightening spectacle. In a climate where winter lasted half the year, wherever they went, the family was cramped together in one or two rooms. Whether Joseph Dix made a drunken fool of himself or was swept up in a bout of religious fanaticism, Dorothea was at his mercy. This brutal intimacy was most trying during Joseph's periodic spells of religious frenzy. People said that during these phases he was overcome with a wild-eyed conviction that the world's salvation hinged on his publishing the Word of God. Possessed, he threw himself into flurries of writing, printing, and binding revivalist tracts, without regard for the well-being of his family.[27]

Meanwhile, the family's needs were growing apace. In October 1812, ten years after Dorothea was born, Mary Dix gave birth to a son whom they called Charles Wesley. Soon she was pregnant again, and delivered her second boy, named Joseph in honor of his father, in January 1815.[28] Both boys were born in Barnard, a Vermont village where Mary had kinfolk. They needed help, because by the time Dorothea's youngest brother was born, the Dix family was in dire straits. "Mr. Madison's War," as New Englanders dubbed the War of 1812, with its embargo of British shipping, had an depressing effect on the New England economy that lasted almost three years. Worried about making ends meet, Mary had persuaded Joseph to take another stab at the book business. Halfheartedly he opened a small store. Handbills he distributed along with his religious tracts advertised "a handsome and useful assortment of miscellaneous books, also schoolbooks, singly or by the dozen," adding that farmers short of cash could trade fresh produce for literature. Unfortunately this new venture soon proved to be another false start.[29]

Three children were considered a small family, and Dorothea's mother was not yet thirty-five when Joseph was born. But in 1815 something happened to Mary Dix, in all likelihood a mishap during the labor and delivery of her last child, that incapacitated her. Prone to various maladies, she had already earned a reputation for frailty. Although rumors circulated that she shared her husband's fondness for the bottle, and even that she suffered from chorea or epilepsy, the only thing known for a fact is that henceforth she was physically unable to care for her children. Sinking into semi-invalidism, knowing full well that her husband could not be trusted to look after his two sons, she frantically pressed Joseph to take the family back to Worcester, where his relatives had the means to help them get back on their feet. Their return to the town of his boyhood was a humiliating admission of defeat. Mary Dix must have realized that the only alternative was the almshouse.[30]

And so in early 1815 the prodigal family slunk back to Worcester. They found lodging in part of a house owned by Joseph's in-laws and, as expected, his kin pitched in to help with Dorothea's brothers. The Dix name still carried weight in town and, had he wished to do so, Joseph might have found regular work through his old family network. But he did not bother to look. Lost in self-preoccupation, he suddenly detected in his plight the mysterious hand of the Lord beckoning him home from the mountains of Vermont to bring the good news of Methodism to the heathen of Worcester County.

When she got wind of her father's scheme, Dorothea was mortified. She was at an awkward, self-conscious age, a month shy of her thirteenth birthday, observant enough to know what her cousins and aunts and uncles were whispering behind her back. Over the years she had withdrawn emotionally from her parents. In Worcester she began to contemplate a physical breaking away. It appears that the last straw came when her father, in one of his extreme religious spells, ordered her to assist him in his holy mission. In preparation for his revival, he set her to work pasting and stitching religious pamphlets, a task she detested, both for its tedium and its meaning. At her wits' end, she decided to sneak away from home and take the stagecoach to Boston, where, it is said, she appealed to her widowed grandmother for refuge in Dix Mansion.[31]

Dorothy Dix, Madam Dix as she preferred people to address her, who abhorred excesses of any kind, had long ago written off Joseph and Mary Dix as a lost cause. Dorothea, on the other hand, she seemed to consider a victim of circumstance. As though to redeem the sins of her impudent son, Dorothea's grandmother, then sixty-eight years old, agreed to take the child under her wing.

There is no indication that her running away from home grieved Dorothea's parents. With their household barely managing to stay afloat, and two young boys demanding attention, they may actually have been relieved to learn that their headstrong daughter was securely ensconced at Orange Court with her grandmother.

On the other hand, it did not take long for Dorothea to realize that the Dix Mansion in which she now found herself was much changed from the magical place she had occasionally visited as a child. There was still ample evidence of Elijah Dix's passion for material acquisition: a black walnut China closet stacked with Wedgewood pottery; chests of polished silver plate; Irish linens, Marseille quiltings, satin antimacassars, laces and chintzes; bookshelves lined with gilt-edged leather volumes, more often than not with their pages uncut; tapestries, carvings, woodcuts, and exotic medical instruments. The merchant had been an omnivorous collector, and the widow's devotion to her husband appeared to have been total. The house was spotlessly clean, the oak floors and wainscoting buffed to a low shine. Everything was in its place, arranged meticulously, as though at any moment the master might walk through the door, drop into his favorite chair, and call for his meerschaum pipe. But he had never returned; and without the Doctor's vivacious presence, his house seemed eerily empty.

Her husband's murder and the debacle of Joseph's career were not the only misfortunes Madam Dix had suffered. It must have seemed to her that a curse of violent death hovered over her family. Her firstborn son had died in his first year. In 1799 she lost her second boy, William, who fell ill aboard one of his father's merchantmen on a voyage to the West Indies. Alexander Dix, the sixth-born son, was killed in 1809 in Canada, just three months before his father's death. Then, two years later, word came from Kentucky that his older brother, Clarendon, had disappeared under sinister circumstances. When Dorothea arrived, all that was left of the once-proud family was her uncle, Harry Elijah, Madam Dix's youngest son, who had graduated from Harvard to study medicine, and her aunt Mary, who had married Harvard's librarian, Thaddeus Mason Harris.

Disappointed with the hand fate had dealt her, Madam Dix grimly set out to ensure that Dorothea would not repeat her father's blunders and improprieties. She replaced Joseph Dix's fire with ice. Discipline, restraint, and self-control were her watchwords, and she had nothing but scorn for idleness and self-pity. At bottom, her values were not inconsistent with Dorothea's, but her personality, glacially reserved and aloof, had a chilling effect on the girl. It did not take long for Dorothea to see that in moving she had not escaped her sorrows but simply exchanged one form of unhappiness for another.

A decade or so later, when she composed a series of moral tales for children, she included thinly disguised portraits of herself during her first stay in Dix Mansion. They are redolent of the isolation that suffering imposes on children. For instance, in one story, "James Coleman; or the Reward of Perseverance," she depicted a hot-tempered thirteen-year-old boy who, when his parents suddenly die, leaves his native village for his affluent grandfather's home some fifty miles away. James Coleman (like Dorothea) is a bookworm. His stentorian grandfather (like Madam Dix), however, seldom opens a book and tends to disdain his reading as idleness. Each night after the lamp has been extinguished, alone in his dark room, she wrote, James "pined in secret for his old home, . . . he longed to join his school fellows in their evening plays; but when he spoke of these things, his grandfather, at other times kind in his rough way, only answered by harsh reproofs at his discontent, and ingratitude in not being thankful that he had so good a home."[32]

Apparently the relationship chafed on both sides. After a year, exasperated by the precocious and stubborn teenager, Madam Dix broached the idea of sending Dorothea back to Worcester. By that time Joseph and Mary Dix had departed for points north, leaving Dorothea's brothers, Charles and Joseph, Jr., in the care of Madam Dix's niece, Sarah Fiske. Thinking it over, Sarah and her mother, Sarah Lynde Duncan, concluded that it would do Dorothea good to help them take care of the boys. She obviously needed direction, they reasoned, and learning how to take care of young children would instill responsibility and help prepare her for the expected role of wife and mother.

She must have had deep misgivings about the move. It promised to reopen old wounds and aggravate her sense of unbelonging, for Worcester was full of disturbing memories and ghosts. But the moment Dorothea moved into Sarah Fiske's commodious, comfortable frame house on a green hill overlooking town, her life brightened. The Lyndes, Fiskes, and Duncans, families whose ancestors had been part of the Great Migration from England to Massachusetts in the seventeenth century, represented the best of old Worcester. They were a genial, close-knit group, as settled and prosperous as Mary and Joseph Dix were peripatetic and poor. Despite her fears about how they would receive her, to Dorothea's amazement, they accepted her on her own terms. Proud of their breeding, her in-laws aspired to the kind of agrarian gentility they read about in the novels of Sir Walter Scott. Unlike Madam Dix, none of them seemed to hold her to account for her parents' shortcomings. Dorothea, eager to put her past behind her, took full advantage of their offer to teach her how to behave like a proper young lady.

It turned out that they expected a lot. Old Sarah Duncan, with whom she spent a good deal of time, was an intensely demanding woman who claimed that she had taught her own daughter to piece together a bed quilt before the age of three. Fortunately, Dorothea was a quick study, an apt student who strove to please her tutors. And she had a sharp eye for the nuances of social relationships.

Shrewd observer though she was, Dorothea could not see her way clear to enter the normal flow of socializing that absorbed most young women her age. Her father, who had been to Harvard and always styled himself as an apostle of moral seriousness, scorned what he considered the Duncans' and Lyndes' frivolous preoccupation with etiquette and polite conversation. Perhaps traces of her father's attitude rubbed off on Dorothea. In any event, she was prepared to do without friends. She professed little interest in the routines that engaged her contemporaries. Garden parties, teas, soirées where powdered and petticoated girls perched at the harpsichord, picking out Clementi and Mozart— this was a world for which her frontier upbringing had ill prepared her. She lacked polish. Her wardrobe, consisting mostly of hand-me-downs from her cousins, and her ignorance of etiquette, made her feel gawky. Painfully embarrassed about not fitting in, she affected a cultivated disdain for other girls' silliness and lack of purpose.[33]

The solution she hit upon to take her mind away from her problems was work. She created a job for herself. Surrounded by people who respected initiative and industry, Dorothea announced her intention to start a school, a plan that encountered no resistance. It was assembled quickly, a few benches, chairs, and cots in a small room in a building one of her uncles owned. No one thought to question her qualifications. After all, a schoolmistress in charge of young children was not expected to know a great deal, and at the outset she served as a babysitter as much as a teacher.

Nevertheless, opening the little school reaffirmed her sense of independence. Although the Fiskes and Duncans were wealthy enough easily to provide for her upkeep, relying on their largesse grated on her. She longed to break free, and an enterprise of her own, however modest, stood for self-reliance. Also it gave her a constructive role in Worcester. Everywhere in New England, young women routinely sought teaching jobs as a respectable way of serving their communities. To a woman who wanted to improve herself, the teacher's role promised intellectual rewards consistent with the maternal qualities society expected in a young lady. Moreover, in a culture imbued with Protestant ideals, teaching had a religious meaning. While churches denied women the ecclesiastical authority of ordination, ministers encouraged them to contribute to the Christian nurture of children through the unassuming work of teaching.[34]

Her school also gave Dorothea a way to augment her own education.

She had grown up loving books and learning. Joseph Dix, for all his waywardness, had taken an earnest interest in her early instruction. He was a bookseller, a pulpit orator, and a writer, and the written word had figured prominently in his home. Along with a thorough grounding in the Bible and *Pilgrim's Progress*, his daughter was schooled in the classics. By the time she returned to Worcester from Boston, she was already laying out for herself an ambitious program of reading and study. If there was any conspicuous failure in her early training, it was penmanship (not a trivial flaw in an age of handwriting). Unlike her grandfather's beautifully precise hand, her cramped scrawl never ceased to perplex her correspondents.

Dorothea's new vocation allowed her for the first time to assume a role of authority, and the school soon became the center of her life. Looking after children was a way of reinventing herself, now in the role of a parent. She appeared before her pupils, they recalled, dressed in "the skirt and sleeves of a grown woman . . . so as to command due respect by a more adult appearance." And she set a tone of utmost austerity and strictness. Despite their youth, Dorothea, unrelievedly serious, demanded that they put away childish things.[35] Conventional wisdom said it was a teacher's duty to mold her students in her own image, a precept Dorothea evidently took to heart. Children recalled being severely caned for the slightest infractions. And when a little girl who had recently been to writing school appeared in class, Dorothea forced her to discard what she had learned there and imitate her own unusual handwriting. When, in its second year, her brother Charles began attending her school, he was "obliged to eat, drink, sleep and wink" at his sister's direction. At age sixteen, having taken responsibility for both her brothers, she had replaced her parents as the head of household.[36]

Sometime around 1820 Dorothea closed her school, left the Fiskes, and, along with her brothers, moved back to Boston, where she shuttled between Dix Mansion and her uncle Thaddeus Mason Harris's modest home in Dorchester. The reasons for the move are not entirely clear. Madam Dorothy Dix, now in her early seventies and no longer in the best of health, probably needed full-time help in Dix Mansion. With her experience in Worcester, Dorothea was capable of managing most of the household. Even more important in the long run, her relatives knew that in Boston, with its brisk marriage market, her chances of attracting the attention of eligible young gentlemen were greatly increased. And eighteen was a perfectly reasonable age at which to commence the search for a husband.

By the time Dorothea returned to Boston she had grown into an imposing young woman, five feet eight or nine inches tall, her ramrod-erect posture making her appear even taller. One glance at her face told that she was tightly wound, an intense person whose sense of humor, if indeed she had one, lay well concealed. A Boston artist who painted an enamel portrait around this time portrayed her as a demure, if not sweet, gentlewoman wearing a lace collar and gold necklace. She wore her brown hair in wispy curls, making her high forehead and nose more prominent; her lips turned up slightly at the corners of her mouth without suggesting a smile. Her early portrait gave no hint of what lay in store for her; and the damage from her childhood lay under the surface. There was a palpable reserve, an aloofness about her. She was by all accounts a striking figure, if not a classic beauty. Some acquaintances, commenting on her watery blue eyes and olive skin, thought her good-looking. Others, noting that her visage was habitually cast in "a very stern, decided expression," used the word "handsome." Emerging from her teens, she reflected all the worries and responsibilities of her broken family that she had taken on her own shoulders. Sensing the hurt and resentment smoldering within her, some people characterized her as "overbearing and dictatorial."[37]

Had it occurred to them they might have called her angry. But anger, one of the seven deadly sins, was rarely an emotion attributed to Victorian ladies. And Dorothea, striving to be a lady, was adept at cloaking her unruly emotions.

Madam Dix was relieved to see that Worcester had smoothed the rough edges of her granddaughter's personality. Under the supervision of Madam Dix's sister and niece, Dorothea had learned exactly the kind of manners her grandmother expected in a young lady. Now she dressed tastefully and displayed a new poise. Sunday mornings, when she walked with Madam Dix along Washington Street to Hollis Street Church, where Elijah Dix had rented a pew during his first days in Boston, she appeared to fit in with her surroundings.

It was at Hollis Street that Dorothea made her unobtrusive debut into Boston society. And it was there, during her first months in the city, that she encountered her first and most beloved friend.

Lingering outside the church after one of minister John Pierpont's marathon sermons, she was introduced to a young parishioner, a likable

*Dorothea Dix at about age twenty. (By permission of the
Houghton Library, Harvard University.)*

woman about her own age whose name was Anne Heath. From their
first meeting they felt a strong personal chemistry between them; and
shortly thereafter, Anne invited Dorothea to her home to visit her family in Brookline, just west of Boston. Anne was everything Dorothea was
not. Her father was the image of a successful old-line merchant,
exceedingly well-off with his commercial and financial interests in the
city and his charming three-story house near the reservoir, where the
clustered maples gave the place a pastoral flavor. While it lacked Dix
Mansion's elegant arches and cornices, the Heath home was always full
of people. Anne had four sisters and two brothers, and, along with her
parents, there seemed always to be aunts and uncles and cousins staying
over. As a family the Heaths were easygoing, close-knit, secure, considerate and gracious, without the least hint of affectation. From her first
visit, Dorothea was drawn to them, marveling at how openly they dis-

played affection for each other and how they warmly they welcomed her as one of their own. Anne's friendship and the cheerful bustle of the Heath houschold were just the antidotes she needed to counteract the emotional sterility of Dix Mansion.

Her sense of solitude worsened in April 1821, for that month Dorothea received word that her father, Joseph Dix, had died. Whether disease or accident cut short his doleful life, she attributed his demise to alcoholic dissipation. With respect to its impact on her inner life, her father's death was bound to have been largely anticlimactic, because Dorothea had already done her best to write him out of her life. As far as the Heaths and her new acquaintances knew, she had arrived in Boston an orphan.

Joseph Dix died penniless and intestate, leaving his widow to fend for herself, relying on her family and in-laws for support. And he left his daughter without a dowry. If she were ever going to lay claim to an inheritance, it would come not from her father but from the estate of Madam Dix; and she had no way of knowing how long her grandmother might live or how much any future bequest might amount to. Without money of her own, nor any firm guarantee of money to come, Dorothea found herself in a bind. The longer she lived in Boston, the more she aspired to gentility. Yet her Orange Court address implied a rank that she could never take for granted. The twin misfortunes of her grandfather's murder and her father's failure to build an estate consigned her not to the hell of poverty but to the purgatory of financial uncertainty and dependence on the whims of her grandmother. In consequence, the ambiguities she now faced were worthy of one of Jane Austen's socially perceptive protagonists. In order to hold her head up in society—worshipping at Hollis Street or dining with the Heaths— she found herself living a deception, silently masquerading as something more than she was.

In Anne Heath's company, Dorothea was torn between the impulse to drop her guard and the desire to protect her unhappy secrets. She desperately needed the friendship of a woman her own age, someone she could trust, someone to whom she could reveal herself, unburden herself, and be accepted for what she was. So, slowly and tentatively, she opened up to Anne. As much as she dared, at any rate. And, in turn, the benefits of their friendship began to change her life all for the good. Anne held a key to the closed world of Boston society, a world that had seemed frighteningly complicated and unapproachable after

Dorothea's years in Worcester. Anne, who moved effortlessly in the best circles, was well established and knew precisely where people fit within the local hierarchy. Both young women liked to talk, and in their long conversations she provided a sounding board for Dorothea's own observations and insights about social behavior. By accompanying her to lectures and teas, Dorothea learned how the bluebloods behaved. Over time, as she worked to blend in, her speech, mannerisms, and personal deportment began to give the appearance that she herself had been to the manner born.[38]

This transformation was slow and onerous work, though, because even as she cultivated new manners and ventured into society Dorothea felt terribly ill at ease. Her discomfort stemmed from seeing how different she was—not just in background but in aspiration—from other young people around her. She felt herself between two worlds, at home in neither.

Trying to find a solid basis for her life in Boston, she used her pen as an outlet. Beginning around age nineteen, Dorothea wrote hundreds of letters to Anne in which she sought simultaneously to express and to control her own turbulent feelings and thoughts. The leitmotif in this correspondence was confession, though exactly what it was that Dorothea wanted to confess was muffled under many layers of sentimental abstraction and grandiloquence. Upon reading a volume of maudlin poems by the deservedly forgotten English writer Letitia Landon, for example, Dorothea exclaimed,

> You say I weep easily. I was early taught to sorrow, to shed tears, and now, when sudden joy lights up or any unexpected sorrow strikes my heart, I find it difficult to repress the full and swelling tide of feeling. Even now, though alone and with not very exciting cause of joy or grief, I am paying my watery tribute to the genius of L. E. L. Oh, Annie! She is a poetess that expresses all the genius and fire of Byron, unalloyed with his gross faults; all the beautiful flow of words which fall like music on the air from the pen of Moore, without his little less than half-concealed consciousness; all the simplicity of Wordsworth without his prosiness and stiffness; finally, in the words of her reviewer, 'If she never excels what she already has written, we can confidently give her the assurance of what the possessor of such talents must earnestly covet, *immortality*.'[39]

Mimicking the melodramatic, florid tone derived from reading popular poetry and fiction, she drifted often into pomposity. This habit was encouraged by the conventions of Victorian letter writing, which when it came to anger, frustration, and rage sought to impose on disruptive emotions the constraints of formal, stilted language.[40]

Anne, a romantic herself, was nonetheless fascinated. A traditional woman in every respect, hers was an innocent and acquiescent frame of mind. Dorothea, on the other hand, burning with an inner fire, seeming so clearly to be a moral visionary, was like no one Anne had ever met. Dorothea's agonizing over the meaning of life led Anne to ponder her own capacity for moral commitment. In their correspondence the two young women poured out their hearts to each other. A short poem Dorothea wrote "To A. E. H." conveys the stilted, lachrymose style they affected:

> In the sad hour of anguish and distress
> To thee for sympathy will I repair
> Thy soothings sure will make my sorrows less
> And what thou canst not soothe, thou wilt share
> Though many are to me both good and kind
> And grateful still my heart shall ever be
> Yet thou'st to me a more congenial mind
> More than a sister's love binds thee to me.
> My own sad fate; no home now waits for me,
> No smiling parents near to greet the wanderer,
> No sister's eye beams on me
> Angel sweet!
> No, on I tread the path of life alone!
> Friendship's voice the gloom is cheering;
> Spirit droop not, Anna's nigh![41]

Madam Dix had no tolerance for nostalgia or bathos. Yet at this stage of her life Dorothea, yearning for the affection she had missed as a child, needed someone to indulge her. Empathy and uncritical appreciation were responses that Anne, raised to believe in feminine submissiveness and her obligation to nurture those in pain, was well suited to provide. And her responsiveness encouraged Dorothea to make heavy demands on the relationship. "My young brothers rest themselves on me," Dorothea told her, "while the feeble frame of my aged grandmother seeks for support from me. I have none to cling to, none that I love in this world hardly. But I persuade myself (like a foolish girl) that I have a sister in you—do not, pray do not withdraw yourself from me quite now Anne." True to Dorothea's wish, Anne stood by her friend, patiently willing to lend a sympathetic ear whenever it was needed. Anne Heath's remarkably selfless power of solace laid the basis for a friendship—the pivotal relationship of Dorothea's life—that survived unbroken until Anne's death more than half a century later.[42]

The bond between the two women depended largely on Anne's admiration for Dorothea's quest for a higher calling. In Boston, quotidian socializing struck her as just as much a waste of time as it had seemed in Worcester. "I have little taste for fashionable dissipation, cards, dancing, the theater and tea-parties are my special aversion," Dorothea advised Anne, "and I look with little envy on those who find their enjoyment solely in such transitory delights." Time idled away on "balls and parties" was better invested in self-improvement. Given her sense of being an interloper on the social scene, her repudiation of ordinary social intercourse as self-indulgence is understandable. While she insisted that the ephemeral pleasures of society distracted one from the higher purpose of life, she also knew that these were pleasures in which she could not participate as an equal.[43]

Finding Boston, apart from her occasional trips to Brookline, a difficult place, Dorothea turned inward. She had an unquenchable thirst for spiritual insight. And if there was one consistent theme between the messages she heard blazoned in the glare of revival bonfires and preached in the dignified hush of Hollis Street Church, it was that life had a purpose that revolved around discovering and carrying out the will of God. In fleeing her parents, she had escaped the formal dictates of Methodism. But she could not avoid the spiral of self-doubt, self-accusation, and religious despair that her evangelical upbringing spawned. This was too deeply ingrained. As she awakened to the world of Boston, her dilemma was how to reconcile her intense ambition, energy, and belief in her own powers with her underlying guilt and shame. How was she, a woman full of anger, hostility, and egotism, to prove she was in fact one of God's chosen people?

Devout Christians from St. Paul on have wrestled with this spiritual conflict. For Dorothea it centered on trying to figure out which aspects of her character were gifts from God, and which were weaknesses or, worse, counterfeit gifts that pride had made her unable to recognize for what they were. Contemplating her own intellect, for example, was an exercise in confusion. "I worship talents almost," she confessed to

Anne, but "I sinfully dare mourn that I possess them not." God had blessed her with a keen mind, she acknowledged; but what good was it? Indeed, it often felt more like a curse, as though she were just smart enough to be disappointed that she were "not endowed with higher and more brilliant powers of intellect." Moreover, too much meditation could be unsettling. At times, she said, her rational faculties burned with "an intentness that threatens to annihilate the little stability that now sustains me." Not that she had any grandiose aspirations for herself, she assured Anne. It was not to "win the world's applause that I would possess a mind above the common sphere," she wrote, "but that I might revel in the luxury of those mental visions that hourly must entrance a spirit less of earth than of heaven; that I might be a fit companion of the virtuous great . . . who 'tread the path of duty,' perfect in the way of righteousness."[44]

Her letters overflowed with pious sentiments about the transience of life, the danger of sensual delights, and the eternal rewards that awaited the soul able to submit itself to the divine will. Underneath all her self-conscious hand wringing though, lurked a deeper anxiety that she was both too bright and too angry for her own good.

Absolute self-mastery, she believed, was the key to bringing her gifts in line with her ambition and her emotions. For her exquisitely sensitive conscience, powered by guilt, self-mastery remained an elusive goal. In daily bouts of soul searching she grew obsessed by her shortcomings. Sin and guilt colored Dorothea's notebooks from the 1820s and 1830s, showing how difficult it was for her to secure even the slenderest basis for self-approval. "Six faults must be abandoned by a man seeking prosperity," she chided herself, "sleep, drowsiness, fear, anger, laziness, loitering." She confessed to suffering from all six.[45]

To rise above her bleak heritage and make something worthwhile of her life meant, first of all, getting a grip on her temper. "To me it seems the highest effort of the human mind to obtain a victory over itself," she told Anne. And most of her letters touch in one way or another on the battle she fought within herself, fending off foes like "ire," "rancor," "vice," "crime," and "guilt." Often she spoke of a malignant principle deep within her, threatening to sabotage her best qualities and noble intentions.[46]

All this tortured self-accusation colored her interpretation of illness and physical infirmity. Like so many Victorians, Dorothea thought of herself as having a fragile constitution, and she painstakingly chronicled her various maladies. "[My] cough, which for a week or two has been becoming less troublesome, returned last night with accumulated violence," she wrote in a typical passage. "I passed one such night with you, Anne, tossing to and fro, seeking in vain for ease: today I am almost sick; the pain in my side and chest is almost constant." Sharing the details of illness strengthened her personal connection with Anne and made their new friendship more intimate. It was also a way of exorcising pain that was as much psychological as somatic. In writing so fulsomely of her illnesses—phrases such as "I may never again enjoy the fragrant airs of spring" flowed easily from her pen—Dorothea elicited those qualities of tenderness and compassion she valued the most in Anne.[47]

The vigorously ill woman was a familiar type in nineteenth-century America. Women were extolled for sacrificing their health for the welfare of their families. At a time when most medical care was provided within people's homes and effective treatments were few, families were large and the vicissitudes of childbirth left many mothers impaired in one way or another. Asepsis and antibiotics lay far in the future, and surgery, feared for its pain, blood loss and potential for infection, was seldom performed unless a patient's life was at stake. People simply endured chronic disorders that later generations would come to see as debilitating. Dorothea's contemporary Catharine Beecher was probably not exaggerating when she said she knew three sick women for every one who was well.

For her part, in her early twenties Dorothea adopted a lifelong pattern of illness and convalescence in which physical symptoms cropped up during times of stress. When she was depressed, the severity of her illnesses increased; in the glow of friendship, progress, or accomplishment, her symptoms shrank into insignificance. A visit to Worcester in 1826, where she was seized "with the prevailing Influenza attended with a considerable degree of fever," was a representative episode. Just as she started to recover, she reported, "again I lost ground, and had a severe attack of Inflammation in my lungs attended with symptoms of Pleuresey [sic]." Each passing year brought new waves of symptoms: asthma, insomnia, dyspepsia, incapacitating headaches, spasms of the heart, rheumatism, and partial paralysis of her right side. At one point, her constant relapses prompted the Reverend John Pierpont to offer his own diagnosis. "I now think that you are sacrificing your life," he observed insightfully, "on what you conceive to be the altar of your duty."[48]

Dorothea ignored her minister's remark, for she thought of her diseases as spiritual tests or, in some instances, deserved punishments. In a passage reminiscent of Samuel Johnson's remark "a man in pain is looking after ease," Dorothea scorned ill health as a mark of human nature's "disposition to indulgence." Sickness, she informed Anne, was more often than not evidence of a "hidden disposition . . . a secret desire to escape from labour." She admitted to feeling within her an insidious force bent on ruining "best faculties" of her mind and paralyzing her "most useful powers." So far, she confided, her dread of falling victim to this "besieger" had given her strength to persevere. But she feared that the struggle was slowly wearing her down, threatening to extinguish the spark of vivacity that had survived her childhood.[49]

In the meantime, she blamed her weak constitution on her parents. The brute facts of genealogy appeared to preordain her vulnerability to disease. Her father was a dipsomaniac who died a month shy of his forty-fourth birthday, and her feckless mother lingered on, enfeebled, dependent on the goodwill of others. Blotting them out of her mind did not make her any less their offspring, nor banish the fear that they had passed along seeds of their own weakness. So she scrutinized her symptoms, noting in her journal the slightest twinge that might be the signal of hereditary corruption. If there was a ray of hope, perhaps it was that the worst disorders, like the terrible affliction that destroyed her father, were thought to take hold only in people whose lives were morally dissipated. Discipline and moral rectitude, medical opinion held, was strong preventive medicine.

Dorothea also tended to project a sense of violence onto the external world. She had been raised in an atmosphere filled with warnings that the end of the world was near, and she never shed her sense of apocalyptic foreboding. "I know the day is drawing nigh," she cautioned Anne Heath, "to fulfill every fearful token." The United States had been lulled into a false confidence, she thought, because the country had managed to avoid the "shocks that convulse every other nation."[50] Nevertheless, in the context of her religious angst, Dorothea's notions of the Last Judgment, the end of time, even heaven and hell, remained vague, more expressions of a personal sense of impending doom that permeated her inner life than of specific theological beliefs. Everywhere around her, she declared, was a swirling vortex of "waves, violently agitated." The only sure way for a person to avoid being pulled under was to live a life *virtuously sacrificed for the benefit of others.*"[51]

Self-renunciation is a fundamental tenet of Christianity. And Dorothea, longing to be reborn in a form more pleasing to God and herself, was drawn to the transforming power of self-denial. Humility and abject resignation to the divine will were, she believed, the keys to divining God's purposes. In this spirit she wrote,

> I will seek his face
> Though thou assign a servant's place
> To me, the meanest round thy door—
> Though humbled, toiling in disgrace,
> Let me again behold thy face
> And eat thy bread—I ask no more. [52]

Earnest as they seem, such passages (and there are many dozens) ring hollow. As her letter about talents revealed, Dorothea did in fact ask for more and, try as she might to rein in her ambition, she would never be satisfied merely with "a servant's place."

If she was at cross-purposes with herself, Dorothea was also in discord with her culture. Beyond her own convictions, she had little upon which to base her dream of carving her niche in the world. Still she believed that if she remained faithful, God would someday reveal to her a great vocation. That the gender conventions of her day, which narrowly circumscribed women's careers, made this extremely implausible did not deter her.

Once settled in Boston, she set about trying to unravel the mystery of God's calling within the citadel of orthodoxy in Massachusetts: the established Congregational Church, whose origins stretched back to the Puritans and their glorious errand into the wilderness. Every morning, before the sun rose over Boston harbor, she was on her knees praying and reading the Scripture, preparing her heart to interpret the will of God. This was a lonely quest, although it was bolstered at every stage by the church.

Despite her religious intensity and her isolation, she was no mystic. From childhood, the minister's daughter had taken for granted the importance of the church—the community of the faithful and professional clergy—in opening the Word of God. While in Worcester she had joined in the Lynde family's traditional commitment to the Second Congregational Society, a progressive group that had split off from the hidebound First Parish in 1786. [53] Its minister was the Reverend Dr. Aaron Bancroft, father of the historian George Bancroft and a pioneer of liberal

Congregationalism who became the first president of the American Unitarian Association at its founding in 1825. Under Bancroft, young Dorothea had discovered for the first time in her life a theology that was reasonably tolerant and humane. Like other liberal Christians, he emphasized the harmony between reason and religion. His message was, according to his eulogist, "a logical consequence of the reaction against " the severities of our Puritan fathers." To Dorothea, Bancroft's views were a refreshing contrast to Methodist revivalism, and she embraced them in the course of putting her father's religion behind her.[54]

When at length she moved to Boston, she took another theological and intellectual step forward. Elijah Dix, and his widow after him, belonged to Hollis Street Church, where John Pierpont had been ordained in 1819. Pierpont, like Bancroft, was a man with broad humanist interests. He had practiced law before enrolling in the new Harvard Divinity School, and had garnered a modest reputation as a poet. What impressed Dorothea as she began attending Hollis Street was Pierpont's "saintlike eloquence" and his manifest devotion to benevolent and philanthropic activities. Pierpont, a paragon of the religious establishment, assumed that his ministry extended beyond the meetinghouse door to include the welfare of all Bostonians. Out of civic concern, he was a long-standing member of the Boston School Committee, a participant in the ministry-at-large to the city's poor, an active supporter of the Children's Mission and the Seamen's Bethel.[55]

Open to new sources of inspiration, and knowing something of poverty herself, Dorothea was captivated by Pierpont's sermons on the social obligations of Christians. Not long after moving to Orange Court she tried to convince her grandmother to let her set up a charity school for poor children in Dix Mansion. "God has placed us here to serve himself in serving his children of earth," she insisted. Echoing her minister's exhortations, she declared herself ready to become "an apostle in communicating the religion of Christ to those who sit in darkness." Perhaps she could emulate Hannah More, the English bluestocking author of moral tales, and rescue "some of America's miserable children from vice and guilt—dependence on the Alms-house" and, ultimately, "eternal misery." The hour was late, she charged Madam Dix. "*We shall not live long*: let us then if possible win souls for our passports into that world where sin and sorrow, and sickness and infirmity cannot come."[56]

The old woman regarded this plan with a cold eye. She had had quite enough religious enthusiasm in her family, and had resolved to turn Dorothea into a proper Bostonian lady whose horizons were confined to child rearing, fancy needlework, and parlor conversation. Little wonder that she disapproved of her granddaughter's scheme to open her beautiful home to urchins off the streets of Boston. But Dorothea was adamant. Pointing to her teaching experience in Worcester, she prevailed on her grandmother to let her furnish a room in the barn behind Dix Mansion and turn it into a charity school. Worn down by her granddaughter's persistence, Madam Dix finally relented, and in 1821 Dorothea began taking students. Over the next few years, she managed to open a second school within Dix Mansion itself that catered to a better class of students who could afford to pay their way.

These schools, at first somewhat informal and loosely organized, helped Dorothea focus her energies. As she attracted more students, she threw herself into her work with an intensity her friends thought compulsive. When Anne complained that their correspondence seemed to be tapering off, Dorothea explained that she was "closely occupied seven or eight hours daily, in school [and] called almost hourly to receive friends." In addition to running her school, she was saddled with the care of her two young brothers. Busy with household chores, and hounded by her grandmother to master the art of fancy needlework, Dorothea found that late evening was the only time she had for her assiduous course of study, and for introspection.[57]

One such evening, she carefully penned the following lines on a scrap of paper:

> *I was*
> *Was born on the 4th year of the century*
> *the 4th day of the month*
> *the 4th hour of the day*
> *My baptismal name of birth was by the initial letter D [which] represents the 4th*
> *letter of the alphabet . . .*
> *I am a 'Sunday Child' and 'child of Morning.'*[58]

Because she so rarely mentioned anything at all about her birth or her age, this fragment stands out. It has an air of idle musing, wistfulness—a little game she was playing with herself—and it entertains the idea of special distinction from birth. She was fond of puzzles and word games, collecting envelopes full of riddles she cut from the newspapers. What makes this fragment interesting, though, is that it misstates her actual date of birth by two years. She was in fact born on 4 April 1802. The note, neatly folded and enclosed in a blank, unsealed envelope, seems to have been written for her eyes only, a trivial piece of self-deception. Yet it reveals a pattern of thought that Dorothea developed early on and that became almost second nature as time passed. By changing her birth date, she was altering the real circumstances of her birth to fit a more appealing fiction.

This coincides with the fabrication that she was an orphan. Imagining oneself as an orphan is, of course, a classic fantasy. And it is easy to see why she preferred the idea of orphanage to the truth. To be an orphan meant she had no choice but to make her own chances, to live with whoever would take her in, to embrace whatever Worcester or Boston offered and use it as best she could. By thinking of herself as an orphan, she could rationalize settling into Dix Mansion while her mother eked out a living in Maine. As an orphan, she had no obligation to worry over the fate of Joseph and Mary Dix. Equally important, she could distance herself from character flaws she had found disgraceful in both parents. An orphan could wipe the slate clean and begin anew. And so she did. Throughout her life, Dorothea Dix was obsessed with an urge to re-create herself—to become more virtuous, more admirable, and more influential than she was. Conceiving of herself as a orphan was the practical first step in becoming a self-made woman.

Liberating as it was in some respects, Dorothea's renunciation of her parents carried a hidden price. It was, after all, tantamount to disowning part of herself. Much as she tried to suppress it, she continued to suffer the consequences of her childhood, never entirely able to banish it from her mind. The memory of Joseph and Mary Dix became her private affliction, and she was never able to enjoy any attainment free from its hurt. Homelessness thus stained the fabric of her identity.

Yet it is a measure of Dorothea Dix's genius that this pain was only partially debilitating. She covered up the hole in the emotional center of her life, and in a remarkable feat of psychological alchemy, Dorothea Dix eventually transmuted her personal heartbreak, and the rage it aroused, into an instrument of power. Eventually, it was her own fierce sense of privation that enabled her to identify so passionately with the mad, whom she unfailingly portrayed as the homeless and abandoned of America.

CHAPTER TWO

The Education of a Liberal Christian

Uncertain about just where she fit in society, and preoccupied though she was with the progress of her soul, still Dorothea was no hermit. The outside world beckoned. In Boston the 1820s were years of vitality and commercial growth, and she could scarcely help being drawn into the city's vibrant social scene. While her reclusive grandmother may have been content with her staying home, Anne Heath, who seemed to be on intimate terms with everyone who mattered, made sure that when invitation lists were drawn up, Dorothea's name was included.

Parlor gatherings, balls, and lavish cotillion parties, with ornately bedecked young ladies and gentlemen contradancing to the music of small string ensembles, were then the rage. Wives of wealthy merchants arranged private balls for as many as three hundred people, outdoing each other with extravagant banquets and elegant decor to attract the most fashionable set. Chefs trained in Paris and London piled sideboards high with roasted game, beef, mutton, poultry, and mounds of fresh fruit and vegetables. Cost seemed to be no object. During winter months they shipped in fresh produce from the South. Banquet tables were customarily decorated with flowers—vases of natural flowers along with delicate silk roses and apple blossoms, which, after supper, the ladies selected to ornament themselves. To Dorothea, who vividly recalled her earlier life on the edge of starvation, such opulence seemed both marvelous and sinfully excessive.[1]

In truth, it was abundant books, not food or finery, that she loved most in Boston. Because of its preeminence in cultivating the life of the mind, the city considered itself the Athens of America, and Dorothea's favorite attraction was the oak-paneled private library of the Boston Athenaeum. Her uncle Thaddeus Mason Harris, a scholar and himself a librarian, procured a borrower's card for her. And every week, roaming from subject to subject, she checked out scores of books. Three or four hours each night, after her brothers and grandmother had gone to bed, she worked pen in hand at her desk by the light of a small brass whale-oil lamp.

She attacked her studies voraciously, if not systematically. She read a smattering of the classics that were the hallmarks of a well-furnished mind—Homer, Virgil, Dante, Cervantes, and so on—and English poetry. Among contemporary poets, she liked Wordsworth the best. Yet she was equally captivated by the physical and natural sciences: astronomy, geology, botany, and entomology. Beyond their confessional aspect, her frequent letters to Anne served as commentaries on her studies.

She was a collector of facts, always preferring the tangible and concrete over abstraction and theory. Not that she lacked a romantic side. Walter Scott's Waverly novels, with their tales of intrigue and derring-do on the Scottish heath, stirred her imagination. By contrast, Washington Irving struck her as long-winded and overrated. John Locke, the epistemological philosopher, she dismissed as too abstruse. Out of obligation she tackled Webber's mathematics, the classic text, but she admitted that it overtaxed her powers of concentration.[2]

Beyond sheer intellectual curiosity, which she certainly had, Dorothea wanted to improve her education as a means to unriddling the mystery of God's calling. Books, she felt, could help lead her to the ultimate purpose of her life.

At the same time Dorothea was encountering men who stimulated her natural bent for idealism and service, and who sparked her confidence. In the period following her move to Boston, her most valuable intellectual influence was her uncle, Thaddeus Mason Harris. Uncle Harris, as Dorothea called him, had in 1795 married Mary Dix, the only daughter of Elijah and Dorothy Lynde Dix. He was the picture of determination and industriousness, qualities that had allowed him to escape the wretched poverty of his youth. His father had died during the Revolutionary War, and although his mother had told him he should reconcile himself to a humble life as a woodworker, he had put himself through Harvard by dint of native ability and hard work. After graduation, he stayed on in Cambridge to study theology and subsequently served for two years as librarian of Harvard College. He had aspired to become a minister in one of Boston's leading churches, but when none beckoned, he agreed to go to the newly developing community of Dorchester. There, over the years, he led his small congregation slowly into the liberal wing of Congregationalism and eventually, though he disliked the label, into Unitarianism.[8]

In the early 1820s, Dorothea regularly trekked south from Orange Court to Dorchester to attend her uncle's church services, and often spent her Sundays with the Harris family. For the first few years, she found this stimulating. Uncle Harris had wide-ranging intellectual interests and, feeling a burden of social responsibility, carried his ministry to the Boston Female Asylum and to the East Cambridge Jail. On occasion, Dorothea and one or two of the seven Harris children accompanied him on these errands of mercy.

Her favorite cousin was the oldest son, Thaddeus William Harris, who had in 1815 graduated from Harvard and in 1820 earned a degree in medicine. Young Harris worked as a physician, but he was a man of erudition whose inquiring mind was absorbed in studies of the natural sciences, particularly entomology and horticulture. Dorothea admired his sizable collection of bottled insects and dried plants, and she fell into the habit of collecting specimens herself that he helped her to identify and categorize. Before he married in 1824, he was her informal tutor—her personal Harvard College—patiently elaborating the standard systems of classification and introducing her to writings of leading scientists.

Meanwhile, Uncle Harris made suggestions to direct her reading and helped her negotiate Boston's network of libraries. He had traveled widely—to the western territories and, in connection with settling Elijah Dix's estate, to England—and was himself a source of substantial learning and intellectual encouragement. In addition, he was a longtime member of the American Antiquarian Society and the American Academy of Arts and Sciences, and later served as the Librarian of the

Massachusetts Historical Society. Undoubtedly his example spurred Dorothea's own tentative efforts at scholarship and writing. Imitating his practiced methods, for example, she formed a lifelong habit of close observation and began to keep notebooks to record her travels.

The longer Dorothea lived in Boston, however, she found herself drifting away from Dorchester. Geography was one obstacle. Despite its proximity, Dorchester was hard to get to, and the community remained a backwater, the public ignoring repeated attempts of land speculators to make it more attractive to new settlers. In consequence, Uncle Harris, whose pastoral style was, as one of his parishioners observed, "tender and affectionate rather than bold and discriminating," presided over a church barely large enough to support his family.[9]

There were also darker clouds. As her social awareness grew, Dorothea was put off by the odor of Freemasonry that lay over Thaddeus Mason Harris's reputation. Freemasonry, a fraternal association based on the principles of brotherly love, faith, and charity, had come to America from England in the early eighteenth century. The movement invited suspicion because it was wrapped in mystery, with reports of its initiates engaging in all manner of secret rituals. Harris not only joined up; while serving as chaplain for the grand lodge in Boston, he had published *Constitutions of the Ancient and Honorable Fraternity of Free and Accepted Masons* (1792), a book that later came back to haunt him. In the 1820s a nasty wave of antipathy to Freemasonry swept Boston, painting the Masons as a dangerous and subversive religious cult. For his part, it was said that poor Uncle Harris was subjected to vicious personal abuse. To Dorothea, this derision, along with her uncle's mercurial temperament, which fluctuated between elation and "seasons of depression and deep despondency," was frightfully reminiscent of her father and the world she had left behind.[10]

It was a measure of her industry and her rising intellectual self-confidence that, after two or three years of study and teaching at Orange Court, Dorothea crystallized her new learning into a book. The form she chose was a children's encyclopedia. Here she was following in the footsteps of her uncle Harris, who twenty years earlier had published a *Minor Encyclopedia* (1803) in four volumes. Dorothea's effort was much less ambitious: a basic lower-school reader and fact book she called *Conversations on Common Things; or, Guide to Knowledge: With Questions* (1824). Still, publishing any book was a remarkable accomplishment for a self-educated woman of twenty-two. Researching and writing it, she managed to introduce herself to a number of prominent scientists and men of letters, greatly widening her circle of correspondents.[11]

To her delight, the little volume quickly caught on with schoolteachers, perhaps because she departed from tired convention and presented her subject matter in the form of a dialogue between a mother and an inquisitive daughter. Since the book was lifted directly from Dorothea's reading notes, the daughter was made to ask her mother improbable questions like "Will you give me a particular description of the salt mines near Cracow?"[12] In any event, however limited its literary merit, Dorothea's first book turned out to be an unexpected financial success, so popular that it went through sixty editions before the Civil War.

Conversations on Common Things was written expressly for teachers— mainly women—by a young woman who was herself full of enthusiasm for learning, who idealized teaching, and who deeply believed in the value of a solid education for women and girls.

Whether or not she had read Mary Wollstonecraft's radical *Thoughts on the Education of Daughters* (1787), she implied a similar argument: namely, that women and men ought to be educated on equal terms. Learning, Dorothea showed, was not intellectual gilding. It was intrinsically useful and rewarding, not to mention socially indispensable, for respectable women. Ladies, no less than gentlemen, the argument went, were obliged to understand the world around them. As the woman and her charming daughter discuss everything from acacia trees to zinc, the good mother shows herself to be well read, thoughtful, and intelligent. Nor does she limit herself to feminine subjects. In the midst of a detailed discourse on mechanics, for example, the daughter asks why her mother has spent so much time studying machinery. "Should I not . . . suffer some degree of mortification," came the reply, "if unable to give any explanation of [the machine's] parts, and the principles upon which they are established?"[13]

Like Wollstonecraft, Dorothea had no patience for the argument, advanced by some of her contemporaries, that nature had not equipped the "weaker sex" for rigorous intellectual pursuits, and that ignorance in a lady was somehow becoming. Accordingly, she had her mother-teacher relate an anecdote about a would-be lady to whom the Duchess of Brunswick presented a dictionary as a gift. Because the pretentious woman was illiterate, she mistook the book for a novel and made a fool of herself in front of the assembled court. The moral was plain.

"Although she had hitherto considered that kind of knowledge which is derived from reading, as unbecoming and unnecessary for a woman of rank," the mother pointed out, "she now saw that learning was valued at court." Taking the lesson to heart, the daughter resolved to study diligently. "What society should I be fit for when I am older," she asked, "if I did not know more about books than she."[14]

Thus, beyond its compendium of facts, *Conversations on Common Things* could be read as a woman's and a girl's book. Admitting no discrepancy between femininity and knowledge, it held that women's intellectual potential was equal to men's, and that ideal womanhood—here embodied in the mother—was well read and articulate.[15]

Dorothea, thrilled by the modest success of her first book, lost no time in producing another volume for children. This time her subject was not the physical universe but the wonders of the invisible world. She titled it simply *Hymns for Children, Selected and Altered* (1825). Her material she gleaned readily from journals and commonplace books she had been keeping for years. Verses of scripture, followed by hymns, illustrated various moral and theological lessons, all meant to enrich the spiritual life of children.

In sharp contrast to the washed-in-the-blood-of-the-Lamb revival songs she had sung as a child, these hymns represented a thoroughly liberal attitude toward to Christianity. Like many Unitarian writers, Dorothea dabbled in newly available English translations of the sacred texts of Buddhism and Hinduism that were in vogue among the liberal intelligentsia. As she tried endeavored to convey a sense of the oneness of God and the brotherhood of humankind, she mixed fragments from Western and non-Western religious sources. She was a compulsive clipper of newspapers, stuffing envelopes with columns that caught her eye. The resulting book was a pastiche, juxtaposing lines from the *Upanishads* with conventional religious poetry she had saved from her reading. Here and there she slipped in a poem or psalm of her own. Readers, though, would scarcely have been able to distinguish her original contributions from the output of dozens of Unitarian versesmiths.

Writing books was a public activity. And convention held that authors of devotional books, particularly women authors, should be demurely self-effacing—invisible behind their work—avoiding personal attention as much as possible. So she published the volume anonymously. The title page simply attributed it to the "Author of *Conversations on Common Things*." Still, she felt vulnerable when she offered up her work to the public. "I expect you to call me self-sufficient, positive and 'Independent,'" she told Anne, "for I am determined to risk publishing the Hymns. It is not a trifle to hazard I know."[16]

When it appeared, though, her book was generally well received, and her confidence soared. The estimable Henry Ware, Jr., commended its design and execution, and applauded her, as he put it, for "devoting yourself to the useful." And her own pastor, John Pierpont, was gratifyingly effusive in his praise. In her own small way, she felt she was beginning to contribute to the life of Boston's respectable religious community, and that its leading lights valued her efforts. At the same time, within the conventions of devotional verse, she discovered a new medium that deepened her own voice and enriched her expressiveness. *Hymns for Children* thus represented an important step in the process of forming a public personality.[17]

Encouraged by small successes during her early twenties, Dorothea imagined she was destined to become a writer. Her first two books received favorable notices, after all, and they had provided an outlet for her restive imagination. Testing various forms over the next several years, she published a good deal of religious poetry, branched out into cautionary fiction for young people, and even tried her hand at writing a botanical book. The religious works after *Hymns for Children* include *Evening Hours* (1825), *Meditations for Private Hours* (1828), and *Selected Hymns for the Use of Children Families, or Sunday Schools* (1833). While none of these works were written as autobiography, they nonetheless contain pieces of a mosaic that reveals Dorothea's spiritual self-portrait. Whatever she wrote to express her personal theology also served to vent the turmoil in her inner life.

Fittingly, the prologue to *Meditations for Private Hours* set the tone for all of Dorothea's devotional writing. In it she thanked God for making Sunday a day of rest, a day to "retire from the perplexities of active life . . . and demand for my soul what progress it is making towards the mark of its high calling in Jesus Christ."[18] Most of the meditations, poems, and hymns that followed spoke of her quietly ferocious straining for perfection—for holiness and complete sanctification.

Although she had long since turned her back on Methodism, she continued to suffer the pangs of its existential dilemma. Feeling that sinful human nature was a constant drag on her soul, Dorothea saw temptations and snares everywhere. Childhood experience had taught her the bitter lesson that the flesh was inveterately weak, ready on the slightest whim to ignore God and one's duties to family and friends. Unlike the Calvinists, her perception of evil was not explicitly developed in terms of the doctrine of original sin. Nevertheless she depicted the condition of humankind as woefully fallen, separated from God by a chasm of Augustinian proportions. Human nature, she reckoned, was by nature hot-blooded, reckless, venal, and predisposed to betray the soul to everlasting shame.

Many of her meditations and prayers were pleas for strength to contain the anger that seethed inside her.

> When in my heart rise angry thoughts,
> And on my tongue are words unkind,
> With what strong chains, by what blest art,
> Shall I the wrathful spirit bind?
> How shall I check the passion fierce,
> My youthful bosom finds so strong,
> Which bids me utter words that pierce,
> And seek to do my brother wrong?[19]

Unless it was held in check by iron discipline, she seemed to say, a destructive impulse lurking within her, just below the surface, was in danger of boiling over.

This helps explain why Unitarianism appealed to her. Because if the Methodism she had known as a child, with its emotionalism and revivals, was fire, Unitarianism was ice. For some people it proved to be too frigid. Over the years, what Emerson called its "corpse cold" passionlessness eventually provoked the Young Turks of Transcendentalism to leave the Unitarian camp in rebellion.

But for a young woman whose upbringing had already contained an embarrassment of religious zeal, and who was convinced that her only redeeming feature was a keen mind, Unitarianism was a perfect antidote for what ailed her soul. To begin with, it was self-consciously cerebral. Although it paid lip service to the value of ecstatic religious experience, Unitarianism derived from reasoned discourse. Intellectually speaking, it was the epitome of restraint and open-minded tolerance. The Unitarians taught that there was no inconsistency between natural religion—those aspects of God that could be deduced from the wonders of creation and formed the basis for all religions—and revealed religion as it was set forth in the Bible. Unitarian ministers held that all types of religious experience were valid, and each had its proper role. Reason led the inquiring mind ineluctably to an awareness of God's existence. Then Christian revelation supplemented reason by sharpening one's knowledge of God's character and purposes.[20]

This convenient marriage of reason and revelation later came to be known as supernatural rationalism. And as a general approach to religion it appealed strongly to Dorothea. Not least, here was a theology that implied she could do something to effect her own salvation. By opening a channel to God, the theory went, the human mind played a crucial part in redemption. This was cause for hope and celebration, as she wrote,

> Awake, awake, my mind!
> Thy reasoning powers bestow,
> With intellect refin'd
> The God, who form'd thee, know.[21]

Ostensibly these words were aimed at children. Dorothea wanted to help them avoid the pain and confusion that had spoiled her own childhood. So she urged them to take advantage of their innocence, to be grateful that their "reason is unclouded," to exploit their natural abilities to learn new things, and to direct their uncorrupted "rational faculties" to "high, holy, and useful purposes" from the beginning.[22]

In distinct contrast to her obsession with impurity, sin, and moral failing, and her pleas for strength to master unruly passions ("Nor be my breath with anger hot"), Dorothea's notions of God and Christ sound platitudinous.[23] Like most of her contemporaries, she simply assumed Christ's role as savior and redeemer as a fact. In this respect, at least, hers was a simple faith. She felt no need to delve into complicated debates about the atonement or the precise character of the historical Jesus. When it came to biblical accounts of miracles, of Jesus' death and resurrection, she accepted the New Testament at face value:

> Diseases at his bidding fled;
> And life revisited the dead;
> He bade the raging tempests flee;
> He calmly walked upon the sea;
> By mighty power he left the grave,
> To which he stooped our souls to save'
> And numerous witnesses record
> The resurrection of our Lord.[24]

Though she grew up in the first age of historical biblical scholarship, a period when the unsettling, skeptical, ideas of German theologians were finding their way into the bookshelves of American intellectuals, she left theological speculation to others.

It was the human side of religion, and especially of Jesus, that transfixed her. She wrote empathetically of the Man of Sorrows, Jesus' example as the suffering servant, his humanity, his faultless obedience, and his horrible humiliation. As a man striving to seek and to save those who were lost, she said, Jesus directly touched human sympathies and feelings. The Jesus of the Gospels was no theologian, in her view, but a man of action. His consummate self-abnegation exemplified, in pure form, the ideal of service to God. He admonished his followers to lift up the weak and helpless. In return, human nature being what it is, he received "malice from men." In a fallen world, he was a divine misfit. As Dorothea imagined Jesus' life and death, his being so despised wrought a psychological torment even more terrible than the agony of crucifixion.

From her understanding of Jesus, Dorothea concluded that the essence of Christianity lay in his simple command to feed the poor and comfort the sick.

> That mutual wants and mutual care
> May bind us man to man.
> Go clothe the naked, feed the blind,
> Give the weary rest;
> For sorrow's children comfort find,
> And help for all distressed.[25]

This was how she interpreted Jesus' words "the poor you have with you always," not as his disregard of poverty but as his direct challenge to the faithful to follow in his footsteps. Or, in his words, "Go and do likewise."

Meanwhile, in an effort to reach a wider audience, Dorothea also experimented with fiction. Making good on her intention to emulate Hannah More, in 1828 she published *Ten Stories for Children* (subsequently revised and published as *American Moral Tales* [1832]). These typical fables, written in flat prose, are didactic parables that dramatize the importance of basic moral virtues. Dorothea, casting about for plots, scenes, and characters, drew upon her own unpleasant memories of childhood. These stories, more than any other biographical material, fill some of the void about the quality of her inner life as a young girl. In the guise of fiction, the moral tales come as close to an autobiography of her childhood as she ever ventured.

Dorothea wrote about two kinds of relationships. In the first type, a stubborn, strong-willed child comes into conflict with parents or relatives. Before long, the parents or guardians die or are otherwise forced to abandon the child, who, as a result of their neglect, ends up a miserable orphan. In counterpoint, a few stories illustrate a happier theme: sketches of lucky children who are in harmony with their virtuous parents. Like the good mother in *Conversations on Common Things*, these parents are at heart teachers who encourage their children's education and moral instruction.[26]

Good parents are exceptions, though, and most of Dorothea's stories are family tragedies. Indeed, they are nightmares about parental neglect and irresponsibility, the powerlessness of children to escape the circumstances of their birth, and the death of parents. "John Williams; or the Sailor Boy," for example, is narrated by a respectable gentleman who comes across an eleven-year-old boy in rags roaming the city streets. It turns out that the boy's father had been a God-fearing man who foolishly left his small woodworking shop for the lure of a better-paying job in a distillery. Before long he succumbed to the enticement of rum, and within a matter months sank into perpetual drunkenness. When he died at last in the local almshouse, his poor son had nowhere to turn. This is where the well-to-do narrator comes upon the scene; but he does not reach out to lend the boy a helping hand. As far as the urchin is concerned, the moral is clear: the poor should expect no deus ex machina to save them. The narrator, a staunch, unsentimental believer in self-reliance, concludes his tale with the pious comment that "as he was very young, something might be done to eradicate the seeds of wickedness thus early sown in his heart, and in their place cultivate virtuous and religious principles."

"Blind Mary" ends, as it begins, with violence and loss, as the poor heroine's mother and father fall victim to fatal illnesses. "Alice and Ruth" watch their father waste away as their frail and ineffectual mother strives in vain to keep the family together. One hauntingly bleak story, "James Coleman," is an obvious reworking of Dorothea's earlier move to Boston and Orange Court.[27]

There was doubtless a therapeutic benefit from to writing these stories. "Write!" the columnist and novelist Fanny Fern exhorted Dorothea's generation of women, "to lift yourselves out of the dead-level of your lives [and] to lessen the number who are yearly added to our lunatic asylums from the ranks of the misappreciated, unhappy womanhood, narrowed by lives made up of details."[28] To be sure, Dorothea's writing was partly an effort to lift herself out of the doldrums of quiet desperation. But it was also something more. In reshaping her memories of childhood into moral lessons, she grappled with her most deeply buried and disturbing ordeal. Transforming her memories into fiction was an important step toward maturity. It gave her a way to bring order to chaos, to assign her demons their roles in a moral universe, and thus to tame them. Fiction enabled her to reconcile the person she was becoming—capable, learned, independent—with her shameful past.

In several of her moral tales, Dorothea introduced characters who represented her maturing personality: young adults who loved books and knew the value of education, who stepped in and took charge of rebellious children, and managed them with just the right combination of firmness and kindness to set them on the right path. This was the kind of nurture that as a child she had sorely missed. Reflecting on her own odyssey, however, Dorothea was coming to understand that while she could not change her past, she could discover ways to put it to good use.[29]

The intellectual quickening that encouraged Dorothea to take up the pen also reverberated in her social and religious life. As she prepared her first books for publication, she found herself bored by Pierpont's interminable sermons at Hollis Street, and quietly began to look around for a church of her own. As her horizons opened up, her grandmother's minister seemed to belong not to the mainstream of liberalism but to the party of the past. "I am greatly changed in sentiment," Dorothea confided to Anne, or "else he is." Younger Bostonians considered Pierpont stodgy. Gradually Dorothea found herself contrasting him unfavorably with younger and more spirited clergymen.[30]

The more she became sensitive to the subtle shades and textures of religious life in Boston, the more Dorothea sensed that she was in the midst of a spiritual revolution. Pillars of Congregationalism like Pierpont were plainly losing their grip, and a new Unitarian elite was seizing the reins, vigorously redirecting liberal Christianity. The Unitarian movement, she came to believe, represented the party of the future.

Looking to make their own mark, its prophets unapologetically announced their liberation from the tired formality and tedious theological hairsplitting of the previous generation. Their voices, full of optimism and hope, captured Dorothea's imagination. As though making up for lost time, she attended every sermon and lecture she could. During a single week in the early 1820s, for instance, she reported hearing Henry Ware, Jr., Nathaniel Frothingham, Ezra Stiles Gannett, and, most important of all, the charismatic father of Unitarianism, William Ellery Channing.[31]

These men were the vanguard of liberal Christianity in Boston. They assumed the name Unitarian because, unlike those whose faith rested on the Trinity (Father, Son, and Holy Spirit), they proclaimed God's essential oneness or unity. From this principle flowed their conviction in the vital connection among all of humankind. If God was one, they reasoned, it followed that in relation to him every person was equal.

Clearly this belief held radical social implications. From the start, since they held that God was blind to social distinctions, Unitarians styled themselves as being on the side of the poor and the unfortunate. That their idealistic commitment to social justice was more rhetorical than practical did not weaken its appeal for Dorothea. Henry Ware, Jr., a genteel Harvard man renowned for his eloquent, extemporaneous preaching, won her admiration with a series of Sunday evening services in his Second Church for the "benefit of the poorer classes." Ware's message was straight noblesse oblige. Yet, if Dorothea's reaction is any indication, his words pricked the conscience of his audience, making them more sensitive to the poverty around them than they had been before.

When it came to stepping off the pulpit and actually rubbing elbows with the city's poor, though, it was not Ware but Joseph Tuckerman who set the standard. Scion of an enormously wealthy merchant family, he had served for twenty years as pastor of the Congregational Church in Chelsea, just north of Boston harbor. Constantly reminding well-heeled Bostonians that Christ would say at the Last Judgment, "as you have done to the least of these, so you have done also to me," Tuckerman impressed the community as a man of personal charisma and extraordinary commitment to practice what he preached. When in 1823 she first heard him speak, Dorothea was transfixed by the inspirational power of his message. "Yes he was indeed eloquent and zealous," she wrote. "I could have listened to the persuasive tones of his voice for hours."[32]

The most persuasive thing about Tuckerman, though, was not his words but the remarkable example he set with his ministry-at-large. During the first four years of what he termed his "permanent ministry to the poor," he logged more than 4,500 visits to people's homes. This immersion in the human reality of poverty was eye-opening. Poor people, he realized, did not match the popular Jacksonian assumption that the destitute deserved their fate and that those who failed to pull themselves up by their own bootstraps were somehow morally deficient. Tuckerman's poor were, by and large, virtuous men and women who, through various, mostly unavoidable, misfortunes, had plunged through the partition that separated ordinary citizens from the abyss of poverty. And the ice was very thin indeed. An illness, a fire, a robbery, the death of the family breadwinner—there were hundreds of reasons why good people had become unable to support themselves decently. A ministry to the poor, he quickly saw, had to go beyond sermonizing. These people clearly needed more than moral instruction. They needed food, clothing, and coal for the winter; and the minister took it upon himself to help supply their material wants.[33]

For Dorothea, who kept her own firsthand experience of poverty in the back country to herself, the most compelling aspect of Tuckerman's work concerned Boston's impoverished children. Much of the impulse behind her teaching came from her desire to save children. She was already providing some free schooling to children who could not otherwise afford it. And whenever she could break away from Dix Place, she spent time collecting old clothes, shoes, and books for Tuckerman to distribute.[34]

Perhaps most important of all, from Joseph Tuckerman's example she saw that an individual working in cooperation with institutions— churches in his case—could make a concrete difference in the lives of the downtrodden. Hence Dorothea began to consider not only how organizations might play a role in channeling humanitarian aspiration into concrete social reform; she began to wonder how she herself could participate more meaningfully in the process.

Increasingly she shunned social functions and made church services, religious lectures, and small benevolent projects into the center of her social life. Like many New Englanders, she became a virtual connoisseur of pulpit oratory. Listening closely and taking notes, she weighed each preacher's sermons and colloquies. Her letters to Anne, and to her friend Mrs. Torrey, many written on Sunday evenings, were packed with minute summaries and commentaries on what she had absorbed during the preceding week. Her correspondence shows that she learned a great deal from the preachers. She knew and understood the finer points of theological argumentation (although when she wrote for the public she carefully avoided points of doctrinal dispute); she pondered various theories of benevolence and philanthropy that were being debated around Boston. In certain ways she began to think like a preacher. With regard to her own rhetoric, for example, she adopted a sermonic style, a habit of stringing together facts and anecdotes to support overarching moral conclusions.

She expected great things of herself. During this phase of her life, Dorothea searched constantly for new inspiration and for new ways, as she put it, to identify "with the virtuous great . . . who 'tread the path of duty.'" When in 1823 she met a young minister named Ezra Stiles Gannett at a party in the company of Ralph Waldo Emerson—an affair at which, according to one of her friends, "she looked sweetly & and was very much admired"—Dorothea thought she had finally met a man who measured up to her ideals. He was charming in every respect. A graduate of the new Harvard Divinity School, Gannett, who was just a year older than Dorothea, was already playing a vital part in forming the American Unitarian Association. Upon first hearing him preach, she imagined Gannett dramatically "shrouded in that mantle 'ere the prophet's flight from earth began / Dropt in the world / A sacred gift to man." Recognizing his gifts, William Ellery Channing, then in the process of shaping the Unitarian movement's organizational structure, recruited Gannett to become his second-in-command at the Federal Street Church. "By nature an organizer, not a seeker, of material," as his son later described him, Gannett was the most genteel of ministers, equally revered for his compassion, his spirit of toleration, his fervor for restoring to Christianity what he called its "first purity," and his conviction that religion should directly engage the problems of society. Gannett's sentiments perfectly matched Dorothea's ideals. In her view, he shone as the embodiment of religious activism.[35]

Drawing on their common outlook and the interests they shared, Dorothea and the young preacher struck up a friendship that some of Dorothea's friends mistook for budding romance. One busybody named Josephine Waters, for instance, provoked Dorothea's consternation by predicting that they would soon be married to each other.

Blithely ignoring Dorothea's protests, she spread the rumor that it was just a matter of time. "If I were a Swedenborgian I should be sure you were spiritually united now," she said, "you are so much alike."[36]

Dorothea scorned such chatter. Nevertheless, she could not help wondering what Gannett's "matrimonial intentions" really were. In one of the rare gossipy references in her letters to Anne, she confided that she expected him soon to marry "a Hingham lady," adding wistfully that the "season has been fatal to Bachelors." Her expectation proved correct. Shortly thereafter Gannett did indeed marry. If Dorothea was saddened, though, she seems to have kept it to herself. She and Gannett continued to move in the same circles, and over the years their paths crossed frequently. He visited Dorothea in 1837 in England when she was recovering from illness and he was embarking on a European holiday with his wife. In 1845, apparently at Dorothea's request, the graying minister sent her a lock of his hair that she saved for the rest of her life in her hope chest.[37]

It is tempting to wonder whether in other circumstances, at age twenty-four or so, Dorothea would have entertained a proposal from

Dorothea Dix in her late twenties.

Gannett. He was, after all, a physically attractive man who certainly conformed to her romantic ideals of genius, gentility, and moral worth. Yet he was by the same token a man of his time who assumed a conventional attitude toward women and the separate domestic sphere in which they were supposed to exercise their capacities. Nothing suggests that he was in the market for an ambitious, driven woman. His published sermons show that he cherished domesticity, the expected constraints of femininity, in the role of the good wife. Perhaps, in this instance at least, when it came to romantic entanglements, courtship, and marriage, Dorothea's aspirations and gifts worked against her.

In the fall of 1827, partly to expand her horizons and partly to avoid the respiratory ailments that the icy Boston winters seemed to bring on, Dorothea traveled south to Philadelphia. At the behest of Gannett and Pierpont, she arranged to stay in the home of the Reverend William Henry Furness, the progressive pastor of the First Congregational Unitarian Church of Philadelphia. A longtime friend of Ralph Waldo Emerson, and one of the first American translators of German theology and literature, Furness was at the time just beginning to think about the relationship between religion and social conditions. Intellectually, he and Dorothea had a good deal in common. Socially, there were many interconnections as well. Furness had been a close friend of Gannet's when both had roomed in Divinity Hall at Harvard, and he remained closely allied with the clique of liberal ministers around Boston who spawned Unitarianism. When she first arrived in Philadelphia Dorothea was uneasy, diffident, worrying that she had been foolish to leave her friends in Boston "to come among strangers." Within a few weeks, though, she warmed up to Furness and his wife.[38]

Unitarianism in Quaker Philadelphia, she learned, was a far cry from Boston. In fact it was a one-man movement. The only Unitarian minister between New York and Baltimore, Furness preached to a small congregation in a brick building on the corner of Tenth and Chestnut Streets. Traditionally, Philadelphia churches were conservative, and for years the local Unitarian society had drifted along without firm leadership. When he arrived in the city, Furness was dismayed to find that Unitarians were "about as obscure and despised as any company of Methodists or such like are in Boston." Even so, in this inhospitable environment, his Philadelphia church quickly became more self-conscious in its liberalism, more activist, and, eventually, more radical in its theology than the Unitarian mainstream in Boston. Alive to the shifting currents of theological change, a lifelong correspondent of Emerson's, Furness rejected orthodox Christian doctrines like the Trinity. Indeed, his later career as a biblical scholar brought him into the orbit of the Transcendentalists, a loose confederation of intellectual ministers and writers so liberal that their ideas sometimes transcended Christianity itself.[39]

Some of his more abstruse theological speculations baffled Dix, and probably most of his parishioners as well. Overcoming some initial uneasiness, however, Dorothea discovered that the real basis of Furness's religion was an idea she was fully prepared to believe: that the Christ of the Gospels was not a spirit cloaked in human form but essentially human. In classical terms, this was a heresy called Socinianism, heretical because the theory seemingly debased Jesus, robbing him of his divinity. Furness argued, however, that since God inhabited the entire universe, the divine spirit flowed through all humans. It was not so much that Jesus was merely human, he declared, but that all humans contained the spark of divinity. Jesus perfectly revealed this latent human godliness. If one went along with this logic, it followed that Jesus' message of enlightenment applied less to the world to come than to the present age.[40]

A message like this might easily have sounded like so much intellectual spectulation had Furness been a less magnetic figure. But people were naturally drawn to the man—handsome, a superb orator, an inspirational teacher with a gift for turning acquaintances into friends.

Within a month he gained Dorothea's confidence and gently coaxed his houseguest out of her shell. First Church was not large but, having survived a stagnant period, it was rejuvenated and had quadrupled in size since Furness had taken charge. For her part, Dorothea, freed from the routine of watching after her grandmother and brothers, began to spread her wings. In the small parsonage's parlor at tea time, during the social hours after church services and Bible studies, amid her perambulations along the red brick sidewalks near the center of town where she walked with the minister's wife and her Ladies Aid Society, Dorothea experienced a sense of freedom, relishing her role as the bright young stranger from Boston. Faced with small groups of curious strangers, she was gratified to find how easily she could command and hold attention as she comfortably held her own in conversation with members of Philadelphia's intellectual and social elite.

The better she got to know it, the city established by William Penn and the Society of Friends appealed to Dorothea, for in its own way it was more committed to charitable pursuits than was Boston. Moreover, its social hierarchy seemed less calcified. In due course, she received invitations to dine with a number of Furness's leading parishioners—scholars, merchants, bankers—and within a few months in Philadelphia, she felt an uplifting sense of freedom and confidence that came from being bid to join a new social circle. People accepted her on her own merits and she quickly made new friends, including an enduring relationship with Rembrandt Peale, Charles Wilson Peale's son and a popular painter in his own right. Her initial fear that she was "unequal to forming new associations" lifted as she met companionable people who obviously shared her ideals of Christian service and social welfare. Above all, Furness's congregation—a "solid phalanx of wealth and dignity," as it has been called—conformed to her notions of gentility. For its members aptly embodied both mercantile success and noblesse oblige.[41]

If she spoke cautiously and chose her words with care, her voice nevertheless carried a tone of authority. Increasingly, as they came to know her better, people solicited her ideas and quizzed her about the state of affairs in Boston. As a teacher and published author, for instance, she could opine on public education with Walter R. Johnson, the principal of the new Franklin Institute High School and a well-known naturalist. And Furness himself, recently appointed director of the public schools, was eager to draw upon her practical experience as a teacher. Realizing that her social opinions carried weight, and suddenly curious to compare how those at the bottom of society lived in Boston and Philadelphia, Dorothea decided to put her days to use by making a field study of "humane institutions of Philadelphia."

So it was that, in the cold, soggy February and March of 1828, she commenced her first survey of the lower orders. Hers was a most modest beginning. To start, she made a survey of infant schools along the lines of the ones she had run in Boston. Next, recalling Joseph Tuckerman's innovative social ministry back in Boston, she checked in on other schools, including one Quaker charity school for the deaf and dumb. Her first instinct was revulsion. Seeing these poor, silent souls, many of whom were thought in addition to their obvious physical handicaps to suffer mental disorders, she wrote that her feelings were at first "altogether painful." Once she got over her initial shock, however, her mood brightened into "a more cheerful state of mind." Pitiful as the scene was, attendants told her stories of how, before the school existed, such children languished in attics and basements, horribly filthy and neglected. And if they were scarcely serene, they had been far worse off in the past. The asylum school had at least cleaned them up and made them as presentable as anyone so afflicted could be. In light of the darker alternatives, she observed, the asylum provided a great service, teaching "so many unfortunate beings . . . so well the good purposes of life."[42]

Interest in institutions like the one she visited was in the air. In 1827, for example, the year before her visit, the Guardians of the Poor of the City and Districts of Philadelphia had appointed a commission to study poor relief along the northeastern seaboard. Following its investigation, the commission had published a report detailing visits to workhouses and almshouses in Boston, New York, and Baltimore. The document painted an ugly picture of urban poverty in the new republic. Everywhere they had gone, the commissioners had come across lunatics and idiots locked up promiscuously with other paupers. While the insane poor were not the main subject of their report, those who read it and the excerpts that appeared in local newspapers were appalled by the commission's findings. To Dorothea Dix, who in her previous charity work had seen enough chaos in Boston's almshouse to appreciate the commissioners' accuracy, the Philadelphia report doubtless suggested a more pervasive problem than she had ever considered.[43]

In Philadelphia, excited to be on her own, she took notes, read, discussed reform, absorbing everything she could. The upbeat atmosphere of the Furness household was invigorating. And she was in a positive frame of mind, eager to take on a new challenge, as she prepared to return to Boston. Over the winter her respect for Furness had increased greatly, she wrote, for she had "never seen the beauty of the truth more beautifully illustrated than in his mind." Even as she departed, already she was planning to return to Philadelphia the following year to visit her newly adopted "second home."[44]

Dorothea admired men like Tuckerman, Gannett, and Furness, but she did not look to them to fill the disturbing void, the hole in the window of her past, left by her father. This role she reserved for William Ellery Channing, the physically frail, spiritually luminous genius of liberal Christianity.

Dorothea first heard him preach under the gothic arches of the Federal Street Church in the fall of 1823, shortly after he had returned to Boston from a grand tour of Europe. He was then forty-three, a youthful, handsome man, slightly built, with fine features, a high forehead, and light brown hair just beginning to gray at the temples. Already he had served as pastor of his church for two decades.

About the time she had first moved into Dix Place, he had come to public prominence by joining a series of theological controversies in which he defended the Unitarian position against the old guard of Trinitarian and Calvinist ministers. Preaching, lecturing, writing letters and pamphlets, Channing rose to become liberal Christianity's moral and intellectual leader. Hungry for fresh ideas, Dorothea devoured his published sermons. At the time, the most notable of these was "Unitarian Christianity," the credo and the definitive document of Unitarianism. Preaching an ordination sermon for a young minister named Jared Sparks, Channing crystallized the movement's main themes: the essential unity of God and Christ, "the moral perfection of God," and the importance of human reason in interpreting the Bible.

When Dorothea began to visit Channing's church, she found it a refreshing contrast to the stodgy congregation at Hollis Street. Channing's oratory, so quietly delivered that listeners strained to hear his words, was mesmerizing. Elizabeth Palmer Peabody, two years Dorothea's junior and just embarking on her own career as a teacher and writer, vividly remembered her first impression of Channing's preaching. He appeared at first unassuming, "a small man, with a rapid, nervous motion, dressed in a traveller's-great-coat," she wrote. But when he ascended the pulpit, took up the hymn book and started to read, everything changed. "Slowly lifting up his large, remarkable eyes," she recalled, Channing's face shone "with the expression of *seeing something*." There he was in their midst, she could not help but believe, "communing with God, face to face." Few could resist his charisma. After hearing Channing deliver Ezra Stiles Gannett's ordination sermon, Henry Ware, Jr., a careful student of pulpit oratory, exclaimed that "to hear such a sermon is one of the memorable things in a man's life. It forms an epoch in his existence." Channing presented a striking contrast to John Pierpont, and Dorothea instantly understood why he never preached to an empty pew. Federal Street Church was crowded each Sunday with many of Boston's brightest and most engaging people. Over her grandmother's objection that she lacked

William Ellery Channing, the father of Unitarianism.

"solidity and seriousness of feeling," and that Unitarianism was just a passing fad, Dorothea told Anne that she had finally found "a church of my own."[45]

Poring over his published essays with a new devotee's fervor, she told Anne she could not believe that she had not earlier placed "a higher estimate upon his writings." She extolled the virtues of his "Sermons on Infidelity," saying "what an admirable writer—how manly and decisive his reasoning!—if we had a few more such preachers, one would suppose there could no such monster as Irreligion exist."

With Channing, James Martineau once observed, "the intensity of the moral sentiment within him absorbed everything into itself."[46] More than any other quality, it was his moral certitude, wrapped in a mysterious delphic aura of personal magnetism, that captivated Dorothea. Nor was she alone. Everyone who wrote about him was in awe of Channing's profound inner calm, a stillness that insinuated wisdom. "He seemed to me a fixed centre," wrote Elizabeth Palmer Peabody, "around which was much revolution of thought in Massachusetts."

Channing's wealth only enhanced his reputation. His wife, née Ruth Gibbs, was the daughter of George Gibbs II, one of New England's richest merchants and great land barons, a man whose fortune Elijah Dix might well have envied. Ruth Channing's inheritance enabled the Channing family to purchase one of the finest brick mansion houses on Mount Vernon Street, at the highest point of Beacon Hill. Like his friend Joseph Tuckerman, though, Channing eschewed the complacency of material comfort. Indeed, he used his freedom from the demands of workaday capitalism to attack what he saw as its disagreeable consequences.

Around the time Dorothea first walked into his church, he had cautiously begun broaching the subject of how the lower orders lived, and what conscientious Christians ought to do to help them. His first step was to appoint a social action committee. Chosen from the church's trustees, its members were charged with defining a mission to the poor and figuring out ways to support it financially. Since the church routinely did the same thing for missions to Indians and heathen in foreign countries, this planning committee was not a radical proposal. When they first convened, the group served as a forum for discussing a broad range of social reforms: educational reform, investigation of conditions in jails and almshouses, and renewed efforts to reduce drunkenness among the poor. By June 1824, what was called the Association of the Members of the Federal Street Society for Benevolent Purposes was endeavoring to organize itself to reach out into the community and play an activist role.[47]

It was at this time—in the early stage of development of the Unitarian social conscience—that Dorothea happened to meet Channing and his wife at the house of a friend. He had just finished delivering a sermon formally to install Gannett as associate minister at Federal Street, reputedly one of his most affecting performances, entitled "The Demands of the Age on the Ministry." The present age, Channing told his audience, was not, as so many of them seemed to think, an age of progress. No, it was an age of sin and moral decline, "obviously and grossly defective when measured by the Christian standard." Young Gannett, about to assume his ministerial post, would go forth as a sheep among wolves. Even so, Channing insisted, this was exactly as it should be, for God never intended his apostles to isolate themselves in "the cell of the monk, and the school of the verbal disputant." A Christian's duty, Channing said, was to press vigorously "into life and society."[48]

These words were not lost on Dorothea. For young, idealistic people groping for ways to change the world, Channing's message was a call to arms. Inspired, Dorothea was eager to talk with Channing about what she herself could do to help solve the burning problems of the age.

Cordially, he told her that he would give the matter some thought and suggested she call on him at home. She did, and a few days later she reported to Anne that she had "spent a pleasant hour with him and Mrs. Channing." William Ellery Channing knew a forceful personality when he saw one, and, sensing her energy, he proposed that if she wanted to contribute to the life of his church she should teach a class in the Federal Street Sabbath School. At first Dorothea demurred, remonstrating that her health was too delicate to add Sunday to her full-time teaching schedule. The following week, though, Channing suggested that she combine her efforts and form a Sunday school class at Federal Street made up mainly of girls from her own school. Eager to please him and envisaging "the great good *Teachers* might effect if they gave themselves earnestly to the labour," she agreed.[49]

Her initial hesitation soon disappeared. The eight teachers she joined in the Federal Street Society were from leading Boston families, the sort of acquaintances Dorothea wanted to cultivate. Within a week, she met Francis Cabot, and the two of them were offered the editorship of a Unitarian literary newsletter. Pleading overwork, she begged off, but she felt a growing pride in being associated with people of Cabot's caliber. At the same time, however, she was bothered by a feeling that she did not fit in with the other teachers. When her Uncle Harris fell ill and she had to move into his modest frame house in Dorchester for a month to help look after him, she had to give up attending the society's weekly evening meetings. In the Harris home, she was still the daughter of Joseph and Mary Dix, and the longer she remained there, she told Anne, the greater were her feelings of isolation and exclusion.[50]

Even so, she managed to see Channing often at church, at his home, and at the homes of mutual friends. The more she was around him, the more Dorothea was impressed by the minister. He possessed all the sophistication, social status, and discipline that Joseph Dix had lacked. And he seemed intuitively, almost mystically, responsive to his young parishioner's inner struggle to find a sense of purpose. Channing's peculiar cool charisma appealed to many young men and women in Boston, and he in turn appears to have enjoyed being the center of a cult of personality.

Occasionally he took bright young women into his home to help with domestic chores and to look after his three children. During the mid-1820s, Dorothea began spending part of her time with the Channings, principally as a tutor. In 1827 she took it as a high honor when the great man asked her to accompany his family as a governess at their summer house near Newport. Putting aside her earlier resolution to take the summer off, she forgot about her weariness and was soon telling friends that, in any case, the Rhode Island sea air would be more therapeutic than idleness. There was also, as her friend Josephine Waters reminded her, "the great privilege you enjoy of intimate association with so great a man as Dr. Channing," including the prospect of contributing her own "testimony respecting his private hours, when his life shall be written."[51]

The Channings summered at Oakland, as their estate was called, every year. When she first arrived in 1827, Dorothea had the impression of stepping into a magical world. The estate had been purchased in 1796 by Channing's father-in-law, George Gibbs II. Beautifully situated, overlooking the sea, the imposing main house sat on eighty acres. The mansion, built in the colonial style of the late eighteenth century, was filled with hardwood furniture, finely detailed cabinets, ceramics, and carpets that its owner had collected from Europe and Asia. After George Gibbs died, the estate remained in the family under the supervision of his daughter Sarah, Ruth Channing's younger sister, who ran Oakland with gracious authority and who saw to it that its wealth was softened by an air of Yankee rusticity. Elizabeth Peabody, a frequent guest at Oakland, remembered that life there was simple and idyllic, devoted to reading and meditation, driving afternoons in a rough wagon for exercise and wading in the surf with "a strong Negro servant . . . on hand for accidents."[52]

Dorothea's mornings were occupied by reading to the Channing children and leading them on walks through the woods, where they collected wildflowers, and along the seashore, where they combed the sand for shells. Her afternoons were her own. But she was unable to relax and was inveterately impatient with leisure. She was driven to do something productive. During her first week at Oakland, she discovered that Aunt Sarah, as everyone called her, had built a chapel on one end of the estate in honor of her parents. Sarah Gibbs was a confirmed Episcopalian, so superstitious, it was said, that she had never entered her brother-in-law's church. Her own small chapel was a jewel. Washington Allston, the celebrated portraitist, had been commissioned to finish the interior with a carved, floor-to-ceiling mural. After visiting the empty chapel, Dorothea decided it should be put to use for the edification of the Newport community. She persuaded Channing to read weekly lessons from the Gospels. Then, with Aunt Sarah's hesitant approval, she went into town and recruited a "class of troublesome men and boys," apparently dockworkers and sailors, whom she brought to Oakland each week. Her aim was to straighten them out by exposing them to a refined atmosphere and by reading them moral lessons and Bible verses. Perhaps they came to Oakland out of curiosity, or for the promise of a meal, or to catch a glimpse of the famous Channing. But once they arrived, according to Channing's daughter, they fell under Dorothea's spell, subject to her "charm of manner and firm will."[53]

During the late 1820s Dorothea continued to teach and to help Madam Dix with the day-to-day management of Dix Mansion. Not that time thawed her grandmother's reserve. A friend of Dorothea's who occasionally visited Orange Court described the old woman stiffly "seated at her little table, with her book by her side, & her knitting in her hands [looking] the very picture of propriety & politesse of the 'old regime.'" As far as her granddaughter was concerned, Madam Dix conveyed a gloomy air of estrangement whose effect was thoroughly depressing. For example, Madam Dix, far from sympathizing with Dorothea during her recurrent illnesses, blamed her for bringing troubles on herself. "She said that you would not let those who love, be happy, because you were constantly making yourself sick by imprudent exertion," Helen Loring, a young woman who sometimes looked after her grandmother, told Dorothea. Madam Dix considered Dorothea's Sunday school activities at the Federal Street Church foolish, even self-destructive. "I do seriously think the knowledge that you are keeping a Sunday School—has destroyed all her hopes of y[ou]r returning strength," Loring continued, "& is the cause of great unhappiness to her."[54]

Dorothea, of course, harbored more than enough guilt and anger without her grandmother's adding to the burden. Under the weight of her persistent disapproval Dorothea lamented to Anne, "I never possessed much vivacity[,] at least since childhood, and I believe the small degree I have of late years obtained has been wholly lost."[55]

Partly it must have been an instinct for self-preservation that prompted her, around 1829, to move out of Dix Mansion. Her brothers were already gone. A few years earlier young Joseph Dix had opened a small dry goods store in Boston. In the business downturn of 1829, her brother Charles, who had yet to settle on a career, was

Dorothea Dix's grandmother, Madam Dorothy Dix, sometime in her seventies. (By permission of the Houghton Library.)

unable to find work. But by the end of the year, after working odd jobs around the merchant fleet in Boston harbor, he had decided to go to sea. Nothing compelled her to remain with her grandmother, so she rented modest quarters on Willow Street.

Channing, moreover, offered an antidote to her domestic melancholy. "Near him you may suppose that anyone may, if they choose[,] be happy," she explained to Anne. "He imparts the peace of his own spirit to those around him." In his company, Dorothea was alive to the beauty of the external world. Recalling their return passage from Oakland to Boston in June 1829, for instance, she described "gentle winds, sunshine and shower; thunder, lightning, rainbows; glorious masses of clouds, and the most resplendent sunset. Oh I shall never forget it. I never so wholly enjoyed a day; it was 'spirituelle'; it cannot be forgotten."[56]

The emotional focus of her life shifted from Orange Court to Mt. Vernon Street, where Channing steadily expanded her duties in his household. By 1830, she had become so much a part of the family that when Channing decided to visit the Caribbean, he naturally asked her to accompany them.

What spurred this trip was Ruth Channing's deteriorating health. Her husband later remarked that she "had long been losing strength under rheumatic complaints, and I resolved to make for her sake one great effort" to alleviate her symptoms. In fact, infirmity was rife within the household. Never robust, the minister himself seemed "too frail for earth," as Dorothea put it. And, for her own part, respiratory congestion and general fatigue had worsened to the point where by the end of summer, she felt she had no choice but to give up her school. Not that this helped much. "Even without the exertion of school duty," one of her friends told her, "how often did your wan appearance & feeble voice excite my fears." In September Channing contemplated a voyage to Cuba, but the next month he changed his mind and arranged instead to stay on St. Croix in the home of a wealthy parishioner until spring.[57]

Beyond its therapeutic benefits, a trip to the Caribbean promised intellectual adventure. For the past year or so, spared the daily drudgery of teaching, Dorothea had been working under the tutelage of her cousin Thaddeus William Harris to improve her knowledge of the natural sciences. At his behest, she approached Benjamin Silliman, whom she had heard lecture in the Boston Lyceum and who was well on his way to becoming America's leading geologist. To introduce herself—apparently without realizing that Silliman was not a botanist—she sent him several envelopes of algae she had gathered around Portsmouth. Her collection was extensive, she said, consisting of "one to two thousand specimens," which she tried to classify using the classic French system of Lamarck, Lamouroux, and Candolle. Heartened by a kind response from Silliman, who encouraged her to write up her discoveries for possible publication in his journal of the natural sciences, she spent weeks in the Boston Athenaeum classifying dozens of bags of rocks, minerals, and quartz she had picked up in her travels around New England.[58]

Her interest in science, unusual for a woman in Jacksonian America, was a serious attempt by Dorothea to improve her education. In the 1820s and 1830s there were no formal channels for young women to study the natural sciences, and even within universities men found most science programs inadequate. Young Harris himself, who aspired to the new chair in natural history at Harvard, conducted most of his experiments at home. If she wanted to study the world around her,

Dorothea had little choice but to do it on her own, reading the chronicles of Silliman and Thomas Nuttall, and, if possible, making contact with people who shared her interests.

Once begun, her correspondence with Benjamin Silliman continued for more than thirty years and demonstrated both her native intellectual curiosity and her methodical approach to observation. Carefully describing eight spiders she had captured and placed in a glass vessel, for example, Dorothea did her best to write like a student of taxonomy. One of her subjects, she noticed,

> is a spider, having a strong similitude to that species designated by Tatricious as the *Aranea aculeata*: I think it belongs to the genus *Epeira*, distinguished by having its eight eyes arranged in this manner. It spins and weaves a geometrical web, remarkably delicate and prismatic. The body of this insect forms a solid equilateral triangle, one plane of which forms the back, curiously marked with chestnut-brown, and yellow, bands, and unequal spots—the angles terminate in sharp thorns. The whole body is encased in a smooth, hard shell, and so singular is the appearance of the insect, that it was some time before I could even decide whether it belonged to the class of spiders.

This sort of minutely detailed explication—not only of spiders but of caterpillars, butterflies, moths, algae, and minerals—went far beyond the secondhand subject matter of *Conversations on Common Things*, and displayed Dorothea's bent for classification and delineation. Also, writing to a distinguished scientist points to a growing measure of self-confidence, at least with respect to her powers of intellect and observation.[59]

As she prepared for her visit to the Caribbean, trying to think of ways to get the most out of the journey, she offered to gather and catalogue tropical specimens for Silliman. "My objects are at once the hope of acquiring confirmed health," she told him; "but while my friends with affectionate care discuss my health I cannot but own I am stimulated to attempt the voyage more in the hope of adding to my knowledge, by the study of Natural Science."[60] To be sure, her expedition was to be educational, though hardly in the way she anticipated.

The party set sail from Boston in early November 1830. The image of her that remained in her friends' minds was of a wan, enfeebled figure, if not exactly at death's door, not far from it either. Dorothea's sickly visage made Josephine Waters think of a sermon Ralph Waldo Emerson preached, "a short time before his wife died." "My friend," she told Dorothea, "if you had sat for the likeness, he could not have portrayed your character more truly, I thought of you all churchtime."[61]

In any event, the voyage—"safe though boisterous," she wrote—did not produce a miracle cure. Instead of finding relief in the southern climes, Dorothea succumbed to a mysterious torpor that made it impossible for her to concentrate on science or, for that matter, on anything else. Entering the Caribbean "torrid zone," she was drained of every ounce of energy, not so much ill, she told her friend Mrs. Torrey, as unwillingly becoming "seriously the subject of inertia." For the past year her friends had been warning her that she was on the verge of collapse. But she had ignored them and continued to press her body to its limit. Now that she had arrived in St. Croix, her energy dissipated, and her spirits plummeted accordingly. Feeling herself slip into a state of mild and then deeper despondency, she mused, "how strangely is the human mind constituted, and strange its deep mysterious motions."[62]

The Channing family had always marveled at her energy, and they now found her unexpected idleness mildly irritating since she sloughed off most of her duties as governess and preceptor. But during her first three months in St. Croix nothing seemed to help her "vexatious *no-disease* that does nothing, thinks nothing, is nothing."[63]

Then, in February 1831, she unexpectedly took a turn for the better and began suddenly to feel healthier than she had in years. She was afraid of examining too closely "the foundations of my almost unbroken cheerfulness," she confided to a friend, lest it vanish. Invigorated after months of indolence, she plotted a strenuous program of study for herself. Starting with natural history, she compiled long lists of the wild and cultivated flora on St. Croix. Its lush tropical vegetation was like nothing she had ever seen. Groves of cocoa palms crowded the beaches. Low divi-divi bushes, whose seeds were prized by chemists as a source of tannin, seemed to take root in every open space. Further inland, she found ribbon-leaved guanatail and immense agave plants, with leaves as long as eight feet, growing in rocky areas where local islanders harvested them for fiber. Fruit trees abounded—banana, mango, orange, shaddock lime, bell apple. And the forests were overgrown with fig, silk cotton, mahogany, campechy, mimosa, and dozens of other varieties she could not name. She learned that more than a thousand different plants had been identified on St. Croix alone. Fascinated, and wanting to share her discoveries, over the course of the winter she sent copies of her catalogues, along with dried specimens, back to Benjamin Silliman and also to the painter and naturalist James Audubon.[64]

The plants that dominated the human and political geography of St. Croix, however, were scarcely exotic. Cotton and sugarcane had been introduced into the Virgin Islands during the seventeenth century. By the time Denmark acquired St. Croix in 1733, it already encompassed 109 plantations, averaging about 120 acres, devoted to these two cash crops. The Danish West India and Guinea Company, which assumed control of the island, looked upon St. Croix purely as a financial investment. Accordingly, in the early 1740s, the company carved it into estates and recruited settlers to manage them. Eventually, at the settlers' urging, the company sold St. Croix back to the Danish crown. Under laissez-faire crown rule, the late eighteenth century became a golden period of commercial prosperity for the Virgin Islands. Unfortunately this affluence was built on the back of the greatest moral and institutional problem of the Age of Revolution: African slavery.[65]

Chattel slavery had been abolished in the northeastern United States before Dorothea was born. The Constitution had outlawed the slave trade, although in the South slavery flourished, firmly rooted in the region's economy. In St. Thomas and St. John, by contrast, the slave trade was unrestricted. (Denmark would extend this policy to St. Croix in 1833.) Accurate data are hard to come by, but it is estimated that during the eighteenth century 123,000 black slaves arrived in the Danish West Indian colonies. Of these, some 53,000 were put to work on the islands' plantations. Most of the rest were shipped to America. Thus the island presented Dorothea with an extraordinary opportunity for a kind of social study that had nothing to do with natural science or religion.[66]

The slave system on St. Croix, organized around the planting and harvesting of cotton and sugarcane, was as onerous and brutal as any in the New World. And its character was glaringly apparent. Of the island's total population of twenty-five thousand, at least twenty-one thousand were black slaves. Two hundred and forty slaves lived and worked on Mount Victory, the plantation where the Channing party spent the winter. As the minister described it, "the piazza in which I sat and walked almost from morning to night overlooked the negro village belonging to the estate. A few steps placed me in the midst of their huts. Here was a volume on slavery opened always before my eyes, and how could I help learning some of its lessons?"[67]

Dorothea's reactions to this lesson are perplexing. With her New England religious heritage, her deep and unremitting morality, piety, and religious conscience, she would appear to have been a perfect candidate for the abolitionist movement as soon as she came face-to-face with the plight of the island's black slaves. Yet her first response to slavery in St. Croix in 1831 was mild and equivocal. In short, Dorothea largely ignored the cruelty, inhumanity, and repression of the human spirit essential to any slave system.[68]

Together with Channing, she strolled around the estate, observing the slaves at work, sometimes stopping to ask them questions. Most of the slaves labored in some aspect of sugarcane agriculture. After their walks, Dorothea often scribbled down notes about the slaves in the manner of her descriptions of local flora and fauna. At first, they made her uneasy. "There is something in a black skin almost analogous to a veil of concealment," she said, but her attitude rapidly softened. In contrast to Puritan New England, St. Croix seemed to her to represent something approaching the romantic, ideal state of nature. While the blacks she had seen in the north were coarse-featured and clumsy, she said, those on St. Croix were generally "handsome, much above the generality of the whites, with very fine figures, and graceful beyond anything I have ever seen." Generally speaking, she reckoned that their physical condition was far better than that of most poor whites on the island. No matter what stories of abuse one might hear in Boston, she told Mrs. Torrey, "I often enter their huts, and assure you that they are sufficiently well clothed, sheltered, and fed." In the sweltering afternoon heat, she claimed to regard "the happy little negroes with a feeling of envy, as they stroll about the plantation with [only] a single slight garment."[69]

Like most of her white contemporaries, North and South, including Channing, Dorothea assumed the basic inferiority of African peoples. In her view, the slaves, no matter how hard they had to work, nonetheless led a simple, carefree, cheerful life, free from the exhausting inner burdens of conscience and moral responsibility that she felt so oppressively. She could not imagine "these subjected beings as *responsible* for *any* immoralities" in their state of natural innocence. On the contrary, she reasoned, it would be a shame to "teach them the distinctions of right and wrong." No, she "would not enlighten them to ensure a tenfold wretchedness *here*, and perhaps not make any progress in aiding them hereafter." They were better off not becoming "*free agents*." In her exploring she had gotten to know two runaway slaves and professed herself "amused by the dexterity with which they elude the hunters . . . those who would take them and receive as the law appoints, the price of blood." Whatever price was to be paid for the slaves' licentiousness, idleness, petty crime, and immorality would ultimately have to be exacted from their white overseers and owners, a class of men Dorothea judged as "very corrupt."[70]

This was her initial response to slavery. Yet it is puzzling that Dorothea did not reformulate her views in the early months of 1831 as she discussed the subject at length with Channing. Upset by what he saw at Mount Victory, he would write later that year that slavery "is truly our foulest blot . . . our greatest reproach. . . . and I fear that nothing will rouse us up to wash it away but the deep, stern, irresistible indignation of the civilized world." Even though he believed that the blacks they watched labored under "the mildest form of slavery," he came to look upon the institution "with increasing aversion" as the winter wore on. But it remained hard for him to speak his mind. As a religious leader and public figure, Channing was uncomfortable with expressing his changing views on such a volatile issue. He and Dorothea talked about the merits of his publishing his thoughts on slavery in the form of an open letter to the South when he returned home. But when news reached them of the furor ignited in Boston by William Lloyd Garrison's radical demand in the *Liberator* for immediate abolition, Channing changed his mind. In the 1830s, in the early phases of the antislavery debate, he tended to side with his protégé Ezra Stiles Gannett, who urged a "prudent, *slow*, solicitous" course, and who called Garrison "one of the most dangerous citizens in our United States." In retrospect, people like Harriet Martineau lamented that Channing was perhaps too slow to recognize "the full merits of the Abolitionists." Given his family history, though, and the prevailing racial assumptions of the era, his ambivalence is not hard to understand.[71]

As Channing explained to Dorothea, his own family had owned black slaves when he was a boy. Moreover, the Gibbs family had grown wealthy from the Caribbean sugar, rum, and slave trade during the American Revolution. He knew full well that the Boston elite, from whom the Federal Street congregation was drawn, would be reluctant to rally to the cause of antislavery. "The slave's toil is the Northern merchant's wealth," Channing succinctly observed, "for it produces the great staple on which all the commercial dealings of the country turn."[72]

This basic economic fact, together with Channing's family background and his dislike of the fiery "fanaticism" and strident rhetoric of the abolitionists, led him to believe that the social order suffered when slaveholders were characterized "as monsters of cruelty and crime." Thus, as the winter wore on, Dorothea found herself assuming Channing's moral approach to slavery, which was really an effort to finesse it. He argued for the compelling force of moral suasion, and Dorothea accepted his contention that direct political action would only antagonize the South and nullify the influence of "a multitude of upright, compassionate, devout minds, which, if awakened from the long insensibility of habit to the evils of slavery, would soon overpower the influences of the merely selfish slaveholder." Perhaps the clearest example of Channing's ambivalence and moral timidity on slavery came five years latter, when he finally summoned the courage to publish an essay on the subject. His first instinct was to include a long description of what he had witnessed in the Virgin Islands, including the story of a slave woman who begged "a friend of mine to buy her and put her in a way to earn her freedom," and whose daughter had been raped by the manager of Mount Victory. Yet when he beheld the visceral force of what he had written, he had qualms about publishing the first-person portion of the essay. The human reality of slavery was medicine too strong for his congregation, and so, rather than risk alienating them, he cut it out.[73]

While Dorothea found it impossible to identify with the blacks on St. Croix, she was as troubled as Channing about the moral status of their white masters. "'His gold shall perish with him,' would seem to be the mildest language of Justice," she told Mrs. Torrey, and "whatever be the form, or however remote the time, sure am I that a retribution will fall on the slave-merchant, the-slave-holder, and their children to the fourth generation." Her condemnation of the slave owners rested on an unquestioned assumption—held by almost every member of the Federal Street Church back in Boston—that blacks were an inferior race. She could not see them as fully human. It was almost as though she ascribed to the West Indian myth that held that blacks could not enter the Kingdom of Heaven until St. Peter waved a divine wand and changed the color of their skin to white.[74]

"These beings," she emphasized, "I repeat, *cannot* be Christians, they cannot act as moral beings, they cannot live as souls destined to immortality." Who then, she asked, "shall pay the awful price for their soul's redemption? Who but those who have hidden from them the bread of life and sealed up from them the fountains of living waters, who have darkened the dark mind and obscured the clouded powers of thought?" Slavery was clearly an evil. "No blessing, no good," she insisted, "can follow in the path trodden by slavery. No door of mercy opens for him whose soul is stained by unnumbered sins committed by *others* through his agency." Though at times she empathized with some of the hundred or so escaped slaves who lived in the forest, a few of whose hiding places she claimed to know, generally she believed that enslaved blacks lacked the capacity for moral judgment. Emancipating these creatures, she feared, would flood society with beings with no internal discipline, no self-management.[75]

Judging from the letters she sent to friends in Boston, Dorothea was troubled less by slavery than by what she called St. Croix's "baneful atmosphere of moral depravity [which] poisons the general springs and taints the whole quality of life." By depravity she meant, in part, an array of petty vices—pilferage, cursing, drunkenness and so forth—that, as she put it, offended "good breeding." These improprieties weighed constantly on her mind. "There is something exceedingly disgusting in the spectacle presented of long drinking at tables before ladies quit the party," she wrote in disapproval after, at one dinner, the host passed around a liquor tray, inviting one and all to "help yourself to the snaps [sic]!"[76]

Much more disturbing than drinking, though, was the rampant promiscuity between the white and black populations of the Virgin Islands. Interbreeding was commonplace. Since few European females had settled on St. Croix, many white masters sexually exploited the black women under their control. These liaisons naturally produced a large and growing minority of racially mixed people, the so-called free-colored population, consisting mainly of black women who had borne the children of white masters, and the racially mixed children from these relationships. When Dorothea arrived in Christiansted, Peter Carl Frederik von Scholten, a Danish civil servant then in his mid-forties, was acting governor-general of the Virgin Islands. Although von Scholten had married twenty years before, his wife had remained in Denmark. In her absence, he enjoyed the company of a free-colored woman named Anna Heegaard, a beautiful, light-skinned woman who had been the mistress of a succession of wealthy planters and merchants before she devoted herself exclusively to von Scholten. In his house she presided as first lady of the Virgin Islands. Apparently, few people in the West Indies considered this unusual. "In these alliances," according to an historian of St. Croix, "it was often customary for young women to progress to the accepted position and social duties of unofficial wives."[77]

Dorothea, who dined at the governor's mansion with the Channings, thought the affair too shameful to discuss. In polite circles in Boston, miscegenation was a taboo subject, certainly not a topic of conversation for a lady. Her revulsion to von Scholten's domestic arrangements, it turned out, blinded her to the governor's progressive racial views. She encountered him about the time he published his "Plan for an Improved and more distinct organisation for Your Majesty's Free Coloured Subjects in the West India Colonies," a legal scheme to break down racial distinctions and create a social basis for emancipation. In retrospect, this document appears a milestone in West Indian history. But Dorothea could see it only as von Scholten's attempt to paper over his own gross immorality. Her ultimate disillusionment with St. Croix was that this Eden, so picturesque and tranquil on the surface, was alive with the lust of the flesh. The governor's flagrant disrespect for piety and morality symbolized a way of life that, at least for the planter class, elevated gratification of appetites over self-control.

In early May 1831 the party sailed for New York City. In no hurry to get back to Boston, Dorothea accompanied the Channings for a few weeks when they visited Philadelphia. Ruth Channing was markedly improved, moving about much more freely than she had the previous fall; her husband, on the other hand seemed tired—"writing wearies him; reading; even eating!" wrote Dorothea—but he had always been a languid soul.[78] Although she held the family in the highest esteem and would remain close to the them for years to come, this Caribbean sojourn represented a turning point in her attachment to William Ellery Channing. Afterward a certain reserve crept into their relationship, and they approached each other with increasing formality.

Living in close quarters with the great man left a slight residue of disappointment. Perhaps she was bound to be disappointed, since her initial investment in their relationship was so heavy.

When she first met him, a year or so after Joseph Dix had died, she had latched onto Channing as a spiritual father. He exuded positive energy. No one in Boston was more respected. He transcended doctrinal quibbling, as well as divisive issues of theology and polity, in favor of a brighter vision, hopeful and immaculate. No one better harmonized the contemplative and active modes of religious experience. Following his example, Dorothea for the rest of her life carefully avoided religious intolerance. She was inspired by his admonition to self-culture and took to heart his conviction that the capstone of creation was "Mind," the intellectual and moral power in all people that could understand the divine will. This doctrine held great appeal for a young woman devoted to self-improvement and convinced that the only reliable gift God had bestowed upon her was a superior intellect. In the early phases of their relationship, his notorious reserve, the impression he gave of being constantly lost in meditation—"Dr. C[hanning] really does not know half the time when a question is being addressed," she wrote in 1831—was counterbalanced by a generous, dedicated commitment to improving society.[79] Though Channing never became an active social reformer, his belief that the Gospel applied to social problems and his confidence in the redemptive power of moral education influenced Dorothea's ideas about religious reform more than any other factor before she was forty.

In his own way, Channing also had a high opinion of the position of women. Looking back, his amanuensis and sometime confidante Elizabeth Peabody thought he believed in "the superiority rather than the inferiority of woman to man, in moral power as well as in sensibility." Channing was a courtly man who naturally displayed "something of the old knightly sentiment, but not a particle of that cheap sentimentality about women, which ignores their equal responsibility with men for all the heroic and stern virtues that are required of all human beings alike." His ideas and principles were thus an inspiration to Dorothea. And a poem she wrote in the late 1820s, "To Dr. Channing," shows how she projected onto him the abstract virtues that obsessed her: "Mine words of fire inflame the soul of youth / With heaven's own spirit—honor, virtue, truth." As if to check herself, however, she jotted at the bottom of the same page that "*it would seem* as though of all *Idolatries* the Infinite God smites with peculiar wrath the *Idolatry of the Affections*."[80]

But gradually during the 1830s it dawned on Dorothea that Channing, for all his high-mindedness and generosity, was not prepared to adopt her into his family as an equal. To be sure, he respected her and liked her. Unsurprisingly, he thought of her as governess and teacher of his children, not as friend. Prominently as he figures in her correspondence, she barely appears in his own letters and papers. There are in fact only two letters from Channing among the thousands Dorothea

Dix saved. One of them advised her not to push herself so hard. "I mean not to reprove you for any of your labours," he admonished her. "You are of age, and have had experience, and have a conscience, and if all these will not keep you right in such a plain matter as the care of your health, your friends will do you little good." Perhaps, he gently suggested, her underlying problem was simply that she was too ambitious. "You must learn to give up your plans for usefulness," he advised, "as much as those of gratification, to the will of God. We may make these the occasion of self-will, vanity, and pride as much as anything else. May not your chief dangers lie there?"[81]

As she worked at the task of molding herself into the kind of person she wanted to be—a person of accomplishment—she discovered an unsettling aspect of her attachment to Channing. Quite simply, he was not her father. He had neither the energy nor the inclination to respond to the needs of such an intense young woman. She was reluctant to complain, but she began to back away from Channing when she realized he would never step into the emotional void created by her estrangement from her parents.

Her disappointment, if more acute, was not unlike that of many young men and women in Boston who admired Channing and competed for his favor. One might argue that Channing's greatest works were his disciples. At different times the notable ministers Ezra Stiles Gannett and Charles Follen, and the future senator Charles Sumner, were among his protégés. And there was a succession of intellectual and literary women—Elizabeth Peabody, Lydia Maria Child, Catherine Sedgwick, Harriet Martineau, and Lucy Aiken—each of whom thought she enjoyed a special relationship with the minister. And like Dorothea, each eventually hinted that Channing's preaching promised something that Channing the man never delivered. His devotees learned that he was, as Henry James said of Emerson, truly a "man without a handle." Underneath his eloquence and quiet charisma, there was something remote and passionless about him, perhaps an inability to translate thought into action, which often led to disillusionment.[82]

Dorothea never complained about the powerlessness and dependence inherent in their relationship. Yet, despite the promise it at first seemed to hold, her relationship with the eminent minister would turn out to be a mixed blessing, aggravating rather than soothing the strain in her inner life. Decades later, after the Civil War, she told a journalist that although she was once "very intimate" with Channing and his family, he had given no direction to her "philanthropic enterprises, for while sympathizing fully with their purpose, he rather opposed her exhaustive exertions on the ground that she would destroy her health." In other words, he never entirely believed in her as she believed in herself. In the same interview, though, she suggested that his resistance spurred her onward, and that "when her resolve had been deliberately formed, opposition only increased its strength."[83]

Channing's legacy to Dorothea was thus mixed. Surely it was from him that she learned, as the archbishop of Paris, Cardinal Suhard, once said, that "to be a witness does not consist in engaging in propaganda or even in stirring people up, but in being a living mystery; it means to live in such a way that one's life would not make sense if God did not exist." Nevertheless, it was no coincidence that she would not awaken to the confidence and self-assurance essential to her public career until 1842, the year she was liberated by Channing's death.[84]

CHAPTER THREE

The English Malady

It seemed evident in the spring of 1831, when she returned to Boston suntanned, rejuvenated, feeling better than she had in years, that Dorothea had come perilously close to breaking down. The previous winter she had been almost paralyzed by fatigue, kept awake by violent fits of coughing—deadly serious symptoms before the invention of antibiotics. In her view, there was no such thing as a minor illness. Influenza, pneumonia, and tuberculosis were leading causes of death. Not unreasonably Dorothea worried that her respiratory ailments might lead to a fatal disease. After all, the death of children, teenagers, and young adults was commonplace; and graveyards were filled with people who had been struck down in the prime of life. Health was not taken for granted, and she, like so many of her contemporaries, was preoccupied by illness, anxiously monitoring her symptoms.

At the same time, she realized that her ailments were as much a matter of mind as of body. The gloomy ruminations reflected in her letters and journals show a woman increasingly depressed by her failure to settle on a suitable vocation, to work out an acceptable relation with society, to decipher God's calling and lead a life worth living. Increasingly, she felt that her existence hinged on discovering this calling. But her path to significance remained elusive.

While serving as the Channings' governess, and breathing the air of the rarefied world they inhabited, was a formative part of Dorothea's sentimental education, she never for a moment mistook it for a career. All along, she continued to think of herself as a schoolteacher and writer. The previous fall she had relinquished her school with the greatest reluctance. And the instant she began to regain her strength on St. Croix, Dorothea schemed to open a new school when she returned to Boston.

Every other young woman in the city seemed to have the same notion. In consequence, Dorothea wrote, Boston was overwhelmed with private schools. Happily, she was so well connected, particularly within the Federal Street congregation, that she had little trouble attracting students. Parents who valued a serious, formal approach to education appreciated her high standards. Elizabeth Peabody, an intellectual Unitarian woman of letters who periodically served as Channing's amanuensis, and who operated a small school of her own, conceded that Miss Dix's students were educated "more nearly to . . . the true principles of education" than any other children she knew. Yet as she looked about for a suitable location, Dorothea suffered misgivings. By this time she knew perfectly well that the horizons of a schoolmistress were limited. Originally she had invested teaching with romance and idealism. "To me the avocation of teacher has something elevating and exciting," she told Anne Heath. "I love to watch the progress of the young being just emerging from infancy when thought first springs into existence." Over the past few years, though, she had also come to see it as a repetitive chore that taxed her health. When Anne started a nursery school in Brookline, Dorothea sounded a note of pessimism, advising her "to take warning from my fate."[1]

Although it scarcely measured up to her higher aspirations, Dorothea's first careers as teacher and writer exploited virtually the only professions open to ladies in Jacksonian America. These pursuits, for all their limitations, were respectable avenues for a woman to keep her mind alive and even exercise a measure of ambition. A schoolroom of her own gave a woman a genuine sphere of influence where, in the words of Catharine Beecher, "she need not outstep the prescribed boundaries of feminine modesty." Despite her hesitancy, Dorothea could see no practical alternative to teaching, so she moved ahead with her school and set about recruiting children from the upper-crust families of Boston. Fittingly, she dubbed her new venture "The Hope."[2]

Education, in due course, might well have become her lifework, as it did for Beecher and many other intelligent women. The 1830s were a time of educational ferment and reform, and Boston, more than any other city, was a center of experimentation and innovation in the teaching of schoolchildren. The classroom was the training ground for citizens of the new republic and, as Emerson remarked on the spirit of the age, everyone seemed to carry in his vest pocket a personal theory of school reform. Emerson himself had earlier tried his hand at teaching, finding the work at first exhilarating, then tedious, at last declaring himself "a hopeless Schoolmaster." His friend Amos Bronson Alcott, an incurable idealistic teacher who would later join the communitarian idyll at Brook Farm, embodied the radical temper of the age, going so far as to require, when his students misbehaved enough to merit physical punishment, that the offending child cane his teacher, rather than the other way around.

Dorothea, however, was decidedly of the old school. One of her first students was William Ellery Channing's daughter, Mary Eustis, who later recalled her teacher's austere demeanor and lockstep discipline. "Strict and inflexible" were the words that seemed to apply to Dorothea as she subjected her scholars to an "iron will from which it was hopeless to appeal." Apparently it never occurred to Dorothea that her demands might have been excessive. The Hope was an expression of her own personality. She instinctively projected onto her children her own exacting moral and ethical imperatives, her own impatience and high expectations.[3]

Sitting stiffly at a small oak table, she put them each day through their paces. Arithmetic, natural science, geography, reading, writing, and grammar formed the core of the curriculum; but Dorothea regarded these subjects mainly as the prelude to weightier tasks. Rigorous pedagogy, in her view, was supposed to nurture personal morality and piety as much as intellectual development. Accordingly, she encouraged self-examination and religious confession, pushing so hard that some of the girls at The Hope grew terribly discouraged about their perceived shortcomings and the futility of trying to measure up to Miss Dix's religious standards. Occasionally students wrote her letters that reflect their teacher's bent for introspection and perhaps indirectly throw light on her turbulent emotional life during this period. Typical of these is the plea of one downcast child who wrote, "I feel the need of some one to whom I can pour forth my feelings, they have been pent up so long. . . . I have a *disease*, not of body but of mind. This is *unhappiness*. Can you tell me of anything to cure it?" Another beseeched Dorothea, "if you are not satisfied in some measure with yourself . . . I don't know what I shall do."[4]

Her unhappy relationship with her own parents, the high value she placed on familial ties, and the fact that she was unmarried with no children of her own led her to invest teaching with a highly charged sense of parental duty and responsibility. Victorian convention, after all, deemed the education of children a suitable feminine calling, ranked just a notch below the culturally paramount role of wife and mother. So if at times her heart was too much in her work, her right to project herself so intently into the lives of her students was justified, Dorothea felt, by the maternalism her society vested in the teacher's role. At thirty, she was certainly old enough to be a mother. Several of her students called themselves "your child," or "your affectionate child"; others addressed her as "Aunt" or "Auntie." Throughout the nineteenth century, Americans used the language of kinship rather more loosely than in later periods. The Hope thus offered Dorothea not only a surrogate family circle but a respectable alternative to marriage.

Some alternative was necessary, because by the late 1820s it was becoming clearer every day that she would not marry. Dorothea did not deliberately avoid marriage. She simply lacked enthusiasm for finding a husband. Without the kind of physical beauty that attracted men in its own right, without the immediate family connections or personal wealth that facilitated unions between members of the upper echelon, Dorothea, in order to marry well, would have needed to plot her course with the shrewdness of one of Jane Austen's heroines. When she read books like *Emma*, however, her thoughts were elsewhere. If she sometimes expressed romantic fantasies about men like Ezra Stiles Gannett, and was flattered by the attention she received from young gentlemen at social gatherings and parties, she nevertheless remained deeply self-absorbed, engrossed less in social relations than in the life of the mind. Most of the time, the small talk, flirtation, and gossip surrounding the rituals of genteel mating seemed to her vulgar.

When her friend Eliza Bellows playfully spread the rumor that Dorothea was engaged to her French teacher, one Mr. Wentz, she scoffed at the idea. "Is it not vexing to be so ridiculously spoken of?" she asked Anne Heath. What vexed her was, in all likelihood, less the silly rumor than the fact that she found so little intellectual and temperamental compatibility between herself and Boston's eligible young men.[5]

Since the reasons Dorothea did not marry are hard to pin down precisely, family tradition conveniently furnished the tale of a blighted romance. Some said that, during her teenage years in Worcester, Dorothea became engaged to Edward Dillingham Bangs, her first cousin and some thirteen years her senior. Then, for some unknown reason, his love turned cold, and he turned his back on the disconsolate young woman and moved on with his career. For her part, Dorothea was left with a broken heart. This was the reason, it was whispered, that she could never love another man.[6]

Certainly, Dorothea and Edward Bangs did know each other well. The diary he kept when he lived in Worcester mentions her occasionally, along with dozens of other in-laws; and in his will he bequeathed her "10$ and a ring." Yet one sifts the record in vain for evidence of passion between them.

Compared with many other young women her age, Dorothea suppressed her romantic impulses; but once in a while they surfaced. In the summer of 1824, for example, she anticipated meeting Lafayette when he made his celebrated visit to Boston. "I could almost kneel to him," she confided to Anne. "I long to see him; to be in the room with him and yet I hardly would trust myself; my feelings, which few would understand, in which none would sympathize, would be under no control; tears and tears only would make my greetings." A few weeks later, George Hayward, a prominent physician whose family she had gotten to know through the Heaths, held a reception for the illustrious Frenchman, and Dorothea was invited. Somehow the event failed to live up to her expectations, though. Wine flowed far too freely and her female friends swooned too unashamedly over the general. In the safety of her imagination, the noble Lafayette was for her, as for any number of her friends, an appealing beau ideal. Seeing him in the flesh, though, made her uncomfortable. When a friend, noticing her standing off by herself, asked what was wrong—"Do you think him handsome?"—Dorothea retorted, "I did not criticize his features—I was thinking of his deeds."[7]

Dorothea linked the idea of meeting this august romantic figure with the prospect of losing control of herself. So hers was a quiescent, apprehensive sexuality, barely developed, and never fully expressed to another person. Self-control was her preoccupation; losing control was from childhood on one of her deepest fears. She could not fail to see, watching the young women she knew marry and settle into domestic routines, that marriage was utterly at odds with her being the mistress of her own destiny. Tocqueville caught the matter succinctly when he observed, "In America a woman loses her independence forever in the bonds of matrimony." To Dorothea, this was an alarming thought. Everything about marriage bespoke giving oneself up to one's husband. There were perhaps a few women who could reconcile marriage with their ideas of a career or calling, but she was not one of them. Moreover, she was visited by memories of her parents' unhappy marriage, which, in the eyes of the Dix family, had ruined her father's once bright promise.

Instinctively she knew, given her personal and material circumstances, that she would not have been able to marry on a basis of equality. The men she knew doubtless recognized that anyone she married could scarcely have escaped being dominated by her. As it happened, the few young men in her circle who measured up to her elevated standards of intellect and moral seriousness—men like Gannett and Furness—chose conventional partners, not women of accomplishment, to be their wives and the mothers of their children.

As almost any man's wife Dorothea would have been terribly miscast. It was impossible for her to think or act conventionally. Over the years, though, she learned to relate to men on her own terms, and the more she did so, the more men found her fascinating and attractive. Once the implicit possibility of marriage had been ruled out, in other words, once Dorothea established a clear identity as an unmarried woman, she would find the world of men far more engaging, and more hospitable, than the sphere of women. By turns she would encounter men who educated her, guided her, ministered to her, praised her, respected her as almost an equal, and, perhaps, even one or two who loved her. She was a strong woman who sought out strong men. What she asked for was their respect, something Andrews Norton, the esteemed Boston essayist and poet, acknowledged she richly deserved "for your judicious and strenuous efforts to be useful, for your triumph over bodily weakness, and for all that constitutes the expression of strong religious principles."[8]

She was finding ways to turn what has been called spinsterhood to her advantage. Not only would she not be stigmatized by remaining unmarried; she was set on using her freedom to open up possibilities she could not otherwise have enjoyed.[9]

The lack of a husband did not mean the lack of emotional nurture. During her twenties and early thirties, Dorothea garnered from her relationship with Anne Heath much of the love and support that women were supposed to get from their husbands. Their attachment was sisterly, not erotic, and it provided Dorothea with a deep psychological mooring from the first year she was in Boston.

The two of them explored the city together, speaking intimately, absorbing the cultural, intellectual, and religious landscape. In good weather they might have been seen walking beside the Boston Common, where cows still grazed, or along the low banks of the Charles River, debating the merits of Sir Walter Scott or gathering specimens for Dorothea's collections of native flora. Dorothea, the teacher, inevitably took the lead. Anne, ever a sheltered homebody, was happy to follow. Anne, like Dorothea, did not find a husband and was also to remain unmarried. Unlike Dorothea, however, she was content to settle into a life of domestic routine in suburban Brookline. Her life revolved around her family. And in maturity she exemplified the traditional figure of the maiden aunt whose sphere was defined by her close-knit family, content (outwardly, at least) to while away her days with sewing, baking, looking after her siblings' children, and endless hours of tea and talk.

Dorothea needed Anne. In her straightforward conventionalism, as much as her companionability, Anne served as Dorothea Dix's alter ego—her adopted "sister" to whom she could always open her heart without fear of disapproval. To the extent she bared her soul to anyone, she trusted Anne with her innermost feelings. Over the years, there would be periods when a distance would open between them. Yet when Dorothea launched herself into the public arena of reform and politics, Anne took on renewed importance in her life: she became for Dorothea what might be called, in T. S. Eliot's phrase, the still point of the turning world. As the stereotypical spinster—the ordinary woman par excellence—Anne defined the point from which Dorothea measured her own progress. More than anyone else, Anne became the person to whom Dorothea could confide how she felt about her experiences in politics. Dorothea, much as she felt that popular acclaim was vulgar, nonetheless needed to share her remarkable experiences with someone who cared about her, another woman who would comprehend the personal magnitude of her success. Anne's esteem was immensely gratifying because Anne had known her in obscurity. Penning a letter to Anne, she could give free rein to her passions and prejudices, could frankly celebrate her own accomplishments without feeling boastful.

For almost everyone else, no matter what she achieved, Dorothea preserved the image of pristine selflessness. But Anne empathized, purely and uncritically, and thus she became the secret sharer in Dorothea Dix's life in the beau monde.

Yet in the early 1830s, a decade before Dix discovered her life's great work, their relationship entered a long period in which Dorothea found herself backing away from their former intimacy. In part she was troubled by a disquieting similarity between Anne's situation and her own. If marriage was not to be her lot, and if she had no family to surround her as she grew older, what in truth was the outlook for a Unitarian schoolteacher and minor author who found herself slowly slipping back into recurrent bouts of illness?

Dorothea could not postpone the question of vocation forever, try as she might to push it temporarily out of her mind. Seeking to lay the groundwork for a new direction, she collaborated with a pair of young ministers, Charles Francis Barnard and Frederick Gray, when, at the suggestion of Channing and the younger Henry Ware, they took over the ministry-at-large while Joseph Tuckerman traveled to Europe. It seemed a promising idea. To her chagrin, however, the men shunted her aside and assigned her the minor task of setting up a Sunday school for pauper children. Disappointed, she realized she would not be allowed to contribute to the innovative social work for which the ministry was known.[10]

As she had occasionally done in the past when she felt unproductive, she renewed her scientific studies. But she had reason to be discouraged, because she had recently received a response to one of her St. Croix letters to John Torrey, a botanist at the University of Pennsylvania.

Along with one letter to Torrey, she had enclosed a copy of *The Garland of Flora*, a little volume she had compiled describing "the most interesting flowers, with striking passages from the ancient and modern poets referring to them." The book's interest is biographical more than literary, yet its pages contain some of Dix's best writing. She showed an erudite, wide-ranging knowledge of the classics, and French and English poetry: Virgil, Percival, Cicero, Plutarch, Chaucer, Shakespeare, Milton, Jonson, Dryden, Spenser, Marvel, and Richardson, among others. She quoted from Johnson's *Rasselas* and Keats's "Endymion," taking pleasure in the sheer beauty of language. A long section called "Vocabulary of Flowers" consists of an alphabetical compendium of floral lore. In discussing "almond," she knew, for instance, that Aaron's rod was taken from an almond tree, that Spenser likened Prince Arthur's plume to an almond tree in the *Faerey Queene*, and that one of Camdeo's arrows is composed of almond flowers.[11]

It was a trifling book, she acknowledged, not "marked by talent or genius; originally written for a circle of young friends, to attract them to Botanical studies, and wider classical readings." Courteously, Torrey answered that he liked the idea of their maintaining "a botanical correspondence." Botany was, in his opinion, the "department of Natural Science [most] admirably suited to the taste and habits of ladies." If she were interested in assisting his work, he suggested that she study some books on algae so that she would know which specimens were likely to hold some scientific interest. She could scarcely have missed the inference that he considered her scientific investigations a pleasant diversion, not serious work.[12]

In April 1832, on the eve of Dorothea's thirtieth birthday, Anne Heath's mother died, and Anne plummeted into deep grief. When Dorothea tried to console her friend, however, what came out was an expression of her own morose depression in the guise of empathy. At least Anne still had her home, Dorothea pointed out in a fit of self-pity, not to mention her father, sister, and brothers. As for herself, she had nobody.

At an age that is classically a time for self-assessment and self-definition, she was sinking into the early stages of a breakdown that would dominate the next several years of her life. Shrouded in a heavy despondency, tormented by her demanding religious aspirations, Dorothea experienced a spreading fatigue. Increasingly she confined herself to her room, unwilling to engage in social life. Spells of weariness overcame her. "We were sent here for action, for constant action," she admonished Anne, as though industry itself could answer the riddle of meaning. But she lacked the energy for action. Daily she chastised herself for inactivity, for wasting time that could be devoted to some useful purpose. She held onto her school, but it felt like a millstone around her neck. Undeniably it would never provide her with the challenge she needed. Nor, apparently, would anything else in the oppressively provincial city of Boston. No other woman in town would have been able so thoroughly to identify with the haunting remark her contemporary Henry David Thoreau confided to his *Journal*: "The society I was made for is not here."[13]

Uncertain about her future, disenchanted with teaching and writing, blocked in her tentative efforts to push into new fields of endeavor, Dorothea began to give in to a debilitating lethargy. She stopped writing books altogether. Her correspondence, ordinarily copious, slackened to a trickle. She saw no one, not her grandmother, not her brothers, not even Channing. Even so, with a kind of frenetic tenacity, she clung to The Hope. In 1833 she had moved her school into an apartment on Washington Street. She continued to hang on to the school even after she became convinced that the stress of teaching was largely responsible for her illnesses. By the winter of 1835, however, the strain was too much. As her friend George Barrell Emerson aptly warned, her weakened body was "pressing its claim upon you in a language which you will not be able to turn away."[14]

Slowly drifting into a more distant orbit around Channing, Dorothea warmed to Emerson, whom she had first gotten to know through his activities in education. He had served as principal of the English Classical School in Boston before striking out on his own with a private school for young ladies in a house on Beacon Street. He was a soft-spoken, intellectual man, part of the circle of scientific Bostonians that included Dorothea's cousin Harris, Asa Gray, her physician, George Hayward, and the prolific naturalist, Thomas Nutall. In 1837, he was elected president of the Natural History Society and was later offered the directorship of the Harvard Botanical Garden. In addition to nature, telegraphs, steam engines, railroads—any new technology—fascinated him. A born organizer, Emerson had played a part in founding the Boston Mechanics Institution and the American Institution of Instruction.

Beneath the mask of depression, he recognized in Dorothea a kindred spirit. He understood the intensity of her drive and self-demand. Emerson was just five years her senior, but he had a maturity and an inner calm beyond his years that inspired trust. Even within a clan that had a reputation for wisdom—George Barrell was the second cousin of Ralph Waldo Emerson—he impressed the historian George Bancroft as "sweet and amiable; always cheerful [and] so regular that he was distinguished from others of his family name as *Pater* Emerson."[15]

Gently he tried to tell his younger friend that she was driving herself too hard, "presuming too far upon the power," he phrased it, she had of self-denial. "I am much afraid that you are doing too much for others and not enough to take care of yourself," he advised her. "You must remember that you cannot do everything." Moreover, she should not dismiss the personal value of her interest in science. "Do not count it time lost to occupy yourself with what will be only recreation to you," he wrote, "the rocks and animals and plants of this beautiful world." Her ferocious impatience reminded him of his own undergraduate days at Harvard College, when he had nearly wrecked his own health working twenty hours a day, impatiently trying to master the entire college curriculum at once. Ambition would have destroyed him, he reflected, had he not been willing to lower his sights and settle for the comparatively modest vocation of tutor and teacher.[16]

She was too demoralized to heed this advice. Physically exhausted, discouraged, and feeling blameworthy for having fallen so short of her goals, she rejected Emerson's suggestion that she had been "enthusiastic, indiscreet, or wilfully rash" in devoting her life to teaching, which she defended as "the cause and work, for which and to which Providence has adopted [sic] me." It had always seemed to her essential to work at some real, productive employment. If she was not up to even such a "quiet round of duties" as running a small school, she bitterly observed, what was her life worth? That her school had not fulfilled her dream now seemed beside the point. Given the state of her health, she feared she would have another chance. "You can doubtless perceive decline since the early Autumn," she wrote to Emerson, adding that her physician painted a bleak picture. "There is a time for everything—a time to live—and also a time to die," she said. "The conviction is, and has long been strong that the veil which divides me from 'my home' would soon fall." In a doleful, rambling good-bye, Dorothea asked Emerson to take over her school after her death in order that it "should be sustained by other and abler minds."[17]

Finally, in March 1836, convinced her life was a miserable failure, she collapsed. Her letters and notebooks from this bleak time are filled with brooding over her physical ailments, chiefly fatigue and congestion in her lungs, and her severely depressed state of mind. Death obsessed her, and her imagination frequently dwelled on thoughts of heaven and eternal bliss. Yet there was a more personally disturbing side to her illness as well. This was a pervasive sense of sin. Her breakdown, she felt, was not a random misfortune but somehow deserved. "In this hour of severe trial there is a prevailing faith that it is *right*," she confessed, "and that I should receive and submit meekly and patiently to the discipline which no doubt I have needed."[18]

Folded in with one letter to Emerson were a few poems Dorothea composed. A "Communion Hymn" for February 1836 portrayed the passion of Christ, in terms that echo her own cries for help,

> *Prostrate upon the ground . . .*
> *In agony of prayer to heaven for help he sues.*
> *Oh Father, let it pass,*

Dejectedly trying to wring some meaning out of her anguish, in the margin she noted that God's "chastisements are inflicted for the soul's health."[19]

Alarmed by Dorothea's deteriorating condition, Emerson and several of his friends—including Channing, George Ticknor, and her physician, George Hayward, who had a long-standing interest in mental disorders—together formed a plan to get her out of Boston. Her only chance for recovery, they concluded, lay in a restorative sea voyage and tour of Europe. Such trips were conventional therapy for well-to-do patients afflicted with illnesses that defied classification and treatment. Since recovering patients could also embellish their education in the capitals of the Old World, vacation cures were doubly attractive. So they quickly mapped out her itinerary. She would follow the same path Channing had taken on his grand tour a few years earlier: spring and summer in England and Scotland, fall and winter in the milder Mediterranean climates of southern France and Italy. During the last freezing weeks of an unusually cold winter, Channing, Tuckerman, Doctor Hayward, and Uncle Harris each wrote her letters of introduction to their English and Continental acquaintances, and secured her passage on the next ship for Liverpool.

Amid these preparations for her tour of Europe, Dorothea, unable to muster the slightest enthusiasm, listlessly withdrew into herself. Feeling hopeless, she wandered about in a trancelike state, writing to no one, hardly speaking except to let people know she had resigned her fate entirely to the hands of others. "I cannot write—and I ought not," she told Emerson.[20]

Such silence and pitiful self-absorption was almost more than Anne Heath could bear. By the time Dorothea embarked, Anne sensed that her best friend had become a stranger. "I feel an uncertainty about your views, plans & health, & this uncertainty renders me exceedingly uncomfortable," she wrote in a touching letter on the eve of Dorothea's departure. If she had somehow, unwittingly, added to Dorothea's troubles, she begged forgiveness: "I acknowledge I have felt distanced by y[ou]r reserve,—but how trifling a fault, when compared to the worth of your character." The trouble was, Anne had to admit, she yearned for an intimacy that Dorothea could not manage. Nothing would have made her happier, she said, than "[that] wh[ich] you denied, y[ou]r own thoughts on paper." She sent Dorothea a gold ring to remind her "how much I love you." Dorothea, trying her best to strike a note of reassurance, responded, "You must think of me as an invalid[,] but not troubled."[21]

But she had never been more troubled in her life. Boarding *The Virginian* on April 22, 1836, she was sick at heart more than at any other time, profoundly estranged from those around her. To make matters worse, she believed she was sailing into a void.

Unexpectedly, the first leg of her journey was somewhat therapeutic. During an uncommonly smooth North Atlantic crossing she was glad to have the company of several acquaintances on board who formed a "pleasant social circle." Removed from the stifling circumstances of her life in Boston, Dorothea found herself feeling more hopeful about her convalescence than she had through the previous winter. Her mood lightened. By the time they docked in Liverpool, she had received invitations from three families—the Lawrences, the Gairs, and the Fessers—to join them on their tours of France and Italy later in the year. While she privately doubted that she had the stamina for such long journeys, she was happy to have been asked. At the end of May, feeling the need to rest, she rented rooms in a small shingled inn in Woodcroft, a hamlet on the outskirts of Liverpool, and there tried to plan the next stage of her trip.[22]

During the first week, as the English rain fell continuously, she felt herself losing ground. Her tiny sitting room was cold and damp. When she tried to read, she was defeated by fatigue. When she tried to sleep, she was kept awake by fits of fever and violent coughing worse than anything she had experienced the winter before. The congestion in her lungs was ample reason to fear tuberculosis. But she was alone in a foreign country and at a loss for whom to call. After all the time she had complained of being alone in the world, her solitude was now a reality. Bedridden, without the least strength to help herself, Dorothea was overcome by the feeling of having at last sunk to the bottom.

At this moment of utter desperation, sorting through the dozens of letters packed in the bottom of her portmanteau, she came across one written by Channing addressed to a Liverpool gentleman named William Rathbone III. It introduced

> Miss Dix, a lady who for many years has enjoyed great confidence & respect as a teacher of the young of her own sex, & who has injured her health by her singular devotion to her work. Her history is one of the most remarkable examples of what may be accomplished by energy & a high sense of duty. . . . she has been a member of our family many months.[23]

When she mentioned Rathbone, her landlady said she knew the name well. Indeed, he was famous: an extraordinary person, a politician, a philanthropist, and the patriarch of one of the first families of Liverpool. Vaguely recalling Channing's description of the family after his last visit to England, Dorothea scribbled a note and sent it to William Rathbone with the letter from Channing and her card.

Upon hearing of the American woman's plight, Rathbone and his wife drove at once to her inn, packed her luggage in their carriage, wrapped her in a woolen shawl, and removed her to Greenbank, their splendid ancestral estate on the banks of the Mersey. There, over the next year, they nursed her back to health with as much compassion and tenderness as they would have lavished on a member of their own family. "She remained," according to Rathbone's son, "about a year and a quarter afterwards, when she was well enough to return to America."[24]

As the Rathbones' fine black carriage passed through the stone gates and entered the drive to the great house, Dorothea was struck with wonder. This ancient family seat, three miles outside Liverpool, with its sprawling grounds, gardens in bloom, a small private lake with a boat, was the original English country house of which the Channing's Oakland retreat had been but a copy. Guests were effusive. "There was a double verandah," wrote one visitor, "and if I live to see all the glories of the sun, moon, and seven stars, I shall never see that verandah equalled." Somehow, though, magnificent as it was, Greenbank struck a balance with its "delicious and elegant comfort . . . plenty without coarseness; exquisiteness without that super-delicacy which oppresses by its extravagance."[25]

Greenbank, the Rathbone family's estate near Liverpool.

Its master was equally impressive. Descended from a long line of Quaker merchants, each more prosperous than the father before him, Rathbone was, by the time she met him, rich enough to abandon commerce in favor of politics and social reform. It was said that at age twenty-two he had begun to set aside two thousand pounds each year to give to charitable causes. Social conscience was part of his pedigree. Dorothea soon learned, for example, that his father, William II, had been active in the late-eighteenth-century antislavery movement, going so far as to refuse to sell timber to builders of slave ships. For his part, William III carried on his father's commitment to abolition and emancipation, and then energetically extended his interests to the new wave of social and municipal reforms sweeping England in the wake of the Reform Bill. Dorothea arrived shortly after Liverpool had voted an overwhelming liberal majority into the city council. Rathbone was chairman of a reform delegation that met in Liverpool to set an agenda of municipal reform, and had already assumed a leading role in the community's political life that would lead in 1837 to his election as mayor.[26]

Each evening after dinner, Rathbone shared with Dorothea, as she put it, "a great deal of interesting information concerning different persons of eminence." Josiah Wedgwood had been a friend of Rathbone's father. The biographer William Roscoe, and John Dalton, the father of atomic theory, were members of an informal circle of liberals who occasionally visited Greenbank, spending long afternoons drinking claret on the veranda. Rathbone enjoyed cultivating people. With his wonderful, old-fashioned manners and his "antique distinction of dress," he seemed to belong to the Augustan, not the Victorian, age.

And despite a reputation for sarcasm, he was generally a warmhearted, charming host. Moreover, he and his wife, Elizabeth, caring little about the opinion of the world, delighted in welcoming "visitors to Liverpool who had some especial opinions or some philanthropic scheme to advance." And should their guest happen to have been socially obscure, or ill, or despised as a heretic or zealot, their welcome was only that much heartier.[27]

Like many British liberal Christians, Rathbone was a great admirer of Channing. In fact, he told Dorothea, he had quietly slipped away from the Society of Friends because he was so attracted to the freedom and openness of Unitarianism. When Channing and Tuckerman had, at different times, visited him, he was delighted to see how much he had in common with them. The Unitarian message, stressing the interrelatedness of humanity, matched his own views and political goals: on parliamentary reform, Roman Catholic emancipation, freedom for the West Indian slaves, and repeal of the Corn Laws. Humanitarianism drew him inevitably into politics. Not that political power for its own sake had any appeal. Rathbone was a man who liked to accomplish concrete improvements, so he concentrated most of his efforts in Liverpool. Over the years, he campaigned passionately for better public schooling, earning the nickname "The Educationist." Likewise, in the wake of the New Poor Law, he pushed to reorganize the administration of poor relief. He also signed on as an overseer of the Rainhill lunatic asylum in Lancashire, among the first generation of English public asylums. It was built to remove the mad from the vicious circumstances of prisons and workhouses, with "the greater object of restoring reason itself." Considering the scope of his good works, Dorothea marveled at her host's self-effacement and discretion. People said that the extent of his private charity would never be known, "for he was emphatically a man 'to do good by stealth.'"[28]

The quiet good the Rathbones did Dorothea is also hard to calculate, but it was very great. Craving filial affection, she was soothed by their concern and feeling for her. Rathbone himself was a father who openly loved his family. Unlike Channing, there was nothing remote, nothing cold about him; and he had deep empathy with those who were ill. Since childhood he had suffered chronic stomach and digestive maladies and thought it his duty to minister to others in their times of infirmity. Shortly after Dorothea returned to America, for example, a family acquaintance named Joseph Blanco White spent his last dying months at Greenbank, nursed "through an illness the distressing accompaniments of which would have appalled and staggered all ordinary friendship."[29] Thus Dorothea, whose condition was grave but not fatal, was given permission to relax into the role of a dutiful invalid.

While she was advised to rest as much as possible, Greenbank presented her with extraordinary social and intellectual opportunities. Under Rathbone's aegis, the great house functioned as a salon of Whig reform. Settling into her comfortable room, Dorothea was astonished by the stream of illustrious politicians and social reformers who walked through the door. "I doubt if one meal is taken when the family circle alone compose the company" she wrote. Over the next several months, she met the acclaimed Quaker prison reformer, Elizabeth Fry; Samuel Tuke, the proprietor of the York Retreat for the mentally disordered; and Robert Owen, the Scottish mill owner whose utopian vision of socialized agricultural communities had led him to emigrate to America, where in 1824 he launched the New Harmony commune. More than the company of notable visitors, though, she valued the way the Rathbones "number me as one of their *own*."[30]

Here, as though she had been transported to paradise, was the family Dorothea never had. "They are all, and everything in themselves, which can render the social and domestic state happy," she rejoiced, "and the contemplation and association makes me feel that there are on earth types of the joys that heaven only can make more perfect." As a convalescent in search of a cure, she became the center of attention. "There is a danger perhaps of my getting a little spoiled," she confessed to her grandmother, "with so much caressing and petting." She spoke of being the "nucleus of long debates," with physicians trying to agree on the best course of treatment. Rathbone's teenaged son liked to bring her peaches and plums to relieve her melancholy. Elizabeth Rathbone, a woman of marvelous vivaciousness and mental acuity, took Dorothea under her wing, begging her to treat Greenbank as her own home.[31]

The first few months of her illness allowed Dorothea to experience a brief second childhood, surrounded by newfound "brothers and sisters" under the guidance of exemplary parents. And the idyll quickly began to give her a new perspective on herself and on her experiences in America. Compared to the Rathbones, with their old money and

English manners, the Heaths (and even the Channings) seemed provincial. For years she had fretted about not being accepted on equal footing among the Boston elite. Yet she now found herself among authentic English gentry so naturally "adopted into this circle of loving spirits that I sometimes forget I really am not to consider the bonds transient." Stronger than any medicine, this feeling of acceptance bolstered her confidence and prompted her to take part in Greenbank's social life. "Your remark that I probably enjoy more now in social intercourse than I have ever before done is quite true," she told Anne. As the resident expert on American life and culture, she was encouraged to voice her observations and opinions.[32]

Her recovery was slow, nonetheless, and even as she extolled "the excellence which shines in [the] lives and characters of the Rathbones," she suffered intermittent bouts of depression. William IV later recalled the impression she made during this period: "a very gentle and poetical young lady, and, in her state of health, without any appearance of mental energy or great power of character." Most of the time she was bedridden. "This is the ninth week that I have no day sat up three hours at a time," she told Mrs. Torrey, "[and have] frequently not risen at all for days in succession." When she heard that Helen Loring, a woman about her own age who was taking care of Madam Dix in Boston, was thought to be dying, she lamented that "it will be her privilege to die in the exercise of ministration to others—strange that it is mine only to be ministered to." Her work ethic made her feel ashamed for abandoning her school, not to mention her unproductive idleness in England. If she dared to "express hope 'for time,'" she confided to Anne Heath, she wanted to get her health back so she could atone for past failings, resume her career as a teacher, "a more faithful one than I have hitherto been." She was still convinced that her only chance for eternal glory lay in saving "all those souls for which I have deserted my powers, in truth and singleness of heart."[33]

Anne urged her to "exert y[ou]rself to live! I know well the world has failed to win you, but . . . are your labours not needed? Do we not greatly want your example?—We do, we do!" In Dorothea's absence Anne said that she had thought long and hard about her friend's character. Dorothea's character, so seemingly isolated and aloof, she finally realized, was the result of occupying a higher plane than other people. "The contrast it presents to all the busy daughters of this age, is striking," she wrote. "Surrounded by numbers, you have hitherto lived without companionship—apart from all, quietly pursuing your course, unmoved by praise or censure, of an unreflecting world."[34]

Wide swings in mood were to be expected in a patient as ill and depressed as she was. Dorothea found, in the flood of emotion that swept her forward, that suppressed feelings about the important relationships in her life rising to the surface for the first time.

To begin with, her correspondence with her grandmother grew overtly hostile. When Madam Dorothy Dix hinted that she probably could have avoided her breakdown altogether if she had just been less ambitious and more properly attentive to her domestic duties back home at Orange Court, Dorothea was furious. Perhaps, she suggested, her grandmother did not grasp the severity of her illness, and that while she had remained in Boston it had taken every ounce of her strength to conceal "my great pain and suffering—for great it certainly was." "How could I allow myself to multiply your sleepless nights?" she asked. Meanwhile, had Madam Dix ever cared about her problems? No, even "when it might naturally have been looked for," sympathy was never forthcoming. Dorothea's grandmother was, at the time, ninety years old and sinking fast. Undoubtedly, what rankled the old woman, and probably the Harris family as well, was the notion of Dorothea in the lap of luxury at Greenbank instead of fulfilling her family duty to the woman who had given her a home. It had been all but a foregone conclusion when Dorothea sailed from Boston harbor that Madam Dix would die while she was abroad. "I trust to see her on earth again," Dorothea told her friend Mrs. Torrey, "but that desire is not unmingled with anxiety."[35]

What reflected worst on her grandmother, as far as Dorothea was concerned, was how she contrasted with William Rathbone's mother, Hannah Mary Reynolds, who was almost as old as Madam Dix but whose temperament was generous and forgiving. Hannah Reynolds outlived William Rathbone II by thirty years and was the matriarch of Greenbank. Perhaps as a monument to her beloved husband, she poured vast sums of money into the property, giving her architects free rein. The final result was an immense structure, mocked by its critics as "Strawberry Hill Gothic," a house so at odds with her Quaker modesty that, not long after the building was finished, she had deeded the place to her son, William III, and moved into a modest cottage on the outer edge of the estate. Dorothea saw her daily when Hannah, well into her eighties, strolled through the garden outside her window. Surprised to find Dorothea "so interesting, and . . . so estimable a character," Hannah stopped often to chat. Sitting in Dorothea's room, a short, stooped, white-haired figure, dressed habitually in dark silk, she exemplified to those who knew her "the quiet nobility of Quaker womanhood." At the end of May 1836, while the great house was being painted, Dorothea moved into Hannah's home. It was Hannah who introduced her to Elizabeth Fry, the unassuming Quaker lady whose single-handed inquiries into English prisons had earned her a national reputation. (While no record of Dorothea's meeting with Fry survives, the Englishwoman clearly inspired her, and later in life Dorothea would often mention Fry's work as a milestone in the march of humanitarian progress.)[36]

Unlike the Rathbones, Madam Dix had come to privilege by way of new money. Even without the terrible stain of Elijah Dix's murder, the Dix family was arriviste and lacked the genealogy and culture to enter the upper reaches of Boston society. Dorothy Lynde had married a promising young man, but after his death her family had disintegrated. From her new viewpoint, Dorothea came to see her grandmother as a misanthrope, insensitive and impossibly demanding, presiding over Orange Court in a narrow world of her own, leading a pathetically isolated life in Boston.

Madam Dix had an uncanny knack for probing the tenderest parts of Dorothea's conscience, making her question her own motives. Slighted by Dorothea's glowing accounts of the Rathbones, Madam Dix accused her of embarrassing the Dix family by living off the charity of others. This provoked Dorothea's sarcastic reply that it was "painful to know you indulged so much solicitude on my part." When Anne Heath reported on a recent visit to Madam Dix in her chamber where she was recovering from a "rheumatic attack," adding that she had spoken of her granddaughter with "animated affection," Dorothea professed her surprise that Anne was able "to summon moral and physical courage to face that Medusa!" Yet the following day, as if to repent, she wrote Madam Dix a note of consolation, closing with the thought that if "we may not meet in time: we may be reunited in the world of spirits." She signed the letter "your affectionate child."[37]

A few months later, in the early spring of 1837, Madam Dorothy Dix died of influenza. "Your Grandmother's departure . . . was so peaceful . . . and the hope to go was at length so strong—it was more than I dared to expect from her sad views of death," wrote a friend. Dorothea's reaction was subdued and coldly ambivalent. "I feel the event as having divided the only link, save the yet closer one of parental bonds, which allied me to kindred," she said, "but in the lot appointed for me on earth I hope to abide in submissive trust." For nearly twenty years she had been much closer to her grandmother than to her mother or father. But just as she had not been able to trust her parents to provide her with a home, she had not been able to trust her grandmother to love her. Madam Dix represented the harshest side of Dorothea's conscience, obsessed with obedience, humility, and an abiding sense of sinfulness. She had been the "iron will" incarnate, and Dorothea was relieved by her passing.[38]

As it turned out, Dorothea's "final link" was broken two months later by the death of her mother, Mary Bigelow Dix, in May 1837. There was "no sickness of suffering," a friend reported, "but a sudden summons to go to her rest after a life of suffering from a lingering disease." For years Dorothea had contributed the royalties from her books to her mother's support in Fitzwilliam, New Hampshire, where she lived as a chronic invalid. Yet they were so estranged that they communicated only through intermediaries. "Let me know if you write regularly to Fitzwilliam," she asked her brother Joseph. "I would rather be deprived myself of your letters than that should be omitted."[39] Despite her friends' efforts to reassure her that she had fulfilled her familial duties and "could have done nothing more had you been home," Dorothea could not avoid remorse for abandoning her grandmother and her mother. Her sense of guilt was undoubtedly sharpened not just because she enjoyed the Rathbone family so much, but because in the process she had denied her own parents. William Rathbone IV, among others, recalled that she represented herself as having been orphaned at seventeen or eighteen, and that she never made any mention of her relatives.

Dorothea kept commonplace books at Greenbank, documents that show how shaky her psyche was in 1836-37, how little she felt in command of her fate. They depict a haunted woman, tormented by self-castigation and loneliness. Her main hope was that by humbly accepting her plight she would receive God's grace. Near the beginning of one notebook she wrote a quatrain that signals her intention as a diarist:

Before my mind the mirror hangs,
Which faithful conscience holds to view;
Her light unflickering there is cast
And brings my secret sins to view.

"Secret sins" refers chiefly to buried anger, spite, failures of love, and unmet responsibilities within her family. So a poem on youth pointedly asks a teenaged girl, "didst thou for thy mother pray? / Didst thou . . . let her find / A comfort, joy, and help in thee?" Her intellectual idiom was steeped in scripture, and she filled notebook after notebook with meditations on biblical passages and characters who interested her.

Her writing conveys a mood of brooding anxiety, most of all a preoccupation with the special suffering and heartbreak that result from straining the bonds of blood and kinship. Abraham's sacrifice, the curse of Cain, Ruth pleading with Naomi to accept her as a daughter, the awful story of David and Absalom were episodes that obsessed her. Ashamed of her alcoholic father, Dorothea, however unreasonably, could not escape a feeling of personal responsibility for her broken home. And to make matters worse, she believed herself to be a victim of damaged heredity. That the sins of the father were to be visited on the next generation she did not doubt.

If her Bible provided myriad examples of penitence and redemption through suffering, occasionally it also offered hopeful parallels to her situation. One little poem she wrote, "Moses in the Bulrushes," begins with the child's mother weeping over the loss of her son, then suddenly becoming cheerful when he is adopted by pharaoh's daughters. The mother eventually reconciles herself to her loss by imagining how much happier her child would be, what great things he was bound to achieve, by virtue of growing up in the royal family. The analogy to her own rescue by the Rathbones is transparent. Dorothea's identification with baby Moses was not altogether encouraging, however, for she also noted that after his great service to God, Moses' fate was "to see the promised land, and die."[40]

In an age still struggling to distinguish mind from spirit, it is unsurprising that Dorothea, herself a woman of the deepest religious convictions, invested her afflictions with religious meaning. Sickness was evidence of evil. So she scrutinized herself, searching for the roots of her condition. At length, she convinced herself that her malady arose from "*within* . . . amid the laws of the affections, the conditions of the intellectual and spiritual life." Unless she could break its hold, she feared that her "hidden disposition" was bound to "overcome and destroy" her. Indeed, death and destruction, the wages of sin, were ever-present in Dorothea's private thoughts. Before the deaths of Madam Dix and Mary Bigelow Dix, she had become too weak even to stand beside her bed. In January 1837, after a few weeks of mild recovery, she began to experience shortness of breath and spit blood, leading the Rathbones' physician, Sir Henry Wentworth Acland of Oxford, to suspect tuberculosis. Bad as her bodily symptoms were, however, she sought to explain her affliction in terms of her underlying depression, or, as she put it, her "morbid condition of mind."[41]

Just as doctors described the physiology of the body, she reasoned, "there is a physiology of mind." The health of both depended on observing certain divine laws that were as firmly established as the laws regulating the physical universe. "God never withholds the train of . . . results he has annexed to wrong conduct," she wrote, "and the pain that visits the involuntary transgression is often our first index to a broken law." Theoretically, this approach suggested a solution to her illnesses. Through reason, she could hope to discover the divine laws that regulated the life of the mind.[42] And if she knew what they were, through the exercise of will, she could put these laws into practice.

The deeper she probed into her own consciousness, however, the more elusive the principles of the mind proved to be. In fact, her mind seemed to be torn between warring attributes. On the one hand was conscience, the faculty that measured personal behavior against God's moral law. "The cold approbation of our own conscience," she said, meant that violating principle caused one to "feel that it is unholy to be happy." The other aspect of mind was reason or intellect. Unfortunately, a strong intellect could create as much mischief as a guilty conscience unless its powers were in proper equilibrium. Imbalance, she felt, was the basis of her own anguish: "such disproportionate education of our complex nature as to leave parts of the fair field of the mind waste and unproductive, whilst a ruinous energy is concentrated onto individual propensities."[43]

Dorothea's indications were consistent with a condition English mad-doctors liked to call "moral insanity." This was a special affliction of the moral faculties or the affections—what later ages would call the emotions. In such patients, according to one leading alienist (as medical experts in madness were called), "the intellectual faculties appear to have sustained little or no injury, while the disorder is manifested principally or alone, in the state of the feelings, temper, or habits." Moral insanity, in other words, sometimes destroyed its victims' minds while leaving their rational faculties largely unimpaired. Cure depended on tracing the sources of imbalance, in body as well as mind, then taking the necessary therapeutic measures.[44]

After her first several months in England, even as her physical symptoms subsided, still Dorothea teetered on the brink, beset by a fear that her mind had snapped and was slipping helplessly into madness. At the time, she thought of her problem not so much as moral insanity as the more familiar affliction, melancholy. Commonly referred to as "the English malady," melancholy (or melancholia) was a general term used to describe a host of depressive disorders. In the time-honored system of classification, wherein mania was supposed to entail "irrationality on all subjects," melancholy was seen as eerily selective, often driving the mind to brood obsessively on single dark theme.[45] "Never give way to melancholy," warned the popular essayist Sydney Smith; "resist it steadily, for the habit will encroach." Its progress unchecked, melancholy might well set the mind on the slippery slope of unreason, eventually producing full-fledged dementia.

Although mad-doctors routinely spoke of melancholy as a serious disease, within the Anglo-American culture of the seventeenth, eighteenth, and nineteenth centuries it had a much broader meaning, something akin to what later ages have called depression. Though dangerous and potentially destructive, melancholy was also thought, in some instances, to be a source of sympathy and power. Indeed, the Romantic poets associated gloom with sensitivity. In an intense, serious-minded woman like Dorothea, a touch of melancholy was not unattractive, for it could be taken as a mark of complexity, depth, even evidence of troubled genius.

Dorothea understood these ambiguities. Certainly she knew Robert Burton's seventeenth-century classic, *The Anatomy of Melancholy*, a brilliant, witty discourse on the emotional vicissitudes of love and religion. Likewise she knew how pervasive melancholy was both in Old and New England. Samuel Johnson, the embodiment of practical common sense, confided to Boswell that he had feared for his sanity, "overwhelmed with a horrible melancholia . . . and with a dejection, gloom, and despair, which made existence misery." For the sons and daughters of the Puritans, Calvinism, proclaiming that a sense of hopelessness was the essential first step toward salvation, bequeathed a notoriously gloomy legacy. Despite their rejection of Calvinism, Emerson, Thoreau, Hawthorne, Melville, Fuller, Dickinson—the New England literary figures who were Dorothea's contemporaries—each struggled with recurrent black moods and mental disquiet.[46]

Frantically, as she tried to get a grip on herself, searching for a way to extricate herself from the bonds of melancholy, Dix got her first exposure to the revolution concerning madness that was sweeping the British reform community.

This movement had originated in late-eighteenth-century England and France around new interpretations of insanity that transformed its whole conception and social meaning. Inspired by revolutionary treatments held to restore the powers of reason in a class of people formerly assumed to have been hopeless, the new advocates of the insane set about creating a new kind of institution: a model domestic environment, a home and family, that would redeem the insane and, in turn, reunite them with the family of humankind.[47] Seen in the light of these new theories of the asylum, Dix's gradual triumph over melancholy under the compassionate care of the Rathbone family could be considered a sterling example of what had come to be called moral treatment. Indeed, as she adapted to her new surroundings, Greenbank turned out to be so wonderfully conducive to her recuperation that this pastoral setting ultimately became her personal frame of reference for the process of curing mental disorders.

At Greenbank she found a means to save her sanity, a way that was to provide a model for others. An English country house was her asylum; and it offered the sensitive New Englander a perfect moratorium.

Trying to grasp what was happening to her, Dorothea researched the prevailing theories of disease from books in Greenbank's library as she had studied natural history ten years before. Victorian medicine was separated by "a kind of geological fault" from the theory and practice that developed later around the germ theory of disease. As Dorothea had learned from Dr. Acland, Victorian physicians did not see diseases as discrete biological entities. Illness, even an epidemic disease like cholera, was thought of as "a protean and dynamic condition" affecting the whole person. Heredity, religion, and morality were seen as no less important to proper diagnosis and treatment than hygiene and environment. As ministers asserted that the spiritual realm interpenetrated the material world, physicians "viewed disease as a changed state of being affecting the whole man and capable of being altered by any of his myriad activities."[48]

In her investigations, Dorothea was especially disturbed by the great emphasis medical writers placed on heredity. Conventional wisdom had always dictated that like begets like, but physicians in the early nineteenth century had devised increasingly elegant theories of the inheritance of acquired characteristics. The consensus was that children inherited a "diathesis or constitutional bent" that shaped their physical, emotional, and intellectual natures. Heredity determined one's proclivity to contract any disease, from tuberculosis to lunacy. And parentage clearly played the most direct part. The mother "was generally seen as contributing temperament, the father intellect; the mother internal viscera, stamina, and vitality; the father musculature."[49] Haunted through her twenties by a "hidden disposition" that threatened "to overcome and destroy" her best qualities, Dorothea confessed to Anne Heath that she could place little hope "upon a fabric the basis of which is insecure."[50]

As the months passed at Greenbank, however, Dorothea slowly emerged from the cocoon of her illness. Even the English winter took on a brighter aspect. Her brother Charles sensed a change in her letters to him. "Your thoughts seem brighter and flow more freely than ever," he told her; "there is no bound, no dimness to the vision of the mind, but light and beauty are always around it." The Rathbones automatically included her in their family life, and the burden of her past seemed to grow lighter. This boosted her self-esteem and encouraged her to begin to take part in their many social, political and religious reform endeavors.[51]

Liverpool in the 1830s, Dorothea soon saw, was undergoing startling population growth, fueled by a torrent of immigrants seeking refuge from Ireland's agricultural crisis. Sadly, the local economy could not support them. And the city's municipal and charitable institutions were unprepared to cope with large numbers of unskilled foreigners. For several years the city fathers had lurched from crisis to crisis: epidemic disease, crime waves, pauperism, and a breakdown in public education. Shortly after Dorothea arrived, a violent controversy erupted between Catholics and Protestants over how the Bible should be taught in the Liverpool corporation schools. William Rathbone, ever the mediator, intervened and helped make peace between the warring factions. Irish immigration forced Rathbone, as he prepared to stand for election for mayor, to articulate his interpretation of the Poor Law reforms that had been enacted by Parliament three years earlier.[52]

All of England was coming to terms with the social and political consequences of the watershed Reform Act of 1832 and the New Poor Law. In 1830, after forty-six years as the opposition, the Whig Party had assumed control of the central government. In short order, the Whigs implemented a series of sweeping political and social reforms. Lord Melbourne's administration vigorously pushed through the Reform Act of 1832, then moved on to establish the municipal corporations, the backbone of local government in Britain.

The aspect of reform that held the most interest for Dorothea was a new civil humanitarianism. Its agenda included abolishing slavery within the empire, improving conditions in factories and prisons, and, above all, reconstructing the Old Poor Law. The later was not a specific statute but a set of loosely knitted policies and procedures that had been on the books since the reign of Elizabeth.

Now that they were in power, the reformers planned to recast the theory of social welfare and reorganize its administration through the structures of national and local government. The Liberal vanguard of Whig reformers to which Rathbone belonged meant to use Poor Law reform as a framework for redefining welfare—especially social welfare for people unable to support themselves. Their goal was a welfare system that would sustain the truly needy without weakening the incentive of the poor to work. The problem they faced was how to decide who among the poor was truly needy. Their solution was, in part, to invent a new social science to sort out who should qualify for help from the state.[53]

The elaborate body of social and economic theory that grew out of this enterprise had no counterpart in America, and to Dorothea it presented a radically new way of thinking about social problems and obligations. Above all, the British reformers sought to ground their policies not in superstition or tradition but in facts. Their appetite for data impelled them to comb the English countryside to find out how the poor really lived in the nation's fifteen thousand parishes. The prodigious efforts of the Poor Law commissioners to compile detailed descriptions from all parts of the country, to synthesize these into reports, and to use their findings to engineer state-sponsored solutions to social problems—all this made a profound impression on Dorothea.[54]

To be sure, their research methods were unscientific, and their findings questionable. But their reconceptualization of poverty, indigence, and human need was nonetheless remarkable. With no preparation in political economy, and having little appetite for abstract social theory, Dorothea never engaged in a systematic study of the Whig reformers' arguments. But she absorbed many of their broader principles.

Putting the New Poor Law into practice was a traumatic process that stirred up fierce debate. As Edwin Chadwick and the commissioners moved to set up a workhouse system and eliminate all forms of outdoor relief, Charles Dickens published the first installments of his scathing commentary on their efforts, *Oliver Twist* (1837). Dorothea, whose only experience had been with private philanthropy, was perplexed by the concept of state-legislated poor relief. "The whole implies a want of healthful social organization," she observed. "The large heart of charity is warmed, and nourished by the heavenly food on which it subsists— but the poor are not made self-relying—raised—strengthened— saved!" Despite her confusion about their new ideas, however, she unconsciously absorbed much of the rhetoric of the Whig reformers, including Jeremy Bentham's famous principle, "the greatest happiness of the greatest number," a phrase she would later incorporate in many of her state and federal petitions on behalf of the insane poor.[55]

In view of her own disease of mind and body, what intrigued Dorothea the most were reports from the York Retreat. Established by the Society of Friends, the celebrated retreat had opened its doors in 1796. William Tuke, its founder, had sought to enshrine the Quaker virtues of gentleness and quietude in "a place in which the unhappy might obtain refuge—a quiet haven in which the shattered bark might find a means of reparation or safety." By the 1830s, under the leadership of William Tuke's grandson Samuel, the York Retreat enjoyed the reputation of being England's most progressive asylum for the insane and was thus the mecca for anyone interested in the study of mental disorders and their treatment.[56]

Dorothea had a natural connection to the retreat through the Rathbones. William Tuke had been a friend of William Rathbone II, and both were members of the elite circle of Quaker reformers whose interests encompassed antislavery, poverty, and prison reform. Samuel Tuke and William Rathbone III continued the friendship to the next generation, and Samuel was a frequent visitor at Greenbank. In addition, around the time Dorothea returned to America an acquaintance of the Rathbones, one Mrs. Glande, underwent the wrenching ordeal of finding care for her insane daughter. At last the girl was committed to the York Retreat, where, Dorothea was told, "we have had satisfactory accounts since."[57]

At the time Dorothea visited England, the retreat, with its Georgian architecture, beautiful gardens, and "most admirable order and refinement," claimed to be able to alleviate and even cure madness by treating the insane with kindness and respect. This was a powerful and attractive idea, especially to a Unitarian schoolmistress fascinated by the development of young minds. In fact Samuel Tuke, in his *Description of the Retreat*, had explicitly compared the education of children and the enlightened treatment of the insane that came to be known as moral treatment or moral management. "There is much analogy between the judicious treatment of children, and that of insane persons," he wrote. "Locke has observed, that 'the great secret of education, lies in finding the way to keep the child's spirit easy, active, and free; and yet, at the same time, to restrain him from many things he has a mind to, and to draw him to things which are uneasy to him'. It is highly desirable that the attendants on lunatics should possess this influence over their minds; but it will never be obtained by austerity and rigour." During the early decades of the century, at least, the Retreat's staff generally tried to take Tuke's statement literally. They eschewed mechanical restraints—chains, muffs, straitjackets, and so forth—and kept corporal punishment to a minimum.[58]

The York Retreat in the early 19th century: lunatic asylum as English country house.

Then and later, Dorothea instinctively responded to the Retreat's therapeutic program, for the premise of moral treatment perfectly fit both the rationalist and the religious aspects of her personality. Regaining the capacity for self-management and moral reasoning was thought to be the key to recovery, which was supposed to be attained through a combination of reflection and hard work. As in ordinary nineteenth-century family life, idleness was discouraged and patients were kept as busy as possible. Organized around the ideals of the Society of Friends—mutual respect, gentleness, the belief that every person has within him or her the spirit of God—the Retreat sought to steep the mad in an atmosphere of humane domesticity. "Nothing has a more favourable and controlling influence over one who is . . . actually affected with melancholy or mania," declared one expert on "nervous affections" in 1816, "than an exhibition of friendship or philanthropy." Accordingly, from the start, the managers of the retreat aimed to heal the "social affections" in the disordered minds of their patients and instill the feeling of family.[59]

It is hard to overestimate the impression these principles made on Dorothea. She thoroughly absorbed the retreat's values and adopted them as the basis for most of her later ideas about asylums and psychiatric treatment.

The retreat exemplified an approach to the treatment of insanity that confirmed her private experience at Greenbank. As she subsequently remarked, Tuke's gentle methods appeared to have proven conclusively that, under the right conditions, madness could be domesticated and treated like any other illness. And the right conditions, as a perceptive student of the retreat has pointed out, embraced a basic ambiguity: "the desirability of humanity towards the weak and the importance of encouraging moral self-discipline in the hope that the weak would become strong." This same tension was also the tension Dorothea experienced in her own inner life.[60]

In the late spring she reported feeling much stronger; and in June she wrote from Greenbank that she no longer needed "medical attention or nursing." With typical caution her physicians continued to prescribe rest. And since they forbade her "to incur fatigue by standing or walking," she was justified in "doing nothing *this* month—but remain at ease."[61]

Her moratorium was drawing to a close.

She had, by virtue of a process she could explain only as providential, recovered her mental health. Because her therapy was largely informal, flowing from the special familial conditions at Greenbank, she would need time to assimilate what had happened to her, and still more time to place it in intellectual and social context. But as she began to consider returning to Boston, she knew her year abroad had transformed her in ways she had scarcely begun to fathom.

Others recognized the change as well. In a letter remarkable for its prescience, an impressionable young Unitarian minister named John Hamilton Thon, who was part of the Rathbone circle, told Dorothea that throughout her illness she had displayed a strong "power over other minds," an exceptional gift. "I have much to hope for you," he wrote, "a life free from suffering it may not be given you to enjoy—but a life irradiated with the consciousness of usefulness, of the graceful ministries of mind, of fulfilled mission, I prophecy [sic] to still be yours."[6]

She would leave England changed in outlook much like American artists—Thomas Cole, comes to mind—who traveled to Europe and studied the old masters at first hand, then returned to see their native landscape with new eyes. Hers was less an aesthetic than a moral enlightenment. She had adopted a new criterion of humanitarianism and in the process discovered unanticipated reasons to be interested in government power. Afterward, in America, she would need fewer than three years to apply her experience to the conditions of her own country, completing the creative process of forming her fresh impressions into a distinctive vision.

CHAPTER FOUR

The Discovery of "Suffering Humanity"

News traveled quickly across the Atlantic, and in June Dorothea was shocked to learn of the Panic of 1837, the financial debacle that resulted when the bottom fell out of the international cotton market. "What a calamitous year this is in the Commercial world," she fretted. "I almost dread yet anxiously anticipate the arrival of the packets." Although she had never showed much interest in business, she could not avoid being caught up in the news. Widespread specie shortages and a string of bank failures in America seemed to prove that reckless speculation and greed had finally taken their toll. She hoped that the painful demands of foreign creditors would teach her moneymaking countrymen "the wisdom and honesty of doing business on a more independent foundation." As the depression deepened, though, she began to worry about its effect on the laboring class, wondering whether mounting unemployment in Boston might lead to the kind of social unrest she had witnessed in Liverpool. Alarmed when she read in May that New York banks had suspended specie payments, Dorothea decided she could no longer put off returning home.[1]

She was a practical woman who understood that her future prospects depended largely on her inheritance. With the American economy in turmoil, and her Boston relatives eager to execute Madam Dix's will, she reluctantly booked passage to Boston. Tearfully bidding the Rathbones farewell, she sailed from Liverpool in August 1837 and arrived in Boston harbor in mid-September.

An extended trip abroad was unusual in those days, particularly for a woman alone, and her return to Boston caused a stir of excitement. Her niece, Mary Harris, recalled her walking down the gangplank and onto the dock at Long Wharf, "a tall slender young woman of erect graceful figure and delicate gentle movements, with an appearance of delicate health. A pair of soft-brown eyes and hair of the same color, a sweet grave face lighted up by not too frequent smiles." Dressed simply in "a plain, one-colored dress of woolen material, probably merino, and a broad plaited white ruffle round the throat which became well the slender neck and delicate face above it," Dorothea climbed into the carriage and disappeared from view.[2]

The Harris family's feelings toward Dorothea were less than warm and enthusiastic. In her absence they had been stuck with the burden of Madam Dix's final illness, and they considered her granddaughter selfish and ungrateful for deserting the matriarch on her deathbed. Dorothea's uncle Thaddeus Mason Harris was at the time gravely ill, and his family had been stretched thin between looking after him and nursing Madam Dix.[3]

If Madam Dix's death was a psychological release for her granddaughter, it meant financial freedom as well. Freedom, but hardly great wealth. Considering the burgeoning family fortune in Elijah Dix's heyday, what remained at the end was astonishingly little. Dorothea's share of the estate, if managed prudently, would produce an adequate income to ensure her independence. The will divided Dorothy Lynde Dix's assets between the Harris family, who received half of the estate, and the three Dix children, who each received one-sixth. In the long run, Dorothea either directly or indirectly benefited from all the Dix money. Her brother Charles went to sea and, five years later, died of a fever aboard a merchant vessel off the coast of Africa. He never married, and his portion of the inheritance reverted to his sister. Dorothea's younger brother, Joseph, followed his grandfather's entrepreneurial example and became a moderately prosperous merchant. Since he did not need the cash, he gave Dorothea his share of the estate with the understanding that she would make loans to him from time to time free of interest.[4]

Combining the royalties from her books, her savings from teaching, a small annuity Elijah Dix had bequeathed her, and the income from her inheritance from Madam Dix, Dorothea could earn perhaps three thousand dollars a year. This was certainly a respectable sum, and her spartan habits helped it to go a very long way indeed. Travel was by far her greatest expense. But compared to later ages, transportation and lodging in the mid-nineteenth century were bargains. For the most part she had enough money to go wherever she wished, staying at the best inns and hotels, without worrying about the cost. Over the years, she learned to use her money as a tool to approach men of social position and influence. The long list of her financial advisers includes names like Kidder, Appleton, Hacker, Randall, and Lamb—bankers and investors in Boston, New York, and Philadelphia who were also influential in politics and philanthropy. Equally important, she had enough money to give some of it away, and she learned to spread around small gifts and donations, helping to cement her relationships with other philanthropists and charitable organizations.

The money was an essential ingredient in her success. Every facet of her career would depend on her being a woman of independent means, and being characterized as a woman of property.

Madam Dix's estate was settled in the winter of 1837. This was for Dorothea a rite of passage, for she knew that while she did not have to worry about money, neither did she have a home in Boston. In her absence her school had dissolved, her students scattered around the city. Her brothers had lives of their own. In contrast with the warmth and gentility she had experienced at Greenbank, Boston felt cold, lonely, empty. Groping for emotional support, instinctively she reached out to Channing, who, despite his failing health, had recently stirred the city with two lectures to the "Mechanics Apprentices," as he called them, the boldest statements he had ever made on the evils of poverty and the urgent need for social reform.

Gravitating to Channing's circle, Dorothea arranged to board with his sister-in-law, Sarah Gibbs, who owned a magnificent brick house on the high point of Mount Vernon Street. The Channings lived next door. Over the course of the next few months, Dorothea tried to re-create something of the domestic ambience of Greenbank. But it was to little avail. Teas, dinners, and other social occasions gave her no more enjoyment, she confessed, "than in days gone by, when parties were contemplated at a distance." Every evening she spent an hour reading to Channing, whose eyesight was failing. Channing loved England as much as she did, loved its history and language, and admired William Rathbone as a saint. While their reading and thoughtful conversation brought her "a satisfaction bringing no alloy," she wrote, this was not in itself sufficient to keep boredom from setting in. After Greenbank, Boston frayed her nerves with "its dull brick walls, throngs of hurrying inhabitants[,] the busy or the frivolous." The city's "noisy paved streets [and] its impure atmosphere have no attraction," she told Anne Heath.[5]

It was during this phase of readjustment, flush with new ideas yet uncertain how to proceed, that she began to narrow her quest for a vocation. She still gave the impression of being self-absorbed, lost, possessed by an aimless dissatisfaction that made it hard to know what she was looking for. She had expected things to be easier. "I was not conscious that so great a trial was to meet my return," Dorothea wrote in February 1838, "till the whole force of contrast was laid before me." She pined for the Rathbones, then chastised herself for her pointless longings. Perhaps she was greedy, she told Anne, "too craving of that rich gift, the power of sharing others' minds; I have drank [sic] deeply, long, and oh how blissfully, at a fountain in a foreign clime."[6]

Anne empathized with her disappointment: "to be shut out from elysium, having abode there with congenial minds, in perfect content and agreement." Perhaps, she mused, it was Dorothea's fate to be "earth's . . . wanderer, doomed to know many a think [sic] of grief and pain." Out of compassion, she urged Dorothea to give up her restless search and join her in Brookline, where the two of them could quietly live out their days together in sisterly affection. Dorothea had complained so often that she had no home. "Why does not someone awake, arise and before you are quite out of reach, offer the inducement which would keep you: a home where your affections may securely repose."[7]

The whole idea of retreating from the world into what she considered idle spinsterhood was so repugnant that Dorothea was convinced that even her best friend failed to understand her. "God help you I cannot feel now like writing," she told Anne, "I have many anxieties which friendship can neither lighten nor share."[8]

Dorothea did not wish to be taken care of; in fact, quite the reverse. She was hungry for responsibility. This was plainly the motive behind her unsuccessful attempt to adopt a young girl named Marianna Cutter.

Marianna's mother was Dorothea's first cousin, and the girl had been one of her students in The Hope before it was disbanded. Sometime during the year before her trip to Liverpool, Dorothea had tried to persuade the mother, bedridden with tuberculosis, to give up her child. She was rebuffed. But in the spring of 1837 Marianna's mother died. At the time the girl, who was probably eleven or twelve, appealed to her "dear Aunt" in Greenbank, telling Dorothea "you are now my only real mother[.] My own dear mother is at rest[;] she is past all trouble and pain and in the home of the blest."[9]

When she first returned, Dorothea assumed her path was clear to adopt the child. Then, to her dismay, she learned that several months earlier, Marianna had been placed in the home of other relatives who apparently had no intention of letting her go, losing the benefit of her share of the Cutter estate. Deeply disappointed, Dorothea tried to gain custody of Marianna, even entertaining the possibility of a lawsuit. At last she accepted the inevitable, though she could not bear entirely to give up her dream of having a daughter. Henceforth she adopted the habit of addressing Marianna Davenport Cutter as "Marianna Davenport Dix Cutter," a practice she continued for fifty years. After Dorothea Dix died in 1887, Marianna (Mrs. Trott after her marriage) recalled that her aunt "sometimes left out the Davenport, sometimes used two initial D's. No one else ever used any name but Davenport."[10]

The two D's were Dorothea Dix's own initials, and they reflect the importance she placed on the relationship. For in her late twenties Dorothea stopped using her given name to sign correspondence, using instead the neutral "D. L. Dix." For Anne Heath she made an exception, usually shortening her name to "Thea." Shedding "Dorothea Lynde" was both a way of putting her family history further behind her and avoiding any confusion with her grandmother, Madam Dorothy Lynde Dix. Asked to account for the idiosyncrasy of using initials rather than her given name in correspondence, she responded to Benjamin Silliman that she could not remember writing her full name "since childhood, disliking it altogether."[11]

Both 1838 and 1839 were years of motion, if not discernible progress. She was constantly on the move, traveling throughout New England, the mid-Atlantic states, and as far south as Virginia. Occasionally she stopped to visit friends and take in local sights, and she spent part of her time trying to track down distant relatives to whom Madam Dix had made minor bequests and people who owed the estate money. The main impulse behind her journeys, however, was simply to get out of Boston. There her psychic state dragged terribly. Old friends failed to appreciate how much she had changed in England. Remaining in their midst anchored her too much to the past, she told Anne Heath, and she knew that if she slipped back into her old pattern of life, say, by opening another school, she risked a relapse of her old melancholy.[12]

The prospect of making some kind of a fresh start, unfettered by the past she felt so stiflingly in Boston, led her to move to Washington in early 1838. Relying on her network of Unitarian friends, she assembled the necessary letters of introduction and easily obtained invitations to visit several prominent families in the capital city, in Alexandria, and in Baltimore.

Yet from the moment she arrived in the capital she was disappointed. Antebellum Washington was more an outpost than a grand citadel of government—"a rude colony [with] unfinished Greek temples for workrooms, and sloughs for roads," Henry Adams disdainfully remarked. Compared to the thoughtful hostesses of Beacon Hill (let alone Greenbank) with their manners and highly cultivated conversation, Washington's parlor culture was crude and vulgar. Her first weeks dredged up Dorothea's old dread of making new friends and her disinclination to waste time in what she saw as idle chatter and dissipation. Brooding about her sense of isolation, her inability to fit in, she worried that she was slipping back into the same ominous melancholy she had managed to shake off the year before. Now, once again, her mind was so gravely darkened by a "morbid sentiment," she confided to Anne, "that perhaps it were wise not to make it a topic of either written or spoken communication."[13]

Before the year was out, however, Dorothea managed to rise above her darker ruminations, turning her gaze away from herself to a variety of tasks to be performed in the community. Her formulation of these tasks shows that she thought of them as antidotes to her own mental anguish. Writing down a list of important duties, she included, "The suffering—to be comforted;—the wandering led home . . . the indolent roused; the over-excited restrained." These were the things she wanted to accomplish, although just listing them did not clarify her approach.[14]

Enlisting the help of two ladies who shared her comfortable lodgings just north of the capital in Georgetown, Dorothea set about visiting schools and orphanages around Washington. She had been interested in educational and charitable institutions for a long time, and she now enjoyed a fresh perspective from her experiences in Liverpool. In 1838–1839, however, she was not sure precisely what she was looking for beyond a chance to do something useful, something to relieve the suffering of society's unfortunates.

In Washington, as elsewhere, most public institutions of incarceration—jails, almshouses, asylums—welcomed visitors. Indeed, many facilities advertised themselves as visitor attractions, charging the curious an admission fee to gape at the criminal, the poor, the mad. So Dorothea had no trouble getting inside. On her informal tours of investigation, she expressed admiration for clean, well-ordered institutions, which were of course the exceptions. One convent school on the outskirts of Washington, for example, impressed her as "the most properly arranged establishment I have ever seen." But she had the opposite reaction to the jails and almshouses of the District of Columbia, with their "black, horrible histories," and evident abuses "from which every sense recoils."[15]

"Studying the aspects of society," as she described these expeditions, collecting facts and impressions without a specific goal in mind, brought to the surface Dorothea's pessimism about human nature. "The history of the human mind" hardly appeared progressive, she observed, when one considered "the multitudes of unreflecting beings who are born, grow to maturity, decline and perish, all the while as little exercising the higher capabilities of their nature as the lower orders of creation." How could one account for the fate of these lost souls? Perhaps it would be a relief, she mused, to adopt the belief "in the intermediate state of Purgatory in that a wider redemption might be hoped."[16]

As she tried to envision a part for herself, a human space she might occupy to exert her moral power to its fullest, she floundered. Alarmed at her aimlessness, her brother Charles asked her to consider coming back to Boston once he had returned from a voyage to Africa and, as she put it, "again renew my pleasant housekeeping life." Anne picked up the idea and urged Dorothea to "gather together under one roof, & form a happy household" with both brothers.[17] But even before she received the news that Charles Dix had died at sea that summer, Dorothea could not abide the thought of returning to Boston. She elected instead to roam through Virginia, Pennsylvania, and New York.[18]

When the cold and rainy season set in, she used an introduction from her old friend William Henry Furness to call on George Washington Burnap, the scholarly minister of the First Independent Church in Baltimore. In many respects, Burnap and his wife, Nancy Williams, reminded her of the Furnesses. He had achieved prominence as a lecturer and man of letters, and was well respected. Like many conscientious Unitarians, and with greater urgency than his colleagues in the free states, Burnap was wrestling with the slavery question, nervously trying to decide how to handle the explosive subject with his congregation. This was not a debate she wished to join, although when she met Burnap's friend Moses Sheppard she was intrigued by his argument that the only permanent solution to the evil of slavery was to ship American blacks back to Africa.[19]

As in the Caribbean seven years earlier, however, Dorothea expressed only a superficial interest in slavery. She was far more engaged by Moses Sheppard's other benevolent projects, above all his plan to build an insane asylum in Baltimore County. Sheppard, a shrewd Quaker merchant who had accumulated a fortune trading groceries and tobacco, reminded Dorothea a little of William Rathbone III, both in his broad philanthropic interests and his absolute aversion to public notice. When Dorothea met him, he was reading every book and pamphlet he could get on mental disease and lunatic asylums. He told her he wanted someday to endow an institution modeled on the York Retreat. In turn, she was able to share with him the view of the retreat she had gained in England.[20] Stimulating though it was, meeting Moses Sheppard did not lead directly to any further action on Dorothea's part. His asylum remained a project for the future. When she left Burnap's house in early 1839, she felt she had no alternative except to return to Boston.

It was at this time, when she was at loose ends, disillusioned, feeling a strong desire to retreat from the world and pursue the life of the mind to the exclusion of all else, that Dorothea drifted into a relationship with a young divinity student named Roswell Dwight Hitchcock.

When Anne Heath insinuated that Dorothea seemed to be encouraging the advances of gentlemen callers in Washington, she was assured that they were nothing more than fellow laborers in the Lord's vineyard. But sometime in late 1838 Hitchcock clearly became something more. When he met Dorothea, he was only twenty-one, fifteen years her junior, a second-year student at Andover Theological Seminary outside Boston. But the difference in their ages did not keep him from falling under her spell. Unfortunately his letters to her are all that remain. By reflection, though, they reveal a seldom evident facet of Dorothea's personality—qualities of charm, attractiveness, vivaciousness she rarely displayed.

They met at the time when Dorothea was just beginning to explore New England jails and almshouses in a systematic way. For reasons that baffled him, the dignified and accomplished lady whom he admired from the moment he met her seemed to delight in his company. What did she see in him, he asked, "immature as I am, and surrounded as you are by some of the noblest and purest spirits in N[ew] E[ngland]." The answer is that she saw the sort of young man she might have married had she been fifteen or twenty years younger—attractive, earnest, a serious student of biblical theology, and, most of all, a captivatingly articulate man who dazzled everyone with his talk. Also, he was a seeker, trying to figure out how to channel his natural gifts into a career.[21]

In the fall of 1839, as they drifted into a common orbit, Hitchcock accepted a tutorship at Amherst, which meant that for two years his relationship with Dorothea would be at long distance. Since the mails were slow and they rarely saw each other, they were free to indulge romantic feelings according to the florid literary conventions of the period without much thought to where the relationship was heading. Encouraging Hitchcock to write as often as possible, Dorothea volunteered to pay the costs of postage; and he sent his letters to her unpaid. Although he was wary of overstepping the bounds of propriety with a decorous older lady, as the months passed the young man was tempted to declare himself with increasing boldness. "To be loved for beauties of heart and life, which you seem to possess unconsciously, is, of course, no merely recent fortune of yours," he wrote in a typical passage. "But I have wished you might know all the love I have had for you since we first met in N[ew] H[ampshire] and found that we had so many sympathies and hopes and aims in common." He declared himself her "*friend*," a word whose meaning he stressed "more fervently than you think."[22]

They kept up their coquettish stream of letters over the next year while Dorothea traveled south, and they arranged at least two meetings in Boston during the winter of 1840–41. By spring of 1841, anticipating a meeting after a long absence, Hitchcock was becoming openly affectionate in his letters. His thoughts of her grew "intenser the more I think of meeting you so soon." Dorothea promised to visit him in

Amherst in May, and he made appropriate arrangements for her to stay in the home of the respectable Reverend Mr. Tyler, confessing that, improbable as their liaison was, his "sturdiest skepticism . . . would be forced to yield to such proof as you lavish on me of your generously continued affection." At the same time, he sensed enough ambiguity in the relationship to warn Dorothea that she "may be in need of the same wholesome caution which you've been dealing out to me for so long a time."[23]

When she postponed her visit to Amherst, he was nervously disappointed, and worried that when they actually met she would find him "far less interesting in every respect almost than you may be dreaming of." He was not far wrong. Dorothea was stepping up the tempo of her survey of lunatics in Massachusetts and taking the first tentative steps toward documenting what she would shortly publish in her *Memorial to the Legislature of Massachusetts*. As this gripping project absorbed more of her time and attention, her interest in young Hitchcock waned. Meanwhile he begged to see her. "You ought to know how desolate I felt for days as I went to my home," he wrote, "and found not your footsteps there to meet me."[24]

When she finally managed to come to Amherst for a few days, he was ecstatic, although he noticed that she was not keeping up her end of their correspondence. "I've longed more intensely than I can describe to hear from you, he wrote in July. Looking into the future "with dreaming eyes," he envisioned that "we have begun to love for Eternity—let this be the one thought to give us bliss." He signed his letter "thine in truest love."[25]

Hitchcock's ardent declaration after their meeting forced an unequivocal response on Dorothea's part. In their moral universe, there was no place for an open-ended affair. Since there was no alternative way to continue their relationship, he forced her to contemplate the idea of marriage. When she did she quickly concluded that such a match was out of the question. Passages in some of her letters to him were surely charged with elements of sexual attraction, but Dorothea never moved to close the distance and would not have welcomed physical passion. In early 1842 she cut him off abruptly and, to his way of thinking, rather cruelly. While she was in Boston, he had written her a letter that assumed she soon expected and would accept a proposal of marriage. He was stunned by the cold severity of reply, which he considered "the strangest phenomenon of the kind which has ever come within my experience. It would be hard to say whether I was more grieved or vexed. [Your] letter seemed to have been designed as a rebuke for my presuming too far upon your affection." This final letter he sent her in an envelope marked "paid."[26]

Hitchcock soon put the episode behind him, married his longtime sweetheart (a woman his own age named Bessie), studied theology in Germany, then served as a Congregational preacher in New Hampshire, where he discovered his natural talent for teaching. In 1855 he accepted a post at Union Theological Seminary in New York City, going on to mesmerize a generation of students with his grandiloquent lectures. He served as president of the faculty from 1880 until his death in 1887.

What he could not have known at the time Dorothea broke with him is that her interest in him had been the last stage of a profound inner transition. Her year with the Rathbones proved that she could win the love of a family; her relationship with Hitchcock proved that she could win the love of a man. In both cases, once she was sure of her acceptance, she moved on with the serious business of defining her lifework. By the time he last wrote to her from Phillipston, she was already absorbed in the early phase of her career and was anxious to get on with it. For a woman who seldom engaged even in mild flirtation, though, their relationship occupied a special niche in her memory. Toward the end of her life, when she burned hundreds of letters she thought too personal to risk saving, she felt his correspondence was too precious to destroy. She would save his letters, but in the spring of 1842 she saw plainly there was no place in her future for Roswell Dwight Hitchcock.

Every published account of Dorothea Dix's discovery of the nether world of madness in 1841 depicts it as a sudden revelation. And she certainly preferred to remember it that way. In the 1850s, asked by a friend, a Baltimore lawyer named Alexander Randall, what had first inspired her to take up the cause of the insane, she described a moment of epiphany. Her road to Damascus, she said, was a brick street in Boston where one day she overheard two gentlemen loudly denouncing the awful conditions in the Middlesex County jail in East Cambridge. Ordinarily she might have sloughed off the matter, but on that morning, she recalled, she was feeling guilty about having become unduly self-centered—so engrossed in the cultivation of her mind and the society of Boston's literary men that she was neglecting the needs of even her closest friends. Her selfishness, she suddenly finally realized, stemmed from an obsessive "improvement of her mind at the expense of her heart." Bereft of family ties or any relationships likely to provide her heart adequate "scope for its affections," she said, she hit upon the idea of going to the jail and finding out whether or not she could be of some use to her fellow creatures.[27]

When she entered the jail and asked to examine it, the story goes, her presence caused the jailer considerable consternation. Unable to fathom why a genteel-looking lady would want to walk through the dirty, stinking facility, he at first suggested that "she must be deranged herself & perhaps ought to be under his control, & not inquiring into the condition of those who were." Undaunted and more determined than ever to get to the bottom of the matter, she inspected the jail and discovered a number of insane inmates in disgusting circumstances, whereupon she immediately approached the Massachusetts legislature and obtained an official inspection commission. As a result of her efforts in Cambridge and Boston, she told Randall, she succeeded in erecting a noble Institution for the Insane in Massachusetts.[28]

This story was a legend. Since Dix's efforts never established a new asylum anywhere in Massachusetts, there is reason to be skeptical about this whole account.

A variant on the same theme—based on an interview with Dix—appeared in an article published after the Civil War in the New York journal *Galaxy*. Ordinarily she dismissed biographical pieces about her as fantasy and fiction, but in this case, after it appeared, she remarked that the story was unusually accurate. Similar to what she had hold Alexander Randall, the piece portrayed her overhearing two benevolent gentlemen outside Dr. Lowell's West Church discussing the East Cambridge jail. Resolving to look into the matter, a few days later she rose from her sickbed and made her way across the Charles River to the institution. Once inside she was unsettled by the babel of prisoners awaiting trial. But what truly shocked her was the spectacle of thirty insane persons in the most wretched state of filth and rags, completely neglected, locked in dingy, malodorous cells. Ignoring the protests of the jailer, she organized Sunday school classes for all prisoners, including the insane, the next week. After a few months, she began to realize that the insane were the lowest of the low and needed her help more than anyone else. Soon it dawned on her that the insane in Cambridge were probably no worse off than other pauper lunatics throughout the

Commonwealth of Massachusetts. Thus simply, the story goes, was her great mission launched.[29]

James T. G. Nichols, a Unitarian minister who had first met Dix when she visited his parents' home in the 1830s, recounted a somewhat different sequence of events. He claimed to have sought her out when he was a student at Harvard Divinity School and begged her to find a wise and experienced woman to take over his unruly Sunday school. When pastoral field work assignments had been handed out, he had the misfortune to draw the twenty women in the East Cambridge House of Corrections. One session with this motley group was enough to convince him that he was out of his depth. Explaining his predicament to Dix, he was astonished when, on the spur of the moment, she proposed to take over the class herself. Her delicate health notwithstanding, he wrote, she appeared at the jail on the frigid morning of March 28, 1841, and taught the class without incident.

Just as she was about to leave, however, she noticed that several cells holding insane prisoners had no heat. Indignantly demanding an explanation, she was told that fire would be an unnecessary hazard because lunatics could not tell the difference between hot and cold. Dix knew better, but she could not convince the jail's officials to change their policy. So she prepared a petition to the East Middlesex court, where it was granted at once. "Thus was her great work commenced," wrote Nichols.[30]

This visit to the East Cambridge House of Corrections, as it turns out, was not her first contact with that notorious jail. Dix's uncle Thaddeus Mason Harris occasionally preached there during the early 1830s, and Dorothea frequently accompanied him carrying a basket of religious books and pamphlets to hand out to the prisoners.[31]

That the institution had been for years a community repository for the indigent insane was widely known by people who had never set foot inside the jail. In the meantime, a growing public controversy had centered on the inhumanity of throwing lunatics in with felons and suspects awaiting trial. Dorothea had followed the issue for a long time, and from England had written her grandmother to ask, "What is the condition of the houses of correction?—Are there any printed reports?"[32]

After her experiences in England, when she revisited the jail she discovered a surprising affinity for the prisoners, sane and insane, and so she decided to continue her weekly teaching through the summer. Seeing the mentally disordered inmates on a regular basis, concerned about the uproar they caused within the jail, and well aware that better arrangements could be made for their care, Dix pondered what she could do. No one had better skills to research and classify. Taking advantage of her abundant connections within the Boston reform community, she began to devote increasing amounts of energy to the problem of the insane poor.

When it came to finding a local alternative to locking up the mad in jails, Dix did not have far to look. In her view, a new hospital for the insane poor, opened in 1839 in South Boston, perfectly illustrated the superiority of hospital care, even for lunatics assumed to be incurable. Previously the city's homeless insane had been housed near the almshouse in a receptacle Dix described as furnishing "such scenes of horror and utter abomination such as language is powerless to represent." Enlightened Bostonians, responding to growing publicity, pressed for the construction of a new facility. "I witnessed with profound interest and surprise," she recalled, as the insane were unchained, "bathed, clothed, fed decently, and placed by kind nurses in comfortable apartments." In its early days the Boston Lunatic Hospital, as it was officially named, was meant to operate according to the theory of moral management, along the lines of the York Retreat. Most of those who were transferred from the almshouse were considered incurable; fewer than one-sixth, Dix said, regained their sanity. But the new institution nonetheless worked wonders. With few exceptions, the inmates "regained the decent habits of respectable life, and a capacity to be useful, to labor, and to enjoy occupation."[33]

Dix's confidence about the new hospital was shared widely. Charles Dickens, on his celebrated tour of America, visited the asylum soon after it opened and concluded that it was "admirably conducted on . . . enlightened principles of conciliation and kindness." Under the considerate and sensitive supervision of the medical director, the patients read, played games, worked in the garden, and moved about freely. "They are cheerful, tranquil, and healthy," Dickens remarked. "Immense politeness and good breeding are observed throughout." When he published American Notes in 1842, he paid extraordinary tribute to the power of moral management. "Every patient in this asylum sits down to dinner every day with a knife and fork," he wrote. "Moral influence alone restrains the more violent among them from cutting the throats of the rest; but the influence is reduced to an absolute certainty, and is found, even as a means of restraint, to say nothing of it as a means of cure, a hundred times more efficacious than all the strait-waistcoats, fetters, and handcuffs, that ignorance, prejudice, and cruelty have manufactured since the creation of the world."[34]

It remained for critics in later times and places—Michel Foucault and his followers—to deconstruct this picture and detect beneath its calm surface coercive power, power all the more sinister for its being cloaked in the rhetoric of humanitarianism and benevolence. Foucault's critique of the York Retreat, for example, turned favorable assessments like those of Dix and Dickens upside down. "Tuke created an asylum where he substituted for the free terror of madness the stifling anguish of responsibility"; he declared in *Madness and Civilization*, "fear no longer reigned on the other side of the prison gates, it now raged under the seals of conscience." Such a statement would have been incomprehensible to Dix (and Dickens, for that matter), not so much because of its later-twentieth-century poststructuralist assumptions, but because under the seals of her own conscience she valued discipline above freedom. Her context for freedom was duty, responsibility, and moral order, not spontaneity. Her struggle was a struggle to suppress her own impulses and subject her whole life to a cast-iron self-control. Thus the order, the apparent civilization within the madhouse effected by moral treatment, appealed to Dix because, in large measure, it mirrored her struggles with her own demons.

The Boston asylum was not the first institution for the mentally disordered in Massachusetts. Indeed it was constructed because the Commonwealth's first institutions, the Worcester State Lunatic Hospital, which opened in 1833, could not keep pace with the city's lunatic population. Dix had, with growing interest, followed the Worcester hospital since the beginning. But it was not until 1841, systematically extending her investigation of insanity in Massachusetts, that she asked her physician, George Hayward, and Walter Channing from the Harvard Medical School to write letters of introduction on her behalf to Samuel B. Woodward, the superintendent of the institution. Woodward, an indefatigable physician, administrator, and student of mental disease, had made a name for himself by advocating moral treatment for the insane.[35] Each year he published an annual recounting the asylum's successes in glowing terms. These he printed in large editions, and sent copies to newspapers and journals in hopes that they would review them and publicize his work.

Worcester State Lunatic Hospital Superinten-
dent Samuel B. Woodward.

Before 1841 Dix probably had not seen any of the original annual reports, but she undoubtedly read the extensive reviews that summarized them in the *North American Review* and the *Christian Examiner*.[36] Eager to build the reputation of his hospital, Woodward maintained that, given the right therapy, mental illnesses could be treated just as effectively as any other serious affliction. As Samuel Tuke had contended two decades earlier in his *Description* of the York Retreat, everything depended on diagnosing insanity early and placing the patient in the proper healing environment. Under a carefully supervised regimen of moral therapy, inmates at the Worcester hospital were recovering at the astonishing rate of eighty to ninety percent. At least this was what the official statistics indicated. And Dix had no reason to doubt them.[37] Even after her first visit to Worcester, however, Dix did not reach the conclusion that the mad were her special calling. In fact for the next several months she looked for a way to get back into education. While she continued with her Sunday school work in East Cambridge, she sounded out George Barrell Emerson on the idea of opening a new school. He told her that his friend Horace Mann was getting ready to open a normal school in Lexington. This would be an academy for training young women to become teachers, Emerson said, and Mann wanted to hire an experienced matron to supervise the students. She asked to be considered for the position, and after hearing a strong recommendation from Emerson, Mann tentatively offered her the job. When, at the end of the summer of 1841, she received his offer, she jumped at the opportunity.

Her excitement was understandable. At the time Horace Mann, a brilliant young legislator with the passion of a revivalist, was waging a campaign to set up normal schools throughout Massachusetts. Long experience had convinced Dorothea that most schoolteachers were ill-equipped for the delicate task of nurturing a child's intellectual and spiritual development. She wholeheartedly agreed with Mann that the only way to develop a cadet corps of capable teachers was to enforce high standards through a system of teacher training schools.

Mann's plans called for a prototype normal school system beginning with three schools in the major population centers of the state. Lexington appealed to Dorothea because the school there was supposed to be a model institution, primarily serving the greater Boston community. Her new position would place her among aspiring young female teachers, the kind of young woman she had been twenty years earlier when she had opened her school in Orange Court. Now, however, she would be highly visible and in a position to enforce her ideas.

Trouble arose even before the school opened in the fall. Without knowing her personality, Mann assumed that Dorothea would be able to get along with the school's headmaster, the Reverend Cyrus Pierce. He was after all a Unitarian minister, an experienced administrator who had served for several years as principal of the Nantucket High School, and by all accounts an excellent teacher. He was also, as Dorothea discovered when she tried to work out the details of her position, extremely nervous about taking on so much responsibility. Mann had given him what he called "plenipotentiary power" to negotiate her salary and living arrangements, and he seemed dead set on getting her as cheaply as possible. When she proposed to hire a steward to manage her house and "also put in a young lady of 24 as a sort of supervisor of the Establishment," Pierce complained about her extravagance. Rather than live at the school, she told him that she intended to stay in Boston most of the time, making weekly trips to Lexington, she said, "to give direction and see how matters go."[38]

This was not at all what the Reverend Cyrus Pierce had in mind. What bothered him even more than the new matron's excessive demands, though, were what he disdainfully called her "nice notions and strait-laced prudery [sic]." He had once heard George Barrell Emerson remark that for all her diligence as a pedagogue, Miss Dix would never "succeed in making her scholars love her." Her views of propriety were too narrow. She announced, for example, that while they boarded at the normal school, young women should admit no gentlemen callers. Indeed, she went so far as to prohibit walks to the town post office, lest her scholars fall into temptation on the way. Knowing full well that his young ladies were at least as interested in finding husbands as in becoming teachers, Pierce feared a full-scale mutiny if Dorothea tried to impose her brand of discipline on the school. Students were hard enough to attract as it was, he cautioned Mann, and if she had her way, the school would fall apart before the spring term. When he tried to rein her in, she openly flouted his authority. In desperation, he at last appealed to Mann to explain to her that as "the earth can have but one sun, so there can be but one head in the administration of the Normalty." Mann agreed. With gentle diplomacy he persuaded Dorothea that his offering her the position had been premature.[39]

Ordinarily she would have been bitter about losing out to Cyrus Pierce, but in the fall of 1841 Dorothea was becoming so wrapped up in her work with jails and other local institutions that she hardly gave the episode a second thought. Her unwillingness to move to Lexington probably stemmed from a reluctance to abandon her interesting work in East Cambridge, where she now enlisted several ministers and divinity students to assist her.

They manifestly admired her example. One young minister, William Moseley, thanked her for helping him overcome the despair he felt when he first tried to preach to "those machines without souls." Following her advice, he had thrown away his prepared sermon and preached extemporaneously to the lunatics. To his surprise this worked and he had been able to elicit a few "feeble indications of their humanity." He was ashamed of his tentative, puny efforts when he thought of Miss Dix working in the midst of such "misery and sin and hypocrisy

. . . with faith unwavering, with zeal untiring and hope undimmed." Joseph Henry Allen, another Harvard Divinity School student and later an historian of the Unitarian movement, told his father that he saw Miss Dix's labors as a "constant rebuke." If he was upset by the squalor of the jail, how must she have felt as "she sacrifice[d] her ease and her refined literary and elegant taste" to work in the House of Correction? The prisoners' responses to this unusual lady were remarkable, he said. Just a few days earlier he had overheard a hardened felon promise Dorothea, "I will be a better man—that's a fact."[40]

These comments suggest that Dorothea was beginning to experience the psychological benefits, and perhaps grasp the potential political usefulness, of being seen as the cultivated lady in the inferno. She cut a striking figure. And when she came to write about her experiences, the shock value of her descriptions of jails and almshouses was intensified by the contrast between squalor and wretchedness and feminine purity and innocence. It was a role to which the duality of her background and personality was well suited. No one realized how well she was prepared by character and temperament to enter the unseemly world of the insane poor. For beneath her apparent frailty, refined manners, and cool reserve, she had a pioneer heartiness and toughness. The hideous spectacle of suffering disturbed but did not intimidate her. Perhaps this was in part because no circumstance she encountered was worse than the remembered misery of her childhood home on the New England frontier.

Meanwhile she wrote letters to jailers, physicians, and local officials throughout eastern Massachusetts. She asked detailed questions about how each county and town provided for its criminals, paupers, and lunatics. When replies came in, she organized them and tried to extrapolate statistics on the general numbers of "idiots and insane persons" in the Commonwealth.[41]

Her first trip outside Boston or Cambridge to inspect a local facility was in the fall of 1841, when she visited the Lowell almshouse. Then she began to drop in systematically on institutions in nearby communities and record in notebooks what she saw. What she collected in these expeditions became the raw material for the *Memorial to the Legislature of Massachusetts*. As her purpose became clearer in her own mind, she rapidly improved her methods. For years she had kept notebooks for natural scientific observations, and she readily adapted this habit to her inspections. From the on-the-spot style of the Massachusetts memorial—and most of her subsequent memorials—her readers might have inferred that Dorothea actually scribbled as she spoke with officials in cellars and almshouses. In most instances, though, her actual procedure was to see and hear as much as she could during a day, then return to her room and spend a few hours by the oil lamp at her desk setting down facts and impressions. Many of her notes were sketchy and fragmentary: "2 violently insane 1 man—1 woman—both exerted a demoralizing influence. . . . one woman violently mad, solitary: could not see her."[42] Only when these copious jottings reached a kind of critical mass did she begin to rearrange her material into a narrative.

The main narrative structure she chose to frame her peculiar tale of lunatics and the conditions they suffered harkened back to her experiences in England. Beginning in 1807, the year a Select Committee of the House of Commons published a survey of the nation's private madhouses, and continuing through the decades that followed, there had been a series of official investigations into the treatment of British lunatics. Ostensibly these inquiries were directed by Parliament. But they relied heavily on a group of upper-middle-class reformers who made it their business to expose the mistreatment of the indigent insane. Certainly, she had read the 1815 select committee's notorious *First Report*, in which a parade of magistrates and philanthropists had testified in lurid detail to the afflictions of the pauper insane. More than anything she had read in her own country, the works of the British lunacy reformers presented a model of investigation and produced a distinct literary genre and an explicit call for state intervention.[43]

Dorothea drew on American examples as well. And for these she went back to the beginning of the century, when the Reverend Jedidiah Morse had published an informal overview of the condition of the insane in Boston for the Humane Society. His report called attention to "circumstances of great wretchedness" among the insane who had the bad luck to land in jails or almshouses, described their physical suffering, and castigated the "terror to female delicacy" their condition presented.[44]

When she was a young woman, every few years some Boston newspaper took up the scandal of the homeless insane for a few weeks, lamented how poorly it reflected in the community, then dropped it. In 1827, about the time Dorothea had returned to Boston after her first stint with the Furnesses in Philadelphia, the Reverend Louis Dwight issued an important report on prisons in which he painted a vivid picture of the condition of several insane prisoners in local jails. The founder of the influential Boston Prison Discipline Society, Dwight was part of the circle of Unitarian social reformers that included Joseph Tuckerman and George Barrell Emerson and that had represented the ideal for religious activism to Dorothea Dix. Dwight's story was famous. Virtually an invalid, he had summoned the energy to overcome his bodily infirmity and become the champion prison reformer in New England. In words that must have had great resonance in Dorothea's conscience, he had declared that there was only one excuse for Christians to allow "such evils to exist in prisons . . . as do exist; and that is, that they are not acquainted with the real state of things."

Accordingly, he used the society's publications to break down public ignorance and complacency, and its *Annual Report* became a bible of humanitarianism. Dorothea, intrigued by prison reform since her twenties, read each report as soon as it was issued. It was in the pages of Dwight's *Annual Report* for 1827, for example, that she first came across a description of the abominable results of confining lunatics with felons. Dwight described one poor madman who "had a wreath of rags around his body, and another around his neck. He had no bed, chair, or bench. Two or three rough planks were strowed [sic] around the room: a heap of filthy straw, like the nest of swine, was in the corner." With economy and precision, Dwight touched on several elements that typified exposés of British and American asylums: the inmate's nakedness, the utter lack of creature comforts, the notion that farm animals were better treated, the human wastes, "the air so fetid, as to produce nauseousness, and vomiting." Elsewhere, Dwight described a lunatic who had left his cell but twice in eight years. Peering through a small hole in an iron door, Dwight had to ask himself whether the creature he saw was human, for "the hair was gone from one side of his head, and his eyes were like balls of fire." While the insane were not the Prison Discipline Society's main subject in the *Annual Report* in 1827, their presence was compelling and unforgettable.[45]

For the insane, Dwight's report had not directly led to reform. It prompted the state legislature to appoint a special committee to study the issue more fully. After a superficial study, the committee proposed building a public facility for the indigent insane near the private McLean asylum (the psychiatric branch of the Massachusetts General Hospital). At the same time, the commissioners drafted a law to pro-

Worcester State Lunatic Hospital around 1840.

hibit the detention of lunatics in ordinary jails and almshouses. Both measures, lacking vigorous sponsorship, died in committee.

Within a year, however, a junior member of the Massachusetts General Court named Horace Mann discovered the issue of lunacy reform. Mann, taking it upon himself to conduct a survey of the state's insane pauper population (he asked overseers and selectmen to count all those receiving public assistance), became the first member of the legislature publicly to advocate a state institution for their welfare.[46] Several years before Dorothea visited England, Mann had studied the latest advances in moral therapy at the American counterpart of the York Retreat, the Hartford Retreat in Connecticut.

With the Hartford model in mind, he triumphantly sponsored legislation, enacted in 1830, that established the Worcester hospital. He helped manage every stage of the project: guiding the site selection, supervising the construction, and drafting the complicated scheme of classifying which types of mental diseases would be treated at Worcester. Even more important, he skillfully negotiated the hot political question of how funding would be shared between the state and local governments.[47] Through his involvement in the project, Mann became a close friend of Samuel B. Woodward, and worked effectively with the Boston medical establishment and state government bureaucracy to name the first board of trustees for the institution.

In bringing the Worcester asylum into being, Horace Mann offered to Dorothea Dix a shining example. By using the right combination of facts, eloquence, and sheer determination, he had been able to marshal the financial resources and legal authority of the state to help the pauper insane. His informed idealism was an inspiration as well. Just after the Worcester hospital opened its doors in the spring of 1833, he expressed his enthusiasm in a letter to his sister. People who had long been shut up in jails and houses of correction, he declared, including lunatics "so frantic and ferocious, that their keepers had not ventured to go into their cells," were converted at Worcester in less than a week's time into quiet and manageable patients. The "reviving influences of good air and suitable diet," he wrote, along with the kindness expressed by the attendants, "transformed them into men" who "declared themselves happy in their new condition."[48]

While he never lost his interest in lunacy reform, Mann subsequently shifted his attention to education and antislavery. For him, building the Worcester asylum finally established a solution to one particular phase of inhumanity.

But to others who followed in his footsteps, it became increasingly apparent the problem was far from solved. And in 1842 circumstances were ripe for a new treatment of the lunacy question. As Dorothea had seen, even with the Worcester hospital filled to overflowing, conditions at the East Cambridge jail were worse than ever. A new wave of concern about mentally disordered inmates crested on August 6, 1842, when the Boston *Courier* published an anonymous column about the jail. Although she did not write it, Dorothea was a source for the piece.

At the time, she and Samuel Gridley Howe were discussing the best way to improve conditions in the facility. Well known in Boston as the director of the New England School for the Blind, Howe had been persuaded to conduct an investigation of his own into the jail. He discovered there, he told readers of the *Daily Advertiser and Patriot*, a "demonic den" that upright Bostonians could have permitted to exist in their midst only because they had never seen it. Like his predecessors, Howe was most disturbed by the spectacle of twenty or so insane paupers who, though not convicted of any crime, were nevertheless locked up with thieves and murderers. Since jailkeepers had no way to make special provisions for these lunatics, "the little light of reason which might be flickering in the mind of the partially insane" was sure to be snuffed out.

Boston reformer, educator, and legislator
Samuel Gridley Howe.

Compassionate enough to want to take on the issue but astute enough to realize that the insane could be a political bombshell, Howe mildly recommended that pressure of public opinion be brought to bear on those who carried out the law, encouraging them to enforce legislation already on the books that discouraged combining criminals and the insane within the same facility. As it had done in the past, the legislature formed a joint committee to recommend what course to take.

Meanwhile, behind the scenes, Howe grew bolder. He solicited opinions on the practice of keeping lunatics in jails from Charles Sumner, from visiting physicians, including the alienist Edward Jarvis, and from Dorothea Dix. Using excerpts from their letters to add weight to his own views, Howe soon found himself in a running battle with local and county jail officials—a dispute prosecuted in the pages of the *Daily Advertiser*.

Predictably, the General Court committee, reluctant to thrust a new tax burden on towns and counties, came back with a toothless suggestion that county authorities be allowed, if it were convenient, to construct separate quarters for insane dependents. As for the East Cambridge jail, the commissioners halfheartedly proposed a bill to erect a small asylum building next to the main facility for prisoners.[49] Disappointed by the committee's report and reluctant to lose the political momentum he had gained, Howe asked Dorothea about the possibility of presenting a fuller report on the indigent insane than had been done before. By that time she had already been studying the matter for twenty months. Any diffidence she might have felt had long since been overshadowed by the horror of her discoveries. Without hesitation, she replied that she was prepared to tell her story.[50]

CHAPTER FIVE

"I plead, I implore, I demand . . ."

As she made her final revisions to have her petition ready when the General Court returned from its holiday recess, Dix realized she had found much more than another worthy reform movement. After so many years of searching, she had discovered a calling—a world of desperate need that offered unlimited moral opportunity. The long struggles in her intellectual, emotional, and spiritual lives, she now realized, had been tests, preparation for this work of unquestionable virtue. Yet, as she discovered from the start, the process of exposing vice and advocating public virtue inexorably drew her into politics. The publication of the Massachusetts *Memorial* launched not only her intended career as a social reformer but an unexpected, incomparable career as a political operative and advocate.

By Christmas of 1842 she had written thirty-two pages. Howe had intended to present the printed document to the General Court when it convened in January. When he read through it, however, he was so moved by the manuscript's persuasive power that he could not wait. He

immediately turned a review he was writing of the asylum superintendent Edward Jarvis's new book, *What shall we do with the Insane?* into a
vehicle for publishing some of Dix's material. He borrowed from Dorothea Dix freely to support his conclusion that a new insane asylum,
devoted exclusively to people who could not afford private care, should
be built in Massachusetts.[1]

Howe's paraphrases attracted scant attention, however, compared
with the extraordinary document Dix finally published, extraordinary
not merely in dramatizing the plight of a neglected class of citizens but
in its vivid conception of lunacy and human suffering.

The raw power of the text was beyond doubt. Dix's method was
simple and straightforward: through unblinking descriptions of life's
grimmest provinces she confronted lawmakers with ghastly facts and
the inescapable conclusions any reasonable person should draw from
them. Over the past year, she had managed to observe at first hand the
thoughtless cruelty that existed in practically every community, and
that no one wanted to recognize for what it was. Yet for all its author's
emphasis on objectivity, the real force of the *Memorial* did not lie in reasoned exposition of facts. Dix was less interested in case histories and
theorizing than in vivid tableaux, allowing readers to draw their own
conclusions. Hers was not so much a scientific treatise as a passionate
appeal to conscience and human feeling.

This much was clear from the voice that addressed the legislature on
the opening page. Suppressing her modesty, her "habitual views of what
is womanly and becoming," as she put it, in favor of "calm and deep
convictions of duty," Dix addressed the gentlemen of the legislature
directly in the first person. To those who might ask what provided her
justification for so boldly stepping outside conventional boundaries of
propriety, she declared that she simply had no choice. The dictates of
her conscience overwhelmed convention. While the horrors she was
about to describe were things from which "a woman's nature shrinks
with peculiar sensitiveness," when she weighed the importance of her
testimony, she finally decided that "truth is the highest consideration."
Hers was thus the testimony of a reluctant witness, inspired purely by a
compulsion to proclaim the truth.[2]

At the same time, Dix's presence as a woman in the first-person narrative that followed vested the *Memorial* with a special moral authority it
could not have had if it were written by a man. Victorian culture placed
womankind on a pedestal, and it was widely assumed that females were

innately impressionable, delicate, and more refined in moral sensibility than males. If the female was a lady, and the lady was genteel, the presumption of rectitude was only that much stronger.

Completely confident of the rightness of her cause, Dix told the legislature that she was coming forward "to present the strong claims of suffering humanity." She asked nothing for herself. For she was merely "an advocate of helpless, forgotten insane and idiotic men and women; of beings, sunk to a condition from which the most unconcerned would start with real horror." To describe their plight, she had to adopt a new idiom, for their misery and degradation could not be "exhibited in softened language, or adorn a polished page."

Her next paragraph was full of fire. "I proceed, Gentlemen, briefly to call your attention to the *present* state of Insane Persons confined within this Commonwealth, in *cages, closets, stalls, pens! Chained, naked, beaten with rods*, and *lashed* into obedience!" Seething with moral outrage, Dix's rhetoric struck a prophetic tone. The alliterative nouns hit the ear like hammer blows, concluding emphatically with the onomatopoeic "lashed." Indeed, "Beaten with rods" recalled St. Paul's account of his sufferings for the Gospel ("Thrice I was beaten with rods"). Yet, just as this fiery outburst promised to stir up strong feelings, Dix immediately moved away from feeling to "cold, severe *facts*."[3]

Thus the *Memorial* was presented as an amalgamation of humanitarianism, colored with religious imagery, and stark facts. The author set it forth as a personal utterance, literally "extracts from my Note-Book and Journal"—but as scenes unfolded, the reader was given a tour of hell on earth. The familiar names of Massachusetts towns appeared in italics, juxtaposed with their unfamiliar residents: a bleak panoply of madmen, madwomen, and their dismal guardians. Dix disregarded chronological sequence, offering instead clusters of raw images. Forcing her readers to gaze into the abyss, she claimed that the scenes she described were only the most terrible examples of distress she had seen in a vast subterranean world of misery, mysterious and threatening.

Concord. A woman from the [Worcester] hospital in a cage in the almshouse. In the jail several, decently cared for in general but not properly placed in a prison. Violent, noisy, unmanageable most of the time.
Lincoln. A woman in a cage.
Medford. One idiotic subject chained, and one in a close stall for 17 years. . . .

Granville. One often closely confined; now losing the use of his limbs from want of exercise.

After several pages, the group portrait Dix painted becomes haunting, sad, and impossible to forget.[4]

Much of her pamphlet's impact resulted from the cumulative weight of facts. But Dix went beyond fact, imaginatively shaping her materials with literary devices and imagery to increase their evocation of anguish and terror.

In overall conception, the *Memorial* was written like a sermon. Cadences and language reminiscent of the evangelical pulpit are everywhere, as when the author charged the men of Massachusetts to "raise up the fallen; succor the desolate; restore the outcast; defend the helpless; and for your eternal and great reward, receive the benediction." Dix's practice of combining personal testimony with overarching moral conclusions was sermonic as well. Since childhood she had been taught that a sermon should use both explication and application, concrete biblical examples and general religious principles, which Christians could use as a guide to life. By the same token, her message carried a two-pronged appeal in which she tried to reach her audience both through intellect ("I state cold, severe *facts*") and through the affections ("that from them you may feel more deeply the imperative obligation which lies upon you"). This double appeal to reason and emotion reflected a convention so deeply embedded in New England preaching that Dix assumed it as readily as she assumed her duty to the poor.[5]

While the *Memorial* sounded like a sermon, it was also infused with other literary traditions whose rhetorical styles and themes go a long way toward explaining its peculiar power.

Of these, the most important was the brutal, unsentimental objectivity of the British lunacy reformers. Outside a small circle of professional asylum doctors, their writings were virtually unknown in America. But Dix owed a large literary and conceptual debt to her British forbears. In England, reading about British asylums while trying to make sense of her own melancholy, she had happened to read exposés of the York Asylum (an institution for paupers not to be confused with the private York Retreat). These, along with published probes into other institutions, provided her with a basic framework for her own enterprise.

By 1842, the body of British asylum reform literature was remarkably rich and suggestive. Since the turn of the nineteenth century scores of reformers had been delving into Britain's hospitals for the insane, county asylums, and far-flung system of private madhouses. In 1807 Parliament sanctioned the first of many official investigations and concluded that, simply shut up without treatment, the insane had no hope of cure and were thus certain "to remain a burden on the public as long as they live." Weighing the evidence before it, the committee resolved that the only way "to ensure the proper care and management [of lunatics] and most likely to conduce their perfect cure, is the erection of Asylums for their reception in different parts of the kingdom."[6]

The concept of public asylum care for the indigent insane, which was to become the idée fixe of Dix's campaign, seemed logical to the 1807 committee because, the committee said, the York Retreat was discharging nearly half of its patients as cured; and St. Luke's Hospital in London boasted even better results.[7] The alternatives to the asylum were plainly unacceptable. In a passage characteristic of the testimony before the committee, Sir George Onisiphorous Paul, principal secretary of state for the Home Department, attacked the practice of confining those with mental disorders in prisons and jails. Prisons were for punishment, he reminded Parliament, and for instilling convicted felons with a sense of order. Lunatics, guilty of nothing, deserved humane treatment; and their presence in prison was bound to disrupt the very order that was essential to its proper function.[8]

Dix advanced the same rationale in her *Memorial*, arguing that Massachusetts law should be changed to prohibit holding madmen and madwomen in prisons.

> Great injustice [is] done to the insane by confining them in Jails and Houses of Correction. . . . This state of things unquestionably retards the recovery of the few who do recover their reason under such circumstances, and may render those permanently insane, who, under other circumstances might have been restored to their right mind. . . . The confinement of the criminal and the insane in the same building is subversive of that good order and discipline which should be observed in every well-regulated prison.[9]

While Dix appears first to have gleaned the logic of removing lunatics from jails and placing them in asylums from the 1807 select committee testimony, it was the next parliamentary inquiry, conducted in 1815–16 by the Committee on Madhouses in England, that influenced her the most profoundly. A far more thorough investigation than their predecessor, the 1815–16 hearings explored how the insane were treated not just in private madhouses but in charity hospitals, county asylums, and workhouses as well.[10] The defining concept and methods of Dix's mission on behalf of the insane poor—her exhaustive collection of data right down to measurements of cells and details of inmates' diets, her attitude of moral affront wrapped in impartiality, her underlying assumption that government, not private philanthropy, was obliged to support those who could not otherwise achieve self-respect—she first encountered in publications of the select committees and the dozens upon dozens of related books and pamphlets that divulged in grisly detail the mistreatment and neglect investigators found throughout the British Isles.

In America, a country with no system of private madhouses and only a few facilities devoted to the care of the insane, these exposés had no direct counterpart. She was transfixed by the hidden world of suffering they unearthed. Once she saw that things were, if anything, worse in her own country than in England, Dix commenced her landmark investigation into the condition of the pauper insane in Massachusetts firmly within the guidelines of this British tradition. To organize their findings, the commissioners outlined nine categories of "observations"—overcrowding, insufficient staff on hand to manage the facility, promiscuous mixing of patients, overrestraint, and lack of treatment, among others. By mid-1816, as the evidence piled up, they further refined their approach. Committee instructions to "the Sheriffs Depute [sic] of the Counties of Edinburgh" and other counties of Scotland, for example, charged local officials to

> state as fully as your means of information will enable you to do, everything relating to the management of these Houses and the treatment of the Patients; whether the medical attendance be sufficient . . . whether any practices have come to your knowledge, which you deemed improper, or indicative [sic] either of negligence or inhumanity; or whether the conduct of the Keepers of these Houses, and their servants, has generally been marked by humanity and an attention to the comfort, health, and cleanliness of the Patients; whether you think these buildings are, in general, of sufficient extent for the number of persons confined therein; whether they are well aired; whether the apartments are kept properly warm and comfortable; and whether the accommodation is, generally speaking, such as has called for your approbation, or the reverse.[11]

Dix set herself an identical task when, in 1840, as she put it, "leisure afforded opportunity, and duty prompted me to visit several prisons and alms-houses in the vicinity" of Boston.[12]

The political aims of the British reformers included a system of public asylums for all their indigent insane compatriots and a state watch-dog agency to ensure that these asylums were carefully supervised so that inmates would not slide back into abuse. Through the 1830s, they were unable to muster enough political support to push their measures through the House of Lords. Not until mid-1842, just when Dix was moving toward the completion of her survey, did Parliament finally enact legislation to establish a national system of inspection for mad-houses. In retrospect, Dix, starting out on her own fact-finding mission in Massachusetts, could see that persistence was essential to the British reformers' success. Her style, no less than her goals, owed a large debt to the commissioners. The format for all the sheriffs' reports was anno-tated journal entries, noting the keeper, location, number of lunatics, and distinguishing features of each madhouse inspected. A typical entry runs as follows:

—Madhouse kept by *David Trench*, Stonehouse.—4 Patients. Remarks:—The apartments of this house are clean, and the state upon the whole creditable to the keeper. At the visit in March, the Reporter had occasion to alter his opinion, as to the conduct of the keeper of this house. No. 1, a pauper he found lying *in bed*, in a wretched apartment, with a broken window and very bad bedding; and it turned out that she had been con-stantly in this situation for the space of *three months* past, solely in conse-quence of having no clothes to put on. It appeared that the only article of clothing of which she was possessed, was one shift then upon her.[13]

Claiming in the Massachusetts *Memorial* to present verbatim extracts from the notebooks she used in the field, Dix used a similar if some-what expanded reportorial style to describe visits such as this one to a poorhouse outside Boston.

Saugus. December 24; thermometer below zero; drove to the poorhouse; was conducted to the master's family-room by himself; . . . thirteen pau-per inmates; one insane man; one insane woman; one idiotic man; asked to see them; the two men were shortly led in; appeared pretty decent and comfortable.

Demanding to see the rest of the facility, though, she discovered an

> apartment ENTIRELY unfurnished; no chair, table, nor bed; neither, what is seldom missing, a bundle of straw or lock of hay; cold, very cold; . . . *On the floor* sat a woman, her limbs immovably contracted, so that the knees were brought upward to the chin; the face was concealed; the head rested on the folded arms; for clothing she appeared to have been furnished with *fragments* of many discharged garments; these were folded about her, yet they little benefitted her, if one might judge by the constant shuddering which almost convulsed her poor crippled frame.[14]

One of Dix's most powerful descriptions, her account of the Newburyport almshouse, relies heavily on the literature of English lunacy reform. Describing her surprise visit to the facility in the summer of 1842, she said that at first she was relieved to find ample space for its eighty inmates and comfortable conditions for its "seven insane [and] one idiotic" charges. Inspecting the grounds, however, she spotted a dilapidated shed that housed a madman. His cell opened not on the yard, she said, but on the local "dead room" or morgue, "affording in lieu of companionship with the living, a contemplation of corpses." Before she could regain her composure, she heard from one of the attendants that there was yet another insane inmate whom no one had wanted her to see: "a woman in a *cellar*."

When Dix asked to inspect the woman's quarters, the master of the house nervously tried to discourage her, cautioning that the madwoman "was *dangerous to be approached*; that 'she had lately attacked his wife;' and *was often naked*." Undeterred, Dix demanded, "if you will not go with me, give me the keys and I will go alone." At last the outer doors were hesitantly opened and she entered the dark staircase. Groping her way down, she was startled by "a strange, unnatural noise [that] seemed to proceed from beneath our feet." When the padlock on the basement door was removed, Dix searched the dim room, but saw nothing until she opened a tiny door beneath the staircase. Peering in, she professed herself horrified. The faint light revealed "a female apparently wasted to a skeleton, partially wrapped in blankets." Her face was withered, Dix wrote, "not by age, but by suffering," and when she saw her visitors, "she poured forth the wailing of despair." Stretching her arms to Dix in a terrible appeal, the mad woman cried, "why am I consigned to hell? dark—dark—I used to pray, I used to read the Bible—I have done no crime in my heart; I had friends, why have all forsaken me!—my God! my God! why hast *thou* forsaken me?" These infernal wailings, Dix wrote, had "come up daily . . . *for years*" in a kind of "perpetual and sad memorial."[15]

In all the previous writings of American asylum doctors and prison reformers, nothing approaches the dramatic power of this passage. Much of its effect comes from the fascination of looking behind the scenes, of accompanying the narrator as she strikes through the veneer of order and tranquility held up by the keepers of the insane and descends into a living hell. Yet the point of view—indeed the basic narrative structure—of this passage depends at least as much on testimony from the 1815 parliamentary hearings as it does on Dix's actual inspection of the Newburyport almshouse.

On the very first page of the select committee's published proceedings, in fact, Dix is certain to have read Godfrey Higgins's lengthy description of his own investigation into the bowels of the York Asylum private York Retreat. Suspicious that the facility was hiding something from him, Higgins, a magistrate of West Riding in Yorkshire and member of the county asylum board, testified that he showed up early one morning to look behind the scenes. "After opening a great number of doors," he said, he noticed a small door "which was in a retired situation in the kitchen apartments, and was almost hid." Demanding to see what was inside, Higgins noticed that "the keeper hesitated, and said, the apartment belonged to the women, and they had not the key." Not to be deterred, he "ordered them to get the key, but it was said to be mislaid, and not to be found at the moment." Indignantly he warned them that if they did not open the door at once, "I could find a key at the kitchen fire-side, namely, the poker." When the door was finally opened, Higgins encountered four madwomen occupying cells "of about eight feet square, in a very horrid and filthy situation." What little straw there was on the floor they had "almost saturated with urine and excrement. . . . The walls were daubed with excrement; the air holes, of which there were one in each cell, were partly filled with it." Sickened by the spectacle and the smell, Higgins confessed that he fled the building and vomited. It took him, he recalled, several days to recover from the experience.[16]

Both the similarities and the differences between Dix's and Higgins's narratives are striking. Culminating in the haunting image of a lost soul, Dix's story is more personalized, more memorable, and far more imaginatively embellished; but its point of view and dramatic movement still bear a strong resemblance to Higgins's. If her reliance on English proto-types explains how she suddenly came to wield such potent verbal weapons, it also makes it easier to understand why the proprietors of the Newburyport almshouse, and other officials around Massachusetts, so vehemently accused her of painting false pictures of their institutions.

Dix's description of the Newburyport almshouse, and many of her other passages, have a richness of gothic imagery and feeling unlike anything one finds in the parliamentary papers. She owed a great deal as well to the gothic tradition. Readers steeped in Romantic modes—just about anyone who read popular fiction or poetry America—would have recognized the gloomy atmosphere and the descent into the infer-nal regions described in the story of the Newburyport almshouse. Bor-rowing techniques used with great success by British gothic novelists and by American writers like Charles Brockden Brown and Edgar Allen Poe, Dix suffused her *Memorial* with an air of gothic terror and mystery. The conventions of gothicism enabled her to shape her incredible experiences, imposing on them a pattern that audiences understood. Ironically, because her narrative sounded in part like popular fiction, she was able to render the unthinkably horrible in terms that were comprehensible and believable.[17]

For thousands of years insanity was thought to be caused by evil spir-its or demon possession. So it is not unexpected that Dix made effective use of the image of demons dragging lost souls down to the Kingdom of Darkness. In Sudbury, for example, she witnessed "paroxysms of mad-ness so appalling; it seemed as if the ancient doctrine of the possession of demons was here illustrated." Case after case provoke Dix's expostu-lations of shock and horror—constantly reminding the reader of her own visceral response to what she has seen—resembling Ann Radcliffe's tales of terror more than the cold-eyed reports of British reformers and asylum physicians. Like many narrators of gothic tales, she often described herself as stunned into silence, gasping for words. Luminous clarity and insight arise from nightmare paralysis. "I know not how to proceed," she wrote, because ordinary language "affords no combina-tions fit for describing" such horrors. This failure of language in the face of unspeakable terror is as much a convention of romantic gothicism as the "walls garnished with handcuffs and chains" that Dix described in Saugus, with one crucial difference. The whole point of the *Memorial* was not that such horrors existed in the pages of a book but that they lurked just beneath the superficial tranquility of Massachusetts.[18]

In town after town, stepping down from her carriage and approaching the buildings that housed the mad, Dix was greeted by blasphemous, indecent shrieks and insults. As often as not these raving voices were the voices of women. Venturing into the shacks and barns and outbuildings where these people lived, her nose was assaulted by the stench, the sickeningly sweet effluvium of urine and feces; then, as her eyes adjusted to dark, she saw the dirt, clumps of wet straw and human wastes, ubiquitous in such circumstances. (Unlike her male British counterparts, Dix used euphemisms for the pervasive excrement in the abodes of the insane.) Bad as this physical degradation was, it was compounded by a moral debasement. Frequently the insane were naked, or nearly so. And the reader is invited to imagine these wild, unclothed beings, mad beyond the restraints of Victorian culture, engaging in debaucheries too horrible to speak of. Toward the conclusion of her pamphlet, Dix told of a pitiful young madwoman in the Worcester almshouse "negligently bearing in her arms a young infant, of which I was told she was the unconscious parent." Though she asked, no one would point out the baby's father, but the powerful image, and the black deed it implied, embodied a powerful plea "for the protection of others of her neglected and outraged sex!"[19]

These sufferings endured by her own sex brought to the surface Dix's searing anger. Her rage simmered beneath the prose surface of the *Memorial*, frequently boiling over in bitterly ironic comments and furious outbursts. Asking about one man in a filthy cage in Wayland so weakened "from cold and confinement . . . that he was often powerless to rise," Dix was told that she was seeing him at his best. "*His best state!*" she exclaimed, "what then was the *worst?*" In Westford she encountered a young woman about whose "*waist was a chain*, the extremity of which was fastened into the wall of the house." The sheer callousness of the poor woman's attendant, she noted, "might have roused to indignation one not dispossessed of reason, and owning self-control."[20] Infuriated by what she witnessed and determined to take action, she was nonetheless keenly aware of the importance of maintaining control and projecting a persona of womanly propriety. She would not let her emotions get the best of her. Nor, interestingly enough, would she directly intervene to help the victims of ignorance. Consequently, there is a strong dramatic tension in the document that comes from witnessing a tragedy she is powerless to stop.

In contrast to the keepers, who appear to have forgotten that their charges were human beings, she was compassionate, always sensitive to the personalities of the insane. Thus while she began her journey ostensibly to gain better shelter and better care for these wretched beings, along the way she asked for much more: she asked her readers to sympathize with them and to acknowledge their dignity. By drawing pictures of real individual men and women with a dramatic intensity usually found in fiction, she transported the insane out of the realm of impersonal phenomena.

Dix not only moved her readers; she had a transforming effect on her subjects. In her brief visits to each town, she opened their almost forgotten qualities as human beings. As she portrayed her encounters with the insane, something in her own manner and personality elicited from them moments of lucid rationality.

Her account of the Ipswich almshouse illustrates her dynamic relation to the human subjects of her story. There, strolling through a dilapidated outbuilding, she came upon three pauper lunatics, two of whom were demented beyond comprehending the wretchedness of their condition. Not so the third, though, a wild madman who glowered anxiously through the bars of his pen. Years before, she learned, he had been a respected gentleman, a newspaper editor, state senator, and judge in the Court of Errors. Then, abruptly, the bottom had fallen out of his world.

> Vicissitudes followed, and insanity closed the scene. He was conveyed to Worcester [hospital]; after a considerable period, either to give place to some new patient, or because the County objected to the continued expense, he being declared incurable, was removed to Salem jail; thence to Ipswich jail; associated with the prisoners there, partaking the same food, and clad in like apparel. After a time the town complained of the expense of keeping him in jail; it was cheaper in the almshouse. . . . How sad a fate! I found him in a quiet state; though at times was told that he is greatly excited; what wonder, with such a [pathetic] companion before him; such cruel scenes within! I perceived in him some little confusion as I paused before the stall, against the bars of which he was leaning; he was not so lost to propriety but that a little disorder of the bed-clothes, &c. embarrassed him. I passed on, but he asked, in a moment, earnestly, "Is the lady gone—gone quite away?" I returned; he gazed a moment without answering my inquiry if he wished to see me? "And have you too lost all your dear friends?" Perhaps my mourning apparel excited his

inquiry. 'Not all.' "Have you any dear father and mother to love you?" and then he sighed and then laughed and traversed the limited stall.[21]

An interview like this—to be sure, a highly stylized portrait of a rational madman—was intended to establish the lunatic's humanity, and bridge the chasm, the strong sense of "otherness," that separated the mad from the rest of society. Pondering their poignant exchange, she remarked, "I do not know how it is argued, that mad persons and idiots may be dealt with as if no spark of recollection ever light up the mind."[22]

The angel of mercy dressed in black is a striking image. Mourning apparel must have overawed not only the lunatics but their guardians as well. Dix was in mourning for William Ellery Channing, who died in 1842, and she felt deeply the loss of her surrogate father. Despite her bereavement, she proceeded unwaveringly in the face of personal pain, assuming a certain dignity while also suggesting that she too was on intimate terms with sorrow and loss. Her empathy for the lunatic sprang from the deeper themes of abandonment, isolation, and broken family ties to which she had always been so exquisitely sensitive.

Episodes like this showed that Dix was not merely concerned for the insane, she was fascinated by them, as though she could see specters of herself in even the most hopeless cases. With a conviction wrung from personal experience, she constantly warned that reason could be dispossessed at any moment. She implored her readers to place themselves "in that dreary cage," deserted by kindred, and imagine how they would want to be treated. How secure, she asked, was anyone's grip on sanity? "Who shall say his own mountain stands strong, his lamp of reason shall not go out in darkness!" Many of her stories, sudden reversals of fortune, showed that the mind was mysteriously fragile, subject to corruption from a thousand sources. If only to protect themselves against unforseen catastrophe, she argued, prudent legislators would ensure a decent provision for the insane.[23]

Dix concluded the *Memorial* with excerpts from letters she had solicited from county sheriffs and other officials that supported her findings and her conviction that no amount of tinkering with the present system of jails and almshouses could adequately provide for the insane. The only practical and humane solution, the authorities agreed, was to remove lunatics from community control and place them in the therapeutic environment of the Worcester asylum. Even when cure was not immediately forthcoming, patients still benefited from the asylum's clinical regimen. To make this point, she recounted the story of one violently mad woman, shut up in a local jail, whose blasphemous ravings "poured forth in torrents . . . giving reality to that blackness of darkness, which it is said might convert a heaven into a hell." Committed at last to Worcester, the madwoman calmed down, her raving mania subsided, and she was, Dix said, "now a controllable woman." So long as state law permitted the incarceration of madmen and madwomen, epileptics, and idiots in prisons and almshouses, she wrote, Massachusetts would be guilty of violating the federal Constitution by subjecting the insane, who had never been convicted of any crime, to false imprisonment and cruel and unusual punishment.[24]

Noting how rapidly the Commonwealth was growing, she told the General Court that it had the power to change the basic direction of social welfare, and thus to "affect the present and future condition of hundreds and thousands."

As it turned out, Dix was right. The Massachusetts legislature's deliberations, which revolved around the issue of incremental funding to enlarge the Worcester institution, would ultimately produce a modest success. But in Dix's mind it was a brilliant victory. It left no room for doubt that she was doing God's work. Nothing else could explain how a woman alone could induce the General Court to rewrite the laws of the Commonwealth. Moving forward, the conviction that she was a special instrument of the divine will laid the foundation for her mission. But she was only beginning to grasp what would be required to accomplish her goals. Until she gained the pragmatic political experience that would come from maneuvering her measure through the fractious legislative process, pure conviction would remain inert.

Women played no visible part in government in Massachusetts in 1843, and ladies seldom entered the stately capitol on Beacon Hill. So Dix was not in the room at nine o'clock on Saturday morning, January 25, when the state House of Representatives met to take up the legislation supported by her memorial. In a letter to Howe's committee, she focused on a point she had made amply in the *Memorial*: "the occupation of Prisons for the detention of Lunatics is subversive of discipline, comfort, and moral order." Since "the qualifications for Wardenship . . . do not embrace qualifications for the management of Lunatics," she declared, there was no way satisfactorily to care for the insane poor in jails and almshouses. She ended with a plea to redraft the statutes so that "hereafter no Prison in Massachusetts be used either permanently or temporarily, for the detention of Lunatics and Idiots, and that all such now therein imprisoned, be speedily removed."[25]

The lawmakers commenced the session by discussing recent complaints about dangerous shootings of hens and turkeys in populated areas, then debated a measure for establishing three houses of correction in the Connecticut river counties. Finally, at Howe's urging, they turned to the main business of the day: what to do with the indigent insane.

Dix had posed the issue in moral terms, but the legislature saw it as a matter of dollars and cents. Based on the Census of 1840, the first census to tally the mentally disordered, Howe said there were 978 lunatics in Massachusetts. The Worcester asylum housed 229 inmates at the time, the Boston Lunatic Hospital 124. Simple arithmetic indicated that 625, nearly two-thirds of the total, were denied the benefits of asylum treatment. Of these, 200 or so were said to be desperately in need of relief. The Worcester superintendent, Samuel Woodward, had testified that it cost about $3,000 a bed to add on to the Worcester facility, or a total of $60,000 for a wing large enough to accommodate all the neediest cases. Admittedly this was a great sum, but fortunately, Howe told the Committee on Charitable Appropriations, there was a potential source of endowment, the Martha Johonot Fund, which could be tapped to avoid a tax increase. It amounted to $40,000 and could be earmarked for any benevolent purpose simply by a majority vote of the legislature. A handful of representatives groused about wasting any money for a state asylum, though they were distinctly in the minority. With a minimum of debate, the house voted to release the Johonot fund, then voted an appropriation of $25,000 of state money to enlarge the Worcester hospital.[26]

Howe was elated. One junior legislator who participated in the debates marveled at his adroit maneuvering and political instincts. To say Howe had managed the business "like an old stager, would be doing him an injustice," Dix was told, for he had carried the day "like a man of humanity, energy, and abundant resources, as he is."[27]

Impressed by the effect her broadside wrought on the normally indifferent legislators, he praised her efforts and encouraged her to press the attack. He advised her to choose one Boston newspaper as her vehicle and write a series of letters or essays to sustain the cause in the public mind. Then, capturing the feeling of the important moment they shared, he told her that when he thought of "the time when you stood hesitating and doubting upon the brink of the enterprise you have so bravely and nobly accomplished, I cannot but be impressed with the lesson of courage and hope which you have taught even to the strongest men."[28]

This kind notice from one of Boston's elite reformers was precisely the sort of approbation Dix craved. Her sense of accomplishment was heightened when Horace Mann wrote to thank her for the *Memorial* "with which you have accomplished the Christian labor of doing good to those who cannot requite you." Apparently they had not spoken to each other since the Lexington normal school misunderstanding, and Mann politely admitted that he was "perhaps too much a stranger to you, *according to the customs of society*, to justify these expressions of my feelings." He was so strongly moved when he read her pamphlet, however, that he knew at once "my heart is no stranger to yours." He completely understood what she had been going through. For when he had conducted his trailblazing effort to found the Worcester hospital, he had felt "as tho' all personal enjoyments were criminal until [the insane] were relieved." Mann closed his letter saying that he was writing out of an "inexpressible impulse" rather than the thought that his note "can be of any gratification to you."[29] Yet no words could have more reassured her, nor more firmly sealed her conviction in her calling.

Reading Mann's letter in her study on Mt. Vernon Street, Dorothea Dix pondered the unexpectedly successful direction her life was taking. Thrilled, yet determined to respond in a dignified manner, she sent back a stilted reply: "To be understood by those we value, those our hearts have long enshrined as the wisest and best, through their lives of disinterestedness and self-sacrifice, is to receive permanent addition to our happiness." Considering his own signal success in founding the Worcester asylum and reforming education in the Commonwealth, she was flattered to think of herself as following in his footsteps. "My painful task is but begun," she wrote, "and I shall feel as I put aside *myself*, and go forth again alone upon that most sad investigation, strengthened and cheered by those lines you have written." Would he allow her to think of him not merely as "the friend of *all*, only, but as one of the very few upon whose minds my thoughts repose with no distrust, and who are garnered in my heart with most sacred affections?" Her solitary pursuit of her mission had released her from her loneliness. It had unleashed resources to unite her heart and mind, to produce the deep affirmation from the likes of Horace Mann that her soul longed for.[30]

Encouragement of a more ambivalent sort arrived in a letter from her friend Anne Heath who, over the past few years, had sensed her relationship with Dix cool. Unable to look upon miserable and unpleasant things herself, Heath marveled at Dix's temerity. The Brookline spinster went on to confide that she secretly empathized with the despair of the insane, "who hardly know which way to pass away the hours. Did I say I had felt this myself?" she asked. With few prospects beyond the material comforts of her home in Brookline, she divulged "that I can form some idea of the trial of being shut up and the feeling of becoming somewhat worthless." Not that she meant to worry her friend in an hour of triumph, Heath added. "This is no serious trouble."[31] But Heath's disclaimer rang false. Dix, who was only beginning to surmount her own dread of marginality, must have shuddered. No one knew better than she how deadly serious these feelings were.

Praise for the lady memorialist, was far from universal. When the General Court met to consider the Worcester asylum appropriations measure, a number of representatives, claiming to have new evidence, openly questioned the accuracy of what Dix had written. Howe, rising to her defense, at first managed to deflect their criticisms. "He pointed out that if there were any misstatements in that memorial," according to one Boston newspaper, "they must have been slight and unintentional, because the motives of the memorialist [were] honest and philanthropic." Nevertheless, the issue of the petition's factual correctness and Dorothea Dix's integrity soon festered.[32]

While the pamphlet, printed in January in an edition of five thousand and circulated around the state, initially attracted favorable reviews, by February Dix was clipping newspaper articles that criticized her procedures and refuted her findings. The *Newburyport Herald*, a paper that had frequently spoken out against conditions in the East Cambridge jail, at first applauded her "plainness of speech" and said that any inaccuracies must have resulted from haste. A few days later, however, a column appeared calling into question both the particulars and the general impression Dix had created in her sensational description of the Newburyport almshouse. If gothicism was a lens through which readers could view her horror story, some questioned how grotesquely the resulting image was distorted. "The statement concerning our alms-house ought not to go forth to the world" the paper said, "without a correction of the erroneous impression it is somewhat calculated to make." The female lunatic in the almshouse, follow-up investigation had revealed, was kept not, as Dix had written, in a dark cellar but in a "cellar-kitchen, not much worse than many kitchens of very genteel city mansions." Admittedly her case was a difficult one, but the almshouse keepers had never tried to hide the woman's condition or prevent outsiders from inspecting any part of the institution. It was a shame, the paper concluded, that Dix's inquiry was so superficial and, in consequence, her account so misleading.[33]

Since her argument hinged on her eyewitness register of facts, Dix was disinclined to back down and acknowledge errors. In Danvers, John Waters Proctor, one of the town's overseers for the poor, became so agitated by Dix's report that he rounded up witnesses to testify under oath to her misrepresentations. "Either some *half a dozen persons*, of fair character and outstanding in society, are *wilfully perjured*," he told her bluntly, "or what is stated in your Memorial . . . cannot be true." Stubbornly refusing to reconsider her story, Dix subjected Proctor to a schoolteacherly scolding. No matter what people claimed, "the statements in the Memorial are *strictly* and *literally* true," she retorted. She could not have made mistakes in Danvers because she had taken notes on the spot. In the same vein, the overseers and selectmen of Shelburne printed the testimony of two physicians who examined a lunatic named Justin Bull—an inmate Dix had described as filthy, half-naked, and freezing—and pronounced his apartment well warmed and him well clothed. As far as the town fathers were concerned, Dix stood guilty of spreading "bare-faced falsehoods, false impressions, and false statements."[34]

To her chagrin, some towns went so far as to publish rebuttal memorials of their own. Officials in Salem, for example, were furious not only because Dix had accused them of mistreating the insane but because when they approached Howe and the young reformer Charles Sumner to protest, they were rudely rebuffed. Dix claimed to have found in the Danvers almshouse, which was under Salem's jurisdiction, a young woman, recently discharged from the Worcester hospital as incurable, who subsequently had fallen into a state of utmost wretchedness. Yet according to depositions from the almshouse keeper, his wife, the attending physician, and several other citizens, the case had been completely and deliberately misconstrued. "Miss Dix was not at the house more than five minutes," insisted Caroline Nourse, "and I do not recall that she asked a single question about her." Everyone involved concurred that Dix had fabricated a story to prove that the madwoman had been better off in the hospital when in fact the Nourses had taken her into their home as though she were a relative. How could anyone say that she was maltreated, they wondered, when "she was permitted to eat at table with us and sleep with our children."[35]

Surprisingly, few people questioned the legitimacy of Dix's mission or complained about the unseemliness of a lady conducting such a macabre investigation.[36] People objected that she used made-up scenes that her deliberate deviations from the more mundane (yet no less terrible) facts of her subjects' existence—and there were many—were mainly for the sake of drama. If Dix had one eye on the mad, her other eye was focused sharply on the public. She was interested in truth, but even more interested in effect. Also, her blurring of fact and fiction took place in a Victorian world innocent of the techniques of investigative journalism, a world with a somewhat looser epistemological standard than that of the late twentieth century. She held that her stories were true because she believed she had not invented people and places. Clearly, however, she did create characters and had them do and say implausible things that some of her more perceptive contemporaries doubted they had ever done. Without retracing her footsteps, her critics produced comparatively little documentary evidence to contradict her descriptions, leaving future generations to speculate about which parts were invented.

In her single-mindedness, Dix was careless and tactless in her portrayals of those who had the responsibility for looking after the insane. Despite her disclaimer that she would "speak as kindly as possible of all Wardens, Keepers, and other responsible officers" and intended only to criticize the Commonwealth's policies, she directly rebuked scores of selectmen, bailiffs, and other petty officials. Rightly feeling themselves maligned by the document, fearful of public opinion and the possibility of losing income, they swiftly counterattacked.

Anson Hooker, the prison doctor at the East Cambridge jail, felt especially betrayed. After answering Dix's formal inquiry about the condition of insane prisoners, he was shocked to read how she had twisted his words. He had plainly told her that visitors were revolted when they saw lunatics "occupying apartments *contiguous* or *similar* to those occupied by the criminals." But she manipulated this to say "occupying apartments *with* or *consigned* to those occupied by the criminal." Moreover, he maintained that despite Dix's pointed references, he had never mentioned anything about "madwomen" in the jail.[37]

Despite the controversy, being a genteel woman helped Dix disarm her attackers. They might carp at the margins of her survey, but who could impugn her motives? She was a lady, and as such could have no political ambitions or self-serving schemes in mind. If she made a few errors, was she not simply overzealous in a good cause?[38] Proud of her methods, proud of the factual basis of the *Memorial*, Dix dashed off a stinging rebuke. Hooker, realizing that she had friends in high places and that he was out of his political depth, backed down and recanted most of his criticisms, trying to patch things up with Dix. He admitted that one lunatic, a man named Hill, who had broken windows "so as to make the room very uncomfortable for others during cold & stormy weather," was brought inside the jail with criminals to keep him warm. Dix noted in the margin of Hooker's letter that "this was not the case—it was that of Browne—whose head was cut" in a fight with prisoners.[39]

The thing that disturbed Hooker and the East Cambridge jailer, Nathaniel Watson, the most was that for all Dix's criticism of their institutions, they mainly agreed with her. Both men supported Howe's efforts to "restore Worcester Insane Asylum to what it was originally assigned to be," and if that failed, to find some other way to get the insane out of the jails. Neither man thought he had the training to manage mentally ill inmates, curable or incurable. So they rightfully felt betrayed when Dix borrowed from their letters wholesale, broadcast their statements as her own conclusions, and indirectly attacked them with their own words.[40]

The weeks between the publication of the *Memorial* and the passage of an appropriations bill by the upper chamber of the legislature were a time of intense activity and learning for Dix. Being identified personally with the *Memorial* and the resulting Worcester hospital appropriations bill, she stepped into the new role of a lobbyist. She began canvasing government officials and writing to superintendents of institutions in several states to corroborate her findings and clarify her ideas about what an insane asylum ought to be. Not only did she have to fend off attacks in the press on her report's credibility; she also had to nullify the efforts of selectmen and other county officials who approached members of the General Court directly to discredit her findings. She spent a good deal of time answering lawmakers' questions about circumstances in their constituent districts.

One wanted to know, for example, whether she had left out of her report "*all the cases* in which you found the insane & idiotic persons properly treated." A politician himself, he intimated that he naturally expected a little exaggeration but wanted to know privately if she had "omitted any circumstances favorable to our state."[41] Whether or not Dix replied is not known, but on February 14 she issued a curt statement to Howe's committee rebutting her detractors' claims that portions of the *Memorial* were false or willfully misrepresented. To clear the air, she called for an independent investigation. She professed herself ready to "render to you personally such evidence of my truthfulness and accuracy in writing as the case demands, and you may require."[42]

When the *Boston Courier*, drawing on "counter-memorials" from Salem and Shelburne, condescendingly cautioned its readers to accept Dix's facts "at a discount of about fifty per cent," a young lawyer named Charles Sumner, destined to lead the struggle for the rights of blacks as a senator from Massachusetts, stepped publicly to her defense. Traveling around the state, he had taken it upon himself to inspect four of the almshouses described in Dix's pamphlet. If her document had any shortcoming, he announced, it was that it did not go far enough. He had seen the Wayland almshouse with his own eyes, and even her graphic description of the lunatic caged there failed to convey the travail he had witnessed. Based on the cases he knew personally, he concluded, the literal correctness of her work "leads me to place entire confidence in her description."[43]

Proclamations like Sumner's gave Dix a new fund of credibility and elevated her standing with legislators who were only marginally concerned with the lunacy issue. She was able to withstand criticism and influence members of both houses in part because Howe and Mann and Sumner were known to be lined up staunchly behind her. Endorsements from the state's political leaders, repeated publicly and reinforced privately in the back halls of the statehouse, were making the lady a figure to be taken seriously. Astutely she wrapped herself in this new mantle of political influence. And in turn she allowed her allies to draw on a fund of disinterested benevolence, moral probity, and self-sacrifice for the sake of principle—precious ideological tender in Massachusetts politics in the early 1840s.

She had a great deal to learn about the tortuous process of passing legislation. Apprehensively she scrambled to meet with as many members as she could, while the lower house of the legislature dragged out its deliberations on what had generally come to be thought of as *her* bill. She was a quick study, able to grasp at once that different legislators could be convinced to support the same measure for different reasons. To a legislator who was involved in the abolitionist movement she argued that it was hypocritical to urge "our Southern countrymen to break the bonds of the slave and bid him free—while here we hold men in dungeons—and chains—and in prisons" simply because "their *minds* are *darkened*." If people worried about the cost of constructing new institutions, she assured another, the cheapest humane solution was a single "Asylum for Incurables."

Constantly she stressed the urgency of the problem. The General Court could not be allowed to put off reform another year, she declared, "another year is not ours." If thirty-two pages of atrocities were not enough to convince leaders to act, then she would have to write another volume, "for darker histories remain as yet untold." Subjected to daily badgering, even politicians who lacked the slightest interest in the lunacy question became convinced that nothing short of a new law would stop Dix's agitation. Although they put it off as long as they could, the legislation finally passed the state senate on the last day of the 1843 spring session and was delivered to the desk of Marcus Morton, the first Democrat to serve as governor of Massachusetts, who signed Dix's bill into law.[44]

❦

CHAPTER SIX

Voice for the Mad

Her unforseen and rousing success in Massachusetts Dix took as a sign from God that she was now an instrument of divine mercy. This knowledge crystallized her sense of purpose; and so she confidently pushed her cause beyond the borders of Massachusetts, continuing to visit the abodes of the insane, to record in minute detail the circumstances of their confinement. Much to the consternation of her critics, she also continued to color and shade her accounts, in the most extreme instances reworking them into a kind of moral fiction, with herself as the intrepid heroine come to redeem lost souls.

In the final months of 1842, even as she was combing the backcountry of western Massachusetts to complete her survey, Dix automatically extended her investigation into New York. She had made her mark in Massachusetts by exposing how the insane were treated in almshouses and jails, and were mishandled by incompetent functionaries entrusted with their care. She meant to apply the same approach in New York. There state law explicitly prohibited the confinement of pauper lunatics in almshouses. But in practice, as she discovered on a memorable visit to Albany in November, the law was widely flouted. For nearly every county house she inspected concealed "its 'crazy house,' its 'crazy-cells,' or its 'crazy-dungeons' and 'crazy-cellar.'"[1]

Even so, at the outset she considered New York a progressive state. It had a long history of lunacy reform dating back to the Quaker Thomas Eddy's efforts to build a lunatic asylum in Manhattan near the Harlem River. A separate department of the New York Hospital had been created for the mad in 1821. This was called the Bloomingdale asylum, and like most of the first generation of American asylums, it was patterned after England's York Retreat. In 1839, to keep pace with immigration, the county of New York had opened a lunatic hospital on Blackwell's Island as a receptacle for the insane who previously had been scattered throughout the region's almshouses.[2]

What was exciting from Dix's perspective, however, was the plan for an immense state insane asylum on a 130-acre site in the central New York town of Utica. Governor William Seward had appointed a special commission to study modern institutions with an eye toward building not merely a hospital but "a monument of the taste and munificence of this age." Although financial realities tended to constrain Seward's and the commissioners' extravagance, the Utica hospital was conceived, like Worcester a decade earlier, as a model institution. And like Worcester, before long it was inundated with pauper lunatics pouring in from around the state.[3]

Opinion was deeply divided about the wisdom of putting up so large a facility. Among those opposed to the idea, McLean's Luther Bell privately assured Dix that Utica was bound to be "the *largest* and *worst* hospital of the world." To design a monster institution for one thousand patients on the premise that its deranged inhabitants could be made to "function in military fashion" was, he said, foolishly optimistic. It was bound to become more like a prison than a hospital. The community would have a measure of confidence in American asylums, he explained, only if they functioned like families. Proper moral treatment called for individual attention and thus required a setting that encouraged familiarity. That had always been his goal at McLean: to live inside the institution as a paterfamilias, able to know his patients' "characters, feelings, connections and interests with a good degree of intimacy." More and smaller asylums were preferable to what was on the drawing board for Utica.[4]

Dix, trying to clarify what principles of therapy and asylum architecture worked best, agreed in concept with Bell "that the curative & custodial treatment of the insane was essentially moral treatment."[5] But she was not yet sure in her own mind of the best way to provide this moral treatment. In a letter to the superintendent of the Bloomingdale asylum, she wanted to know whether larger asylums could really serve "the well being moral and physical of the insane," and whether it was best to place curable and incurable patients alongside in the same environment. In response, William Wilson told her that his experience had demonstrated the efficacy of smaller institutions.[6]

After her revenue bill for the Worcester asylum was passed, Dix crisscrossed New England and New York, using her contacts and her growing celebrity to gain access to institutions wherever she traveled. She wanted to see for herself what worked best. On the one hand, personal experience—above all, pleasant memories of Greenbank—biased her in favor of small, homey facilities. On the other, she realized there were a host of new theories on both sides of the Atlantic regarding institutional architecture, including some that argued for both the cost-effectiveness and the therapeutic power of large hospitals. Obtaining a partial list of New York almshouses from Dr. Theodore Beck, one of the physicians at the Utica asylum, she mapped out a route that would take her through every county in the state. He and the other managers of the new state hospital encouraged her to pursue a similar investigation to the one she had conducted in Massachusetts and present the results to the governor and the assembly. They hoped that a fresh voice would help persuade the legislature to open the state treasury and increase the level of funding for their institution.[7]

By November 1843, putting everything else aside to "traverse New York in length and breadth," she set out to gather the information to write her next memorial. It was hardly the season for extensive travel. She told George Barrell Emerson that she had between sixteen hundred and eighteen hundred miles yet to cover before the end of the year, "through mud-sloughs in . . . lumber wagons—or breaking roads through snow drifts." Unlike most people, though, the prospect of adversity cheered her up, and she exuded growing confidence: "I encounter nothing which a determined will, created by the necessities of the cause I advocate, does not enable me to vanquish."[8] This optimism was a far cry from the pathetic malaise that had crippled her during her late thirties, when she had desperately reached out to Emerson and his wife for help. Now the tables were turned. When she asked him for copies of his lectures to hand out to the teachers in the almshouses she visited, Emerson replied that her whirlwind energy made him feel slothful. The example of "your perseverance in this angel work," he wrote, "strengthens me in my poor & distant imitation." He envied her newfound verve; she envied his sanguine hopefulness. Indeed, she told Emerson that he seemed to be the only genuinely happy person she knew. As for her own happiness, trudging the long, slow road from Lake Erie to Barcelona and Silver Creek, she was as much at peace with herself as she had ever been in her life.[9]

Dix officially reported her findings in the *Memorial. To the Honorable the Legislature of the State of New-York*, published in January 1844, in the proceedings of the state house of representatives. What she had learned in a year is remarkable. The document marked a new sophistication in Dix's grasp of lunacy reform and the politics that surrounded it. From the first page, her presentation was more self-assured, more balanced, with a firmer grasp of legal distinctions and legislative issues than what she had written in Massachusetts.

The New York county-house system was the main target of her inquiry, but in each town and county she heard innumerable stories of lunatics and idiots kept in private houses, living often, she was convinced, in circumstances more degrading than anything she was allowed to see. This thought led her, in the opening section of the memorial, to make one of the favorite arguments of the English parliamentary reformers: to wit, that all insane paupers, by virtue of their "total incapacity for self-care and self-government," should be designated wards of the state. New York, she allowed, had taken promising steps in this direction. The Utica hospital, a central state institution, was predicated on the theory that the severely mad ought to be wards of the state. Whether or not one agreed that massive institutions on this scale were a good idea—and Dix continued to have her doubts—the underlying principle of state responsibility seemed to her irrefutable. Everywhere she had seen men and women "sinking in the prime of life into irrecoverable insanity"—people whose only hopes of recovery lay in a therapeutic environment. Given the prevalence of mental disorder and the complexity of building a curative asylum, local communities could not begin to solve the problem.[10]

She believed it was the responsibility of the state to save the insane poor. But how should it go about this difficult task? In contrast to Massachusetts, New York's state government had been reasonably generous in its spending for the poor. Many public institutions around the state were clean, orderly, and comfortable enough for their inmates, but this was not enough for Dix. Having learned her lesson in Massachusetts about appearing too one-sided, throughout the New York *Memorial* Dix mentioned examples of decent, well-run almshouses. In the Westchester county house near White Plains, for example, she had found that some of the rooms, scrubbed clean and freshly painted, even had "an air of cheerfulness." If anything could have convinced her that community-controlled asylums would work, Westchester would have done it. "But nothing can," she maintained, because the root principle of local organization was flawed.[11]

Expanding haphazardly without any plan for over a century, the county-house system had generated a patchwork quilt of "*complex* and *compound*" institutions. Surveying these, she described "*alms-houses*, or retreats for the aged, the invalid, and helpless poor: *houses of correction* for the vicious and abandoned; *asylums for orphaned and neglected children; receptacles for the insane and imbecile;* extensive *farming*, and more limited *manufacturing establishments*." Who could expect places in which outcasts of all kinds were promiscuously thrown together, regardless of their needs, to provide lunatics with moral treatment and education? The supervisors of Erie County mocked the therapeutic ideals of the asylum movement when they simply painted a new sign that said "County Hospital for the Insane" and plastered it on a few cells in the local almshouse. Curative treatment, she said, was more than window dressing. It depended on calm, well-appointed surroundings, well-trained attendants, and expert medical supervision. These were available only in institutions specifically devoted to the care and cure of the insane.[12]

Judging from the fifteen hundred lunatics and idiots she had seen in her investigation, Dix estimated there were at least three thousand scattered throughout New York. To accommodate them all, she told the legislature, would probably require between four and six new "asylums in convenient sections of the State" designated for "incurables." She reasoned that building and operating elaborate facilities like the Utica asylum for incurably retarded and deranged patients would cost more than the state could afford. Such "curative" institutions should be reserved for people with the best chances for recovery. Hopeless cases, on the other hand, needed only decent, custodial care, which could be provided simply "on the plan of the celebrated establishment of *Ghiel* [sic], connected with the hospital at Antwerp." For centuries lunatics from all over Europe had come to the cottages of Gheel in hopes of divine healing. During the Victorian period, the Flemish town formed an administrative structure to manage its system of small facilities for the insane, and by midcentury this system was celebrated as a worthy example of moral treatment in action. (Dix was ahead of her time in recommending the Gheel model. The American alienist mainstream did not begin to debate its merits until the 1850s.[13]) If this seemed overly ambitious and costly, she argued that in the long run it was really cheaper to take care of the chronically insane in such asylums than any- where else.[14]

Although generally more restrained than her first memorial, the New York *Memorial* also relied on gothic images and evangelical exhortations to duty for its effect. The most richly embroidered scene in the docu- ment came from her first journey to Albany, the first draft of which was composed while she was working on her Massachusetts *Memorial*. As in her description of the Newburyport almshouse, she complained that the Albany almshouse master was suspiciously reluctant to let her inside to see the insane inmates. He insisted that the male inmates were "naked, in the crazy cellar," in no condition for a lady to view. Using all her persistence, over his objections, she was finally ushered to the insane women's apartment. This was a miserably uncomfortable room, overheated, "foul with noisome vapors," and she could stand it only for a few minutes. Walking outside for a breath of air, however, she over- heard talk of "the dungeons." Immediately she demanded that her guide escort her to see them. Intimidated by her authoritative tone and manner, he found the turnkey and convinced him to open the cells. "I affirm that the dungeons of Spielberg and Chillon, and the prisons of the Court of Inquisition before their destruction," she wrote, "afforded no more heart-rending spectacles than the dungeons (not subter- ranean) of the Albany alms-house." As she had expected, inside she encountered a horrible spectacle: a madman, wild, unclothed, encrust- ed with filth, who, she felt compelled to remind her readers, was "dis- gusting it is true, but no less a human being—nay more, an immortal being, though now the mind has fallen in ruins." One of God's chil- dren—a human soul—he endured a living death, his debasement equally a reproach to his keepers and the state that employed them.[15]

From the outside these almshouses looked peaceful enough. But each one housed its physical and psychic tragedies. Visiting the Oneida county house at Rome, Dix quoted from Dante's *Inferno*: "so by my *subject, is my power surpassed, / What'er I say compared with truth seems weak!"*[16] The Rome almshouse had earned a local reputation for sexual impropriety that, she saw when she inspected it, was entirely deserved. "The history of these unfortunate females is shocking to relate. No more than brief allusion can be made of it. *They have become mothers!"* The deplorable spectacle of pregnant lunatics and madwomen with infants proved that they had been subjected to "the lowest vices." If one were looking for a more scathing indictment of the "culpably indifferent and inefficient" county-house system, Dix could not imagine what it would be.[17]

Dix had by this time, seen and read enough to know that sexual abuse of the mentally incompetent, male and female, was commonplace in local institutions. The rape of madwomen had surfaced a generation earlier as a most serious problem in the British parliamentary inquiry on madhouses in 1815–16. Madness often left its victims defenseless against the sexual depredations of the petty criminals and beggars who congregated around such establishments. More disturbingly, it also left them vulnerable to their guardians. And the New York practice of employing almshouse paupers and hangers-on as attendants for mentally disordered inmates increased the likelihood that women and children would be sexually molested.[18]

With such outrages being perpetrated every day in their own communities, Dix chided would-be reformers who devoted their attention to foreign missions "to Asia and the South Sea Islands," or spent their time trying to push "the cause of emancipation in the slave-holding States." Why did they not begin by addressing the gross injustices right under their noses? As she saw it, antislavery agitation was hypocritical so long as the North continued to shackle its own innocent victims. A good example would be much stronger than a "reiterated precept," she declared. Only after "having plucked the beam from our own eye, we can with a less pharisaical spirit, direct our efforts to clearing the mental vision of our neighbor."[19]

This biblical language suited her purpose well, for she thought of her work as a divinely commissioned errand into the wilderness. Lamenting the "great neglect of the moral and religious instruction" in county houses, she remarked that Jesus had preached to the poor and there was no reason to believe that paupers, whatever their mental capacities, "cease to need the benign influences of christianity."[20] In fact the whole concluding section of the New York *Memorial* was a lay sermon meant to convert the legislature to her way of thinking. Their "duty to the Most

High God," Dix admonished the lawmakers, demanded that they seek "sanctification in the exercise of the higher charities, and the ennobling acts of life." Responsibility to provide for the poor was part and parcel of the state's religious obligation. For God "ordained that nations, not less than individuals" were accountable for the welfare of the helpless and downtrodden in their midst. With a well-orchestrated crescendo, Dix concluded by urging the legislature to act on her findings and her plan, and thereby make good on the lofty promise of the New York state motto, "Excelsior! Excelsior!"[21]

Her religious and humanitarian reason for speaking out so boldly needed no justification. The essential rightness of delivering the suffering captives was an easy argument to make. But in several scenes, she suggested another rationale. Something needed to be done not only for the insane poor but for the sane poor was well.

Dix was concerned that the flood of immigrants pouring into New York City in the early 1840s would produce serious social problems that, left unchecked, would end in crisis. On her first visit to Albany in 1842, for example, she had concentrated on the sufferings of the individual lunatics in the almshouse "dungeons." Returning a year later she was at first pleasantly surprised to find that a new master had cleaned up the facility, and that the insane inmates were much better treated. Her initial enthusiasm waned, however, when she noticed that the total pauper census of the almshouse had swelled to more than five hundred, "a large proportion of these able-bodied foreigners, who here are idle for want of work. . . . as well as idle in many cases from choice."[22]

While the county-house welfare system had not provided adequately for the insane, the state had, in her judgment, been too eager to untie its purse strings for the undeserving poor. Knowing they could fall back on public relief, she said, foreign paupers had too little incentive for honest labor. Her recommendation for separating the deserving from the undeserving poor derived from what she had seen in England in the wake of the New Poor Law: she suggested that New York State set up workhouses in the new urban centers that were already inundated with immigrants, starting with Albany, Rochester, Buffalo, and Utica. These compulsory establishments would exemplify the work ethic that all foreigners, beginning with the Irish, were expected to adopt. "Let them know certainly, that if they do not support themselves abroad," she urged, "they will, by law, be required to do so in a work-house." Within a few years of implementing such a system, she predicted that the idle poor would cease to be a problem, and the few remaining almshouses would see their populations "dwindle down to cases of the aged, the infirm, and to children without parental guardians."[23]

In the larger scheme of things, she argued that workhouses might be thought of as preventive medicine for insanity. A year earlier, in the Massachusetts *Memorial*, Dix had been unwilling to speculate on the causes of mental illness. But now, after reading what the asylum doctors had to say about the roots of mental disease, she was convinced that "imperfect or vicious social institutions" were among the chief culprits. Heading her list of causes were "revolutions, party strife, unwise and capricious legislation, causing commercial speculations and disasters; false standards of worth and rank, undue encouragement of the propensities and passions, social rivalry, social intemperance; some fashions and conventional usages; religious and political excitement."[24] Exposed to these discontents of civilization, many foreigners (and American citizens as well), she believed, stood in danger of mental disintegration. Not that she had a well-thought-out theory of the etiology of madness and its biological and environmental determinants. If she had learned anything from her own experience in England, however, it was that the only certain way to protect oneself from the bewildering upheaval of the modern age was to submit oneself to the discipline of hard work. If the path of idleness did not lead the lower orders to the workhouse, she was afraid it would lead them to the asylum.

The New York *Memorial* was published in January 1844 In some measure, its arguments resonated with the legislature because many of the same points had already been made by Governor Enos Throop, who, during the early 1830s, invoked moral outrage, Christian compassion, and state pride in his imprecations to build a state asylum. In fact, the legislature produced six asylum bills between 1830 and 1837. In each instance, though, these measures failed to make it through the legislative process. During this period, the State Assembly was in a phenomenal state of flux. Turnover was high; in some years as many as nine out of ten lawmakers were freshmen, most of them with no prior legislative experience, who had won election on promises not to raise taxes.[25]

Unlike the document Dix had published a year earlier, however, it neither stirred vigorous political response nor resulted in significant legislative action. The state had already poured far more money than expected into the new Utica facility, which was supposed to concentrate patients with curable disorders, treat them with compassion and efficiency, and return them to productive lives in their communities. Dix's plan of building "four or six" smaller institutions for incurables—the chronically insane paupers she had surveyed in the county houses—was sure to be expensive and had little appeal. At the same time, in New York politics she was on unfamiliar ground. There she lacked the predisposition and dedicated sponsorship of political leaders. Equally important, she had few connections in New York society who could help her advance her agenda in Albany.[26]

She also lacked support within the medical establishment. After trying unsuccessfully to lure Samuel Woodward away from Worcester to take the helm of their flagship institution, the Utica asylum trustees had turned to a physician named Amariah Brigham. He had impressed them with his professional pedigree: medical training at the College of Physicians and Surgeons in New York, then to Paris for advanced study, followed by private practice and a few years as medical superintendent of the Hartford Retreat. There he continued to publish prolifically on mental disorders and their treatment. Up to the time he came to Utica,

Amariah Brigham, Superintendent of New York's Utica asylum and founding editor of the American Journal of Insanity.

The enormous New York State Lunatic Asylum at Utica in 1850.

Brigham, like most American asylum superintendents, assumed that moral treatment required a small institution. But when he received an enticing offer to head up Utica, he began to have doubts about his old views. It did not take him long to see how narrow they had been, and that a large hospital possessed certain virtues owing to its scale. The offer to come to Utica had been generous, but when he arrived Brigham realized how difficult it was going to be to thread his way between the legislature's towering expectations for cost-efficient cures, on the one hand, and its miserly unwillingness to increase his operating and capital budgets.[27]

He had a reputation as a careful man, circumspect and disinclined to stir up trouble. So he was angered and annoyed by Dorothea Dix—a woman from another state with no claim to expertise in an area in which he had spent his entire professional life—as she scoured New York for scandal and petitioned the legislature to adopt a policy that might divert money away from Utica to several new institutions.

To make matters worse, she did not share her findings with Brigham until her survey was already in press. This was a serious political blunder. At the time, he was taking the first steps to organize his profession by founding the Association of Medical Superintendents of American Institutions for the Insane, and to launch the country's first professional journal devoted to psychiatric subjects, *The American Journal of Insani-*

ty. At this point, she was still inexperienced and in consequence naive about the importance of quietly lining up support before issuing public pronouncements.

After the publication of her New York *Memorial,* he sent her a well-reasoned explanation of why he disagreed with her proposal for "hospitals *solely* for the incurable insane." First of all, he wrote, "who can say which patients *are* and which *are not* incurable?" At Utica, with a population of four hundred or so, Brigham said he would have found it impossible to classify at least one-third of his patients along such rigid lines. Moreover, he argued that sending a borderline patient to an institution for incurables would surely crush the slightest hope of recovery. Gazing rather presciently into the future, he predicted that if they were instituted, hospitals for chronic cases "would soon become objects of little interest to anyone, and where misrule, neglect, and all kinds of abuse would exist, and exist without detection." He had once visited such an institution in Genoa, "where the clashing of chains, the howlings, groans and curses, give to the place the appearance of the infernal regions. Where no patient is ever expected to leave until dead—where hope never comes." The asylum was supposed to restore the mad to circulation, not serve as a dead letter office for lost souls.[28]

Professional circumspection kept him from publicizing his criticisms, but Brigham privately expressed dismay at Dix's cavalier disregard for accuracy in her *Memorial*. The following year, when she was busy with a similar survey in Pennsylvania, he confided misgivings about her methods to his friend Thomas Story Kirkbride, the superintendent of the Pennsylvania Hospital for the Insane. "I see Miss Dix has been over your state & *Memorialized* your legislature," Brigham wrote. "I hope good will result from it—& trust that her experience in this state may make her more cautious in observing & publishing. In this state I am afraid she did hurt by *coloring* & by not accurately observing. She was often mistaken & this has thrown a doubt over all her statements with many."[29]

Dix had become so thoroughly enchanted with the feasibility of her program that literal accuracy was of little concern. Simplifying the complicated issues of poverty and madness, and dramatizing the huge suffering they brought, she had created a personal vision. This tended to make her very selective when it came to reporting facts. Indeed, for her, facts existed to be used, not to be enshrined in their own right.

In Massachusetts she experienced a rapid upward spiral of her reputation and influence. In New York she experienced the limits of influence without power. As a woman, she had no direct means to assume the power she needed to advance her cause. Working in New York, however, and at the same time becoming involved in Rhode Island's policies, she began to understand more clearly than before the need to master the inner workings of politics and government. Prisons and asylums, both institutions in a state of flux in the early 1840s, were high priorities on most states' legislative agendas. If she could focus her energy, intelligence, and moral convictions through the channel of politics, as she had managed to do with surprising ease in Massachusetts, she saw that she might find a way to realize her ambitions for the insane. The next and most vital phase of her career awaited the joining of her personality with a new mastery of the subtle techniques of the political process in antebellum America.

Her father had been an itinerant lay minister who proclaimed the Methodist gospel ardently yet ineffectually across the New England frontier. In September 1843, more than twenty years after his death, his daughter might have been seen retracing Joseph Dix's footsteps as she boarded "the stage for Boston to *Keene through Fitzwilliam*," the New Hampshire village where her mother, Mary Bigelow Dix, had died. Succeeding where her parents had failed, Dorothea Dix traveled across northern New England, through upstate New York, and back to Rhode Island, preaching her own increasingly powerful message of repentance and salvation. Invigorated by her recent triumph in Massachusetts and what appeared to be good prospects in New York, she now revisited the northern New England she knew from childhood.

She was pleased to find the "alms-houses in New Hampshire in generally excellent condition."[30] Not long after the first state facilities for lunatics opened in Connecticut and Massachusetts in the early 1830s, New Hampshire, Vermont, and Maine began planning their first state mental institutions. The reformers who founded the Worcester hospital were linked by common religious and benevolent associations to their counterparts in other states. And the same arguments that influenced policy in Boston were easily adapted to its northern neighbors. As Dix soon discovered, however, northern New England, full of staunch independence, was far more skeptical of state institutions than was Massachusetts. Legislatures readily approved the concept of central lunatic asylums, but they were reluctant to ask towns to raise the necessary taxes. Not surprisingly, financing was a constant source of contention. Dix's conviction that the state, rather than unreliable localities, should manage the care of the insane poor had deepened. If a state could not raise enough money on its own, she advocated supplementing public funds with private philanthropy to capitalize asylums. Based on this concept of joint public-private financing, her work in Vermont in 1843–44 was a catalyst for a measure that secured the first state funding for the Vermont Asylum for the Insane.[31]

Meanwhile, her single-minded efforts to publicize the lunacy issue in each state she visited drew her into a bitter controversy in Rhode Island. The Massachusetts *Memorial* had been widely distributed and reviewed in Rhode Island, and by early 1843 Dix was besieged by requests to look into all manner of abuses in local institutions there. Sometime in mid-1843 she heard from Thomas G. Hazard, a well-connected humanitarian, who told her about an atrocious case of a madman confined in the Rhode Island town of Little Compton. As soon as she found time, between frequent trips to New York and ongoing efforts to lobby the Massachusetts legislature, she assumed a personal interest in a lunatic named Abram Simmons.[32]

Brattleboro Retreat, 1836, asylum as country inn.

Dix first saw Simmons in early September 1843 in the Little Compton poorhouse. "What do you say to finding me in a cage," she asked George Emerson, with a pathetic creature "confined for *thirty years*—out three times during that period!" Upbraiding the mistress of the house about Simmons's condition, she was blithely told, "don't know, as he's been there so long if it's worth while to have him removed!" Shocked at his condition—his body twisted, his skin sallow and covered with sores—Dix wanted him removed at once, but told Emerson that she was afraid to press for Simmons's release unless he could be taken directly to an asylum. At large, she feared that he was bound to suffer even worse indignities at the hands of the callous local townspeople than he had in the poorhouse.[33]

In the fall of 1843, Dix was so preoccupied with New York that she gave little thought to Simmons. In the middle of putting the finishing touches on her New York *Memorial*, however, she received a request from a member of the Rhode Island assembly asking her to forward to him a report on any facts she had gathered regarding the condition of the insane in his state. Her correspondent, William Giles Goddard, reminded her that Nicolas Brown, a Providence merchant who had contributed so handsomely to the local university's endowment that it was renamed Brown University in his honor, had in 1841 bequeathed $30,000 to endow an asylum for the insane. Having some idea of what it cost to build a hospital, the assembly understood that this was not remotely enough money to build an asylum consistent with the increasingly elaborate architectural standards in the early 1840s. But Brown's bequest did set the wheels in motion. With his money available to start work on the project, Rhode Island lawmakers discovered a new interest in the building of a state asylum.[34]

After the lackluster reception of her New York *Memorial*, with nothing further to do there, Dix was anxious to get back to Rhode Island. The state was no larger than many individual counties in New York, and she thought she could survey it in a matter of weeks and draft a memorial along the lines of what she had published in Massachusetts.

Before taking up anything else, however, she wrote an account of Abram Simmons for the *Providence Journal*. Published in April 1844 under the heading "Astonishing Tenacity of Life," Dix's column purported to describe not her own visit to Little Compton the previous fall but rather a story she had got from a gentleman she had run into accidentally that morning. "He stated that he had visited the cell of Abram

Simmons during the past winter," she said, and had discovered an appalling scene. The poorhouse dungeon was dark and unventilated.

> At that time the internal surface of the walls was covered with a thick frost, adhering to the stone in some places to the thickness of half an inch, as ascertained by actual measurement. . . . Thus, in utter darkness, encased on every side by walls of frost, his garments constantly more or less wet, with only wet straw to lie upon, and a sheet of ice for his covering, has this most dreadfully abused man existed through the past inclement winter. . . . His teeth must have been worn out by constant and violent chattering for such a length of time, night and day, "Poor Tom's a-cold!"

Dix went on sarcastically to say that if the inhabitants of Little Compton worshipped as Christians, they must not have been praying to "poor Simmons' God . . . that Almighty Being, in whose keeping sleeps the vengeance due to all wrongs."[35]

Unlike the comparatively restrained approach she had taken in New York, this overwrought account of a Shakespeare-quoting lunatic is reminiscent of the hyperbole and dramatic rhetoric she had used in Massachusetts. A short time later, however, in a different version of her encounter with Simmons, she revealed a new and important theme in her career as a reformer.

For at least two years she had been researching the history of the insane asylum in Great Britain and on the Continent to refine her own ideas about insanity and its treatment. In 1844, as she came to grips with the personal implications of her mission to the mad, Dix was beginning to identify more and more with the late-eighteenth-century heroes of lunacy reform. In all her reading, nothing gripped Dix's mind more firmly than the luminous image of Philippe Pinel, the physician to the insane at Salpétrière and Bicêtre, entering the dungeon and, to the astonishment of all, fearlessly unshackling the lunatics. Crediting the celebrated French physician with the "first great triumph of humanity and skill, over ferocity and ignorance," she translated passages of a memoir Pinel's son had delivered before the French Academy. One of the most memorable passage had to do with Pinel's encounter with a reputedly vicious lunatic.

> The experiments commenced with an English captain whose history was unknown: *he had been in chains forty years!* As he was thought to be one of

the most dangerous, having killed, at one time, an attendant with a blow from his manacles, the keepers approached him with caution; but first Pinel entered his cell unattended. "Ah, well captain, I will cause your chains to be taken off; you shall have liberty and walk in the court, if you will promise to behave like a gentleman."

Unfettered, the lunatic limped out of his "dark dungeon," beheld the sky, "Ah," cried he, "how beautiful!" Over the next two years at Bicêtre, the story went, the mad Englishman was transformed and "had no recurrence of violent paroxysms, and often rendered good service to the keepers in conducting the affairs of the establishment."[36]

The transforming power of the courageous healer, able to restore at least a glimmer of reason to the lunatic simply by acknowledging his humanity, enthralled Dix. And in her second account of Abram Simmons, she repainted the picture of her encounter with the madman. Now she appeared to have inherited the mantle of Pinel. Simmons became a terror, a monster locked in a tomblike strong room, secured by *two* "strong, solid iron" doors. Descending by the light of a single candle into the horrible den, she dimly made out a wild creature, "emaciated to a shadow, etiolated," more resembling "a disinterred corpse than any living creature." Undeterred by this fearsome sight, Dix reached out and gently rubbed his hands to warm them— "notwithstanding the assertions of the mistress that he would kill me." Making no concession to his mental dissolution, she "spoke to him of release, of liberty, of care and kindness." Although the maniac could not summon words to answer her, she wrote, "a tear stole over the hollow cheek." For a flickering moment, her touch had restored his emotions and thus his latent humanity.[37]

Who was to say it had not happened thus?

In early May 1844, she prevailed on several members of the Rhode Island State Assembly who met with her in Newport to take the Simmons case directly to the floor of the legislature. For almost a year, Little Compton had done nothing to make the madman more comfortable and had resisted Dix's efforts to send him to an asylum at town expense. When the issue was presented at the assembly's next session, however, suddenly the member from Little Compton arose and announced the death of Simmons. After a moment of shocked silence, the assembly, without further discussion, voted to appoint a state lunacy commission. "I told them some plain truths which they received not illy," Dix wrote to George Emerson, although many were "startled at my imputing to the townspeople—the crime of murder in the second degree."[38]

Up to this time, Dix had reshaped her experiences and materials mainly to dramatize the plight of the insane. But in Rhode Island, she shifted into a more active mode. She began to envision herself not merely as an witness and chronicler but as an actor with a vital part to play. Characterizing herself as a latter-day Pinel helped justify direct intervention on behalf of the helpless and helped justify her increasing involvement in politics. Her image as a woman with extraordinary power over disordered minds served to create a personal mythology. Madness frightened most people and made them feel helpless but not her. She seemed to relate to the insane on a different level, as though they were confused children who would soon grow out of their illness, not forlorn objects who should be abandoned.

Just as important to her work as her affinity for the mad was her special gift for influencing men of wealth and power. At the same time as the Abram Simmons affair, Dix met with Cyrus Butler, a Providence business magnate. She apparently went to see him at the urging of the Reverend Edward Brooks Hall, a local Unitarian minister who hoped the irascible Butler might be persuaded to contribute to building an asylum in Rhode Island. A self-made millionaire in the mold of Elijah Dix, Butler was one of the wealthiest men in the state and by all reports a skinflint of the first water. To Dix fell the difficult task of persuading him to make a donation that, when added to Nicolas Brown's original $30,000 bequest, would fund the construction of a new hospital for the insane.

Exaggerated accounts of their meeting began to circulate almost immediately. According to the traditional version, Dix looked Butler squarely in the eye, brushed off his attempts to change the subject, and delivered a spellbinding description of the condition of the insane in Rhode Island. When she finished, a converted Butler was supposed to have asked, "'Miss Dix, what do you want me to do?' 'Sir, I want you to give $50,000 toward the enlargement of the insane hospital in this city!' 'Madam, I'll do it!' was his answer."[39]

When it was circulated in the press, this act of squeezing "milk out of a stone," as Dix's nineteenth-century biographer put it, further enhanced her growing reputation. In the subsequent rush to take credit for founding the new institution, however, there arose questions about what her real contribution had been. Pliny Earle, for example, an eccentric and splenetic alienist who was leery, if not jealous, of Dix and disliked her methods privately suggested that her part in founding the institution had been exaggerated.[40]

Judging by her subsequent successes in other marvelous feats of persuasion, though, it is certainly plausible that Dix sparked Butler's exceptional act of philanthropy. In any event, whether or not she single-handedly solicited Cyrus Butler's gift, she was widely credited with a miracle. The magnate donated $40,000 toward building an asylum, contingent on an additional $40,000 being raised from public subscriptions. That Dix refused to confirm rumors or talk to the local press about what her role had been only enhanced her mystique for the public. Perpetually wary of personal publicity, she believed that an attitude of feminine self-effacement helped keep her work above reproach. After the Butler Hospital for the Insane was incorporated in January 1844, Dix pitched in to help its trustees raise sufficient matching funds to begin construction of the new asylum building. Two years later they had collected pledges for more than $125,000.[41]

Upon the recommendation of Luther Bell, Cyrus Butler (who became president of the new institution) and the board of trustees hired Isaac Ray, a bright and capable physician who had managed a similar facility in Augusta, Maine. During the month of December 1847 forty patients moved into the half-completed main building, twenty-nine of whom were paupers transferred from the Providence almshouse with the understanding that the new asylum would be paid two dollars a week for their upkeep. As it turned out, this was not nearly enough. Dr. Ray was beset by money woes from the start, and by 1849 the institution was embarrassingly near insolvency. Only an emergency gift of $20,000 from Cyrus Butler's son-in-law kept it afloat.[42]

By this time Dix, following the upward arc of her crusade, had long since moved on to other states. Had she revisited Rhode Island in 1850, however, she would have been dismayed to find how little the creation of the Butler Hospital for the Insane had really improved the lot of the state's homeless insane. Her old friend Thomas Hazard, who took it upon himself to act as a one-man lunacy commission, sadly told the General Assembly in its opening session in January 1851 that things remained as bad as ever. In three visits to the town of Coventry he had come across a handful of lunatics "in the most deplorable condition imaginable." Among them, huddled in a dirty, dilapidated poorhouse, was a "an insane woman, who had recently been removed by the town from the Butler Hospital." When Hazard arrived, this woman was ordered by the keeper "from her filthy lair (where she was confined by the corner of a bedstead being pushed against the door) in a tone of voice such as keepers of wild beasts use in colloquy with tigers. At the stern summons she came forth and stood silent and motionless, to be gazed at—a caricature of despair clothed in filth and rags. No sign, look or token indicated that she noticed aught that was said, until at the keeper's bidding, she quietly retired to her den." The whole scene was, he wrote, "heart-sickening."[43]

Rhode Island had its asylum, filled with 115 destitute patients, shipped there by cities and towns and maintained until money or good-will ran low. But town after town, as Hazard sadly concluded, still had its Abram Simmonses awaiting redemption.

CHAPTER SEVEN

The Perils of Politics

In the Northeast and elsewhere, as word of her extraordinary mission spread, the name of Dorothea Dix was rapidly becoming synonymous with lunacy reform. Stepping up the pace of her travels, in fewer than eighteen months she covered all the major prisons, jails, and almshouses of New Jersey and Pennsylvania. In those states she found herself moving beyond being a witness and a reporter to drafting amendments to legislation and contributing to asylum design. Some politicians deferred to her on those matters because she was so well informed; others were intimidated by her intensity. Few could ignore her.

The strangeness of finding herself in the midst of political life was not lost on Dix. Politics, with its brute aggression in pursuit of power, was, everyone agreed, the antithesis of woman's sphere. The door to the statehouse was seldom opened for ladies, and Dix never intended to become embroiled in the masculine business of government. What perplexed her was that, early on, she saw that her issues would continue to be ignored unless she met face-to-face with the people's elected

representatives and persuaded them to rewrite the law. Personal confrontation was her most powerful weapon against denial.

How she justified stepping outside the narrowly circumscribed role
that Victorian America had outlined for women's participation in public life is suggested by an essay Dix treasured. It was entitled "A Lesson
for Woman from History." Although it did not mention her by name,
the article, published in the Boston *Monthly Religious Magazine*, presents
an accurate summary of Dix's views on women and the public sphere.
Its author was a friend of hers, Caroline Wells Healy Dall, a Unitarian
whose feminist interests led her to organize the Boston Woman's
Rights convention in 1855. Dall began with a quotation attributed to
the Irish novelist, Lady Sydney Morgan, "This is the age of great events,
and not of great men." She noted that some publication had recently
criticized a book about "the Sphere and Duties of Women" by asking,
"Why does not some one write upon the Sphere and Duties of Men?"
The answer, she asserted, was because the sphere and duties of men
and women amounted to the same thing. "The great aim of life, to perfect the individual and the race, is the same in both sexes." (Here Dix
made a mark of approval in the margin.) Dall went on to say that no
two individuals were given the same means to pursue their lifework,
but that no matter what some men with old-fashioned notions argued,
the great questions of duty were equally important for men and
women. The trouble, she wrote, was that "women have not so been
accustomed to regard their own vocation." Then in a fascinating passage about Dix's work she urged woman to "look facts in the face, and
though for the instant they turn heart to stone, they will nevertheless
give her the power of the Medusa."[1]

The prospect of wielding such power was frighteningly ambiguous
for Dix and her contemporaries. Medusa, after all, was a killer. For her
part Dix was certain she would not have chosen to seek such power—
to enter the political arena—had the decision been hers to make. She
might well have suspected that God had thrust her into politics in a fit
of malice; in many respects, she found it emotionally easier to visit the
almshouse and the prison than the statehouse. But politics was so integral to her mission that she could not avoid it. She would have preferred to avoid the institutional politics and professional intrigue that
surrounded the rise of new medical institutions if a strong leader had
emerged within the world of asylum superintendents. But none had.
She forced herself into state politics and the politics of an emerging

profession because she came to the conclusion that if she did not carry the standard, her cause would fail.

Leaving Rhode Island in mid-1844, she intended to pursue her work southward directly into Pennsylvania, where she had a reliable network of Unitarian friends. But her exploration of New York crossed over into New Jersey, a state, she discovered, with only the crudest provisions for the insane. Following the geographical contours of railroads, canals, and stage routes, she ignored state boundaries and cast a widening net over the Middle Atlantic States. Methodically she mapped out her routes, visiting every almshouse, poorhouse, jail, and prison in her path. Witnessing so much misery so rapidly weighed heavily on her. "You should look on the poor afflicted beings," she told George Emerson, "see them thrust into prison God help them, *because* they are crazy—see them beaten to inspire terror."[2] There would be time during the coming winter, when travel was more difficult, to determine how best to use the information she was compiling.

From the first day, her work in New Jersey seemed to be divinely orchestrated. Passing through Jersey City one fine June morning on her way to Bordentown, she asked the first gentleman she met about what provision the community made for the poor. This stranger turned out to be an overseer of the local almshouse and an alderman who gladly directed her to the old town jail a few blocks away. Her good luck continued when she rang the doorbell of an imposing mansion. Presenting her card to a servant, she was invited in and greeted warmly by the owner and his wife, "Ah you are then Miss Dix." When she explained her mission, they said they were delighted to hear that she wanted to reform New Jersey's overburdened public institutions and offered to do whatever they could to help her. It was not until she boarded her train later that morning and ran into the owner of the mansion, his briefcase bulging with official documents, that she learned from the conductor that her host was the richest man in the county and the city's mayor. As the car rolled through the countryside they talked, and he assured Dix that he would put her in touch with New Jersey's political and social leaders, promising to furnish her with "letters to the Governor—and other persons of influence and distinction."[3]

While her overarching goal was political, she was frequently drawn into individual cases of madness. She liked to strike up conversations with fellow passengers on trains, and on the way to Newark she found herself sitting beside a well-heeled lady who, when she realized her companion was the celebrated lunacy reformer, said that one of her servants had recently been struck with insanity. Her physician, perplexed by the man's symptoms but determined to act forcefully, intended to shave his head, then blister and bleed him. Dix expressed her disapproval. The only hope for a cure, she explained, was to place the servant in an asylum as soon as possible. Taking matters into her own hands, she accompanied the woman to her mansion, where, to everyone's surprise, she succeeded in calming the patient. Next she borrowed the family coach and driver, ordering him to take her and the lunatic to the home of one of the trustees of a small asylum near Schuylkill. Within a matter of hours the necessary admission papers were signed and she personally conveyed the bewildered man to the hospital.[4]

She entered New Jersey at the perfect moment to exert maximum effect. Beginning in 1837, the State Medical Association had begun to press for a state lunatic hospital, and in response the New Jersey legislature had appointed a committee to study the matter and make appropriate recommendations. Its report came back at the end of February 1839, and its conclusions were typical of similar committees in different parts of the country. Until recently, the commissioners said, "lunatics and idiots of every grade have been regarded as incapable of cure, their malady beyond the reach of hope, their sufferings without the pale of sympathy." But advances in medicine now rendered these assumptions old-fashioned. "Modern science has dispelled this illusion [and] it is ascertained that mental maladies are as susceptible of cure as corporeal, and that when the disease cannot be healed, the suffering may be alleviated." The encouraging rates of cured patients discharged from hospitals in other states were convincing enough to persuade the commission and, in turn, the legislature to take the first steps toward building a state institution. In 1839–40 the New Jersey governor's commission, polling doctors who belonged to the medical association, compiled statistics on the total number of insane and idiots in the state, and, after the results were in, recommended allocating $20,000 toward a state asylum. Two of the commissioners had spent a month in Boston studying the McLean and Worcester facilities, along with the Massachusetts General Hospital and Boston Penitentiary. They returned home convinced that the Worcester hospital should be New Jersey's model.[5]

Governor and legislature alike agreed that an asylum was warranted on humanitarian grounds. As always, though, there was the quandary of how to pay for it. The hospital question had already been several times before the legislature, one supporter told Dix. "I was informed by one of the members three years since, that there was nothing in the way of a resolution being passed authorizing the erection of such an Asylum, but the want of being countenanced by publick opinion."[6] This same correspondent noted that in her own town of Salem the local poor house had kept a madman chained by the leg in a barely heated cell for more than twenty years. Examples of affliction abounded. This news energized Dix because, from her experience up to this point, she believed that the only obstacle to gaining public support was to show people specifically how the insane were being mistreated throughout the state. Thus the stage was set, and in the second half of 1844 she embarked upon the methodical survey of New Jersey that formed the basis for her *Memorial Soliciting A State Hospital For The Insane*.

By this time she had a formula. She had learned a great deal from the reception of her first two petitions, and her appreciation of what it took to win lawmakers' support for a given measure had been sharpened by her personal dealings with dozens of representatives and state senators in Massachusetts, New York, and Rhode Island. First she flattered the legislature by reminding its members how forward-thinking they had been to appoint commissions, research asylums in other parts of the country, and assemble estimates of the number of lunatics and idiots within their borders (338 and 358, respectively). So far they had done everything right, she said. Everything, that is, except to demonstrate the courage of their convictions.

In the document she submitted to them, the wildness and vituperation of the Massachusetts *Memorial*, with its lurid images and passionate outbursts, were gone. In place of gothic drama, the author offered calculation, professional opinion, and legal argumentation. The dark terrors that she exploited so adroitly in her previous writing—fear of abandonment, of being stripped of one's humanity—gave way to a more logical appeal. At the outset, perhaps to blunt criticism that she was too much the bleeding heart, she explicitly disavowed her intention to play on feelings. She was, she explained, simply an advocate. Her essential purpose in "showing the existence of terrible abuses," she quietly began, was to "ask *justice* of the Legislature of New Jersey, for those who . . . are incapable of pleading their own cause, and of claiming redress for their own grievances." In Massachusetts and Rhode Island, political process was peripheral to Dix's dramatic vision of the outcast insane, and she had allowed her literary contrivances to rage out of control. Possessing a much clearer concept now of how to pass a money bill through a fractious state assembly, in New Jersey she self-consciously drafted a kind of legal brief to advance the human rights of her voiceless clients.[7]

Unlike most of its neighbors, New Jersey had yet to determine how far the state's jurisdiction should extend over pauper lunatics and other classes of deviants. When Dix began her investigation, she found no hospital or asylum, public or private, devoted to the mentally ill. The absence of an adequate facility, as it turned out, proved to be not only a hardship for New Jersey's own "Idiots, Epileptics, and the Insane Poor," it shifted the burden of caring for them to New York and Pennsylvania. Hospitals for the insane in those states, Dix discovered, were housing dozens of inmates from New Jersey, displacing the citizens for whom they originally had been built.[8] At the same time, she said, a population explosion in the middle states was making this state of affairs untenable. Public facilities for the poor, swamped by newly arrived Irish and German immigrants, were alarmingly inadequate. Four years had elapsed since the state council and assembly had declared the need for a state asylum. During that time, New Jersey had slipped further behind, and now teetered on the brink of a public health crisis.[9]

Expecting private charity to solve the lunacy problem missed a critical point. The insane were not a group who appealed to most philanthropists. Dix knew how few social reformers wanted to bother with homeless lunatics, let alone befriend them. "This affecting christian duty devolves on *the state*," she declared, "and the state will cancel this sacred obligation, only by acknowledging the wardship of these, the *Pariahs* of our country, and establishing an asylum for their protection."[10] State sponsorship was the only prudent and just solution, a point borne out by what she had heard from citizens everywhere she traveled. In town after town she had "heard but one and the same opinion and wish:— 'We need a hospital; we desire its immediate establishment.'"[11]

In a day when public opinion polls, apart from official elections, were unknown, politicians knew little about the views of voters except what they read in the newspapers or learned by talking to constituents in their own districts. Consequently, Dix's appraisal of the mood of the electorate, based on her own extensive, documented, grassroots investigations, were not taken lightly.

Originally it had been her intention, she said, to make a new, more accurate estimate of the number of idiots and lunatics in New Jersey. Previous surveys, however well-intentioned, had been flawed and obviously underestimated the mentally disordered population. But over the past four years their numbers had swelled so ominously that no one needed to be convinced of their magnitude. Instead of statistics, she said, for the purposes of her petition, she was content to substantiate in each locality "*facts* at present existing, and scenes to which I have lately been witness."[12]

By and large these facts differed little from what she had reported in Massachusetts and New York. In each county she described the condition of pauper lunatics and idiots, and usually interviewed their keepers. Using an ideal conception of the curative asylum—again something along the lines of the York Retreat—as her standard, she faulted local institutions for their failure to respect human decency and their utter incompetence to provide therapeutic care.

As she had done in Massachusetts, Dix tried to frighten the legislature by showing them that they and their families were just as vulnerable to the threat of mental disease as immigrants and the lower orders. In her pitiful tale of a visit to the Salem County poorhouse, she wrote about coming across a bedridden old man muttering, "*the mind*, the mind is going—almost gone." Inquiring about his background, she was told that Judge. S. had been for years a distinguished jurist and member of the state assembly. A man of honor and respect, he had suddenly and inexplicably gone mad. His "insanity assumed the form of frenzy; he was chained 'for safety:' in fine, he was committed to the county jail for greater security!" As time wore on, he became less violent and was given to the care of a local family. Unfortunately, when his money finally ran out there was no alternative but the poorhouse. "For men such as Judge S., is no hospital needed?" Dix pleaded.[13]

Most people assumed that the ideal setting for troubled minds was home and hearth. Hospitals were mainly for the urban poor, the homeless; few families with sufficient means would have considered turning loved ones over to such institutions. But Dix, amplifying an argument that was being propounded by asylum superintendents, insisted that in the case of insanity, hospital treatment was the best medicine. If poorhouses and jails were inadequate to meet the needs of the insane, she asserted, families and private houses were often worse. Insanity was not like other illnesses. It confounded laypersons, and their bafflement, in turn, prompted them to improvise all sorts of cruel and inhumane measures. While she avoided mentioning names, she cited several example of men and women isolated by their relatives in cellars and outbuildings, including one madwoman locked in a smokehouse, and a northern New Jersey farmer known to keep his mad son "chained up like a ferocious dog."[14]

In her memorials, Dix asserted the authority of comprehensiveness, and her New Jersey petition was no exception. Who could fail to be impressed by such a dense collection of facts and impressions listed methodically under the names of counties, towns, and local institutions of incarceration? Much of the document reads like a catalogue with Dix herself standing outside the narrative, an invisible witness objectively reporting what she saw, as though she were an explorer returned from a strange land describing its geography, people, and customs.

But the most interesting scenes are the ones in which she describes herself stepping into the picture and bringing a human touch to her subject. "I always remark that, however insane a man may be, the humiliation of being loaded with chains, and wearing manacles and fetters, is deeply felt," she wrote. Few lunatics were entirely bereft of mental faculties or insensitive to the attitude of their keepers. The stock in trade of jails and poorhouses—"*severity, unkindness, blows, and the use of chains*"—only aggravated mental disease with physical distress. In a telling episode, she described one maniac "whose fetters and manacles I caused to be removed, and whose aching, bruised limb I chafed and bathed." Looking hopefully into her face, the madman said, "'Ah, now I am treated like a human creature. God is good—He sends you to set me free; I will pray for you forever.'" Not from the mouths of babes, but in the voices of the mad she heard ringing confirmation that, as she interpreted it, "God's spirit bids this message to you, saying, it is his work you are doing; lo, it shall prosper in your hands."[15]

Dix, firm believer in the puissance of moral management, repudiated the idea that the brutal methods of confinement and punishment the insane endured in almshouses and jails were necessary to maintain order. Physical abuse derived not from rational desire for order, she explained, but from primitive superstitions about lunacy. Ancients considered insanity "a judicial infliction from the Supreme Being—hence tortures, chains, and incarceration in gloomy dungeons" were just measures to reinforce God's chastisement. Over the centuries, Europe gradually adopted more enlightened views. St. Vincent de Paul, for example, "traversed vast regions, sustained by a holy charity, teaching men, that to be humane, was to be allied with the Deity." But the humanitarian breakthrough in managing lunatics "by the influence of *firmness* and *kindness*" awaited the appearance in revolutionary France of the great Pinel.[16]

In the modern age, she said, the spirit of Pinel and Tuke was exemplified in the Hanwell Asylum, England's largest public institution for the insane, which was famous for its policy of nonrestraint.[17]

Her reading of the historical record placed her mission within the larger sweep of the progress of civilization. "The establishment of hospitals for the insane has, within the last century, become so general among all civilized and christianized nations, that the neglect of this duty seems to involve aggravated culpability," she wrote.[18] It was perhaps to have been expected that at the turn of the nineteenth century, America, busy shaping itself into a new nation, had lagged behind the Old World's advances in lunacy reform. The present generation heralded a new era, though. With new asylums sprouting up each year and old ones being refurbished, she asserted that the United States was catching up with Europe. Indeed, she thought the best American institutions compared favorably with what the Old World had to offer. The point was that none of these admirable hospitals existed in New Jersey. And Dix bluntly told the legislature that unless the state built a modern facility, it would remain in the dark ages.[19]

The argument, often advanced, that the state had recently invested heavily in a modern prison system, which was good enough for the insane poor, completely misconstrued the nature of insanity. Jails were built "to detain *criminals*, bad persons, who willingly and willfully [transgress] the civil and social laws." Lunatics, in contrast, were innocents, guilty of nothing "*but labouring under disease.*" Madness was not a crime. Although its immediate causes were often social and moral, the underlying condition in mental disorders, she believed, was a biological malfunction of the brain. Throwing a person who had a lesion of the brain in with common criminals made about as much sense as imprisoning people for contracting tuberculosis or, for that matter, catching a cold.[20]

Dix acknowledged that the legislators were pragmatic men. So having briefly covered the history of humanitarianism, she turned to what she saw as the only legitimate objection to a state asylum: doubts about the curability of the madness and the merits of hospital treatment. Thirty years earlier such skepticism may have been plausible, she allowed, but now an overwhelming body of evidence supported the asylum. She devoted the closing section of the New Jersey *Memorial* to expert testimony. From Maine to Ohio, asylum superintendents were publishing impressive records of their successes in curing insanity. Dix used her *Memorial* to broadcast their claims. She cited Dr. William Awl, the superintendent of the Ohio Lunatic Asylum, who claimed that out of 473 insane men and women committed to his asylum in its first five years, 221 had been discharged as cured, and those who remained had been redeemed from wretchedness and needless suffering.[21]

Persuasive as this argument sounded, Dix realized it would be far more powerful if she could draw a solid connection between humanitarianism and economics. The New Jersey assembly, after all, had voted in 1839 to build an asylum, then stumbled on the caveat, "*as soon as the finances of the state will warrant a sufficient appropriation* [Dix's emphasis]."[22] No matter how convincing arguments for the asylum sounded, the practical obstacle was to justify its cost. If one looked closely at the facts submitted by asylum superintendents in their annual reports, however, it appeared that a strong argument for the cost-effectiveness of asylum treatment was already being advanced.

Annual reports for the Worcester hospital and the Ohio Lunatic Asylum featured elaborate tables illustrating why proper hospital care was ultimately cheaper than other alternatives. These schedules illustrated that a limited course of moral therapy in an asylum, with the likelihood of curing the patient, cost far less than supporting chronic lunatics for years at public expense. In the long run, it was cheaper to heal than to sustain. Unfortunately, the asylum superintendents' ignorance of statistics and accounting, together with their eagerness to count any discharged patient as cured, led them to vastly overstate their case. Dix, who herself had no feel for numbers and who was strongly biased in favor of institutional treatment, enthusiastically embraced their conclusions. She calculated, for example, from the Ohio Lunatic Asylum report of 1840 that "the number of *years* [emphasis added] that the twenty-five old cases had been insane, was 413; the whole expense of their support during that time, $47,590; the average, $1,903.60." By contrast, the 25 recent cases had been institutionalized a total of 556 *weeks*. The aggregate expense for them was $1,400, or an average of just $56 per patient.[23]

Here was the argument she had been looking for. And it seemed to be such good news that she was disinclined to examine it too carefully.

Depending on the institution, old cases meant people who had been insane for at least ten years and had little hope of recovery. New cases, by contrast, were measured in months. The sooner the mad were hospitalized, the more likely they were to be cured and not to need continuing public assistance. Viewed in this light, the standard practice of paying almshouses and jails to confine lunatics was like throwing good money after bad. "I will not dishonor you by urging this suit on the moneysaving principle," she declared. But she tried to show that any honest legislator who considered how much the state spent on jails and almshouses, even if he did not believe that an asylum was necessary on humanitarian grounds, would have to vote for it sheerly on the basis of fiscal responsibility.[24]

Dix's *Memorial* was completed in time for the January 1845 legislative session. State Senator Joseph S. Dodd, who had vigorously supported the original recommendations of the governor's commission in 1840, introduced it to his colleagues on January 23. Dix herself made the rounds, earnestly explaining to members in the halls of the capitol and on the courthouse steps how important their vote was. "I am so tired I can hardly hold my pen," Dix told Harriet Hare, but her efforts paid off. Within a few days, she marveled, "the ice melted from their hearts," and they voted to print 2,000 copies of the document in English, 500 in German. Subsequently they appointed a select committee of members from both houses to draft appropriate legislation.[25]

Keenly aware that previous efforts to build a state hospital had never made it through the budgetary gauntlet, Dix mounted a tenacious personal lobbying campaign to win the votes of assemblymen and senators. "You cannot imagine the labor of conversing and convincing," she told her friend Harriet Hare. "Some evenings I have at once twenty gentlemen for three hours, steady conversation." With her vision for saving the insane poor at stake, she could summon the fire of a camp meeting revivalist. Faced one evening with a rough country representative who loudly exclaimed that the "wants of the insane in N. Jersey were all humbug," she delivered an eloquent, impassioned account of the misery she had witnessed, including a number of shameful abuses in his own district. Riveted by her speech, which lasted more than an hour, the lawmaker suddenly stood up, walked to the middle of the room, and declared to all assembled: "I do'nt [sic] for my part want to hear anything more; the others can stay here if they want to; I am convinced, and you've conquered me out and out; I shall vote for the Hospital; if you'll come to the House and talk there as you've done here, no man that is'nt [*sic*] a brute can withstand you; and so when a man's convinced that's enough." In her telling, this account of a conversion sounds like Charles Gradison Finney's conversion of the backcountry heathen. Afterward, full of inspiration, she rode to the railroad station with the speaker of the house and the president of the senate, bound for Harrisburg, continuing to hammer home her message every mile of the way.[26]

If the New Jersey legislature needed a portent to influence its deliberations, the week after Dodd presented Dix's *Memorial*, Salem County's large poorhouse, which Dix described at length in her memorial, burned to the ground in a spectacular fire. Miraculously none of the eighty paupers confined there, including "several epileptics and persons of infirm minds [and] eight insane," was killed.[27] But the fire underscored Dix's root-and-branch indictment of the county almshouse system.

With just three weeks of discussion, a joint legislative committee endorsed her *Memorial*, taking the unusual step of substituting her document for the customary committee report. Confronting no serious opposition, "An Act to Authorize the Establishment of the New Jersey State Lunatic Asylum" breezed through both houses of the legislature and was signed into law by the governor on 20 March 1845.

The New Jersey State Lunatic Asylum at Trenton, the first state institution built as a direct result of Dix's work.

Sweet as this legislative victory was, Dix saw that it only cleared the way for establishing a state asylum. The practical matter of how it would be built and who would run it was still undecided. New Jersey had no private asylum within its boundaries, no internal sources of psychiatric or institutional expertise. After the state bill passed, although it was not exactly what she intended, individual counties began to act on Dix's findings. "I have *four* new county poor houses *going up*," she wrote in April, and "twenty-one Jails on a reformed plan."[28] At the state level, meanwhile, everything was funneled through a new committee of the legislature appointed to find a site for the proposed asylum and supervise the complicated business of construction. Because Dix had earned the respect of New Jersey's political leaders and was considered the only purely disinterested expert on matters pertaining to hospitals for the insane, they turned to her for assistance. Although her knowledge of asylum architecture and management was quite limited, she knew as much or more than anyone else in New Jersey. Realizing this, she reasoned that if she could master the nuances of state politics, she could apply the same principles to the professional environment of the insane asylum.

Indeed, she could apply her mastery in two states at once. Moving on to Pennsylvania, her original destination, she did not abandon New Jersey but continued to advance rapidly on both political and professional fronts.

She slept only five or six hours a night. In the morning she breakfasted on coffee and a muffin or a crust of bread; at midday she liked a small piece of meat, perhaps with a potato or some other vegetable; evenings she rarely consumed more than a bowl of soup and, later as she read and answered correspondence late into the night, a cup of weak tea. If she dined on richer fare or lingered over any meal it was because she was transacting business. Moving at a pace that astonished anyone who knew her, Dix was now in full stride.

Her work had become her life.

Yet the nature of her work was changing, taking her down an unanticipated path. As she shuttled between New Jersey and Pennsylvania in 1845–46, Dix came to realize that if she were to hope to play an active role in creating state institutions, she would have to work more closely with lawmakers within the day-to-day world of government. Yet to do so went against the grain. Most assemblymen seemed to regard the statehouse as nothing more than a place to gather power in order to advance their own selfish purpose. Their petty local concerns failed to interest her, and she hated their constant bickering and cloakroom deal making. "You cannot exactly comprehend the miserable anxieties that beset me in being *obliged* to act *with* others," she confided to George Emerson.[29]

Given the formality that governed relations between Victorian men and women, at least in higher circles, much social distance was inevitable. She was now operating in a public sphere inhabited almost entirely by men, and ambitious men at that. As a lady, she was entirely excluded from the masculine good fellowship that provided the informal basis for most political decisions. Moreover, she possessed little sense of humor, no fondness for political give-and-take, no qualities of mind or temperament to leaven the weighty moral seriousness of her cause. When the budgetary axe threatened her asylum bills, she could barely tolerate what she saw as politicians' willingness to sacrifice principle to expedience. Their readiness to compromise made her feel she had nothing in common with the men around her.

Yet they had a great deal in common. The most complicated aspect of her expanding political role in the asylum movement is that she felt compelled to suppress her own needs and desire for leadership to conform to her culture's model of womanhood. A female political leader was a contradiction in terms. Women, everyone knew, were meant to follow. Nevertheless, as a supremely devoted follower of God, she claimed to be his representative, pronouncing his will to lawmakers. In doing so, she exercised the requisites of leadership—vision, willpower, focus, sharply defined goals—and without their realizing it, turned these men into her followers.

Privately she paid a price for exercising her authority. The whole sordid business of politics estranged her, she complained, almost to the point of turning her into a "*humanity-hater*." Whenever she could, she avoided dinners and other social obligations, because, as she told Emerson, "intercourse with society . . . crushes and depresses me." Only when acting alone did she feel her inner being rise toward God and spiritual reward. No one had ever fully understood her calling; she complained, the success she had achieved so far had been based on self-reliance. Since childhood, she had learned never to place trust in anything outside herself. On the other hand, she acknowledged that the danger of trying to maintain her aloofness, to avoid depending on anyone else, isolated her from the natural flow of human relations.[30]

To steady her turbulent inner life during this period of relentless effort, Dix turned to her old friend "Pater" Emerson, who, with his common sense and serene confidence in human nature, became her sea anchor. She was confident that, because he had stood staunchly beside her seven years earlier during her breakdown, he would appreciate the emotional ambivalence that accompanied her recent success. At this point she had eclipsed him as a social reformer and as a public figure, a fact he freely acknowledged and genuinely celebrated. She was living up to their shared religious ideals. Her example of selflessness, he confessed, "preached to me more loudly than any sermon I ever heard or read." Dix, captured by his generosity of spirit, came to feel that Emerson was the one man with whom she was secure enough to relax her guard.[31]

Exhausted after a ten-week excursion in late 1844 through western Pennsylvania into Ohio and Indiana, she reached out despondently to him, describing herself as a weary child in need of "caressing and aff[ectionate] parental voices." Only with the greatest reluctance did she divulge how alone she felt, how much an orphan. "It may be a woman's weakness," she conceded, "[but] my strength of will threatens, as at this hour, to be insufficient for my stern purposes of self-extinction." Usually her work left her no time to brood over the emotional emptiness that had resulted from her privation of family ties. Although she was ashamed of herself, she said, because she thought it

George Barrell Emerson.

selfish to bother Emerson with her unresolvable problems, she had to ease the pain of her troubles by talking about them.[32]

Her despondent tone alarmed Emerson, who vividly remembered Dix's mental and physical collapse in 1837. "I hardly know what you mean by your 'stern purpose of self-extinction,'" he replied. He warned her to pay attention to her health and sent her a copy of the educational reformer—Catharine Beecher's plan for educating young ladies in the western territories. Perhaps, he suggested, realizing that there were other women like Beecher working on their own to improve the world would help Dix feel a bit less alienated. He reminded her of their deep friendship and offered her, whenever she was weary, "a cordial welcome . . . a seat by our table & fire-side, and a room & fire of your own, so that you shall be with us or by yourself, as you please." He was a model family man with a loving wife and two adolescent daughters, and Dix's confessions of vulnerability brought out in him the same protective impulses he had for his own children. Seeing her so low, he told her that he wanted nothing so much as simply to take care of her, to shield her from the harshness of the world.[33]

Dix replied that she could imagine nothing more profoundly important to her than his use of the word "paternal" to describe his feelings for her. And so she agreed to take some time in early 1846 to visit the Emersons in Boston and renew their friendship. The week she spent with them proved to be restorative. And all her best expectations were confirmed. Having seen so many unhappy families, torn apart by madness and crime, she considered the Emerson household her personal island of tranquility. In addition, Emerson was a fount of information: on the latest developments in the Boston philanthropic community, on natural history, on arts and literature, on immigration, and on prison reform. Time in his company meant an infusion of new ideas. Several months later, trying to convey the importance of their relationship, Dix told Emerson that he was a necessity for her, an essential ingredient in her success. For her own part, though, "I am necessary to none— except the world at large." At the most critical junctures in her life, she had found in him a surrogate father. Now that she was fully embarked on her mission, she told Emerson, "you have taken the place of Dr. Channing in my respect and affections."[34]

Spending her days in the thick of politics was depressing her already low opinion of the human race, since even its "civilized" leaders were so conspicuously lacking in higher aspiration. Only by shutting her eyes to what was going on around her, turning inward, and thereby aggravating her sense of aloofness and detachment did she feel she could preserve her ideals. The further she thrust herself into the worlds of politics and professional organization, the higher the wall she had to build between herself and other people.

Though disheartened from time to time by her inability to fit in and by sheer fatigue, Dix did not allow herself to sink into despair. Travel, she realized, was the best remedy for discouragement. On the road, her spirits lifted, her diffidence vanished, and she became a different person: the famous lady selflessly pursuing her crusade for the downtrodden. Understandably, this image appealed to the public imagination. Wherever she went, Dix found the unexpected growth of her reputation immensely satisfying. Touring western Pennsylvania on her way to Ohio, she boasted of being universally recognized and welcomed. "I see all the best minds; physicians, lawyers, judges &c." Letters of introduction, unused, lined the bottom of her portmanteau, for "not one place yet have I reached, however obscure, but I find them saying—'Oh, we know you.'"[35]

Her circuit was prodigious. In September she covered prisons on Long Island and in New York City, New Jersey, and eastern Pennsylvania. After two weeks in and out of Harrisburg, preparing to lobby the Pennsylvania legislature for a state asylum, she left for Baltimore "and so on as far as Pittsburgh." By the end of October in addition to touring Maryland and Virginia, she had traversed all the southern, western, and many of the northern counties of Pennsylvania, and had ventured into Ohio as far as Lanesville and Columbus. The month of November found her in Kentucky, and then, hearing that the Tennessee legislature was in session, to Nashville to influence debate about redesigning the state prison.[36]

The sheer difficulty of covering so much ground was a source of pride, and Dix, a spellbinding raconteur, enthralled her friends and acquaintances with her adventures in the back country. At a crossing on the Allegheny, for example, she had to choose whether to ride the next sixty-nine miles in a ramshackle wagon without springs or board a tiny skiff, alone with a boatman clad in "sulphurous garments and [who] would not be noticed for acquaintance either with comb or razor." Worried about being stranded with this Charon-like figure in the trackless forest, she took the wagon. Nineteen hours and four breakdowns later, she found herself, together with the United States mails, in Franklin, thirty-nine miles from Warren, "inhaling miasma from a stagnant marshy lakelet." Just when it looked as though she would have to risk spending the night in the forest, a horseman appeared out of nowhere and managed to carry her to a hotel in the next town.[37]

On this westward trek, Dix followed routes that were channeling unprecedented numbers of Irish and German immigrants through western Pennsylvania into the less settled regions of Ohio, Indiana, and Illinois. Seeing their impact on the social and cultural landscape during the months when she was preparing her next memorial, she began to ponder the meaning of this rapid demographic and ethnic transformation. Everywhere she went, Irish and Germans seemed to be straining public institutions. When she heard news that the state militia had to be called into Philadelphia to suppress ethnic riots in which sixteen people were killed, she began approaching her work with an even greater sense of urgency. Thus she started looking for new methods to upgrade the disconnected and disorganized almshouses she saw throughout the state of Pennsylvania. She knew from experience that the machinery of state government was slow and cumbersome. At best, a legislative solution would yield no tangible results for two years. Perhaps she could circumvent much factious and bureaucratic process, she reasoned, by personally taking her war to individual counties.[38]

The county courts had legal jurisdiction over almshouses, and county newspapers printed on cheap paper and distributed widely offered a convenient medium to arouse public indignation. So throughout the northern and western counties of Pennsylvania, she commenced a one-woman editorial publicity campaign. At every opportunity, she wrote letters and columns in local papers calling local officials to account for abuses within their jurisdiction.[39]An example of this local-oriented campaign was her frontal assault on the almshouse in Washington County. There she directly petitioned the county grand jury to remodel the local almshouse and simultaneously aired her charges of mistreatment in the press. Seven lunatics inhabited the facility the day she visited, Dix told the court. Among these were three insane women, two of whom were coiled up in a bunch of straw inside wooden packing boxes. When she approached, "they suddenly threw aside the straw and stepped out upon the floor entirely naked—nor was there any garment in the place which could be used to cover them." How much longer, she angrily demanded, would local citizens tolerate such indecency? Unless the county grand jury took immediate action, it should be held to account for criminal negligence.[40]

It soon became apparent, however, that she had miscalculated. Her indignant tone, which was a staple of political speech making, was too emphatic and struck county commissioners as high-handed and exaggerated. The grand jury briefly looked into the matter and concluded that while conditions in the county jail and almshouse could certainly stand improvement, things were hardly as bad as Dix described. With the community solidly behind him, the Washington County almshouse master issued a rebuttal that cast doubt on Dix's methods and regard for the truth. At the county level, people tended to place more trust in the explanations of local officials than in the criticism of outsiders, even when the outsider was the famous Dorothea Dix.[41] Frustrated with this apparent parochialism, Dix once again focused on driving policy through the state government, for despite her misgivings that was the arena in which she could work to greatest effect.

Since her mid-twenties, when she had spent winters with the Furness family, she had come to feel more at home in Philadelphia than in Boston. Through George Emerson and her cousin Thaddeus William Harris, both well established in the Boston scientific community, she had been introduced to Robert Hare, a distinguished professor of chemistry at the University of Pennsylvania, and his wife Harriet. The Hares were cultured and intellectually vibrant people who insisted that whenever she was in Philadelphia, she stay with them as their guest.

From its Quaker beginnings, the city had the richest history of lunacy and hospital reform in America. As early as 1811, the Philadelphia Society of Friends, in close contact with English Quakers, had envisaged an asylum patterned on the York Retreat.[42] Well ahead of developments in other parts of the country, in 1813 they had printed an American edition of Samuel Tuke's *Description of the Retreat* and given it wide circulation. Relying on Tuke's theories of nonrestraint, the Philadelphia Friends bought fifty-two acres ten miles outside the city and in 1817 opened a small asylum called the Frankford Retreat. This was exclusively a Quaker institution until 1836, when, formally at least, the religion of prospective patients was no longer taken into account.[43]

Apart from the Frankford Retreat, the legislative history of lunacy reform in Pennsylvania parallels the sequence of events in New Jersey. To address the growing problem of the homeless insane, two Pennsylvania legislative commission reports were published in 1839 and 1840. Hoping to gain support in the state senate and house of representatives for a public asylum, both had emphasized instances of misery and abuse. The 1839 report pressed the governor to appoint three commissioners empowered to select a site for "the Pennsylvania State Lunatic Asylum." For fiscal reasons, the governor, who claimed to support the measure in his heart, subsequently vetoed a funding bill passed by both houses of the legislature.[44]

During the winter months of 1844–45, frustrated by her experience in county politics, Dix hurried to complete her Pennsylvania *Memorial Soliciting a State Hospital for the Insane*. There, as in New Jersey, legislative support for a public asylum seemed within reach if lawmakers could simply be made aware of the breakthroughs in treatment already well accepted by the emerging professional brotherhood of asylum superintendents. The form and substance of the Pennsylvania *Memorial* borrowed freely from asylum annual reports and a variety of other public documents. Dix presented testimony from several asylum superintendents that summarized the state of psychiatric medicine and emphasized the importance of early treatment of insanity.

What distinguished the Pennsylvania *Memorial* from her previous memorials was its more foreboding sense of a social order cracking under pressure. She did not replace her moral argument with a call for social control, but she did shift her emphasis. At the same time she worked on this memorial, Dix was writing a pamphlet about the American penal system called *Remarks on Prisons and Prison Discipline*. Thus her awareness of violence, crime, and the jurisprudence of insanity were heightened.

As she made her way through each county's jails and almshouses, she was alarmed to see around her mounting evidence of danger and chaos. Lunacy, her survey demonstrated, besides being a dire personal affliction for the insane, had the potential to erupt violently and harm anyone in its path. In Adams County she described a chained axe murderer; in the Fayette County jail, a maniac who bludgeoned his drunken cell mate and later set fire to a building; in Crawford County, a madman who, "driven to frenzy by his street-tormentors, threw a stone at random, which killed a child." There were not the hapless victims portrayed in her earlier memorials but the terrifying criminally insane.[45]

Meanwhile, spending time inspecting penitentiaries was giving Dix a new perspective on institutional order. She had already made up her mind that the mad belonged in asylums, though she was unclear on how order inside these institutions should be maintained.

Her description of the Blockley almshouse—the main receptacle for Philadelphia's pauper lunatics—was a set piece illustrating why the state had to abolish the practice of committing the insane to county facilities. Gathered there in one huge room, wrote Dix, was a "great, monstrous, horrid company . . . crying, shouting, laughing, screaming, moaning, complaining, rolling on the floor, moping in the corners, assuming all attitudes, and rousing each other to higher and higher exasperation." In the midst of this chaos "was sent the pauper musician, with the sharp, shrill, dissonant fiddle, adding discord to discord, and commingling the war of words, with the war of sounds, in rivalry of Babel!" Completing the wild scene, Dix described a beautiful raven-haired girl who alternated between fits of frenzy and moments of passivity. Bound head to foot, the poor girl looked on from the confines of a "tranquilizing chair," a kind of swing whose motion was supposed to calm its occupant's mind.[46]

Scenes of bedlam like this, Dix warned the legislature, were far from uncommon. Of Pennsylvania's fifty-eight counties, twenty-one routinely consigned people with mental disorders to almshouses or poorhouses. The remaining thirty-seven counties followed the old practice of auctioning off the pauper insane to the lowest bidders. What incentive did these contractors have, she asked, except to keep their charges alive at the least possible cost? She found it strangely inconsistent that the state with the best penitentiaries in the country continued to condemn its "needy citizens to become the life-long victims of a terrible disease" rather than "provide remedial care in a State Hospital."[47]

As she had done in New Jersey, Dix contended that building a state asylum would prove economical as well as humane. Accordingly, she cited the argument of Thomas Kirkbride, influential superintendent of the private Pennsylvania Hospital for the Insane, that when people falling into the first stages of insanity were quickly hospitalized, the progress of their disease was arrested and they were usually returned to their families within a few months. Untreated, according to the consensus of asylum professionals, these same people would have inevitably required support for the rest of their lives. If they were heads of households, Kirkbride noted, their families would also depend permanently on public welfare. Costs compounded geometrically. A few simple calculations from Kirkbride's patient register demonstrated the savings that resulted from early institutionalization and a regimen of moral therapy. Since Kirkbride's claims were similar to what most heads of asylums in England and America were saying at the time, it did not occur to Dix to question his statistics. Nor did she doubt whether Kirkbride's recent experience in a well-endowed private hospital, filled with patients who could afford expensive treatment, could be replicated in a state-funded institution for those at the bottom of the social order.[48]

As she was finishing the Pennsylvania *Memorial* in January 1845, Dix simultaneously concentrated her energies on gaining political support for its recommendations. She began by approaching a rich Quaker congressman named Thomas P. Cope, a man with abundant political connections in the state capital and philanthropic interests in Philadelphia, and asked him about the propriety of her petitioning the legislature. Cope confided to his diary that, even though she impressed him as the Elizabeth Fry of America, he discouraged her. Pennsylvania, through years of deficit spending, had accumulated a public debt exceeding $40,000,000, and he considered it unlikely that the state would dig itself further into debt to build a lunatic hospital.[49]

Refusing to take no for an answer, she bombarded Cope and other opinion leaders with letters and copies of her memorials. In early March, as a spring snowstorm swept across Pennsylvania, she traveled to Harrisburg, the state capital, to attend sessions of the legislature. Her best chance, she felt, was to apply as much personal pressure as she could. Gradually the campaign made headway, although its progress seemed to her sluggish and unpredictable. The worst impediment, she complained, was the dishonesty and unreliability of the lawmakers themselves. Politics, not the actual merits of issues, dictated their opinions and decisions. "Sordid influences" were, to her dismay, "openly admitted [and] bribery and corruption stalk through the Capitol unmasked and unabashed."[50]

Initially Dix hoped to win support for the total cost of building an institution. But it became apparent that several influential members failed to appreciate the enormity of what she had uncovered and the urgency of building the new hospital. Quickly learning the practical art of legislation, however, she saw that reaching her ultimate goal would require compromise. Recognizing that an insufficient appropriations bill was still better than none at all, she shrewdly revived an old tactic. The state, she proposed, could fund only $15,000 of the estimated

$30,000 it would cost to build an asylum. The remaining money could subsequently be raised by private gifts. When she asked Cope to pledge $10,000, however, which she called a modest tax on his estate, he demurred. If the new hospital was for the insane poor, he wrote, the state should fund the whole thing. Yet even if public charity were slow, Dix realized that any tangible commitment from the state could be used to start the long process of asylum building: site selection, architecture, determining governance and management. In addition, supervising the public subscription fund would also keep her involved with both the political machinery of the state and the influential community of private philanthropists.[51]

By mid-March this strategy worked to produce a financially conservative bill that passed the lower house on March 12. When, a fortnight later, it sailed through the senate by a margin of two to one, Dix was told "that no man nor woman, other than yourself, from Maine to Louisiana could have passed the bill under the discouraging circumstances with which you had to contend." As she had planned, $15,000 was appropriated for the facility; nothing for the land. Through dogged persistence she enlisted Thomas Cope to head a subscription drive to raise the necessary money for a site. He sympathized with her goal. And he grudgingly admired her unwillingness to be dissuaded, though he privately remarked of her single-minded zeal that "constant pursuit of even a praiseworthy object may warp the judgement & impair the intellect." Despite her best intentions, he feared that if the enterprise fell into the hands of greedy politicians, it was likely to fall far short of its purpose. "Men will probably be appointed as physicians, &c. to have charge of it, who will have an eye to their own gain, rather than the comfort & cure of the patients."[52]

To keep this from happening, the asylum bill established a commission to oversee the project. After Governor Francis Shunk signed the bill into law on April 14, Dix was asked to assist the committee as a consultant whenever her schedule permitted. By virtue of her superior judgment and experience, the chairman proclaimed, in matters of choosing a site and designing structures, her wishes would be taken as law. Over the next year, worried that unless the commission began construction of a building the legislature would change its mind, she pieced together a coalition of private philanthropists and the Dauphin County Commissioners. Together they contracted to purchase the land for the Pennsylvania State Lunatic Hospital at Harrisburg. Still the process dragged. Not until four years later, 7 April 1849, was the cornerstone for the facility laid, with a copy of Dix's memorial placed underneath it.

During the steamy summer of 1844, Dix made use of the rail lines to explore beyond western Pennsylvania into Ohio, Indiana, and Illinois. Everywhere she went she inspected local institutions and, when she stumbled onto particularly egregious cases, wrote petitions to grand juries and published exposés in the papers. In Lanesville, Ohio, for example, she publicly upbraided the citizens of Muskingum County. Their almshouse, she said, contained three lunatics: one man and two women in appalling condition. "One especially, I was told refused to be clothed; both summer and winter she is in a state of complete nudity; the other idiotic from continual fits is equally incapable of possessing any forms of decency: yet in these small, close cells they must be kept . . . grossly exposed to observation from without." If the county was too parsimonious to protect its women, albeit insane women, from such indignity, in her view it deserved notoriety.[53]

On this trip, as she looped back through Pennsylvania, Dix began to realize that the institutional landscape of the United States was substantially more complicated than she had realized. Her travels were taking her not just through count jails but also through state penitentiaries. Up to this point, her views about prisons had been formed mainly from the perspective of their glaring inadequacies to serve the needs of the insane. Despite the efforts of reformers, New England jails and prisons lagged behind the times. The county jails she had surveyed in New York were little better. Now, however, spending all day at Philadelphia's Eastern Penitentiary—a famous institution considered to be a model for the future—and leaving only when "I could no longer use my voice for following out the questioning investigations I am making in the cells of the prisoners," Dix reexamined her ideas about the functions and structure of American prisons.[54]

Why, busy as she was with her asylum politicking, was she drawn to this new subject? In part it was because of overlapping personalities and relationships within the lunacy reform and prison reform movements. Samuel Gridley Howe, George Emerson, Charles Sumner, the political scientist Francis Lieber, William Henry Channing (William Ellery Channing's cousin, an influential Unitarian minister in his own right)—each of these men, who were Dix's friends and supporters, deeply involved himself in the debate over what prison system would best address the country's rising wave of crime. Knowing of her exhaustive inspections of state, county, and local places of incarceration, they automatically sought out her opinions. And her responses added to her fund of credibility with them.

On a deeper level, though, her contact with prisoners stirred some of the same emotions that caused her to identify with the insane. A convict by the name of John Beadel whom Dix met on a visit to Pennsylvania's Western State Penitentiary wrote her a letter in August 1844 drawing a close parallel between crime and insanity. "Crime is a madness," he said, "and Madness is a disease." The roots of criminal behavior, she and her contemporaries strongly believed, stretched back to early childhood. She underscored the words of William Henry Channing who, in 1844, in the introduction to his first annual report of the New York Prison Association, declared that criminal tendencies stemmed from "an evil organization derived from bad parents. Bad germs bear bad fruit." The sins of the fathers were visited on their offspring, making the criminal in large measure a victim of heredity. By the grace of God and an uncommon gift of willpower, Dix had managed to throw off the dead weight of her parentage. But few other people, she believed, could manage by themselves to do what she had done. Increasingly impressed by the shaping power of environment over mind and character—which was the premise of the curative asylum—she regarded penal institutions as having the potential to remold men and women whose family lives had warped them early on. This was a program with which she thoroughly empathized.

So, propelled forward by a desire to master the personalities and facts of prison reform, she enlarged the scope of her investigations. The last week in July, just returned from West-Chester prison and almshouse, she was on her way to Baltimore, Washington, and Richmond, places she felt she had to visit before taking up the prison question.[55]

When Dix returned from her forays to Philadelphia, she worked intermittently on her New Jersey and Pennsylvania memorials, and devoted increasing effort to a long piece on prison reform. *Remarks on Prisons and Prison Discipline in the United States*, as she titled her treatise, was already mushrooming into a full-fledged study of more than one hundred pages, twice the length of her previous memorials. Originally she had intended to publish it as an article in the *North American Review*, but Ezra Stiles Gannett told her it was too long for a periodical. Samuel

Gridley Howe, who saw in Dix's report an argument that would advance his own agenda within the Boston Prison Discipline Society, then suggested that the group would probably sponsor the publication of her pamphlet.[56]

She took up the issue in a highly charged atmosphere. During the past decade prison reform, like so many other humanitarian movements in antebellum America, had become increasingly polarized. And she knew that trouble had long been brewing in the Boston Prison Discipline Society. Howe, along with Charles Sumner, who had seized upon penal reform with his characteristic zeal, disliked the society's secretary, Louis Dwight, and had for years tried to oust him. In 1844, a disagreement about which of two rival schemes of prison discipline— the Pennsylvania plan or the Auburn plan—the society should endorse erupted in an acrimonious battle for control. Dwight carried the banner for the Auburn system, in which prisoners were isolated individually in their cells at night but worked days in groups, in strictly enforced silence. Howe, Sumner, and George Emerson, on the other hand, championed the Pennsylvania system: complete solitary confinement with no interaction whatsoever between convicts. Inflamed mainly by Sumner, the debate soon reached a level of personal invective that startled the Boston reform community.[57]

Dix added fuel to the fire when she claimed that from everything she had seen Dwight's annual reports for the Boston Prison Discipline Society were grossly inaccurate and misleading. "I see every prisoner," she wrote, "I converse with all freely." She had not intended to take up the subject of prison reform, but she had seen so much in the past few weeks in favor of solitary confinement that she felt obligated to set the record straight about the Pennsylvania system and its merits. Meanwhile, George Emerson confided that he had long suspected the accuracy of Dwight's reports "since I know of the indolent life of the author."[58] In October 1845, disgusted by the wretched conditions she encountered in New York State jails, she approached the county grand jury in Utica with a bill of particulars and was subsequently asked to testify in person.[59]

Cautious about publicly taking sides in the controversy, Dix claimed to present a neutral analysis of what she called the Auburn and Pennsylvania *"experimental systems."* But she naturally sided with her political friends and the wing of the Boston Prison Discipline Society that advocated keeping incarcerated felons separate from one another. Anyone familiar with the issues knew that *On Prisons and Prison Discipline* was an argument for the separate system. Remarking that Dix was "in herself alone a whole Prison Discipline Society," Sumner admitted that he wanted to trade on the authority of her name to support his views.[60]

Her thought of the penitentiary envisioned a well-regulated school-room in which the moral lessons criminals had missed as youngsters could be taught anew. Just as society had an obligation to take care of the insane who were incompetent to care for themselves, so the state had the responsibility to reshape and reform the criminal character. Solitary confinement, supplemented by a pure diet of moral and religious education, seemed the most humane and straightforward way to accomplish this. Teachers and chaplains stood a better chance at remolding criminals if they were isolated from all contaminating influences.[61]

The elaborate procedures at Eastern Penitentiary to prevent even the slightest contact between prisoners fascinated Dix. Prison architects had designed long wings of cell blocks, radiating outward from a central hub structure that housed administrative and support services. This ingenious design was intended to prevent inmates from catching even a glimpse of one another. Prison administrators took every precaution against the growth of a criminal subculture within their walls. Keepers outdid each other in finding ways to baffle walls and pipes to block the tapping of coded messages. New prisoners were blindfolded and hooded before being marched to their cells to reinforce their sense of anonymity and isolation.

Dickens, on his American tour in 1842, spent a day interviewing prisoners at the Eastern Penitentiary and afterward pronounced its "rigid, strict, and hopeless solitary confinement . . . to be cruel and wrong." He conceded it was immaculately clean, orderly, and quiet, but the insidious practice of depriving men and women of social inter-course produced "an anguish so acute and so tremendous that all imagination of it must fall far short of the reality." In their revulsion for physical punishment, the well-meaning architects of the solitary system had unwittingly instituted a "slow and daily tampering with the mysteries of the brain . . . immeasurably worse than any torture of the body." Precisely *because* this process of burying people alive left no ugly marks on the flesh, he wrote, its true destructive potential exceeded any type of physical punishment.[62]

Dix thought this was nonsense. "His pages are certainly written with effect," she scoffed, "but belong to the fancy sketches which have so

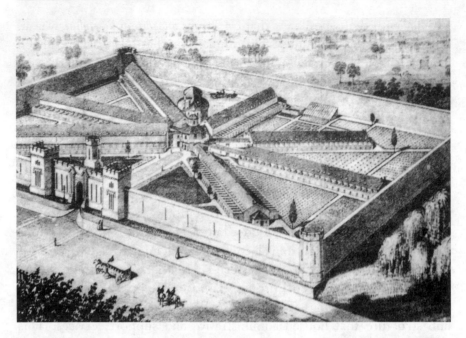

Pennsylvania's Eastern Penitentiary, the citadel of solitary confinement, around 1845.

much interested the readers of his attractive works." Introverted and sharing few of Dickens's empathetic social instincts, she was able to imagine solitude not as torture but as a kind of blessing, a time for reflection, prayer, and repentance.[63] In any event, Dix delivered not a polemic so much as remarks and observations. Judging from her experience, she thought the spate of books, pamphlets, official reports, and newspaper articles that, ever since the visit in 1831 of Alexis de Tocqueville and Gustave de Beaumont, had been celebrating American advances in penology were overly idealistic. "We claim too much for our prisons," she wrote, "on whatever system established." The time had come, she declared, to "courageously state the truth in plain terms," regardless of who might take offense.[64]

In her view prisons, by their very nature, no matter which procedures they followed, were bound to contain extremes of cruelty and injudicious laxity. "What do you think of more than *seventy floggings* of from 6 to 40 strokes with the *cat* p[er] month, each stroke giving *nine cuts* at one of our *model northern* prisons?" she asked George Emerson.[65] This was Auburn penitentiary, the epitome of discipline, lockstep organization, and congregate silence. Prisoners were forbidden to exchange so much as a word, and most lashings were meted out as punishment for talking. Dix's visit in November 1844 to Sing-Sing, an enormous congregate facility in New York State, left no room for doubt that the guards maintained order only by liberal use of the lash. Reading from the prison's annual report, she figured that 1,195 lashes with the "cat o' nine" meted out in 1844 for various infractions actually yielded "*ten thousand seven hundred and fifty-five strokes*." This was serious corporal punishment; the severity of these beatings was well known among inmates. Guards stripped the victim and tied him fast to a post or bench. The first whack ordinarily tore the skin; multiple blows caused even strong prisoners to pass out in shock. When this happened, they were revived with smelling salts before the flogging was completed. Permanent scars on their backs, not to mention serious psychological trauma, were the result.[66]

Nevertheless, Dix's dislike of whipping did not stem from hesitation to discipline and punish. She condoned the Eastern Penitentiary's practices of withholding food, darkening the cells of fractious inmates, and, if drastic measures were called for, chaining them to the stone floor in solitary confinement. In place of the cat-o'-nine-tails, she recommended that prisons adopt "the shower-bath, (not the *douche* or bolt-bath) [as] a very effectual means of procuring submission to proper rules and regulations." This procedure involved chaining a prisoner to the wall and dousing him with buckets of cold water. While Dix acknowledged that wardens needed to be able to use harsh disciplinary measures, in the end she argued for the mildest effective punishments. For criminals, she was convinced, were not fundamentally to blame for their misdeeds. The roots of crime were partly hereditary, she maintained, but the catalyst in creating a life of crime was to be found in "the defects of our social organization."[67]

Those born with the slightest moral weakness or criminal predisposition were, she thought, likely to be influenced by "this business-tossed phase of society," obsessed as it was with the pursuit of wealth and material gratification. Like most educated Americans, Dix saw all varieties of human weakness—crime, poverty, disease—as moral failure. Even the terrible cholera epidemics of 1832 and 1849 were interpreted, by doctors and laity alike, as evidence of social corruption.[68]

The aspect of society that had the deepest resonance for Dix, owing to the memories of her own upbringing, was the family. Sharing the opinion of virtually every writer in her day who had tried to explain the origins of criminal behavior, Dix lamented the breakdown of family ties and the lack of moral culture in childhood. Evidence for this view was not hard to find. Of 778 inmates at Auburn, the prison chaplain told her, "331 lost one or both parents at an early age; 252 left their parents before they were 15 years of age." Percentages were similar in prisons everywhere. Dix grieved for the young men and women in penitentiaries—she noted that half the prisoners at Auburn were under thirty—victims of broken homes and orphans who, unlike her, had never discovered the inner strength to rise above their heritage and surroundings.[69]

For most of them, it was already too late. From what she had seen and heard from prisoners, Dix held out little hope that any scheme would have much success with hardened criminals. Wardens in some institutions boasted about their successes. But who, she wondered, had followed released felons back to their communities to know whether or not they had permanently exchanged crime for honest industry? She believed that unless insanity were arrested early it was likely to become a chronic condition. And the same principle held true for criminal deviance. The solution to crime was to be found not in prisons but in "*radical* changes in the *early and later* instruction of all children and young persons; in domestic life more wisely regulated; schools more perfectly taught."[70]

From her early days as a schoolmistress in Orange Court, Dix had maintained this same sense that a well-disciplined moral education, based on the teachings of Jesus, would inexorably "decrease those wrongs and follies, and miseries; those errors and vices, and crimes, which deform society, and break its peace." At bottom, her argument for Pennsylvania-style solitary confinement was that in removing criminals from their environment, it cleaned the slate and permitted their guardians to educate them according to Christian precepts without interference.

This notion comes through clearly in a pamphlet she wrote, "An Address by a Recent Female Visiter [*sic*] to the Prisoners in the Eastern Penitentiary of Pennsylvania." The address is essentially a lay sermon, a call for conversion. To secure their temporal and eternal welfare, she beseeched the prisoners to feel in their hearts "that you have offended against the laws of society, that you have sinned against your own souls, that you have transgressed the laws of God." In the same way that divine power flowing through her seemed to touch the insane, she felt that her presence had a soothing effect on even the most hardened felons. As she passed from cell to cell, she could remember no instance of "a disrespectful or improper word or act, amongst the many hundred persons I have seen." Her quiet, dignified presence heightened their sense of sinfulness. In many cases they broke down and professed a change of heart so earnestly she had hopes of their restoration.[71]

To prove her point, she related the story of her visit to one particularly vicious prison. When she arrived the guards told her she was wasting her time with the prisoners for they were incorrigibly bad.

> And what have you done to make them better? I asked:—"Nothing, that is not our business."—"Well, then it shall be mine."—I will go now and make my first attempt. The doors were unlocked, and I passed first into the men's prison. . . . I advanced quickly and firmly to the noisiest group. I raised my hand to secure silence, and whilst the sense of wonder yet remained, at my appearance in such a place, I said, "Friends they tell me that I shall find only very bad people here, and that they have only bad purposes and feelings:—I do not believe this. I know you are guilty:—I know you are often wicked in your thoughts and acts, but that you are wholly abandoned to evil, I will not believe. I have come here as your friend:—I am sorry for you. . . . Will you listen to me or shall I go away?"—a dozen voices said, "We will hear you."

What she told them was that they were responsible for their own reformation. Evidently they had nothing constructive to do, so she distributed books, writing materials, and slates. She singled out the most notorious inmate, a thug named William, and asked him to help the other prisoners with their lessons—arithmetic, geography, composition, and so forth. As time passed, she checked up on their progress and professed herself delighted to find that several of them were released and after three years "are still pursuing an honest and respectable mode of life." Most surprising of all, William, the "most turbulent and oftenest punished, the drunkard, the thief, the burglar,—is reformed; in a retired part of the country he is now established with his family; endeavoring as he can, to make some amends for the injury he has done to them, to himself, and to society." Just as she had found a spark of reason in the most degraded lunatic, Dix insisted "there is *some good* left in those who are most debased,—I am *sure* of that."[72]

She reasoned that solitary confinement with its opportunity for uninterrupted meditation gave miscreants the best chance of finding that spark. Prisoners in the Eastern Penitentiary had an advantage over inmates in less disciplined surroundings because, removed from all distractions and temptations, they could concentrate purely on improvement. "Ponder well the great goodness of God in granting you space for repentance," she urged them, "in permitting you to possess so many aids in this great and solemn work of reformation." She believed that no convict seriously inclined toward rehabilitation could fail to appreciate his good fortune to be protected from bad company—the tavern, the gambling table, the brothel.[73]

Still, she salted her celebration of the virtues of the separate system with a large measure of caution. In any prison system she suspected that recidivism was rampant, despite the best intentions and the best-managed programs. At the same time, judicial sentencing was notoriously irregular. Pardons were doled out capriciously. The certainty of punishment—something that she thought really worked to deter crime—scarcely existed. She could not, moreover, entirely dismiss the uncomfortable paradox symbolized in American prisons, a paradox well expressed by Tocqueville's remark that while American society embodied the world's greatest example of liberty, "the prisons of the same country offer the spectacle of the most complete despotism."[74]

Although Dix believed that asylums could cure insanity, she questioned the power of penitentiaries to reform a whole life of wrong. She was sympathetic to her friend James Dunlop's argument: "I look upon the Culprit as a constitutional enemy of the human race who should be punished as an example or deprived of his liberty for the protection of society." After all, in the book of Romans St. Paul had speculated that some men were made for dishonor. No penitentiary could change that. Perhaps, she mused, the best way to reconcile the shortcomings of prisons with their lofty goals was to think of them as bold experiments. The present age was a time of innovation and "daring enterprise. . . . The restlessness and excitability of our people must have some escape valve; it is therefore well that the thousand projects and theories of the day should have their experimental life."[75] She noted that American penal institutions were serving as models for the Old World, translating liberally from the French minister of the interior's 1844 report on efforts to introduce the Pennsylvania penitentiary system into France. Also she touched on developments in England, where the Pentonville Prison had established a solitary confinement regime, and other European nations in which noble minds were fighting crime and restoring offenders "through moral culture and religious influence to duty and a better life."[76]

Although it admittedly did a poor job of deterring crime or reforming lawbreakers, the penitentiary played a critical role in maintaining social order. As a last resort, it occupied an important position in an emerging continuum of institutions that included public schools, hospitals, asylums, poorhouses, reformatories, jails, and prisons. Each of these was at a different stage of development. But together, Dix hoped, they were means by which "noble minds, in all enlightened countries [are] reaching to the real good of mankind." While she maintained a general faith in the progressive improvement of such institutions, she slowly discovered that her heart was not in prison reform. Unlike her friends, who spent most of their time in Boston or Washington (and little time inside prisons), she had visited every penitentiary on the eastern seaboard. From what she saw, she grew increasingly skeptical about the efficacy of any system of confinement to remedy the dissolution of family ties that she believed from her own experience to lie at the root of all social evil. Nor could she see clearly how to reconcile grand theories of prison reform with the functional failings of institutions. So in early 1845, having published *Remarks on Prisons and Prison Discipline*, she preferred to return to the one mission about which she felt no twinges of ambivalence.

CHAPTER EIGHT

"The Brethren"

When Dix moved onto the battleground of prison reform, she paid little heed to how her published opinions would be received by asylum superintendents. These physicians, preoccupied for the most part with the day-to-day problems of their institutions, seemed to concentrate on madness to the exclusion of all else. Because she had done so much to help their cause, she was taken aback when she read a scathingly negative review of her book on prison discipline in their official periodical, *The American Journal of Insanity*.

The problem was that she had unwittingly put the asylum doctors in the wrong company. Because they craved respect and prestige, they bitterly resented any suggestion that their cherished asylums resembled prisons, jails, and other places of incarceration for criminals. Dix had gained a wide popular following. Her mingling of prison reform with lunacy reform, they feared, might alienate the better-off clientele they were struggling to attract. "No greater good scarcely can be done to those who are insane, than to have the public generally convinced that Asylums for the insane are not merely comfortable places, but that it is in no respect more discreditable for a person to reside in one a few months on account of insanity, than at any other boarding-house for the purpose of obtaining the services of a skillful physician," wrote Utica's Amariah Brigham. "But such an opinion will never become general, if accounts of these Asylums, the number of inmates, &c., are published in connection with accounts of the prisons and prisoners in the country."[1]

Despite Brigham's hopes, as far as most Americans were concerned in the 1840s, hospitals, along with almshouses and prisons, were mainly places for society's castoffs. A few medical institutions, like the famous Pennsylvania Hospital founded in the mid-eighteenth century by Benjamin Franklin, did admit paying patients along with indigents. But these remained rare exceptions. A decade after the Civil War there were only 125 or so medical and surgical hospitals in the United States. Throughout the Victorian period doctors preferred to call on patients at home, treat them there, and leave them to recuperate in familiar surroundings where their families could attend them. Generally speaking, the same attitude applied to the treatment of mental disease. Unless they were utterly destitute, lunatics were kept at home. Thus, Brigham and his colleagues faced ingrained prejudices, for the mainstream of physicians and the lay public shared a deep bias against institutions. It was becoming clear to the asylum professionals that Dix could be an effective ally in the effort to build asylums for the mad; but it was far less clear whether her campaign on behalf of the homeless insane would serve their professional aspirations and raise their standing within the professional hierarchy of medicine.

Since they were ambivalent about her, mistrustful of her methods, and nervous about a woman wielding influence, a number of them, including Brigham and later editors of *The American Journal of Insanity* tried simply to ignore Dix. From the scant attention the journal paid to her work, its readers might have inferred that she was a peripheral figure in the asylum movement. In its pages asylum after asylum springs into being with no mention of her surveys, her petitions to legislatures, no acknowledgement of her personal involvement in drafting laws and lobbying government officials for their passage. During the 1840s her remarkable public success in the legislative arena made it increasingly hard to disregard her. Since she had no discernible self-interest, legislatures and politicians trusted her more than they trusted asylum superintendents. They considered the measures she recommended as coming from an unbiased source. So in Pennsylvania and elsewhere they readily turned to her for independent professional and technical advice.

From the outset of her career, Dix earnestly held that the medical superintendents of asylums represented the only practical, medical solution to the problem of insanity. From her first tentative discussions with Samuel Woodward and Luther Bell in Massachusetts, she had relied on medical men for clinical and therapeutic judgments. In principle, she committed herself to work on their behalf. Despite being snubbed by several of "the brethren," as the superintendents privately referred to themselves, still she remained a strong advocate for their institutions and ideas. These were unselfish, generous men, she wrote, who "devote themselves without reservation" to curing the insane. To judge from her public statements, no other group of professionals was so earnestly devoted to its humanitarian work.[2]

As her practical experience and her self-confidence grew, however, she began to assert her own ideas, based on her own experience, with increasing vigor. At the same time, because many of them wanted a friend in high places to support their institutions, she was inevitably drawn into their professional politics and personal rivalries.

To concentrate their energies and open new fields of professional endeavor, in 1844 thirteen leading asylum administrators organized the nation's first medical society of any kind: the Association of Medical Superintendents of American Institutions for the Insane.[3] This group included, among others, Samuel Woodward, Luther Bell, Amariah Brigham, Isaac Ray (soon to head the new Butler Hospital in Rhode Island), and Thomas Story Kirkbride. They were, for the most part, determined men, firmly committed to the principles of moral therapy and the advancement of their own professional reputations. Like most physicians, they were also socially conservative, in most respects amazingly parochial, their administrative frame of mind having no place, as one of their leaders put it, for "abolitionists, bloomers, free-lovers and come-outers in general."[4] As they began to see the immense potential of the groundswell of lunacy reform for their own institutions and the careers they wanted for themselves, they closed ranks. Their aim was to promote the asylum by asserting the curability of insanity. They were, in Andrew Scull's fine phrase, "moral entrepreneurs" who sought to elevate themselves above the mainstream of American medicine.[5]

During the 1830s and 1840s the stock of the entire profession had fallen to an all-time low. In contrast to the situation in Europe, domestic medical education was slipshod and perfunctory. Most medical colleges functioned as trade schools, serving more to facilitate physician apprenticeships than to ground students in wider medical science. It became distressingly obvious as the bodies piled up in the cholera outbreak of 1832, for example, that the medical profession was powerless against the epidemic. Reluctant to admit they were helpless when faced with diseases like diphtheria and tuberculosis, physicians bled and blistered their patients, dosed them routinely with a chalky mercury compound called calomel, immersed their bodies in ice water, shocked them with electric current, prescribed copious quantities of laudanum, administered purgatives and diuretics for almost any symptoms. Despite physicians' professed confidence in such measures, many people realized how ineffective they were. Nevertheless, professional ethics did not seem to moderate doctors' appetite for fees.

Changes in law reflected declining confidence in the American medical profession. While Dix was conducting her surveys, states from New York to South Carolina were relaxing medical licensure requirements. By 1850 twenty-three states had little or no legal restriction of the practice of medicine. As barriers to the profession fell, laypersons rushed in headlong. Alternatives to orthodox medicine mushroomed. Self-help medical advice filled the columns of newspapers and popular journals. Quacks and homeopathic healers offered the public a bewildering variety of cures and medications, many of them do-it-yourself remedies, which, even if they did nothing to cure patients, at least seemed less harmful than the prescriptions of regular doctors. If the upper classes in cities like Boston and Philadelphia, who could afford the services of the best-trained physicians (generally from socially respectable backgrounds themselves), never lost faith in the profession, most other Jacksonians were skeptical.

Against this backdrop of general professional decline stemming mainly from regular medicine's powerlessness to remedy disease, psychiatry as a discrete medical specialty made its first appearance. The asylum physicians wished to invent a distinct professional identity as doctors to the mad. The basis for their aspirations was not that they enjoyed any special scientific or theoretical advantage over their peers. If anything, their intellectual horizons were remarkably low. Rather they envisaged a new role for themselves as masters of a powerful new technology—the asylum—capable of producing cures. Hence their conception of mental disorder, its causes, its cure, and its meaning, was influenced far less by science than by quotidian experience within the walls of their institutions.[6]

Accordingly, a large proportion of their published papers and professional journal were devoted to the minutiae of hospital operations. Above all, they were obsessed with the physical plants of their institutions, seemingly convinced that what one historian has called "moral architecture" could project prestige and ultimately establish the legitimacy of their profession. Narrowly focused on managing their staffs and patients, all the while convincing their boards of trustees that they were doing worthy work, asylum superintendents inevitably slipped into institutional provincialism. Their letters and papers reveal a claustrophobic world not far removed from medieval court politics. To them, Dix was a formidable woman of whom most of the superintendents were a little afraid. While they often benefited from her sponsorship, they feared that her influence was uncomfortably powerful. In many cases she was directly responsible for the construction of their institutions. In several instances she literally named the doctor to his post. Since they were consumed with professional rivalries, fears of losing their jobs, and schemes for improving their lot in private practice or other hospitals, she constantly figured into their calculations.[7]

Important as she was, she remained an outsider. A woman who was neither a physician nor the administrator of an asylum, Dix could never have been a candidate for membership in the new association, even though she was the main stimulus for its growth. After 1845 membership in the association soared as the proliferation of state-funded mental institutions—many of which Dix herself started—created the need for dozens of new superintendents and asylum doctors. Yet as the superintendents commenced their formal organization, she understood that she would not be invited to their meetings. If this rankled, she accepted her exclusion without comment, continuing to correspond and meet with each of them individually. They related to her as a missionary and, in some cases, as a friend. But these Victorian men were unprepared to see that a woman could be a political animal. She understood their prejudice; in many respects she shared it. Yet she had the satisfaction of knowing that despite being legally barred from electoral politics, she had carved out channels to assert her interests.

Dix knew that in the realm of politics she was the doctors' superior.

The asylum superintendents, much as they hated to acknowledge it, needed her as their representative in the statehouse. None of them came close to owning her political instincts nor, as time passed, her political connections. More important still, they lacked her sweeping vision of a new moral order in the world outside their hospitals. In practical terms, however, she could accomplish nothing without them. Their asylums were essential to her purposes. And Dix realized she lacked standing when it came to strictly medical matters, and thus appreciated how much her goal of building state mental hospitals depended on helping this group of physicians to enhance their medical authority. In short, Dix and the asylum doctors needed each other.

Their mutual dependence did not make for a smooth relationship. With her asylum bill supported by both houses of the state legislature in 1845, Dix had naturally assumed that Thomas Kirkbride, the respected Quaker physician leader of a model private hospital, would join her cause. But she was disappointed. From the outset, he was conspicuously absent from the planning sessions in which she formed her Pennsylvania lobbying strategy. When she tried repeatedly to arrange a private conference with him, Kirkbride put her off. Finally, in exasperation, she sharply chided him for his apathy, even threatening to show up unannounced at his Pennsylvania Hospital for the Insane to see what account he could give of a ladies' benevolent society fund that had been granted to the hospital.[8]

All through the spring of 1845 she continued to wonder about his motives. She could think of no reason for him to be hostile. Indeed, she admired Kirkbride, an appealing man, five years her junior, with a high forehead, muttonchops, and large, sensitive eyes. She had no wish to work around him. State leaders looked to his hospital as an example of what an asylum should be. Politically, she wanted his support for her program. Technically, she needed his help when it came to the design and staffing of the new facility, for he was America's leading authority on asylum design.

Seeing no alternative but confrontation, in July she finally asked him to explain rumors that he had been working behind her back to scuttle her proposal for a new asylum and, instead, persuade the legislature to expand the campus of his own Philadelphia Hospital for the Insane to include a new division: a state-funded asylum directly under his control. She expressed regret, as she put it, "that so many misrepresentations"

*Master of asylum architecture Thomas Story
Kirkbride in his sixties.*

surrounded her hospital plan. In view of Pennsylvania's size and far-flung population, she told him, her ultimate goal was actually to build two mental institutions: one in Harrisburg and another in the western part of the state. Kirkbride, she was sure, had "too good a heart, and sound understanding" of the value of a state institution to oppose her scheme, even if he was disappointed that her bill would not enlarge his hospital. Embarrassed by her suggestion that he was more interested in empire building than in what was best for the insane poor, he promptly dismissed her charges as a silly, malicious rumor. Even so, he remained on the sidelines until well after the legislature adopted Dix's proposal for the Pennsylvania State Lunatic Hospital in Harrisburg.[9]

She was quickly learning that professional politics could be as disagreeable a business as working between Democrats and Whigs. Clearly she and Kirkbride had got off on the wrong foot, and for a while she worried that their estrangement might harden into enmity.

When she was called to Harrisburg to help design the Hospital, though, she hit upon a way to close the rift between them. Recognizing that it would be far easier to work with Kirkbride than against him, she peppered him with technical questions about his favorite subject: asylum architecture and construction.[10] It was an approach that he could not resist. She presented herself as his willing pupil, ready to learn everything about building an asylum. What were the wages of master carpenters, masons, plasterers, and plumbers? she asked. How much should the best brick cost, or one thousand panes of window glass?[11] The task of creating this important new structure, she let it be known, would be impossible without Kirkbride's active participation. Among the asylum superintendents, everyone looked up to him as the supreme authority on hospital architecture—the man who had worked out an elegant theory of the relationship between physical surroundings and moral treatment. He could hardly turn down an opportunity to implement his theories. Over the next few years, while Dix was busy campaigning in the South, Kirkbride sketched ideas for Harrisburg and published his ideas. "Remarks on the Construction and Arrangements of Hospitals for the Insane" secured his reputation as an expert, and he was soon asked to help the New Jersey and Pennsylvania commissions design their new state facilities.[12]

When he saw how much she could do for his professional career, his attitude toward her softened. Coming to regard Dix as his ally, Kirkbride lauded her efforts. When the Tennessee legislature passed an asylum bill she had sponsored, he congratulated her success, "so complete and so well deserved." They began to exchange confidences. He was pleased when she confided to him her suspicion that Dr. Boyd McNairy, the Nashville Hospital superintendent, was rather too fond of the bottle. "Brandy can [n]ever be substituted for water" by a conscientious asylum superintendent, Kirkbride responded with mock solemnity. Conveying bits of gossip, information, and speculation, Dix gradually assumed a role as a go-between for Kirkbride and several other key superintendents. Information was power, she knew, and by collecting and distributing news of what was happening in asylums from state to state, she insinuated herself into the center of the superintendents' informal professional network.[13]

At their fourth annual meeting, the Association of Medical Superintendents unanimously voted to adopt a resolution, offered by New Jersey's Horace Buttolph, to honor Dix's achievements. Kirkbride, as the association's secretary, was responsible for transmitting the news to her. And he took the opportunity warmly to declare his own "admiration of such long continuous, devoted and valued services." His letter reached Dix during a low period and immediately lifted her sagging spirits. She took his personal addendum as a signal that he wanted to mend fences and put their differences behind them. What meant more to her than anything else, she replied, was "the friendship and esteem of intelligent persons, whose position and abilities qualify them peculiarly to comprehend and judge the vocation to which my energies have been devoted." Sheer celebrity counted for nothing compared with the respect of one worthy man.[14]

Her ability to negotiate between the macrocosm of state politics and the microcosm of the asylum physicians invested her with special power. In 1847–48, for example, she grew increasingly impatient with the Pennsylvania legislature's sluggish progress toward moving her hospital completion. In her absence, the project had been assigned a lower priority than other public works such as repairing the state canal system. The hospital commission, originally charged to hire a superintendent and get on with the construction of the facility, proved timid and ineffectual when it came to asserting itself with stingy lawmakers. When she assessed the situation in Harrisburg, Dix realized that although they were perfectly willing to drag out the process of building the asylum, the state's leading politicians had no wish for lunacy to become a public issue. Far better known at this point than when she had first entered the state three years earlier, Dix privately pressured the party leaders who really controlled state government to make a renewed commitment to finishing the state hospital. Otherwise she threatened to take her case public. Then, taking matters into her own hands, she promised to identify a qualified superintendent for the facility and personally to oversee the project to keep it within budget.[15]

This self-imposed assignment automatically increased her standing with the asylum superintendents. They were as a group nervous about holding on to the jobs they had, and most of them did not want to rock the political boat in their hope of finding new positions with higher pay and more prestige. Beginning around 1850, Dix seldom missed opportunities for recruiting and recommending men to head new institutions. She guided the career of R. J. Patterson from 1847, when he asked her where he should look for his first asylum job, through stints as secretary of the board of commissioners for the Indiana Hospital for the Insane in 1850, and superintendent of the Iowa Hospital for the Insane ten years later. When rumors circulated about changes at New York's Utica hospital, Dix was told by one job seeker, "no recommendation would have more weight than your own."[16] By the Civil War, many of the superintendents depended on her goodwill for their jobs, or feared that they did. In consequence, their often obsequious professions of gratitude carried an undercurrent of resentment. In a revealing letter from the association secretary at the time, John Nichols wrote in 1855, while Dix was in Europe, "Our Association has never met without many grateful recognitions of your invaluable services to humanity." Then he added, stumbling into unintentional irony, "and though, at the late meeting, you and ourselves were much more widely separated than ever before since we became an organized body, I can assure you that you never held a higher place in our most respectful consideration."[17]

The extent to which Dix involved herself in the professional aspects of asylum affairs may be seen in her dealings with John Curwen. Assistant physician for several years to Kirkbride at the Pennsylvania Hospital for the Insane, in the late 1840s Curwen hounded her to find him an asylum of his own. He was certain, he told her, that he would be chosen to run the new North Carolina facility if she would only say the word. After three years of searching for a position, Curwen finally convinced Dix and Kirkbride to sponsor his candidacy to head the new state lunatic hospital at Harrisburg. Curwen's dream—a dream shared by Dix and Kirkbride—was to pattern the new state institution after the corporate Philadelphia hospital. Unlike Dr. Kirkbride's expensive, private hospital, however, the Harrisburg facility was supposed to serve a mixed clientele of paying patients who were not wealthy enough to afford the Pennsylvania Hospital, and the indigent insane who would otherwise end up in the almshouse.

Proudly Curwen and Dix opened the Pennsylvania State Lunatic Hospital in 1851. In its grand design, the four-story central building, with two-tiered wings extending on either side, rivaled the nearby state capitol. Standing beneath the grand Tuscan portico that framed its entrance, they had an unobstructed view of the Susquehanna River, the canal, the railroad that stopped at the village of Dauphin, and beyond, the beautiful Blue Mountains.

For both of them it was a dream come true.

In the asylum's early months of operation Dix took the train to Harrisburg several times to see how things were going. By Thanksgiving, a dozen patients—six men, six women—had been admitted. Strict order prevailed. Mornings at five o'clock the asylum steward sounded the alarm bell. Attendants made sure the inmates were clean and properly dressed for the day ahead. The matron supervised the hospital's kitchen and the two dining rooms—the two genders were always segregated at mealtime—where inmates sat down to a breakfast of buttered bread and eggs. Afterward, those who could work, according to their skills and preferences, spent part of the day in the wood shop or the vegetable garden. Women retired to the library, where they read or knitted. Everyone was gathered back in the male and female dining rooms for lunch. Then the same pattern of work or purposeful relaxation obtained in the afternoon, until it was time for dinner.[18]

But there were problems from the start. Even during the first few months, it was apparent that the physical plant was inadequate. In February 1852, Curwen said he needed an additional $20,000 to make it habitable for its fifty-five inmates. This was only the beginning. He soon discovered that the architect and builder had been practically incompetent. "A northwester is roaring around, making the windows rattle and throwing in an abundance of cool air through every crack and crevice," he complained to Kirkbride. "The windows are so fitted that in many of them an opening through which your finger may be pushed is found." The facility's defects left him in the awkward position of constantly begging for increased appropriations from the legislature. With little sense of operating budgets herself, Dix, who had helped direct the asylum architecture, suggested a variety of expensive improvements. In 1852 she proposed adding on a museum and reading room, noting that construction expenses could be cut if Curwen's staff could quarry their own stone. Frequently dipping into her private "Philadelphia fund for the comfort and relief of Insane patients in the State Hospital at Harrisburg," for which she had been soliciting contributions since the mid-1840s, Dix regularly bought extra items for the asylum: "$312 for a carriage," "$312 for a pair of horses," "$70 for bookcases," and "$50 magic lantern slides."[19]

Visitors to the institution, expecting austerity, were struck by its handsome appointments: a well-equipped conservatory, oiled hardwood bookcases, and even a large stained glass window boasting the Pennsylvania coat of arms. No matter where the money to pay for these items came from, they seemed bizarrely inappropriate in a state madhouse. Irritated by two years of what seemed like throwing good money after bad, the state legislature finally called Curwen on the carpet to defend his expenditures. In a panic, he told Dix that rumors were flying around the state capital that she was so displeased with his management that she had boycotted the hospital and refused to give him access to her "Philadelphia fund."[20] He had at first thought of the legislators as "very clever men and disposed to help on the interest of the Institution," but he quickly came to fear, as he told Dix, that they thought they knew "more about our business than we do ourselves."[21]

Ironically enough, though he was an inept practitioner of state politics, Curwen was also a victim of the unrealistic expectations Dix had created when she sold the legislature on the benefits of a state hospital. Legislators who remembered her arguments or who bothered to refer to her Pennsylvania *Memorial* would have recalled its argument that, between producing cash crops for market and quickly returning lunatics to their communities, an asylum would virtually pay for itself. Obviously if Dix's cost-benefit claims were correct—and who had reason to doubt them?—Curwen should have had little trouble meeting his expenses. Unfortunately, like most of his fellow physicians, Curwen had no aptitude for finance or politics. "I have so strong a repugnance to any thing which has even the appearance of a connexion of any of our Hospitals with the troubled arena of politics," he wrote, "that I would rather submit to a very great inconvenience than be suspected of a leaning in that direction."[22] This was a common sentiment among superintendents, yet it was also a dangerous weakness since most of their asylums depended on continuing financial support from state or local political bodies.

In the case of the Pennsylvania State Lunatic Hospital, neither Dix nor Curwen was able to explain that the original economic rationale for the asylum was faulty. It was inevitably a magnet for the state's worst chronic cases, not the sort of patients who returned home after a few months of moral therapy, nor people who were capable of farming and light industry. Cures and patient-generated revenues failed to materialize. To cut his losses, beginning in the 1860s, Curwen began to admit paying patients. This practice reduced the hospital's operating deficits, but not enough to erase the hostility of the legislature. A respected physician of meager managerial and political talents, Curwen continued for years to call on Dix to bail him out of troubles with the state legislature and the asylum's board of trustees before he was finally ousted in 1880.[23]

Ordinarily, Dix did not work where asylums were established, so her contact with the leading superintendents was sporadic and conducted mainly through the mails. In a few cases, however, she took special interest in an established institution, and her interest had dramatic consequences for its superintendent. Take, for example, Dix's assault on New York Hospital and Bloomingdale Asylum. Charles H. Nichols was its superintendent, a post he had inherited from the estimable Pliny Earle in the late 1840s. Perhaps because he professed to admire her so ardently, Dix took a shine to Nichols and soon set about trying to orchestrate the young man's career.

In 1850 he began to complain to her about the difficulty of trying to get the Bloomingdale asylum to live up to its therapeutic mission, given that the old facility was falling into "decrepitude." He was hamstrung, he claimed, by the asylum's divided and meddlesome board, which constantly interfered in its operations. His predecessor had encountered the same problems. "None but they who have learned from experience can comprehend the amount and the variety of evils which in its practical operation, flow from this system," Pliny Earle remarked a few years later. The source of their problems was the Bloomingdale board of directors, a mixed body of general physicians and community laymen, each with his own idea of the institution's mission and the best way to accomplish it.

Ever since she had first toured Bloomingdale in 1843, Dix had been critical of its inadequacies. Visiting New York in 1850, she found that the institution had changed but little in seven years. It was still "relatively for the rich," she wrote, and hardly provided a resource for the pauper lunatics of New York City. All in all, she told Kirkbride, there was "more to reform in New York than any other part of the United States at the present time."[24]

In the fall of 1851, with Nichols in the background feeding her information, she wrote a brief memorial for the asylum's board of governors. Through a New York congressman whom she knew from her work in Washington, Dix approached one of the most prominent trustees and asked him about presenting her critique. Since she was personally acquainted with several of the trustees, she said, she had hoped to remedy serious "grievances which are so serious as to *demand redress*" in private conversation.[25] To buttress her position, she tried to draw Earle, who at the time was serving as visiting physician in the New York Lunatic Asylum at Ward's Island, into the quarrel. Prudently he demurred, telling her that her purpose "will best be effected by your own influence."[26]

Bloomingdale Asylum in 1821.

Her Bloomingdale petition bluntly criticized every aspect of the hospital, its facilities, and staff. The building's ventilation, heating, water supply—indeed, every detail of its architecture, she said—made it impossible to ensure the supply of fresh air and pure water essential for moral therapy. Mortified by stories of sexual improprieties, she upbraided the staffing plan and suggested employing male and female keepers to prevent any contact between inmates, especially at night. Beyond this, she concluded that the root of all evil at Bloomingdale was the institution's system of governance. Advocating the Association of Superintendents' position, Dix admonished the board to limit its role in hospital operations and give Nichols, who was a physician after all, a free hand to run things as he saw fit.[27]

Not unexpectedly, the board disagreed. Apart from the matter of governance, the trustees thought that Dix favored undue extravagance within a public institution. She was accused of blowing trivial deficiencies entirely out of proportion. "I am no advocate of frescoed halls and vaulted roofs; for couch of velvet and stain canopy," one trustee wrote in reply to her memorial. "Well painted, plain walls, warm comfortable blankets . . . and clean coarse sheets such as I like and use myself; meet my ideas of unexceptionable, common sense treatment." To make matters worse, another trustee accused Dix of an egregious breach of manners because she had publicly aired her views. The Board of Governors had met with her at length, he noted, and had given her carte blanche to examine the asylum and its records. Just because they took exception to her "undeserved censure of the Asylum" and failed to go along with her recommendations was no justification for her public statements. After careful review, the chairman of the board wrote, the committee he appointed to consider Dix's charges concluded that the "institution possess merits which entitles [sic] the confidence of the community."[28]

Nichols initially supported Dix's brief. As he saw its potential to create a backlash on the part of the board, though, he told Kirkbride that what she might accomplish was "I fear not the best thing by far." To Dix, he proclaimed the memorial "admirable" and assured her her language was not too strong for the task at hand. The board was split into factions, and the old guard, according to Nichols, needed a jolt. He was right, nonetheless, to worry that Dix's criticism might have unintended consequences. Indeed, how could anyone have read her report without seeing it as a reflection on his administration? When it became apparent that the trustees, who were less than enthusiastic about Nichols in the first place, meant to use her charges as an excuse to dismiss him, Dix belatedly came to his defense. "Possibly I ought to have urged more in his favor," she told the board. "Allow me to suggest that if you lose Dr. Nichols your chances to say the least are not in favor of securing a better man."[29]

The Bloomingdale trustees were unpersuaded. Some of them even hinted that Nichols had manipulated Dix, inciting her investigation with an eye toward securing more power over the board. To avoid the embarrassment of firing him outright, they picked up on Dix's findings of moral impropriety and instituted a new policy that required the superintendent to be a married man. Nichols was unmarried and in January 1852 was forced to resign. Needless to say, it did not take long for word of this episode to reach his fellow superintendents, who could not have helped but wonder what might happen should Dix take a like interest in their institutions.[30]

When it came to convincing lawmakers to build state asylums, Dix played the role of a moral visionary, ready to seize any argument or example that would help sell her plan. It was a noble vision, charged

with passion and high expectation. The men who were left to implement it, however, were often chagrined to find that they were saddled
from the beginning with an impossible task. After they had been in the
job for a while, most superintendents learned that there was a deep gulf
between the high-flown rhetoric used to convince politicians and the
public of the merits of asylum treatment and the difficult, often
depressing reality of running a mental institution.

In due course, learning this unpleasant lesson made many of them
uneasy with Dix. To her detractors she seemed to skim the surface,
constantly visiting and comparing institutions, and thus failing to
understand the dark waters in which they spent their lives. She was, her
friend Robert Hare said, "Philanthropy in a Female form, which like a
meteor flies from one end of the civilized American world, to the other
so as to require the dexterity of Death, or Cupid to hit the mark."
Moving always at high velocity, without a hospital of her own, and thus
with little appreciation for the depressing banality of life inside a single
institution in which the physicians and staff confronted the same problems every day, she seemed to overlook the human realities of institutional management. How, for instance, was a doctor whose wards were
crammed with the most wretched cases supposed to motivate his staff
to convey the bright and cheerful attitude she expected? How was he to
justify subjecting his wife and children to life inside an asylum?[31]

It was not that Dix was blind to these issues, nor was she unsympathetic. For example, in the case of Horace Buttolph, whom she helped
to move from his position as assistant physician at Utica to medical
superintendent of the New Jersey State Lunatic Asylum, she became a
close friend, stayed with his family over the years whenever she was in
Trenton, and finally in old age took up permanent residence in the hospital itself. It was more that hers was the outlook of an evangelist, constantly moving on to proclaim the Gospel to new souls, not a parish
minister tending a flock.

In her ability to secure state funding to build and improve the superintendents asylums, she was indispensable. Though they respected
Dix's energy and her power within the legal and legislative system, they
remained wary. Letters between superintendents reveal that they treated her gingerly. In mentioning to Kirkbride that Dix intended to
inspect the strong rooms in the Philadelphia Hospital for the Insane,
for example, Horace Buttolph casually warned him, "by the way, she
threatens to make a presentment to the grand jury of [the strong

Horace A. Buttoph.

rooms] in Taunton, if they do not pull them down at once." As a group, they depended on her to advocate their profession at the highest levels of government. "How much more remains to be done which no one but you can do!" Luther Bell told her. By taking up the pen, she had the capacity to marshall the facts that could show the country's leaders how the "awful concomitants of civilization and prosperity . . . can be grappled with." For too long "the public mind [has] been utterly perverted by morbid, shortsighted philanthropists," he declared, who stirred up popular emotions without considering "an awful retributory re-action hereafter."[32]

She was their utterly devoted, unpaid lobbyist in state capitals and in Washington. She was the link between their institutions and their ideas and the larger world. No theorist or critical thinker herself, she borrowed generously from the professional writings of asylum doctors, enthusiastically and uncritically recycling their claims: that insanity was a product of social organization, that it was reaching epidemic proportions, and that their profession and their hospitals offered the only effective, economical cure. She asserted their professional prerogatives and argued that only the efforts of asylum physicians should be sanctioned by law and supported by public funds. They readily supplied her with the materials she needed to advance their cause. And simply by being at the seat of power, she connected their work to the larger national issues of the day.[33]

"We owe a majority, perhaps, of our largest and best institutions for the insane to her efforts," wrote Luther Bell in 1849. "Her information as to the condition of the insane and the measures for their relief is probably more extensive than that of any person in our country. I must say further that in social position she ever has moved among our highest circles." While her critics among "the brethren" of asylum physicians shared private doubts about whether or not she was, as Bell claimed, "a pure disinterested promoter of the interests of the unfortunate," none would have denied that she was among "the extraordinary women of the age."[34]

"The day was when she was the virtual Queen of the Asylums of the land," declared Dix's nineteenth-century biographer in a phrase that accurately, if unintentionally, caught both her imperiousness and her lack of real institutional power. In retrospect, Dix's advocacy of the new psychiatric profession suggests a certain irony. Stripped of scientific jargon, the fundamental goal of the asylum superintendents was to lay claim to insanity and its treatment as their exclusive province within the emerging world of medical specialization. With respect to their careers, the asylum doctors hoped to become the captains of flagship institutions like Kirkbride's prestigious private hospital in Philadelphia. But those who paid closer attention heard an ominous theme in Dix's message that the state asylum was for the indigent insane: those so ill and so destitute that their presence outdoors was a threat to social morality. What real hope was there for curing such patients? And what prestige would attach to those physicians who spent their time treating the lowest order of society? Her success both expanded their profession and limited its prestige. By popularizing the concept of the *state* hospital for the insane, Dix inadvertently and permanently undermined the professional status of the group she sought most fervently to promote.

❧

CHAPTER NINE

Conquest of the South

Dorothea Dix's career was never identified strongly with the South. In so many ways she was the archetypal New Englander: a Unitarian descended from Puritans and Yankees, a woman who would go on to serve her native North as superintendent of women nurses during the Civil War. Her touchstone memorial was a petition to the Massachusetts General Court; her most ambitious program was a land grant scheme for the federal government. Yet in the major phase of her career, between 1845 and 1860, Dix gravitated to the South, and it was in the slave states that she achieved the majority of her legislative victories. From Mississippi to Maryland, she won over governors and assemblies against what were thought to be impossible odds. And in the process she won the hearts of the Southern people—at least the hearts of the white middle class and planter aristocracy. In regard to her larger political agenda, moreover, as she began to advance federal lunacy reform, support from leading Southern congressmen was essential to her effectiveness in national politics.

In the fall of 1845, as President Polk set his sights on war with Mexico and the first 4,500 copies of a book called *Narrative of the Life of Freder-*

235

ick Douglass quickly sold out in Boston, Dix carried her providential campaign below the Mason-Dixon line. Although she was slow to realize it, she entered the South at a time when the political bargains of the past were beginning to fray. During her twenties and thirties the Missouri Compromise of 1820, which divided the nation slave and free along the 36°30, parallel, seemed to have settled the question of how slavery would be permitted to enter the new territories. Even as abolitionist voices grew more strident in the early 1840s, like most of her contemporaries Dix assumed that America could muddle along divided indefinitely. She had passed through the upper South several months earlier on her first Southern tour, briefly visiting the State Penitentiary of Kentucky at Frankfort, in preparation for writing her prison reform pamphlet. In what was to be the first leg of a sweeping survey of the South, she now returned to Kentucky, planning to work her way carefully through the whole state. "Considering it is almost unknown here for one lady to make a journey by herself," she proudly told Harriet Hare, "I have made my way quite successfully." It was purely a matter of conveying the right attitude. On the road, she thought that a woman was her own best protector. Proper manners and high self-regard broadcast an aura of invincibility, so much so that she felt comfortable in traveling alone all the way through the so-called black belt to New Orleans.[1]

Most Northerners who visited the South took a keen interest in slavery, the presence of large numbers of African Americans offering the most striking contrast to the North, where free blacks generally represented a tiny minority. But Dix's mind was not on slavery. The focal point of her thinking about the South was her newfound interest in institutional architecture and organization, and how these factors related to treatment and rehabilitation. So in Kentucky she wrote two petitions to the state legislature: one about lunacy reform and another about prisons. With a rare note of approval, she confessed that she had less to say about the insane poor than in any Northern state she had visited, because "*in the jails and poor-houses of Kentucky there are no insane.*" In law, if not always in practice, the state explicitly assumed responsibility for pauper lunatics and idiots, and mandated that anyone who was to be cared for at state expense had to be sent to the Kentucky Eastern Lunatic Asylum.[2]

The Kentucky asylum had been established in 1824, Dix learned, but until its first medical superintendent arrived in 1844, it had been noth-

ing more than an almshouse for the insane. The situation confronting
the new director was grim. Most of the inmates were chronically
deranged, "generally of the most hopeless character." There was no pre-
tense of providing moral therapy; nothing in the spartan facility was
designed to treat insanity. Attendants were unfamiliar with their
patients' case histories and were out of touch with the great strides that
had been made in treatment. The result had been bedlam: "a promiscuous and heterogeneous assembly" echoing with "the discordant sounds
of maddened ravings."[3] But a year after the new medical superintendent
arrived, and by the time Dix inspected the asylum, the place had been
revitalized. The asylum's commissioners, physician, and staff won her
confidence and respect by providing humane care, albeit within the confines of an overcrowded, poorly constructed facility. It was the facility
itself, she concluded, not the laws of Kentucky, that needed reforming.

Thus in her Kentucky *Memorial*, Dix catalogued the myriad defects
within the Eastern Lunatic Asylum's physical plant. Its kitchen was
poorly designed and had the wrong kind of stove. The layout of rooms
made it impossible to keep patients properly separated according to the
type and severity of their illnesses. There were no "bathing-rooms"; the
water system was completely inadequate; the laundry could not regularly supply clean bedclothes. The asylum had no infirmary to quaran-
tine and treat patients with fevers or infectious diseases; the sick often
got sicker. Mortality was disturbingly high. Although the hospital was
pleasantly situated on thirty acres on the outskirts of town, Dix
observed, the site was nonetheless far too cramped. The facility would
benefit greatly from "owning a farm of one or two hundred acres," she
maintained, on which patients would benefit from agricultural work
outdoors and, in the process, offset some of the institution's operating
costs by growing cash crops.[4]

Compared with her previous petitions the Kentucky *Memorial* was
brief, just fourteen pages, but it heralded a departure from the pattern
Dix had followed elsewhere. In place of an exhaustive survey of the
state's counties, she set forth general observations on the causes of
insanity, the human suffering it inflicted, the history of humanitarian
treatment, the importance of getting lunatics into hospitals at the first
sign of disease, and, of course, the economic argument for hospital
treatment over any other approach. Short on facts about individual
cases of lunacy in Kentucky, and long on references to the optimistic

claims of asylum superintendents around the country, the Kentucky *Memorial* represented Dix's refinement of her political formula. Like most formulas, it could be easily adapted to local circumstances.

Her prison survey, on the other hand, *A Review of the Present Condition of the State Penitentiary of Kentucky, with Brief Notices and Remarks upon the Jails and Poor-Houses in Some of the Most Populous Counties*, was more thorough and better researched. She narrowed her subject to the construction of jails and the feasibility of building "work-houses, or *houses of correction*" in the state's most populous regions. In far greater detail than any memorial she had written to date, the Kentucky *Review* analyzed physical plants and institutional operations. She measured the dimensions of buildings, rooms, cells, and the thickness of walls. She made inventories of the furniture in cells, noting what kind of clothing prisoners wore and its condition. She researched prison diet—bread, bacon, beef, rye coffee without sugar, Irish potatoes, turnips, and cabbages—and pronounced it "coarse, but substantial, and wholesome." Well rehearsed in the running debates about prison and asylum architecture, she recommended improvements in water systems, ventilation, and organization of prison industries. Finally she suggested new policies to limit visitors (she eschewed the popular practice of charging sightseers an admission fee to gawk at prisoners or lunatics) and to encourage religious instruction.[5]

Interestingly enough, the approach she took in her *Review* seems partly to have been influenced by the debate over slavery, especially the writings of Southerners who deployed the "facts" of slaves' material lives to prove that they were well clothed, well fed, and, for the most part, content. Southern newspapers regularly printed inventories—the dimensions of their dwellings, pounds of meat in their diet, pairs of shoes per capita—meant to show how well on average their masters provided for black slaves.

Dix had always liked facts, but here her purpose was no longer to describe minutely the condition of people. She was guided more by her ambition than by empathy for the incarcerated. For she was looking ahead to the role she would play in the design and construction of the Trenton and Harrisburg asylums. She was going to school in Kentucky. It never occurred to her that in the process of making inventories of entities and concentrating on buildings she might run the risk of overlooking the humanity of her subjects in favor of the institutions that housed them.

She felt free to spend her time sketching improvements in Kentucky's prisons and jails because she thought that in most other respects the state was doing pretty well by its citizens. Nowhere else in the past five years had she seen so little "human privation, misery, and suffering in any form . . . and so wide a diffusion of general cheerfulness and contentment." Of course, pockets of backwardness and cruelty remained. Seeing the Greensburg County jail's massive iron "man-cages," for example, she exclaimed, "I had supposed we had at this period of civilization, outlived the *iron age* of dungeons." Even this pun hinted at her brighter mood, though. Indeed, her description of the Lincoln County jail came as close to finding humor in her subject as anything she wrote. Thereafter asking the jailer to open a trap door, she wrote, "the dungeon is disclosed—no, not disclosed, unless total darkness is a revelation." She was unable to descend into the hole, "as there were neither steps nor ladder, and I have not action enough as a Gymnast [*sic*], to swing myself down into a depth of seven feet or more." Lest she make too light of her subject, however, she added a local physician's opinion that consigning any man to that dungeon "was no other than judicial murder."[6]

The change in tone and the gallows humor apparent in her Kentucky prison *Memorial* are clues that point to a gradually shifting sensibility—a widening emotional distance—between Dix and her subject. She had begun her mission as a chronicler, but along the way she was learning much more than facts about the homeless insane. She was learning to feel comfortable encountering people whose existence was gruesome beyond telling. (Clearly she was right to say that the words of her memorials were pale substitutes for the ugly truth they portrayed.) She was learning to weigh and sift the raw data of human experience with an eye toward its political use. She was learning, as she was drawn into technical issues of incarceration and treatment, not to think of the insane as people but as a category, a social problem that demanded a political solution.

This tendency did not keep her from involving herself with individual lunatics, especially when the patient was socially prominent. She valued her reputation for discretion as much as she prided herself on knowing what to do in cases of madness. When she got to know members of Virginia's eminent Lee family, she discovered that one of General Light-Horse Harry Lee's grandsons (and a nephew of Robert E. Lee), a boy of twelve, was hopelessly insane. Charles as a young child had been an amazing prodigy. At seven his parents sent him to a special high school in New Jersey to study with a professor renowned for getting the most out of boys with special gifts. Unfortunately the professor was overly impressed, praising the child constantly, and failed to heed the early warnings of lunacy, above all, a mean streak that was turning Charles Lee into a bully and a thief. Dix confided to Harriet Hare that the foolish teacher

> in his pride and ignorance made the boy his companion to New York during a vacation when he himself was to give lectures. Charles Lee was placed beside him on the platform and during the exercise the Professor eulogized his pupil and invited any person present to test his abilities[.] A difficult theme was proposed—the boy wrote instantly—was applauded, and poor child, intoxicated with ill-timed praises. The Professor proposed his making a speech—the subject was given by one of the audience[.] For a little time he was coherent and wonderfully powerful—but in less than half an hour was a raving *mad* child.

This was by far the worst, though not the only, case she could recall of a mind ruined by an inept teacher. When the Lee family asked her advice, she arranged for the lad's admission to the Kentucky state asylum, where he proved to be the most disruptive inmate in the place. "A total wreck, morally and physically insane," she lamented. "The D[octo]r has *no* hope for him."[7]

Discretion prevented the name of Charles Lee from figuring in her memorial. But she needed human examples. Despite its emphasis on buildings, not people, Dix knew her report would attract more notice if she publicized a particularly shocking case. So before she submitted her petition to the legislature, Dix wrote up some of her findings for the newspapers. And when she did, the Kentuckians expressed their annoyance at what they regarded as false assertions and sloppy reporting. In a typically sensational piece entitled "Dreadful Inhumanity," Dix had depicted a madman in private hands in Wayne County, caged in an outbuilding, filthy and naked. In response, sixteen leading citizens from Wayne County signed a letter to the editor of the *Louisville Journal* in which they "plead not guilty to the wicked and inhuman outrage which they for the first time stand charged before the public." Knowing their county well, they maintained that no person resembling Dix's lunatic was to be found there. In this case, Dix thought it best to apologize for her error, writing that she had mistaken the name of the county. She insisted, nevertheless, that such a person did exist in Clinton County, and that his miserable condition argued for the establishment of a hospital.[8]

Both the asylum and the prison documents were published by order of the legislature in February 1846. For the Eastern State hospital at Lexington, Dix wanted an adequate appropriation from the state treasury to place it "upon a suitable foundation." At the same time she called for a new asylum to be built in the Green River country. Dix concluded her prison *Report* not with any specific call to action but with several pages of excerpts from her recent pamphlet on prisons. In shifting the basis of her argument for the asylum from the concrete to the abstract, Dix was abandoning a reliance on human facts, which had long formed the substance of her moral vision, in favor of broader generalizations and the expert testimony that politics seemed to demand. Her most recent foray into publishing human facts—at least as she understood them—had backfired. She had learned her political lesson.

The Kentucky legislature, for its part, accepted Dix's report with little debate. To her delight, she succeeded in gaining an appropriation for improvements in the old Eastern Lunatic Asylum facility as well as a modest financial commitment toward a Western Lunatic Asylum, which was finally opened in Hopkinsville in September 1854. Since the new hospital needed year-to-year support to fund its planning and construction, Dix found herself repeatedly called to Frankfort over the next eight years to shepherd the new facility toward completion.[9]

During all her years in New England and the Middle Atlantic States, Dix had given little thought to the South. After her pleasant experiences in Kentucky, however, she was convinced that many Northern prejudices about the South were unfounded. Thus in December 1845, when temperatures dropped to seven degrees below zero and a freak blizzard rendered the roads in Indiana and Illinois—the next states on her itinerary—virtually impassable, she readily changed her plans to take in the cities of the South: Birmingham, Baton Rouge, New Orleans, Vicksburg, Jackson, and Little Rock. By the spring, she expected to pass through St. Louis and Jefferson City on her way back north to Indianapolis.

Commencing this long journey, Dix marveled at the beautiful Southern landscape in springtime, pausing often to pick azalea blossoms and wisteria, which she dried and pressed between the pages of her letters and journals. Flooded with delightful impressions, she remarked on how easy it was for her to travel alone in the South, and how much better ordered Southern institutions were than those in the middle and western states. The prim, genteel Southerners she met scarcely conformed to abolitionist caricatures of slaveholders; they were open, friendly, and remarkably accommodating. Plantations of the upper class, with their tree-lined entrances and white-columned manor houses, brought back memories of Greenbank and her time with the wonderfully civilized, patriarchal Rathbone family. There was the same sense of aristocratic tranquility and cultivated ease, all in the midst of boundless affluence. The furniture was finely crafted cherry, mahogany, and black walnut, oiled and polished to a low sheen. The food was rich—pheasant, quail, fresh fish, and garden vegetables—served on English china. Servants—in this case, black slaves—were everywhere, waiting on their masters' distinguished guest hand and foot. In its pockets of wealth, the homes of planters in which Dix was often asked to spend a few nights or a week, the South was a romantic country, a sanctuary of conservatism and order, where everything flowed in equilibrium.

This at least was her first impression. It would take time and many return visits to the South for her to appreciate the deep fissures that divided the slaveholding rulers from their social and economic inferiors, to say nothing of the black slaves who formed the basis of the Southern labor system.

Over the next several years Dix developed a special affection for South Carolina, in part because she thought its asylums and almshouses were excellent, and in part because she enjoyed the companionships of Francis Lieber, a friend of George Emerson, Howe, and Sumner who had moved there for an academic post at South Carolina College. Lieber had for years tried to no avail to distinguish himself as a prison reformer, first in New England and later in the South, and he thoroughly admired Dix and all she had accomplished. On visits to South Carolina, she stayed with Lieber and his family, and he rapidly became her guide to the culture of the planter aristocracy as well as to prisons and asylums.[10] In New Orleans, feeling "as much at ease here as I should in any place in which I had spent two years, instead of two days," she wondered how it was that Southern hospitals, prisons, indeed "all the public institutions [are] in a better condition than I was led to anticipate."[11]

Wherever her stage stopped to pick up passengers, she took the opportunity to visit county jails, which she described as "generally large, commodious, and well kept." The prisons and jails of Alabama and southern Georgia were so well ordered, she felt, that they put Massachusetts and New York to shame. Over the years she visited the insane department of the state hospital at Milledgeville, Georgia, on many occasions, and remarked that "the Legislature has been liberal but has grumbled a little while giving—yet on the whole has really been open-handed." Of course, not all Southern institutions were perfect; many were awful. The Hospital for the Insane in Augusta, for example, she described as "a terrible Receptacle, not a hospital . . . worthy of Georgia, and Georgian justice."[12] There was no shortage of work to be done. Seeking to begin fruitful cooperation with Southern legislatures, Dix was pleased to find that her name continued to open doors. Once inside, though, she found that Southerners were lukewarm to humanitarian arguments for prison and asylum reform. Since most Yankee and Quaker prison reformers were also active in the antislavery movement, Southerners suspected their intentions.[13] By the same token, though, they justified slavery on the grounds that unruly people should be disciplined for their own and society's good—a logic of coercion that could be extended to prison reform. Also, experience with the institution of slavery helped sell the idea that well-organized and well-managed penitentiaries were both more humane and cheaper than the alternatives. It did not take Dix long to understand why Southerners generally advocated the harsh Auburn system of prison discipline, with its emphasis

The vast Georgia State Sanitarium at Milledgeville.

on silent collective labor enforced by the lash, to say nothing of the obligation of prisoners to produce industrial goods to offset their upkeep. The slave states suffered from chronic labor shortages, and the notion of forcing miscreants into productive labor had terrific appeal.[14]

Having written a tract in favor of the separate system just a year earlier, Dix might have faced an awkward problem had she been unwilling to bend her ideas about prison organization to conform to Southern tolerances. But working alone, outside the empire of religious and voluntary associations she had known in the North, she was free to accommodate any aspects of Southern society and culture she wished.

In the fall of 1847, just at the point when she was beginning to think of hers as a truly national reform movement, Dix turned her attention to Tennessee. Like Kentucky and South Carolina, Tennessee had started work on its first state asylum in the 1830s, several years before she arrived on the scene. Each year, as part of the state budget, the asylum received some state money, though barely enough to meet its growing needs. In Dix's view, the legislature had paid too little attention to the defective hospital facility itself. A primitive stone structure with dank underground cells, it was, she insisted, "not fit for any human creature," much less people recovering from disease. Since 1840, the few improvements that had been made were disastrous. For instance, an expensive new furnace had proved a failure when, instead of warming the asylum, it filled the patients' rooms with noxious fumes.[15] A well-run lunatic hospital, Dix told the legislature, should function like a self-sufficient village; but they had created "no bakery, no meat house, no smoke-house, no ice-house, no corn-crib nor meal bin, no spring-house, milk-house, nor sheds for storing coal, wood, &c&c." The water system was unworkable and dangerous. Therapy, moreover, was a mockery. The dilapidated facility was dangerously understaffed, with a skeleton crew of three attendants trying to care for as many as seventy patients.[16]

Citing specific sections of the original asylum legislation, in lawyer-like fashion Dix told the state assembly that the new measure she was sponsoring went well beyond the statutes they had passed in 1839–40. She called for proper staffing (one attendant for every ten inmates), for exercise grounds, gardens, a library—in brief, for all the means to offer moral therapy that regularly graced the pages of the *American Journal of Insanity*. If the legislature wished to fulfill its moral responsibility "to secure the *greatest good for the greatest numbers*," she urged it to put up a single state institution to serve the curable and incurable insane. The place to begin was with a suitable site, she wrote, preferably one hundred to two hundred acres of arable land. It should lie just outside a city, "not too remote from the steam boat landings, and stage-coach offices" by which patients and visitors would arrive. With respect to construction, the state could economize by using brick instead of stone, by elevating the basement to ensure ventilation, and by installing hot air heaters instead of steam boilers. Windows were important for light and fresh air, but care was to be taken to disguise the bars. Nothing, she advised, should suggest "the *appearance* of a prison." Cleanliness being essential to treatment, there should be bathrooms on each floor. And the entire structure "should be so placed as that the sun's direct rays, at all seasons, may, during some portion of the day reach all occupied apartments."[17]

She went into great detail. Perhaps her specifications seemed tedious, Dix allowed, but the qualities and operations of an asylum's physical plant played a far more important role in the cure of madness than most people realized. Healing the mind required healing the body. And the apparatus of the lunatic hospital was designed to work from the outside in. In the absence of reliable drugs or procedures for working directly on the brain, she remarked, "we certainly do most wisely adopt all those rules of hygiene which modern science and intelligence supply."[18]

She did not include a survey of Tennessee's indigent population, its almshouses, and prisons. Beyond her prescriptions for the new asylum bill, she merely gave a boilerplate review of the march of medical progress in treating insanity, and the now customary recitals from medical superintendents around the country. Though there was little to distinguish the substance of the Tennessee *Memorial* from memorials Dix had written in other states, it was presented to the state government in dramatic circumstances and soon captured the imagination of all Nashville. Armed with letters of introduction to the governor, Dix persuaded him to call a special joint session of the legislature to hear her appeal. He agreed, and on a rainy November evening she was introduced by the governor to a packed audience in the old state capitol. According to one witness, "the spectacle of a woman addressing a public body was a novel one . . . and many of her auditors perhaps came with prejudices on that occasion." Every bit equal to the challenge, though, Dix soon dispelled all doubts. After her eloquent speech, building a hospital incorporating modern ideas of science and philanthropy seemed to the legislature so clearly justified that she was asked immediately to put pen to paper and, relying on her experience in other states, draft an appropriate law.[19]

This was heady business. Women were hardly supposed to understand the statute books, let alone write them. Dix settled into a commodious furnished apartment in Nashville's Sewanee House, for which she paid $8.75 per week. Confined to her room for several days by an attack of bronchitis, she still had enough energy to outline the legal path to a hospital through the state's legislative maze. At her request, the legislature ordered the printing of four thousand copies of her *Memorial* and arranged to send them to county courts, grand juries, justices of the peace, sheriffs, newspaper editors, and leading citizens throughout the state. Privately she expressed doubts about her prospects for success. But she could not help but relish her celebrity, influence, and ready invitations into the parlors and dining rooms of Tennessee's best homes.[20]

In January 1848, just before the legislature reconvened, a group of twenty-five of the city's most prominent ladies approached her with a flattering offer. To commemorate what they called her "disinterested & persevering philanthropy," they sought out a sculptor named Hall who had earned a regional reputation for his statues. Bronze figures in the statehouse and marble figures adorning family crypts in the local cemetery attested to his talents. With her permission, they proposed to commission a bust to pay her homage. It would take all his artistry, they suggested, to capture in stone her "countenance expressive at once of feminine delicacy, a heroic firmness, sensibility & strength, compassion & courage." Taken aback, Dix tactfully declined to sit for Mr. Hall, telling them that she would "rather to *dwell in your hearts*" than be immortalized in marble. It was not a woman's place, she said, to occupy a public pedestal between the likenesses of, say, a governor and speaker of the house.

> To us, women, it peculiarly belongs to reveal in its holiest aspects the spirituality of Religion; to bring consolation upon the troubled earth; to sanctify and perpetuate by our lives and through our actions remembrance of our existence which shall cause many to feel that the world is the *better* for our having lived therein.

Beneath this pious sentiment, Dix felt deeply ambivalent about receiving accolades for her accomplishments, because she understood that publicity brought with it vulnerability. Her role in politics, if scrutinized closely, could well have raised questions of propriety. In this instance the Nashville ladies unintentionally touched on the unusual combination of masculine and feminine qualities that she embodied. Indeed, they made special note of her heroic firmness, strength, and courage—not qualities conventionally associated with a lady. Dix undoubtedly saw this. She was extremely sensitive to any suggestion that her work diminished her femininity, for her image as the quintessential highborn lady was indispensable to her career. Thus she objected to being characterized, however benign the intent, as anything more (or less) than a lady; and she was at pains to remind the Nashville ladies that she was really no different from them. They all shared the same humanitarian aims, she said, and the same distinctly feminine obligations.[21]

On another level, Dix shrewdly saw that rejecting the token of honor they proffered was politically useful. Turning down the bust was an act of conspicuous self-denial, a way of reminding everyone of her position on the moral high ground. After this, who could accuse her of glory seeking? Her decision was made easier because the Nashville ladies tried to bestow a brand of recognition that she had long held in low regard. Secretly, she held a low opinion of the way most Victorian women, especially in the upper classes, spent their lives. Abhorrence of idleness was, since childhood, her obsession. But many of the ladies she encountered considered well-turned-out leisure as a fitting entitlement of their gender. They professed, in what Dix thought sheer self-delusion, to be terribly busy with managing their households. In the North as well as the South many of these women flaunted their complete ignorance of business, politics, and public policy as though these subjects were beneath them, too complicated or too worldly to deserve their attention. Such women, in their own view and in the opinion of most men, defined what has been called the cult of true womanhood. To the degree she found it useful, Dix wore the mantle of this cult, but she realized how little her life had to do with theirs. In this respect she stood far outside the mainstream of her own sex, even as she was held to embody its most noble ideals.

Meanwhile, the result of her working with men was to adopt many of their values. Several days after she rebuffed the Nashville ladies, their husbands approved a budget of $40,000 to purchase a site and begin planning a hospital for 250 patients in line with her specifications. In acknowledgement of her part in the process, the legislature passed a special resolution of thanks, proclaiming that "her disinterested benevolence, sublime charity and unmixed philanthropy, challenge alike the gratitude and admiration of our State." Printed on silk cloth and signed by the speakers of both houses, this resolution became a prized possession among her memorabilia. Later, when construction of the Central Hospital for the Insane at Nashville began, the legislature conferred upon her an even greater honor, which she also graciously accepted, setting apart a chamber for her use in the administrative wing of the asylum. She had no antipathy for the right sort of recognition: leaders honoring her concrete personal achievement.[22]

Dix's ambivalence was rooted in an ambivalence about being a woman in a man's world. In 1850 Sarah Josepha Hale, the well-known editor of a popular journal called *Godey's Ladies Book*, approached Dix for a biographical sketch of her life and work. Hale was compiling material for her encyclopedic *Woman's Record*, a collection of "Lives and Characters of Distinguished Women" from Cleopatra down to the present day, and planned to include Dix as a modern exemplar of female achievement. Hale was stunned by Dix's response. "Nothing could be undertaken which would give me more pain and serious annoyance," she retorted, "or more seriously interfere with the real usefulness of my mission." The whole idea of publicizing women, "however unblemished their lives, noble their aims, or successful their deeds," struck her as unsuited to "the delicacy and modesty which are the most attractive ornaments of their sex." At bottom her deeds and reputation were not personal accomplishments; they belonged to her country. She wanted no personal approbation for merely doing her duty. When Hale protested, arguing that she should think of her story in terms of its potential to "assist women to educate themselves to perform their own part in life," Dix insisted that even her name should be omitted from the book.[23]

Dix's thunderous reaction to Hale's innocent request was due, in part, to the fact that she did not consider her work distinctly feminine. Surveying jails and almshouses, writing memorials on insanity and lunacy policy, and lobbying legislatures—the essential activities of her career—did not conform to the received wisdom about woman's sphere. Aiming to carry out a mission for humankind, she had no wish to see her vocation diminished by being lumped together with what she considered the marginal accomplishments of Dolly Madison and Elizabeth Peabody, let alone a literary hack like Sarah Josepha Hale. Her reaction also included a bit of playacting, again intended to build her political capital. At a time when she was increasingly engaged in the masculine struggles of national politics, Dix saw a chance to reinforce her moral position and affirm her femininity. She lost no time in circulating her letters to Hale within her circle of Washington friends, who were duly impressed by her selflessness and modesty. In her view, she stood the best chance of preserving the integrity of her achievements and the moral force of her feminine identity by standing aloof, even from history's outstanding women. So she manipulated her status as a woman, using it implicitly to raise herself onto the high moral pedestal-women were supposed to occupy, but denying that she should be grouped with other distinguished women.

A counterpoint to this episode occurred when, traveling in east Florida, she received word that the trustees of the Massachusetts General Hospital wished to rename one of the McLean asylum's wards in her honor. Joseph Lee, a wealthy Boston merchant, had bequeathed more than $30,000 to the institution, and the trustees had intended to designate one of the hospital buildings with his family name when his heirs stepped forward and asked "to suggest the more appropriate name of *Dix*." She professed herself to be overwhelmed by the honor. "While I would avoid all distinctions of a personal character and retreat from notoriety," she replied, "I am myself profoundly moved and gratified, by this mark of esteem and appreciation of my efforts in behalf of . . . the insane." She accepted their recognition, though had someone suggested naming a female wing of the asylum for her, or putting her name on a female academy, in all likelihood she would have demurred."[25]

After her signal success in Tennessee, followed by a summer of frustrating stalemate in Washington after she had unveiled her first federal land bill, Dix decided to unfurl the banner of her cause in North Carolina. Throwing herself headlong into "ten weeks' most fatiguing journeys and labors," she seems on this occasion to have been motivated not only by her ambition to pass lunacy reform legislation in yet another state, but a renewed, almost prophetic, conviction that she was the voice for a silent and invisible constituency.[26]

The result was her North Carolina *Memorial*, the zenith of Dix's effort to present herself as the pure embodiment of her cause. The insane were people bereft of the ability or resources to mobilize and assert themselves within representative government, so she pronounced herself, a similarly powerless woman, their advocate. She beseeched the general assembly to look through her to see the underworld of faceless, suffering beings whom she represented. "I am the Hope of the poor crazed beings who pine in the cells, and stalls, and cages, and waste rooms of your poor-houses," she proclaimed in biblical cadences. "I am the Revelation of hundreds of wailing, suffering creatures."[27]

Each memorial she wrote touched on different aspects of madness, and what she revealed in North Carolina was a shocking propensity for the insane to engage in acts of random violence. The dangers of mixing lunatics and common lawbreakers in jails were illustrated with gruesome anecdotes including the images of an "insane murderer covered with gore, and exulting over the reeking remains of his victim," and a knife-wielding maniac slashing and almost decapitating his cell mate.[28] In Surry she saw a man who had threatened to murder his wife, and who expressed "an almost uncontrollable desire 'to see blood run.'" In Wilkes she came across a middle-aged woman who had used a large granite stone to beat her sleeping husband to death. Virtually all of the homicides she had seen were instances of domestic violence: husbands murdering their wives, parents abusing children, people suddenly turning on their closest friends. In seemingly innocent circumstances, she warned, insanity might leap out with deadly effect. "An insane man, left in the room where a little girl three years old was sleeping," she reported, "threw down the Bible which he was reading, seized an axe, and deliberately chopped the little victim into five pieces." Even if one lacked compassion for the insane, she implied, stories like these proved that lunatics were too dangerous to be left at large.[29]

Public safety was a different argument than human decency, but she tried to connect them by relating accounts of regeneration. Even the most violent, she suggested, could be reclaimed by asylum care. To this end, she told the story of a gentle and industrious man who was plunged into religious melancholy by the death of his mother. In a fit of furious madness, he killed one of his own children, along with a neighbor who tried to intervene. Committed to a hospital for the insane, though, he gradually recovered and was returned to society with no lasting effects from his disease. The best candidates for rapid recovery were men and women "whose minds have been cultivated, and who had habits of active industry and employment." For those with histories of immoderate behavior—drinking, using tobacco, even eating highly seasoned food—chances were decidedly slimmer.[30]

Using a rule of thumb alienists often applied in England and America, Dix estimated that the ratio of insane to sane people in the general population was about 1:1,000. This meant that there were at least twenty-two thousand insane out of a total United States population of twenty-two million. Rescuing this helpless minority, she wrote, ought to be viewed as a moral opportunity for the state. Adapting the words of the Gospel, she admonished the legislature, "As ye would that others should do for you in like circumstances, so do ye for these helpless ones." And she pointed out that her good news would not create an onerous financial burden. At the cost of "a few dollars and dimes, gathered from each citizen," the state could fulfill its moral obligation to the insane, which she likened to "*a particular rent charge upon the great family of mankind.*"[31]

Several North Carolina Whigs, who cared little about the asylum issue, conferred with Dix the day she finished her document and delivered a discouraging message. "They say, 'Nothing can be done here!'," she reported afterward, but her response had been to say, "'I know no such word in the vocabulary I adopt.'" Deciding that the Whig party was in disarray and would be useless, she carried a personal appeal to the state Democratic leadership. Interrupting a caucus meeting, pressing her *Memorial* into the hands of John W. Ellis, the majority leader in the lower house and a popular figure, she demanded that he read it and then present it to the full assembly. Turning to the whole delegation, she virtually ordered them "to sustain the motion this gentleman will make to print" the document and open the question to public debate. As she hoped, the motion was made and carried to print the *Memorial* and distribute twelve copies to each legislator. In the same session, a joint committee consisting of seven members from each branch of the legislature was appointed to meet with Dix to draft an asylum bill to be read before the general assembly before the end of the year.[32]

Following the pattern Dix had used in other states, the bill that emerged from the committee proposed to build and commence operations of an asylum. Naturally, it encapsulated the latest prescriptions for asylum building: a site of at least one hundred acres, a dependable supply of water, plentiful supplies of wood and coal, good drainage, sunlight, a modern kitchen and laundry, and elaborate apparatus for heating and ventilation. The trouble was the proposed cost of $100,000, an enormous sum equal to nearly half of the state's annual budget. No matter how they felt about the insane, neither Democrats nor Whigs saw political advantage in sponsoring a measure that would sharply spike the state's tax rate. Several lawmakers, unhappy with the whole business, openly questioned whether the Northern lady with the extravagant hospital scheme really knew her business. While her supporters managed to push through a joint resolution thanking her for her efforts in North Carolina, when the appriations measure reached the assembly floor, her asylum bill was soundly defeated. Unless she could invent an innovative funding scheme, hopes for the asylum proposal were doomed.[33]

At the eleventh hour, when she had all but given up hope, a leading member of the House of Commons, James C. Dobbin, breathed new life into the project by delivering an impassioned speech to the full legislature. During the previous month, while Dix had been Dobbin's houseguest, his wife, Louisa, had fallen gravely ill. Dix was drawn to the unfortunate woman. As her condition rapidly worsened, Dix did what she could to make her comfortable, quietly knitting seated in a rocking chair in the corner of her sickroom, giving her small words of encouragement and reading to her from the New Testament late into the night. But nothing seemed to slow the course of the disease. Toward the end, just before she died, Louisa Dobbin summoned her husband to her bedside and told him that it was his solemn duty to discharge her debt of gratitude to Miss Dix by doing whatever was in his power to pass her asylum bill. Dobbin, a loyal and chivalrous soul, appears to have been deeply moved by what his wife said. After several discussions with Dix, who accompanied him to his hometown of Fayetteville to help make arrangements for Louisa Dobbin's funeral, he decided to return to Raleigh before the end of the session and reopen debate on the asylum bill. The measure had been introduced on the floor of the legislature on 21 December 1848 while they were still in Fayetteville. Two days later Dobbin returned to Raleigh, demanding to speak on the issue. He was a celebrated orator, and when he walked onto the dais everyone in the chamber knew he had just returned from burying his wife. The heartrending oration that followed—many people called it the best speech he ever made—reduced his audience to tears. The emotional moment seemed to overwhelm all opposition, according to Dix, and the bill finally passed by a vote of 101 to 10.[34]

Compelling as this speech was, it is clear that the final passage of asylum legislation in North Carolina was largely a function of Dix's and Dobbin's proposal to reduce a special land tax and poll tax that had been the financing mechanism in earlier versions of the measure. The legislature, however much they were inclined toward Dix's humanitarian arguments, were not prepared to ask their constituents to bear any significant tax burden to pay for an asylum. So they finessed the financial issue by approving for an appropriation of only $7,000 in the next fiscal year. This modest sum, they reasoned, would be sufficient to select a site and draw up preliminary plans. If the work proceeded favorably, new appropriations would be forthcoming in the next budget cycle. The legislature was unwilling to underwrite the new Insane Asylum of North Carolina prospectively and tried to ensure that construction would move forward only on a pay-as-you-go basis, relying only on revenues specifically earmarked for that purpose. Underfunded from the start the hospital was perpetually a bone of contention, and was not completed until 1856.[35]

Despite the reduced allocation, Dix read the episode as a signal triumph. To Governor William A. Graham she predicted that his name, along with her bill's legislative sponsors, "would be associated with the cause after we have passed away." In her own case, at least, this turned out to be true, for at Graham's behest the legislature subsequently designated the site of the proposed asylum as "Dix Hill." A century later, their descendants would rename this institution the Dorothea Dix Hospital.[36]

At the end of 1848 she was, she told her friend Harriet Hare, "not well, though perfectly happy." An almost constant exhaustion, she believed, made her more vulnerable than most to the epidemics that coursed through the South with frightening regularity. "This year I had an attack of cholera on the Cumberland River, coming to Nashville from New Orleans," she later wrote to Elizabeth Rathbone, which made her "feel more than usually sensible that my own life was held by an increasingly slight tenure." But she could not doubt that her sacrifice was worth the price. "I leave North Carolina," she said, "compensated a thousand fold for all my labors by this great success."[37]

Between 1848 and 1853, as she spent an increasing amount of time in Washington, Dix returned regularly to her work with Southern legislatures and men of influence. Motion itself relieved her nervous energy, and journeys into the deep South were wonderfully exhausting. Traveling east to west, in one instance from Baltimore to Montgomery, was almost literally a contest of endurance. The staggering difficulty of a trip like this, in which she covered 1,100 miles in five days, was hard to convey to her friends. To reach the town of Marion, 105 miles west of Columbia, South Carolina, for example, she had to travel first to Charleston, "embark on a freight *flatboat* steamer, drawing two and a half feet water, put to sea (in fine weather), run for the mouth of the Pedee river and ascend till Marion is reached, for *positively, except* on *foot*, there is no other way of reaching that part of the state." To journey 105 miles as the crow flies required a serpentine route of 510 miles, and "this is no quick time," she added, since she had to avoid "the night air on the river as a pestilence."[38]

Travel in the South was an ordeal everywhere but on the Mississippi. In New Orleans she could board a magnificent sternwheeler like the famous *Missouri*, 306 feet long with seven boilers, outfitted with mahogany furniture, a piano, and the finest Brussels carpets, and watch from her stateroom as the country changed from sugar plantations, to cotton, to hemp and tobacco, and at last on a northward journey to minerals, lead, and iron. In contrast, Southern railroads, her preferred means of transportation, were slow, unreliable, and astonishingly disconnected. Many of her destinations—New Orleans and Montgomery, Alabama; Mobile and Jackson, Mississippi—had no railroad connections at all. Thus she found herself patching together trains, steamboats, and horse-drawn carriages in a land where cities set their own time zones, and schedules notoriously changed without notice. Since people were unaccustomed to a lady traveling alone, Dix's mastery of transportation added to her mystique.[39]

In her first sweep through the lower part of the Cotton Kingdom in 1848, Dix was warmly received in New Orleans. The spectacle of the city—its burial grounds, its enormous slave auctions, its French market teeming with a mixture of races—was like nothing she had ever seen. Standing on the vast levee, with its endless string of ships and steamboats, she had the sense of having stepped into another world. But she did not allow her sense of wonder to distract her from her business. Quickly getting her bearings, she used letters of introduction from her network of Southern influentials to set up meetings with local planters, legislators, and physicians.

With the blessing of the city fathers, who gave her a written pass to present in case local functionaries were suspicious, she set about touring the city's institutions for criminals, the homeless, the aged, and the insane. Mentally disordered paupers were supposed to be cared for in a separate building on the grounds of the New Orleans Charity Hospital, a sprawling omnibus facility that was part almshouse and part asylum. In 1847 the state legislature, unhappy with reports of crowding and abuse of the insane, had voted to build a separate state lunatic asylum near

Jackson, Louisiana, some thirty miles outside Baton Rouge, the state capital. Dix visited the new facility shortly after it opened, and privately told Thomas Kirkbride that she was appalled by its poor organization and how its architects had utterly ignored new theories of light and ventilation. The heavy, moist air that flowed off the Gulf seemed to bring a pervasive miasma. The last time she had seen so many insects had been in the Virgin Islands. Here mosquito nets draped the beds, but the patients were too deranged to make use of them and in consequence suffered terribly. Yellow fever was endemic. The legislature was proud of its accomplishment, however, and Dix withheld criticism. They were not about to tear down what they had just built at great expense. Looking to say something positive, she publicly praised its bucolic setting. Amid the magnolia, holly, and pine, she wrote, "flowering plants and shrubs diffuse an agreeable perfume, while . . . the eye is charmed by the beauty and variety of these vegetable productions." After a few weeks, miserable in the humidity and convinced that she could have greater impact elsewhere, she decided to leave Louisiana, she told Kirkbride, content to meet with the city council and board of health to recommend changes in the workhouse, a library for the prison, and "more fit provision for the fever patients in the City Hospitals."[40]

When she returned to the deep South in 1849, Dix chose to focus her energies in Alabama, where, during her first passage through the state the year before, the *Mobile Register and Journal* had waxed effusive on the moral grandeur of her mission. Lest anyone suspect that she was just another Yankee reformer (and probably mixed up with antislavery), the paper pointed out that "she is connected with no society. . . . She is in fact alone—relying for success upon the strength of her cause, the good sense and justice of the public, and her own unwearying spirit of self-sacrifice."[41]

Alabama, overwhelmingly rural and agricultural, had, up until Dix's visit, given little thought to the state's insane population. Rather than make her way through every county as she had done elsewhere, Dix simply stitched together a compendium of incidents and testimony she had used in other states. This made her Alabama *Memorial* her least original work. But to most of her readers her facts and arguments, even if they did not involve local abuses, rang true. Like their neighbors in other states, they knew of cells and outbuildings where isolated lunatics were kept. To drum up public support for building a state institution, Dix published excerpts of her memorial in local newspapers. But this was largely a symbolic exercise, for she had privately solicited the support of the governor, the president of the senate, and the speaker of the house before the document was written. When the motion to print two thousand copies was introduced in the legislature, wrote Dix, it passed "without a dissenting voice or vote!" By now, though, she expected state funding of her proposed asylum to come grudgingly, if at all. To make matters worse, most of the assembly consisted of freshmen who had been swept into office after a series of financial debacles and political scandals had soured voters on the incumbents. Only sixteen of one hundred legislators had been returned to office in the lower house. Unsurprisingly, they feared any new tax measure. Thus she would have to "combat 84 in the popular body whose interest it is to oppose me."[42]

As the holiday season approached, she lost herself in her work. In effect she served as staff to a legislative select committee, single-handedly drafting a hospital bill, lobbying the committee members to win over their colleagues before the question came to a formal vote. Naturally everyone agreed that taxes were already too high, declared one Senator Stewart, just as they agreed that the family, not an institution swarming with employees on the state payroll, was the best place to care for the insane. But Dix had illuminated a different side of the issue, he continued. She had demonstrated that the homeless insane represented "a moral obligation resting on the State . . . which she cannot evade, and which she ought not if she could." Jesus had told his followers, "as ye do unto the least of these, so ye do also unto me," words that she applied to those in Alabama too poor and too disordered to care for themselves. Were not the mad, Dix asked, precisely those defenseless children whose treatment was evidence of Christian charity? How could Alabama afford not to make an investment in civic virtue? Putting pencil to paper, one of Stewart's colleagues calculated that $100,000 over five years, divided by the numbers of citizens in the state, worked out to just twenty-five cents per person. "This class mindless, but not soulless," he adjured, "has claims upon us which cannot be neglected."[43]

During the period set for debate, the bill's prospects, fueled by Dix's moral argument, brightened. But before her measure could be presented, the state capitol caught fire and burned to the ground. Records, documentation, draft statutes were destroyed. Confusion reigned for months. Since the structure was uninsured, everyone knew that rebuilding the statehouse would place a heavy burden on Alabama taxpayers. Even before the fire Dix had been reluctant to get her hopes up because there were so many regional and party disagreements among lawmakers. Afterward, with a state asylum seeming a very low priority, she estimated that her Alabama bill had "just one chance in a hundred." In exasperation she complained that politics resembled "the gambling table—or any games of chance" in which one's prospects for success swung according to "unlooked for and often trivial balances." Once her present work was completed, she resolved, "I shall certainly not suffer myself to engage in any Legislative affairs for a year."[44]

This was not a resolution she copuld keep.

She could not resist returning to the state when a coalition of doctors, ministers, justices of the peace, and judges wrote her a letter formally asking her to survey Alabama and suggest how they should provide for the insane poor. Dix, busy with projects in several other states and in Washington, recalled that in England Parliament had from time to time asked local officials to inspect institutions within their purview and send their finding to London. So she asked the president of the state medical society to send out circulars to physicians in every county asking for their help in identifying cases of insanity. She also contacted county sheriffs, religious denominations—especially the Methodists, whose itinerant circuit riders had firsthand knowledge of how the lower orders lived, including those who were insane, even in the remotest parts of the state. She prevailed on editors of Whig and Democratic papers in most of the larger population centers to publish "information respecting Hospitals for the Insane" in order that "the subject [be] kept before the public till the next biennial session of the Legislature."[45]

Building on the framework of Dix's *Memorial*, in December 1850 the Medical Association of the State of Alabama pulled together the findings of its survey into an exhaustive petition of its own. An energetic Mobile physician, Dr. A. Lopez, assembled more than sixteen thousand pages of evidence, replete with a history of insanity and asylums from ancient times, arranged to have it printed in eight volumes, and, at the beginning of the 1851–52 legislative session, laid copies of the document on each lawmaker's desk. Confronted with this evidence, the legislature finally drew up an asylum bill, settled on a site, and appropriated $100,000 for construction of a two-hundred–bed hospital. When this proved insufficient, Lopez, struggling in Dix's absence to keep the project on track, talked the legislature into increasing its original investment to $175,000, and, when the budget was vetoed by an unsympathetic new governor, to override him. Over the next several years, while construction on the facility continued, the Alabama Insane Hospital regularly overspent its budget. Its advocates were caught in a constant fiscal tug of war between the governor and the legislature, and it was not opened until the beginning of the Civil War.[46]

"These back and forth journeys are terrible," Dix complained as she tried to keep pace with sessions of legislatures simultaneously in South Carolina, Tennessee, Pennsylvania, and Louisiana. Across several states, she confided to Anne Heath, she was asking for "more than a third of a million *dollars*; and may perhaps get it all."[47]

When she turned her attention to Mississippi, she met a prominent gentleman, one J. O. King, aboard a steamboat out of New Orleans. There was something about her manner so "remarkably dignified," he recalled, that he impulsively invited Dix to his house to spend a few days with his family. No sooner had she arrived than she had King and his wife accompanying her to county jails in search of insane inmates. At her request, he invited the leading citizens of his town to meet her in his parlor. There she clearly and eloquently explained her mission. Using King's home as her base, she took field trips in a one-horse buggy, visiting each county in the region, talking to people and making careful

State Asylum for the Insane at Tuscaloosa.

notes of cases of insanity. Personal comfort meant nothing to her. When they explored the back country, Dix thought nothing of sharing a small room with three young children. And her facts, collected at first hand, served her well. In Lewiston, challenged by a physician who said that it would be the height of folly for a state $14 million in debt to build a hospital for seventy lunatics, Dix retorted that she herself had already counted three hundred. "It was her practice to greet people kindly that she met and present them with some little book or tract," King wrote. Every morning, before she started out, Dix read aloud a chapter from the New Testament and one of the Psalms. King's brother, who accompanied her for part of her journey, admiringly remarked that "it seemed to him [he had] never heard the Scriptures before."[48]

A year and a half before Dix entered Mississippi, the state legislature had passed the original bill to found a state mental institution. Only $10,000 had been appropriated, however, an amount so pitifully inadequate that Dix assumed the lawmakers must simply have been ignorant of how much a modern hospital cost.[49] When she returned from the field after gathering information about the scope of insanity in the state, she could be found seated at an enormous oak table in the state capitol library, poring over scores of annual reports, folio statute books, and transcripts of debates within the assembly. She aimed to prove how expensive it was to build an asylum, and to justify the expense, showing good reasons why states continued to pump money into institutions for capital improvements. Many times a day she was interrupted by members of the legislature to whom she preached "the noble privilege of ameliorating the suffering of the unfortunate." As word of her worthy projected spread, even the local clergy temporarily put aside its denominational rivalries to unify behind her plan.[50]

Since her main goal was education, the Mississippi *Memorial* was a primer in asylum construction costs and the principles for efficient operations. While a hospital should never be expected to make money for the state, Dix cautioned, once it was up and running it should be able to meet its operating budget. Agriculture, along with modest industrial activities like woodcraft and sewing, she liked to point out, contributed to patients' recoveries and produced quantities of cash crops and dry goods that could be sold on the open market. People recuperated as part of a process that prepared them to rejoin the economy. Even so, Mississippians were foolish to imagine that a hospital could be built cheaply. At least $80,000 would be needed to get the project off the ground. Her scrutiny of state documents revealed that the state asylum commissioners had already used the original $10,000 allocation to buy 140 acres outside Jackson. Her job, she decided, was to push through a bill to pay for a building and staff.[51]

Her principal tactic was an appeal to state pride. How long, she asked, would Mississippi allow its humanitarianism to be outstripped by its neighbors? With surprising ease lawmakers proclaimed themselves willing to incorporate the most modern improvements into the new asylum. They designated $50,000 for the new Mississippi Lunatic Asylum, the full amount she had requested. In just four weeks she had been able to pass an asylum bill and, for good measure, to convince the legislature to rebuild the penitentiary. With a copy of the legislature's resolution of thanks in hand, she pronounced herself "quite satisfied," and boarded the Mississippi steamer, *America*, to begin the long trip back to Washington.[52]

Curiously enough, in her Southern sojourn the one aspect of Southern life she loathed was, above all as she put it, the pervasive "*smoking, chewing, snuffing*, and . . . that most disgusting, injurious, and obnoxious practise [*sic*] of *dipping*" tobacco. The Methodist Episcopal Conference convened while she was in Mississippi; and at the invitation of the presiding bishop, she dashed off a *Memorial on the Use of Tobacco*. Speaking as an expert on insanity, she asserted that beyond its messy "*outward, palpable* results," tobacco had invisible effects. For it worked on "that delicate and sensitive organ . . . the *brain*." Sometimes the assault was swift and fatal. More often, though, tobacco was a slow poison, its evil spreading internally so that victims seldom suspected the underlying cause of "palsy, epilepsy, palpitation of the heart, apoplexy, organic lesions," and a variety of other maladies. Every asylum had inmates, she contended, "whose insanity has been traced directly to the use of Tobacco alone." Citing dozens of authorities to support her position, Dix called on the clergy to carry her message to the countryside.[53]

Much as she felt that using tobacco was a nasty habit, this unusual memorial held a deeper and more personal meaning for Dix. The daughter of an intemperate Methodist minister (a personal detail she kept to herself), she warned the assembled circuit riders that the original purity and self-sacrificing spirit of their Methodist forefathers like Wesley and Whitefield was being corrupted by intemperance. It was thus incumbent on clergymen, she insisted, to set an upright example in their own lives by avoiding low habits and immoderation. "The

Teacher, though he speak with the tongue of angels," she admonished the conference, "if he have not control over his own habits" was certain to do more evil than good.[54] It was of course the failure of example that most disturbed her memories of Joseph Dix, an eloquent preacher who was never able to master his baser appetites. So her antitobacco memorial—a sort of lay sermon to the traveling clergy—was in part a veiled lamentation for her father.

Rounding out Dix's conquest of the South was her work in the state of Maryland. There were close social and economic interrelationships between Maryland's agrarian elite and upper-class merchants in Philadelphia and New York, and Baltimore was conveniently connected by rail to middle-Atlantic mercantile centers. During the 1830s and 1840s Dix had made dozens of trips through the state, usually staying with a socially prominent Unitarian minister named George Washington Burnap. Through Burnap she had been introduced in to the Baltimore reform community, and met R. S. Stewart, who had been working with the city's indigent insane for a generation. By 1851 she had come to believe, as she told Kirkbride, that "things are in a bad way in Maryland." In November of that year Stewart spoke to Dix of his frustration in trying to raise philanthropic support for a new hospital. Experience elsewhere had taught her that private charity could never raise enough money to build and operate a state hospital. But she welcomed Stewart's enthusiasm, hoping that it could be put to use to bring the asylum question to the attention of the governor and state assembly.[55]

After a brief survey of Maryland, Dix swiftly composed what was to be her last state petition. She reviewed the history of the state's mental institutions: the establishment of Baltimore's public hospital in 1797, its complicated evolution into the Maryland Hospital, the Sisters of Charity Mt. Hope Hospital, and the Baltimore almshouse and penitentiary. This growth was largely unplanned. As a result, Maryland's institutions were inadequate to cope with the spiraling increase in the rate of insanity over the past decade. Comparing the Census of 1840 with the newly released Census of 1850, Dix pointed out that while the state's general population had risen from 470,019 to 583,035 (a 24 percent increase), the insane population had jumped from 550 to 946 (a 72 percent increase). She looked to the peculiar composition of Maryland society to explain what was happening.

The most notable difference between Maryland and most other

Southern states Dix had surveyed was that in Maryland slavery was on
the decline and the state was home to a large free black population. In
practice, while they were not officially slaves, they were not really free
either. In 1832 the legislature had proscribed people of color from vot-
ing, from holding public office, and from serving on juries. Frederick
Douglass liked to remind his Northern audiences about Maryland's
vagrancy statutes: laws that paid county sheriffs to capture unemployed
blacks and auction them off for a year's involuntary servitude. To rid
the state of free blacks, many Marylanders (including Dix's old Quaker
friend Moses Shepard) actively supported the idea of transporting them
back to Africa. Beginning in the 1830s, the Maryland Colonization
Society raised hundreds of thousands of dollars toward this end.

Dix, like many other reformers, felt that unless free black people
were removed, there was no way to control racial mixing. She had been
thoroughly disgusted by rampant miscegenation when she visited the
Virgin Islands in the early 1830s; and she was no less disturbed by the
idea in 1850. Indeed, she now viewed it as a source of pathology, suggesting that "the *wickedness and ill-consequences of the intermarriage of blood-
relations*" was a particularly vicious "cause of cerebral disease." Racial
mixing created a miasma of moral depravity, an atmosphere in which
even prudent people could lose their bearings and drift into madness.
"No truth in ethics is more surely established," she claimed, than the
principle that every human being, "whether high or low degree, strong
or weak, learned or unlearned . . . but is vulnerable to the attacks of
maniacal insanity."[56] To support her point, she noted that only 63 of
Maryland's lunatics were of foreign birth, 96 were slaves, and 104 were
free blacks. The remainder were white Anglo-Americans, she said,
many of them between fifteen and twenty-five years old, "evidently
belonging to middle and higher walks of life."[57]

With this in mind, she stressed the importance of early institutionalization to cure insanity in young people. And again she emphasized the
importance of rendering the incurable at least comfortable. Because
many legislators were worried that any expenditure to help the insane
would prove unpopular among their constituents, she devoted one-
third of her *Memorial* to economy. "It is not *occupation* alone," she
wrote, "but *useful employment*, that so eminently assists other remedial
moral means of the restoration of the patient."[58] When she was told
that the state was simply too deep in debt to finance an institution, Dix,

undaunted, argued that the economics of a properly managed asylum would soon lighten the state's funding burden.[59]

The Maryland *Memorial* was presented on February 24, and three months later, after extensive lobbying and committee work to shape the asylum bill, Dix rejoiced that her "Maryland Hospital Bill has passed— $100,000 prospectively[;] $10,000 in hand to begin this summer." But as in other Southern states, it was a partial and incomplete victory, because $100,000 would not go very far. Before the end of the year the men entrusted with building the new asylum, who had themselves grossly underestimated its cost, were back before the legislature to ask for more money. The $5,000 appropriation for a 100-acre site, they protested, would force them to locate the asylum on the outskirts of Baltimore, unduly remote from transportation and services. This was a likely prescription for failure. Dix remained nonetheless optimistic. She had learned from practical experience that, once started, major hospital construction projects took on lives of their own. As she expected, Maryland's state asylum proved to be no exception.[60]

"I have marked on the map of the United States with a cross thus *x* points where I have had hospitals built," she proudly wrote Elizabeth Rathbone in England, "and a double cross where I have had additions to old hospitals equivalent to previous accommodations." Her marks covered Trenton and Harrisburg, where she had been the driving force, as well as states like Alabama and Missouri, where her presence served mainly to raise public consciousness. Wary as she was of publicity, in private she exulted over her role in reshaping the institutional geography of her native land. Confident that God had used her as his instrument to accomplish so much so rapidly, she now had the self-possession to storm the main gate of the United States government.

CHAPTER TEN

Slavery and the Limits of a Moral Vision

The inexorable fact of Southern life, as every politician from Thomas Jefferson to Abraham Lincoln realized, was its peculiar institution: slavery. Dix knew this too; and yet, during all the time she spent in the South—against what would seem to have been undeniable evidence—she turned her back on the prejudice, hate, and violence of the slave system. She screened it out so thoroughly that, while she traveled as extensively throughout the antebellum South as any Northerner, one finds no description of slavery in her private papers or published writings. For her, the black slaves seem barely to have existed.

When she first entered the South, Dix, always sensitive to the attitudes and prejudices of the elite, was careful not to offend Southern sensibilities. Not that she actively suppressed criticism of how blacks were treated out of obligation to her hosts; she simply saw little to criticize. In contrast to the horror stories she had heard in the North, she was pleasantly surprised to find a quite different scene than the stereotype of plantations and slave gangs presided over by a decadent planter aristocracy pictured by Northern newspapers. The more she came to know Southern society, in fact, the more she doubted that the North occupied the moral high ground its intelligentsia and politicians took for granted. In fact, she shared the values of the Southern elite. She shared their contempt for laissez-faire capitalism, their suspicion of individualism in Northern society, and she liked their gentility and affectation of English manners. Clearly the South was not the evil empire its critics depicted, Dix mused, so perhaps the North had things backward and "the slave states really are in advance of us when the charities of life are called into exercise?"[1]

If Dix was drawn to the South, it is nonetheless surprising that Southerners responded so favorably to her. During the antebellum period, social reforms of the sort she sponsored were generally on the wane. Moreover, even if Northerners, alarmed by urbanization, immigration, industrialization, and other vexing social conditions occasionally described the asylum as a mechanism of social control, in states like Alabama and Mississippi these problems simply did not exist. The slave states never construed Dix's message as an answer to the problem of social disorder. For during the antebellum period their socioeconomic hierarchy was remarkably stable. Controlled at the top by a wealthy, politically powerful planter elite, the Southern social order was firmly secured at the bottom by the institution of chattel slavery. Founded on the quintessential system of social domination, a predominantly rural, agricultural Southern society scarcely needed expensive penitentiaries or state lunatic asylums to stabilize itself.

Nor was the South especially responsive to the professional aims of physicians and asylum superintendents. Even larger Southern cities like Charleston, Atlanta, and New Orleans were comparative backwaters when it came to the theory and practice of treating mental disease. Well into the era of Reconstruction, Southern asylum doctors played only supporting roles within the Association of Asylum Superintendents. The picture of the American asylum movement as a program of social control led by a powerful new breed of entrepreneurial doctors has little to do with the reality of Southern life.[2]

Yet Southerners were exquisitely sensitive to the moral dimension of Dix's message. It was her overarching moral argument—presented in her memorials, published in local newspaper articles, and argued eloquently from the statehouse floor—that won them over. Oddly and unexpectedly, her message presented then an opportunity. Under mounting pressure from Northern and Southern critics of slavery to justify the labor system that formed the socioeconomic bulwark of their society, by the late 1840s Southern political leaders were grasping at straws. Since they professed to honor the Declaration of Independence and the Constitution, they were at pains to prove that, slavery notwithstanding, they were humane states, organized on natural principles of racial hierarchy, whose social institutions worked to the good of all. In no uncertain terms, Dix offered Southern leaders a chance to demonstrate their compassion, to confirm their humanitarianism.

There she was, a Northern saint, the leading authority on treatment of the mad, the homeless, and the prisoner, proposing that insanity—not slavery—posed the greatest moral threat to society. When she urged that the insane be treated compassionately, and that compassion could be applied scientifically within the modern asylum, she invited the Southern states to affirm their morality and progressiveness. As soon as they grasped the startling fact that antislavery was not Dix's concealed agenda—indeed, that she tacitly accepted slavery—they eagerly espoused her mission.

She, in turn, was gratified by her warm reception. In December 1859, even as the likelihood of a war over slavery approached certainty, Dix wrote from Columbia, South Carolina, about having been "greeted and welcomed on all sides by private friends and public authorities." One state senator in a telling statement promised her on behalf of his colleagues, "We will prove our regard for you by our acts in behalf of those for whom you plead." This was political symbolism, since helping Dorothea Dix automatically conferred an aura of humanitarian integrity.[3] Thus a citizen of Jackson, Mississippi, scanning the front page of the *Weekly Southron* in 1850, might have seen a column headed "Attention is called to the sale of twenty negroes belonging to the State," alongside a story applauding Dix as a "noble hearted philanthropist and accomplished lady." The paper's editors, commenting on her state asylum bill, noted that "while it will prove a blessing to that unfortunate class, [the insane]" on a loftier level her hospital "will serve as a monument to the liberality of the State, and the humanity of the people at whose expense it will be built."[4]

Human equality, particularly racial equality, had never been part of Dix's vision. The moral imperative that the black slaves should be free was lost on her because she did not accord them the same degree of dignity that she accorded her own race. Even so, her deliberate avoidance of the slavery question raises questions about the limitations of her mental and moral approach not only to blacks but to those dependent classes in whose welfare she was most actively interested. Of a woman so thoroughly inspired by moral conviction, one must ask why the dictates of her conscience moved her to speak out boldly on asylums and prisons, yet evaporated when they confronted the most profound and bitterly divisive moral issue of her century.

First, it is important to remember that American slavery and the moral problems surrounding it look, in retrospect, far simpler in the late twentieth century than they appeared to Dix and her contemporaries in the mid-nineteenth.

Unlike the monolithic slave power painted by abolitionists, the real South, Dix discovered when she first toured Kentucky, was a patchwork quilt of subregions. These were remarkably diverse in agricultural base, social organization, and culture. Broadly speaking, slaveholders were a minority. No more than a quarter of the white population owned slaves, and most of these owned fewer than ten. Large plantations with slave gangs were the exception. Yet the contour of Southern politics and social policy, even in the border states, tended to be shaped by the elite planter class. In her work, Dix focused on state lawmakers, and it was the planters and large slaveholders who constituted state legislatures in the 1840s and 1850s, as well as making up their states' congressional delegations. In the South, as elsewhere, land and money were the raw ingredients of political power. And the nonslaveholder majority was willing to defer to the wealthy, educated slaveholder elite only so long as they remained convinced that any shift in power threatened the republican order of their world. So this was a world that depended on a delicate balance of deference and compulsion. As far as the majority of white voters were concerned, the continuing success of the South's privileged leaders depended on their demonstrating that they were indeed the proper guardians of society.[5]

Dix started her Southern crusade in Kentucky, a border state far from the center of the Cotton Kingdom. In the majority of its forty-four counties, she discovered, slavery was of marginal interest to the entrepreneurial traders and small-time farmers who, after seven years of economic depression, were experiencing an unprecedented boom. In 1845 black slaves represented about one-fifth of the state's population, but they were heavily concentrated in the agricultural Bluegrass region, a diagonal belt running southwestward from Lexington to Bowling Green. With the influx of white settlers during the Jacksonian period, slaves had actually been declining as a percentage of the state population for two decades. Kentucky provided her introduction to slavery, yet the state's comparative whiteness enabled Dix to overlook the black population in a way that would have been impossible in the deep South.[6]

It was, moreover, a moderate state populated by moderate people, many of whom expected slavery gradually to wither away in the natural course of social and economic progress. Dix's asylum work was founded on progressive assumptions: a faith that America was moving steadily toward toward a more perfect vision of its ideals. When she addressed the legislature in her Kentucky petition on prisons, she expressed her shared confidence that in Kentucky "*progress, advancement*, and rectitude, are in the ascendant." Too often, people gazed "steadily and anxiously upon the shadows, rather than upon the lights of the picture," she said, and failed to realize that "the shadows are dispersing, and the lights breaking into fuller radiance." No matter that in Washington the extension of slavery was being pushed on the territories by some of the nation's most powerful leaders. Believing, as many Southerners did, that in time slavery would somehow fade away as part of the process of enlightenment, Dix chose to look on the bright side. Her survey of Kentucky and what she saw of black slaves there did nothing to shake her faith in progress.[7]

Finding so much that was pleasant, even admirable, in Southern society, Dix regretted that the attitudes of Northern writers and politicians were so glaringly prejudiced and misinformed. Well read in the literature of atrocity, she thought the abolitionist press dismayingly irresponsible. Frederick Douglass's accounts, constantly repeated in antislavery tracts, of black women whipped until the "warm red blood came dripping on the floor" served, she felt, to do nothing except to excite passions, and thus aggravate sectional discord. She despised what she called "the company of young sentimentalists, nor *ultra-abolitionists*." She attributed much of the responsibility for the slavery controversy to power-hungry politicians from both sides. "I have no patience and no sympathy either with northern [*sic*] abolitionists or Southern agitators," she told Heath with unusual asperity. "I am quite sure that neither the one nor the other party would willingly see the question of Slavery determined[,] as in that case they would lose the whole political capital which they possess, or are likely to command."[8]

For most moderate Northerners, disunion was the worst imaginable result of the slavery controversy. Dix shared this fear, but because she did not feel strongly about the issue, she could not believe that the Union was in serious jeopardy. One result of her status as an outsider in the sectional debate was that she was constantly surprised at how seriously politicians seemed to take slavery.

When Dix visited Francis Lieber in Charleston in 1851, for example, she was shocked to see how far down the road to secession the Palmetto state had traveled. At the time, South Carolina was buzzing about the Southern convention and the secessionist conspiracy of 1850–51, eliciting her remark that "the delusion of the citizens seems fairly to entitle them to be classed with the insane." She saw no possibility that any state could hold its own against the might of the federal government, but she sadly acknowledged that people were "possessed with the most ultra and heathenish notions of *honour*, and will plunge into the gulf when they only look to stand on the pinnacle of Fame." Through the 1850s, nevertheless, she sloughed off portents of disaster. When the wife of a wealthy planter fretted to her about the fulminations of Robert Barnwell Rhett, the state's most uncompromising secessionist, Dix assured the woman that he was "weak as a puny infant to disturb the Union."[9]

Blind to the moral dimension of the conflict over slavery, she slipped into traps formed by her own prejudices. The country's sectional turmoil she saw not as a struggle over principle but as the machination of "political demagogues," Northern abolitionists, and Southern fire eaters who stirred up the masses. She expressed shock that "the most insulting papers are secretly gotten into [South Carolina] and circulated." Abolitionism only hardened Southern resistance and diverted people of good hope from the incremental reform that conscience would inevitably lead them to adopt. In addition, she felt personally endangered. To this end she related an incident in which an abolitionist in Ableville "managed to get up a conspiracy amongst the negroes—who have been urged to assassinate their Masters' families indiscriminately." At the last moment, someone in the house in which she was staying got wind of the plot. It was "really wonderful," she exclaimed, "that I got forward unmolested *under these* circumstances." The worst thing about the episode, she said, was that "the instigator had fled, leaving his poor ignorant tools to suffer for what he ought to pay a severe penalty."[10]

This was hardly an unusual point of view. Many Northern leaders, including Presidents Millard Fillmore and James Buchanan, loathed the antislavery vanguard and would have agreed with Dix's assertion that "people have serious ground of complaint against the unjustifiable proceedings of northern unprincipled abolitionists." Even Abraham Lincoln, who during the same period called slavery "an unqualified evil to the negro, the white man and the State," also maintained that "the promulgation of abolitionist doctrines tends rather to increase than abate its evils."[11]

The pressures of partisan politics eventually forced many Northern antiabolitionists into the antislavery camp. But Dix could choose her own political battles. Up to the day Fort Sumter fell, she chose to remain aloof. Indeed, when the Supreme Court in early 1857 announced its incendiary Dred Scott decision, she expressed her hope that it "shall prove as designed, a quietus to all political wranglers on the Slave question." Even as late as 1859, in Charleston, the citadel of secession, she could say with astonishing equanimity that "the Abolition fever seems declining, and Southern Citizens may have time to improve the condition of the Negro population, if not disturbed by indiscreet Northern interference."[12]

In the South, perhaps more than anywhere else, being a lady made it easier for Dix both to speak boldly about lunacy and to equivocate on slavery. The political scientist Francis Lieber told her that "with the firmness, courage and persevering strength of a male mind, you unite the advantage of a woman." Because of the Southern code of chivalry, he observed, a lady would not arouse the kind of political opposition a man would have encountered. "No one can suspect you of ambitious party views." One Southern jailkeeper, learning of a letter Dix had written to the governor criticizing his ability, expressed this code of chivalry more bluntly. "If a man had said what Miss Dix had [said]," he fumed, "he would shoot her."[13]

Northern men were under constant pressure to declare their positions on the slavery question. But Dix, standing outside parties and outside the formal channels of American politics, did not have to declare herself. When necessary, she could conveniently plead that a woman had no business getting involved in party politics. It was possible for her to finesse her position on this critical issue in a way that would have been impossible for any other political figure. No one dared press a lady to step over the line.

At the same time, within her own immediate circle, Dix looked on with dismay as her old friends, Samuel Gridley Howe and Horace

Mann notably among them, each struggled long and painfully with his stand on slavery. Howe, reticent and reluctant to be distracted from his experiments with deaf-mutes, tried in vain to sidestep the issue. But he could not avoid it. In 1834, the radical abolitionist William Lloyd Garrison had attacked him for refusing to admit a black girl to the Perkins Institution, and continued to snipe at him for years in the pages of the *Liberator*. During the fiery controversy over admitting Texas to the Union, Howe was unable to straddle the fence any longer and finally, in the fall of 1846, publicly announced his antislavery stand. And he paid a high price, going down to defeat in a hopeless effort to unseat the Whig leader Robert C. Winthrop.[14]

From the mid-1830s, Horace Mann also had sought to avoid the political perils of antislavery. For more than a decade he hung back, fearing that the Garrisonians, with their single-minded demand for immediate emancipation, would splinter the Massachusetts reform community into rival factions, and very likely deprive him of his political base. Not until 1848, when he campaigned for John Quincy Adams's old seat in the United States House of Representatives, did Mann publicly seek to reconcile his conscience with the conflicting demands of his constituency. Prodded by Charles Sumner, for whom antislavery was not merely a position but a calling, in 1849 Mann finally declared himself. That year he delivered before the House his celebrated broadside against the constitutionality of slavery in the District of Columbia.[15]

After the Civil War, in the cool light of retrospect, most Northern politicians liked to remember how early they had joined the antislavery cause and taken their place on the side of the angels. Yet many had done so not out of conscience but because they had had no choice. The example Dix saw in the moral odysseys of her two oldest political allies was one of temporizing, followed by taking a clear position on slavery only when it became politically untenable to do anything else.

Despite her Methodist childhood and Unitarian adulthood, and despite her deep admiration for the Rathbones, paragons of the English antislavery movement, Dix continued to rank the evil of slavery low. She could not imagine placing slavery on the same plane as madness. In varying degrees, other antebellum reformers in the North concluded that the underlying principles of their programs included conceptions of human rights that extended ineluctably to blacks; and even Dix's memorials themselves reverberated with the language of human rights. Constantly she beseeched those in power to remember "the bond of our common humanity," and to use the law to dispense justice on behalf of the powerless. But where madness posed an imminent threat that demanded an urgent response, she submitted, chattel slavery could be tolerated while it gradually succumbed to the forces of social progress.[16]

Ironically, her uncompromising demand for immediate and decisive use of state power to effect lunacy reform closely resembles the immediatism of the radical abolitionists. If there was one antebellum reformer whose attitude, methods, and sheer passion could be compared to hers, it was William Lloyd Garrison himself. Dix used the same arguments on behalf of the insane poor that abolitionists used to condemn slavery. In her accounts of lunatics, Dix spoke passionately of how thoughtless and brutal treatment degraded the image of God in man, destroying self-respect and potential for self-management. Adopting the structure of the abolitionists' arguments, Dix maintained that the poor and the criminal were victimized by their environment, and she hammered at illiteracy and the need for moral instruction to redeem them. So too she described how madness broke up families, leaving lunatics friendless and cut off from their loved ones. In her 1848 *Memorial* to Congress and elsewhere, she lamented the common local practice of selling the insane at auction to whoever would contract for their upkeep at the lowest rate, a practice sure to expose its victims "to the tender mercies of the most worthless of society." These, of course, were the persistent themes of antislavery. In thousands of pamphlets, books, and newspaper columns, abolitionists capitalized on the pathetic image of black families torn apart by callous slaveholders.

Dix's failure to connect the rights of society's deviants—the poor, the criminal, and the insane—and the rights of all other people, black and white, worked in the long term to her disadvantage. Fixed on the narrow institutional attributes of the prison and the asylum, she accepted a self-imposed isolation from the broader currents of liberal democratic thought that transformed men like Howe and Mann.

Yet Dix turned her back on slavery not only because she was preoccupied with reforming prisons and creating asylums, convinced that the slightest hint of abolitionist sentiment would destroy her standing with Southern whites, but for the more basic reason that she did not identify with the slaves. When she traveled to England in 1854, free from any Southern political exigencies, she castigated Harriet Beecher Stowe for spreading "the most absurd and often mistaken notions of America and American life." Asked for her own thoughts, Dix wrote, "the slavery question I positively ignore."[17] Blacks did not interest her. The insane did. That fierce concentration of moral vision and willpower that enabled her to fight for the human rights of lunatics and prisoners deserted her when it came to blacks.

From her early days in the Caribbean with Channing, she had assumed that dark-skinned peoples were somehow inferior beings. Later she continued to think of the Southern blacks she saw as "gay, obliging, and anything but miserable," while privately she expressed contempt for these "thoughtless and impossible" inferiors. In a private letter to her brother, written from Raleigh, North Carolina, she ridiculed the thick dialect she heard from a slave at the post office who helped her with her mail: "Missus got all mail 'spect—Pos'-massa tink lady do good heap ob bussiness [sic] for Uncle Sam—take missis heap of time to read all these." This was not a sympathetic caricature. When her friend Millard Fillmore in 1854 asked her advice on traveling in the South, she offered to procure a slave for him if he wanted a reliable ser-vant. Thus in the 1850s, increasingly well regarded in the milieu of Southern legislators and the planter class, her racial views calcified.[18]

In keeping with generally accepted theories of mental disorder in her day, she argued that the South clearly had a lower incidence of insanity than the North because "the negro and the Indian rarely become sub-ject to the malady." Lunacy was a disease of "civilized and cultivated life, and of sections and communities whose nervous energies are most roused and nourished."[19] Africans were a backward race, predisposed to idleness and generally unmotivated toward discipline, self-culture, and higher moral aspirations. Slavery was the most orderly, most humane system for ensuring their health, happiness, and, above all, their productivity. The failure of British emancipation in the West Indies, she believed, had recently illustrated the dangers of liberating people who were unprepared for freedom.[20]

Her assumptions about blacks led Dix to conclude that the racial organization of the South was necessary, if not entirely benign. Strange-ly enough, apologists for slavery might readily have pointed to evidence within Dix's own publications to demonstrate that enslaved blacks were materially better off than Northern wage slaves. Proslavery writers like George Fitzhugh claimed that black slaves were well fed, well housed, well supplied with medical care when they needed it, and well exposed to religious instruction. They liked to lay out tables of statistics showing the per capita consumption of cereal, vegetables, and meat among slaves, as though this were proof of the slaves' happiness. To Dix's way of thinking, this method of measuring a human being's condition was plausible. She had used it herself to evaluate prisons, almshouses, and asylums. Accordingly, she told one asylum superintendent, "I suspect that even now in New York, Connecticut, Ohio, Pennsylvania, and in Massachusetts there is more actual suffering at present than in all other States beside."[21]

The picture of society that emerged from her memorials and letters closely resembled the Northern moral and economic jungle painted by proslavery writers. From Boston to Philadelphia, in almshouses and prisons she had encountered alarming numbers of free blacks, people who appeared even less well-equipped to cope with the ruthlessly competitive economy of the North than working-class Irish and German immigrants. With her vast experience among Northern paupers, prisoners, and madmen—with the castoffs of the free society of the North—Dix was more ready than were most Northern reformers to tolerate coercive measures to control backward racial groups. Having little enough faith in the inherent moral capacities of the white population, she could not imagine what would become of four million black slaves, in whom inner discipline and respect for moral order had never been inculcated, if the national institution of racial control were suddenly removed. Dix never went so far as to sanction chattel slavery, yet so deeply had she come to admire order that she had no room for conflicting doubts about liberty.[22]

The supreme irony in her toleration of slavery lay in her inability to see the psychological and human damage it wrought. More perceptive antislavery writers realized, as the diarist George Templeton Strong put it, that slavery entailed "the systematic murder, not of the physical, but of the moral and intellectual being; blasphemy, not in word, but in systematic action against the Spirit of God which dwells in the souls of men to elevate, purify and ennoble them." In short, slavery forced upon its victims a kind of madness. One former slave described his years of involuntary servitude as "the graveyard of the mind," a state that necessitated mental vacancy in order to survive it.[23] Because Dix, like so many of her contemporaries in both sections of the country, could not see that a black was a person like her, she overlooked the pervasive moral insanity around her.

As the national debate over slavery progressed toward its violent conclusion, Dix carried her campaign to the South, finally deciding in

1847–48 to move to Washington. There she could travel easily to Virginia, North Carolina, Tennessee, and other Southern states as opportunities to further her cause presented themselves. But the moralist who had set out from Boston five years before was, through her immersion in their world, coming in one critical aspect to resemble the politicians she distrusted. She was becoming a pragmatist. For all its rhetoric about liberty and justice, Dix's plea on behalf of the insane poor had became an argument for a tighter, more rational method of incarceration than the haphazard system of jails, almshouses, and family care that had existed in the past. Her dream of unchaining the lunatic insane had become not a dream to set them free but to transport them to a perfect confinement—an asylum under the supervision of medical professionals.

In 1843, in Massachusetts, she had made her public debut with an emotional, evangelical plea to lift up and save the fallen insane. Five years later, while she continued to use religious phrases, she was shifting her emphasis away from the plight of individual people toward the utilitarian and cost-benefit aspects of hospital care. Little by little she was exchanging the romantic language of the heart for the practical language of political economy.

As it so often does, the shift in language betrays a deeper change in sensibility. By 1850, she all but stopped writing about the sufferings of individual men, women, and children in any kind of detail, concentrating her attention instead on the mechanics of prisons, asylums, and, most of all, the purely political and professional processes of creating and managing new institutions. In her transcendent belief in the goodness of these institutions, she lost some sense of human scale. Her failure to include blacks in her grand scheme, even as the Civil War approached, shows how restrictive her conception of human rights had become.

❦

CHAPTER ELEVEN

"I bask in court favor"

When she first arrived in Washington in the spring of 1847 Dorothea Dix, forty-five years old, vibrant with the energy of her success, was approaching the height of her powers. No letters of introduction were needed to confirm her reputation as a woman of extraordinary intelligence, talent, and moral determination. It took little effort to attract attention; now people sought her out. Her legislative accomplishments in the North and South had given her political seasoning and practical experience working the machinery of government unique among women of her era. And she had widespread grassroots support as well. In fewer than five years she had built a national following. After much prayerful reflection, she wrote, she had decided to go to the seat of the national government because she was prepared to chart a new course for "objects and aims [that] now reach the length and breadth of the union."[1]

Important as she considered her ongoing state and local campaigns, they paled in the dawning brightness of a new vision, a cause that would gradually become the supreme goal of her ambition and eventually bring her to the climactic moment of her career. For the next seven years Dix would pursue, with desperate intensity, an heroic struggle to commit the resources of the federal government to the welfare of the indigent insane.

Hers was a singular vision. Even as General Winfield Scott marched into Mexico, capturing Vera Cruz and Mexico City, Dix described her dream of an American nation that achieved its manifest destiny not through commercial enterprise, territorial expansion, or military con-

Dorothea Dix in 1846. (By permission of the Houghton Library, Harvard University.)

quest but by meeting the deep moral obligation to make decent provision for its most disadvantaged citizens. This conception of government's role, she realized, was contrary to popular opinion. During the Jacksonian period it became clear to her that, unlike the English, Americans had little enthusiasm for centralizing power within the general government. Washington was expected to foster the country's economy, not define and manage its social welfare. Nevertheless, precisely because of the unevenness of her experience with state legislatures, she came to believe that her submerged constituency of the mad constituted a truly national problem that demanded a federal solution. Not incidentally, she felt that properly addressing it offered a perfect opportunity for America to live up to its founding principles of justice and equality.[2]

To her way of thinking, a national policy of lunacy reform need not be a radical innovation. Indeed, it seemed merely a logical, and necessary, extension of the work she had already started in several states. Unschooled in the vagaries of national politics and the fundamental differences between federal and state government, she did not foresee that a federal scheme would inevitably raise underlying issues of the constitutional rights, responsibilities, and proper limits of the national government's authority. Dix, despite her natural instincts and well-honed political skills, had little appreciation for political theory and no feeling for congressional debates about federalism and states' rights.

While her insensitivity to the larger themes of national politics stemmed partly from her single-issue agenda, in forming her national agenda Dix was strongly influenced by events on the other side of the Atlantic.

She remained a persistent student of British reform. She kept up a steady correspondence with her old friends in Liverpool, who applauded her work from afar. As her publications became known to the British lunacy reform community, its leaders made sure to send her their books, pamphlets, and annual reports. Meanwhile, beginning in 1844, the *American Journal of Insanity* regularly featured summaries of British reports, as well as firsthand accounts of American asylum superintendents' travels to the Old World. There was no shortage of information. Thus she had followed the development of Poor Law policies and watched with keen interest as a national system of state-financed institutions for the mentally disordered took shape in England and

Wales. This system was well entrenched by the time she reached Washington. In reviewing its course, she was struck by the fact that, beginning in 1807, when a House of Commons Select Committee completed the first survey and census of the insane in Britain, Parliament itself guided lunacy reform. In fact, up until the 1840s the House of Commons and its various select committees performed in England a role quite similar to the one Dix tried single-handedly to play in America. Parliament, of course, enjoyed an overwhelming advantage: it could write the law of the land. For example, in 1844 the English Metropolitan Commission initiated legislation requiring counties to establish public asylums. Dix considered this action a landmark in advancing state responsibility for the insane.[3]

In short, just as English institutions like the York Retreat had presented the model for the first generation of American asylums, Dix reasoned, the British government's aggressive national asylum program could be imported into the United States.

Her innocent faith that Congress and the president could be persuaded to enact a national welfare scheme for homeless lunatics flowed from a mistaken presumption that the American and British legislatures were comparable institutions. She assumed that they could be made to function in similar ways to effect domestic policy. Moreover, her experience with state assemblies—American legislative bodies that did facilitate the growth of institutions like schools, prisons, and asylums—misled her when it came to understanding Washington. Since the nation's capital was in the 1840s and 1850s a small, unprepossessing city, it was easy for her to think that it operated more or less like the state capitals with which she was so familiar. To be sure, there were attempts at magnificence. The grand domed Capitol, restored after the fire of 1814 by Benjamin Henry Latrobe and, later, Charles Bullfinch, commanding the brow of Jenkins' Hill, she thought oddly isolated, rising out of the thick forest like a Greek temple in the wilderness. Boston and Philadelphia were, on balance, far more impressive. So her impressions and experience conspired to make her misconstrue the federal government as more provincial, more manageable and, paradoxically, far more powerful, than it actually was.

In the smaller arena of statehouse politics, Dix was accustomed to identifying a handful of key legislators, enlisting them in her cause, and using their power as a channel for her own influence. With this tried-and-true strategy in mind, she found her initial reception in Washington encouraging. "Fortunately I bask in court favor," she remarked in May shortly after her arrival. "Mr. Polk is all attention." Her presence in the corridors of power elicited no untoward comment. During the Jacksonian period, women flocked to the Capitol. One Washington hostess, for example, described the Senate Chamber as it filled up before the 1830 Webster-Hayne debate, "every seat, every inch of ground, even the steps were *compactly* filled, and yet not space enough for the ladies—the Senators were obliged to relinquish their chairs of State to the fair auditors who literally sat in the Senate." In 1835 the Senate resolved to reserve one-third of the red-draped semicircular gallery exclusively for ladies. This prompted one highborn woman to remark that "our government is becoming every day more and more democratic, the rulers of the people are truly their servants and among those rulers women are gaining more than their share of power." If, as some said, a woman's status in Washington depended on how frequently she was seen in the halls of Congress, Dix occupied a high rung indeed.[4]

She remained scrupulously nonpartisan, most congressmen claimed to hold a high opinion of her mission, and it seemed to her that she shared "the good-will pretty equally of Democrats and Whigs." Ironically she thought that if there were any weak spots in her network of political support, they would be "opposition from the New England Delegations." Her native region was a bastion of abolitionism, she knew, and its politicians were so riven by factional rivalries within the Whig party that they seemed to have no interest or sympathy for any important national issue. Even if she failed to win them over, she believed she could succeed without their support. Clearly, lunacy reform on the federal level was a lofty goal, but God and science alike were on her side. Once she laid out the raw facts of human misery and showed how a national welfare could put an end to untold suffering, how could Congress not vote for a plan that would obviously work for the good of all?[5]

The unhappy answer, she quickly discovered, was slavery and the violent sectional strife it spawned. The period 1846–50 saw an unprecedented deadlock as partisan political maneuvering brought government action to a standstill. After several months in the capital, the scales fell from her eyes and Dix's estimation of the federal government sank. Day after day, John Calhoun stood on the Senate floor and introduced resolutions affirming the right of any American citizen to take slaves into any territory of the United States. Until the Compromise of

1850, this question of slavery in the territories wrought a bitter paralysis in Washington. The more clearly she grasped the government's predicament, the more Dix denigrated lawmakers. Given "so much apathy and so strange want of a consistent and wise policy," she wrote, who could expect Congress to solve the Country's problems?[6]

Perplexed about how to proceed and needing a break from the sweltering Washington summer, Dix accepted Sarah Gibbs's invitation to escape to the cool tranquility of Oakland, Rhode Island. This was supposed to be an interlude, a time for relaxing and cultivating the private side of her personality with trusted friends. But in her room in the old seaside mansion, shadowed by the ghost of William Ellery Channing, she was ill at ease. Politics preyed constantly on her mind. "The peculiar duties and obligations associated with extended public objects," she complained, kept crowding out meditation and personal intercourse. When Anne Heath, in an attempt to rekindle their old friendship, admiringly asked her to share "something more about how you obtained the strength within," Dix was too preoccupied to respond. She had succeeded in losing herself in her work almost to the point of being empty of anything else.[7]

The only diversion Dix allowed herself as she planned the first stage of her federal campaign was a brief correspondence with Laura Bridgman, a young deaf-blind girl who had been painstakingly educated by Samuel Gridley Howe. To nineteenth-century Americans, Laura Bridgman was a symbol—as Helen Keller was a century later—exemplifying the power of enlightened educational techniques and their capacity to transform seemingly hopeless cases. Her letters to Dix, written in a fine, neat hand, combined childish naïveté and insight. For example, she extolled Dix's "sacrifices to do good to the poor crazy so they all love you." For her part, Dix, in describing how this young girl had found the strength to overcome such severe handicaps, unconsciously drew a parallel between Laura Bridgman's triumphs over suffering and her own. But where Dix was restless, she admired Bridgman's serenity. "The thought of God's presence and love," she wrote, "occurring in moments of irritation and discontent, has soothed her into placid peace and content." The following year, as she composed her first federal memorial, Dix took time out to draft a brief "Memorial in behalf of the Blind and the Deaf and Dumb." But she did not want to press their claims herself. Instead she handed it to Horace Mann, suggesting that he surface it in the House of Representatives. Dix told him that she did not want this issue, important as it was, to distract Congress from her main work. For reasons of political focus, she "could not combine the claims of the uneducated Blind etc." with the completely different needs of the insane.[8]

She possessed the gift, extremely useful in lobbying a cause through a fractious legislature, of singleminded focus. She was determined to pursue her crusade and to ignore most of the great political issues of the day. So on the one hand, she could privately express dismay over the Mexican War, remarking in disgust that "it has surely disgraced our country long enough." On the other, she could share the elation of her "southern and western friends" over the territorial expansion created by the Treaty of Guadalupe Hidalgo. Not infrequently her assessment of politics and political figures tended toward gossip. As the election of 1848 neared, for example, she told her brother, Joseph, that Henry Clay, who was reputed to be something of a rake, was incompetent for anything beyond being "President of a *kissing* association."[9] Her hazy impression of the larger, outstanding national controversies of the late 1840s was an image of stormy political crisis brewing not just in Washington but in all of nature. "The world universal is sorely tossed in civil as in physical conditions[,] strifes and rumors of War," she warned in apocalyptic tones, "while cyclones, floods[,] conflagrations, earthquakes, & volcanic fires rule the earth with fearfully destructive power."[10]

Against this backdrop of impending disorder, Dix began to gather material for a memorial to the general government, a document intended to make Congress see the plight of the indigent insane not as an inevitable, if unfortunate, blot on the American landscape but as a crisis threatening the health of the body politic.

Specifically, she meant to prove that however rapidly the American population was growing, insanity was galloping at an even faster pace. The epidemic was spreading. Her starting point was to pull together the most reliable data she could find for the numbers of insane in the United States over the past few decades, then calculate these numbers as percentages of the country's total population. This was not hard to do. Since its inception, the *American Journal of Insanity* had regularly published estimates.[11] But sloppy methods combined with the problem of defining who should and should not be classified as insane tended to raise doubts about the accuracy of these estimates. In response to her query about the number of insane, McLean superintendent Luther Bell soberly advised Dix that "the statistics are all mere guesses, except the [1840] United States Census, which was an aggregation of fraud and blunders." Using a ratio that was commonplace in England, he estimated that there was one lunatic or idiot for every thousand white citizens. Although many of these had mild or transient disorders, he said, fully one of three was either dangerous enough or helpless enough to need hospitalization. When he went on to apply his formula to the American population, however, Bell proceeded to make a careless mathematical blunder. In a population "say of 15 millions of whites," he wrote, "that is 150,000 insane." Not realizing that he was off by a factor of 10 and that the number should have been 15,000, he calculated that one-third of the insane—"50,000 white citizens"—stood in need of asylum care. According to reports from his fellow superintendents, he knew there were fewer than 4,500 people presently in mental institutions around the country. With just "one-twelfth of your lunatics provided for," he exclaimed, "my dear Miss Dix, you have got work enough for twenty lives instead of one." Dix, taking Bell's arithmetic at face value, repeated his mistake in her published petition. She asserted that "*about eleven twelfths of all the insane who absolutely require fostering and remedial care are wholly unprovided for in this country.*" It was an egregious and embarrassing slip, because this error in a basic premise of her argument would lead careful readers to wonder whether or not other data were grossly exaggerated as well.[12]

In any event, Dix's first congressional petition, *Memorial of D. L. Dix, Praying A grant of land for the relief and support of the indigent curable and incurable insane in the United States,* was printed on 17 June, 1848. She would vouch for the facts it contained, she confided to Harriet Hare, but feared that "as a literary effort it is open . . . to severe criticism." A nasty bout of influenza had kept her from putting forth her best effort.[13]

In essence, she argued that madness was a social disease, a by-product of modernity. The recent histories of America and Europe demonstrated beyond a doubt that the incidence of madness rose with the refinement of civilization. Countries with "the largest civil and religious liberty," whose citizens freely competed for wealth or "high literary and scholastic attainments," were in greatest jeopardy. Indeed, she warned, "statesmen, politicians, and merchants, are peculiarly liable to insanity." Religious freedom, which often led to uncontrollable religious enthusiasm, was another source of peril. She was certain, as were most of the asylum doctors, that "the Millerite delusions prepared large numbers for our hospitals." Because it was often a disease of nervous excitement, Dix argued, insanity disproportionately afflicted the educated and "the highest classes of society." Fortunately these were people who, in the throes of madness, at least possessed means to protect themselves from "the grossest exposures and most cruel sufferings." The "toiling millions," however, had little recourse but the almshouse.[14]

The American lunacy epidemic was, she claimed, not exceptional. It was typical of the spread of insanity experienced in advancing nations. France, Canada, and especially Britain, she reported, had all seen similar trends in the growth of their lunatic populations. She cited Sir Andrew Halliday's 1829 *Report on the Number of Lunatics and Idiots in England and Wales*, which claimed that insanity in Britain had tripled in twenty years.[15]

Having sketched the dimensions of the issue, Dix plunged into a lengthy state-by-state catalogue of atrocities. Most of the examples she cited were taken from earlier memorials. She selected the most shocking stories, images intended to stick in the legislators' minds: a madman in Maine who *"tore out his eyes"*; a woman in New Hampshire confined so long in a low cage that "she grew double" and was reduced to walking on all fours"; the horrible Simmons case in Rhode Island. By the time she was finished, few states were unscathed. On the positive side of the ledger, she touted the miraculous cures and marvelous cost efficiencies being reported by asylum superintendents. She also emphasized, however, that *"cure* alone, manifestly, is not the sole object of hospital care." Of great, if not equal, importance was to make the incurable comfortable and as useful to society as they could possibly be.[16]

As she had done in the states, Dix based her crusade on the premise that morality made economic sense. The asylum, in effect, promised something for nothing: savings from cured patients who no longer needed to be maintained at public expense would more than make up for the initial capital and operating costs of institutions. And she could cite detailed evidence from lunatic hospitals around the country in support of this rationale.

But why was this any business of the federal government? Dix knew from the outset that her strongest opposition would come from those who argued for leaving it to the states to fashion their own welfare policies and finance their own institutions according to their tastes and means. She believed, however, that her survey proved conclusively in this case that the states had shirked their duty. Also, the national government had established precedents for assisting states "in the accomplishment of great moral obligations" by granting land to colleges and to two institutions for the deaf and dumb in Hartford, Connecticut, and Danville, Kentucky. It should do no less for the mad. Now, she argued, Congress had a chance to rise above sectional interests and enact a law that promised equal benefits "for the east and for the west, for the north and for the south." Legislators were admonished to put aside their parochialism and remember that they were representatives of the whole nation, obliged to "contribute to the moral elevation and true dignity of a great people." In the race among nations, she announced with rhetorical flourish, America would ultimately establish its preeminence not through territorial expansion "or mere physical prosperity" but rather through the exercise of "incorruptible integrity and justice." These principles, she maintained, were the only true foundations of national greatness. Through the mysterious workings of divine providence, Dix concluded, the insane were intended to be "*wards of the nation*," their affliction representing both a personal tragedy and a test of civic virtue. Henceforth, ignorance would no longer serve as an excuse. Now that she had broadcast their plight, the United States would have to provide for the insane if it wished to confirm its manifesto of moral hegemony.[17]

Trading on her relationships with senators from states in which she had already demonstrated her political clout—senators like John Bell from Tennessee and Gerrit Davis from Kentucky—Dix was welcomed into the Senate chamber. Often, when they were in session, she sat in the gallery, where, owing to the room's small size and excellent acoustics, she could hear every whisper. She liked the semicircular chamber with its ornamented dome, its Ionic columns, its walls with fluted draperies hanging between marble pilasters, its rows of platformed armchairs and mahogany senators' desks. Despite the increasingly rancorous tone of debate—not to mention the spittoons adorning every desk in the chamber—the Senate sought to retain a formal, aristocratic atmosphere. Dix relished their decorum. Most senators arrived dressed in dark, swallowtail coats, though she once saw Daniel Webster sporting a blue coat, blue pantaloons, and a buff vest. Dressed in dark silk and a starched white collars, she felt at home in the Senate. The senators seemed naturally to recognize this and welcome her participation without hesitation. But, after all, this was a body comfortable carrying on debate while a group of Cherokee chiefs stood in their midst watching Senator Sam Houston, attired in his panther-hide waistcoat, purple and blue serape, flaming-red vest, and sombrero, whittle miniature wooden hearts from pine logs and send them to women in the upper gallery. And Dix herself had by now seen enough of life to take such things in stride.[18]

As soon as her petition was completed in late June 1848, the Senate, rather than assigning Dix's petition to one of its standing committees, appointed a select committee to study it and, if feasible, draft an appropriate legislative response. Dix was asked for her recommendations on the committee's membership. At her request, Missouri's Thomas Hart Benton consented to serve as its chairman and to formally introduce her memorial to the Senate. Once Benton had time to ponder the implications of Dix's demands for federal land, however, he decided to distance himself from her. The evening before he was due to introduce her report, Benton was stricken by a politically convenient illness. At the last minute, Dix's petition was presented instead by New York Senator John Adams Dix (no relation to Dorothea).[19]

Surprised and gratified by how receptive political leaders seemed to be to her ideas, she at first anticipated enough support to be able to push through not just one but two bills before Congress adjourned: "one asking for 5 million [acres] of the public surveyed lands for the curable and incurable, indigent insane, and the other . . . for 2 million for the Blind and Deaf and Dumb." On her most recent visit to Boston, Charles Sumner, a brilliant young lawyer who was then battling to win his first election to the House of Representatives, advised her that in Washington it was always better to ask for too much than for too little. With Providence blessing her and her cause with increasing popularity, she told her friends, she was determined to strike while the iron was hot.[20]

In mid-July 1848, meeting daily with members of the select committee, Dix labored strenuously to hammer an acceptable bill into shape. The result was an ambitious measure that boldly designated at first five and then ten million acres of the public domain as a special reserve that could be gradually sold off to finance "a perpetual fund for the care of the indigent insane." Cash, she reasoned, was perpetually hard to come by, but land was plentiful and cheap. The value of the national domain was unknown; indeed, there was no basis for estimating it. Carving out a portion of this vast common asset would not add one dollar to the federal budget. And, logically speaking, if the insane were the nation's providential burden, the public lands could be thought of as a commensurate national treasure that might justly be tapped for their relief. She made these arguments a dozen times a day to committee members as she caught them on the Capitol steps, cornered them in the hallways, and stood over their desks in the Senate chamber. One by one they offered to help her. On 21 July 1848 she reported that "the whole committee, even the impracticable Colonel Benton, concurred in my 5,000,000 acre bill." It was reported out of committee that morning and read on the Senate floor.[21]

The problem, she knew from experience, was that her special committee had been handpicked. Getting a majority in the full Senate would require her to engage a much broader set of prejudices and objections. Thus she continued to feel that the support expressed in the halls of Congress could easily slip through her fingers. And although she was on good terms with President Polk and his wife, having been introduced to the first couple by family friends in Tennessee and North Carolina, and believed that Vice President George M. Dallas was "warmly in favor of the bill," she also suspected that the administration might well pose an obstacle to her initiative. Not long before, Polk had threatened automatically to veto any land bill that, like hers, omitted provisional payments to the federal government. Most worrisome of all, the House of Representatives was to her largely terra incognita. Ruled far more than the Senate by Northern and Western men, it remained unpredictable. Parties and alliances changed like quicksilver. Even before a House version of her bill was introduced, she fretted that "the new Democratic movement in the Northern States has threatened the safety of the whole measure." With political alignments shifting apace, few legislators were entirely reliable allies.

Concerned about her measure, Dix did not allow herself to grow discouraged. When she heard rumors that Benton was waffling, for example, she decided that it was best to confront the senator directly and settle his position on the lunacy bill once and for all. Because he had been effusive in his support for the measure, she decided Benton had no right to change his mind. During their meeting he was eager to soften his position and, according to Dix's account of it, "put me off with promises to do for *me* all that was feasible under the circumstances." Stubbornly she refused to let him off the hook. She reminded the senator that she had not come to ask even the smallest favor for herself. He was a Democrat, was he not, who professed "to support the interests of the people, the multitude, the poor?" Her lunacy bill would give him the chance to practice what he preached. "Reject this measure," she exclaimed, and "you trample on the rights of the poor, you crush them; sustain it, and their blessings shall echo round your pillow when the angel of the last hour comes to call you to the other life of action in progress." At the end of the interview, as Dix described their meeting, a chastened Benton sighed, "My dear Miss Dix, I will do all I can!"[22]

It turned out that he could do very little. For his days in the Senate were numbered. Unlike Dix, Benton—a unionist on the verge of being ousted from Congress by a coalition of Missouri Whig and Democrat disunionists—quickly saw the ideological and political significance of the land she asked for. Adopting any federal land policy would strengthen the hand of the federal government and thus strengthen the Union. Because she overlooked the gravity of the sectional conflict over slavery, Dix continued to think of land not in terms of its political meaning but simply as a cheap national resource. Dismissing all other explanations, she was convinced that those who opposed her could do so only out of ignorance or selfish interests. So when her bill, failing to fit into any group's broader legislative agenda, languished in committee debates, she immediately blamed "the Southern Democrats" with their seemingly disingenuous "cry of 'the Constitution must be preserved inviolable,'" or the equally obstinate "new States men," who did not want portions of their lands to fall into the hands of the more populous old states. Dix had been warned that on every issue of consequence sectional and party preferences defined the boundaries of political possibility in Washington. Up until now, though, she had thought of these divisions as ephemeral and had been confident that they would evaporate in the heat of moral principle. As the weeks and months passed, she clung to her belief in the righteousness of her cause, yet she found herself wondering whether anyone in Washington could carry the battle of principle over politics.[23]

"Miss Dix is here laboring with all her might," wrote Horace Mann from the House of Representatives in the winter of 1849 to his wife, "but it is a matter of doubt where she will accomplish any thing during this session." Amazed at what she had been able to achieve in six years, though, Mann was of a mind to vote for anything she wanted. Dix knew she could count on him. She also knew that, in regard to her bill, his congressional colleagues were distracted and divided. In January, Washington was preparing for the presidential inauguration of Zachary Tay-

lor, a Louisiana Whig, a war hero, and a large slaveholder. While the
city buzzed with speculation about the new administration, Dix wondered whether she was wasting her time. Cynical about the intractable
sectional crisis of the late 1840s, she remarked that "the members [of
Congress] are in general a good deal more occupied with party politics
than . . . the duties of Statesmanship."[24]

Juggling legislation, asylum construction projects, and professional
politics in several states, Dix consciously tried to adopt an aura of neu-
trality whenever she was in Washington. Acutely sensitive to the difficulty of building a coalition to support her bill without touching off
regional hostilities, she resented it when the papers branded her proposed as the product of a "Massachusetts citizen." In too many minds
Massachusetts was a code word for abolitionism, a movement she
despised. "I scarcely think I can be called of Massachusetts," she insisted, "where for eight years I have not resided."[25]

Meanwhile, when a member of the Pennsylvania legislature brought
up the idea that she might "procure the adoption of a joint resolution
of our legislature instructing our senators & representatives to support
the measure," Dix demurred. Drawing on the advice of her Washington friends, she concluded that it would be a mistake to force legislation through "interposition of the State legislatures." The states could
agree on nothing, and she feared that a state-based process would
polarize her bill. As she saw it, a principle binding together the common good of all states was at stake. To accomplish this goal she preferred to take her chances with the "'uninstructed' deliberations and
acts of the two branches of Congress." In other words, she tried to
sidestep political organizations, placing trust only in herself to build a
coalition across party lines.[26]

While she impatiently waited for congressional actions, Dix managed
to acquire perquisites unusual even for an elected official. These included a private committee room in the capitol library to use as her office
and "a little good-tempered lad [who] is my page and attendant." In the
most hierarchical and status-conscious city in America, she told her
brother that she enjoyed "all the advantages any one can possess here in
relation to social position and public fame." Yet the thrill of being a
woman of influence at the center of power was offset by her perpetual
disgust with the ignoble realities of political life. Much of the time
Washington was for her an unpleasant place. In public and in private she
saw a pervasive masculine crudeness, a brutal cynicism about power,

and a moral climate that grew unrelievedly depressing. Knowing all the inside gossip concerning "the private characters and habits . . . of our most prominent statesmen," she was convinced that the new president—whom she sarcastically called the "great and good man"—could not possibly form an able cabinet "from the class of active politicians."[27]

The sustained assault on her idealism through the spring of 1849 darkened her mood. Whenever she visited the capital, her correspondence slackened, and what few letters she did write were gloomy. In a typical passage, she described herself to Horace Mann as "dragging a weary way through unmeasurable depths of mind, and bathed in the steadily falling rain."[28]

Her letter basket held a plaintive appeal from Anne Heath, to whom Dix tended to confide her bouts of depression, begging her to quit public life and join her back in Brookline. With Dix's work in the South completed, "this house is the place for you now," Heath wrote. "I feel the need of you, even more than at any time in my life." But entreaties like this, suggesting that Dix should abandon her vocation, served only to stiffen her resolve. Much as she harbored fantasies of intimacy and mutual affection with others, Dix dreaded inactivity and the prospect of her own uselessness. What she craved, she confided to her brother, was not to abandon her work but simply to receive some parental concern for what she was going through. She told him, "I rest upon your affections as a tired child, worn with its exertions[,] casts itself confidingly, and without apprehension on a parent's care,—resting there without fear and doubt." She had pushed self-denial to its psychological limit. Her exhausting work in asylums and exhilarating involvement in politics satisfied her intellect and her objective sense of duty. But nothing banished her deep emotional isolation.[29]

Her sense of isolation was compounded in Washington because she was excluded not only from formal participation in government but, perhaps more important, from most of the informal interactions among politicians. Public speeches rarely changed anyone's vote. In reality, she saw that bills were amended in the cloakroom before they reached committee, and that the private deals and alliances legislators hatched over bottles of Madeira in the boardinghouses of Washington set the ultimate course of legislation. Political success depended on one's fund of relationships. So realizing she could not join them at the whist table, Dix made, in her own way, strenuous efforts to cultivate friendships with lawmakers. In doing so she not only relied on her considerable intelligence and charm; she also learned to confer what might be called moral patronage. This was a lesson she learned in the South. By enrolling themselves in her mission, politicians were privileged to work for a cause of pure virtue. Being identified with a celebrated humanitarian was always good for a politician's reputation. And allying oneself with Dix carried little cost—no partisan implications, no new taxes. (This, Dix shrewdly discerned, was the beauty of a land bill in contrast to any measure based on taxes.) If a member of the House or Senate had the tiniest shred of idealism, Dix sought to draw it out and recruit him to her side.

Of course the streets of Washington were paved with shattered ideals. Disillusionment, cynicism, and pessimism were endemic in the capital, the burden of those who had come to Congress with high hopes that they could accomplish some worthy goal.

Charles Sumner was a case in point. Indeed, Dix found in Sumner someone with a moral consciousness at least as sensitive and as burdened as her own. After his arrival he confessed to being sick at heart with the low tone of society and political debate in Washington. He had never wanted to come to Congress in the first place, he rather disingenuously complained to Dix, adding that he regretted "the fate which has launched me on this career." In words that echoed her own ambivalence about struggling for achievement in the world of political power, he lamented that he had no choice but to try to endure what he could not change. But in relief to the odious business of factions and parties, he singled out Dix's work as a noble labor. "I cannot forbear saying how much higher I regard y[ou]r triumphs than any in this Mexican war," he said, and endorsed her land bill wholeheartedly as a force for good throughout the entire country.[30]

Watching Dix operate in the practical art of politics as skillfully as any statesman, Samuel Gridley Howe openly expressed his amazement at how far she had come in so short a time. He had followed her career closely. And he recalled clearly how conflicted and uncertain she had been in 1842, "the time when the whisperings of maiden delicacy made you hesitate about obeying the stern voice of conscience." Looking back to those days, remembering "what you were then," he was amazed. If he had one wish for himself, he told her, it would be "to look back upon some three years of my life with a part of the self approval you must feel."[31]

Power, then as now, was the official currency of Washington, and Dix's

Charles Sumner, Senator from Massachusetts.

personality and reputation attracted a widening circle of powerful male acquaintances. Some of these, like Tennessee Senator John Bell, saw value in identifying themselves with her humanitarianism. For others, like New York Senators John Adams Dix and Millard Fillmore, cooperating with her political aims was an entrée into a more intimate relationship.

She had initially turned to Senator Dix for help presenting her federal memorial. Not long afterward, as the result of many hours of listening to her stories and arguments, he confessed "a paternal feeling on my part," and asked for assurances of a reciprocal feeling on hers. Mildly disconcerted about the peculiar energy she conveyed, he imagined that some inscrutable purpose of Providence had brought them together. Now, he soberly advised her, "it seems to have been ordained that the more than ordinary interest we felt in each other without avowing it should become mutually known."[32]

For upper-class Victorians sexuality often smoldered under heavy masks of formality. Unsurprisingly, the senator's paraphrastic missives suggest that he was unsure how he should handle his attraction to Dorothea Dix. He was married, but like many men in Congress, lonely. Back in New York his devoted wife, a delicate woman who never completely recovered from a breakdown several years earlier, oversaw his household and the upbringing of his children. Completely unlike his wife, Dorothea Dix, astonishingly bold, self-possessed, and wise in the ways of public life, was unlike any other woman he had ever met. What were the right words, he kept asking her, to describe his "incomprehensible feeling" that there was an important connection between them? It was as if in the person of his namesake friend, he had finally met his kindred spirit. Not exactly his better half. Searching for the right footing—a path to continue their relationship without its becoming overtly sexual—he assured her he was confident that he could bridle his "constitutionally rebellious spirit [and] fairly match my prudence with yours." Befitting what was to remain a long-standing platonic relationship, Senator Dix adopted Dorothea as his "machire soeur" and began signing his letters "your newly-found brother." This was a game she enjoyed. Bereft of her own family, she played along with the innocent fiction of joining the senator's distinguished family.[33]

It was not lost on Dix, as she encouraged this flirtation, that John Adams Dix appeared to be heading toward a position of leadership in Congress. Unexpectedly, though, his career was cut short. His imprudent alliance with the Barnburner Democrats in 1848, and his subsequent decision to join the Free-Soil Whigs, meant that by 1850 he was neutralized in the Senate. Blocked by his political enemies in attempts to secure a cabinet post or an ambassadorship, in 1854 he retired from politics. He would return to Washington six years later, when he served briefly as postmaster general and secretary of the treasury under James Buchanan. Through all this he corresponded with Dorothea Dix, facilitated introductions within his wide circle of friends, and provided her with political advice. Even out of office, he proved a valuable friend to his adopted sister, and they remained in close contact for the next twenty years.

To stay on course amid the swirling crosscurrents of Washington politics in the late 1840s and early 1850s, Dix relied most of all on Horace Mann. His common-school crusade completed in 1848, he had resigned as Massachusetts secretary of the board of education to enter the House of Representatives in 1848. Fifty-two years old, he had assumed the aspect of a monument: prematurely white hair receding from a high, wide forehead; deep-set eyes under a chiseled brow; prominent, regular nose; wide, firm mouth and lantern jaw. Over the past year, his zeal for education had been subsumed by a passion against slavery. An ardent Free-Soiler, he carried the new party's standard, "no more slave states and no more slave territory," and now held the seat long occupied by John Quincy Adams. His brand of antislavery did not bother Dix. She had known Mann too long to lump him in with Garrison and the wild-eyed abolitionist fanatics. He remained one of the few people whom she trusted implicitly. No one in Congress had a keener appreciation of the asylum movement nor, it seemed to her, acted from purer motives.

On Christmas eve 1849, Dix asked Mann to take whatever steps he thought wisest to keep her measure alive in the House. She had heard rumors that states' rights advocates were about introduce a law "*demanding* of the Government the relinquishment to the several States, all the public lands within their respective boundaries." Much of the public domain lay within state boundaries, so this would have ruined her scheme. He reassured her that there was nothing to worry about, and discouraged her from leaving her work in Alabama and Mississippi to return to Washington. "People are thinking here of only one thing," he

Horace Mann.

wrote: "Who shall be Speaker[?]" Still, after conferring with the Massachusetts delegation, he guessed that the chances for any federal land bill along the lines she proposed were slim. He thought the best strategy was to keep it alive in committee until the political climate improved enough to reintroduce it in both Houses of Congress simultaneously.[34]

Mann tried to help Dix understand why Congress could not think of land without thinking of slavery. The momentous issues of popular sovereignty, of the Fugitive Slave bill, of whether or not to extend slavery to California all in one way or another affected the status of the territories and federal lands. In January 1850 he advised her to "retouch" her Congressional *Memorial* and bring it up to date, but he continued to feel that her presence in the capital would be useless "until this all absorbing question of the territories is abandoned." Unless, he added in jest, she could work miracles. If she could bring that power, he urged her to come as soon as she could.[35]

Based on her experience, a miracle did not seem out of the question. But she was put off by the prospect of individually lobbying each member of Congress to achieve it. "I *cannot* proceed to visit 'the Fathers of the land' myself," she told Mann, "but if they will come to me, not for my sake or because I desire it,—but for the sake of suffering humanity, I will be glad to receive them."[36]

In day-to-day legislative matters, Mann found himself treating Dix like a colleague. He was her inside source, keeping her up to date on personalities and intrigues that lay underneath the public utterances of congressmen. She asked him to run interference for her. Would he find out whether she were entitled to use Capitol stationary when she wrote on public affairs? And if she were, could he "direct the suitable messenger to bring me some Note paper, letter paper, wafers, and correspondence envelopes." Surely this was a reasonable request, she said, particularly in light of the Senate's custom of paying for wine out of its appropriation for "House Feed."[37]

Because several House committees claimed jurisdiction over federal land policy, whenever Congress was in session, her bill became a moving target. With Mann's help, she plotted moves and countermoves based on the interrelated proceedings of these committees. When a vote seemed imminent just before a recess, she charged him to find out whether Southern Whig opponents of the bill were absent. If they had departed for their districts and he could quickly rally her supporters from New England, New York, and Pennsylvania, she knew her measure would be in safe hands. In the event the Senate Land Committee offered an unacceptable report, she had already prepared an alternative memorial and bill. These she kept locked in the drawer of her writing table, ready for use at any moment. She told Mann that he had only to pick up her key from the librarian. When her 1850 federal *Memorial* was ready for distribution, it was Mann who carried the freshly printed pamphlets up from the Document Room and placed a copy on each member's desk.[38]

His support was compassionate as well as practical. In the summer of 1850, when she worked and worried herself to the point of exhaustion, it was Mann who realized what she was doing to herself. He drew her aside for a frank, serious talk. Several times she had mentioned being so severely afflicted by *"palpitation of the heart"* that she could not walk up a flight of stairs without pausing to rest. In the course of their conversation, he confided to his wife, Mary, Dix opened up and let him "see deeper into her soul than I was ever permitted to do before." Despite her physical ailments, she demonstrated profound conviction. She said "that while she lives[,] she will never cease to prosecute this petition of getting a grant of land for the insane." The steadfastness of her resolve moved him to declare, "She is a glorious woman." Nothing was wrong with her spirit. Her problem was just that she was worn out and badly in need of rest.[39]

What shone through her fatigue, Mann thought, was an extraordinary charisma, "her divine magnetism," he called it. Her life was vivid testimony, he thought, to "how much women could do if they would! When will they be well and good enough to use their power!"[40] Her power—a blend of intellectual intensity, insight into human motives and weakness, and absolute moral certitude—set him to thinking about women's place in society more generally. In Mann's view, Dix personified "'Women's Rights' in the highest sense of the word." Like most of his fellow politicians, he thought it went against nature for a woman to aspire to be "a politician or soldier, a judge or a President." Women were created instead to inhabit "that glorious sphere of Benevolence which Nature has opened, but which the selfishness and shortsightedness of men have hitherto clouded up."[41]

Life in the "glorious sphere" was evidently killing Dix. For he himself admitted that she looked terrible, and that he would "not be surprised if she were to die suddenly on any day."

The familiar rhetoric of woman's sphere obscured the stark fact that she was living her life in a man's world. Beyond the direct strain political life exerted, she had to cope with the contradictions now enshrined in her vocation. Fighting a major political battle while professing to be nothing more than a humble woman doing God's will, she feared that her health might crack under such constant pressure. She knew full well the risk that came with rising anxieties, but neither her conscience nor her drive would accept her slackening the pace. At one time she had promised herself that after ten years of public toil she would retire. But when she considered how "God in his benignity blesses and advances the cause by the Instrument he has fitted for the labor," she foresaw no end to her labors as long as she lived. No one else, woman or man, could take her place.[42]

By 1850 she acknowledged that her long siege of Congress would require a greater commitment to being in Washington than she had been willing to make in the past. Unwilling to be tied down, she reluctantly weighed an invitation from her friend Joseph Henry, director of the new Smithsonian Institution, to stay at his comfortable house in the city. Impressed with Henry's straightforward manner and knowing his reputation for high moral and religious principles, she finally agreed to board with the professor and his wife until her bill passed. It was an ideal arrangement. Henry was a scientist, not a politician, and the thought of running an institution whose funding depended on Congress gave him pause. When Dix moved in, he was pleased to see that, in effect, he had his own lobbyist on Capitol Hill who never tired of singing the praises of Professor Henry's Smithsonian Institution. What truly astonished him, though, was his genteel houseguest's interest in science and technology. Unlike the hostesses and society ladies he encountered, she was fascinated by discussions of mechanics, cyclonographs, and water spouts. Much as she liked the Henrys, however, Dix decided that she preferred to be independent, and so began to search for a place of her own.[43]

While temporarily lodged at Professor Henry's house, she received a constant stream of visitors. Before long she had several envelopes filled with cards of senators, congressmen, diplomats, officials of the administration, local physicians—all who came to pay their respects. Even Daniel Webster called on her, wholeheartedly agreeing that her land bill should be as ambitious as possible. Since she would have, at best, only one chance with Congress, he boomed, "one may as well ask 10,000,000 [acres] as one or five."[44]

Then, suddenly on 9 July 1850, whatever progress she had made during the winter and spring was jeopardized by the death of President Zachary Taylor. The thought of changes in the administration filled her with "great anxiety and confusion" as she guessed at their political consequences.[45] It soon became obvious that the new president, Millard Fillmore, was not the strong leader the country needed, and had neither the capacity nor the desire to take on Congress. The only encouraging thing about Fillmore, she thought, was that if Congress passed her bill, he would automatically sign it into law. A Fillmore veto was unthinkable. When the House, thrown into disarray by the president's death, delayed naming its own special committee to take up her *Memorial*, she found it hard "to possess my soul in patience—very hard!" She had already drawn up a list of her choices for committee members, which she passed along to Horace Mann. She wanted him, as she put it, to take over as "Captain to the Cause" in the House, so that she could concentrate entirely on the Senate. Leaving on one of her innumerable brief trips—this time escorting two young deaf-mute orphan girls to a special school in Staunton, Virginia—Dix admonished Mann to "gather all the forces and work with a *will*."[46]

While she labored in Washington, Dix had every reason to expect some show of political support from the official Association of Asylum Superintendents. Federal asylum legislation would have given a huge boost to their profession. And the way she structured her bill, with proceeds from the sale of public lands flowing back to state asylums, was ideally designed to pump new money into their institutions. But to her chagrin, the first notice she received from the Association was bluntly negative. In its review of her 1848 *Memorial* to Congress, the *American Journal of Insanity* reprinted an ill-informed, unfavorable notice of her work taken from the *Boston Medical and Surgical Journal*. Completely misunderstanding her argument and the legislative solution she proposed, the reviewer thought that Dix was calling for the creation of "a mammoth hospital, into which the States might send their incurable insane." She replied that her plan involved nothing of the sort. She merely wanted to secure a permanent source of financial support for state institutions. But Amariah Brigham and the editors of the *Journal*, even when they finally acknowledged that the earlier review had misrepresented her position, still maintained that they concurred "in the views expressed by the writer in the *Boston Journal*, and hope and believe Congress will do nothing upon the subject." Adding insult to injury, they included in the same issue a "Memoir of Elizabeth Fry," unstinting in its praise for the Englishwoman's efforts on behalf of prisoners and lunatics.[47]

Fortunately for her, before the Civil War the asylum doctors were unknown in Congress, no member read the *American Journal of Insanity*, and there were no squadrons of staff assistants and legislative aides combing obscure journals for policy analysis. The harm done by Brigham and his colleagues was merely personal.

At the same time, however, Dix was beginning to fear she might fall victim to her own success. Several Southern legislators claimed that the rapid adoption of her state-by-state reforms showed that no overarching federal program was necessary. States were best positioned to care for their own; a federal program would only undermine states' autonomy. Her congressional *Memorial* carefully refuted this argument, showing how even the most progressive states lagged behind what medical science had shown to be beneficial. Despite the official attitude of the Association, she urged the leading superintendent in each state to send a copy of her petition to his state's senators to debunk the myth that "the Hospitals which already exist are sufficient for the public necessity."

When the Association met in July 1850, with Brigham now out of the picture, it finally occurred to the members that in fact they had much to gain if Miss Dix's land bill passed. Belatedly, they endorsed a tepid resolution of support. By this time it was apparent that whether or not they backed it, the measure had a real chance of passage. "It was unanimously resolved," Kirkbride reported, "that this association regard with deep interest, the prospect of the magnificent project, which has been and continues to be urged by Miss D. L. Dix." Her project met with the group's "unqualified sanction." Yet, to a man they were leery of any direct political involvement on its behalf. Everyone at the meeting had agreed, Kirkbride told her "that it must be yourself, and your own Christian weapons" that will carry it forward. The message was clear: Dix was not to expect any real political help from the professionals who stood to gain most tangibly from her efforts. Disappointed first by their opposition, then by the feebleness of their support, Dix simply remarked that she could not understand the reasoning of those who "have set themselves against me these last 2 years."[48]

"**D**o you know how provokingly I lost the passage of the Land Bill yesterday?" she fumed to Mann. Fifty senators agreed to vote on the measure without debate when New Hampshire's Charles G. Atherton, chairman of the Ways and Means Committee, stood up to oppose it. Furious, Dix could not resist castigating Atherton's opposition to her bill on principle. "For an unprincipled man," she snapped, "his is rather a strange position."[49] The tortuous process of legislation had foiled her one more time. Nothing more would happen in Washington on her bill until 1851. "The National affairs are recorded historically in two brief syllables," she wrote: "Delay." As she had feared all along, her bill was not popular among the Massachusetts delegation. Practically speaking, the Bay State contained comparatively little federal land, and it had more asylum beds per capita than any other state in the Union. Bitterly she remarked to Horace Mann, "I do not seem likely to be burthened with obligations to my own State."[50]

In addition to lobbying congress, Dix also found time to exert her own influence on the executive branch. Dix had first met the new President Millard Fillmore, a New York Whig and Unitarian, in 1849 in Washington when he was vice president. Shortly after he assumed his duties and began to organize his cabinet, Dix sent him a long letter opposing the nomination of Richard H. Bayard for secretary of the interior. Bayard, she warned, had "a very *mediocre* reputation" and was little more than a tool of the scheming Henry Clay. Since her private correspondence, she told the president, showed that Fillmore's stock was rising in the capital, surely he would not want to compromise his independence by drifting too close to Clay. Then, paying back a political debt, she encouraged Fillmore to consider instead New Jersey's James Gore King, a supporter of her land bill and someone she had proposed for her select committee. She closed by saying that if the president would listen to her, she was willing to help lead him through the political thicket, giving him her unbiased opinion of which men might be trusted.[51]

Throughout the fall and winter of 1850–51, Dix's relationship with the president grew warmer. Although she had a firm policy of never receiving gifts, she readily made an exception for Fillmore. She sent the president a lithograph of the planned Central Hospital for the Insane in Nashville, and frequently sent him flowers. He reciprocated in kind. Over the months, she found it easy to make appointments to see him.[52]

Fillmore liked Dorothea Dix; liked her honesty, her unexpected insights into public figures, leavened by a dry wit, and her gripping tales of what she had seen; liked her remarkable commitment to a cause she believed in; indeed, he liked almost everything about her except that she was neither rich nor beautiful. He praised her conversation, so animated and eloquent, as a moral relief from the long agony of bitter and seemingly intractable disputes over slavery.[53] Although he knew that Dix thrived on political talk, Fillmore, when he addressed her, felt compelled to step up to a higher plane of moral concern and political discourse. Unlike his letters to male colleagues, his letters to Dix are full of stilted diction, pious clichés, and awkward syntax—the affectations of trying to strike an appropriately lofty tone. In one instance, when her land bill squeaked through the House only to be tabled in the Senate, he urged her not to despair. "Hope on—Hope ever!" he wrote. "My philosophy is, that all things are for the best," and she should "rest assured, that where we have done our duty, God will eventually bless our work."[54]

As her relationship with Fillmore became more familiar, Dix enjoyed the role of presidential confidante. Besieged by office seekers, men he described as rushing "from the remotest corners of the republic to the Capitol like famished wolves," he concurred with her view that it was hard to say whether politicians were, as a class, more ambitious or self-ish. Admitting this was to reveal "*state secrets*," he joked, but he felt free to share confidences with her, for he never doubted that a woman could keep a secret. Although he at first mistook her gift of her early devotional book, *Private Hours*, for an Episcopal prayer book, in matters of religion he told her that they were kindred souls. He hated sects and denominational hairsplitting as much as she did. When he sent her a Bible as a New Year's present, it was meant as a token of sincere friendship.[55]

Her standing with the president helped Dix overcome some of her disaffection with Washington society. Since Jackson's time, the advent of the spoils system had vastly increased the value of access to the president. Recognizing this, Dix found herself in a position to influence the course of men's careers with a few well-chosen words. When for example she heard that her friend Titian Peale needed work, her first impulse was to ask Fillmore to help along his application for a position in the patent office. Since returning from Trenton and Harrisburg in early December, she had gotten into the habit of returning calling cards and left about fifty cards in a month's time. With evident pride, she described for Anne Heath dinners at the White House, at the mansion of the secretary of the navy, and "a very select party—given by the

Hon. J[ames] G[ore] King to the Heads of the Departments, leading officers and families of the Army and Navy—and the Foreign Ministers." She could not help being impressed by these extravagant feasts, in which notorious quantities of food were consumed and wine flowed freely. White House dinners were especially lavish affairs. One evening's menu might begin with mock turtle soup and move on to rockfish, duck, chicken fricassee, lamb chops, young pigeons with olives, croquette of chicken, larded sweetbreads with mushrooms, fillet of veal with spinach, roast chicken with salad, and end with five desserts, fruits, coffee, and liqueurs. Characteristically, she claimed to be unfazed by the attractions of the gay life in Washington. Society's pleasures had not grown on her, she told Anne Heath, adding, though, that "if any person has reason to be satisfied with [social] compensations[,] perhaps it is myself."[56]

To prove that hers was not a life of idle dissipation, she outlined her disciplined routine, a pattern of constant motion. She rented rooms in a commodious house, centrally located near the corner of 12th and E Streets, owned by a man she called Professor Johnson. When Congress was in town, nearly every waking hour was devoted to her bill. Rising in the dark at 4:15 A.M., she spent mornings at her writing desk until 8:30. Then she breakfasted with her knitting in her hand while Johnson read aloud the newspaper. At 10:00 she repaired to her alcove in the Capitol's congressional library, where she received people and worked most days until 3:00 P.M. Returning home, she read the day's memoranda, the recorded speeches in the *Globe*, and incoming correspondence until she joined the family at six o'clock for the evening meal. After dinner she repaired to her room, writing letters until eight, when, she said, "I return to the parlour, take tea and remain with Book or work-basket till 10." Some evenings, she said, she worked for an additional hour or two, "but not often."[57]

In the dog days of the Washington summer of 1850, Dix pushed herself to the limits of her endurance. An outbreak of cholera threatened to become an epidemic and break up the present session of Congress prematurely. Much as she would have welcomed a holiday in Rhode Island or Nova Scotia, "the Committees and friends of the measure say [that I should] not by any means leave Washington." She asked Anne Heath to find her a dress of light fabric "sufficiently dressy to wear at any time in company and in public." For she was constantly engaged, taking her post daily in the Capitol Library to explain, cajole, or plead with any legislator who would lend an ear. "In truth," she confessed to Anne Heath, "none can tell what a mountain will be lifted from my heart if my Bill pass."[58]

Emboldened by her friendship with the president, Dix finally asked him to use his influence with his close friend, Maryland Senator James A. Pearce, to push the measure through before the session ended. Pearce's power in the Democratic-controlled Senate was apparent from his success in leading the move to break up Henry Clay's omnibus bill just six months earlier. The strength of the South and the Democrats, Pearce advised Dix, boded well for her cause. When he finally submitted her bill on 11 February 1851, Dix stood by in her library alcove, following the action from notes carried up to her from the Senate floor. "I am perfectly calm and as cold as ice," she wrote as she learned that a test motion to table her bill had just been defeated thirty-two to fourteen. After a day of terrible suspense, she heard at four o'clock in the afternoon that "the Bill has passed the Senate beautifully [by] a large majority [of] more than 2 to 1."[59]

The House of Representatives, on the other hand, was a political swamp. There the South commanded 40 percent of the votes, and the Democrats 48 percent. Just before Dix's measure could be introduced in the House, however, Congress suddenly erupted in furious debate over federal enforcement of the new Fugitive Slave Law. For the remainder of its short winter session, Congress transacted little other business.

In mid-February, Dix learned, Boston abolitionists, led by Theodore Parker and Wendell Phillips, had flagrantly defied the new Fugitive Slave Law. Freeing a runaway slave from federal officials who had tried to uphold the onerous law was, according to Parker, Boston's noblest deed since the destruction of the tea in 1773. But Dix, tired of hearing about the slavery issue and irritated with the abolitionists, saw it as a disaster. "I put away thoughts of Massachusetts generally," she remarked with disgust, for it now seemed that her own state was ruining her lifework. Congress was at once deluged with antislavery and proslavery petitions that sought to repeal or toughen the Fugitive Slave Law. The remaining weeks of the session were dominated by fierce sectional debates. The devil was having his day. "As for political life," she wrote, "I have never seen so much that illustrates the life of sin." When her bill was tabled, she tried again to pin the blame on Atherton, the Ways and Means

Committee chairman, consoling herself with the thought that he was a lame duck and would not return to do more mischief.

"Defeated but not conquered," as she described herself to President Fillmore, she had nothing to do in the capital until Congress reconvened. Grimly she packed her bags, preparing to travel south for Virginia, South Carolina, and Georgia, taking up once again, she said, "my accustomed labors of searching into the condition of the insane."[60]

CHAPTER TWELVE

"The poor weak president has . . .
lacerated my life"

She was a driven woman, a tireless evangelist for her cause, always seeking fresh converts. Seldom was she too busy in Washington to rush off on a moment's notice to some distant quarter to proclaim the good news of the asylum. For she thrived on the idea of there being limitless need for her intervention. So even as she assiduously assembled the coalition of Whigs and Democrats she would need to steer her bill through Congress, she also took on all manner of additional legislative and professional burdens. If a congressman had a lunatic nephew, it was Dorothea Dix who quietly made arrangements for admission to a private hospital. If a prison warden could not convince his board of overseers that the institution's chapel needed refurbishing, Dix swooped in to convince the state's governor and party leaders that nothing was more critical to rehabilitating felons than regular religious instruction.

Between 1850 and 1854, beyond her extensive work in the South, errands of mercy took her as far north as Nova Scotia. There she was the catalyst for Canadian lunacy reform legislation. At the same time, she adroitly used her relationships with men in government and in the medical profession to found the Government Hospital for the Insane in Washington, D.C., which would come to be known as Saint Elizabeth's Hospital.

But these achievements, substantial in their own right, seemed incidental to the passage of her land bill. It became her constant obsession. Against the advice of politicians who warned her that the exigencies of politics and the policies of the new president boded ill for its passage, she persevered. She continued to dismiss all opposition as irrelevant intrusion of partisanship on moral principle. To her the land bill had become far more than another political contest. It had turned into a test of her faith and of her nation's moral resolve.

Nevertheless, even though she viewed her mission to Canada as an interlude, she made a significant mark. At the outset of her career in the early 1840s, when she had surveyed upstate New York and northern New England, Dix had occasionally gone farther north. "Visiting the Canadas in 1843 and 1844," she wrote, "I found the jail at Toronto thronged with insane patients, held in detention for their own protection and the public safety. In the jail at Montreal were above 70 of the most suffering and mismanaged patients I have ever seen." In 1848 she visited St. John's, Newfoundland, where she met a young doctor, Henry Hunt Stabb, who was doing his best with limited resources to build a provincial hospital for lunatics. At the time she had donated £100 to help him, and allowed him to use her name in efforts to raise additional funds. Returning to Canada in September 1849, she found forty-four madmen and madwomen terribly mistreated in the Halifax poorhouse. She was too busy to do anything for them. But she made the acquaintance of Hugh Bell, the mayor of Halifax, a conscientious man who had for three years been calling for a regional asylum for Nova Scotia, New Brunswick, and Prince Edward Island. After she returned south, he did everything in his power to convince her that the time was right to bring her cause to Nova Scotia.[1]

With the United States Congress in session, she told Bell that she was uneasy about a prolonged absence from Washington. By December, however, he persuaded her that unless she intervened, Nova Scotia would remain in the Dark Ages. "The effort will fail—if I do not come," she wrote as she dashed off "a Memorial for both State and Province." In sixteen pages written in the manner of her previous memorials, she described the abuses she had seen on her several visits to Canada. Her description of lunatics in Quebec is typical. "Left to pine in dreary solitude, without recreation or employment; without fire for warmth in winter, and imperfectly defended from the cold by scanty apparel, they become maniacal or idiotic, some piercing the heavy poisonous air of their filthy cells with loud cries, rending their clothes, or uttering low, meaningless babblings of idiocy." Having dozens of American asylum annual reports at her fingertips, she peppered her "Memorial" with the usual statistics showing high rates of cure. Canada's was an agrarian economy. So Dix emphasized how American asylums had developed farms whose sales of cash crops offset their costs. She appealed to their pocketbooks more than their hearts. "The age of experiment has passed," she told the provincial legislature, "the age of facts is in the present. The question then is, not whether you will appropriate funds for a hospital, hoping good may thence ensue, but whether you will venture . . . to *refuse* what you *know* will heal the sick and restore those whose reason is shattered through physical maladies."[2]

She completed this petition sitting before a fire during a rainstorm in Montgomery, Alabama, on 10 December 1849. Immediately she sent it off to Hugh Bell, who, the following month, presented it in Halifax. Earlier Dix had "half-promised" to make the journey and deliver it herself, for she was uncomfortable leaving it to others. It failed. Afterward Bell assured her that her presence would have been to no avail. "I fear even the thunders of Demosthenes would scarce disturb our apathy," he lamented. Insanity was rare and not viewed as a pressing social problem, as evidenced by the lack of support for printing Dix's "Memorial" at government expense. What little publicity it received was in the newspapers. Lacking public support, the £20,000 asylum appropriations proposal appended to the petition was rejected with little discussion. For her trouble Dix received a ceremonial resolution of gratitude from the legislature, which Bell dismissed as "a mere compliment." This resounding defeat humbled Bell. Henceforth he came to believe that his only hope of building an asylum was to entice Dix to come to Nova Scotia. No one else but her, he conceded, would be able to get the legislature's mind off railroads and onto hospitals.[3]

The course of events over the next several years was to prove him right.

For in 1853 Dix decided to take a kind of working vacation away from the Washington summer. In mid-June she sailed from Boston harbor for Halifax aboard the sleek *Europa*. With Congress in recess, she had ample time to tour the peninsula, help Bell stir the provincial legislature to action, and still get back to Washington before it reconvened in the fall. Several months before Dix arrived, in response to Bell's persistent pleas, the legislature had scraped together £5,000 as a start toward erecting a special structure for the mad. Although this was scarcely enough money to construct a facility, this seemed to prove that the provincial government's heart was in the right place. Indeed, the legislature had underwritten its commitment to the project with government securities.[4]

In the meantime, Bell had gotten himself appointed chief commissioner for the proposed asylum—an empty title unless Dix could loosen the government's purse strings. He confessed that with all the inertia in the provincial legislature he had never really expected to get the project off the ground, but that her recent "unflinching resolution shame[d] away doubt, and inspire[d] confidence." Acknowledging that he was woefully ignorant about the technical side of asylum construction, he was relieved to let her take the lead in choosing a site and hiring an architect for the new hospital. All he cared about was to make sure that the building was "useful and necessary, rather than ornamental." Rarely shy when asked to take the initiative, Dix reported after a week in Nova Scotia that she was busy "surveying farms—selecting points for sites . . . looking into Granite quarries &c&c." For the moment, at least, merrily engrossed in the tasks at hand, she was able to put Washington out of her mind.[5]

Searching for local allies, Dix made a trip to St. John's to revisit Henry Stabb's fledgling provincial asylum. He was astonished when she appeared unannounced, bearing a crate of religious books for his library. As one of the few physicians in eastern Canada who made any claim to being a mad-doctor or alienist, Stabb was an opinion leader within the medical community. Over a pot of tea they discussed the latest innovations in asylum architecture, and he was at pains to show her that, isolated though he was, he was nonetheless abreast of modern medical science. He intended to banish the term "lunatic" as old-fashioned and demeaning, for instance, and hoped that if the province erected new homes for the mad, they should be designated "Hospitals for Mental Diseases."[6] Dix agreed. Because she had in mind to show the governor and his council that Nova Scotia needed not merely a warehouse for the chronic insane but "a *curative* institution." This would require designing two wings: one for violent and furiously mad patients, the other for depressed and otherwise quiescent cases. Judging from recent experience, she estimated this would cost just £3,500 more than a hospital with a single ward. To demonstrate her personal commitment to the project, she met with the governor and the legislature, together with a group of several leading citizens. She promised that if they could raise £2,000 by private subscription, she would secure the remaining £1,500 from philanthropists in England and America.[7]

While she was working with the government to plan the new facility, Dix saw a chance to make a different kind of benevolent contribution to the province. Sable Island was then, as it is today, a notorious hazard for the Halifax fishing fleet. It formed "a solemn rock-girdled monument," Dix said, "marking the ocean-grave of unnamed thousands." In fair weather, though, the rocky coast was a tourist attraction, a place of bleak solitude and rugged beauty. Curious to see it, Dix sailed to Sable Island one day in late July. Her expedition was picturesque and uneventful. The next day, however, a handsome new boat call the *Guide* ran aground in dense fog and sank. Thanks to calm seas and quick work by the island's lifeguards, all the crew and passengers were saved. But the incident lingered in Dix's imagination. She had recognized the potential for disaster, remarking after her visit that the rocky archipelago had "no Life-Boats, no Fog-bells, no Lighthouses." On a personal level, the near-catastrophe of the *Guide* haunted her all the more because, fifteen years earlier, her younger brother, Charles Wesley Dix, had perished at sea off the coast of Africa.[8]

Resolving to do what she could, Dix asked a few of her wealthy friends to establish a fund whose proceeds would be used to pay for six new lifeboats stationed on the island. John Adams Dix, then in the private practice of law in New York, helped with the subscription fund, while Dorothea Dix squeezed the lifeboat manufacturer for a fifty-dollar discount on each boat.[9] Though they were not donated to advance the cause of lunacy reform in Canada, the Sable Island lifeboats were a perfect gesture in a province whose economy and imagination faced the sea. Shipwreck was a danger everyone understood, and the boats were a practical and obviously needed precaution. "A gallant woman," was the sentiment from the Admiralty House, and this opinion was widely shared within the government. Hugh Bell, who took on the role of "Superintendent of the Metallic Life Boat Manufactory," organized the delivery and placement of the boats. Before the end of 1853, he incredulously reported that the legislature had revived Dix's asylum bill and that "£15,000, equal to $60,000[,] has been appropriated unencumbered with the condition to have £5,000 more subscribed."[10]

Three more years were required for the government to arrange the financing of "Mount Hope," an asylum in Dartmouth overlooking Halifax harbor. Then it took another two years, until May 1858, to institute "An Act for the Management of the Hospital for the Insane," which enabled the new facility to commence operations. The site that Dix had selected was charming. But in practice it was so weirdly configured, running a mile long and six hundred feet wide, that it was extremely difficult to adapt to its stated purpose. Also, the problems of the site were compounded by Dix's architectural recommendation. To draw up plans for the buildings and grounds, she convinced the provincial commission entrusted with overseeing construction of the hospital to retain her friend Charles Nichols, the medical superintendent of the new United States Government Hospital for the Insane in Washington. With scant sense of design and no knowledge of what building materials were available locally, he tried to translate the design of his immense gothic structure to Nova Scotia. The result was an imposing brick edifice with a pretentious façade and insufficient capacity. In 1859, when it was vastly over budget, the commissioners complained that Mount Hope could accommodate only 90 of an estimated 350 provincial lunatics who needed hospitalization. Owing to continued shortfalls in the institution's year-to-year operations, the asylum was not completed until 1874.[11]

Her miscalculation in suggesting Nichols grew out of the complex history of her relationship with him.

During the late summer of 1853, while she was occupied in Nova Scotia, Dix also found time to carry on a flirtatious correspondence with the erstwhile superintendent of the Bloomingdale asylum in New York. The main subject of their letters, however, was not romance but the intrigue and professional politics surrounding Dix's proposed Government Hospital for the Insane. Earlier, her clumsy plan to help the ambitious Nichols gain more autonomy from the Bloomingdale trustees had backfired. Now she hinted to him that his ouster from Bloomingdale might have been a blessing in disguise. Perhaps he could move up in the world. Feeling a little guilty about the damage she had unintentionally done to Nichols's career, she promised to use her influence to help him find a position in an institution that would offer him a fuller opportunity to exercise his professional talents than he had had in New York.[12]

A portion of the imposing main building, Nova Scotia Hospital.

After leaving Bloomingdale in the summer of 1852, Nichols headed west for a vacation. Traveling around the Great Lakes trying to decide what to do next, he was surprised to come across an item in the *National Intelligencer* reporting that the United States Senate, at Dix's behest, had appropriated $100,000 "for the establishment of an Asylum for the Insane of the District of Columbia & of the U. S. Army and Navy." Reading on with great interest, he was astonished to notice how small was the "amount of land authorized to be purchased by the Secretary of the Interior"—a mere fifteen acres. He reminded Dix of his own availability and pointedly asked her whether she or anyone with experience in asylum construction and management was being consulted about the planned facility.[13]

The project had of course been Dix's idea in the first place. A government hospital in Washington was a corollary of her national land bill. Its presence in the capital would be symbolic as well as practical. Figuring that an asylum was needed, at the very least, to house mentally disordered members of the army and navy, she envisioned the new institution as a demonstration on a small scale of the principle that the federal government should assume responsibility for the well-being of its citizens. In the process of redrafting her federal *Memorial* in 1850, she had added a proposal for the government hospital. Henceforth she vigorously lobbied Congress and President Fillmore to approve it. Subsequently the hospital legislation was detached from her land bill. In the summer and fall of 1852, Dix prevailed on Fillmore—by that time a lame-duck president comparatively unconcerned with political consequences—to get the project under way before he left office. She urged him to bypass Congress and issue an executive order designating a site and naming a superintendent for the new facility.

Fillmore had been deeply frustrated by his ineffectiveness with Congress. Perhaps as a reaction, he did what Dix asked. In September, the president instructed Secretary of the Interior Alexander Stuart to authorize Dix to recruit Nichols to head the asylum.

Nichols, trying to avoid seeming too anxious, responded that he would be glad to consider the job "provided the conditions are liberal." But he grew more anxious when it suddenly dawned on him that Fillmore had failed in his bid for renomination, and that the next administration might well have its own notions about the hospital. He told Dix he needed to receive an official appointment "*at once*" so that he could "assist in devising the plan of the Institution and *Superintend its construction*." He even floated the idea of visiting Europe at government expense, where, he noted, "they have some fine small asylums." Since his dream, and Dix's, was to erect "*a model hospital*," he did not miss any of the latest developments abroad.[14]

Writing on executive chamber stationary, Dix officially notified Nichols of the "unanimous" decision to bring him to Washington.

> By direction of the President of the United States, I have the honour to acquaint Charles H. Nichols, M. D. with his appointment by the unanimous decision,
>
> the Nominee—D. L. Dix
> Assenting voice—A. H. H. Stuart
> Executive—Millard Fillmore, President of the United States

The appointment was a consummate insider political maneuver. Fillmore trusted Dix's judgment on such professional matters, and no one was in a position to question the president. No sooner did Nichols accept the appointment than he began to look for new ways to ingratiate himself with Dix. He needed no reminding how important his relationship with her was to his career.[15]

The initial Government Hospital appropriations bill, allocating $25,000 for the acquisition of land, was signed in early November 1852. In an unorthodox arrangement, even though it was initially chartered to receive mentally disordered patients from the army and navy, the new hospital fell under direct control of the secretary of the interior (not the secretary of war). Whether or not this was Dix's doing, in practice it left the way open for the hospital to admit private patients from the District of Columbia. Nichols immediately traveled to the capital to assume his new post. No sooner did he arrive in Washington, however, than he discovered that the proposed asylum was already freighted with political controversy. Furious that they had not been consulted on Nichols's appointment and had in effect been passed over, leaders of the local medical community were up in arms and complained loudly and publicly. One local physician who had lobbied Congress for a District of Columbia hospital was furious that he had not been chosen for the job. He was enraged that a superintendent would collect a large salary for nothing more than supervising the building of the asylum. Seemingly this was a position "much better suited to an architect than a medical man." The whole matter, he carped, smacked of a plot by "Miss Dix and her friends, who feared that the application of a lunatic asylum here, might endanger her plan for the several States."[16]

Even before Nichols was confirmed, Dix herself had already preempted the superintendent's first prerogative and chosen a site for the facility—a charming pastoral tract of land overlooking the confluence of the Potomac and East Branch Rivers. Nichols when learned of her plan, was taken aback. But unfamiliar with Washington, he had no alternative but to agree, particularly after she told him that she had persuaded President Fillmore and Secretary Stuart that no other site would do. As a newcomer, Nichols was disconcerted to find that when he met with congressmen on the District of Columbia Committee, he was told that "Miss Dix ought to be here to talk to Members of Congress." This was a blow to his pride. Yet he had little choice except to work through Dix if he wanted lawmakers to budget the funds for his new institution. Not that he had any inclination to turn his back on her. They shared a grand vision of a monumental institution that would ultimately become a showcase for the nation and, perhaps, for the world.

When he got wind of their majestic scheme, Charles Sumner acknowledged that it was a worthy goal, although he quipped that "the grade of
civilization in Washington is too low to accomplish it."[17]

Realizing that Dix's sponsorship was essential to his success,
Nichols, pushed their relationship toward greater personal intimacy. In
early 1853, addressing her as "my dear, good Mentor Sister," he even
went so far as to bring up the subject of marriage, albeit in a rather
abstract way. A man of his qualities would make the best husband in the
world, he mused, "but I have pretty much come to the conclusion that
getting married is not my forte—I am right—Am I not?"[18] Over the
next year he adopted an ingratiatingly intimate tone. He invented pet
names for her: "my dear Christiana, Angelina and Sandora." He called
her "my best friend" and frequently asked about her health "for my
sake," as he put it. "Am I merely deceiving myself when I . . . fancy you
like me a shade better than the other Doctors?" he wanted to know.
Her affection for him, he wrote, was doubtless "all I deserve, tho' not
more than I covet." Dix did nothing to discourage this kind of playful,
suggestive intimacy. She rather enjoyed it. Flattered by the young doctor's attentions, confident of his personal loyalty, and satisfied with his
professional reputation, Dix thought of Nichols as her junior partner in
carrying out her plans for the Government Hospital.[19]

Combining her lobbying for the new Government Hospital funding
bill with her federal land bill, Dix in 1854 managed to get the Senate's
unanimous consent to a $100,000 measure for construction of the
hospital building. As cost overruns mounted, though, this sum was not
enough for Nichols to realize his model institution.[20]

When Dix departed Washington in the summer of 1854 and left
Nichols to his own devices, it became apparent that his troubles were
only beginning. She had given him indispensable support to build the
facility, and he was now expected to operate in keeping with everyone's
inflated expectations—expectations symbolized by the institution's
gothic portico with its tile roof and massive columns. By the time the
Government Hospital opened in 1855, Nichols had grown increasingly
irritated by the intransigence of Congress and the Department of the
Interior, and troubled by the prospect of fighting annually over every
item in his budget. Soon his differences with the institution's board of
trustees called to mind his worst memories of Bloomingdale.

Owing to its unique federal charter and its prominence in the District of Columbia, the Government Hospital would, over the years, receive microscopic scrutiny from lawmakers and the local medical community. In early 1855 a board of overseers was selected. This body, consisting of five physicians, three attorneys, and a minister, was supposed to report back yearly to the Department of the Interior to ensure that the fiduciary and medical management of the facility lived up to its charter. As they commenced their work, the critical question in their minds revolved around the central goal of the institution. What rate of cure or discharge should it aim for? To address this issue, they studied the reports of the York Retreat. The Retreat had been operating for sixty years, they reasoned, and it was generally held to be the gold standard for moral treatment. In its best year, the Retreat calculated, two-thirds of its admissions were cases in which the onset of insanity had been within the past twelve months. Of these, it claimed a 61 percent rate of cure. For established cases, on the other hand, the rate plummeted to 18 percent.[21]

Nichols, under increasing pressure to prove his capability, prepared a report for the secretary of the interior in October 1855, ten months after the Government Hospital for the Insane admitted its first patient. He asked for appropriations to build a library; a large barn, cow house, and piggery; a two-story brick mechanics' shop complete with sleeping quarters for farmhands and machine shop workers; a brick-and-blue flagstone wall capacious enough to enclose forty acres. To carry out his entire plan, he projected the costs of the completed asylum at $214,784, an enormous sum. The problem he faced from the beginning, however, was that his patient population was the worst of the worst. Of his first sixty-three patients, he estimated that only nine had the slightest hope for improvement. The rest arrived at his new institution from Baltimore, where they had long been incarcerated at government expense "in various stages of chronic dementia." Since the first stage of the hospital's growth would necessarily involve collecting insane members of the military and residents of the District of Columbia, Nichols tried to lower expectations. His first priority was to make room for one hundred white patients and a separate lodge for twenty blacks. Until he could begin to bring in patients in the early stages of madness, he insisted, "recoveries, in proportion to the number of residents, must continue to be very small."[22]

As elsewhere, the expected recoveries never materialized. For the

The massive portico of the Government Hospital for the Insane in Washington, D.C.

next twenty years, with the local medical community nipping at his heels, he was constantly hampered by his inability to win the full confidence of his board. If Nichols, as most of his fellow superintendents believed, was professionally talented, he nonetheless continued throughout his career to tread on thin ice with those above him. In several instances Dix's support proved invaluable. On the eve of the Civil War, for example, Secretary of the Interior Robert McClelland seriously questioned whether Nichols should continue in his position. Cost overruns and disappointing rates of cure were impossible to deny. Dix herself informed Nichols that she had often heard people remark on the low standard of patient care provided in his institution. To save him, she lined up leading citizens from around Washington and five superintendents, "his oldest and well known professional brethren," to bear witness to his character and professional qualifications.[23]

After the war, his administration was investigated several times—notably in 1869 and 1876—after he was accused first of disloyalty to the Union and later charged with mismanagement of asylum funds. At the conclusion of the 1876 investigation he told Dix, with whom he maintained a steady correspondence, that he was nearing a nervous breakdown. Beleaguered and feeling he had no choice but to resign, Nichols finally left St. Elizabeth's dispirited, a broken man. As fate would have it, the only position he could find was a post at the Bloomingdale asylum. In the end, even his close friendship with Dix could not save him from the proclivity to invite suspicion, which eventually caught up with him wherever he went.[24]

For all her importance to his career, Nichols was a minor player in Dix's life. In the fall of 1853, she returned from Nova Scotia to Washington not to work on the Government Hospital but to press Congress to enact her land bill for the indigent insane. If she was to triumph, though, she felt it would be because her cause was divinely inspired, not because the lawmakers were receptive. Social welfare was not part of their legislative agenda. Divided by worsening sectional hostilities that eroded party discipline, the Congress of 1854, Senator Charles Sumner predicted, "promise[d] to be the worst—since the Constitution was adopted."[25]

But Dix realized she had no alternative to working with Congress. It was overwhelmingly the dominant branch of government. Stephen Douglas of Illinois, hero of Young America and chairman of the Senate committee on territories, was its leader. Dix had a hard time reading Douglas and worried that since he had no moral interest in her cause, he would manipulate it for his own political purposes. There were Democratic majorities in both houses, a fact that masked the reality of splinter factions and competing interest groups lurking just beneath the surface.

Of immediate concern to Dix, the thirty-third Congress was besieged by conflicting requests, schemes, and claims involving the public lands. Exponential growth of the railroads, the country's first big businesses, was pushing lawmakers to try to formulate federal land policy to manage their expansion. Westward migration likewise put pressure on the public domain. A long line of settlers and speculators, seeking to capitalize on the territorial expansion that followed the war with Mexico, appeared on the steps of the Capitol, each group shoving to stake its claim. Many congressmen, especially in the Northwestern states and in the territories, favored federal land grants to settlers. Immigration would increase their tax base and political clout. "Miss Dix's bill," as it was commonly known, was thus debated in the context of homestead legislation and a controversial measure for granting 160 acres to war veterans and their families. Few members of the Senate or the House of Representatives shared a clear vision of the limits and responsibilities of the federal government, so the disposition of the public lands inevitably raised basic political conflicts.[26]

To Dix's consternation, the basic humanitarian intent of her legislation tended to get lost in the shuffle. Congressmen from newer states in the West complained that her measure threatened to hit them with a hidden tax. Old states like Virginia and Massachusetts contained little or no public domain, whereas states admitted into the Union after the Northwest Ordinance encompassed a great deal. Where was the justice in a law, they wanted to know, that allowed "the states which have no federal lands within their borders [to] acquire such land in the states which have." Worse, if federal land were auctioned off to pay for lunatic hospitals, its sale would likely glut the market, automatically driving down the value of real estate in private hands and lands owned by the states themselves. To ease such worries, Dix and her supporters pointed out that the bill should really be viewed as a preliminary step toward transferring the federal lands to the states. As long as land remained in the public domain it was, for all intents and purposes, frozen and of no real benefit to the states.[27]

Between 1848 and 1853, overcoming the politics of land appeared to represent Dix's most formidable obstacle. Virginia's Francis Stribling, who wished her success, privately expressed fears that even if her bill were enacted, his state's legislature would "oppose such disposition of the public lands [and] probably would reject the donation."[28]

Still, despite the unpredictability of the states and the fragmentation of Congress, during Fillmore's administration Dix had at least felt confident of White House support for her bill. While he had not explicitly committed himself, Millard Fillmore, she believed, would have signed the bill into law the moment it reached his desk. But Franklin Pierce was another matter. Dix was baffled by Pierce, an attractive, insecure man of considerable personal charm and few discernible principles. He came to the presidency as a Democrat with a long history of political experience in New Hampshire state government and in both houses of Congress. Yet from the day he took office Pierce found it impossible to gain control over his own party. To his growing exasperation, this failure crippled him in his subsequent efforts to rein in a disorderly and intractable Congress.[29]

On December 7, 1853, when at last it seemed likely that both houses of Congress would bring her bill to a vote, Dix, acting on the advice of Fillmore, paid Pierce a call. She found him at home in the recently refurbished Executive Mansion, "wavering and hurried" between meetings. Obviously distracted, he politely listened to her case for the

Ten-Million Acre bill. "He said it had his warmest sympathies," Dix told Fillmore after her interview, "but he had not well considered the question of such landed appropriations." Determined to pin the president down to a tangible commitment, Dix told him that she intended to tell the Senate committee on the public lands that her cause enjoyed the president's "interest and good will." According to her account, he listened and replied: "More than that Miss Dix, more than that, I sincerely regretted that it had not passed the last session." Although he admitted that he had not really looked into the subject, he wished her success, then said that he would "be glad if it passes now." That was the extent of her interview. No matter how hard she pressed, he refused to say anything more definite. So Dix, who had by this time been in politics long enough to know the difference between firm endorsement and diplomatic evasion, left the meeting deeply disturbed by the president's "air of restless half uncertainty."[30]

When he read her description of the president's demeanor, Fillmore acknowledged that it may well have been a telling episode, and that her alarm was indeed warranted. Even at second hand, an experienced politician could decipher the writing on the wall. From his own experience, Fillmore inferred that Pierce "really and truly sympathises with the object which you have in view, but he had not fully satisfied himself, that as President he can constitutionally approve the measure." Pierce would try to avoid vetoing the bill, Fillmore predicted, by quietly prevailing on congressional Democrats to bottle it up in the House and keep it from ever coming before him. To Dix this was a depressing prospect. But she had now invested far too much in the bill to ponder what would happen if the president's views clashed with her mission. Practically she knew she needed White House support, but she could not bring herself to believe that Pierce would veto a measure that embodied both high moral principle *and* the will of the people as expressed by their representatives.

Moreover, if Fillmore's surmise turned out to be correct and the president thought he could quietly undermine the bill in Congress, Dix knew that she was far more popular than the president among the members of both houses. If it came to that, her battle with the president would be waged on friendly territory. She could, if need be, beat Franklin Pierce at his own game.[31]

As the debates in Congress got under way again, her confidence in the popularity and the irresistibility of her cause grew apace. Vermont's

Solomon Foot, the chairman of the Senate committee on public lands, began by calling relief of the insane "an object of the highest national concernment." And for Dorothea Dix he expressed only glowing praise. She had documented the condition of more than twenty-three thousand insane Americans, he declared; and of these, seven out of eight were utterly without access to treatment or custodial care.[32]

Except for a hard core of perhaps a dozen senators who implacably opposed the federal social welfare legislation on constitutional grounds, the Senate was predisposed to approve Dix's measure. The breakdown by party was thirty-six Democrats, twenty Whigs, two Free-Soilers, and four vacant seats. She believed she could count on most of the Whigs, whose concept of government, like her own, was that it should be a positive force for ensuring social welfare. The Democrats, on the other hand, were divided, the party containing a strong contingent of strong states' rights advocates.

Schemes for turning the proceeds from the sale of federal lands over to the states had been circulating ever since Henry Clay's Distribution bill first surfaced in 1831. In 1837 Congress had distributed a surplus $27,000,000 to the states, and much of the money had gone to support public schools. But no previous proposal had linked the states' fiduciary interests with the idea of the nation's moral obligation to the destitute. The proposed law called for 100,000 acres of the public lands to be distributed directly to each of the thirty states. Another 7,000,000 acres was to be set aside and allocated to states according to a complicated formula based on geographic area and population. There was also a provision, which Dix had unsuccessfully tried to keep out, for an additional 2,225,000 acres for the benefit of the deaf dumb and blind. All in all, Dix ended up asking for 12,225,000 acres of the public domain.

Critics noted that the plan was not without its problems. To be sure, Congress had made a few small land grants for charitable purposes. But a scheme of national proportions had no precedent. Nor did there exist the bureaucratic apparatus to implement it. If land were simply allocated to each state without some mechanism for regulating its use, the land would be left in the notoriously untrustworthy hands of state politicians. Land speculators, who enjoyed strong influence in most statehouses, were understandably delighted by this prospect. And what of the money generated by the sale of land? Haggling over "the difference between appropriating *land* and *money*, and the distinctions between giving it for the education of the *sane* and for the *insane*" produced "some singular casuistry," the *National Intelligencer* commented. Should income from the appropriated lands simply be handed over to the states, one state legislator asked Dix, "leaving the particular disposition of the funds to the good pleasure & wisdom of each?" If this happened, each state would invent its own method for allocating funds to the public institutions it deemed most worthy of assistance. Depending on the status of its insane asylums, a state might or might not choose to funnel money to them.[33]

In the meantime, editorial opinion expressed in leading newspapers and periodicals around the country had long supported the bill. Writers in several states favored any reasonable plan that would unlock the riches of the public domain and thereby ease the burden of taxation for their citizens. Considering the "millions of acres [that] have been noted [*sic*] away to corporations, from which local and personal benefit will only ensue," the *North American* had observed when the bill first passed the House, "this proposition is as broad as the sphere of humanity, and invests one of the most beautiful charities that philanthropy ever conceived." Dix, who had carried forward her work with the expectation of "no reward but the approval of a pure conscience," was such a perfect embodiment of noble self-sacrifice that "even her gratification might be urged as a reasonable inducement to support such a measure," if the desire to validate America's destiny as a Christian people were not enough.[34]

So dozens of issues were debated but not resolved. Presumably the technical administration of the law was a matter to be settled after its passage. After six years of indecision, Congress suddenly seemed of one mind. Informally counting the votes, Vermont's Senator Solomon Foot confided to Dix that her measure had solid majority support in the Senate. William H. Bissell in turn assured her that if the Senate approved the legislation, the House would follow suit. Such confidence had been expressed before, Dix warily told Fillmore, but if the bill passed in the present session Pierce could veto it only at the risk of incurring the wrath of Congress.[35]

Then in January 1854, as the Senate committee on public lands ordered the printing of five thousand copies of Dix's federal *Memorial* in preparation for sending the measure to the House of Representatives, Stephen Douglas introduced a bill for organizing the Kansas-Nebraska country. Once debate commenced on January 30, this measure reopened the whole question of slavery in the territories that had been deferred by the Compromise of 1850. Dix, seeing the collective gaze of Congress shifting once again to slavery, lashed out at Douglas, sarcastically remarking "that fine specimen of a great man and gentleman, Senator Douglas . . . demeans himself like the tom-tit, which fancied itself an Eagle."[36]

At first Dix was sure that the rekindled slavery debate would have dire consequences for her bill. But it soon occurred to her that a measure for the relief of the indigent insane afforded politicians of various sections and parties the opportunity to prove that, despite their political differences, they were men of humanitarian principles. Indeed, it was a measure of Dix's powers of persuasion that many of them were captivated by the picture of the ideal asylum that she so convincingly painted. Richard Yates, a congressman from Illinois, maintained that each state could use its portion of the public lands to "erect a magnificent edifice, with comfortable and spacious apartments, adorned with decorations of art and every pleasing embellishment; surrounded by large inclosures [sic] of forest tree, beautiful shrub, and blooming flower." In his mind, the asylum became pastoral and even utopian. Forgetting that the bill was for pauper lunatics, he asked his fellow members of the House to vote for it in case "your wife, or daughter, or mine, should ever fall victims to insanity." With Dix's measure in place, "instead of being confined within narrow apartments and prison-houses, she may walk forth in the light of God's glorious sun, breathe Heaven's pure air, and, if her fancy chooses, pluck a flower by the wayside."[37]

Ohio Senator Salmon P. Chase captured the perceived disinterestedness and simplicity of Dix's appeal. "Who is the lady in behalf of whose measure we are appealed to to-night?" he asked from the Senate floor. "She has no power or patronage. She controls no vast money claims with which to approach Congress." On the contrary, he maintained, "her clients are the poor, the friendless, and the wretched." Since her only goal was "to dispense blessings and consolations" to these unfortunates, could the Senate "deny a simple vote on her bill?" His view of Dix, like that of his colleagues, assumed that she could not possibly have been motivated by any of the personal ambition that consumed them. She and her cause were pure, untainted. In the face of the unresolvable question of slavery and worst political conflict the nation had yet faced, Dix's bill gave congressmen the opportunity to imagine that they were rising above politics.[38]

Nowhere in the congressional discussion and debate over this extraordinary measure, nor in the press coverage devoted to it, was there the slightest suggestion that Dix's cause and the Ten Million Acre bill were viewed as antidotes for social disorder. The meaning of the asylum, at least as it was articulated in the speeches of congressmen, had nothing to do with controlling a deviant element that threatened their world. For the most part they agreed with Dix's argument that lunatics and idiots defined the lower boundary of the human condition. In making salutary provision for these unfortunate souls, the state would assert not its coercive power but realize its republican ideal.

"**M**y bill has passed the Senate by more than two-thirds majority, 25 to 12," wrote Dix on March 9, already tallying the margin she would need to override a presidential veto. Nineteen senators had been absent. "Had every senator been present," she declared with unwarranted optimism, "the vote would have been maintained exactly the same." As it happened, Whigs voted unanimously for the measure; Democrats split, twelve for and eight against. Still reluctant to get her hopes up too much, she rejoiced "quietly and silently," and thanked "the Lord who has made my mountain strong." Her prudence was justified when the House voted on the bill in April. There the margin of victory was frighteningly slim: ninety-eight to eighty-four. After six years of unrelenting effort Dorothea Dix was in reach of her objective. The bill now needed only the signature of the president to become law. Yet this brought up the unnerving possibility that no matter what she said or did, her glorious political accomplishment could be deflated by a stroke of the president's pen. To head off a veto, she apparently had met with Pierce again sometime in the early months of 1854, and had left that meeting certain, she later wrote, that he had given "his positive assurance that the Bill for the relief of the Indigent Insane had his approval and sympathy and would not be vetoed!"[39]

Believing that she had at last carried the day, her friends and supporters were ebullient. "A thousand congratulations on the success of your nobel, disinterested and persevering effort!" enthused Kirkbride in a typical response. "There is some virtue yet in Congress, and large hope for the Republic!"[40]

By constitutional design, however, the arbiter of republican virtue was the president, in this instance a staunch Unionist convinced that executive power was to be exercised chiefly to preserve the constitutional rights of the states. Understood in the context of the power struggle between states and the federal government, Dix's land bill proposed an important extension of federal power into an arena controlled entirely by the states. To counter criticism, she had pointed out that Congress readily offered millions of acres in railroad subsidies to capitalists whose only motive was to make a profit. But Pierce refused to accept the analogy. Faced with an array of forces that threatened the political relationship between the federal government and the states, he sought to avoid conflict by limiting Washington's role in domestic policy. Pierce vetoed Dix's land bill for the same reasons he vetoed any measure that weakened states' prerogatives.[41]Ironically, his vetoes were among the strongest acts of an otherwise weak and indecisive president. Aware that he was antagonizing an unusually broad coalition of Free-Soilers, Whigs, and members of his own party, North and South, Pierce took the unusual step of drafting a lengthy defense of his unpopular action.

Beginning with an expression of his personal sympathy for the humanitarian spirit of the bill, the president insisted that he was obligated to suppress his own better instincts in order to consider the issue purely on legal grounds. Thus he opened with the question of "whether any such act, on the part of the federal government, is warranted and sanctioned by the constitution." If one accepted the principle inherent in Dix's bill, where was the general government then to draw the line? If Congress had the power to "make provision for the indigent insane" any place outside the District of Columbia, he warned, it could claim with equal authority "to provide for the indigent who are not insane, and thus to transfer to the federal government the charge of all the poor in all the States." By signing Dix's bill into law, he claimed that he would have been opening a Pandora's box, and that there would have been no end of demands for federal aid. The federal government would become a giant social welfare agency, supplanting the states and undermining the national economy.[42]

This much said, Pierce attempted to leave himself some latitude to support the several land-grant railroad measures he expected to sign over the next few years. Despite his constitutional scruples, he said, he did not mean to cling to a foolish consistency in land policy. There were many times when the federal government was called upon to act as a responsible property manager or a prudent proprietor working to enhance the sale value of its real estate.[43]

Franklin Pierce from an oil portrait in 1853.

The dangers of Dix's approach, however, both to constitutional order and to the fabric of federalism, he could easily predict. By providing charity the federal government would dry up private philanthropy. Even the states themselves would likely become "humble supplicants" for federal aid and turn their "true relation to this Union" upside down. He said that in its exhaustive debates over founding a national university, the Constitutional Convention had determined once and for all that land grants for public institutions were properly the business of the states. He knew that supporters of the measure had pointed to numerous precedents for federal land grants—from the "sixteenth sections" provision of the Northwest Ordinance to small grants of land for deaf and dumb asylums in Connecticut and Kentucky. But it would be foolhardy to compound these mistakes of the past. Congress needed to learn to operate within the limits of its constitutional powers.[44]

Pierce's veto of the land bill, for all his constitutional justification of it, was largely a tactic to assert some measure of authority over an unruly Congress in the midst of the Kansas-Nebraska fight. But as a power play it was a dismal failure. If anything, his unpopular action, which became front-page news around the country, served to widen the rift between Congress and the administration. Outside the halls of the Capitol, the *National Intelligencer* expressed outrage that Pierce had paid so little heed to the wishes of the people clearly voiced by their representatives. Denying that any legitimate constitutional issue existed, the paper added that "it is generally agreed that the veto power was not given to be interposed except on constitutional questions."

Inside, North Carolina Senator George E. Badger voiced the opinion of dozens of his colleagues when he rose to urge them to override the president. Citing Thomas Jefferson's principle that the presidential veto should never be exercised to subvert the will of the people, Badger insisted that "the Constitution consists not in that printed book. . . . it is in the meaning of that book." Dix's bill plainly complied with the spirit of the nation's fundamental law. Indeed, it represented "the first time in the history of the country [that] a measure has been passed through both Houses of Congress to do an act of general benefit and justice to all the States of the Union, to allow all to have some beneficial interest upon fair and equal terms in what is the common property of all." If the president sincerely believed the bill raised an issue of constitutional law, Senator Foot remarked, he ought to have left the matter for the federal courts to decide. Mississippi Senator Albert G. Brown, irritated by what he saw as Pierce's usurpation of congressional authority, declared that he thought that Dix's was the "first land bill ever brought forward in the true spirit of the deeds of cession." If the Constitution, moreover, gave Congress the right to grant land to railroads and veterans of the War of 1812—as Pierce acknowledged it did—how could the same principle fail to apply to the insane poor?[45]

In an extraordinarily long-winded speech that took its listeners back to the Magna Carta, Delaware Senator John M. Clayton pointedly asked Pierce, "how is the country to be . . . corrupted by the building of roads and establishment of asylums for the indigent insane?" Supporters of the Homestead bill seemed to him to be perfectly willing to dole out millions of acres to speculators, squatters, and "every jailbird flying from Europe." What principles did the president apply when he decided whether or not federal resources should be used to save the perishing? Would he support a federal rescue effort for twenty thousand people aboard a sinking ship, or who were held captive by the Turks?[46]

Pierce had never been popular with the press, and newspapers pounced on the veto as an example of presidential arrogance and abuse of power. Against the argument that the measure would set the government on the slippery slope of increasing intervention in the internal affairs of the states, the *Boston Daily Advertiser* reminded its readers that by the terms of the bill, the states would retain "exclusive jurisdiction . . . for the care of the indigent population." Money from the sale of the public domain was to provide adequate funding for new or existing state programs, not direct federal control. His more extreme opponents accused Pierce of a high-handed "attempt to act the tyrant." The veto message, according to the Whig *Atlas*, represented a declaration of war "not only against justice, but also mercy" that was "totally unworthy of the President of the United States."[47]

The president's supporters were equally vehement. No one questioned the pure motives of its standard-bearer but to its opponents, Dix's land bill threatened the Constitution and rights of the states. For Stephen Douglas, who strongly endorsed the veto, apart from any questions of humanitarianism, the measure "open[ed] a door to the extension of the power of the Government and its jurisdiction, in derogation of the rights of the States to a wider and more fearful extent than any bill or proposition which I have ever known to be presented." Illinois, where Dix herself had worked with the legislature, was, he noted, already establishing a good system of institutions without federal aid. Dix's memorials seemed to show that other states were rapidly following suit. This was fitting. The care of dependent classes was rightly left to the states. Because Douglas did not believe for an instant "that the condition of the insane, or of the deaf, of the dumb, or the blind, of the poor, will be benefitted by withdrawing them from the jurisdiction of the States, and placing them under the Federal Government." Along the same lines, the most extreme criticism of the bill came from an editor named Alfred Nicholson, a close friend of the president. "The tendency to loose legislation is a monster evil of our times," he declared. "All these attempts to legislate for a class, or to encourage expenditures of the public money, or to nullify the practical meaning of the constitution [*sic*]," he editorialized, are "made the more dangerous by the pretext, or the belief, (we care not how false or how sincere the motive,) that the particular proposition is intended to help the masses, or to carry out some benevolent project." He was thankful for the president's "lucid, straightforward" veto message, which he called a superb defense *against the blandishments of those who unwittingly ask its violation in the name of humanity*."[48]

Since Dix had personalized the Ten Million Acre bill so intensely, those who knew her worried that the veto and the rhetoric that had supported it would exact a heavy toll on her spirit. New York congressman James G. King had been concerned for some time that she had virtually staked her life on the bill and that its failure would bring on a fatal *"heart sickness.*"[49] When Anne Heath first heard news of the veto, she told Dix, it "fell on my spirits like a weight of ice." Pierce, she added, "was undoubtedly drunk . . . the poor tool." She feared Dix might lapse into depression, given so deep a disappointment, but was soon relieved to see that her old friend was stronger than she imagined. "The Evil eye must fall on a more faltering character," she wrote, "to have any withering effect."[50]

In fact, Dix's first reaction to the veto was anger. She was outraged, seeing that on the threshold of her supreme political triumph she stood repudiated by the leader of the system she had all but mastered. Bitterly she accused Pierce of having gone back on his promise to her, and her first instinct was to mount a direct assault by writing "a publication showing that the President had declared himself in favor of the bill." While Pierce had claimed that "his *'conscience'* would not suffer him to make the bill a law," Dix remarked, "all here know it was Jefferson Davis who would not suffer it." She was not without solid grounds for suspecting Pierce's secretary of war, Davis. In 1851, when he was a senator from Mississippi, he had raised the same objections to Dix's proposal that Pierce now voiced. To dispense charities to any class, whether the insane or "the whole range of paupers whose provision is now confined to the communities to which they belong," he had insisted, "the objectives are all left to the Sovereign States." When Dix, trying to reconstruct how things had gone awry, placed Pierce's message alongside a transcript of Davis's earlier tirade from the Senate floor, she found striking similarities. But whether or not the president was a pawn of Davis, the deed was done.[51]

In the wake of the president's action, Dix still held out a small hope that the veto might be overridden. "In this game of abstract Chess I am waging with the President," she wrote, "thus far I hold all the advantage." As the Congress continued to debate Pierce's veto message, however, she became discouraged. "I cannot *Bribe*[,] and absenteeism I cannot control," she remarked with disgust. The political system awarded few advantages to those who stuck to a losing cause. By midsummer she realized it would be impossible to marshal the two-thirds majorities she would need. When the vote came in the Senate, the veto was sustained twenty-six to twenty-one, some of her Democratic supporters falling back into party line. She saw her congressional coalition disintegrate, she thought, before the question was fairly settled. In many ways, the president's act was consistent with her view of how unprincipled and incompetent the "fathers of the land" were when it came to accepting the moral leadership that was offered to them. In a battle between politics and social justice, politics had triumphed. When several senators who had originally voted for the bill succumbed to pressure from the White House to uphold the president, Dix sarcastically commented that "the price for their forfeited honour is not shown; probably [Pierce's] bid for so poor a commodity was not high." Pierce, a devil to whom she attributed only the darkest of motives, she singled out for special scorn as an unprincipled weakling, saying "I would certainly not exchange either mental, moral, nor social states with the President, poor man!"[52]

Her righteous indignation and anger, however, could not alleviate her sadness and sense of loss. "The poor weak President has by an unprecedented extremity of folly lacerated my life," she confided to Heath shortly after the Senate voted to uphold the president. "May God forgive him—and I will try to forgive and to forget him also." How unsuccessful she was in carrying out this resolution is apparent from her correspondence in later years. For example, when in 1857 she learned that the city of Savannah had presented Pierce with a plaque for his distinguished public service, she acidly quipped that "one seems to see inscribed on it Judas the Younger."[53]

The Pierce veto was a devastating affront not only to her ego, which was completely wrapped up in the measure, but also to her sense of optimism for the republic. As she would gradually discover, the veto defined for the first time a limit to the ascent of her work, and thus symbolized a dark deprivation of possibility that was forced on her. Watching her ephemeral political coalition dissipate as she vainly tried to mount a campaign to override the president, Dix foresaw the demise of her own political career and, with it, her dream of a more virtuous society.

Her opinion that the failure of her crusade could be reduced to the capricious action of one man, while psychologically comforting, was rooted in a basic misreading of the political situation in antebellum America.

Pierce vetoed her measure halfway through a year that produced, among other things, a spate of spectacular Know-Nothing election victories (which heightened anti-immigrant tensions), the Kansas-Nebraska bill (which repealed the slavery-extension provisions of the Missouri Compromise, touching off unprecedented violence in the territories), the publication of George Fitzhugh's vigorously proslavery *Sociology for the South*, and the early phase of organization of the Republican party. These movements and events, when she noticed them at all, Dix regarded as examples of political folly, not evidence of fundamental moral or social ills. Ignoring the deepening sectional conflict over slavery, she stubbornly pushed the Whiggish idea of extending the constitution into the realm of social welfare. In doing this she was out of step with a nation marching not toward utopia but disunion. The national, more centralized kind of government her policy implied could not have existed in a country that was rapidly coming to see itself as two separate nations. Before the government in Washington could effectively legislate the essential interest of any group, it had first to settle more basic question's of national identity, above all, the question of slavery. Thus, the impending crisis of the Union rapidly made all other national issues seem unimportant.

Yet in the longer sweep of American history the significance of the issue Dix first posed to the nation stands out. For her mission worked against the American grain, and against the laissez-faire parochialism of her contemporaries, to commit the state to the welfare of its least able constituents. Americans in the 1840s and 1850s understood this as a novel proposition. They considered it skeptically and implemented its central institution—the asylum—tentatively, attempting at every stage to cut expenditures to the bone. No one knew better than Dix how parsimonious her countrymen were when it came to the economics of compassion.[54] Not surprisingly, their solutions to the evils of insanity and poverty proved to be inadequate from the beginning, for they lacked the political will to address these problems in their full social context. Using the resources of the national government—even on the limited scale that Dix's data suggested was necessary for the basic social welfare of a single class of dependents—was inconsistent with the whole direction of American policy.

Americans have never favored redistributing wealth on a scale large enough to make a decent provision for the poor, sane or insane. Yet for one woman to have made any mark on the national conscience was an admirable failure. Sadly, in the course of the next century and a half, the nation has done little to improve upon it.

CHAPTER THIRTEEN

The American Missionary to the Mad

She had failed in her greatest fight. And for a time, as she tried to decipher what the defeat meant for her career, she wondered whether Pierce's atrocious veto had sapped her of the energy, the will, the nerve she needed to regain the battlefield of politics.

Disappointment of this magnitude, so public and undeniable, was something Dix had never faced. She hardly knew how to respond. Out of habit she spent the summer of 1854 going through the old motions, inspecting asylums, conferring with medical superintendents and legislators as though nothing had changed. Beneath the façade of routine, though, she was dangerously foundering. Dulled by a general lassitude, heavy with fatigue, she now knew herself well enough to seek some catharsis for her spirit to keep from spiraling into a breakdown. Earlier that year she had turned down an invitation to accompany John Adams Dix and his family to Italy. Tourism for its own sake had scant appeal. At the end of August, however, after a few consoling, domestic weeks in Boston with Anne Heath and George Barrell Emerson, she caught her friends by surprise with an announcement that she intended to sail immediately for England. Yearning for some source of vitality, she had decided to pay a visit to the "dear old home," as she called her first sanctuary, William Rathbone's Greenbank.[1]

Leaving Brookline hurriedly to meet her ship in New York, she boarded the *Arctic,* one of the Collins Line's fast new paddle steamers that had cut the crossing to Europe from weeks to days. It weighed anchor on 2 September 1854, bound for Liverpool. A dockside society columnist for one of the local dailies remarked on Dix's feeble demeanor, concluding that "her nervous system is completely prostrated." As the voyage began, despite rough seas, Dix's spirits soon rallied. In honor of her public service—and, not incidentally, as a public relations gesture meant to encourage ongoing federal subsidies of the Collins line—E. K. Collins, the principal owner, had offered her a first-class stateroom of her own, free of charge. With nothing to do for nine days during the crossing, she relaxed as much as she could, chiding herself all the while for feeling so listless.[2]

Before the Civil War a sojourn abroad was still the prerogative of the rich; and it was soothing for her to find that her well-turned-out fellow passengers were engaging, respectful, and politely curious. "I know most of those on board," she said as they pulled into port, "and never was associated with a pleasanter circle of persons on any vessel." Whenever it suited her, she could become the center of attention, entertaining them with tales of insanity on the American frontier and imbecility in Washington. And even at sea, she could not resist seizing small opportunities for philanthropy. Noticing several gamblers setting odds on the steamer's time of arrival, for example, she waited until their bets were settled. "I . . . then asked the winner for the winnings," she proudly told Anne Heath, "which I put into the Captain's care for the benefit of 'the Home for the children of Indigent Sailors now Orphans' at New York." By asking each of the seventy-five passengers to make donations of a dollar or two, she reckoned that she could collect at least a hundred dollars—a sum almost substantial enough in itself to justify her excursion.[3]

Before she returned to Liverpool, she had an image of England in mind, a misty picture of Greenbank as she had left it in the mid-1830s. As she discovered almost immediately, though, another England had taken its place—a country whose sociopolitical climate had undergone profound changes, doubly magnified because she herself had changed even more. She returned not as the provincial Bostonian of her younger days but a woman of accomplishment and wide public experience. Now she beheld Britain and its peoples through the lens of her own career.

She had known no greater happiness than her first encounter with the Rathbones and had subsequently exalted them as mythical figures. Accordingly Dix ran the risk of serious disillusionment had they fallen short of her expectations. Yet when she became reacquainted with the family, despite everything that had happened over the years, time seemed to have stood still. In their early sixties, William and Elizabeth Rathbone, however they had changed, still lived up to her fondest memories. And they welcomed her affectionately, genuinely proud of her achievements, as though she were their prodigal daughter. For the first several days they did nothing but catch up, conversing animatedly through dinner as servants quietly shuffled in and out, then moving into the carpeted sitting room, where the Rathbones and their visitors talked late into the night. "It gives me pleasure to think you are at Green Bank," a British alienist and occasional dinner guest once told her. "There is something always encircling the family of Rathbone which is not of this vulgar world, but half-divine."[4]

Perennially engaged in reforming society, from improving the corporation schools to raising money for Liverpool's charity hospital, the Rathbones set about reintroducing her to their world. A sense of that world appeared in the *Liverpool Mercury* many years later, in April 1868, after William Rathbone had died. On the afternoon of his burial, one hundred carriages had followed his coffin in the rain to the family plot. "His house became almost a sort of refuge," the newspaper observed, "for men who had made any sacrifice for the sake of conscience or principle." And, it might have added, for women. In a letter of eulogy to his son, Dix mused on the meaning of Rathbone's example. His was a long and honorable life, she wrote, "marked by the daily exercise of enlarged liberality; care for national faith, public and local institutions of both learning and charity, and rare disinterestedness, unto good-works from which was banished all self-aggrandizement and self-elation." He was a worthy father.[5]

Inasmuch as she had an itinerary, she had planned to proceed, after a short visit to Greenbank, directly to the Continent. But England and the Rathbones proved far too interesting to leave. "I am still here with dear friends," she informed Heath after a week, "much occupied with charitable institutions and the meetings of the British Scientific Association." Science and technology always fascinated her. In England her

William Rathbone III.

renown, and her acquaintance with the American scientists Benjamin Silliman, Joseph Henry, and Robert Hare, brought her to the attention of Sir Walter Calverly Trevelyan, an amateur geologist and botanist who owned agricultural estates from Scotland to Sussex. Finding her intelligent and charming, Trevelyan and his wife included her in their circle and invited her to visit them in northern Scotland. She was naturally flattered and intrigued. Even if one were not overly fond of socializing, the attraction of the landed gentry with its vast wealth and social preeminence was hard to resist.[6]

The England to which Dix returned had rebounded from the economic upheavals of the 1830s and 1840s, and had entered a phase of comparative political stability that has since been dubbed "the age of equipoise." Barely underneath the surface, however, was an ominous turbulence. Throughout the industrial centers of England, the mid-Victorian period witnessed a rapid shifting of the population as workers streamed in from the countryside in search of new factory jobs. The result was a series of social dislocations that overwhelmed local philanthropic agencies, rooted as they were in the old preindustrial order. Factories were notoriously crowded and dangerous; the urban infrastructure, choked with soot and sewage, deteriorated; public services were swamped. Living conditions for industrial workers and their families were horrifying and, as they were brought to light, assaulted the nation's sensibilities and principles of common decency. In consequence, bourgeois complacency was assailed by more diligent and searching explorations into poverty, crime, and insanity than any conducted earlier in the century.[7]

Beginning in the autumn of 1849, for example, the journalist and amateur social scientist Henry Mayhew published a bellwether series of articles in London's *Morning Chronicle* that formed the basis for his four-volume *London Labour and the London Poor* (1861–62). Reading Mayhew, as every English reformer did, Dix must have been struck by certain resemblances between his mission and her own. For he styled himself as a "traveller in the undiscovered country of the poor." Here was another unflinching witness who sought to startle his compatriots out their self-satisfaction by bringing to life scenes of poverty, as he put it, "in all their stark literality." Mayhew's interest in exposing the lot of the poor echoed in diverse quarters—in the works of the Christian Socialists F. D. Maurice and Charles Kingsley, social commentators like Thomas Carlyle, and most famously Charles Dickens, who had just published a novel called *Hard Times*.[8]

Because poverty and its consequences never received the quality of intellectual attention in Victorian America that they commanded in England, Dix, like most of her countrymen, failed to appreciate the profound anxieties that suffused the debate over how to deal with the poor. Her focus was narrower. Theories of economics either failed to interest her or went over her head. So did matters like the exploitation of workers, Chartism (an early movement to organize English labor), and the fears of working-class violence and revolution the Chartists spawned.

To her bafflement the English seemed obsessed by poverty. Welfare had grown into a major industry. Nothing had prepared her for "the vast number of Charitable Institutions in all towns and cities," each with its special constituency and its own peculiar theories. It was one thing to create jobs so the poor could become self-reliant, she said, but quite another "to put a premium on Pauperism," as she thought the English had done. "To give to the idle or to the unoccupied *establishes* beggary." It alarmed her to think that many English philanthropists, including the Rathbones themselves, considered their largesse a fulfillment of Christian duty. On matters like this, as when she was queried about where she stood on Catholicism, though, Dix was circumspect and kept her own counsel. "When any good can be done through a knowledge of disagreeable facts or the discussion of unwelcome topics I would never turn away," she told Anne Heath, "but as it is I think ignorance is the best discretion."[9]

But silence had its limits. She found it all but impossible to refrain from scolding her British cousins for what she deemed preposterous and unmerited enthusiasm over the recent visit of Harriet Beecher Stowe. With much fanfare, the author of *Uncle Tom's Cabin* had been acclaimed as the finest flower of the American conscience. On behalf of American antislavery, the Liverpool Negroes' Friend Society had given Stowe 130 gold sovereigns raised mostly from the working class by penny subscriptions. Not to be outdone, Scottish abolitionists had presented her with "1,000 gold sovereigns on a silver salver," collected in the same manner. "I have been really mortified to find an American taking collections, as a *personal relief fund*, in Ireland, Scotland and England," she confided caustically to Fillmore, "under such influences as those used by Mrs. Stowe. I am afraid I hardly excuse this sort of pauperism."[10]

As the weeks and months passed, though, careful observation began to sharpen her picture of England, and she found herself unsettled by a side of English society that she had been unwilling to believe existed until she saw it with her own eyes. Her interest in the insane brought her, in due course, to explore the bleak workhouses of England, Ireland, and Scotland. Within their walls she saw huddled the losers in the market economy's inexorable laissez-faire competition. "There are so few ways in which the laboring classes can benefit themselves in this country," she finally conceded. "There are no middle classes as with us—and the rich control the poor beyond any power of the laborer to shake off." She was disgusted by the abject filth everywhere in the factory slums, the pervasive intemperance, the crude language. Still, the Rathbones and their genteel friends assured her that present circumstances, bad as they might look to an outsider, represented real progress over the past—a thought that prompted her to remark, "I do not know what they could have been—once." She told Millard Fillmore that if the miserable subjection and suppression of the lower classes she witnessed in England was, as the upper class routinely argued, an inevitable product of free-market capitalism, it boded ill for American society. Seeing where it all led, she felt she saw early signs of the same inequalities already forming in New York and elsewhere.[11]

In light of her recent political experience in Washington, struggling against the tide to persuade lawmakers that the national government ought to face up to its responsibility for the social welfare of its con- stituents, she found that England presented a striking contrast. Broadly speaking, Britain was in the midst of a transformation of its public institutions that was nothing less than a revolution in government. Despite a body of theory, advocated prominently at different times by Robert Peel, William Gladstone, and other politicians, that government should be pruned back, its role strictly limited, Whitehall had become more than ever the focus for social welfare reform. What was Parlia- ment's role, it was asked, if not to secure the commonwealth by eradi- cating social evils? In the decades after the Reform Bill of 1832, reformers' efforts to guide government policy and state institutions were gathering momentum on all sides.[12]

Nowhere did opportunities for state intervention appear more allur- ing than within the British asylum movement. Building on the early nineteenth-century tradition of parliamentary investigation and regula- tion that Dix knew so well, by the early 1850s lunacy reformers were achieving a high degree of central control. Through Parliament, the British asylum physicians actively pushed measures to restrict the care of lunatics in private institutions, tighten the government's administrative grasp of qualifications and licensure, and thus consolidate the medical profession's sovereignty over the realm of madness and its treatment.

As the government was induced to take an increasingly strong stance in asylumdom, the British medical profession alertly reorganized itself to capitalize on changing social policy. A full generation earlier than their American counterparts, British physicians had consolidated their position as licensed practitioners and had begun formally to segment their profession into fields of specialization. This clever and very effec- tive tactic of subdivision, heralded every step of the way by proclama- tions of medical quality, worked to suppress competition. Quacks and unlicensed practitioners were painted as a danger to the public. Those asylum doctors and professional alienists who had the right credentials welcomed an increasingly active role for government. And this, in turn, connected with a tradition of inspection and medical supervision that went back to the late eighteenth century. Since then, calls for strong state intervention in asylum affairs had resounded in the recommenda- tions of the Parliamentary Select Committee on Madhouses. Had mea- sures proposed in 1815–16 been enacted, England and Scotland would then have adopted a compulsory asylum system for all the insane poor, along with a regimen of national inspection. Even so, by midcentury British asylum physicians, with growing parliamentary support, asserted a dominance over their field that American asylum superintendents could only envy.[13]

Nothing illustrates the political differences between the American and British lunacy reform movements more clearly than the attributes of their respective leaders. Both were lay reformers who focused their efforts on legislation and government power. But in America, Dorothea Dix remained an outsider: a woman with no official standing, operating alone on the periphery of government. In England, on the other hand, the chairman of the Parliamentary Lunacy Commission was a consummate insider: Anthony Ashley Cooper, the seventh earl of Shaftesbury, a conservative ideologue with evangelical sympathies, an aristocrat, a conservative, a lion of the reform establishment, who had served in Parliament for twenty-eight years. Reaching instinctively for the levers of government, Shaftesbury had been instrumental in passing the watershed laws of 1845 that empowered Parliament to create a network of county asylums. This was intended to be the first step toward eliminating Britain's private madhouses—the far-flung cottage industry that reformers disparagingly termed "the trade in lunacy." In words similar to the language Dix used in her state and federal memorials, Shaftesbury had closed his Lunacy Report to Parliament in 1844 with a call for bold new legislation. "These unhappy persons are outcasts from all the social and domestic affections of private life," he insisted, "and have no refuge but in the laws." It was government's solemn duty, he implored his fellow members, to "soothe the days of the incurable [insane] and restore many sufferers to health and usefulness." He hardly needed to add that his motion was not for himself but was "made on behalf of the most helpless, if not the most afflicted, portion of the human race," thus summoning up the same mixture of disinterested morality and rationality Dix employed.[14]

The British aristocracy was its own tiny, closed universe. As important as anything, Dix had in William Rathbone a friend and sponsor who was, if not quite Shaftesbury's social equal, someone who moved in the same circles and who could provide her with the requisite introductions. Greenbank's pastoral charms, enhanced by an unusually mild fall, prompted Dix to reconsider her original thought of moving on when the weather turned cold to tour France and Italy. "I have avoided the Continent this Winter altogether," she later told Millard Fillmore.

"Here I am gratified in the midst of highly cultivated society. . . . Here I *learn*, abroad on the Continent, I should *see*."[15]

Despite her intention to stay, after a few weeks at Greenbank her native impatience began to show. With a spate of energy, she visited the asylum and the thousand-inmate prison in Liverpool. They were hardly model institutions; in fact the Royal Asylum at Rainhill, just a few miles from Greenbank, verged on the disgraceful. Whether or not its filthy, overcrowded state had something to do with the Irish immigration that continued to choke Liverpool, she did not know. Nor was she by any means prepared to start making waves in a foreign country and risk embarrassing her hosts. Nevertheless, having read so much about Britain's asylums, she was beset with the idea of studying them. How did they compare with the institutions she had helped to found? This was a question American asylum superintendents, many of whom toured Europe, constantly debated. Daily she heard stories that piqued her curiosity. England itself, by most accounts, was generally at the forefront of modern asylum care. Other parts of the kingdom, however, were rumored to harbor places that were throwbacks to the Dark Ages. Ireland, Scotland, and Wales, each had its detractors, but there were little reliable data. She reckoned that in a kind of working holiday, without calling attention to herself, she could put her travels to use. With little idea what to expect, she would simply go forth as she had done for years, walking through hospital wards, exchanging a few words of consolation or encouragement with inmates. It was none of her business to stir up trouble, she explained to Heath, but merely to "gather up a store of knowledge for future use."[16]

Setting a heroic pace, she combed Ireland from south to north, moving briskly from one town to the next, rarely spending more than one night under the same roof. Part of the time she traveled alone, and part of the time with a group of Quakers who had convened to inspect the island's schools. The Rathbones had furnished her with introductions to a number of the country's leading families, and she had letters from the archbishop and lord chancellor as well. "The educated inhabitants," by which she meant the island's Protestant elite, she pronounced "a most interesting people." Whenever people got wind of who she was, they hailed her as a visiting dignitary. And in a nation of storytellers she was a great talker, uncommonly knowledgeable, opinionated, and adventuresome for a woman. While visiting the 150-bed Ballinasloe asylum, she procured an invitation to dine at Parsontown

Castle, where Lord Ross had installed a renowned telescope. The lord's manservant escorted her from her hotel to the castle, where, after dinner, she and the rest of his party spent the clear night, until four o'clock in the morning, "swinging in mid-air, sixty feet from the ground . . . on a massive gallery, by turn, looking through the most magnificent telescope in the world."[17]

Yet beneath the veneer of wealth and education, she confronted another Ireland, a country she described as made up of "the lowest class[,] squalid, ignorant, and with only one wish stimulating their dull lives; viz. the hope of emigrating to America." Left to their own devices, these human dregs of the Emerald Isle posed a threat to the United States and its institutions for the insane. "We reap the course of a vicious population—sent over to people our now fast corrupted and overburthened country." This xenophobia hardened her prejudice against the Irish and, by extension, against Catholicism. Subsequently she would go so far as to propose that Irish lunatics were a lower order of beings, and that they should be separated within hospitals from other patients. Upon returning to America, she quietly asked a handful of asylum superintendents to tally their Irish patients with an eye to displacing them in favor of "our citizens." (When doctors pointed out that only a small minority of patients—37 out of 247 in the case of the Pennsylvania State Lunatic Hospital—were "Irish, German, Welsh & English," it did nothing to soften her preconceptions.) Paranoia about Irish immigration was endemic in Boston, infecting many otherwise sound minds. Even as genial a soul as Dix's friend, George Barrell Emerson, could be found attacking a proposal to build a new asylum in Massachusetts on nativist grounds. "If the contemplated palace should be built, it would not long want occupants," he warned. "The news would quickly reach Ireland. Pictures of the building would be sent there. Families liable to insanity would be invited and aided to come to Boston, and the squalid, unhealthy habitations which would receive them would soon complete the work of developing the inherent insanity."[18]

To her surprise, however, she had to admit that Ireland's native "Institutions, as Hospitals, Work-Houses, schools, and Prisons, are in the main excellently directed." Other visitors to Ireland remarked on the same thing. Harriet Martineau, for example, distressed as she was about pauperism in the Irish countryside, called the modern asylum at Killarney a palace. A Toronto physician named Joseph Workman who visited Ireland and published his impressions in the *American Journal of*

Insanity was likewise astonished. "Certainly had I not seen it," he wrote, "I could never have believed that contiguous to such a den of filth, laziness, and unaspiring poverty, as the old town of Killarney presented to my organs of sight and smell, so pretty, clean, and comfortable insane asylum could be established." Beginning in the 1830s, Ireland launched a concerted effort, bolstered by strong national legislation, to segregate the mad in institutions of their own. Considering the country's abysmal poverty, its elaborate provision for small numbers of lunatics seems vastly out of proportion. Between 1825 and Dix's visit in 1854, the Irish state, in a centrally managed construction program, put up at least fifteen new facilities. At midcentury, increasingly under the aegis of the medical profession, Dublin castle's asylum program far outshone any other social welfare enterprise. Dix seldom weighed the costs of hospital construction against other social reforms, though, so it is little wonder she approved of Irish priorities.[19]

Scotland proved to be another matter entirely.

She did not travel north on a mission. Lord Trevelyan had invited her to visit his immense estate in northern Scotland, where he was busy experimenting with new breeds of cattle. The Rathbones, trying to slow her down a bit, suggested she make it a leisurely trip and first spend a few weeks in the majestic city of Edinburgh, where they arranged for her to lodge with a wealthy widow they knew. Dix seldom paused for the merely picturesque, but the venerable city moved her, she said, beyond her powers of description. She told Heath that she had seen nothing in Britain or America to compare with it. Sir Walter Scott was one of the few novelists she had ever read with pleasure, and to walk by his fine house, to imagine his valorous heroes riding across the blue-green heath, touched in her a romantic chord.

Between her hostess, a formidable woman named Carnegie, and letters from the Rathbones, she gained entrée into Edinburgh's best society, and there was no shortage of invitations to teas and dinners. As usual, she was far less interested in socializing than in strolling the city's narrow, cobbled streets and making casual inquiries into how the community provided for its mad.

It did not take her long to detect the scent of scandal. After just two days' perambulation, she knew beyond a doubt that something was gravely amiss in local madhouses. "Of those," she wrote, "none are so much needing quick reform as the *private* establishments for the insane."

Although she had barely unpacked her luggage, she had already reached the conclusion that God meant for her to take a stand against exploitation of the insane in Scotland. The prospect of resuming her work in Edinburgh galvanized her. "I am confident that this move is to rest with me—and the sooner I address myself to this work of humanity the sooner will my conscience cease to suggest effort or rebuke inaction," she told Heath. "It will be no holiday work however—but hundreds of miserable creatures may be released from a bitter bondage—which the people at large are quite unconscious of. It is true I came here for plea-sure[,] but that is no reason why I should close my eyes to the condition of these most hapless of all God's creatures. These most afflicted of living beings."[20]

At first glance, Dix's impulse to bring reform to Scotland would seem to have been the moral equivalent of carrying coals to Newcastle. The ancient city, with its distinguished medical school and large asylum, was hardly a backwater.

In fact, the roots of lunacy reform in Scotland went back nearly four decades. Whether or not Dix remembered it, Parliament's 1816 Select Committee on Madhouses had devoted the bulk of its *Third Report* to conditions in Scotland. To compile this survey of the country, the commissioners had charged Scotland's county sheriffs with visiting each madhouse north of the border and detailing "the state and condition of these Houses, both the public and the private ones." Under a statue of 1815, the sheriffs were given sole responsibility for licensing madhouses, inspecting them every six months, and collecting affidavits from physicians to ensure that no sane inmate was pronounced mad and locked up under false pretenses. The result of the first parliamentary inquiry was a painstaking chronicle covering all Scotland. Among other parliamentary documents, it was a source for Dix's own *Memorial to the Legislature of Massachusetts*.

In the early days, between 1816 and 1819, Parliament disappointed the reformers because it failed to pass the sweeping legislation they favored. Still, despite the absence of government sanctions, Scotland continued to produce its share of charity asylums and reform-minded asylum doctors. In 1837, for example, William Alexander Francis Brown, the medical superintendent of the Montrose asylum and a former president of Edinburgh's Royal Medical Society, published an influential and widely quoted *summa* on behalf of moral treatment, *What Asylums Were, Are, and Ought to Be*. This book had a vogue in America as well as England. Dix deemed it a masterful work. Two years later, Browne assumed the helm of the Crichton Royal Asylum at Dumfries. The new institution, enjoying generous private philanthropic support, was meant to exemplify moral treatment and to provide Scotland's mentally disordered with the best care that modern medicine could offer.[21]

Beyond a superficial similarity, though, the asylum systems in England and Scotland had evolved along quite different lines. Their differences stemmed from an underlying political tension that had deep sociocultural roots. The Union of 1707, incorporating Scotland into the United Kingdom, had never resolved vital differences of national character. Scotland continued to retain a large measure of legislative autonomy, and its leaders proudly resisted parliamentary encroachments into the nation's domestic affairs. Above all, Scottish leaders, proud of their conservatism, disdained England's New Poor Law reforms of the 1830s. The Scots had decidedly un-Whiggish ideas about how to deal with poverty and indigence. In principle they eschewed a public, tax-based welfare program as overgenerous, indiscriminate charity, feeling sure that it would sabotage the work ethic among the able-bodied poor. Rather than extend the Poor Law northward, Scotland tenaciously held onto its voluntary parish-based system of poor relief. It was not until the mid-1840s, when a schism within the Church of Scotland finally made it impossible for the church to continue to perform its time-honored administration of welfare to the unemployed, that things began to change. In political terms, social welfare policy was extremely important, for it led directly to the proper role of Whitehall and the reach of Britain's national government. Whether or not Dix realized it, lunacy reform in Scotland would raise fundamental questions about to what extent and for what purposes Whitehall should make policy and concentrate power.[22]

Presbyterian belief in its own frugal poor law practices, as well as a basic fear of opening the way for increased English meddling in its internal affairs, had prompted Scotland to attack the 1818 Scottish lunacy bill. This law, along with similar legislation proposed for England, constituted the lunacy reformers' first major attempt to create a national asylum system. The bills before Parliament in 1818 and 1819 failed; and in Scotland the matter was put to rest for almost forty years. In England, by contrast, there continued to be sustained agitation for government intervention. As the result of successive rounds of parliamentary inquiry, between 1828 and 1845 the key elements of a new state policy were put into place. The moment of triumph came in 1845 in the form of laws that authorized the building of county and borough asylums for the insane poor. These laws also instituted the powerful Lunacy Commission, a national board charged with inspecting and regulating all types of institutions for the mad. Scotland remained conspicuously outside the fold. So in 1848, shortly after the English laws were passed, Shaftesbury and his fellow parliamentarian reformers drafted a new bill to extend the county asylum act to Scotland. But Scottish opposition proved so fierce that the measure was withdrawn before the House of Commons could vote on it.

From the other side of the Atlantic, Dix had watched these events with more than casual interest. In many respects England had furnished her with an example for her own crusade. Now, strangely enough, her work in Scotland broached constitutional issues similar to those she had unwittingly raised in her failed land bill.

The Scots remained skeptical of English reform. Just as they scorned English poor relief, they opposed what they saw as a heavy-handed, compulsory English asylum system. Why abandon local control of local institutions? Few Scots saw any compelling reason to change their traditional community-based approach to dealing with the mad. Depending on the severity of their illness and the amplitude of their means, lunatics could have been committed to one of Scotland's seven royal asylums—modest charity facilities, for the most part, called "royal" because they had received corporate charters from the Crown. Those whose symptoms were more manageable were normally placed with citizens who contracted to provide them room and board. If the afflicted could fall back on people in the community, most counties encouraged the time-honored practice of placing them in homes of friends or relatives. Over the years, some guardians of the mad made a business of home care. Some of them took on groups of boarders and became proprietors of so-called licensed madhouses—a broad term that covered a multitude of arrangements. At the time Dix visited, Scotland was officially estimated to have a total insane population of 7,403 souls, 3,904 of whom were listed as impoverished. Technically speaking, a board of supervisors based in Edinburgh (analogous to the Poor Law Commission in London) was responsible for overseeing their welfare.[23]

For all its gaps and imperfections, there was little if any sense that the Scottish system was in dire straits. The city's Royal Morningside Asylum, with more than 450 inmates, was the largest such facility in Scotland. Dix, when she inspected it, found the place generally above reproach. By contrast, the licensed houses fit perfectly into the pattern of her previous work. They operated on a familial, not a medical, model. Thus, in her eyes, they were a throwback to what she had discovered throughout villages and counties of her own country in the preasylum era. Home care and private ministrations, even though provided with wonderful tenderness and the best intentions, could never, she insisted, measure up to the curative environment of the medically supervised asylum. To be sure, the licensed madhouses were held to regulatory standards. But Dix considered licensure of nonmedical institutions a sham. It was common knowledge that the Scottish supervisors and sheriffs had long since flouted their obligation to rigorously inspect facilities for the mad. Happy enough to pocket a licensing fee, sheriffs regarded subsequent inspection as inconvenient and a waste of time.

Inspection was of course Dix's forte. Motivated by what she called "an exhaustless fund of compassion," she lived to expose what others tried to sweep under the rug. "I am not naturally very active and never do any thing there is a fair chance other people will take up," she wrote to Elizabeth Rathbone from Edinburgh. "So when you know I am busy you may be sure it is lending the 'forlorn hope'—which I conduct to a successful termination through a certain sort of obstinacy that some people make the blunder of calling zeal; and yet the greater blunder of naming . . . philanthropy." (It was not philanthropy, she claimed, because she had no love of her fellow beings in general.) In the winter and spring of 1855 she cast a widening net, visiting a large number of Scotland's public and private establishments. "The *Public* Institutions for the treatment of Insanity are good—*very good*," she told Mrs. Torrey in reference to the royal asylums. "I have visited all these, namely, Dumfries, Marston, Glasgow, Perth, Dundee, Aberdeen, and Edinburgh." But the scores of private madhouses she had seen and, she suspected, dozens more she had been prevented from seeing were simply horrible. "It is pretty plain that I am in for a serious work in both England and Scotland," she observed. "I don't see the end of this beginning."[24]

Hers was not a story Scottish officials were eager to publicize. Dix met her first official resistance when she tried to bring to light the condition of a few "very ill ordered" houses in Musselburgh, six miles outside Edinburgh. Noting that the keepers of the Musselburgh madhouses were negligent to the point of savagery, Dix appealed for a warrant to investigate these and other private establishments. She was told, however, that they fell within the jurisdiction of the sheriff of Mid-Lothian. And as it happened, he was the man who had himself originally issued licenses for the facilities, and who also functioned as the chief justice of the county court. According to the licensure statute of 1815, madhouse proprietors were obliged to open themselves to semiannual inspections by the sheriff and, at his discretion, a consulting physician. In practice, Dix discovered, the sheriff was in connivance with local madhouse keepers. He permitted them to hire their own physicians, then he accepted the doctors' certification at face value. To Dix this represented an obvious conflict of interest. Madhouse keepers were "people of the lowest grade of character, and very ignorant," she complained, and although "the law required them to report abuses, if abuses existed; their pecuniary interests urged them to pass in silence—in fine, the proprietors had the thing all their own way, and they were intent on making money."[25]

This was hardly an exaggeration. Since the proprietors received a fixed annual payment, economics favored not compassion but cutting costs. Without responsible inspection, the patients were in no position to complain. In a case that seemed to typify the evils of perverse incentives, an official investigation into the Musselburgh houses two years later uncovered "one proprietor whose previous occupation had been that of a victual-dealer; another had been an unsuccessful gardener; and the last person who obtained the sheriff's sanction for a license was a woman keeping a public house, who had taken a second house of the reception of lunatics, with the view, as we were told by her daughter, of keeping both for a while, and continuing that which should prove the most successful speculation."[26]

Armed with notebooks full of wrongdoing, Dix met with the sheriff, who, when she reviewed the conditions she had seen "trifled, jested, and prevaricated." Stung by his condescending attitude and annoyed by his indifference to his duty, she left the interview seething, and more determined than ever to expose the whole rotten system over which he presided. The trouble was, when it came to the insane in Scotland the sheriffs were the law. Nevertheless they were not entirely unaccountable, for they were in fact officers of the Crown and, as such, ultimately answerable to Whitehall. Intently searching for a way to foil the sheriff of Mid-Lothian, Dix conferred with a handful of reform-minded physicians in Edinburgh. Unable to agree upon any less drastic remedy, they concluded "that nothing would do but to demand of the Home Secretary, Sir George Gray [sic], in London, a Commission for Investigation."[27]

It would be a bold (and very likely unsuccessful) gamble. No one in Edinburgh was prepared to risk it. So Dix, whose only credentials were her devotion to her cause, her force of personality, and her independence as a foreigner, stepped forward to volunteer. A sense of crisis with high stakes enlivened her; and she had never been one to shrink from storming the main gate. Clearly excited, buoyed by the encouragement of her new acquaintances, she telegraphed Lord Shaftesbury, informing him that she would be on the first train to London and wished to meet with him at three o'clock the following afternoon.

Passing a sleepless night on the royal mail express, she arrived the next morning at King's Cross Station, where a messenger from Shaftesbury met her to confirm their appointment. London was new to her; she had only the haziest idea of times and distances, but she had to go somewhere to refresh herself before her meeting. Fortunately George Douglas Campbell, the eighth duke of Argyll, and his wife were intimates of the Rathbones, and had given Dix a standing invitation to call on them in Kensington. Her cab driver informed her that Argyll Lodge was not far from Whitehall. "[I] threw off my traveling cloak in the cab for a velvet I had in my hand," she said, "folded a cashmere shawl on, and believe I did not look so much amiss as one traveling so far might look." As expected, the duke and duchess graciously received her. Once she had explained her mission, moreover, Argyll told her, "I can easily procure your admission to the House of Lords." He also offered to contact the home secretary on her behalf and arrange for her to meet with key legislators individually.[28]

Had a daguerreotypist been on hand that afternoon of 4 March 1855, posterity might have glimpsed an extraordinary moment in the history of medicine: the grande dame of the American asylum movement face-to-face with the British Lunacy Commission, Lord Shaftesbury presiding. She had not slept; her left arm, seized by an acute pain, hung in sling; and she was in the throes of "a pretty serious attack of inflammation of the muceous [sic] membrane of the throat and stomach, and an Influenza." The following day, her friend Argyll would call in Sir James Clarke, Queen Victoria's personal physician, to look after her. But on that afternoon she was willing to pay the price for having worked herself into this state.[29]

If lunacy reform had a high priesthood, it was now assembled in its inner sanctum. The board consisted of six full-time members—three physicians and three barristers—who were paid the substantial salary of £1,500 per annum. America had nothing like it. Its scope and powers were national. Through a rigorous regimen of inspection, it was supposed to enforce standards of medical certification, ensure that asylums were managed according to what the law required, and maintain high standards of care for all patients. At the same time, in concert with the home secretary, the commission conferred on asylum legislation and directed the site selection, building, and staffing of the county asylum system. Until now it had not sought to impose its standards on Scotland.

The board beheld her, at once so obviously feeble and so unexpectedly poised, with a sense of wonder, not least because her fervent plea for Scotland was delivered precisely in the commissioners' own intellectual idiom. Although an American, she reflected their sensibility, their ambitions, even their words and images. Her vivid evocations of the stench, the filthy straw, the rusty manacles, the jabbering maniacs shivering with cold, ignored by their uneducated and callous keepers, echoed the litany of familiar evils that they themselves had publicized and finally been entrusted to eliminate.

Above all, Shaftesbury was in many ways Dix's kindred spirit. They shared the same preoccupations, the same values. He prized cleanliness, order, and tranquillity; urged the separation of the sexes within institutions; and he was strongly opposed to private madhouses, even threatening at one point to eliminate their licensure wholesale.[30]

Speaking to the commission in favor of the need to regulate the private madhouses of Scotland was preaching to the choir. Dix already had gained their support before she spoke. And why should they not have backed her? As a Scottish friend of Elizabeth Rathbone astutely explained, "Nothing but her quiet resolute forbearing spirit could have so penetrated into abuses and disarmed all resistance. And our nation was so vain and ignorant, that had the abuses been pointed out by any commissioners or officials, there would have arisen a party of defenders. She being a woman and a stranger went on her quiet way undisturbed." Her celebrated expertise coupled with her autonomy from British asylum politics made Dix an unassailable messenger.[31]

That the board might extend its powers northward with little or no expenditure of political capital seemed a godsend to the commissioners. Convincing Sir George Grey, the prudent and exceedingly deliberate home secretary, that London should intercede in Scottish affairs, though, would take a bit of doing. Grey, who was admired for having outmaneuvered the Chartists in 1848, had originally entered the House of Commons in the thirties in the wake of the Reform Bill. There he earned a reputation for integrity, good judgment, and flawless mastery of administrative detail that brought him to the attention of Melbourne and, later, Lord John Russell, who, in 1846, appointed him home secretary. Grey was a tall, distinguished-looking gentleman, genial, socially charming, a diplomat to his fingertips.

When Dix, accompanied by the fascinated Argyll, delivered her charges, the home secretary listened attentively. Her story was certainly plausible enough. Recent investigations, he knew, had unearthed similar conditions in English asylums. No one needed to remind him, though, that Scottish politicians were prominent in Parliament, and that there was little enthusiasm for any action that would give the appearance that Whitehall was trying to run Scotland. Compulsory registration of Scots for the Crimean War, enacted at the beginning of the year, had gone against the grain. He certainly had no intention of following Dix's initial suggestion that he set up a secret commission and conduct a covert probe of Scottish institutions. Taking stock of the situation, the home secretary told Dix in a note that evening that it would be premature to consider a commission before discussing the matter with Scotland's lord advocate, James Moncrieff.[32]

To that end he immediately telegraphed Moncrieff, a man whom Dix characterized as "selfish" and had heretofore avoided because of his purported "social and political interest [that] would hinder the right action." She suspected Moncrieff of being a crony of the sheriff of Mid-Lothian, the latter "a bad man, wholly despotic," she inveighed, "[who] ridicules the entire idea of reform." But if she expected a confrontation when Moncrieff arrived from Edinburgh on March 8, it never materialized. While she had wanted Grey to exact some retribution for past abuses, he quietly urged her to "let it be sufficient that the condition of the insane will be ameliorated." They met privately with the home secretary for the better part of the day. At the end of the meeting, Dix exulted, "I got the promise from him that the Commission of reform for all Scotland should at once be formed."[33]

Not knowing the rules, written and unwritten, of the British political game, Dix had consulted Shaftesbury, the parliamentary authority figure, on what to ask for. He was wonderfully helpful. Relying on his agenda, she negotiated with confidence and moral authority. The result was an agreement with Sir George Grey and James Moncrieff—an agreement that was the genesis of the Scottish Lunacy Commission—that could not have suited the head of the Lunacy Commission better if he had drafted it himself. Not forgetting her personal score to settle with the sheriff, she had insisted on two commissions: "one of inquiry, one of investigation in Mid-Lothian." She envisioned sweeping changes: "first, reports into the condition of all the insane in Scotland. Next the *entire* modification of the Lunacy laws, the *abrogation* of all *Private* establishments; the establishment of two or three new general hospitals, etc." Attentive to winning legislative backing, before boarding her train to Edinburgh, she made sure to spend several hours "securing the interest and votes of members of Parliament for the [commission] Bill soon to be introduced."[34]

"The whole business prospered to my heart's and mind's content," she boasted with a faint air of disbelief that things had fallen into place so easily. She returned to Edinburgh invigorated, intent on paving the way for the Scottish Lunacy Commission by conducting a new round of inspections and committing her findings to a written report to give them a head start on their task.[35]

Word of her astonishing coup in Whitehall won her a new flock of allies from the ranks of Edinburgh's leaders, including the city's powerful duke of Buccleuch. Meanwhile, in London Shaftesbury swiftly orchestrated the selection of the new commission. Queen Victoria signed the Order of Commission on 9 April 1855, superseding the Great Seal of Scotland, directly appointing the commissioners under the authority of the Crown. Along the lines Dix suggested, they were charged "to be her Majesty's Commissioners for the purpose of inquiring into the state of the Lunatic Asylums in Scotland, and also into the present state of the law respecting Lunatics and Lunatic Asylums in that part of the United Kingdom."

Suddenly, to her delight, Dix found herself in a pivotal position. There had been suggestions that she continue her crusade in Scotland, working in some official capacity with the new commission. She brushed this idea aside. Instead, she aggressively used her influence to shape the form and content of the Scottish Lunacy Commission.

Three of its original four members—William George Campbell, James Coxe, and Samuel Gaskell—owed their appointments directly to her. The fourth, James Moncrieff, was selected by the home secretary for political reasons beyond her control. She championed Campbell, who was a barrister, protégé, and nephew of the duke of Argyll. She lobbied on behalf of Coxe, a young physician whose main distinction was his friendship with Sir Walter Trevelyan, friend of Dix and the Rathbones, who was a strong supporter of the young man. To his surprise, Coxe heard about his appointment from Dix before he even knew that he was being considered for the prestigious appointment and a week before he was officially notified by Shaftesbury. Samuel Gaskell, brother of the well-known novelist Elizabeth Gaskell, was a physician who, a decade earlier, had served as medical superintendent of the Lancaster Moor Asylum. Dix regarded him as a forward-thinking alienist, in part because he had abolished the use of cuff, muffs, and straitjackets in his institution. She interviewed him at St. James Place and emphasized how important it was for the commission to include a doctor committed, as he was, to moral treatment and the principle of nonrestraint. He told her that he wanted to participate. But he worried about giving up his position at Lancaster Moor. Perhaps she could persuade Shaftesbury to hire him as a consultant, he suggested, "in such a way that I could give help when needed without interfering materially with my duties here." She saw Shaftesbury the next day, and Gaskell joined the commission.[36]

From the outset, the group's goal was, after conducting an initial investigation, to set up a permanent board along English lines and answerable to the Lunacy Commission in London.

For obvious reasons, the idea of such a powerful new tribunal alarmed the Scottish medical community. When he learned what Dix had done, W. A. F. Browne, Scotland's leading asylum physician, was incensed. "You must permit me to express my great & deep regret that your sense of duty has led you to induce Government to open a Commission of inquiry," he told her. "In this country such a proceeding indicates the existence or the suspicion of abuse or maladministration." Despite his "twenty-five years of humble toil," public opinion would, he feared, turn against him, along with other directors and medical officers of public institutions. After his initial reaction, however, Browne calmed down. He realized that the inquiry was moving ahead whether he liked it or not. "I shall not . . . prosecute what is to me a distressing contemplation," he said, "nor offer observations which may not be acceptable to you." And so he swiftly patched things up with Dix, ensuring that he would become part of the movement she had set in motion.[37]

After she returned to Edinburgh, Dix met with the newly appointed board and marveled at its rapid progress. They officially commenced their investigation of Scotland on 1 May 1855. For background, Coxe asked Dix for her notes. "Any papers connected with the subject I will carefully copy & return immediately," he promised. They would start where she had left off. For her part, she could become involved as much, or as little, as she wished. "I shall not fail to keep you *au courant* of our proceedings at all times," Coxe assured her, "so that you will be in a position to decide on the necessity of your presence." Since Dix keenly appreciated the value of information, particularly inside information, she tried to orchestrate her communications with Coxe, Gaskell, and Campbell along separate lines. Campbell saw the dangers of this approach and declared that he would correspond with her only if it were clearly understood that their letters would be shared among all four commissioners.[38]

Working through the spring and into the summer, the commissioners systematically validated Dix's impression of Scottish institutions. Campbell was a disappointment, exasperatingly plodding and legalistic. Gaskell, though competent, was preoccupied with his asylum in England. This left Coxe and Moncrieff, sometimes together, often separately, to perform most of the actual inspections. In early August, Coxe informed Dix that "Mr. Moncrieff & I have now managed to visit nearly all the public & private asylums in Scotland." Undoubtedly, he continued, "the whole system requires remodelling. Every Sheriff is a little despot in his own county, and it depends too much upon his individual character than upon the law whether the Lunatic meets with proper attention or not." Wholesale reform, based on centralized administration and inspection, was precisely what Dix had imagined all along. She was gratified with what she had accomplished. "You will be glad dear to know that my Commission works well," she told Heath, "that all is just as I would have it in Scotland, reforming all abuses gradually and putting things right that are amiss."[39]

A year earlier, amid the shambles of legislative defeat in Washington, Dix could not have imagined becoming a force in Britain.

But she had. By mid-1855, her constituencies included a widening circle of British reformers, including the Lunacy Commission itself. In Parliament, Shaftesbury lavished praise on her. Informed opinion, typified in an article by John Charles Bucknill, held that her energy and "American audacity" were the keys to her success. "We doubt whether any English lady would have had sufficient influence upon the English government to induce it to appoint a royal commission," he remarked. "We English certainly do entertain a general aversion to ladies whose mission extends itself beyond the home circle, and who have a propensity to set people to rights; we are apt to ascribe it to restlessness, impatience of control, and other unwomanly motives." But unlike most of her contemporaries, "Miss Dix is not a mere weaver of philanthropic phrases, she is a true worker [who] has obtained enough success to convince us that she has not entered upon her arduous course under mistaken impressions of her own ability; enough also to elevate her far above the smally fry of female philanthropists or *philanthro-pests*."[40]

By the same token, to Americans in Europe her accomplishments became a source of national pride. "Tell her I kiss the hem of her garment," wrote the wife of the American ambassador to France. "Such a woman is to be worshipped, if anything human could be worshipped." In congratulating her success, seemingly wrung from the deliberate sacrifice of bodily health, William Rathbone compared Dix to Christ. "God . . . has *tried* you in the success of what you have undertaken beyond what I have ever known," he said, "or, as far as my recollection serves me, have read of any other person, male or female—far beyond that of Howard, Father Matthew, Mrs. Chisholm, or Mrs. Fry." These were the words she lived for. Such praise from the patriarch of her adopted family, a man whom she revered as a spiritual father, had inestimable personal value.[41]

Still, the burden of illness lay very heavily upon her. In May, suffering from exhaustion and another bout of influenza, she journeyed to the venerable York Retreat. There, within the ivy-covered walls of the Quaker institution that had become the prototype for her movement, she allowed herself to collapse under the care of Dr. Daniel Hack Tuke. She had been looking forward to meeting him, the youngest son of the institution's celebrated proprietor, Samuel Tuke, and grandson of William Tuke, its legendary founder. Hearing of her arrival in town, he had driven at once to her hotel, gathered her and her trunk in his carriage, and removed her to the Retreat. When she arrived, she discovered that, in addition to madness, death was in the air. For Daniel's father was then fatally ill, wasting away in the room next to hers. But this did not depress Dix, for whom death was no stranger, and who thought the old man fortunate to pass his last days in an environment so pleasant and nurturing. The staff was wonderfully solicitous, she wrote. "I am tended as carefully and tenderly as if I were a sister."[42]

Officially, Young Tuke, twenty-eight years old, was visiting physician to the Retreat. He had recently returned to his native Yorkshire from Heidelberg where, taking advantage of the best medical education in Europe, he had earned an M.D. degree. An erudite student of the literature on mental disorder, he was interested in expanding the intellectual and historical horizons of his profession. At the time he met Dix, he had just written a substantial historical inquiry, "On the Progressive Changes in the Moral Management of the Insane" (1854). Dix was, for her part, a living encyclopedia of American developments. Her visit stirred his interest in the New World and set him on the long road that would eventually bring him to America, where he conducted the field research for his most influential publication, *Reform in the Treatment of the Insane* (1892).

Hers was for both of them a most stimulating convalescence. After a week or two in bed, she arose with renewed strength and, in the company of Tuke, proceeded to comb the fourteen madhouses and asylums of Yorkshire. The stamina of the woman nearly twice his age astounded him, as did her compassion for all God's creatures. "I remember that on our driving in a hired vehicle to one of them," he recalled three decades later, "she showed that her sympathies were not restricted to the insane by remonstrating with the driver for his mistreatment of the horse."[43]

It was while she was recuperating at York, exhilarated by her victory in Scotland and anxious to move on to her next battle, that the "*leads of Providence*," as she put it, drew her to the Channel Islands. A few months earlier, back in Edinburgh, she had been told that the islands of Jersey and Guernsey were notorious for "great abuses to which the insane were there subject." But she was so busy at the time she let the matter slide. At York, as chance would have it, Tuke had assembled a library of books and pamphlets on asylums and the treatment of insanity, many collected during his years abroad. Among these, he gave her a few articles to read written in French by D. H. Van Leuven, a young Dutch physician then living on the Island of Jersey. Her interest piqued, Dix asked Tuke to contact Van Leuven; and when his response came by return mail, Dix read it as evidence of God's will that, she wrote, "determined my *duty and next work*."[44]

Like Tuke and the managers of the York Retreat, Van Leuven believed in the principles of moral management and abhorred the notion of external restraint—the ropes, manacles, and chains that symbolized the primitive past. And he had written a series of exposés in the Jersey *Chronique* to call attention to backward practices around the island. What caught Dix's eye when she slowly translated his account of Jersey was the way he brought to life human tragedies wrought by insanity on the island. It was as though he had copied her own methods. For instance, Van Leuven reported the case of a dairy farmer with an insane son whose disease had all but ruined his family. Trying with increasing desperation to keep the boy in check, the father had neglected his business to the brink of bankruptcy. Still there were spells of violence, so unmanageable that he did the unthinkable: "I was forced to resort to iron chains," he confessed, "yes, sir, I had to chain up my own son! My heart was broken under such misery!" Van Leuven sympathized with the poor man and looked forward to the day when Jersey would have its own asylum with "no more frightful cells, nor iron bars, nor any shapes of mechanical restraint." In short, an English asylum like the York Retreat or Hanwell.[45]

Van Leuven's story stuck in Dix's mind. Then came an incident that fired her indignation. Not only was there no decent asylum, Van Leuven wrote in a letter to Tuke; things promised to get even worse. He claimed to have been approached by a diabolic figure, with the Dickensian name of Isaac Pothecary, who was the keeper of an infamous private asylum in Grove Place near Southampton. Pothecary had a reputation for ruthless indifference to the sufferings of his hapless charges, and he was well known to Shaftesbury and the Lunacy Commission, who had long since set their sights on putting him out of business. His solution, he told Van Leuven, was "to escape or avoid all this nonsense in England" by transporting twenty or so patients to the Island of Jersey, "where even no license is required."[46]

Private asylums, strategically placed offshore beyond the jurisdiction of the Lunacy Commission, represented a common and profitable practice. Pothecary's lunatics and others like them were generally private patients who paid handsomely—more than £500 a year in some cases. Whatever standard of care they provided (and it varied from excellent to horrible), the private establishments offered one important advantage over any institution in England: discretion and privacy. Insanity was a shame that many families of moderate and substantial means wished to hide. Even Shaftesbury himself arranged for his own epileptic son to be cared for not in England but in a private asylum in Switzerland.

Whatever commercial sense he possessed, Pothecary badly misjudged Van Leuven. Originally he had tried to hire him on attractive terms to serve as his visiting physician and make the rounds of his Jersey facilities twice a week. Though repulsed by this "odious *Insanity Trade*," the Dutch doctor told Tuke that the offer put him in a quandary. If he declined, Pothecary would simply turn to one of the local Jersey physicians, a uniformly mercenary lot, he noted, and the defenseless lunatics would be the ones to suffer. Officials on the Channel Islands cared nothing for the insane, he said, so there was no legal recourse unless something could be done to change the law. This was where the lady from America might help. "Could Miss Dix persuade the English Government," he wondered, "to [establish] an Asylum in Jersey, Guernsey, or Wight, but under the same laws as [obtain] in England?"[47]

It was an appealing prospect. A few years before she had gone on a similar errand to Nova Scotia, where she had not only passed asylum legislation but had procured lifeboats for Sable Island—boats, she recently learned, that had rescued passengers and crew from the wreck of the *Arcadia* in December 1854. Who could tell what good might come in this case from heeding the still, small voice of Providence? On a warm afternoon on 1 June 1855, as she sat convalescing in the cloistered garden of the York Retreat, now recovered enough to travel back to Greenbank, she had a vision. She would bring deliverance to the captives of Jersey, "helping out of dismal dark dungeons those whose only crime is that they are sick—insane—and so feared and brutalized till they are really what the sane would call them[:] madmen and madwomen capable of outbreak." Recalling Van Leuven's pathetic anecdote of the father and his manacled son, and thinking at the same moment of Greenbank, her own refuge and asylum, Dix told Anne Heath, "I shall saw their chains off[;] I shall take them into the *greenfields* and show them the lovely little flowers—and the blue sky,—and they shall play with the lambs and listen to the song of the birds—'and a little child shall lead them.' This is no romance—this all will be if I get to the Channel Islands, Jersey and Guernsey, with God's blessing."[48]

She sailed from London the second week in July. "My success I think depends much on great prudence in this movement," she confided to Millard Fillmore. Before her departure she revealed her intentions to Shaftesbury, and with his staunch endorsement secured a letter from the home secretary authorizing her to inspect whatever establishments for lunatics and idiots she might find. No local functionary would brush her off this time. After she arrived, Van Leuven eagerly escorted her around the island. The hospital seemed every bit as bad as he had written. Within its walls some forty insane patients languished "in a horrid state, naked, filthy, and attended by persons of ill character." The insane kept in private homes scattered throughout the island fared little better, she thought, and presented "a sad—a very sad scene." Plainly they needed to be gathered into an asylum. And to this end the Dutch doctor, evidently interested in his own career, had already selected a site for a new hospital. Fittingly enough, this parcel had reverted to the Crown when its former owner, an insane woman, had died without heirs.[49]

Although Van Leuven had hoped Dix could bring Jersey under the wing of the Lunacy Commission, the Channel Islands, like other parts of the United Kingdom, enjoyed a great deal of practical independence. Realizing this, and suspecting that Parliament might be loath to intervene on her behalf so soon after the episode in Scotland, Dix decided to resolve the problem at the local level. Long accustomed to working with state and provincial governments, she saw no reason to drag the matter back to Whitehall if the local government would consent to the reforms she proposed. Had officials in Edinburgh heeded her, she reasoned, there would have been no appeal to London and no Scottish Lunacy Commission. When the regional governor and his council convened, she offered them a bargain: "I consented to . . . *not* present the subject to the *Government at Home*, if they would do the work without."[50]

After some wrangling the Jersey legislative committee unanimously passed her resolution to build an asylum, she added, "with the least possible delay." To prove they meant business, the governor ordered the attorney general to place the oily Isaac Pothecary in the custody of the high constable. Dix was assured there were laws on the books sufficient to protect any lunatics he had so far transported. Meanwhile, the council appointed a subcommittee to accompany her and Van Leuven on a search for a location large enough to accommodate a building for one hundred patients. "I have got a farm for the hospital that I hope shall be," she wrote to Elizabeth Rathbone, "and the hospital I will call La Maison de l'Espérance" (The House of Hope). There is no way of knowing, when she wrote this, whether she remembered the little school in Boston that she had abandoned two decades earlier when she first sailed to Liverpool, the school she had named "The Hope."[51]

Despite a promising start, her optimism proved to be premature. The hospital that was eventually constructed was not called La Maison de l'Espérance, although that name would have been ironically suitable. For all the good intentions expressed by the governor and council, Dix had an inkling that government support was shallow. For this reason she lingered in Jersey, trying to get the project under way, worrying that without her around to apply pressure "the building will not be finished till next century." Her suspicions were well founded. Despite Tuke's confidence that in her absence Van Leuven would be able to see it through to completion, the hospital was not built until thirteen years later.[52]

When Dix left England for the Continent at the end of the summer of 1855, her achievements in Scotland and Jersey seemed wonderfully conclusive. But clouds of ambiguity were not long in gathering.

Dix's contribution to British lunacy reform was, as it turned out, fraught with ironies. After she had safely returned to her own country, in May 1857, James Coxe sent her the hefty report of the Scottish Lunacy Commission, filling some 838 closely printed pages. "We are quite surprised at the sensation the Report has produced," he told her, adding that the commissioners were not prepared for the popular outcry. "Throughout the length and breadth of the land the press is ringing with it."[53]

The commission's revelations were shocking news to Scotland, "the terrible and unvarnished truth" averred the *Glasgow Herald*. It was reported that in one private madhouse after another, "the patients were scantily fed and clothed; that they were subjected to mechanical restrain and to seclusion; that they were occasionally stripped naked, and sent to sleep together upon straw; that no means of recreation were provided for them; that the number of attendants was insufficient; that no provision was made for religious exercises." In sum, all the traditional abuses—only the geography had changed. When she read it, along with the scores of press clippings sent by her English and Scottish friends that reported the surrounding parliamentary testimony and debate, she was dismayed. "The report of the commission was entirely due to the exertions of a lady," declared the *London Times*, "Miss Dicks [*sic*] experienced great difficulty in penetrating into the lunatic asylums of Scotland." This much was true. But while the Scottish commissioners, along with the English and Scottish press, credited her with pulling the thread that unraveled a tightly shrouded national disgrace whose reform was long overdue, they also warped her findings.[54]

The search for villains to blame for the maltreatment and negligence unearthed by the commission focused more on English officialdom than on Scottish madhouse proprietors. "As much blame was imputed in Parliament to the magistracy of Scotland, indiscriminately, for permitting such a state of things to exist," one writer maintained, "on the magistrates of burghs Parliament has conferred no power of licensing, regulating, or inspecting private lunatic asylums." That authority was jealously guarded by officers of the Crown, who misused it. How did it happen, the *Edinburgh Daily Express* asked in tones of sarcasm, that James Moncrieff, the Crown's lord advocate of Scotland and the man plainly responsible for the country's institutions, should have blithely allowed his duties "to be performed by an American citizen, and that citizen a lady!" Considering the mismanagement that was going on behind the scenes, it seemed absurd to pay country sheriffs £1,000 and the lord advocate £5,000 per annum. Since he "has already abdicated his functions of public prosecutor, guardian of the laws, in favour of Miss Dix," the paper declared, "why should not Miss Dix receive a fair proportion of the salary of the Lord Advocate for having performed one portion of his duties with such great ability?"[55]

In hearings before Parliament, Sir George Grey, scurrying to keep the peace and align himself with the right side of the issue, swore that he had been a proponent of Dix's cause from the first day they met. When Dix read his testimony, she was incensed. To Elizabeth Rathbone she confessed that she was "struck with the strange misrepresentations of my course of action both uttered in Parliament, and published in the Newspapers in Edinburgh." Cooperation from the home secretary, and even the duke of Argyll, had come after the fact; and then only grudgingly. They had been afraid to sanction her probe into the private madhouses, and had responded to her entreaties only after she had presented them a prima facie case for intervention in Scotland based on her own prior investigation. Making use of her contacts within the Edinburgh medical community, Dix leaked parts of her story to the press. "The plain English of the matter," an Edinburgh doctor named Duncan McLaren wrote on her behalf in the *Daily Express*, "is that Sir George Grey, and [the Lord Advocate], and their subordinates, *REFUSED TO MISS DIX ALL ACCESS TO THOSE ASYLUMS; AND YET THEY LED THE HOUSE OF COMMONS AND THE PUBLIC TO SUPPOSE THAT IT WAS SOLELY THROUGH THEIR INSTRUMENTALITY THAT SHE ACQUIRED ALL HER INFORMATION!*"[56]

What troubled her more deeply than distortions of how the investigation had come about in the first place were the machinations of British politicians to subvert the commission for their own purposes. To begin with, the commissioners had little influence on the form and content of the reform legislation ultimately introduced. "The Scotch Commissioners, I am sorry to say, have not been consulted regarding it," James Coxe complained to Dix, "& there is then fear that it may not be well adapted to remedy the many grievous evils we pointed out." Since Scottish members of Parliament were deadset on blocking encroachment of the English welfare system, they were uniformly hostile to the commission and its findings, and deadset on opposing any lunacy reform bill. They enjoyed the support of their compatriots. "Already on every side is heard the din of preparation for resistance," Coxe said. Town councils, county meetings, parochial boards, along with the proprietors of Scotland's hundreds of private madhouses banded together, "all animated with the desire to avoid legal interference." But the lord advocate, seizing the moment to tighten the reins, moved ahead with his own legislative agenda.[57]

The bill he introduced set up a permanent Scottish board along the lines of the British Lunacy Commission to regulate all establishments for the insane. It would succeed, in part, because quietly, behind the scenes, W. A. F. Browne and James Coxe—one the paragon of Scottish asylumdom, the other a commissioner with close connections to Shaftesbury and the home secretary—skillfully lobbied for Browne's "appointment as Commissioner under a new Lunacy Act for Scotland." This was obviously an abrupt about-face. But his seeking the post, Browne assured Dix, "was dictated rather by a desire for rest and for change in the exercise of my faculties than from any vain aspiration after either rank or riches." What made it worthwhile for him to leave the Chrichton institution, he continued, was the chance to enact the two great principles of the Scottish asylum law: "liberal accommodations for the pauper Insane and systematic Inspection of all classes of the insane."[58]

In the meantime, the press, unaware of Browne's coup, was sharply negative. Had not an unresponsive English bureaucracy been the problem all along? Was not the condition of the mad largely a problem of individual communities? How would diluting local responsibility for the insane even further produce better treatment? Taking her place on the side of the critics, Dix was quoted in Edinburgh's *Daily Scotsman* as asking "what can be done to reach the evils the Commission was appointed to control?" When she thought of the brutalized patients at Musselburgh, she worried that the commission's findings, which only corroborated what she had seen at once, did nothing to ameliorate their plight. They continued to suffer "the same miseries and ignorant management as when I first saw and declared their injuries," she wrote in exasperation. "I am anxious on this question, and if my aid could avail, which, however, is not probable, I would recross the Atlantic, and throw into the cause all the energy I possess."[59]

Her initial impressions had changed. Earlier, back in Liverpool and in London, she had remained an uncritical admirer of the Lunacy Commission, trusting its judgment, envying its parliamentary mandate to regulate English institutions. Confident that a strong-government approach to the management of insanity was best, she had automatically united with Shaftesbury to clean up Scotland.

Not long after the Scottish commissioners had commenced their investigations, though, she became aware of circumstances in England that gave her a nagging sense that Shaftesbury and the board were too complacent. Delving into Yorkshire's private madhouses with Daniel Hack Tuke brought her up against a perplexing truth she had first glimpsed at the Rainhill asylum: to a startling degree English madhouses themselves concealed cases of barbarous cruelty comparable to the worst she had seen in Scotland. She began to wonder whether the Lunacy Commission was truly committed to its charter. If it was, given its civil authority, why did it tolerate flagrant abuse? She had come across the keeper of a private madhouse in Newcastle-upon-Tyne, for example, who was reputed to have flogged an unruly lunatic and ordered his teeth removed. Outraged, she told Horace Buttolph and Thomas Kirkbride that, had she the power, "I would have applied the Jewish law of retribution, like for like . . . then I would have sent him to hard labor in the Central Prison."[60]

Dix admired the work of the Tukes, John Connolly, and other advocates of nonrestraint, and she praised institutions like the York Retreat and Hanwell asylum in Middlesex. What she could not tolerate, however, was a double standard between the management of lunatics in the newer, progressive county asylums, on the one hand, and workhouses and private madhouses, on the other. "The Public County Hospitals for the Insane in England are for the most part good," she wrote, "the Private for paying patients for the most part are detestable—that much is certain. I trust we in the United States shall never be cursed with such vile mercenary brutal establishments." As the dispute in Scotland ran its course, and she was identified as the outsider unafraid to tell the truth, she asked Elizabeth Rathbone to help her plant a story in the English newspapers divulging "what has not been said, that some of the private houses in England are *worse* than any I saw or heard of in Scotland."[61]

In her mind the whole episode turned out to be a vicious betrayal. The more she thought about it, the angrier she grew, and the more disgusted with the Lunacy Commission. "I cannot excuse Lord Shaftesbury," she indignantly told the Rathbones. He had all the information he needed, and surely possessed the power, to "crush the Hydra-headed monster . . . those bad private hospitals." She confessed that "this horror haunts me like an ill-dream. . . . If I could have authority, I would not let one circling moon pass her changes, before I was upon that field of toil." When it came to stamping out England's most scandalous mistreatment of the mad, she regarded "the Lunacy Commission as next to useless, indeed it does harm; for the people at large trust in its efficiency, and so abuses lie concealed and perpetuated." The commissioners "are too indolent to exert the influence their official station gives to remedy, at least in large measure, what their criminal sufferance makes them participant in maintaining." What could one expect from the new commission in Scotland, cut from the old cloth, but ongoing dereliction?[62]

Beyond a doubt she was right about the unevenness of English reform, although this was hardly ignored by the commission. In its report for 1856, for example, the board demanded "further provision for the care and treatment of the Insane Poor," based on its finding that "in nearly every County the accommodation provided in Asylums is, at present, or shortly will be, inadequate." The commissioners asserted that while the metropolitan licensed houses had manifestly improved since coming under their jurisdiction in 1845, facilities "for patients of the middle and humbler classes, both in the metropolitan and provincial districts, do not keep pace in the march of improvement by which the [county] asylums of the first class are distinguished."[63]

Her reaction expressed the pain of wounded idealism. By temporizing on the issue of private madhouses, the Lunacy Commission abused what Dix considered its essential moral obligation to the insane. Shaftesbury, who formerly had seemed so uncompromising, she now despised as a mere politician acting from personal and petty motives.

Perhaps, in view of the way she had phrased her grand vision of freedom and redemption from madness, disillusionment was inevitable. Perhaps, too, her experience in Britain, separated from America by distance and time, made possible a degree of detachment that opened her eyes to things she screened out in her own country.

For there was always a dark, ugly side to the treatment of the mad, whether in Scotland or America, that even the most modern, most enlightened asylums could not paper over. When the Scottish Lunacy Commission was instituted as a permanent board, its chairman was the distinguished Scottish alienist W. A. F. Browne. As he prepared to take on his new responsibilities, in his final annual report from Crichton Royal Asylum, Browne wrote a chilling portrait of life inside his admirable hospital. He described not a comfortable and tranquil domestic environment in which disordered minds were gently nursed back to health. Even within the confines of his model institution, he wrote, one was assaulted by the spectacle of frenzied maniacs, "glorying in obscenity and filth; devouring garbage or ordure, surpassing those brutalities which to the savage may be a heritage and a superstition." Far from passing their time in morally therapeutic endeavors, the inmates "wash or plaster their bodies, fill every crevice in the room, their ears, noses, hair, with ordure."[64]

Dix had visited Crichton Royal Asylum and could not reconcile this true portrait, let alone the corrupt domesticity of the private madhouses, with the pure utopian ideal she had envisioned at Greenbank. She was forced to agree with the American asylum superintendent who in 1859 wrote that Americans' national conscience of our own deficiencies could be eased by the knowledge "that in [Scotland] under a government whose efforts to relieve the wants of the insane are well worthy of imitation, so much should yet remain to be accomplished."[65] Reluctantly she concluded that England had abandoned its moral leadership. This conclusion was only confirmed when the Select Committee on Lunatics delivered its report to Parliament in 1859, replete with horror stories to match anything described forty years earlier. In the future, Dix would no longer look across the Atlantic for ideas or inspiration.

Earlier, contemptuous of mere sightseeing, Dix had brushed off Anne Heath's suggestion that she visit the dungeons of France and Italy. But at the end of July 1855, when the Rathbones invited her to join them in Switzerland, she decided to travel to the Continent. In the weeks that followed, flush with the apparent success of her work in Britain, Dix decided that when the Rathbones returned to Liverpool at summer's end, she would embark on a grand tour of Europe.

It was to be a journey unmatched in the annals of travel. The Europe of the guidebooks with its museums, courts, and castles would not be her subject. Instead, as she had done in her own country and in Britain, she proposed to explore the subterranean suffering of the mad throughout the Continent. Her version of a grand tour would turn out to be a kind of *via dolorosa* threading its way through the prisons, hospitals, and asylums of each country.

There was then a certain vogue among tourists for visiting famous prisons and asylums. But, for its incredible scope, taking in virtually all of Europe, Dix's undertaking would seem nearly as daunting to modern tourists as it must have appeared in her own day. Setting out from Liverpool, in the space of a year she would cover perhaps ten thousand miles using every conceivable means of transport: deluxe steamers, crude barques, rowboats, trains; carriages, wagons, and carts pulled by all manner of beasts; and sometimes the beasts themselves, donkeys, horses, and even a camel. Since the places she wanted most to see—madhouses, hospitals, prisons—were off the beaten track, she often made her way on foot, walking until her feet were as blistered as a penitent's. And only penitents traveled lighter. With her valise and small trunk packed with linens, an evening dress, her Bible, and a few volumes of edifying discourses, she was poised to change direction at a moment's notice. English and, according to William Rathbone IV, a smattering of "very bad French" were her only languages.

In the eyes of Europeans, American tourists had already earned their reputation for frenetic bustle. But even the hardiest would have found it difficult to keep up with Dix. In Paris, armed with "a full Police and Magisterial sanction under seal," she dashed about at a lightning pace. "In the morning I saw the Church and the statues of Joan of Arc," she told William Rathbone, "and then visited the great hospitals and the farm for the insane; took the train at 12 'clk for Blois—stopped at 2 3/4[,] saw the large excellent hospital for the insane, regained the station in time for the express to Tours, and at 6 PM took a carriage and spent two hours in the Hospital for the insane and drove to Mittrey arriving at 9 o'clock."[66]

France was, in its own way, as much a bastion of lunacy reform as

England. Long ago, Philippe Pinel had been her first hero of humane outreach to the mad, so it was with the deepest reverence that she made pilgrimages to Bicêtre and Salpêtrière. Though more than half a century had passed, she needed little imagination to picture the scene that French artists had so often celebrated: the noble doctor striding through the gloom of Bicêtre, his countenance illuminated by a shaft of light, striking off the chains of the ragged lunatics imprisoned there. As though still moved by his example, the French government liberally supported the country's charitable institutions. And they were, she concluded after a long, hard look, generally excellent. Of course she had criticisms. There was poor ventilation in French asylums (she shared Kirkbride's obsession with fresh air), which she thought accounted for their "amazing mortality." In place of moral treatment, the French displayed a dangerous tendency to set medical interns loose to conduct an array of experimental treatments. And then there was the Catholic Church in the form of its pervasive "Sisters of Charity, and nuns of various orders," along with priests who looked like they could use a dose of moral therapy themselves.[67]

Dogged by foul weather on her journey south through Provence, she reached Italy in January 1856. Friends had warned her about the perils of a woman traveling alone in Italy, but to her relief it was no harder than in England, and she found the Italians wonderfully helpful and engaging. Despite the dirt and the unavoidable poverty that disappointed most English and American visitors to Naples, she found the city pleasant. She assured her skeptical correspondents that she could find little to improve in the local hospitals. "Strange as it is," she remarked, "I found a better Institution there for the Insane than has been founded in all southern and central Italy." In Rome, however, she encountered distressing circumstances. It was not simply a matter of squalid conditions in a hospital here or a prison there, she maintained, but of a debased system, corrupt to the core. Within sight of St. Peter's, she thought it intolerable that "6,000 priests, 300 monks, 3,000 nuns, and a spiritual sovereignty joined with the temporal powers had not assured for the miserable insane a decent, much less an intelligent, care." Ecclesiastical power intimidated Dix no more than political power. She had after all operated effectively in Washington and London; and so she saw no reason not to follow the lines of authority in Rome to their ultimate source. "I have the idea of removing these mountains," she wrote, "and seeing if Protestant energy cannot work what Catholic powers fail to undertake." With the assistance of the American ambassador, she contacted the Vatican to arrange an audience with Pope Pius IX.[68]

She was inspired by the knowledge that a month earlier her friend Millard Fillmore, on the eve of his being nominated the anti-Catholic American party's presidential candidate, had traveled to Rome and met the pope. He had done so despite his prejudices—the thought of kneeling to "kiss the hand of the Pope, if not his foot," made him shudder, Fillmore confessed, and if it leaked out, he knew, his political opponents would have made hay with the image. He was immensely relieved that, when the moment of truth arrived, the pontiff remained seated, "neither offering hand or foot for salutation." For her part, Dix had no such qualms and, when she met the pope, kissed the proffered hand in a businesslike, if not reverent, gesture of good faith.[69]

In Pio Nono she came face to face with the most important pope of the nineteenth century. He was a man whose dominion over the Papal States (which he ultimately lost) invested him with a political importance in European affairs far beyond his religious leadership of the universal church. In the Europe of 1848 and Napoléon III, he was a central and perplexed figure of the Italian risorgimento, a would-be reformer who, nonetheless, blithely proclaimed the doctrine of papal infallibility. The brilliant American writer Margaret Fuller, who as a correspondent for the *New York Tribune* reported his ascent to the papacy, characterized him as a first-class soul with a second-class mind. "He is a man of noble and good aspect, who it is easy to see has set his heart upon doing something solid for the benefit of man," she wrote, "but pensively, too, must one feel how hampered and inadequate are the means at his command to accomplish these ends."[70]

Unknown to Dix, apart from his renowned humanitarian instincts, the pope was for the most personal reasons inclined to be receptive to her plea for the insane. Almost fifty years earlier, when he was seventeen, he had been stricken by a debilitating nervous disorder. Most notably, he was tormented by fits of depression. The original diagnosis was epilepsy, a disease customarily classified as a form of madness. This illness rendered him for several years a social outcast. Eventually, as he struggled to control his mind and emotions, it led to his decision to enter the priesthood. When he first joined the Jesuits in Rome, in an effort to expiate his self-preoccupation and master his great ambition the young man had devoted himself to Tata Giovanni, an asylum for homeless boys in Via Giulia on the banks of the Tiber River. Several years later, Pope Leo XII appointed him director of the Hospital of San Michele, an enormous institution with several hundred inmates, which served as a workhouse, reformatory, and lunatic asylum. All this was in the distant past when Dix confronted him in early 1856, for at the time Pius IX was embroiled in the politics of Italian nationality and the Congress of Paris. Even so, preoccupied as he was, the gravity of his personal history gave her message a weight he could not disregard.[71]

Apparently he and his advisers listened attentively, but the details of Dix's dealings with the pope, and later with his Machiavellian secretary of state, Cardinal Giacomo Antonelli, remain sketchy. She told Horace Buttolph that they promised to purchase land and build a new lunatic hospital, and that she meant to hold them to their word, even if it meant returning to Rome and staying there until the work was completed. In the early spring, after she had left Italy, the pope reaffirmed his commitment to build an asylum in central Rome near the Villa Borghese. Dix's banker assured her that the project was well begun and that there was no need for her to return. She was confident that with the pope's blessing she had unleashed the forces of reform in the asylums of Rome.[72]

As was often the case, though, beyond expressions of concern and good intentions, the concrete outcome of her work in Italy is hard to know with certainty. In 1876, twenty years after her audience with him, Pius IX still occupied the papal throne. In accordance with his word, he had taken steps to palliate the suffering of the insane. As promised he had acquired land near the Villa Borghese and built a new department of the mammoth San Spirito Hospital. Visiting Rome that year, an American hospital superintendent and his wife, in hopes of verifying the fruits of Dix's labors, found 650 patients, mostly paupers, in the asylum "in very unsatisfactory condition." They blamed the unsettling conditions on Italy's lax culture and its poverty, factors that bothered most newly arrived Americans. "There can be no question that a great revolution in the care and treatment of the insane was effected by the organization of this present Institution," Dix was told, "in comparison with former methods." But this faint praise had a hollow ring that Dix found disappointing.[73]

In April, with the weather unseasonably chilly, she sailed among the Greek isles, enchanted by Athens and the sight of Mt. Parnassus glistening with snow "as white and cold as Mt. Blanc." Yet it was never natural wonders, however grand, that truly moved her. If she were obliged to write a book about her travels, as she told Anne Heath she was planning to do, it could only have been a chronicle of the world of pain. With the end of the Crimean War she pushed on to Constantinople, going out of her way to inspect the English hospitals at Smyrna and Scutari. Contrary to expectation, Constantinople itself boasted a hospital, founded by the Ottoman Süleyman the Magnificent, that put Italian hospitals to shame. "The insane of Constantinople are in *far better condition* than those of Rome, or Trieste," she told Elizabeth Rathbone, and in many ways better off than anywhere on the Italian peninsula. "The provisions for the comfort and pleasure of the patients[,] including music, quite astonished me. The Superintendent proposes improvements—and I had *substantially* little to suggest—and *nothing* to urge!" She marched from one prison or hospital to the next until a pain in one of her feet lamed her. Covering every ethnic institution in the intensely heterogeneous city, in the end she was most disappointed with the English prison, which she called an embarrassment to the Crown. "So far as the Christian hospitals are concerned," she asserted, "those of the Mahometans [*sic*] are *better*, to my surprise."[74]

Had she, as she intended, composed an account of what she saw during these months on the Continent, Dix would have left the world an unmatched record of European institutions at midcentury. Unfortunately she fell into the habit of sending her correspondents little more than inventories, lists of dozens of cities and towns, and the names of the institutions she surveyed. Largely missing is the eye for detail, caricature, and anecdote that made her memorials so powerful. At this stage, she lacked the energy and desire to compose a focused narrative.

Heading north, she proceeded to take the steamer *Franz Joseph* up the Danube, through Hungary, to Vienna, scrambling to explore every place of incarceration she could locate, bringing whatever flaws she detected to the attention of the highest officials around. Perpetually in motion she swept through central Europe, eastward into Russia, often surprised to see that otherwise backward nations showed singular compassion for the mad. Hospitals in St. Petersburg and Moscow, for example, treated lunatics kindly, using very little mechanical restraint, she said. "I really had nothing to add." In late summer she made her way through Scandinavia, circled southward through the Low Countries—where she interviewed physicians and municipal authorities in Rotterdam—then once again to France.[75]

In Paris she was introduced to the poet Robert Browning and his wife, Elizabeth, who was putting the finishing touches on *Aurora Leigh*, a long, mannered "novel-poem" that Dix, when she later read it, pronounced a "work of wonderful originality and merit." In the meantime, her bankers had accumulated thirty-one letters informing, beseeching, complimenting her on various matters. Without breaking stride, she raced on to Rouen, where she "saw all the noble ancient edifices in that city, the large hospital for aged men and women, 1,000 patients; 'the Colonie' for young offenders at Quilley [and] the great Hospital for 700 insane women." This was the end of her continental journey. She told William Rathbone that she was on her way back to Liverpool, intending to stay only long enough to catch her breath before booking passage on the next steamer for America. She had seen enough of the Old World. "It is quite time I was on my own ground," she said.[76]

In considering Dix's two frenzied years abroad, it is hard not to think of her as a woman on the run, afraid to stop, as though her life depended on perpetual motion. Her compulsion to create a peripatetic and disordered existence alarmed her friends. None of them could understand the centrifugal force that impelled her outward, away from any center, away from home. Not infrequently they offered her a home. Anne Heath, the Rathbones, and Daniel Hack Tuke, among others, begged her to slow down, to stay with them as long as she wished. To their consternation, even as she complained about exhaustion and the physical toll her labors exacted, the moment she was able, she moved on.

Yet impatience, hyperkineticism, and wanderlust, which appear at first to have been obsessive, are perhaps not as outlandish as they seem. Or rather, they would not seem outlandish had Dix been a man. From Daniel Boone to Theodore Roosevelt, American men were celebrated for their vitality and wanderlust. Boone felt cramped, and ready to move his family ever deeper into the wilderness, the moment he could detect any wisp of smoke from a neighbor's chimney. Roosevelt's notorious hustle took him from New York to the White House and then to the jungles of Africa in search of ever bigger game, which he shot, stuffed, and mounted as testimony to his own vigor. The problem for Dix, no less restless than Boone nor less ambitious than Roosevelt, was that she was expected—and to some degree expected herself—to conform to the feminine ideals of Victorian culture.

These ideals revolved around domesticity. A woman's duty was, above all, to preside over the domestic sphere of her home, a place where the rest of the world was shut out. "There is nothing like staying at home for real comfort," Jane Austen wrote in *Emma*. By midcentury the bourgeois home in England and America had been transformed, refined, and feminized to make it as different as possible from the workplace. Home was a place to experience comfort, tranquillity, and ease. On the level of theory, it was supposed to be a retreat. This ideal, with its emphasis on cleanliness and comfort, inspired Dix's concept of the well-ordered asylum: a home for the homeless insane.

Though she built homes for the mad, Dix continued to think of herself as homeless in the sense that she never presided over a domestic realm of her own. While she enjoyed her connection to the upper class, she personally despised ease and comfort. In fact she was often conspicuously austere. Creature comforts meant nothing to her. On the road, she slept as often on floors or cots as on mattresses. Typically she looked down on the pampered wives of men like William Ellery Channing, Thomas Story Kirkbride, and Horace Mann as people without accomplishment or interest. It was the husbands whose achievements formed the framework of her aspiration. But this was a truth that she could never voice. Because, according to her age's assumptions about gender, female ambition was sinister and went against God's will. The only way she could exculpate her ambition was to sacrifice precisely the comfort and leisure to which her position would have seemed to entitle her—to renounce the feminine ideal of home by becoming homeless herself.

CHAPTER FOURTEEN

Into the Tempest

Although it had been but two years, it seemed that a decade had passed since she had arrived in Liverpool, sick, demoralized, despondent about her career. If English reform had failed to live up to her expectations, Greenbank at least had again worked its healing magic. In September 1856, despite a week of seasickness from violent storms in the North Atlantic, she approached America hopefully, refreshed, her spirits rekindled. From her stateroom on the *Baltic* she jotted a note to Heath. "I have hardly in life experienced more vivid emotions than when 'land, land' was the cry from the quarter deck," she told her faithful friend. "I really felt myself nearer to you and near to the time of reunion as through tears that would not stay back." Having had ample time alone to reflect on her work in America and the restorative power of friendship, she was looking forward to rededicating herself to the insane.[1]

When she returned, her breadth of experience made Dix the Western world's leading authority on mental institutions. No one in America or Europe could rival her sweeping comparative perspective, gained not from reading articles but from direct observation. Europe had opened her eyes to a rich and complicated diversity of arrangements for the insane. On balance, she believed she left the Old World better than she found it, having set in motion the forces of enlightenment in Rome, in the Channel Islands, and, most important of all, in Scotland. She hoped to be able to apply her new insights to the conditions of her own country.

As she tried to decide how best to refocus her career in America, she resolved to avoid James Buchanan's Washington. A fire had ravaged the Congressional Library, effectively eliminating her office in the Capitol. Perhaps, she thought, this was an omen, pointing her away from Washington back to the states, where she had been much more effective.

And so she eagerly plunged back into asylum affairs. Within days of her arrival in New York City, she showed up without warning at the Bloomingdale asylum, where she had a few years earlier stirred up the trustees and provoked Charles Nichols's ouster. She strolled about the old building with an air of proprietorship, making notes, listening to complaints about the medical staff, and consulting with the doctors on cases. It was gratifying to see that despite her long absence, reports of her endeavors in Europe had drifted back across the Atlantic, serving to enhance her reputation. Partly out of respect and partly out of fear, everyone treated her like a full-fledged trustee of the institution.

From Bloomingdale she headed upstate, winding her way north to Toronto. In many ways this difficult winter expedition beyond the frontier of her own country was a continuation of her European wandering: a brooding, soul-searching ordeal in which Dix, through the process of extreme self-denial, affirmed the meaning of her labors. The weather was unusually bad. Heavy snowfall and ice storms closed the roads and interrupted train schedules. "I have no experience of so stormy and severe winter weather that I can recollect since my childhood," she mused, "and the somber impressions made are deepened by the scenes of various trouble and misery which I meet in many places—side by side with joy and prosperity." Temperatures dropped to twenty-eight below zero. Yet as the cold and the obstacles to driving herself onward multiplied, she said in biblical cadence, "in proportion as my own discomforts have increased, my conviction of the necessity to search into the wants of the friendless and afflicted has deepened—if I am cold they are colder—if I am weary they are distressed—if I am alone they are abandoned, and cast out." To gain the approval of her reproachful conscience she had to subject herself to physical suffering. This was the price for reclaiming her cause and regaining her voice.[2]

At this time, in her fifty-fourth year, Dix's experience of loneliness was all the more acute because she felt she had missed out on a chance to marry Millard Fillmore. Three years earlier Fillmore's wife, Abigail, had died. Because of the friendship Dix had already established with the president, the possibility of their relationship moving toward romance and intimacy was not out of the question. Circumspect and always within the formal bounds of propriety, she wrote him enough notes and letters to fill a small volume. By the time she left for Europe, a subtle sexual tension had crept into their correspondence. When, less than a year after Abigail Fillmore's death, Washington gossip had linked Fillmore to a thirty-two-year-old socialite from western New York named Elizabeth Porter, Dix had publicly risen to his defense to refute what she assumed were malicious rumors. Her overwrought defense of the president's honor barely concealed a hope that their friendship might blossom into a deeper relationship. "If I wound you," she had written in a letter she asked him to burn, "recollect only that I would *prove* my friendship something more than a profession." She was attracted to him because Fillmore was one of the few eligible men she knew whose personality, views, and social status were compatible with her own aspirations. Unfortunately, she lacked the assets of youth, beauty, and wealth that, events would later reveal, were his criteria for matrimony.[3]

In the course of her northward trek, she paid a call on Fillmore, at home in Buffalo in comfortable exile after finishing a distant third in the presidential election of 1856. He was still unmarried, though by this time Dix's hopes had dimmed. She knew she had given him many opportunities in Washington, and then in England, where they had met on a handful of social occasions, to put their relationship on a new footing had he wished to do so. In his parlor, their talk remained on neutral ground, personal enough to be polite, nothing more. He seemed to take his poor showing in the election with equanimity, blaming it not on personal failings but on the splintering of the Whig party. She contended that he should reform his strategy and regroup for another run in 1860. By then the tedious Buchanan would surely have exhausted the voters' patience. But Fillmore knew that national politics had passed him by. Saddened that such an honest and capable man had been pushed off the national stage, Dix left Buffalo with all her old pessimism about American politics restored.

Later that year Fillmore announced his engagement to Caroline McIntosh, the daughter of a fabulously wealthy tycoon who had built

Millard Fillmore from an oil portrait in 1847.

the Mohawk and Hudson Railroad. Like so many politicians whose earnings fail to keep up with their taste for the good life, Fillmore had for years fretted over his bank account. His marriage to Caroline instantly made him a rich man, an icon of Buffalo society who was free to travel and to spend summers in Saratoga. The couple, it turned out, would need Caroline's money. To their dismay, Caroline was prone to neurasthenia and violent paroxysms that neither travel abroad nor the costly ministrations of doctors could more than temporarily relieve.

Still, Dix envied Caroline Fillmore, or at least she envied the younger woman's prosperous conventionality and secure social position. For there was a side of Dorothea Dix that longed for the home and family she never had, that yearned to be a genteel Victorian lady, that dreamed of settling down and living a normal life. It was never anything more than a dream, though, because this aspect of her personality was overpowered by her need for independence and her ambition to make something of herself. Throughout her life, when the meaning of her lifework was called into question, as it was when President Pierce vetoed her land bill, she was tormented by the split between submissive gentlewoman and aggressive activist, feeling that domesticity must be better than the hardship she endured. But such moods were evanescent. As she was to acknowledge to Elizabeth Rathbone, she was cut out for the life she lived, and no other.

Putting the past out of her mind, Dix traveled from Buffalo to see the New York State Lunatic Asylum at Utica. There the superintendent, a plodding and sickly doctor named Nathan Benedict, had recently been toppled by his ferociously ambitious twenty-nine-year-old assistant, John P. Gray. Eager to make a name for himself, Gray had seized editorial control of the *American Journal of Insanity*, the official organ of the asylum superintendents' association, which Utica's Amariah Brigham had founded a decade earlier. When Dix sat down with Gray, a corpulent, massively bearded character who looked far older than his years, and listened to him hold forth on his theories of madness and his plans for restructuring Utica, she realized she was witnessing a changing of the guard.

Gray's was a new generation of medical superintendents, steeped in anatomical methods, who believed that the key to mental disease must lie within the gray tissues of the brain itself. This concept reflected a broader shift in medical thinking that moved increasingly toward trying to find a somatic basis for mental illness. If one could look closely enough through a powerful microscope, according to this school of thought, mania, dementia—all forms of madness—would be seen to have an observable pathophysiological basis. The corollary to this view was that the absence of structural abnormality would suggest that a person was sane. No lesion, no madness. Performing autopsies on hundreds of asylum inmates and carefully scrutinizing sections of their brains, Gray reached the conclusion that bona fide clinical madness was far less prevalent than the forefathers of psychiatry like Woodward and Brigham had thought. Above all, behavior that they readily diagnosed as proof of moral insanity seemed to Gray not evidence of disease at all but of willful, thus culpable, crime. Styling himself as a master at smoking out phony mental illness, the formidable Dr. Gray was acclaimed for his regular appearances as an expert witness for the prosecution in murder trials.[4]

Like most superintendents, he had an unlimited appetite for hospital construction. While Dix had been in Europe, Gray, together with his colleagues, the keepers of a number of local asylums and almshouses in different regions of the state, and county overseers of the poor, had petitioned the New York legislature to build two new hospitals, including one exclusively for chronic patients. Reciting the familiar chorus of overcrowding at Utica, they hoped to persuade Albany that continuing to house pauper lunatics in local facilities was intolerably inhumane. Dix certainly agreed. It had been fifteen years since she had surveyed the state's jails and almshouses and published her New York *Memorial*. Returning in early 1857, she was painfully disappointed, especially when she noted "the intelligence and ability of the communities considered," that so little had changed. "The want of system, prudent expenditure of funds, and humane care of the poor, the sick, the aged, the insane and the helpless are astonishing." But there was a new dimension to her critique. Dix now saw the problem as more than simply a matter of setting up asylums in eastern and western parts of the state as the legislation proposed. "That which is of at least equal importance is yet to be considered and matured," she told Fillmore, "*viz.*, revision of the Pauper Laws." Her experience in England had taught her that poverty, crime, and mental disorder were profoundly interrelated. An institutional solution imposed before the underlying problems were better understood struck her as simplistic and premature. What was called for, she said, was a thorough and penetrating review of all New York's penal institutions.[5]

Opening the Pandora's box of crime and welfare policy was not something lawmakers welcomed. They looked to Dix, as they had in the past, for a concrete solution to the problem of indigent insanity.

But the world was quickly becoming more complicated. In the late 1850s she could not help but sense the growing crisis in the first generation of public institutions. A decade earlier, many physicians and reformers had insisted that properly constructed prisons, reformatories, and asylums would be self-regulating. On the eve of the war, it was becoming apparent that such optimism had been naive. As overcrowding, indifference, neglect, and all the old abuses began to surface inside the institutions she had founded, Dix was vexed. It was the same kind of institutional decay she had witnessed in England. When she shared her frustration with George Barrell Emerson, he consoled her with the thought that such failings stemmed from the basic imperfection of human nature. "Do you think that the time will come, before the millennium, when charitable institutions, schools and religious societies will cease to need occasional oversight and reestablishment?" he asked. "Will almshouses, churches or Normal Schools ever take care of themselves?"[6]

Faced with spiraling censuses in most state institutions and irrefutable evidence that most mental illnesses severe enough to warrant hospitalization turned out to be persistent disorders, superintendents reconsidered the question of whether they should build separate facilities for long-term custodial care. In Washington, Charles Nichols, for whom magnitude symbolized success, argued strenuously that the only way to make "scientific and benevolent" asylum care affordable for the masses of insane paupers was to spread the medical administrative overhead across large hospitals for chronic incurables. Most of his colleagues were reluctant to give up their faith in curability. The world of men like Thomas Kirkbride was centered on their commitment to moral treatment. They were troubled by the idea of writing off any portion of humankind as beyond hope. To Horace Buttolph the idea of segregating lunatics by their apparent prospects for recovery seemed to fly in the face of humane treatment. "Why," he demanded, "should any person, however hopeless may be their mental disorder, be deprived of such reasonable accommodation and comfort as is afforded by the best State institution in the country?" Also, chronic cases were seldom troublemakers, John Curwen told Dix. Many of them adapted to institutional life quite well, and if their disease were not debilitating they often helped keep acutely mad patients in check.[7]

The reason for considering custodial institutions, Dix knew better than the superintendents, was money. When she later accused R. L. Parsons, the chief medical officer of the New York City asylum, of presiding over an institution that was "custodial rather than curative in its uses," he pleaded no contest. With patients of every diagnosis spilling into the corridors, he explained, the attendants could barely maintain order, let alone administer treatment. In its early days the asylum had boasted a forty-two percent rate of cure. As the census climbed, the rate fell below thirty. He attributed most of the drop to sheer volume. In just five years the average yearly census had climbed from 368 to 628. Unless he were provided resources to meet increased caseloads, he insisted that it was unreasonable to expect anything more than a warehouse for the mad. No state institution was immune to these pressures. Population growth always seemed to outstrip a state's tax base. Over the years even the model Worcester State Lunatic Hospital would find itself transformed into an institution for chronic lunatics.[8]

In 1857 Dix, who had long argued that the state of New York should build several small-scale institutions in which incurables could be cared for comfortably but cheaply, decided that the time had finally come for a two-tiered system. A former Utica Hospital physician named John Chapin backed her plan; indeed, he had himself published an article along the same lines in the *American Journal of Insanity*. To her astonishment, though, the hospital bill she proposed, seemingly a fait accompli, sank in the lower house. Convinced that the need for new asylums was self-evident, she had left it to the measure's legislative sponsor to line up the votes. "I will next year take the subject up without *sharing* responsibility," she told Fillmore. "This year it was Mr. [Spencer's] measure; next year I claim it for mine." As it turned out, however, the financial Panic of 1857, and later the Civil War, would push hospital measures off the legislative agenda until the later 1860s, when the Willard asylum, a separate institution for chronic patients, was finally established. When she moved on to other pursuits, Dix's idea of opening up a fuller debate on New York social policy fell by the wayside.[9]

Turning to Pennsylvania, she found familiar roles to play. At her request, the legislature assigned her to find a farm the state could purchase to build a "school for Imbecile children." Meanwhile, John Curwen, whose control over the State Lunatic Hospital in Harrisburg was shaky at best, needed her help to raise money for equipment and to keep his trustees at bay.

More important, in May 1858 Harriet Hare summoned Dix to Philadelphia, where her seventy-eight-year-old husband, Robert Hare, lay dying from pneumonia. Dix had known the Hares for thirty years, from her first trip to Philadelphia. A professor of chemistry at the University of Pennsylvania, Robert was immediately struck by the young woman's intensity, intelligence, and phenomenal work ethic. Looking back, she realized he had been the first man who ever believed in her. And over the years he constantly reminded her how proud he was of her, and how everything she had done justified his original faith. Putting everything else aside, she moved into their fine house at 917 Chestnut Street, and for a month served as the old man's private nurse. Mornings she read to him from the New Testament. Afternoons, sitting in a rocking chair with her lap full of knitting, she listened as he expounded in a low voice his weird scientific theories concerning chemical manifestations of spiritual phenomena. Evenings, after he had fallen asleep, she sat quietly with Harriet, assuring her that her husband had lived a noble life and was indeed a great man. Had it not been for him, she said, she would never have had the courage to pursue her own career of public service. And when he died, Dix did her best to memorialize him, even urging Benjamin Silliman (unsuccessfully) to write Professor Hare's biography.

Shortly after Hare's funeral, she received a request from the commissioners of the Western Pennsylvania Hospital in Pittsburgh. In 1847 they had endowed a charity hospital in the middle of the city that had grown apace, and, by 1854, along with a patient population of several dozen sick paupers, housed fifty-two insane patients. That year the board, bowing to pressure from the medical community, agreed to charter a separate department for lunatics. Dix had helped raise part of the hospital's original endowment and, in the process, had come into contact with John Harper, the president of the Bank of Pittsburgh and one of the city's leading philanthropists. Harper, a man who admired accomplishment, was so taken with her that he prevailed on the board to allow Dix to select the site for the new asylum. She was delighted. Then he proposed that they name it in her honor, a thought that made her uneasy because she believed it would make her appear self-promoting. Harper good-naturedly told her she had no choice in the matter, although he did agree to her request to call the place Dixmont, the name of the Maine town her grandfather, Elijah Dix, had founded a half-century earlier and in which he was buried.[10]

During the late 1850s Dix gathered steam, never allowing her pace to slacken. None of the medical men could understand how her frail body withstood the marathon pace she inflicted on it. Everyone else slowed with age, Isaac Ray told Kirkbride, but she was wondrous, her powers undiminished. Recognizing this, in 1859 Horace Mann, who had left Congress for Yellow Springs, Ohio, to become president of Antioch College, asked her to join him there to organize "the Ladies Hall," in effect to become dean of women.[11] Recalling her experience with Mann's school in Lexington, she demurred. In any event, she had no desire to stay in one place.

In 1859, for example, she started off the New Year in Philadelphia, left in mid-January for Maryland and North Carolina, then on to

Columbia and Charleston, South Carolina, where she spent two weeks inspecting prisons and hospitals. February she continued on south to Millidgeville, Savannah, and Macon. Taking the six-horse post hack from Gladstone to Tuscaloosa, she was in an accident; one of the hack's cars demolished when the track under it gave way. The forty-mile trip took fourteen hours. Next to New Orleans. There, on a typical day in March, she scrawled in her green leather notebook, "New Orleans Bible Society; Mayor's Office; Recorder's Office; Charity Hospital; House of Refuge; House of Correction; Orleans Parish Jail," and also mentioned a visit to a local madhouse where she saw fifty patients. Arriving in Benwick Bay she boarded the *Magnolia* and, despite a violent storm at sea, steamed across the Gulf of Mexico. Landing at Galveston, astonished to see camels on the beach, she lost no time in booking passage on a ship for Houston. "Texas is not the Australia of the United States as it once was," she grandly declared, "but a great and soon to be influential state." In Austin she met the governor and the state's leading politicians, along with prominent members of the city's medical community.[12]

Everywhere people welcomed her. Eating supper in a small public house on "a wide lonely Prairie," she wrote, she was approached by the stagecoach ticket agent who eyed her strangely. She assumed this was because she was a lady traveling alone, an oddity on the frontier. When she drew her purse to pay for her ticket, however, he protested: "No, no by [sic] take money from you,—why I never thought I should see you, and now you are in my house;—why you've done good to every body for years and years;—make sure now there's a home for you in any house in Texas . . . here wife this is Miss Dix,—shake hands and call the children." By April, back in New Orleans again, she figured she had been on the road thirty-two out of ninety-seven days. Vicksburg and St. Louis in May; Springfield, Cincinnati, Harrisburg, Trenton, and New York in June; Philadelphia, Baltimore, and Boston in July; then on to Maine and Nova Scotia. By year's end, making more than a full circuit, she was again in the deep South.[13]

On this perpetual odyssey, as a way of quantifying her progress, she kept a running tally of the asylum appropriations bills she was instrumental in passing. Like a businessman taking stock of his investments, she told Heath, "I ask this winter more than a third of a million."[14]

Her attraction to the South remained and, despite evidence of the region's growing bellicosity, grew stronger than ever. She told Mrs. Torrey that the incident with the friendly stagecoach driver in Texas was only "one of a thousand all through the South." In contrast to the North, she was "constantly surprised by spontaneous expressions of the heartiest good-will—and I may well be careful what I ask for hospitals, etc., for my work is unquestioned, and so I try to be very prudent and watchful." There more than anywhere else in the country, as one Texan told her, "You are a moral autocrat; you speak and your word is law."[15]

Her moral discourse continued to omit slavery. But by the fall of 1859, when Dix was in Jackson, Mississippi, absorbed once again in politicking for the state asylum, slavery and its repercussions were growing too ominous to overlook.

She had been called to Mississippi on routine business. Her presence was needed to help straighten out the management of the State Insane Hospital, an institution she had set in motion nine years earlier with a memorial to the state legislature. Its predicament had become disconcertingly familiar. Strapped for operating funds, the asylum was on its third superintendent in the space of five years. The legislator who begged Dix to intervene claimed that the issue was bottled up in committee because his opponents were accusing him of politicizing the asylum to advance his own purposes. Everyone knew that she was above politics, he said, and if she came to Jackson, none would dare impugn her motives. Sizing up the situation, she was confident that the newly appointed administrator, Robert Kells, would prove capable enough if the state assembly and its various oversight committees would stay out of operational decisions, vote him an adequate budget, and leave him alone to do his job. In this instance, she figured that the hospital, together with the additional capacity it obviously needed, would amount to $140,000. Subjected to "much talking" and some vigorous arm-twisting, she told her friends, "the Governor, the Committees and those I have seen of the Senate and House are on my side of the question."[16]

On October 16, though, events in Virginia had eclipsed every other political question. On that day John Brown, bent on touching off an armed uprising among slaves, led his ill-fated attempt to seize the federal arsenal at Harpers Ferry. Brown and his band were swiftly defeated. But news of the assault electrified the slave states. "A kind of insane anxiety gripped the whole population," wrote a friend of Frederick Douglass's. "A lightning bolt had awakened Virginia and the whole South." Indeed, Harper's Ferry fueled extremism and whetted the appetite for violent confrontation on both sides. Abolitionists like Theodore Parker instantly canonized the zealot; and in "A Plea for Captain John Brown," Thoreau, as thoughtful a man as lived in New England, prophesied that Brown, sentenced to hang for treason, was an exalted martyr who merited comparison to Christ himself.[17]

Dix was revolted by such talk. Long sympathetic to Southern antiabolitionism, she shared the view that aggressive antislavery activity risked inciting a slave insurrection that would destroy Southern society. "This mad scheme of Brown's is the strangest illustration of mistaken feelings overruling judgment and practical common sense that I have ever heard or read of," she declared. "All in all the Southern people are as moderate in their opinions under such press of danger as could possibly be expected." Like many moderate Southerners, she held on to an ingenuous hope that the slave system, unmolested, was destined gradually to wither and die a natural death. Northern meddling would bring only divisiveness and hostility. In addition, as much as she believed in moral suasion and in government action based on moral principles, violence distressed her. She found it incomprehensible that Unitarians like Parker, Worcester's Thomas Wentworth Higginson, and her old friend Samuel Gridley Howe, could actively encourage an uprising of the African savages whose condition, she believed, they had never studied at first hand and therefore completely misrepresented.[18]

The Southern elite understood that few Northerners sympathized with their values more instinctively than Dorothea Dix. Consequently, at a time when virtually every Yankee in the South came under suspicion, she continued to be not only accepted but revered.

Yet, if as she felt at home in the South, when it came to taking sides, she had too much of Old and New England in her blood to be a woman of divided loyalties. At the marrow she was still a Unitarian, a protégé of Channing, an almost-adopted daughter of the devoutly antislavery Rathbones, a friend of Horace Mann and even that bête noir of the slave states, Charles Sumner, now recovering from the savage caning the slaveholder Preston Brooks had given him on the Senate floor. Nor could she help but recall that when it had come down to a vote on whether or not to override Pierce's veto of her land measure, Southern congressional support had evaporated. In her hour of need, men like Sumner had supported her against the president. In contrast, she had strongly suspected ever since the early 1850s that Jefferson Davis, the future president of the Confederacy, had been a Machiavelli working behind the scenes at every turn to sabotage her beloved bill.

For the better part of two decades, she had prided herself on occupying a moral high ground that was also a middle ground set off from the sectional politics of slavery. After Harpers Ferry, however, in the election year of 1860, the idea that there could be a neutral zone large enough to accommodate even one woman and her narrow cause was losing its plausibility.

Since her return from Europe, it was apparent that the South had played into the hands of the extremists. Even more than the righteous dictates of the abolitionists, the increasingly strident, inflammatory rhetoric of the fire eaters, drowning out all tones of moderation, alienated her. Up to the day Abraham Lincoln was elected president, however, she tried to dismiss their deeds as harmless bluster and downplayed the possibility of armed conflict. "All this nonsense about dissolution of the Union is to me absurd," she told Government Hospital Superintendent Charles Nichols on 4 November 1860. After the election, even she could no longer ignore the portents of disaster. Within weeks, South Carolina voted to secede from the Union. To explain and justify their position, state political leaders drafted "An Address to the People of South Carolina." In reading this manifesto, what saddened Dix more than anything else was the flat declaration that "all fraternity of feeling between North and South is lost, or has been converted to hate."[19]

She was in Washington when she read these fateful words. She was just returning from a trip to the deep South and was stopping over for a few days to visit friends and check the pulse of the capital. Truculent and bewildering, the secessionist contagion was spreading. "I have never read anything in the history of any people more extraordinary than that which is characterizing the people of the gulf states," she lamented, "but South Carolina in particular."[20]

She was there briefly in December, when she met with legislative committees to review a proposal to add two new wings onto the State Hospital for the Insane. As always, aristocratic South Carolinians had striven to make her feel at home in their world. Charleston, so quaint and well ordered, with its three-story brick houses dating back to colonial days, its cobblestone streets, and its picturesque harbor, reminded her in some ways of the Boston of her youth, before it was swamped by immigration. In Charleston and Columbia, however, she realized that the antebellum South was disintegrating before her eyes. Her old friend Francis Lieber himself, a moderate man long evasive on slavery though a fervid believer in the Union, had in mid-1856 been ousted from his professorship at South Carolina College on drummed-up charges of harboring abolitionist sympathies. Reason was giving way to hysteria.[21]

An inexorable series of events seemed to be forcing everyone, inside and outside government, to take sides. Traditional politics and law counted for nothing. It was common knowledge, for example, that in anticipation of armed conflict President Buchanan's secretary of war, John Floyd of Virginia, was transferring federal munitions to Southern arsenals as fast as he could. Such behavior by a cabinet official, young Henry Adams remarked, would have cost him his life in any other country. But in what he called "the Great Secession Winter of 1860–1861," Adams noted acidly that with Flood heading the War Department, dead-set on using any means, no matter how despicable, to destroy the government, it was easy to understand why the citizens of Washington believed themselves lost. And so it seemed to Dix. The city, she said with disgust, was rife with disloyalty and anarchy. The vibrant "seat of Gov[ernmen]t that was[,] is all but a city of the Dead. [Not] literally a shrouded corpse, but dead in action[,] intellectual force and resource." Its malaise seemed to her evidence of how a people bereft of sound "religious education . . . may plunge in a moment of hot-headed excitement to [the] verge of ruin." Despite evidence to the contrary, she held out a faint hope. Possibly the rumors of war were overstated, and were only the death throes of the old Democratic party, shattered in the election of 1860, trying to piece together the fragments of its power.[22]

Dix's dream had been a Whiggish dream that encompassed the nation. Thus sectional schism, by weakening the national government and dividing the public domain on which her land bill had been based, ran contrary to her republican ideal. Hers was a vision of one country, and she was in consequence a Unionist. Arguments about slavery and freedom never resonated within her. Black slaves remained invisible and never became factors in her moral calculus. Her Civil War would never be about slavery, but the Union was in her mind no abstraction. She knew it state by state; knew its counties and towns; had ridden its railroads, crossed its mountain ranges, navigated its rivers; and knew its leaders and its ordinary citizens, as well as those who had fallen beneath citizenship into the realms of madness, poverty, and crime. She would have agreed with Walt Whitman that "the war of attempted Secession," as he preferred to call it, was at bottom a test of "Solidarity." "What is any Nation, after all," he asked, "and what is a human being—but a struggle between conflicting, paradoxical, opposing elements—and they themselves and their most violent contests, important parts of that One Identity and of its development?" Dix possessed none of Whitman's intellectual flair, but when the war came she expressed her own hope that the "great national trouble will work out a benefit to national character—that the fires of tribulation may act like the refiner's fire and purify from sin and wickedness!"[23]

Powerless to influence the great forces at work, in January 1861, while the fate of the Union floated in limbo, Dix decided to pursue her state legislative agenda as long as the South welcomed her and the railroads remained open. On her desk were four letters from members of the Kentucky legislature begging her to help them pass legislation to rebuild the Western Lunatic Asylum, which had recently burned to the ground. Helping them was a matter of pride, she told Heath, because the hospital had been built at her behest and was therefore "*one of mine.*"[24]

And so the next week she boarded a train for Frankfort. When she arrived in the state capital, despite the worsening political climate in Kentucky, she was greeted warmly by the governor and leading members of both houses of the state assembly. Francis Montgomery, the hapless asylum superintendent, impressed her as a blundering fool. Against his protests, she more or less ignored him and took matters into her own hands. Time was running out in the legislative session, and the proposed hospital reconstruction bill was in sorry shape. To meet the deadline, she worked like a demon, up at four o'clock every morning, recalculating the capital budget, arguing the advantages of an iron roof rather than one made of tin, figuring out, item by item, what could be cut and what was essential for rebuilding the facility to meet the latest standards of care. No one dared stand in her way. The bill, presented at the last possible moment, sailed through the legislature.[25]

When she had time to look up from her work, though, she was shocked by how the secession fever was advancing unchecked even in the border states. From what she heard in the corridors of the statehouse, it was plain "that the South is *determined* on a *Revolution*." Mississippi and South Carolina were simply mad, she lamented, what with their proposals to renew the slave trade and divide the country. Perhaps, in other circumstances, a strong leader might have risen to the challenge, but "there seems no wise great man to lead the bewildered people to a safe position," she ruefully wrote. Before the election she had professed herself most "deeply mortified to see [Stephen A.] Douglas in the Presidential Chair." On the other hand, she observed, "we have suffered so many humiliations as a Nation, that we dare not be sanguine of a better result than the last *choice* of the people afforded." Buchanan weakened her admittedly feeble faith in democracy. "Revolutionary movements of plotting Secessionists have held the mind in suspense," Dix told Fillmore. "The poor, imbecile and base President [Buchanan] has helped on the present crisis by folly and treason alike, I believe, and there have been quite enough persons to take advantage of his infirmity as well as his real unfaithfulness to himself, his Oath of Office, and to his Country." A leader with firm principles and moral resolution could have "cauterized the head of the Hydra," she believed, before the secession monster could spread its poison. Instead, she was convinced that Buchanan, in league with the Southern members of his cabinet, had hatched a conspiracy the previous summer to elect his vice president, the Kentuckian John C. Breckenridge, to the presidency. Had their man gained the White House, she speculated, they would have been free to "perfect as silently as surely the scheme for Southern rule."[26]

A lame duck throughout the tumultuous winter of 1860–61, Buchanan hedged and equivocated. In her opinion, his hollow professions of dismay at secession, claiming all the while that the Constitution gave him no authority to interfere in the affairs of the Southern states, smacked of the same hypocritical legalism Pierce had used to veto her land bill.[27]

In February 1861, as President-elect Lincoln was preparing to leave for Washington, Dix was summoned to Springfield, Illinois, to lobby for capital appropriations for the Illinois State Hospital for the Insane in Jacksonville. The asylum's origins lay in her 1847 Illinois *Memorial*, but the institution had been managed in a slipshod fashion from the day it was incorporated. In exasperation, the trustees finally recruited Andrew McFarland in 1854. He had been for years superintendent of the New Hampshire Asylum for the Insane and had a reputation as a man who could whip things into shape. Once on board, he loudly criticized his predecessors for so overcrowding the asylum with chronic cases that it would be next to impossible for him to create the therapeutic environment they expected. If there was skepticism about his indictment of the facility's inadequacies, in all likelihood it dissipated in 1860 when an epidemic of typhoid broke out. Thirty cases were reported and three deaths. Worried about the political repercussions of their failure to honor the institution's charter—which, among other things, called for "a never failing supply of water"—the trustees quickly brought in a hydraulic engineer who proceeded to design a reservoir and pumping system that tied into a nearby creek.[28]

This was an exorbitantly expensive undertaking. But McFarland, along with the trustees, concluded that if they could persuade Dorothea Dix personally to approach the legislature on their behalf, she could pry loose the needed funds from the state budget. They all recalled her earlier work in Illinois—how intrepidly she had worn down her opponents and at last had her way.

When she received McFarland's urgent telegram, imploring her to save his asylum and thus keep alive her own original purpose for the Illinois asylum, Dix came at once to Springfield. This was the work, accomplished at high speed and under pressure, that she loved. As expected, the Illinois State Senate responded to Dix's eleventh-hour appearance by passing the measure before it. When she informed them that McFarland, competent as he was, had nevertheless omitted a few state-of-the-art features of asylum architecture, the senators suspended their rules of order and permitted her to introduce additional legislation to bring the facility fully up to her standard. The ink had barely dried on the new bill, she rejoiced, when they passed it unanimously, "saying I no doubt represented the right work for them to do." Understandably she agreed that they should congratulate themselves. In a world of looming disaster, a comparatively trifling appropriation for the state asylum rendered a tangible benefit that was of graspable human scale.[29]

For the weary legislature, as for Dix herself, such work served as a diversion from the cataclysm about to engulf the nation. "I think God I have such full uses for time now," she confided to Heath, "for the state of our beloved country would crush my heart and life." Only once before, "when the 10,000,000 Bill was killed by a poor base man in power," she confessed, had grief so nearly overwhelmed her. But in 1854, she realized, her sadness had been solitary, rooted in personal anguish over her lost cause. The tribulation of civil war would spare no one.[30]

With better insight than most of her fellow citizens into the nature of sectional disagreement, Dix had a sense of the calm before the tempest. Everywhere she went, an eerie unreality prevailed. "It is singular how little people realize the facts of this momentous period," she told Heath. "I see no changes in things, people, or business—but for the distant echoes we should not know that this great cloud is gathering its stormy terror." By her count, two-thirds of Southerners were for the

Union. Like Henry Adams she believed that no one really wanted war. And so she continued to look for something that would jolt them to their senses and preserve the border states at least from "the punishment South Carolina and Mississippi merit." But at this point she intended to be realistic. If war were to break out while she was in the South, she was confident she could secure a military pass for her return trip north. Indeed, the head of the South Carolina railroad had already given her a rail pass valid through the end of 1862.

By January 1861 Charleston was swarming with men in new gray uniforms; ships were sailing under the guns of Fort Sumter, palmetto flags streaming from their masts; a permanent Confederate constitution was being drafted; and politicians were speculating whether or not President-elect Lincoln would use force to defend the federal forts. James Buchanan confirmed his reputation as a nervous appeaser, refusing to take federal action after the *Star of the West* had been fired upon. In contrast the president-elect, whom Dix vaguely thought a trustworthy man, was a steadfast Unionist, committed, as he would declare March 4 in his inaugural address, to wield executive power "to hold, occupy, and possess the property and places belonging to the government, and to collect the duties and imposts."[31]

For those attuned to politics, it was a season of conspiracy theories. Although she probably did not link it directly to Buchanan, Dix had for a while been overhearing frighteningly sober talk of a scheme to murder Lincoln and derail his Republican administration before it could take the reins of government. She remained tight-lipped about the whole affair, but her unique position as a lady and a trustworthy friend of the South within the statehouses and drawing rooms of South Carolina, Mississippi, and Kentucky made her privy to the malevolent details of at least one such plan.

There was indeed more than ample cause for concern. In the weeks leading up to the inauguration, Lincoln, faced with the need to affirm his leadership and keep the border states from pulling out of the Union, was conducting a whistle-stop tour. Starting out in Springfield, Illinois, he proposed to parade through Baltimore and arrive triumphantly in Washington in time to take the oath of office. Everyone knew it was a dangerous itinerary. Threats against his life had been circulating since the election. And the final leg of his journey southward, the passage through Baltimore, was the most perilous. For Baltimore was a city nearly out of control, aflame with anti-Northern feeling fanned by secessionist and slaveholding interests.

Dix was sure that a conspiracy to murder Lincoln existed and that she possessed important intelligence that could foil it. She was uncertain in whom to confide, though. Finally, in mid-January, after Alabama, Mississippi, and Florida had followed South Carolina out of the Union, Dix took her story to Samuel M. Felton, the president of the Philadelphia, Wilmington and Baltimore Railroad. Felton was a gimlet-eyed businessman and a staunch Unionist who did not relish the prospect of an independent South slicing his railroad empire into pieces. From time to time he had made contributions to Pennsylvania hospitals and had earned Dix's gratitude by presenting her with a free rail pass. So one Saturday afternoon in January 1861 she arranged to meet him, and in the privacy of his office told him her tale of intrigue. It took her a full hour to lay out all the details, he later recalled, but the main point was "that there was an extensive and organized conspiracy through the South to seize upon Washington, with its archives and records, and then declare the Southern Confederacy de facto the Government of the United States." Teams of thugs, she said, had already been assigned their various roles and were awaiting the signal to burn bridges, cut telegraph lines, and sabotage Felton's own railroad's Washington and Annapolis line when the president-elect's train appeared.[32]

What made Dix's warning fully credible was that Felton had been hearing the same story in bits and pieces for some time. Without delay he passed her information on to Allan Pinkerton, the private detective he retained to police his railroad and help him with labor problems. Expecting trouble of some kind, Pinkerton already had planted informants inside Baltimore's political organizations and gangs. Based on further investigation, his detectives reported back that there was indeed a plot to assassinate Lincoln when he switched trains in Baltimore. This intelligence was soon confirmed independently by the War Department's spies. As a result, Lincoln changed his schedule at the last moment and passed through Baltimore, unheralded, in the early morning hours. Although the president subsequently regretted his decision to slink into Washington "like a thief in the night," the evidence suggests that the conspiracy was real enough. Baltimore was, as events were about to prove, a powder keg awaiting a match, and his prudence was hardly unwarranted.[33]

For his part, Felton thought that Dix's revelation had, by saving Lincoln's life and thwarting Confederate plans to seize the capital, changed the course of history. Years later, long after the guns on both sides had fallen silent, he tried to persuade her to reveal her part in the episode. To his dismay, she stubbornly objected with "a point-blank refusal to have any use made of her name."[34] Her unwillingness to accept the laurels he thought her good deed deserved baffled him. Unaware of her deep-seated ambivalence toward the South, he had no way of knowing that she recoiled from the whole affair as an inglorious betrayal of the confidences bestowed upon her by her Southern friends—an obligatory evil, no doubt, yet also a violation of her personal code of honor. At the same time, in the war's aftermath there was a torrent of cheap potboilers, tales of wartime adventure and derring-do, many of them scribbled by women (or men writing under female noms de plume) who claimed to have been spies, or battlefield nurses, or both. This pulp genre Dix detested. She may not have regretted what she told Felton, but neither was she prepared to name names and acknowledge that there was a time when she had spied on her friends. Even after the war, she knew that Southerners continued to esteem her as one Northerner whom they could trust.

CHAPTER FIFTEEN

"Our Florence Nightingale"

After smoldering for so long the war burst into flames in the early morning of 12 April 1861 as the Confederates began bombarding Fort Sumter in Charleston harbor. Even though all the signs had pointed to war, when the conflict finally erupted, Dix, like most of her compatriots, was caught by surprise. Around the country, the immediate response to Sumter was less dread than exhilaration. Northerners and Southerners alike, unaware of the horror ahead, blithely took to the streets, declaring themselves now literally to be two separate nations. Northerners had been divided among themselves; but now, as one New York woman put it, that time felt like a different century: "It seems as if we never were alive till now; never had a country till now." The change in popular sentiment was instantaneous, something akin to a miracle, a New York merchant wrote in awe. And if anyone doubted the new president's resolve, without delay Lincoln issued a proclamation asking the states for seventy-five thousand militiamen to quell the rebellion. With a confidence born of innocence, young men on both sides of the Mason-Dixon line rushed to enlist in local regiments. And the women followed.[1]

At that moment, the idea that Dorothea Dix, fifty-nine years old and never in the best of health, was about to embark on a second career would have seemed incredible. But, then again, no one envisioned the magnitude of the Civil War, and how the great contest of national self-definition was shortly to redefine almost every public figure in the country.

And, as it did for the nation, the war proved to be for her a wrenching experience. Long afterward, reflecting in old age on her role, Dix tried to downplay it as a minor episode, of little consequence in the grander sweep of her accomplishments. "This is not the work I would have my life judged by," she is supposed to have said.[2] But such misgivings were all in retrospect. Although she had not anticipated, let alone welcomed, the war, the moment it erupted she realized that it presented a unique opportunity for public service. Every fiber of her being was intent on rising to the occasion. Considering what she had accomplished in peacetime, she had every reason to hope that her service in wartime would be her crowning achievement.

The easy thing, of course, would have been to remain back on the home front. This is what her friends urged. When Heath heard that fighting had broken out, her protective instincts were aroused, and she beckoned Dix to come to Brookline for a long, restful visit. Predictably, Dix shot back that the notion of rest in the midst of a great crisis was unthinkable. "Do you realize at all that we are in the whirlpool," she responded with evident excitement, "the Scylla and Charybdis of Civil War! Pray to God that our great National sins do not bring their full desert in a destruction of the Republic."[3]

She did not have long to wait. In April 1861, fresh from her legislative work in Kentucky and Illinois, she was the houseguest of Horace A. Buttolph and his wife at the well-appointed New Jersey State Lunatic Hospital. Massachusetts Governor John Andrew, responding at once to President Lincoln's request for troops, sent the 6th Massachusetts Regiment on its way to Washington. Wedged between hostile Virginia and potentially hostile Maryland, the capital was in dire need of reinforcement. Unfortunately for the Massachusetts 6th, there was no direct railroad between Boston and Washington. When the troop transport reached Baltimore, the Yankee soldiers were faced with unloading their equipment and marching across the unfriendly city to board the train for their destination. They arrived at the east station on the morning of April 19 to find secessionist gangs already busily ripping up the tracks.

As they began their march, a crowd of hecklers surged around them. Within minutes the crowd became a boisterous mob. Stones and bricks began to fly, then somewhere in the melee shots were fired, inciting the terrified militiamen to turn their rifles on the crowd. Scrambling in disarray, the 6th Regiment ran the remaining mile or so, just managing to climb on board the Washington train. Four of them had been killed in the riot, along with at least a dozen Baltimoreans. In their wake they left a city lawless and enraged.

By midday, news of the fighting, sensationalized and wildly exaggerated in its estimates of casualties, was all over the telegraph. Dix, who for months had been anticipating some violent outbreak, took this as her signal. Briskly, without a moment's hesitation, she packed her valise and left the Trenton station the same afternoon. "I followed in the Train three hours after the tumult in Baltimore," she noted the next day. "It was not easy getting across the city—but I did not choose to turn back—I reached my place of destination." Now Washington, the seat of government, was where she wanted to be. Rumor had it that armies from Maryland and Virginia (Virginia had officially seceded a few days earlier) were preparing to lay siege to the capital. If this happened, as most insiders including Lincoln himself, expected, Washington would be awash in wounded and dying soldiers. "I think my duty lies near the Military Hospitals for the present," Dix confided to Heath. "This need not be announced, I have reported myself and some nurses for Free service, at the War Department, and to the Surgeon General—wherein we may be needed."[4]

Yet if Dix seemed to be swept up along with everyone else in the headlong enthusiasm and confused drama that marked the first days of the war, she knew the difference between swift deliberation and sheer impetuosity. Her decision to join the war effort and the personal meaning she invested in it were not simply reactions to the present crisis. Unbeknown to anyone else, the seeds of her wartime demeanor had been sown several years before when she was in Europe. Since her return they had awaited only the right conditions to germinate.[5]

When she arrived in the capital she set about outfitting herself for the task ahead. Curiously enough, the first thing she did was to request a sartorial favor of Anne Heath. Could she, perhaps with three or four friends, get together and make a dress, Dix asked, a simple black dress of "glossy comfortable plain summer silk?"[6] This black silk dress—its

measurements carefully detailed in her first war letter from Washington—was to be Dix's uniform, a trademark often recalled by the nurses who served with her. The interesting thing about the dress, though,
is that it provides a clue to the part she intended to play in the war. Her
model was to be Florence Nightingale, the young British nursing heroine "always handsomely and nicely dressed, but perfectly plain," her
aunt wrote, "[in] a black gown and black shawl."[7]

Dix's preoccupation with Nightingale was not, as it was for so many
other American women after Sumter, a product of the Civil War. It
went back to 1855 and 1856 when, traveling south from Naples, she
had followed Nightingale's trail to her famous Scutari hospital. Subsequently, in August and September 1856 after her tour of the Continent,
Dix had happened to be in England when Nightingale returned from
the Crimea. In fewer than two years, the young nurse captured the
popular imagination and at the same time appealed to the aristocracy in
a way that Dix had not managed to approach in two decades. To Dix,
the popular response to Nightingale was a revelation. No woman in
Europe or America had ever received such a homecoming. Bedridden,
half-dead from fever, she was acclaimed as the purest embodiment of
self-sacrifice the world had seen; and Victorian England gained its outstanding saint. Photographs from this time show a gaunt, weary young
woman—with hints of that peculiar combination of delicacy and
toughness that made her so compelling—wearing in each picture her
distinctive dress of black silk.

Dix had first read about Florence Nightingale in the British press in
the fall of 1855, shortly after she arrived at Greenbank. From the
beginning, she was extremely curious to meet this young lady of wealth
and privilege who had ignored convention and the disapproval of family
and friends to venture off on her own to the battlefields of the Crimea.
In April 1856, Dix sailed to Constantinople, where, in addition to surveying prisons and hospitals, she hired a rowboat to cross the
Bosporous to Scutari. There the British had transformed an enormous
Turkish barracks into a makeshift military hospital. There Nightingale
had arrived the year before, bearing the largely ceremonial title,
"Superintendent of the Female Nursing Establishment of the English
General Hospitals in Turkey." What she had discovered in the hospital
made her furious and, when reports reached England, outraged the
nation. Scutari was squalid beyond belief, physically and morally. Rats
and other vermin swarmed throughout the filthy building; and the cel-

Florence Nightingale shortly after her return from the Crimea.

lar was home to some two hundred women, many of them drunks and prostitutes. Resolving to clean things up or die trying, Nightingale was prevented from taking any action during her first months in Scutari. Army medical officers were undisturbed by their sordid surroundings, and they jealously guarded their authority. Nothing could be done without their approval, she discovered, and they approved nothing.

The tide turned during the dreadful winter of 1855–56. Over the course of a few months, more than ten thousand soldiers died, most of them in an epidemic of cholera. Shrewdly pulling strings with her old family connections back home, Nightingale circumvented the army doctors by quietly sending reports directly to London. Her objective

The converted Turkish army barracks at Scutari.

was to press Lord Shaftesbury to call for the appointment of a sanitary commission with blanket authority to investigate and reorganize the military hospitals.

With press coverage of Scutari and its horrors reaching a crescendo, Whitehall was forced to act. Florence Nightingale's sanitary commission, the first of its kind, was swiftly appointed and shipped off to Constantinople. When the commissioners arrived at Scutari, they offered Nightingale an official channel to government through which to pursue her work. And work she did. Witnesses described her as a holy terror. Cleanliness, order, pure water, and fresh air—these were the watchwords of her credo. She and the commissioners swept out the dirt, purified the water supply, ensured that wholesome food was available. From Dorothea Dix's perspective, they effected exactly the kind of sanitary reforms that she had spent her career instituting in prisons and asylums. Dix came on the scene just after most of the commission's major reforms had transformed Scutari. But to her disappointment, Nightingale had since carried her crusade to the field hospitals of Balaklava, where she was said to be bedridden with fever. So the two women did not meet. It hardly mattered, though, for the impression of Nightingale's transfigured infirmary—the military hospital as therapeutic asylum—was etched permanently in Dix's mind.[8]

Dix believed that events most people dismissed as coincidence were often reflections of a divine scheme. And there was no denying the resemblance between her work and Nightingale's. Like Dix, Nightingale was neither a physician, a scientist, nor a theorist but a self-appointed humanitarian missionary. Equally important, she was a natural politician with a genius for symbolism. Just as Dix prevailed on legislatures to reconsider the treatment of the insane and erect a new generation of institutions to care for them, Nightingale reinvented the general hospital for her age. Like Dix and the English reformers before her, Nightingale learned how to marshal statistics (on infection rates and hospital mortality, and so forth) to buttress her arguments. Both Dix and Nightingale believed that a hospital was not merely a building but a moral institution. Disease, more than biological malfunction, was in their view a matter of moral deprivation. Architecture, sanitation, administration, and therapy were each elements in a spectrum of care whose chief purpose was to synchronize the patient's body with God's laws regulating sickness and health. "Nature alone cures," Nightingale firmly insisted. From this dictum it followed that the purpose of hospital care was to place the patient in an environment where nature, shielded from corrupting influences, could purely exercise its healing power.

This emphasis on the palliative power of the hospital environment redefined nursing. Nurses, Nightingale declared, were to think of themselves as nature's allies. Conceived in these terms, theirs was both a moral profession and a high calling. If nature were really the essential agent in healing, why could not nurses assist nature just as well as physicians? Perhaps even better, it was insinuated, since they were less likely to subject patients to aggressive treatments. This subversive implication was not lost on the medical profession. Threatened by her ideas and her personality, doctors, first in the Crimea and later on in England, stubbornly resisted her reforms, and she repeatedly locked horns with surgeons in "her" hospitals.[9]

When Dix returned to England from the Continent in the late summer of 1856 and heard that Nightingale, gravely ill with the Crimean fever, was convalescing at her family's estate, she tried again to visit her. She prevailed on the Rathbones, who knew the family, for an introduction. But to her dismay, she was told that Miss Nightingale was too ill to see anyone. There was as yet no published biography, so Dix pieced together an account of her background from newspaper clippings and conversations with friends of the Nightingales.

Born into an upper-class family but ill at ease with leisure and luxury; inveterately anxious and plagued by neurasthenia; consumed with a desire to improve her mind; convinced that God had created her for some great humanitarian purpose—Nightingale had gone to the Crimea in a desperate attempt to tear through the curtain of conventionality. Seasoned by the harrowing spectacle of Scutari, lucky to have survived at all, she had returned to England with absolute confidence in her program of hospital reform. The impossibility of what she had done clearly confirmed that she was doing God's work; she was his instrument. And so she led an extraordinary public life, taking on the medical and political establishments with unwavering confidence. Nightingale had no inclination to suffer fools—or anyone who disagreed with her, for that matter—and notoriously few qualms about quarreling with doctors and lawmakers. Zealously she practiced her own brand of political inconvenience.

The more Dix learned, the more she was struck not only by the affinity of their ideas but by certain uncanny parallels in the paths their lives had taken. It turned out that the teenaged Florence had been a devoted reader of Channing's sermons. At fourteen she had met Samuel Gridley Howe when, on his way home from touring Europe and studying surgery in Paris, he had been a guest at her family's estate. Howe had encouraged her, against her parents' wishes, to pursue her interest in nursing.[10]

In Dix's mind, the most important concurrence of all was that, like herself, Florence Nightingale had become a favorite of the Rathbones. In the late 1850s William Rathbone IV, determined to follow in his father's footsteps, was inspired by the example of Florence Nightingale in the Crimea. Upon her return, he enlisted her help provide nurses directly to the sick paupers of his community. "I went to Miss Nightingale," he wrote, "who told me that we ought to train our own nurses in our own hospital, the Royal Infirmary." Seeing that Rathbone had the means to follow through, she agreed to help inaugurate what she called his "district nurse scheme," agreeing that it could be a model for "every town and district in the kingdom." The plan called for the recruitment and training of a new breed of professional nurses. Their charge was to visit poor patients at home to dispense low-cost (and in many cases free) medical services. Rathbone and Nightingale's collaboration resulted in the new Liverpool Training School and Home for Nurses, an institution that became the touchstone for district nursing in England.[11]

Nightingale proved for the first time that a lady could become a nurse, not to mention wonderfully famous, without sacrificing a shred of femininity or dignity.

Her example had widespread appeal. Nightingale's transformation of nursing into a calling of high moral deportment was undreamed of in the days when Dix had been searching for a godly vocation. What, she asked herself, were the peculiar qualities of Nightingale's genius? What in her elicited such unbounded reverence and awe? A partial answer to these questions was that the Englishwoman had made her mark not by bringing relief to the poor—that would come later—but by valiantly coming to the rescue of her country's men at war. Her persona was defined by her dramatic expedition to the Crimea. Unquestionably it was the aura of martial glory that made her accomplishments shine so much brighter than everything Dix had achieved on behalf of the home-less insane. In addition to her lofty reputation, Nightingale enjoyed other advantages Dix envied. She had a devoted family, wealth, and social position; her gentility was not her own creation but her birthright.

Americans adopted Nightingale, and all that she symbolized, as readi-ly as the English. There was Longfellow enshrining her in popular verse:

> Lo, in that house of misery
> A lady with a lamp I see
> Pass through the glimmering gloom
> And flit from room to room.

"In all that adorns the female character," Millard Fillmore tactfully told Dix, "she has no parallel but yourself." The press reported that she had a regal air and seemed to mingle with royalty as an equal. Recovering from her battlefield illnesses, she wrote books, *Notes on Hospitals* (1859) and *Notes on Nursing* (1861), that instantly became bibles of hospital administration and professional nursing. By the time she read *Notes on Hospitals*, Dix seems to have been chagrined by the ongoing public fuss. "I have seen her little book," she told Elizabeth Rathbone. "On the whole it did not meet my expectations,—but it may be useful."[12]

It was not the book, as it turned out, but the author's example that Dix took to heart. Dix had never been a woman of original ideas. Her eclectic genius lay in seizing on the ideas and methods of others, rein-terpreting them in her own language, infusing them with her own pas-sion, and applying them within the context of her own experience. This is why travel, the new people and scenes it brought, was so integral to her career. In view of the British inspiration for her first career as a lunacy reformer, there is an ironic symmetry in the fact that her second visit to Europe inspired her second career. Her careful observations of Scutari and insight into Nightingale's little-noticed political maneuvers—which she gleaned from the Rathbones and her friends within the English political establishment—equipped her with a unique fund of experience. It was on this fund that she drew heavily during the first chaotic days of the Civil War, and it was the example of Florence Nightingale that enabled her to exhibit such a clear sense of direction.

After the war, Dix let stand an account of her life that included a fictional meeting with Nightingale. The story, based on a postwar interview with a New York journalist, described Dix "in the military hospitals of the Crimea, where she made careful observations and became familiar with a new phase of active benevolence, little dreaming how soon she was to dispense the same kind offices among the sick and wounded heroes of her own country." And then came the picture of "these two sisters of the world's charity, representing two hemispheres, the old and the new, meet[ing] face to face and shak[ing] hands." A beautiful dream, the two of them meeting on equal footing, too beguiling for Dix to deny.[13]

Envisaging her part in the war—America's supreme nurse—Dix instinctively decided to operate as independently as she could. In Washington and elsewhere, her credentials inspired confidence. When the war started, the leading state lunatic asylums were as advanced as any medical institutions in the country. Hence she could plausibly claim that she knew more about hospitals and medical organizations than any other woman in America. Reshaping the military hospitals seemed a task ideally suited to her experience.

And they cried out for reform. In many ways, the primitive state of the Medical Bureau and what passed for hospitals reminded her of the haphazard approach to the mentally disordered before the advent of the asylum. The Medical Bureau itself was an anachronism, ill-equipped, poorly staffed, barely adequate to serve a peacetime army of sixteen thousand men. In 1861 the largest army hospital had forty beds; there was no ambulance service, no established channel for distributing medical supplies, no system of inspection, and no professional nursing corps. "The agony and suffering endured during the first nine months [of war]," wrote the Sanitary Commission's official scribe, "owing to the delay in construction of proper General Hospitals, can never be accurately known, but it is not easy to over-estimate it." Immediate, radical reorganization of the whole system was essential. In her own view and in the opinion of many who knew her, Dorothea Dix seemed to have spent her whole life preparing for this job.[14]

The first question she faced was where to apply herself. In the first phase of the war, chaos prevailed. To shore up the Medical Bureau, Northerners began to form voluntary associations. Virtually every community spawned a ladies' aid society oriented toward the aid and comfort of its local volunteers. The largest and by far the most important of these myriad relief organizations was the United States Sanitary Commission. The Sanitary, as it was called, knitted together dozens of local and regional benevolent societies and tried its best to coordinate their efforts. The Sanitary sprang from the exertions of Elizabeth Blackwell, who a dozen years before had become the first American woman to earn an M.D. degree, and Henry Bellows, whom Dix had known for years as the pastor of All Souls Unitarian Church in New York City. On 25 April 1861, as patriotic enthusiasm crested, these two presided over a meeting of some three thousand people, most of them women, at the Cooper Union in Manhattan. This meeting was the genesis of the Women's Central Association of Relief (W.C.A.R.), a group that was supposed to organize the activities of its member relief agencies and oversee the training of women nurses. At the time, no one imagined the scope and scale of the effort that would be required. The war, after all, was expected to last no longer than a few months.

Dix had already been busy in Washington for the better part of a month when Bellows, accompanied by a small entourage of medical men, arrived. There was nothing lighthearted in her attitude. She was all business. Knowing her way around Washington, during her first week in the capital she skillfully used her connections in Congress and her access to the president's cabinet to secure for herself an official appointment from Secretary of War Simon Cameron. According to the secretary's original commission:

> The free services of Miss D. L. Dix are accepted by the War Department and that she will give at all times all necessary aid in organizing military hospitals for the cure of all sick and wounded soldiers, aiding the chief surgeon by supplying nurses and substantial means for the comfort and relief of the suffering; also that she is fully authorized to receive, control, and disburse special supplies bestowed by individuals or associations for

the comfort of their friends or the citizen soldiers from all parts of the limited states; as also, under action of the Acting Surgeon-General, to draw from the army stores.[15]

In addition, she was granted responsibility "to select and assign women nurses to general or permanent military hospitals [and] they need not be employed in such hospitals without her sanction and approval, except in cases of urgent need." By offering to work without pay, Dix both claimed a certain moral advantage and practically exempted herself from a key lever of management and control. Her position was nearly unassailable.[16]

Within two months she managed to secure the title she wanted: Superintendent of Women Nurses. This was, she knew, a title without portfolio. What few nurses the army employed were mainly convalescent soldiers, "so sick themselves," according to one observer, "that they ought to be in the wards." (Throughout the war no more than 20 percent of nurses on either side were women.) The army was a male institution, and medical officers resented the intrusion of women on their turf. Dix, who had spent her life evading the ingrained sexual prejudices of the political system, was annoyed by the assumption that women lacked the stamina and the stomach to serve in battlefield hospitals. Judging by the present state of the hospitals, she reasoned, could women do worse? For her own part, despite the respiratory ailment that was a chronic affliction, she remained vigorous. Unintimidated and undeterred, she plunged in to organize a female nursing corps. She was confident that practical success would overcome bias. She had made a career of overcoming opposition.

So she viewed the army's disorganization as an opportunity. She was a master of improvisation. Without waiting for approval she took her commission as sufficient authority to begin pulling together teams of women volunteers under her command. At the beginning they came in droves. The general euphoria for military duty affected women as much as men, and she turned her attention first to stemming the tide of nursing applicants and weeding out those who were obviously unsuitable. "No young ladies should be sent at all but women who can afford to give their services and time and meet part of their expenses or the whole, who will associate themselves by twos to be ready for duty at any hour of day or night—those who are sober, earnest, self-sacrificing and exercise entire self-control," she warned W.C.A.R. president Louisa Schuyler. In other words, she wanted women more or less like herself.[17]

Not unexpectedly, she soon encountered resistance from the Army Medical Bureau. General Robert C. Wood, the doddering, taciturn, septuagenarian army doctor who was acting surgeon general, despised meddlesome civilians. Initially he tried to keep her at arm's length, asking her to help supply his bureau by procuring lint, bandages, and five hundred hospital gowns. Knowing that women in Boston had converted the Union Hall into a factory to make uniforms, Dix made a requisition for five hundred hospital shirts, one Boston paper noted, and they were ready the following day. No one had a larger network of philanthropic contacts. Through local and regional newspapers she appealed to ministers of all denominations to take special offerings for hospital supplies and send them directly to her in Washington. When it came to handling large quantities of cash, her trustworthiness was beyond question.[18]

Procurement and fund-raising, however important, was not the primary work she felt called to do. When Bellows met with her on May 16, he found her fuming at Wood's incompetence and his connivance with the surgeons to keep her out of the real action. She made it clear that she had no intention of letting the army's hidebound traditions stand in the way of her plan to establish her nurses directly within the military hospitals. Asylums had used women matrons and attendants for years, she pointed out, generally with good results. Using her own money, she rented a large town house near the center of the city to be used as a clearing station for nurse recruits who were streaming by rail into Washington. Making efficient use of the telegraph, she sent notices to newspapers throughout the North urging women who wanted to serve their country to contact her rather than strike off on their own.[19] Owing to the fragmentation of every aspect of the military, however, this turned out to be impossible. A rational procedure for integrating her efforts to provide nurses to the army with the scores of organizations encompassed by the W.C.A.R. remained an elusive goal. No one wanted to surrender control. Moreover, Surgeon-General Wood had no budget to pay Dix's nurses, and Henry Bellows had no intention of assuming such an enormous financial burden.

Had she been willing to work within an organizational structure, she might well have joined forces with Bellows and cooperated with the

Sanitary. Their principles and aims were mutually consistent. Recognizing this, Dix publicly endorsed Bellows's proposal when he and his delegation met with the president and Secretary Cameron to make the case for an official civilian arm of the Medical Bureau. And in June she rejoiced when Lincoln, overcoming his skepticism that the Sanitary would become a "fifth wheel to the coach," signed the executive order that officially recognized the United States Sanitary Commission. Like Dix, during the first year of the war, Bellows and his colleagues also pondered the lessons of the Crimean War. They had borrowed their name from the original British Sanitary Commission and tried earnestly to incorporate its precepts. In many ways, their mission was complementary to Dix's inclination to pattern herself after Nightingale.

But her impatience, her eccentricities, and her passion for autonomy were too great. Not about to change her ways, Dix behaved as she had for twenty years, working outside established lines of authority, cutting through red tape, a pure moral force answerable only to God. As far as the Sanitary was concerned, she was an enigma—well intentioned and utterly capricious. No one could keep her from veering off on wild tangents. Hearing that soldiers were in need of havelocks—a kind of flannel-and-linen wrap to protect the ears and neck from wind and sun—she urgently enjoined the W.C.A.R. to make twenty thousand of them, nearly all of which were finally thrown away as useless.[20]

A few months later, in late July, the first real test of the Medical Bureau and the new Sanitary Commission came after the disastrous Union defeat at Bull Run. Battered remnants of General Irvin McDowell's army arrived in Washington helter-skelter, clogging the rutted thoroughfares with wagons full of wounded and dying soldiers piled in, it was said, like so much firewood. The weather turned viciously hot and humid. A virtual a plague of flies and mosquitoes clouded the air. Hastily, Dix, the Sanitary, the Medical Bureau, and scores of private groups set about converting churches, taverns, schools, warehouses, and private homes to make room for the casualties. Dix had previously prevailed on Charles Nichols to open part of the Government Hospital for the Insane, when the need arose, to shelter the most seriously wounded. Throughout late July into early August she worked frantically to increase the flow of food and medical supplies into Washington. Telegrams requesting that contributions be sent to her house on H Street went out to dozens of community leaders all over the North.

Surveying the scene in early August, though, the treasurer of the

Sanitary Commission, George Templeton Strong, making his way through the city's provisional hospitals overflowing with soldiers wounded in the battle, confided to his diary, "Miss Dix has plagued us a little. She is energetic, benevolent, unselfish, and a mild case of mono-mania. Working on her own hook, she does good, but no one can cooperate with her, for she belongs to the class of comets and can be subdued into relations with no system whatever."[21]

Dix's own anxiety, coupled with absolute confidence in her priorities and principles, amplified those patterns of behavior that made her almost impossible to work with. And to aggravate matters further, she soon developed an inflated conception of her office. As the war dragged on, she invested herself with ever greater clusters of authority. "This dreadful civil war has as a huge wild beast consumed my whole life," she told William Rathbone in a letter that described the towering responsibilities of her position. "You cannot realize I have the Hospitals over this wide Northern Country—to provide qualified nurses." She went on to say that "in trust under government Seal as a Free Service to my Country" she had been given the authority to procure and dis-tribute medical supplies, foodstuffs, and clothing from the various vol-untary associations. This was only partly true. But even afterward she continued to hold onto the notion that "she had almost plenary power conferred upon her in the administration of the hospitals, removed and appointed nurses at will, and had general supervision of this depart-ment of the service."[22]

Such grandiose interpretations of her commission undermined her relations with the Sanitary and with the Medical Bureau itself. Strug-gling for power, Bellows, Strong, and Frederick Law Olmsted were doing their best to streamline control of all medical services. To this end, they met with Lincoln in an all-out effort to get rid of Clement A. Finley, who had taken over from Wood, and replace him with William Alexander Hammond as surgeon-general. Meanwhile, at every turn, they tried to rein in the manifold regional aid societies, each with its own agenda, whenever these groups splintered off on their own.

On this front, Dix appeared to be working against them. In Septem-ber 1861, she traveled to St. Louis, where she aided General John C. Frémont in setting up the Western Sanitary Commission. Strong and his colleagues worried that such maverick actions would turn their own fragile organization into a rope of sand. Bellows, furious at the breach, did everything in his power to quash the Western group's independence. At length he was told that the real impetus behind the separate organization was not Dix at all but William Greenleaf Eliot, a Harvard Divinity School graduate and minister whom Dix had known back in Boston in the 1830s. The frail and zealous Eliot (who was T. S. Eliot's grandfather) had gone as a Unitarian missionary to St. Louis, where be built schools, poor relief funds, a university, and, when the war came, a sanitary commission. When she returned to Washington, Dix denied that she had ever encouraged Eliot to break away from the fold. But even the fact she could produce a telegram from Frémont, summoning her to "come here and organize these hospitals," did not cut much ice with Bellows. Her independent streak was too well known, so suspicion lingered. From that time forward the Sanitary treated her gingerly when it did not bypass her altogether.[23]

That she was a moral visionary with no talent for administration is a truth Dix never grasped. Managing people and matériel had, of course, always been part of her experience as a reformer. But she did not naturally think in managerial terms. Balancing costs and benefits, setting priorities among competing goals, motivating subordinates—such activities were foreign to her. Qualities of temperament and personality that had served her well during her meteoric political career—especially her stubborn self-assurance and her zeal—scarcely lent themselves to the day-to-day business of nursing administration. She personalized every issue, every decision. She trusted no one to act on her behalf, so she delegated almost nothing. Aloof by nature, she frequently said things that the rank and file took as evidence of icy insensitivity. The Civil War required that she exercise not just moral but administrative leadership. Since her skills failed to meet the needs of her nurses, she slowly became out of touch, irrelevant—a commander with nobody to command.

Many women suffered disenchantment with her regimen when they read her infamous bulletin to prospective nurses. In it she set down her qualifications for recruits in the most tactless and unflattering terms imaginable. "No woman under thirty need apply to serve in the government hospitals," she tersely announced. "All nurses are required to be plain looking women. Their dresses must be brown or black, with no bows, no curls, no jewelry, and no hoop-skirts." Nursing had long been dishonorable work, associated with charity hospitals, almshouses, and asylums—institutions for the lower orders. So Dix went out of her way to remove the odor of moral license and promiscuity. Even Walt Whitman, who generally liked older women nurses, agreed "that few or no young ladies, under the irresistible conventions of society, answer the practical requirement of nurses for soldiers." But Dix's style, rigid and confrontational, alienated many women who were looking for encouragement and inspiration.[24]

She succeeded in persuading the War Department to issue a general order that barred women from military camps and required any woman who presented herself for nursing service to provide certificates from two physicians and testimonials from two clergymen. For a salary of forty cents per diem, her nurses were to "be in their own rooms at taps, or nine o'clock unless obliged to be with the sick; must not go to any place of amusement in the evening; must not walk out with any patient or officer in their own room except on business." At the same time, she published a stern warning in leading Northern newspapers to "women of any age in search of employment." They were to stay away from Washington unless they were specifically called upon. "The expense for providing [for] these ill-counselled but well-intentioned and helpless persons in Washington," she wrote, "falls inconveniently on individuals who are not willing to witness needless exposure or suffering."[25]

In Washington, handing out field assignments in her parlor and scurrying from hospital to hospital, Dix was in her element. Most of her nurses, however, in the capital for the first time, let alone in a state of war, were awestruck. To keep them in line, she stage-managed her appearances. In a telling incident, Sophronia E. Bucklin, a vivacious young schoolteacher from upstate New York, remembered falling asleep on the job in the Judiciary Square Hospital and being awakened by "a strange woman in black." Possessing an air of implacable authority, the unknown woman grilled her about her background, then lectured her on the importance of diligence and duty. At sunrise the following morning she was summoned to meet Miss Dix, who, as it turned out, had been her mysterious inquisitor. Their interview took surprising twist, with Dix revealing an unexpected munificence. Before their meeting, Bucklin had reasonably feared that the superintendent was about to dismiss her for laziness. But the young woman, officially too young to qualify for nursing duty, touched a chord in Dix, who must have admired her gumption. To her astonishment, instead of reprimanding her, Dix opened a drawer in her table, took out a five-dollar bill, and handed it to her saying, "This is not pay—only a little present from me." At the going wage, Dix's gift amounted to nearly two weeks' pay.[26]

Women who came to Dix with education or claims to social status often marveled that she took a personal interest in them and helped them find their bearings within the rough-and-tumble medical system. Immediately after Sumter, for example, Mary Phinney, baroness von Olnhausen, asked Dix to find a place for her in the nursing corps. For some reason, Dix took a shine to her, brought her to Washington, and personally escorted her to Alexandria, where after the battle of Cedar Mountain the old Mansion House hotel had been converted into a hospital. "She was a stern woman of few words," Phinney recollected. On the ride to the hospital she was told that the surgeon in charge of the hospital detested Dix and "was determined to give her no foothold in any hospital where he reigned." When she walked into the Mansion House Phinney learned, much to her dismay, that she was the only nurse there from Dix's organization, and that the surgeons were conspiring to make her life so miserable that she would flee. "They seemed to me then," Phinney wrote, "the most brutal men I ever saw." Given no room of her own, she slept on a straw mat on the floor of one of the other nurses's rooms or in the ward among the wounded soldiers. Whenever she protested to Dix, who made regular rounds, she was told to keep a stiff upper lip. "'My child,' (I was nearly as old as herself)," Dix flatly ordered her, "I have placed you here and you must stay." Eventually this almost inhuman tenacity paid off, Phinney remarked, for Dix outlasted her enemies and replaced every female nurse at Mansion House with women from her own corps.[27]

As a taskmaster, though, Dix was more often tough than tender, and her blunt manner did not sit well with many women under her jurisdiction. "Dragon Dix . . . won't accept the services of any *pretty* nurses," Ellen Wright (the future wife of William Lloyd Garrison II) wrote in typical complaint. "Just think of putting such an old thing over everyone else," she confided to a relative. "Some fool man did it, so now . . . his sex must suffer from it." Doggedly pursuing what many considered a foolish consistency, Dix dismissed out of hand applications from such superbly well-qualified candidates as Esther Hill Hawks and Elisha Harris, both female physicians who failed to meet her exacting standards of homeliness or submissiveness. Not long after Appomattox, an appealing young woman named Cornelia Hancock wrote about her own encounter with Dix. Having heard reports of the awesome carnage at Gettysburg, she had joined a group of nurse recruits at the Baltimore train station, headed for the battlefield. Just as they boarded the car, "Dorothea Dix appeared on the scene." Like a general inspecting his troops, she looked them over; but when she came to nineteen-year-old Cornelia, she stopped. "In those days it was considered indecorous for angels of mercy to appear otherwise than gray-haired and spectacled," Hancock wrote, adding that Dix was "a self-sealing can of horror tied up with red tape." The superintendent would have removed her from the train, she added, had it not been for the intervention of an older nurse who agreed to take responsibility for her. Nevertheless, looking back on the whole episode, Hancock concluded that Dix had taken on an impossible job, and would have been criticized in some quarters no matter what she actually did.[28]

In her *Hospital Sketches*, Louisa May Alcott distilled the ambivalence many nurses felt about their leader. Recovering in Washington from a serious bout of illness that took her out of the war, Alcott recalled the welcome ministrations of her colleagues. More than anyone else she remembered Dix. "Daily our Florence Nightingale climbed the steep stairs," she wrote, "stealing a moment from her busy life, to watch over a stranger, of whom she was as thoughtfully tender as any mother." Alcott conceded that she was eccentric. No matter what others might say of Dix, though, she remained thankful for the older woman's kindness. Of all her memorabilia, she claimed to treasure most of all "the little book which appeared on her pillow, one dreary day; for the D. D. written in it means to [Alcott] far more than Doctor of Divinity."[29]

During the war and after, the most disturbing charges leveled against Dix's administration stemmed from her prejudice against Catholic nurses. Oddly enough, her anti-Catholicism seems to have increased markedly as a result of her wartime experience. Before the war, particularly during her travels in Ireland and France, she had divulged hints of religious bigotry. Of the Sisters of Charity and various orders of nuns in the hospitals of Paris, for example, she had tartly observed, "Some of them are very self-denying, not many. As for the priests, they should for the most part occupy places in houses of correctional discipline." As a Unitarian since early adulthood she was caught between an intellectual desire to preserve a nonsectarian spirit of religious toleration and an emotional disdain for Romanism and the ethnic groups she associated with the Catholic Church. She found no occasion to criticize the upper-crust British, French, and Italian Catholics she met. In 1856 she had been flattered by her reception in the Vatican and her dealings with Pope Pius IX and Cardinal Antonelli. On the other hand, her friend Millard Fillmore had allied himself with the vehemently anti-Catholic Know-Nothing movement and had run as the presidential candidate of the movement's American party in 1856. Like Fillmore and so many of her friends, North and South, Dix worried that immigrants were packing America with luckless Catholic foreigners, many of whom would lose their minds and "swell the amount of those who crowd the incurable wards of hospitals." In this spirit she confided to Fillmore, after he lost the election, "my sympathies have been from the first, with the American party."[30]

It was one thing to harbor anti-Catholic sentiments, quite another to act upon them. Within the Civil War medical establishment, her intolerance was neither popular nor widely shared. The Sanitary, from its earliest days, followed a policy of inclusion and refused to discriminate against benevolent associations on the basis of religious denomination. In characteristic praise of Catholic nurses, the Sanitary leader Mary Livermore later proclaimed that "the world has known no nobler and no more heroic women than those found in the ranks of the Catholic Sisterhoods."[31]

What evidently galled Dix was that this favorable view of the nuns was also the view of the army doctors. Living under vows of poverty, chastity, and obedience, Catholic sisters, in effect, had already formed prototype nursing organizations within their orders before the fighting began. Their religious training and personal discipline, along with their practiced ability to treat soldiers with a compassion that remained devoid of sexual energy, won the respect of most people who came in contact with them. Also, absolute hierarchical authority was nothing new to the nuns. To most of them it seemed natural to humbly take direction from the male physicians.[32]

It was one thing to submit to the authority of priests, another to obey the officers of the medical corps. The surgeons' arrogance and rudeness was legendary. Georgeanna M. Woolsey, a young nurse from a proud and well-heeled New York family, said that it was hard to name a single surgeon who treated women with common courtesy. In many instances, their nastiness appeared to be a protest against the official policy of hiring women nurses. "It seemed a cool calculation," according to Woolsey, "to make their lives so unbearable that they should be forced in self-defence to leave."[33]

This lack of respect brought out the worst in Dorothea Dix, who earned a reputation for taking direction from no one. To be sure, she paid lip service to the principle of physician authority. But in practice she expected to give her own orders and to have them carried out. Writing of a visit he made to the infirmary in Washington on C Street, managed by the Sisters of Charity, Samuel Gridley Howe reported that "Miss Dix, who is the terror of all mere formalists, idlers, and evil-doers, goes there, as she goes everywhere, to prevent and remedy abuses and shortcomings." Her ideas on proper regimen, however, impressed many physicians as bizarre. "Dr. A. was in a state of indignation with Miss Dix," one nurse wrote in her journal. "She has peculiar views on diet, not approving of meat, and treating all to arrowroot and farina, and by no means allowing crackers with gruel." For two decades she had been accustomed to descending upon prisons, almshouses, and asylums, inspecting them, and presenting her findings to people in power. To her chagrin, the military, along with the Sanitary, proved to be far less responsive to her demands than legislators and asylum physicians. "She came upon us in breathless excitement to say that a cow in the Smithsonian grounds was dying of sunstroke," George Templeton Strong sardonically wrote, "and she took it very ill that we did not adjourn instantly to look after the case."[34]

Worse, she sometimes used her official rank and title to humiliate doctors who challenged her. She felt herself to be far too confirmed in dignity and elevated in stature to subordinate herself to officers, many of whom were inexperienced and half her age. So she refused them the thing they most desired: deference. She did everything she could to curry favor with the high command, even sending gift baskets of fruit to generals in the field. But she thought of herself as a superior to the ordinary army surgeons, whom she regarded as barely competent hacks. She sternly disapproved of their drinking and harped on them to clean up their foul language. On a visit to the field hospital in General Benjamin Butler's encampment, the story goes, she happened to see three injured soldiers who had been strung up by their thumbs for some infraction. Outraged, she sought out the medical officer who had ordered their punishment and charged him to cut them loose. The offending surgeon, apparently provoked by the thought of a woman ordering him around in his own unit, pugnaciously refused. As was her habit, Dix went straight to the top and demanded that General Butler settle the question of who outranked whom. Butler, presumably delighted to put the medical officer in his place, decided the matter in Dix's favor.[35]

She might have been able to weather some dissension within the nursing ranks; every successful officer must. As the war blazed out of control, however, spreading epidemics of trauma in its path, she could not be effective without the support of the army doctors. And if she sometimes had the last word in disputes with them, her victories were pyrrhic. During 1862, with casualties mounting and the Medical Bureau struggling to integrate itself with the military chain of command, a number of army surgeons complained that, unlike the Catholic sisters, Dix and her nurses were unmanageable. Increasingly, doctors rejected the nurses under her supervision and chose other nurses for their hospitals and battlefield units. Disconcertingly, the Sanitary sided with the doctors.[36]

Politicking with his supporters in Congress, Bellows had finally been able to discredit Surgeon-General Finley, the quibbling, officious bureaucrat who presided over the department. Apart from the secretary of war, he had few supporters. For a year Dix had roundly denounced his ineptitude. Strong called him "ossified and useless"; Frederick Law Olmsted, the secretary of the Sanitary, went even further, saying of Finley that "it is criminal weakness to intrust such responsibilities as those resting on the surgeon-general to a self-satisfied, supercilious, bigoted blockhead, merely because he is the oldest of the old mess-room doctors."[37]

Two weeks after Dix turned sixty, on 18 April 1862, Bellows and the Sanitary Commission finally won their most important battle. With Lincoln's cautious approval, they passed "An Act to Reorganize and Increase the Efficiency of the Medical Department of the Army." This bill unhinged the Medical Bureau's rusty seniority system, reformed arcane practices in hospital administration and transportation of patients, and charged the surgeon general with establishing eight medical inspectors to ensure compliance with departmental policy. As he signed these wholesale changes into law, Lincoln appointed William Alexander Hammond to head the department. Hammond, a tall, handsome, thirty-three-year-old army surgeon, had been the Sanitary's favorite candidate all along. Over the past year he had worked closely with commission leaders to reorganize military hospitals at Baltimore,

Wheeling, Hagerstown, and Chambersburg. He was the man best qualified, it seemed, to weave together the loose threads of military and private medical organization into a single fabric.[38]

At first Dix was elated by Hammond's appointment. The new surgeon general impressed her as energetic, fair-minded, and responsive to good ideas. To her way of thinking, he was bound to support consolidation of all women nurses under a single superintendent—her paramount goal. In July she seemed to make headway toward achieving it when the new surgeon general issued a circular meant to clarify her official role and "to give greater utility to the acts of Miss D. L. Dix." In effect, medical officers were put on notice that "except in cases of urgent need" Dix and her delegates were exclusively in charge of all recruitment and assignment of women nurses. To carry out her orders, she was authorized to appoint deputies to administer each city or military district under her jurisdiction. The surgeon general, knowing that many medical officers sought to exclude women nurses, bluntly asserted the supremacy of his own office, commanding his subordinates to hire one female nurse for every two males and "to organize their respective hospitals accordingly."[39]

There was one exception. Hammond retained personal jurisdiction over the Sisters of Charity. Like many of his fellow surgeons, he had the highest regard for the nuns. The previous month he had sent one hundred Sisters of Charity to Robert E. Lee's Virginia "white house," which had been commandeered by the army, to tend the wounded. Subsequently he ordered a large contingent of them to staff the infirmary at Fortress Monroe. Throughout the course of the war, ever responsive to the wishes of officers in the field, he actively promoted the use of Catholic nurses.[40]

Throughout the winter of 1862–63 the friction between Dix, who took Hammond's commission as a vindication of her regime, and the doctors intensified. While they repeatedly urged Hammond to clip her wings, he feared that a dispute with the eminent reformer would generate bad publicity and, quite possibly, negative political consequences for him and his department. The fine carriages of senators, congressmen, and other dignitaries, parked conspicuously in front of her house whenever she was in Washington, had not escaped his notice. Nor had she been subtle about exercising her influence. She was on good terms with President Lincoln, whom she occasionally met in the White House. The moment Hammond had been appointed, she had persuaded the outgoing secretary of war to reaffirm her official title as Superintendent of Women Nurses. On tours of inspection, she often arrived at military hospitals brandishing a letter of introduction addressed to the medical director and signed not by Hammond but by the president himself.[41]

At the same time, there were fissures in Hammond's own political base. Edwin Stanton, Lincoln's brusquely efficient secretary of war, had preferred a rival candidate for surgeon general and had taken a dislike to the strong-minded Hammond from the start. The two men were to cross swords on many occasions over the next few years; and Hammond suspected that Dix had already curried favor with the new secretary. By the fall of 1863, however, after the battles of Gettysburg and Vicksburg, Hammond had established his competence and solidified his authority. He was prepared to take on Dix. On October 29, under the signatures of Stanton (whose officers supported Hammond) and E. D. Townsend, his assistant surgeon general, he issued General Order 351. On the surface, the order appeared merely to clarify the rules for women nurses in military hospitals. But its true intent was to diminish Dix's powers and, implicitly, to deliver a stinging personal rebuke.

The order set forth four provisions. First, any nurse Dix hired was required also to obtain a "certificate of approval" from the medical director of the department to which she was assigned. Next, all nursing assignments were to be made by hospital surgeons and medical directors; Dix and her associates were relegated to the role of employment agents. And any nurse currently working in a hospital who failed to obtain physician certification by year's end could be immediately dismissed. Finally, while they were on job, nurses were to be unequivocally "under the exclusive control of the chief medical officer, who will direct their several duties." In addition, the surgeon general reserved the right personally to appoint nurses at his own discretion—a right he liberally exercised to appoint Catholic sisters and other nurses recommended by his officers.[42]

It was a mortifying blow to her power and to her pride. Everyone could see that the War Department and the surgeon general had conspired to strip her of authority and had left her with no recourse. Given official sanction to do so, the army surgeons turned a deaf ear to her imprecations. Before the order was issued, there were about one hundred and fifty nurses under her direct control in Washington. Elsewhere, she told Heath in the spring, she had "delegated my authority to parties I have believed to be responsible."[43] But everywhere her nurses, who had primarily staffed military hospitals, were subsumed without delay by the Medical Bureau's hierarchy. In two strokes of the pen, Dorothea Dix had become a superintendent in name only.

If the domineering aspect of her personality had led to her downfall, in the end of 1863 it was sheer grit, along with a large measure of denial, that kept her going. Partly to fight off the depression that threatened to swallow her, she decided not to resign but to continue in office, insofar as possible, as though nothing had changed. That she had, for all intents and purposes, been fired diminished neither her sense of duty nor her confidence that she was ordained to be a divine instrument. She had never drawn a salary from the government, and nothing prevented her from continuing on her own. But she shuddered to realize how powerless she had become and how the nurses she had formerly commanded mocked her behind her back. "We had a good-natured laugh over a visit from Miss Dix," wrote Georgeanna Woolsey in August 1864, "who, poor old lady, kept up the fiction of appointing all the army nurses." Dix "descended" upon the Beverly Hospital outside Philadelphia where Georgeanna and her sister Carolina were working and served them with printed authorization from the "Office of Superintendent of Women Nurses" to perform the duties to which they had already been assigned by the hospital's medical officer. Yet many nurses did remain loyal to her and willingly went where she assigned them; and some medical officers continued to receive them gratefully.[44]

In retrospect, she could see that everything she had accomplished for the insane had been done on her own, with no title, no official confirmation. It was the only way for a woman to make a real difference. This lesson was driven home by newspaper accounts of other Civil War nurses who aspired to the mantle of Florence Nightingale. Clara Barton—who would later go on to found the American Red Cross—had been an unknown forty-year-old clerk in the Washington patent office when the war began. Preferring to work independently, she formally allied herself with no association. She went directly to the battlefields and threw herself into the work at hand, deftly publicizing her efforts through her connections in Washington.[45] By the same token, Mary Ann Bickerdyke, who became famous as "Mother" Bickerdyke, had waded, uninvited, into the grisly field hospitals that followed Grant, and later Sherman. The war was a particular kind of hell; and both generals accorded Mother Bickerdyke the same kind of grudging respect that Dix herself had once earned for boldly entering the little-known hell she had illuminated in her memorials.

These women became war heroines, and Dix did not, because they connected with the soldiers as powerfully and compassionately as she had empathized with the mad. They came to believe that nursing the wounded of God's battalions was holy work—the fulfillment of their own personal quests—and they took it up with missionary fervor. For her part, Dix, who never wholly subscribed to the idea of the war as a conflict between good and evil, was incapable of matching their faith. She never gained the strength of convictions to devote herself with abject selflessness to the Northern ideology. There was also a purely physical difference. At sixty-one she simply lacked the physical strength and stamina that field nursing demanded. She could not match the intensity of the war's female heroines who worked in the operating tents drenched in blood.

She was conscious of her waning vitality. Contrasting the image she saw in the mirror with an engraving of a daguerreotype made when she was younger startled her. People told her she looked "'frail and attenuated'—and this with much truth," she admitted. "My weight is 99 1/2 lbs—When the rebellion first broke on our Holy Peace it was 139[,] the maximum of my solid proportions." The war had left her no time for anything beyond the barest necessities of life, she told Heath. Sitting in her house in Washington, she sadly looked upon herself "as much a sojourner in my domicile as are the soldiers in their tents."[46]

As long as the war continued, she refused to slacken her pace. More and more she confined herself to the hospitals within range of Washington, especially those around Fortress Monroe at the mouth of the Potomac. One young nurse named Anne T. Wittenmeyer recalled meeting her on board a steamer running down the river to City Point. She was the stateliest and most dignified woman Wittenmeyer had ever seen, "tall, straight as an arrow, and unusually slender. . . . Her dress was plain and neat and her linen collar and cuffs immaculate." When they arrived at the hospital, the two women were told that the whole place had been taken over by delegates from the Christian Commission, and that there was not even one cot to spare. At last a vacant spot was found in a storeroom. There, piling up some straw and shavings for a bed, Wittenmeyer made a place for herself and Dix to spend the night, marveling that "that stately woman with all her dignity upon her was glad to find even such a shelter as that."[47]

Using whatever vestigial influence she could muster, Dix worked among the hospitals until the end of the war. There was little hope of resuming her career as a lunacy reformer so long as state legislatures were entirely preoccupied with "the great labor of reorganization and recuperation" that would come to be called Reconstruction. Washington as much as anywhere was now her home. And in a city that revolved around rank and official position, she still possessed both. Not until September 1866, when the War Department finally got around to dismantling the bureaucratic apparatus of the army medical services, did she officially relinquish her title, and then only with the greatest reluctance. Trying to put a good face on the inevitable, in a letter to Heath she claimed she had "resigned in August the place of Superintendent of Women Nurses—to take effect the 1st of Sept[ember,] but thereby did not relieve myself of labor." In fact she wrote this letter on the same day she had been informed rather tersely by the surgeon general that the office of Superintendent of Women Nurses had been discontinued and all women nurses remaining on duty were discharged."[48]

Peace turned Washington into a vast terminal, and Dix enjoyed watching the stream of soldiers flowing north. She took it as her own special task to help lost and wounded soldiers and nurses find their way home. At sixty-four she had no intention of slowing down. When she mentioned her age at all, she usually took off ten years, and people usually believed her. She prided herself on keeping up the same pace she always had. Still powerfully connected throughout the North and South, she had become a one-woman relief agency. Up before sunrise every morning, she toiled at her letter desk until ten or eleven o'clock each night writing notes and letters, mostly requesting small favors for people she barely knew. This was, she knew, a transitional time. As soon as she could, she wanted to begin inspecting her cherished asylums and renewing her relationships with their superintendents, most of whom she had not seen since Sumter. But before she could attempt to step back into her antebellum career, she felt the need to do something to resolve the inglorious chapter of her life that was now drawing to a close.

Fittingly her last substantial public service was to erect a monument—a monument to the Union dead, chiseled from granite she per-

sonally selected from quarries in the state of Maine. By mid-1866, raising funds by asking her friends for modest contributions, she had raised
$8,000 to build an obelisk forty-five feet high "in a cemetery in
Fortress Monroe in which," she told Elizabeth Rathbone, "are interred
the remains of 6,000 American soldiers who laid down their lives in
defence [sic] of the Constitution and to maintain the laws of their country." It was meant to memorialize self-sacrifice. She had witnessed
untold suffering and death in the hospitals around the fortress and
heard there "the countless last messages of hundreds of dying men . . .
martyred to a sacred cause." The government purchased the land, but,
according to her wishes, the design and construction of the monument
were left up to her. And she was the ideal woman to select the architect
and contract with the necessary masons and other craftsmen. She had
always had a knack for getting the attention of the men at the top of any
organization. General Grant himself readily approved her request for
"1,000 muskets and bayonets, 15 rifled guns, and a quantity of 24-
pound shot, with which to construct my fence." Secretary of War Stanton, who had granted her request for a "stand of arms of the United
States colors" to commemorate her wartime service, professed himself
pleased by her efforts. The monument, he acknowledged to her delight,
was irrefutable testimony to her "arduous, patriotic, humane, and
benevolent labors." It was at least a partial redemption.[49]

CHAPTER SIXTEEN

A Buried Life

While the hellish war was winding down, Dorothea Dix, her nursing administration a humiliating shambles, longed for the day when she could return once more to the work she knew and loved. By the time the troops went home, however, she found it impossible to summon the same vehement stamina that had always driven her onward.

Reunions with old friends left them with the sad impression that the war had taken a heavy toll on her. "The terrible suffering she had witnessed & the constant privations she endured, to say nothing of the trial on her nervous system, left an impress from which she never fully rallied," Trenton's Maria Buttolph observed. Her deteriorating health made Dix a patient of the physicians she knew best: the asylum doctors. They had all been trained in general medicine before taking up their specialized careers as alienists, and they naturally took it upon themselves to treat her various maladies. In 1870, for instance, when William Peck examined her at the Central Ohio Lunatic asylum, he described her as a walking textbook of symptoms. She appeared alarmingly thin and fatigued. His diagnosis included a "malarious fever accompanied with severe Bronchial disease . . . rheumatic neuralgia" and circulatory problems he attributed to advanced arterial disease.[1] Dix, nearing the biblical span of three-score-and-ten, was inevitably succumbing to the ravages of old age.

Still, she came from rugged Yankee stock. Mastery of bodily suffering was deeply ingrained in her character—a life without pain would have been inconceivable. Indeed, she had long believed that the paramount goal of life was to conquer her own human proclivities, subjecting the flesh to the spirit. For her, the essence of life was motion and service. So she made no concessions to her body. She would fight or deny decrepitude every step of the way.

Her dignity and authoritative presence remained firm, as did her sense of compassion and responsibility to the unfortunate. Until her strength ran out, she decided to become a roving one-woman relief agency and lunacy commission, intervening on behalf of the helpless, inquiring into institutions throughout the country, and holding them to account, weighing in on the side of local institutions whenever she thought she could be of help.

To be sure, people needed her. In the chaotic wake of the war, many wives and mothers solicited Dix for assistance in finding lost loved ones reported missing in action. A clearinghouse for information in herself, she was unfailingly helpful, scribbling notes and queries to her vast network of contacts late into the night. She helped soldiers collect back pay from the army. She distributed food and clothing to poor veterans and their families. And she did her best to find homes for the war's legions of orphans. "If you think I am idle any part of the working time for the twenty-four hours," she told Anne Heath, "you are mistaken."[2]

If her body was exhausted, her mind remained clear and her capacious memory held strong as ever. Often her efforts to locate missing persons paid off, as they did in the case of Mary Bickerdyke. "Mother" Bickerdyke, as she became popularly known after the battle of Shiloh, was one of the Civil War's best-known nurses. She had entered the conflict in 1861, not through Dix's nursing organization but on her own, in Cairo, Illinois. There, without official sanction, she leaped into the fray, a human whirlwind, cleaning, cooking, soliciting supplies, and, above all, tending the wounded and dying soldiers as compassionately, survivors said, as if they had been her own boys. She toiled around the clock in the grisly hospital tents that sprouted behind Sherman's march to Atlanta. And when the fighting ceased, she ministered to the living skeletons released from the South's infamous Andersonville prison.

Like Dix, she tangled with the surgeons; unlike Dix, she stayed out of politics. By the war's end she had won the earnest admiration of several top commanders, among them Sherman, Logan, Hurlburt, and Grant.

Battlefield nursing brought her national fame, but the peace of Appomattox robbed Mother Bickerdyke of her profession. Most nurses went home with the troops. Army hospitals were dismantled; the wounded returned to their families.

After a few years of struggling in vain to apply her nursing skills to piece together a career within the benevolent empire of postwar social welfare organizations, Mother Bickerdyke vanished. Rumor had it that the horrors of war had been too much for her, finally pushing her over the brink. She had been involved with the Kansas Pacific Railroad in an abortive homestead relief scheme to help indigent war veterans. Her son James thought that if she had lost her mind, the blame lay on the railroad for cruelly foreclosing on her mortgage. Seething at the injustice of it all, he implored Dix to canvas her connections in the North to trace his mother. Dix systematically passed the word. And two months later she heard from a former nurse named Anne Gilkison that Mother Bickerdyke, disoriented and mildly demented, was working the graveyard shift in New York's Bethany Institute for the Insane. "It makes my blood run cold when I hear my mother relate her straightened circumstances in New York City," James Bickerdyke told Dix, "and how she had to struggle the past five years there to make a lively hood [sic]."[3]

For her part, Dix doubtless saw in Mary Bickerdyke—abandoned, hanging on by a thread—a nightmare reflection of herself. Despite her abject selflessness, her acknowledged heroism, the poor woman's moment of honor had been evanescent. Her bravery and humanitarian accomplishments quickly became irrelevant. The moment she was no longer of use, the erstwhile heroine was discarded.

Dix was determined not to let herself slip into inconsequence. Her mission had not come to her fortuitously, and she knew how to make herself useful in the public sphere.

Realizing, for example, that the wealthy state of Connecticut had not yet built a public facility for the mad, she scrawled a brief memorial to the legislature. It was boilerplate, culled from her earlier petitions. Nevertheless, her document, supported with letters from asylum superintendents around the country, formed the basis for the General Assembly's efforts over the next two years to organize a state hospital. She made a dozen trips through the state to call on legislators to remind them of the project's urgency. Insiders knew that purely her personal effort had brought the asylum to completion. Somehow, pitifully frail and worn as she looked, Dix managed "to do great and noble things in public assemblies without a lobby or the use of money," marveled Yale's Benjamin Silliman when the Connecticut General Hospital for the Insane building was at last dedicated in 1868. "And it was all done so quietly!"[4]

Within the asylum community she became notorious for her surprise inspections of institutions. For those who knew Dorothea Dix only by her august reputation, her stealth could be disconcerting. The superintendent of one small Pennsylvania school for feebleminded children was astonished to find her hovering on the edge of the grounds one chilly morning at 5:00 A.M. silently scrutinizing the school's procedures as the day began. Initially fearing her wrath, he was pleasantly relieved to find that her critique was accurate, evenhanded, and generally constructive. Miss Dix was the epitome of discretion, his wife recalled, an impressive, tight-lipped gentlewoman who "never gossiped about the weakness or faults of others." She conveyed an aura of dignity and power, "her language, voice, and manner were thoroughly gentle and lady-like, yet so strong was she in intelligence and womanhood that at times I ranked her alone, and above all other women."[5]

Trying to regain her bearings in America's turbulent postwar realignment, Dix frequently had the feeling of being an expatriate in her native land. Whatever hopes she had once held that the war would purify America quickly dimmed. Even in its early stages, the era of Radical Reconstruction dismayed her, confounding her dream of a more just America. Far from reforming the nation as she had hoped, the war seemed to have fueled an unprecedented, unprincipled cupidity.

Briefly returning to New York City to visit former Senator John Adams Dix and Sarah Platt Doremus, a wealthy activist who supported the city's Home for Discharged Female Convicts and had recently become president of the board of the New York Women's Hospital, she was amazed to see how many in the highest circles had enriched themselves during the war. She had always been drawn to people of wealth and high standing, but she was put off by this new money. There was talk of men who had made millions—millionaires, people had taken to calling them—whose financial power was symbolized by Jay Gould's brazen attempt in 1869, apparently with the connivance of the White

Dorothea Dix at her writing desk in her sixties. (By permission of the Houghton Library, Harvard University.)

House, to corner the gold market. Two years later the breathtakingly pervasive corruption of Boss Tweed's New York, exposed in the press, became a national scandal

The profiteering, the shameless greed, and the gaudy excesses spawned by the city's shady fortuncs repulsed her. Not that urban life had ever held much appeal. But the chaos of New York City, its population surging toward a million, was something new and frightening. She abhorred the ferocious commercial marketplace more than ever. Thinking back to her grandfather's fleeting fortune, she cast a cold eye on the arrivistes' stone mansions, sprouting like mushrooms up the east side of Fifth Avenue. When she rode by carriage along the cobbled streets, she shuddered at the boisterous traffic, the sulphurous air filled with plumes of coal smoke streaming from hundreds of smokestacks along the river. Her experienced eyes were drawn to the details of the seamy underside of the city that most of her friends screened out. She saw the hovels, the clusters of ragpickers, the filthy derelicts slumped in doorways, so many of them amputees wearing soiled regimental jackets and tattered uniform trousers. And she counted the homeless insane—street people, as they were to become known—roaming the cityscape, as common as sidewalk vendors.

But what saddened her the most were the children, throngs of urchins, heartbreakingly young, peering furtively from every passage-way and alley. Their faces, desolate, suspicious, drained of joy and inno-cence, were not the faces of children at all. What kind of republic, she mused darkly, could one imagine when this generation of citizens reached its maturity?

Many of them were immigrants. Foreigners were pouring into the city as if a floodgate had been opened. Of these newcomers, the Irish worried her the most. Passing through the slums of Hell's Kitchen, she lamented their presence. More than any other group, she despised them, with their low-class habits, their swearing, their drinking, their crowded, filthy tenements. If possible, she told George Barrell Emer-son, lunatic hospitals should find ways to segregate the Irish, lest they contaminate the moral atmosphere of entire institutions.[6]

Even in the case of the Irish, though, in no way did she believe that any group should be left unaided to sink to the bottom. Charles Dar-win's revolutionary theories of evolution and natural selection had sparked a lively debate about social welfare. But Dix gave no credence to modern social theorists who, citing Darwin's principle of the sur-vival of the fittest, insisted that to save those not strong enough to sur-vive on their own violated the laws of nature and thus weakened society.

Like Henry Adams and others whose world view had been formed in antebellum Boston, Dix sensed that the modern world was speeding away from her, accelerating in an unforeseen, unsettling direction. Her earlier faith in universal progress shaken at its foundation, increasingly she satisfied herself with discrete acts of human compassion.

Using her money, she found satisfaction in good deeds: $500 to a relative for a new piano; $400 loaned to William Greenleaf Eliot to see him through a difficult year; $100 to an acquaintance in Oregon for books; $20 to the Widows and Orphans of Deceased Fisherman; dozens of gifts of $10 or $20 to nurses who had served under her during the war; and always money to asylum superintendents for lithographs, furniture, and even a milk cow. After receiving a gift box full of books and fancy needlework Dix had donated to the inmates of the Kansas State Insane Asylum, the superintendent's wife wrote to say that one of the insane women, impressed by Dix's kindness, remarked: "She is building a monument more lasting than marble or stone and one that will reach even to the very heavens." When she made a contribution to the Women's National Temperance Union, Frances Willard, understanding the personal passion behind the gift, responded that she looked upon any money given by Miss Dix as "sacred."[7]

The old schoolteacher never lost her faith in education. Quietly she told officials at Vassar College that she would contribute regular support to educating young women, and that they should send her the names and background of individual candidates. Her only criterion was that candidates were to be intelligent and extremely self-sufficient.[8]

Her altruism was not limited to humankind. All her life she had loved animals, reacting indignantly whenever she saw any creature being abused. Accordingly, she decided to pay for a water fountain for beasts of burden in downtown Boston, in the financial district, not far from the site of her grandfather Elijah Dix's apothecary shop. When it was almost finished, she asked the poet John Greenleaf Whittier to write an inscription to be engraved on its base. He gladly complied, telling her he would not charge her for his literary services. After all, he said, such a gift was fitting for a lady who "all her life has been opening fountains in the desert of human suffering." The lines Whittier finally wrote were his reverent tribute to a woman he had come to see as a spiritual paragon.

> *Stranger and traveler!*
> *Drink freely, and bestow*
> *A kindly thought on her*
> *Who bade this fountain flow,*
> *Yet hath for it no claim*
> *Save as the minister*
> *Of blessing in God's name.*[9]

In such ways she gradually spent down the equity in her estate. By 1878, a good share of her principal depleted, her annual investment income dropped to around $1,000—about the annual salary of senior civil servants in Washington. In addition to cash reserves, she retained equity interests in real estate and several noninterest-bearing notes to friends and relatives. The "benevolent fraternity" of eastern Unitarian ministers, assuming her wealth to be much greater than it really was, and knowing of her generosity, bombarded her with eleemosynary schemes. Baltimore's Jonathan Ware, among others, furnished her with inventories of good causes, each acutely in need of funding. He even asked her to place a Dorchester house that she had inherited from her uncle's family in his judicious hands. She demurred, but there was no end to requests like this. Since she needed very little to get by and had a reputation for philanthropy, she was able to respond to a great many entreaties, not with large sums but with small matching grants, along with references to private endowments and rich friends whose bequests she could influence. She was, in her own right, a minor philanthropist. Yet, because she knew the personalities and details of charitable programs, and was accepted in the parlors and drawing rooms of the elite, she became a kind of moral impresario—a role for which her public career had prepared her perfectly.[10]

In her late sixties and early seventies, whenever she felt up to it, she continued to travel. Curious to see the one part of America she had hitherto missed, in 1869, not long after the Golden Spike signaled the completion of the Transcontinental Railroad, she made her way by rail to the West Coast, dropping in on jails and asylums from Oregon to California. While seldom attentive to creature comforts, she was grateful for the innovation of the Pullman sleeping car.

California was booming. And the inescapable result of the state's skyrocketing population growth was an increase in mental illness. She had expected to find the insane subject to primitive conditions, and so Dix was surprised to see that, by and large, California was progressive and up to date. Its facilities for the mad, like the one she visited in the gold-rush town of Stockton, were typically small, clean, and as well managed as any in the country. On the California frontier, community-based institutions appeared to be doing a good job. She saw no need to petition the legislature in Sacramento.

With time on her hands and little to reform, she spent a few weeks exploring the majestic natural landscape between the Pacific Ocean and the Sierra Nevada Mountains. It was a dramatic, sparsely settled, unspoiled land. And she took it all in: the immense open landscape, the ancient pines forests and cathedral-like redwood groves, the glaciers, granite cliffs and ice-blue lakes. The craggy beauty of the California landscape reawakened her interest in natural history. She filled her notebooks with sketches of flowers, fish, and wildlife. Transforming her enjoyment of nature into work, she clipped pages of the popular science magazine, *The Naturalist,* describing rare species (*Sequoya sempervirens,* for example) and loaded crates with specimens—shells, fossils, minerals, dried flowers—that she shipped off to the Peabody Museum in Salem, Massachusetts. This project brought back pleasant memories of her expedition with the Channing family to the exotic island of St. Croix nearly forty years earlier.[11]

When at last she returned east, invigorated by her western tour, she found the Grant administration ineffectually trying to restore order to the national government. Reading through the stacks of letters that awaited her, she saw that Reconstruction had overwhelmed the South with waves of dread and anxiety. Dix's desk was papered with desperate appeals from old friends, now mostly powerless and dispossessed, imploring her to apply her influence in Washington.

The Civil War had decimated Southern state governments and bled state economies dry. Even in flush times, asylum funding was an uphill battle. Judging from how much ground the asylum movement had lost during the past several years, she told a friend "that all my work is to be done over so far as the insane are concerned." In Charleston one of the founders of the city's lunatic asylum begged her "for succor and for help" to stay the hand of the dreaded carpetbaggers. Could she somehow step in and prevent them from firing the superintendent? Likewise John H. Callender, a young Tennessee asylum doctor who had just commenced experiments using drugs to pacify unruly patients, pleaded with Dix to take his case to Washington. The Tennessee hospital was in imminent danger, he warned, unless she could intervene with Congress and the administration to ensure "that no feature of the 'reconstruction' threatened shall be made applicable to charitable institutions."[12]

Preserving welfare spending turned out to be impossible. Dix entertained each of these pleas seriously and in several cases met with state officials in attempts to protect individual institutions. Washington was another matter, though. In truth, she had little political capital in the Grant administration and even less desire to return to the capital where her friends in Congress like Charles Sumner were so thoroughly

engrossed in the larger issues of Reconstruction that preserving Southern asylums was the least of their concerns. Moreover, the prevailing
doctrine of laissez-faire held that the most effective program of Reconstruction was simply to let the laws of economics take their natural
course with a minimum of interference from Washington. Anything
suggesting a federal welfare scheme for the decimated South was
denounced as incipient socialism. As Yale's William Graham Sumner
succinctly put it, "It is not necessary to have Washington exercise a
political providence over the country. . . . God has done that a great
deal better by the laws of political economy."[13]

Dix, judging from what she had seen of the losers in America's economic struggle, was much less willing than Sumner to attribute their
misery to divine law. But her experience was at odds with informed
opinion in the North.

As it turned out, immediately after the war she was more popular in
the South than in the North. Her role in the army had done nothing to
lessen her popularity among the Southern ruling class, and when she
toured the region in 1870, she was one of the few welcome faces of
Yankeedom. In Raleigh, North Carolina, visiting at the invitation of the
state asylum's superintendent, Eugene Grissom, she was escorted to the
capitol by the governor himself, who, when they entered the building,
ushered her to a seat on the floor of the senate. Moving a little stiffly
under the full burden of her sixty-eight years, she cut a striking figure,
and as she passed along the aisle the lawmakers rose in silent tribute.[14]

Later, appearing before a joint committee of the Tennessee legislature trying to help them pick up the pieces of their state asylum program, she was as articulate, fluent, and forceful as ever. Dignity
incarnate, she sat there in her plain black dress, a white gauze scarf
around her neck fastened with a gold pin. Her long hair, braided and
gathered tightly behind her head, was, despite her years, more brown
than gray. Besides the pin, she wore no jewelry except a small gold
watch chain and a ring—the nuns' precaution—which strangers naturally mistook for a wedding band. In an interview with a statehouse
reporter she trimmed eight years off her age. Asked where she lived,
she remarked with good humor that she had traveled so constantly
among the states that she could not really call any of them home.[15]

When Dix beheld the devastation of the Southern landscape, not to
mention the region's social turmoil, like many of her Southern hosts
she considered the emancipation of three million slaves a disaster in the

making. Since few blacks owned land, and their former owners were often unwilling to hire freedmen on reasonable terms, she expected "a terrible result from this winter's destitution." Not that the Fourteenth and Fifteenth Amendments' extension to the freedmen of the full rights and privileges of citizenship either changed or softened her inveterate racial prejudice. While she was loath to see any of God's creatures suffer, she continued to believe that the Negro had no future in the United States. In her basic racial pessimism she resembled most of her white contemporaries. Unlike them, however, as she had done in the past, she actively worked toward what she believed to be an appropriate solution to the problem of race: she gave money, and continued to solicit her friends among the asylum superintendents for contributions, to African American colonization in Liberia.[16]

When she returned to the North, over the next several years, one by one, the asylums she had founded honored her. After she spent a few days with the trustees of the handsome new Dixmont Hospital in Pittsburgh, John Harper, the financier who had been instrumental in its original funding, told her, "The Hospitals are your children; and if Dixmont is not the first-born I know she is well-beloved."[17] Elsewhere, the trustees of the New Jersey State Lunatic Asylum, noting that her work had "rendered her name a household word throughout the christianized world," commissioned her portrait to be placed near the entrance of the institution.[18] Similar portraits, most of them based on a daguerreotype made two decades earlier, were installed at St. Elizabeth's, Harrisburg, and perhaps a dozen other institutions throughout the southern and middle states.

Dix's visage, known through reproductions of this painting to asylum doctors and inmates alike, seems if anything to confirm an impression of somber and dispassionate severity. She was the one who selected the image. And she chose to be portrayed as a self-possessed lady of a certain age in whose face wit and vivacity—qualities she possessed in abundance—were eclipsed by a patina of suffering.

Her likeness adorned the entryways and libraries of institutions along the eastern seaboard and throughout the South. And although her direct political role had diminished, Dix's public reputation continued to make her a useful advocate for asylum programs. When she visited, William Peck tried to entice her to weigh in with the local press to support his plan to move the Columbus, Ohio, asylum to a more pastoral setting two miles outside the city. Meanwhile, in Dayton, she helped the Southern Ohio Lunatic Asylum gain the support of the State Board of Charities and the State Medical Society to fund an expensive new steam heating system.[19] Daniel Brower, the superintendent of Virginia's Williamsburg asylum, beseeched her to petition the legislature to set aside $100,000 for renovating his facility. The following year she helped him raise money to buy an organ for the asylum choir, then to refurbish the whole chapel. When in 1876 he fell out of favor with his board of directors and was fired, Dix diligently wrote letters on his behalf in an attempt to place him at another hospital.[20]

Judging by the two dozen mental hospitals built between 1865 and 1880, it would seem that Dix's cause sustained its momentum, succeeding even as she cut back her active involvement in politics. In some ways, particularly in the South, the war turned back the clock, and there was a phase of scrambling during Reconstruction simply to rebuild institutions. This was borrowed time, though. Public money was scarce. Private philanthropy, much as conservatives extolled its power—then as now—was trifling compared with the magnitude of the social problems it confronted.

Perhaps more important, the basic premises of the antebellum asylum movement were increasingly being called into question, opening the door to a new level of scrutiny from state governments, prompting lawmakers to reexamine the earlier reformers' whole approach to madness. Since the early part of the century, the asylum was supposed to present an unquestionably superior alternative to older community-based methods of dealing with the insane. Ideally it was supposed to cure them. Starting in the 1850s, however, unmistakable evidence began to surface showing that the early confidence that medical science had developed means to restore the mad—under any circumstances—was naive.

By the 1860s, the inflated statistics on rates of cure that superintendents had habitually published in their annual reports had been officially discredited in the pages of the *American Journal of Insanity*. Figures had been blatantly manipulated to overstate asylums' effectiveness. Critics pointed out, for instance, that some superintendents counted any discharged inmate as "cured"—even though the patient was merely shifted to another institution. In some cases, the same patients were reported as cured several times because they had been repeatedly released and readmitted. Out of simple self-preservation, the second generation of asylum doctors was forced to repudiate the heroic optimism of their predecessors. "The claims of earlier Sup[erintenden]ts, that 80, 90, or even a higher per c[en]t of the insane could be cured is not and was not earnest," Barnard D. Eastman, a man of the new generation, informed Dix.[21] Three decades of experience showed that even in an elite private institution like Thomas Kirkbride's Pennsylvania Hospital for the Insane, the result of asylum treatment was more to care for inmates than to rehabilitate them.[22]

This was not necessarily a fatal flaw. Dix, more than most alienists, had long since realized that there were many types of mental disorder whose victims rarely if ever recovered and went on to live productive lives. One of the striking things about the last chapter of her career is that the word "cure" virtually disappeared from her vocabulary. In her realism concerning the intractability of mental illness, she had more in common with the new generation of asylum doctors than the old. She knew the truth of John B. Chapin's remark that the medical profession remained in the dark about what actually caused insanity, and that in the absence of scientific comprehension, "the majority of the insane are not likely to, and, as a matter of fact, do not recover."[23]

Diseases later generations would call severe retardation or schizophrenia, to name two, tenaciously defied moral treatment as they resisted every other approach. Nevertheless, it was Dix's passionate conviction that people afflicted with disorders like these deserved a well-managed sanctuary to escape the gross forms of physical distress and mistreatment that obtained in jails, almshouses, cellars, and attics. In light of everything she had seen of madness—and no one had seen more—she believed custodial care to be the only sensible idea. Whether or not their disease was curable, who would argue that those incompetent to support themselves should not be decently clothed, fed, and maintained in a place where their basic humanity was respected?

The problem was, as they grew in size, few if any of the state hospitals for the insane Dix founded conformed to this basic ideal. Those who actually bothered to walk through asylums realized how far short they fell from their charters. A blue-ribbon committee investigating conditions in Massachusetts's Worcester asylum, a bellwether facility in its day, left with an oppressive feeling of sadness. In their survey, visitors encountered "so many persons of each sex, in the prime or middle of life, sitting or lying about, moping idly and listlessly in the debilitating atmosphere of the wards, and sinking gradually into a torpor, like that of living corpses."[24]

Dorothea Dix herself could not have written a more poignant repudiation.

Despite mounting evidence of the asylum's insufficiency, officially the Association of Medical Superintendents remained opposed to creating any institution whose goals were not explicitly therapeutic. Their commitment to the vision of a curative institution, rooted in their confidence that medical science would defeat madness, prompted them to resist asylums for incurables. The superintendents' organization continued to press for more resources, certain their therapeutic mission could be accomplished if they had enough money. But there was never to be enough money. As urban centers grew, the numbers of homeless lunatics grew apace. In the view of policymakers, the appetite of immigrants and those on the lowest rung of the economic ladder for all manner of state-financed welfare seemed insatiable. Few politicians saw any political gain in raising taxes to fund programs for the foreign-born poor, no matter how pitiful their circumstances.

Trying frantically to impose some order on the spreading claims of the needy—widows, orphans, cripples, feebleminded children, the deaf, dumb, and blind, along with the insane—state lawmakers took note that their English cousins had long since grappled with the same problems. Across the Atlantic, Parliament had instituted government commissions to administer the Poor Law, lunacy reform—indeed, the whole spectrum of British social welfare policy. Hence, roughly following the British example, a number of states set up welfare commissions. Boards of charities they were generally called after Massachusetts inaugurated its State Board of Charity in 1863. These panels were typically made up of laymen and leading physicians appointed by governors in consultation with legislatures.

They were meant to be watchdogs and, as such, were suspicious of the asylum superintendents. During the 1870s, one after another, superintendents were subjected to official inquiries. Under the best circumstances these were uncomfortable affairs. Driven by a desire to cut costs, state boards wanted data, and they tried to reconcile institutional claims and budgets with clinical outcomes. In a typical letter, the medical director of the Taunton hospital complained that the head of the Massachusetts Board of Charity "seems ambitious to gain favor with politicians by cheapening everything and would reduce the expenses of our Hospitals to poor House Rates. It is like a wet blanket to all our institutions. I have not known him to commend a single thing that has been done here to increase the comforts and make more cheerful the daily lives of our patients. The burden of his inquiry is, 'how much is it costing you this quarter?'" In almost every instance, the results were disappointing, and in some cases scandalous. Maine's H. M. Harlow complained that "the party now in power here in Maine is disposed to prostitute the Hospital to the slums of party politics."[25]

Dorothea Dix might have told him that it had never been otherwise.

Pressure built steadily, and in 1877 the dam broke. That year Northampton's Pliny Earle, one of the founding fathers of the superintendents' professional association, published a withering critique of the asylum movement. Citing the statistics in his colleagues' annual reports, piece by piece he dismantled the argument that their hospitals had been effective in curing insanity. Even the most distinguished alienists, men like Samuel Woodward and Thomas Kirkbride, he argued, had been intellectually dishonest. They had systematically overstated recoveries not to help the insane but mainly to further their own professional interests.[26] When she read Earle's indictment Dix was profoundly torn. She knew what he said was true. Yet his indictment came at the worst conceivable time. What, she asked herself, would happen to these institutions if they abandoned the prospect of cure? Cure was as much a political as a scientific concept. Bereft of its original therapeutic promise, what would the asylum become except a warehouse for the mad?

Beneath the rhetoric of therapeutic intent, this was exactly what was happening. In Massachusetts, shortly after Dix helped William Whitney Godding land his position as superintendent of the Taunton asylum, he told her he was admitting an unprecedented forty new cases per month. He was all for growth, he said, but the trouble with this influx was that it consisted mainly of the state's most "active and violent" patients. The impulse to rehabilitate them was overwhelmed by the immediate need to maintain order. In overcrowded facilities like Taunton, superintendents found themselves dusting off restraining chairs, handcuffs, leg irons, and straitjackets—precisely the emblems of cruel and unenlightened confinement that Dix's movement had sought to eradicate.[27]

When she criticized the New York City Lunatic Asylum for being "custodial rather than curative," its chief medical officer, R. L. Parsons, tried to explain to her what he was up against. In the five years before 1865 the asylum's census had averaged 368; between 1865 and 1870 it swelled to 628. There were not enough rooms, and the corridors were so overcrowded that inmates constantly annoyed one another. It was a raucous, brutal place. Attendants were swamped and had scarcely enough time to maintain any semblance of order, let alone read to the patients, take them on nature walks, and render the soothing ministrations integral to moral treatment. Unsurprising, he said, given these chaotic conditions, the percentage of patients discharged as cured was plummeting. And the situation was aggravated because the asylum, which formerly admitted only patients who were deemed curable or so violent as to threaten the community, was now officially the repository for the large class of "quiet incurables" who used to inhabit the almshouse.[28]

Even in the most tightly regimented facilities, patients remained unruly, constantly fighting among themselves and frequently provoking their keepers to cast aside theories of moral management and enforce obedience by any means at hand. Since the early 1840s when she launched her crusade, Dix had believed there should be two types of asylums: one for chronic, "incurable" cases, another for those with a likelihood of being restored to reason then discharged. The asylum population explosion after the war forced her, along with many of the superintendents, to reconsider this issue.

Still, the old guard, because it assaulted their ideals, continued to dismiss the concept, as they dismissed Earle's allegations, out of hand. Kirkbride told Dix that writing any patient off as beyond hope undercut the principles of the emerging psychiatric profession, whose goal was the recovery of each patient. "I would say that no finite mind can determine in all cases, which are and which are not of this class," Trenton's Horace Buttolph said of her suggestion to segregate incurables, "and why they should be deprived of their remaining hope of recovery." Ever since Hippocrates, medical ethics had revolved around the sanctity of the individual physician-patient relationship. The notion that costs should enter into treatment decisions struck most doctors as anathema. As far as Buttolph was concerned, no one, "however hopeless may be their mental disorder [should] be deprived of such reasonable accommodation and comfort as is afforded by the best State hospital of the country."[29]

Unfortunately this high-minded aspiration flew in the face of fiscal reality. Increasingly costs dictated policy. Although John Curwen assured Dix that combining acute and chronic patient made economic sense because "when the two classes are treated together much work may be done by the chronic insane and much mischief prevented by their watchful care," a growing number of his colleagues, along with members of the Pennsylvania State Board of Charities, thought otherwise. Charles Nichols, under constant cost pressure at St. Elizabeth's, advised Dix, "It is only by *increasing the size of the institutions and their diminishing cost per head of superintendence, that you can keep the chronic insane out of mere receptacles—mere houses, mad-house dens*, because that is the *only way* in which a scientific and benevolent care can be made to cost less than its does now." If economies of scale had brought improved efficiency to munitions plants, could not the same principle apply to asylums?[30]

Dix's experience in monstrous Civil War hospitals, crammed to overflowing with wounded soldiers, made the idea of massive asylums repugnant. Instead, the Gheel system—clusters of small cottages where the insane could live "family style" (though segregated by sex)— appealed to her as the architectural ideal. The problem was that hospitals were inundated. "We are admitting patients now at the rate of one a day," J. P. Bancroft wrote from the New Hampshire asylum. Rapidly rising patient demand, fueled by wartime trauma and immigration, meant that Dix's human-scale cottage system would remain unaffordable.[31]

One by one, the hospitals Dix had built ran out of room. In Harrisburg, Curwen's trustees set a limit of 350 inmates, and ordered him to turn away all new patients until his census dropped below that number. Since it no longer seemed acceptable to permit severely deranged people to roam at large—incarceration was viewed as the most appropriate response to their condition—jails, prisons, and reformatories were reopened to serve as intermediate repositories for the mad. The bitterest irony embedded in the loss of the previous generation's therapeutic ideal was a movement to identify incurable patients and transfer them out of the asylum back to the almshouse. Would patients with no hope of recovery really be worse off, H. M. Quinby asked Dix, in an almshouse than in a hospital? In a world of limited resources, would not the greatest good for the greatest numbers result from weeding out the incurables, and reorganizing asylums so as to give *curable* patients a chance?[32]

By the 1870s stories of abuses *within* mental hospitals were becoming so rampant that neither the medical community nor state legislatures could ignore them. "All our newspapers, the best as well as the worst," wrote Isaac Ray, the superintendent of Rhode Island's Butler Hospital, "take intense satisfaction in pitching into hospitals on every occasion, with an utter lack of intelligence, fairness, & honesty."[33] Every year seemed to bring fresh revelations of how sane patients were committed against their will, or how patients who suffered from temporary disorders were slapped into locked cells and subjected to terrible mistreatment by fiendish keepers. The story of Mrs. E. P. W. Packard, an Illinois woman who claimed that her husband had nefariously conspired with Andrew McFarland, the superintendent of the state hospital, to shut her up was only the most sensational of many cases in which former patients portrayed themselves as victims of a system run amok.[34]

Dix's asylums had been constructed as symbols of hope and progress. Yet in the last quarter of the century, their reputations had become badly tarnished. Popular fiction represented them as hell-holes and the doctors who ran them as conniving medical villains. Doctors whose professional lives were wrapped up in their asylums naturally resented that society held them and their institutions in such low regard. They had aspired to great things, had carved out their personal fiefdoms in which they hoped to profit from doing good. But the mad, especially the insane poor who occupied public institutions, were seldom a vehicle for brilliant careers. As time passed, few superintendents could avoid a growing despair about the value of their work and a disturbing sense of how inadequate their institutions were as a response to the intolerable problem of mental disease.

More than any of the asylum physicians, Dix grasped the abhorrence with which the American public and, for the most part, their elected representatives regarded the insane. From the start she had realized how the primitive specter of madness haunted society, how the maniac and the idiot existed as a sinister presence, posing a threat to the security of their rational compatriots. Clearly and unmistakably, the nation indicated that it wanted the insane to vanish. Just as plainly, it signaled that it wanted to effect their disappearance as cheaply as possible.

A half-century earlier, before Dix thrust them forcibly into popular consciousness, they had been invisible; that is, no one thought of them as a class of citizens whose interests needed to be protected. She exposed this mass of "suffering humanity" to the full light of day, and, in the process, created a interest group. At the same time, though, even as she illuminated the plight of the insane, she also proposed an economical way to remove it once again from sight. One of the most attractive promises of the asylum was its segregation of these undesir-

ables out of sight and thus out of the public mind. Compassion facilitated evasion, making Victorian asylums, in America as in England, less
hospitals than "museums of madness."[35]

In her seventies, her thin frame stiffened by arthritis, Dix no longer
traveled into the backwoods. She wrote no more memorials. Nevertheless she hoped to accomplish one last goal before time ran out—to publish a memoir of her life. Her desire was not to increase her eminence,
though a passion for appropriate fame—what Alexander Hamilton once
called "the ruling passion of the noblest minds"—had inspired her from
the beginning. But she already had a worldwide reputation. Insofar as
she had a final ambition, it was to set the record straight.

Her friends constantly pressed the matter. "I never cease to regret
that thee did not keep a journal of thy life and labors," Whittier told
her. "The world needs it." John Adams Dix insisted that to share her
dramatic story with the world was nothing less than a solemn duty.
"You cover up your tracks so carefully wherever you go," he chided her,
"and as I think most improperly, that no one knows, at least beyond a
limited circle, the meritorious things you do." When friends offered to
help her sort through her voluminous correspondence, notebooks, and
publications, she rebuffed them. For she intended to approach her
autobiography as she had approached every challenge throughout her
life, she said, "solely by myself . . . quite unaided, by *labor* or *compensa
tion* in any other way, or form."[36]

Considering her wealth of experience and what she had witnessed,
Dix's autobiography is surely one of the great unwritten books of the
nineteenth century. Yet during a period of life when she did little else
but write, she could not write her own story because she was overcome
by an inexpressible block. It was not just her passion for privacy, her
unease with opening any part of her inner life to public gaze. Of course
she had long resisted popular exaltation. And the thought of being
pawed over by the popular press as a mere curiosity—one of Barnum's
human oddities, as she put it—struck her as deplorably unfeminine
and vulgar. Nor was she paralyzed by her long-standing lack of confidence as an author. True, with herself as the subject, the possibility of
making a poor impression was especially worrisome. But she had published dozens of books and pamphlets.

In fact, George Barrell Emerson wanted to honor her by printing a
new edition of her early devotional book, *Meditations for Private Hours*,

with a preface explaining that it was a precursor to its author's brilliant career. "I would like to say in how many different states you have furthered your blessed work, and how many different Hospitals or Asylums you have assisted in erecting, how many different times you have worn yourself out, how many times you have risen from what anyone else would have considered a sick bed, from which it was impossible to rise, and have gone away to a work which you felt the Father had given you to do. I want to express my profound conviction," he continued, "that it is only from such meditations and prayers as these that you could have gone to your Father's work, only with that entire faith and trust that he would have given you the strength that you needed. This my dear friend I have learned from your own mouth and seen with my own eyes."[37] Dix treasured this pious assessment, characterizing her not as an ambitious woman but simply as God's vessel.

Her story was well worth telling. But as she sorted through her letters and papers, reflecting on the unusual course her life had taken, she could not decide where to begin. Looking back over her sweeping career, she was overcome by the apprehension that, write what she would, no one was really going to understand her. "There is no relative standard of contrast or comparison," she told her friend Alexander Randall. "The whole of my years, from the age of ten to the present, differ essentially from the experience and pursuits of those around me."[38] Her achievements, and the praise they elicited, had never really dispelled her deep sense of isolation. She felt so singular and alienated from the polite mainstream of Victorian America that she was certain no one could fathom what she had lived through or where she had been.

For those who knew her best, like Emerson, her life crystallized the Christian ideal of transcendence through self-denial. She knew what they thought of her, yet she knew what a partial and incomplete truth this was. Seeing no way to formulate or expound the inner significance of her life, she was relieved when she abandoned the autobiographical project once and for all. A few times before her death she made half-hearted and fruitless attempts to find a biographer to whom she could entrust her papers. But in the end she resigned herself to the thought that, except for the public record of her accomplishments, her life would remain a closed book.[39]

Autobiography is difficult under any circumstances. And because Dix was more a woman of action than a woman of thought—of deeds more than words—telling her own story demanded a kind of objectivity about the shape and meaning of her life that was beyond her powers. Moreover, she was acutely aware of how much more there was to her story than founding lunatic asylums. While the condition of the mentally disordered was her public cause, she had privately faced another unspoken social problem that has troubled women in every age. This was the question of how a woman excluded from society's central political and economic institutions could carve her niche in the world. If society assigned women to marginal roles, should she suppress her desires for public life? Or should she resist society's prescriptions?

Among vigorous women in Dix's era, Susan B. Anthony, Elizabeth Cady Stanton, and the first generation of American feminists had come to reject the legitimacy of a society whose politics excluded the majority of its citizens. Their solution was to mount a collective effort to assert women's rights and tear down the barriers to full participation. Never able to identify with women as a class, Dorothea Dix had invented a different approach. While she never directly questioned society's definition of woman's place, she devoted much of her life to overcoming the barriers posed by her gender. The secret of her career lay in combining a professed acceptance of the limitations of woman's sphere with an unexpressed, yet radically expanded conception of personal political action.

In trying to live up to her age's image of a modest lady who devotes herself entirely to others, she instinctively raised a banner of selflessness whenever she challenged society's prescriptions. This let her use her natural reserve and her aloofness to great advantage. As she realized at the beginning of her career, the idea of a genteel lady single handedly battling the world's injustice was a source of power. Politicians and the public, she learned, were prepared to sanction a woman working ambitiously in the public sphere so long as she labored on behalf of others and revealed no *personal* aspirations beyond the pursuit of high principle. Most of Dix's contemporaries, convinced that she was not overstepping the boundaries of propriety laid down for her gender, saw her as a shining example of self-denial: a martyr for a noble cause.

People seldom paused to consider her motivation, beyond her own explanation that she was following God's will. Certainly no one understood how profound her self-renunciation actually was.

This is evident in a hundred incidents. George Jelly, the superintendent of Boston's McLean hospital, recounted a brief encounter one snowy winter night when Dix, then in her late seventies, visited his home. Though she was obviously ill and shivering with cold, she refused his arm when he offered to help her up the staircase to her room. Afraid that she might come down with pneumonia, Jelly and his wife gave her some hot tea, turned up the furnace, stoked the fire in the grate, and placed several blankets over their guest. At dawn the next morning, with a blizzard raging outside, she got up, dressed, and announced that she had already sent for a carriage to continue her rounds of inspecting asylums. Jelly, sure that she was going collapse at any moment, begged her at least to let him accompany her to the railroad station. "No! she would go alone," she told him sharply. "She was used to such things . . . and as soon as she got through with her work in New England, would go farther South, where she always became better soon."[40]

From childhood onward, self-sufficiency was her supreme virtue; indeed, it was her identity. Her accomplishments sprang from her extraordinary self-reliance, yet the more she achieved, the more she felt compelled to protect her private personality and to mask the relentless ambition that drove her onward. To write a true autobiography, she would have needed to connect her public and private selves. And this brought her face-to-face with the uncomfortable paradox implicit in her active pursuit of political power. For she knew full well that her career was only partly a parable of self-denial. The other part was a plot about political and institutional power that did not conform to the conventional language of feminine values and disinterested benevolence. Dix realized that the character traits required to wage political campaigns—toughness, persistence, determination, realism, and even a measure of cynicism—were not the qualities society was prepared to accept in a lady. So when it came to self-revelation, faced with the prospect of betraying her most cherished values, she lapsed into silence.

Her silence ensured that she would remain an enigmatic, if familiar, figure among American reformers. The anonymity she wished for herself endured. Devoid of flesh-and-blood personality, her name would fade into an outmoded crusader; her face would be consigned to a penny postage stamp.

It was her fate to outlive her friends and relatives, and thus to confirm her basic self-conception as a woman alone in the world.

Old age meant that black-edged cards announcing the deaths of people she had known for half a century piled up in her letter box. Mostly these death were expected—blessings, she felt, that removed sufferers to a better world. But others were poignant. In the muggy August of 1871 she learned that her old friend, the Unitarian divine Ezra Stiles Gannett, one of the brightest spiritual stars during her formative years in Boston, had been killed in a train wreck in Lynn, Massachusetts. His untimely death hit her especially hard because she had identified with him as a kind of spiritual sibling. His open-minded, undogmatic, socially aware Christianity was her religious model. She mourned him more than she mourned her own brothers.

Later in the decade, 1878 saw the deaths of her brother Joseph Dix and her dearest friend, Anne Heath. As she set about the process of putting her own estate in order and drafting her will, she wrote, "I have never had any nephews or nieces—no sisters; 2 brothers, both deceased, no near kindred whom I should know if I were to meet them." Her closest surviving family members were her in-laws, Joseph's wife Sarah, and their adopted daughter, Eva Clara Dix, neither of whom Dorothea Dix liked. Perhaps it was money that soured their relationship. She had made her brother a number of loans over the years, amounting to as much as $50,000. Neither he nor his wife had ever paid interest, nor showed any inclination to pay her back.[41]

The will she finally handed over to her adviser and executor, Horatio Appleton Lamb, was designed mainly to benefit not the insane but people of sound mind. She left instructions to invest her entire estate until its principal reached $50,000. Then the lion's share of it she instructed her executors to disburse "for training and education of American youth of both sexes best qualifying them for self-support and loyal good citizenship . . . much preferring educational training of journeymen and women in such mechanical, or all industrial works." She wanted girls to learn practical arts: dressmaking, horticulture "fruit, flowers, and vegetable culture grafting, and general charge of all domestic fowls." In addition, she made small bequests: $500 to the Society for the Prevention of Cruelty to Animals to build another fountain for thirsty creatures in Boston; $100 to the African church in Washington, and $100 to the Old Women's Colored Home in Boston. And she left $100 each to several of the nurses who had served under her. Finally, in an oblique memorial to her father, Joseph Dix, who had failed at Harvard, she bequeathed the university her Civil War memorabilia: her official parchments and her flags to be placed in the monumental Memorial Hall. As a gesture toward the memory of Mary Bigelow Dix, there were small bequests to relatives of her mother in Fitzwilliam, New Hampshire.

It is undoubtedly a measure of her disenchantment with the postwar asylum movement that she left virtually nothing to the institutions she had created. They had changed so much that she could no longer identify with their purposes.

In the fall of 1881, several months after the death of the Butler asylum's Isaac Ray, as though circumstance had conspired to impose on her life its own ironic symmetry, Dorothea Dix, now seventy-nine, moved into the last home she would ever know, the New Jersey State Hospital at Trenton, the institution she was said to have called "her first-born child." Realizing that she had nowhere else to go, her old friend Horace Buttolph, who in 1876 had resigned as superintendent of Trenton to head a new state asylum near Morris Plains, lobbied the New Jersey legislature to designate a suite for her private use as long as she lived. So she passed her invalid days under the asylum's massive Greek Revival portico propped up in bed or seated in her birch-and-wicker wheelchair. From her windows the long wings that housed the institution's six hundred or so lunatics were invisible. She could see only a broad expanse of lawn, bordered by well-tended flower gardens, sloping down to the Delaware River in the distance.

A visitor who occasionally called on her toward the end was aston-

New Jersey State Hospital, Morris Plains, where Dix spent her declining years.

ished to find that she was in good spirits and still the Victorian mistress—bright, sociable, interested in life, and beyond everything else, hard at work. Dix made light of her infirmities. Apparently her helplessness did not extend either to her head or hands, and despite her handicaps, "from her sick room lines of communication ran in every direction to the outside world." Traveling vicariously, in her illegible hand she wrote packets of letters every day. On occasion, a distinguished visitor would call, as when Hack Tuke called on her in the early fall of 1884. Dix took special pride in a letter from Arinori Mori, Japan's first chargé d'affaires in Washington, describing how she had inspired him to build an asylum in Kyoto. Her eyesight failing, half-deaf, she clung tenaciously to life, convinced, she said, "even lying on my bed I can still do something." When pain came, which it did with distressing frequency, she refused the offered laudanum. She would face death as she had faced life, she told John Ward, the asylum's medical superintendent, with nothing to fog her mind. "The doctor does not encourage me to hope that I shall ever be better," she said with evident good cheer, "but he comforts me with the assurance that I am in no danger of ever losing my reason."[42]

She remained lucid until the midsummer evening when she died, 17 July 1887. According to her instructions, her body was placed in a plain casket, carried, in keeping with her instructions, by railroad to Boston, and then by carriage hearse across the Charles River to Cambridge for burial in the idyllic Mount Auburn Cemetery. She had specified nothing more elaborate than a granite headstone simply bearing her name to mark her grave. The funeral ceremony was equally modest. A small group including Ward, Charles Nichols, and Horatio Lamb stood at graveside, sharing the sense, as Nichols said, that they had "laid to rest in the most quiet, unostentatious way the most useful and distinguished woman America has yet produced."[43]

And so the flesh-and-blood woman entered the pantheon of feminine icons: "That heroine of mercy, that Christian philanthropist—one of the noblest specimens of woman—'last at the Cross and first at the grave'—in every good work—whose name is as a household word in every state;—I need scarcely mention the name of Miss D. L. Dix."[44] The rough facets of her personality Victorians considered masculine were elided. And what remained was less Dorothea Dix than an angelic caricature. "She sympathised so completely with their sorrow," one English writer said of her work on behalf of the insane, "that she pleads their cause like a heartbroken wife, an affectionate sister, a weeping child."[45] One old friend told Lamb that like the Man of Sorrows himself, "her life was surely sad—unutterably so." Yet as if by some miraculous alchemic principle, the appalling horrors she witnessed were transformed and purified by her inner fire, so that her travail confirmed her life as "a romance of the Christ-spirit."[46] Dix would not have been displeased with such acclaim. She knew that with respect to her ideals, her life was far less romance than tragedy.

Madness itself, she felt, was strangely tragic. It is the nature of insanity to offend sensibilities, to disrupt the rational social order—in short, to subvert the sympathies ordinarily due those suffering from any other disease. Accordingly she likened the insane to a kind of awful moral tax that God assessed on society. She argued that how society paid this tax was the most valid test of a its principles—that is, to make what Dr. Johnson called "a decent provision" for those incapable of attaining decency on their own. Where Dix failed, and where every other reformer has failed since, is in making this humanitarian ideal tenable within the perpetually self-interested scheme of American politics. While modern society frets about visible madness in the streets, now as then, it seems resigned to tolerating a mentally ill underclass whose condition thwarts treatment, palliation, or control.

The institutions that Dix built are, for the most part, still standing. But most people have long since come to view them as part of the problem of what to do with the mad, not the solution. "Asylum" brings to the popular mind not the clean, cheerful retreat Dix envisaged but the snake pit of B movies and Frederick Weisman documentaries.

Meanwhile, the demise of the mental hospital has been fueled by the work of historians who, beginning with Michel Foucault's landmark *Madness and Civilization* (1961), characterized the invention of the asylum as the exercise of "social control." In dozens of books and articles, removing the insane from cellars and jails and placing them in special asylums, which had generally been seen as benevolent and valorous, was castigated as a subtle form of oppression. The reformers, according to social-control theory, were afraid that traditional American society, buffeted by waves of immigration and urbanization, was falling apart, and that they were about to lose their privileged place. Out of selfish class-based interests, not humanitarianism, they fought back. To impose "authority, obedience, and regularity" on the unruly lower orders, middle- and upper-class Jacksonians hit upon the idea of incarceration. Pious rhetoric, in this view, barely concealed the iron fist of coercion. Thus, gravely flawed in its most basic premise, the asylum movement was described as having set American social policy on the wrong path, making it all the harder to resolve the nation's continuing problem of mental illness.[47]

Dorothea Dix's life suggests that social control is not very useful as a tool for interpreting the midnineteenth-century impulse to rescue the insane. Her institutions failed not because they were so powerful but because they were so weak; not because their goal was domination of the mad, but because the medical profession could not produce effective therapies; not because they were institutions of central social and political importance, but because they were marginal and, as such, starved to the point of financial breakdown. The asylum movement never received enough funding, and enough intelligent management, to settle the question of whether or not institutional care could be made to work under modern conditions.

On the other hand, America has now had more than twenty years to experiment with decarceration, the policy of moving the mentally ill out of institutions, back to local communities. It is an attractive concept, and one that saves money: removing people from federal or state custody, placing them in halfway houses, or treating them on an outpatient basis. Yet by all indications, this policy has been an abject failure. Instead of welcoming former inmates, friends and families withdrew. And few communities had facilities to handle the patients who needed care. The word "dumping" entered the national vocabulary, used to describe what happened when mentally ill patients were discharged from mental hospitals with nowhere to go but the streets.

Dix, had she been able to look into the future, would surely have been crestfallen, though not astonished, to read a recent survey of American jails that revealed, among other things, that nearly one-third of all jails regularly hold people with serious mental disorders on trivial charges or no charges at all. Including people who *have* been charged or convicted of a crime, 85 percent of jails report confining people who are mentally ill. The old asylum has been dismantled; but the policy of decarceration is a notorious failure. With the breakdown of the community health system that was supposed to replace the state mental hospitals, the jail becomes the refuge of last resort—what one official calls "the substitute institution of our neglect." By default the Los Angeles County Jail, violent and overcrowded, has in the late twentieth century become the nation's largest mental institution.

Of course Dix was a woman of the Victorian, not the modern, age. And within the context of her time, her most original and striking contribution was to apply the moral and religious ideals of the early republic to a class of people whose interests had long gone unrecognized. In effect she discovered their humanity and demanded that a government founded on principles of justice redefine its obligations to its citizens. This is precisely the meaning Congress understood during the late 1840s and early 1850s when the House and Senate vigorously debated her land bill. Her dream was public policy that was broad (if not universal) and nonstigmatizing, a policy meant to be social insurance against catastrophic mental disease. In the case of the insane poor, Dix rejected the idea that medical welfare was charity. She insisted that it was a right.

In the end, it was framing her asylum bill broadly in terms of rights that led to her political undoing. In his message to Congress explaining why he vetoed Dix's land bill, Franklin Pierce pointed out its underlying principle. If the general government takes responsibility for the insane poor, he wrote, someone would be bound to argue that it should also take responsibility for the poor who are not insane. In Pierce's view, and the view of many in Congress, Dix's land bill threatened to set federal policy on a path toward a welfare state. And that is a path, despite everything that has happened since, that still runs against the American grain.

❦

NOTES

The following abbreviations are used in the notes.

AAS American Antiquarian Society, Worcester, Massachusetts

BPL Boston Public Library, Boston, Massachusetts

HL Dorothea Lynde Dix MSS, Houghton Library, Harvard University, Cambridge, Massachusetts

IPH Institute of the Pennsylvania Hospital, Philadelphia, Pennsylvania

MHS Massachusetts Historical Society, Boston, Massachusetts

PHS Pennsylvania Historical Society

Prologue

1 *Boston Evening Transcript*, 30 January and 6 February 1843.

2. [Dorothea Lynde Dix], *Memorial to the Legislature of Massachusetts* (Boston: Monroe and Francis, 1843), 4; Samuel Gridley Howe to Dorothea Dix, n.d. [January 1843], quoted in Francis Tiffany, *Life of Dorothea Lynde Dix* (Cambridge, Mass.: Houghton Mifflin, 1890), 89.

3. Dix, Massachusetts *Memorial*, 3, 5.

4. Jonathan Messerli, *Horace Mann: A Biography* (New York: Knopf, 1972), 122–37.

5. Gerald N. Grob, *The State and the Mentally Ill: A History of the Worcester State Hospital in Massachusetts, 1830–1920* (Chapel Hill: University of North Carolina Press, 1966), esp. chaps. 1–3.

6. Boston Lunatic Hospital, *Annual Report*, 1 (1840); Henry M. Hurd, *The Institutional Care of the Insane in the United States and Canada*, 4 vols. (Baltimore: Johns Hopkins University Press, 1916–17), II:645–46.

7. Ralph Waldo Emerson to Walt Whitman, 21 July 1855, in *The Collected Writings of Walt*

Whitman: The Correspondence, ed. Edwin Haviland Miller, 6 vols. (New York: New York University Press, 1961–77), 1: 41.

Chapter 1: The Making of an Angry Young Woman

1. Levi Lincoln and Isaac Davis, *Reminiscences of the Original Associates and Past Members of the Worcester Fire Society* (Worcester: Charles Hamilton, 1870), 22–23; William Lincoln, *History of Worcester, Massachusetts, From Its Earliest Settlement to September, 1836* (Worcester: Charles Hersey, 1862), 214, 221.

2. Timothy Dwight, *Travels in New England and New York*, ed. Barbara Miller Solomon, 4 vols. (Cambridge, Mass.: Harvard University Press, 1969 [originally published 1821]), I:272.

3. Dorothy Lynde, Dorothea's namesake grandmother, was one of seventeen children of Joseph Lynde (b. 1705) and Mary Lemon. See "Wheeler Genealogy, Worcester, Massachusetts Families" [1823], AAS.

4. The apt phrase "moral entrepreneur" was coined by Andrew Scull. See, for example, "From Madness to Mental Illness: Medical Men as Moral Entrepreneurs," in his book *The Most Solitary of Afflictions: Madness and Society in Britain 1700–1900* (New Haven and London: Yale University Press, 1993), 175–231. Caleb A. Wall, *Reminiscences of Worcester from the Earliest Period, Historical and Genealogical* (Worcester: Tyler and Seagrave, 1877), 182; Nathaniel Hall, *An Address Delivered in the First Church, Dorchester, Thursday, April 7, 1842, At the Funeral of Rev. Thaddeus Mason Harris, D.D.* (Boston: B. H. Green, 1842), 3 ff.

5. Wall, *Reminiscences of Worcester*, 226–27.

6. Quoted in Justin Winsor, *The Memorial History of Boston, Including Suffolk County, Massachusetts, 1630–1880*, 4 vols. (Boston: James R. Osgood, 1883), IV:211.

7. *The Diary of Isaiah Thomas, 1805–1808*, ed. Benjamin Thomas Hill (AAS Transactions and Collections, IX, 1909), 56; Lincoln, *History of Worcester*, 221.

8. Walter Muir Whitehill, *Boston: A Topographical History*, 2d ed. (Cambridge, Mass.: Harvard University Press, 1968), chap. 3.

9. [Caroline A. Kennard], *Miss Dorothea L. Dix and Her Life-Work* (Brookline, Mass.: [privately printed], 1887), 1.

10. Ava Harriet Chadbourne, *Maine Place Names and the Peopling of Its Towns* (Portland, Me.: B. Wheelwright, 1955), 322–27; *Maine, A History*, ed. Louis Clinton Hatch (Somersworth: New Hampshire Publishing Co., 1974); Joyce Butler, "Rising Like a Phoenix: Commerce in Southern Maine, 1775–1830," in Laura Fecych Sprague, *Agreeable Situations: Society, Commerce, and Art in Southern Maine, 1730–1830* (Kennebunk: Brick Store Museum, 1987), 25; "Elijah Dix," in Isaiah Thomas Manuscript Collection, AAS.

11. Lincoln and Davis, *Reminiscences of the Worcester Fire Society*, 23; Tiffany, *Life*, 6.

12. Elizabeth Harris to W. R. Thayer, 7 February 1915, Harvard University Archives.

13. This is written in a fragmentary note in the Dix MSS, HL. Worcester's vital records record the birth of the second Joseph Dix on 29 March 1778, three days later. *Lists of Temporary Students at Harvard College* (Cambridge, Mass.: Charles Wilson and Sons, 1914), 278, establishes Joseph Dix's matriculation. His disciplinary problems are recorded in the University Faculty Records VI (Harvard University Archives, 1788–1797): 249, 268, 275, 306, 310, 318, 328, 339, 343, 352.

14. Dix MSS, HL; the accuracy of Dix's manuscript is confirmed by the *Vital Records of Shrewsbury, Massachusetts, To the end of the Year 1849* (Worcester: n.p., 1904), 17, listing Mary Biglo, born 15 July 1779, as the daughter of Charles and Lucy Biglo. Dix spelled her mother's family name "Biglow." Andrew H. Ward's *History of the Town of Shrewsbury, Massachusetts, From Its Settlement in 1717 to 1829* (Boston: n.p., 1847) settled on the standard spelling of "Bigelow," while noting variants (e.g., Biglo, Bigluh, Biggely), 231. In her biography, Helen Marshall concluded that Mary Bigelow was eighteen years older than Joseph Dix because she researched the vital records of the wrong town, Sudbury, instead of Shrewsbury. See Helen Marshall, *Dorothea Dix: Forgotten Samaritan* (Chapel Hill: University of North Carolina Press, 1937), 6, 25.

15. Ward, *History of Shrewsbury*, 230 ff. For a discussion of the demographic transformation of New England, see Kenneth Lockridge, "Land, Population and the Evolution of New England Society," *Past and Present* 39 (April 1968): 62–80, and James A. Henretta, *The Evolution of American Society, 1700–1815: An Interdisciplinary Analysis* (Lexington, Mass.: D.C. Heath, 1973), 5–40.

16. Lincoln and Davis, *Reminiscences of the Worcester Fire Society*, 58; *Diary of Isaiah Thomas*, IX:172.

17. For an overview of backwoods Methodism in New England during this period, see William H. Pilsbury, *History of Methodism in Maine, 1793–1886* (Augusta: Charles E. Nash, 1887), 5–30, 62–68, 88–89. The social opprobrium associated with Methodist revivalism is discussed in David M. Ludlum, *Social Ferment in Vermont, 1791–1850* (New York: Columbia University Press, 1939). The radical theological and social tendencies of rural splinter groups, including the Methodists, are portrayed in Stephen A. Marini, *Radical Sects in Revolutionary New England* (Cambridge, Mass.: Harvard University Press, 1982). Although Joseph Dix was reputedly a Methodist minister, he left no lasting impression. Frontier ecclesiastical organization was notoriously loose, which may explain his absence from George Claude Baker, Jr., *An Introduction to the History of Early New England Methodism*, 3 vols. (Nashville, Tenn.: Abington Press, 1964). Emerson on the Methodist was quoted by Andrew Delbanco, "The Art of Piety," *New Republic* (26 October 1992): 38.

18. Lincoln and Davis, *Reminiscences of the Worcester Fire Society*, 59.

19. *Boston Sunday Herald*, 20 October 1901.

20. William B. Sprague, *Annals of the American Pulpit* . . . (New York: Robert Carter & Brothers, 1873), VII:308.

21. On Susanna Wesley's letter, see Philip Greven, *Spare the Child: The Religious Roots of Punishment and the Psychological Impact of Physical Abuse* (New York: Knopf, 1991), 19–20. Sereno Dwight's comment comes from Philip J. Greven, ed., *Child-Rearing Concepts, 1628–1861: Historical Sources* (Itasca, Ill.: Peacock, 1973), 78.

22. Roe, *Dorothea Lynde Dix*, a Paper Read before the Worcester Society of Antiquity, November 20th, 1888 (Worcester: Franklin P. Rice, 1889), 9.

23. Dix to Anne Heath, no date [1824?], HL.

24. John Owen King III, *The Iron of Melancholy: Structures of Spiritual Conversion in America from the Puritan Conscience to Victorian Neurosis* (Middletown, Conn.: Wesleyan University Press); Greven, *Spare the Child*, 135. A useful overview of depression in historical context is Stanley W. Jackson, *Melancholia and Depression: From Hippocratic Times to Modern Times* (New Haven: Yale University Press, 1986).

25. The consequences of physical punishment are outlined in detail in Greven, *Spare the Child*, 121–212.

26. Social and family pressures on adolescents to demonstrate visible signs of religious conversion are discussed in Joseph R. Kett, *Rites of Passage: Adolescence in America 1790 to the Present* (New York: Basic Books, 1977), 62–85, and Nancy Cott, "Young Women and the Second Great Awakening in New England," *Feminist Studies* 3 (1975): 15–29. The story of a girl who was as intelligent and sensitive as Dorothea, and who stubbornly resisted the religious conversion expected of her, is well told in Kathryn Kish Sklar, *Catharine Beecher: A Study in American Domesticity* (New Haven: Yale University Press, 1973), esp. 29–42.

27. Tiffany, *Life*, 2.

28. Dix MS genealogy, HL.

29. Quoted in Marshall, *Forgotten Samaritan*, 7.

30. "Of the mother unpleasant stories were told," wrote Alfred Roe, "of excesses which would be inexcusable in the eyes of her more than puritanic daughter" (*Dorothea Lynde Dix*, 6).

31. Tiffany, *Life*, 2.

32. Dorothea L. Dix, "James Coleman; or the Reward of Perseverance," in *American Moral Tales, For Young Persons* (Boston: Leonard C. Bowles, and B. H. Greene, 1832), 105–6.

33. The most reliable account of this phase of her life is a short narrative written shortly after her death, see Roe, *Dorothea Lynde Dix,* esp. 7–8.

34. Cott, *Bonds of Womanhood*, chap. 3, offers an excellent overview of women and schoolteaching in New England during this period. The pattern of schoolteaching was commonplace among women who later engaged in organized benevolence. See Anne M. Boylan, "Timid Girls, Venerable Widows and Dignified Matrons: Life Cycle Patterns among Organized Women in New York and Boston, 1797–1840," *American Quarterly* 38 (Winter 1986): 779–97.

35. Quoted in Tiffany, *Life*, 12; Roe, *Dorothea Lynde Dix*, 9.

36. Roe, *Dorothea Lynde Dix*, 10.

37. Ibid., 10–11.

38. Despite her diffidence, Dorothea favorably impressed her contemporaries as an attractive and socially adept young lady. See, for example, A. L. Barnett to Dix, 2 December 1883, HL.

39. Dix to Heath, n.d. [1823], HL.

40. The Victorian impulse to suppress anger is discussed in Carol Zisowitz Stearns and Peter N. Stearns, *Anger: The Struggle for Emotional Control in America's History* (Chicago and London: University of Chicago Press, 1986), 18–68.

41. Dix to Heath, n.d. [1823?], Dix MSS, HL.

42. Dix to Heath, n.d. [1825], HL; the long, fervent, friendship between Dorothea Dix and Anne Heath conforms to the pattern of nurture and psychological support that has been described by Carroll Smith-Rosenberg, "The Female World of Love and Ritual: Relations between Women in Nineteenth-Century America," *SIGNS* 1 (1975): 1–29.

43. Dix to Heath, n.d. [1823?], HL.

44. Dix to Heath, n.d. [1823], HL.

45. Dix to Heath, n.d. [1823?], HL.

46. Dix to Heath, n.d. [1824], HL.

47. Dix to Heath, n.d. [ca. 1824], HL.

48. Catherine Beecher, *Letters to the People on Health and Happiness* (New York: Harper Bros., 1855), 129; Dix to Heath, n.d. [ca. 1825] and 5 March 1826, HL. For an overview of the social context for women's illness, much of the analysis based on contemporary medical sources, see Carroll Smith-Rosenberg and Charles Rosenberg, "The Female Animal: Medical and Biological Views of Woman and Her Role in Nineteenth-Century America," *Journal of American History* 60 (1973): 332–56. Elaine Showalter has demonstrated the continuity of sociocultural subjection, psychological stress, and physiological symptoms in Victorian England. See *The Female Malady: Women, Madness and English Culture, 1830–1980* (New York: Pantheon, 1985), esp. chaps. 1–4.

49. Dix to Heath, 23 June 1829, HL.

50. Ibid.

51. Green leather commonplace book, MS no. Am 1274, HL.

52. Ibid.

53. The history of the Parish Church is detailed in Lincoln, *History of Worcester*, 166–74.

54. William B. Sprague, *Annals of the American Unitarian Pulpit*, 2 vols. (New York: Robert Carter and Bros., 1865):II 132–40, esp. 139–40.

55. Samuel A. Eliot, *Heralds of a Liberal Faith*, 3 vols. (Boston: American Unitarian Association, 1910), II:185–92.

56. Dix to Dorothy Dix (grandmother), n.d. [ca. 1822], HL.

57. Dix to Heath, n.d. [ca. 1823], HL.

58. Miscellaneous MS No. 956, HL.

Chapter 2: The Education of a Liberal Christian

1. For a sketch of elegant socializing during this period see Joseph P. Quincy, "Social Life in Boston," in Justin Winsor, ed., *The Memorial History of Boston, Including Suffolk County, Massachusetts, 1630–1880*, 4 vols. (Boston: James R. Osgood, 1883), IV:1–24.

2. Dix to Heath, three letters, n.d. [early 1820s], HL.

3. The history of the Parish Church is detailed in William Lincoln, *History of Worcester, Massachusetts, From Its Earliest Settlement to September, 1836* (Worcester: Charles Hersey, 1862), 132–40, esp. 139–40.

4. William B. Sprague, *Annals of the American Unitarian Pulpit* (New York: Robert Carter and Bros., 1865), 132–40, esp. 139–40.

5. Samuel A. Eliot, *Heralds of a Liberal Faith*, 3 vols. (Boston: American Unitarian Association, 1910), II:185–92.

6. Dix to Dorothy Dix (grandmother), no date [ca. 1822], HL.

7. Dix to Heath, no date [ca. 1823], HL.

8. Harris's life is chronicled in Samuel A. Eliot, *Heralds of a Liberal Faith*, 3 vols. (Boston: American Unitarian Association, 1910), I, 205–12; Nathaniel L. Frothingham, "Memoir of the Rev. Thaddeus Mason Harris" (MHS Collections, 4th ser., 1854), II:130–55; *Proceedings of the Most Worshipful Grand Lodge Ancient Free and Accepted Masons Commonwealth of Massachusetts, 1824–1844* [n.p., n.d.].

9. Frothingham, "Memoir," 150–55; Dix to Heath, n.d. [1826?], HL.

10. Nathaniel Hall, *An Address Delivered in the First Church, Dorchester, Thursday, April 7, 1842, At the Funeral of Rev. Thaddeus Mason Harris, D.D.* (Boston: B.H. Greene, 1842), 10–11.

11. See, for example, Dix to Convers Francis, 8 February [1823], HL.

12. [Dorothea Lynde Dix], *Conversations on Common Things: or, Guide to Knowledge: With Questions* (Boston: Monroe and Francis, 1824), 34.

13. Ibid., 14.

14. Ibid., 121.

15. Barbara Welter has argued that the Victorian idea of "pure womanhood" was distinctly anti-intellectual. See "The Cult of True Womanhood, 1820–1860," *American Quarterly* 18 (Summer 1966): 151–75, and "Anti-Intellectualism and the American Woman, 1800–1860," *Mid-America* 48 (1966): 258–70. Yet if one looks beyond the prescriptive literature, most of it written by men, on which this argument is based, it is clear that Dix's ideas of female intellect and education were well accepted. See, for example, Susan P. Conrad, *Perish the Thought: Intellectual Women in Romantic America, 1830–1860* (Seacacus, N.J.: Citadel Press, 1976), 3–44 and passim.

16. Dix to Heath, no date [1825], HL.

17. Henry Ware, Jr., to Dix, 10 November [1829], HL.

18. [Dorothea Lynde Dix], *Meditations for Private Hours* (Boston: Monroe and Francis, 1828), 6.

19. [Dorothea Lynde Dix], *Selected Hymns for the Use of Children in Families, and Sunday Schools* (Boston: Monroe and Francis, 1833), 102–3.

20. Dorothea Dix's beliefs fit the pattern of "supernatural rationalism" described in C. Conrad Wright, *The Liberal Christians: Essays on American Unitarian History* (Boston: Beacon Press, 1970), 1–21.

21. Dix, *Selected Hymns*, 12.

22. Dix, *Meditations for Private Hours*, 29.

23. Ibid.

24. Dix, *Selected Hymns*, 45.

25. Ibid., 79.

26. Dorothea's model for this kind of writing was Hannah More. An excellent review of moral and didactic pamphlet literature in the New Republic is Paul Boyer, *Urban Masses and Moral Order in America, 1820–1920* (Cambridge, Mass.: Harvard University Press, 1978), chap. 2.

27. [Dorothea Lynde Dix], *American Moral Tales, For Young Persons* (Boston: Leonard C. Bowles and B. H. Greene, 1832), 10–11, 154–55, 105–6.

28. Sara Willis Parton [Fanny Fern], *New York Ledger*, 10 August 1867, quoted in Ann Douglas Wood, "The 'Scribbling Women' and Fanny Fern: Why Women Wrote," *American Quarterly* 23 (Spring 1971): 24.

29. The connection between Dix's publications and her past was more than psychological. According to one of her acquaintances, "the proceeds of Miss Dix's writings were settled as an annuity on her mother," who lingered in poor health in Fitzwilliam, New Hampshire, until death in 1837 (Mariana D. Trott to Francis Tiffany, 19 February 1890, HL).

30. Dix to Heath, n.d. [ca. 1824], HL.

31. Dix to Heath, n.d. [1824?], HL.

32. Henry Ware, Jr., and Tuckerman were prominent in the Association for Mutual

Improvement, a Unitarian group formed in the early 1820s to take on the issue of urban poverty. See Eliot, *Heralds of a Liberal Faith*, II:225, and Daniel T. McColgan, *Joseph Tuckerman: Pioneer in American Social Work* (Washington, D.C.: Catholic University of America Press, 1940), 66–68. Dix to Heath, n.d. [ca. 1824], HL.

33. Jane H. Pease and William H. Pease, "Whose Right Hand of Fellowship? Pew and Pulpit in Shaping Church Practice," in *American Unitarianism, 1805–1865*, ed. Conrad Edick Wright (Boston: Massachusetts Historical Society and Northeastern University Press, 1989), 181–206.

34. Dix to Heath, n.d. [1825], HL.

35. A. L Barnett to Dix, 2 December [1883], HL; on Gannett see Eliot, *Heralds of a Liberal Faith*, III:138–47, and Charles C. Forman, "Elected Now By Time," in C. Conrad Wright, ed., *A Stream of Light: A Sesquicentennial History of American Unitarianism* (Boston: Unitarian Universalist Association, 1975), 31. The quotation is from William Channing Gannett, *Ezra Stiles Gannett: Unitarian Minister in Boston, 1824–1871* (Boston: Roberts Brothers, 1875), 141.

36. Josephine Waters to Dix, 29 December 1827, HL.

37. Dix to Mrs. Torrey, 24 January and 23 April 1837, HL.

38. Eliot, *Heralds of a Liberal Faith*, III:134–35; Dix to Mrs. Torrey, 29 November and 31 December 1827, HL.

39. William Henry Furness to Mary Jenks, 20 September 1825, quoted in Elizabeth M. Geffen, *Philadelphia Unitarianism, 1796–1861* (Philadelphia: University of Pennsylvania Press, 1961), 121; on Furness's theology see R. Joseph Hoffman, "William Henry Furness: Transcendental Christianity" (unpubl. seminar paper, Harvard University, May 1978). Furness is also discussed in William R. Hutchison, *The Transcendentalist Ministers: Church Reform in the New England Renaissance* (New Haven: Yale University Press, 1959), 46, 50, 198 and passim.

40. On the changes in Dorothea's views on Christ, see Dix to Mrs. Torrey, 19 February 1828, HL.

41. Geffen, *Philadelphia Unitarianism*, 122, 126–83; Dix to Mrs. Torrey, 31 December 1827, 19 February and 3 March 1828, HL.

42. Dix to Mrs. Torrey, 3 March 1828, HL.

43. *Report of the Committee Appointed by the Board of Guardians of the Poor of the City and Districts of Philadelphia, to Visit the Cities of Baltimore, New-York, Providence, Boston and Salem* (Philadelphia: Samuel Parker, 1827). The community interest stirred by this report inspired the Quakers, who operated the Friends' Asylum for the Insane, to issue *Rules for the Management of the Asylum. Adopted by the Board of Managers, Ninth Month 8th, 1828* (Philadelphia: Conrad, 1828).

44. Dix to Mrs. Torrey, 8 January 1828, HL.

45. On Channing's religious ideas see Andrew Delbanco, *William Ellery Channing: An Essay on the Liberal Spirit in America* (Cambridge, Mass.: Harvard University Press, 1981), 1–32, and C. Conrad Wright, "The Rediscovery of Channing," in *The Liberal Christians*, 22–40; Elizabeth Palmer Peabody's remark is quoted in Arthur W. Brown, *Always Young for Liberty: A Biography of William Ellery Channing* (Syracuse: Syracuse University Press, 1956), 125; Ware's comment is quoted in Jack Mendelsohn, *Channing: The Reluctant Radical* (Boston: Little, Brown, 1971), 199; Dix to Heath, n.d. [ca. 1824], HL.

46. Dix to Heath, two letters, n.d. [1824], HL; quoted in John White Chadwick, *William Ellery Channing: Minister of Religion* (Boston: Houghton Mifflin, 1903), 428.

47. Elizabeth Palmer Peabody, *Reminiscences of Rev. Wm. Ellery Channing* (Boston: Roberts Brothers, 1880), iii; William Henry Channing, *The Life of William Ellery Channing, with Extracts from His Correspondence and Manuscripts*, 3 vols. (Boston: Wm. Crosby and H. P. Nichols, 1848), III:15–16.

48. Channing, *Works*, III:144–45; William R. Hutchison, *The Modernist Impulse in American Protestantism* (Cambridge, Mass.: Harvard University Press, 1976), 17.

49. Dix to Heath, n.d. [April 1824] and 31 May 1824, HL.

50. Dix to Heath, 16 June 1826, HL.

51. Josephine Waters to Dix, 4 July 1829, HL.

52. George Gibbs, *The Gibbs Family of Rhode Island and Some Related Families* (New York: privately printed, 1933), 16–17, 104–8; Elizabeth Palmer Peabody, *Reminiscences of Rev. Wm. Ellery Channing* (Boston: Roberts Brothers, 1880), 328, 335.

53. Mendelsohn, *Channing: The Reluctant Radical*, 130–31; Mary Eustis Channing to Francis Tiffany, n.d., quoted in Tiffany, *Life*, 34.

54. M. T. Torrey to Dix, 7 December 1830; Helen Loring to Dix, 23 July [1829], HL.

55. Dix to Heath, 23 June 1829, HL.

56. Dix to Heath, 8 July 1829, HL.

57. William Ellery Channing to Lucy Aiken, 4 March and 22 June 1831, in *The Correspondence of William Ellery Channing and Lucy Aiken, From 1826 to 1842* (Boston: Roberts Brothers, 1874), 60, 70; Helen C. Loring to Dix, 2 October [1829?]; Dix to Heath, June 1826; Josephine Waters to Dix, 1 March 1831, HL.

58. Dix to Benjamin Silliman, 9 September 1830; Silliman to Dix, 16 January and 17 June, 1830 HL.

59. Dix to Silliman, 3 June 1830, HL; for a discussion of the limitations women faced in pursuing science in the nineteenth century, see Sally Gregory Kohlstedt, "In from the Periphery: American Women in Science, 1830–1880," *SIGNS* 4 (Autumn 1978): 81–96.

60. Dix to Silliman, 9 September 1830, HL.

61. Josephine Waters to Dix, 1 March 1831, HL.

62. Dix to Mrs. Torrey, 23 January 1831, HL.

63. Dix to Mrs. Torrey, 27 January 1831, HL.

64. See Charles Edwin Taylor, *Leaflets from the Danish West Indies: Description of the Social, Political, and Commercial Conditions of these Island* (London: Wm. Dawson and Sons, 1888), 194–203; Dix to Torrey, 28 February 1831, HL.

65. William M. Boyer, *America's Virgin Islands: A History of Human Rights and Wrongs* (Durham, N.C.: Carolina Academic Press, 1983), 10–13.

66. Ibid., 13–33.

67. A brief survey of the Caribbean islands during this period is Waldeman Westergaard, *The Danish West Indies under Company Rule (1671–1754) with a Supplementary Chapter, 1755–1917* (New York: Macmillan, 1917), 252 ff.; see also Gordon K. Lewis, *The Virgin Islands: A Caribbean Lilliput* (Evanston: Northwestern University Press, 1972), 29; William Henry Channing, *Life of William Ellery Channing, D.D.*, 522.

68. Dorothea fits the type of religious young woman who took up abolitionism. See, for

example, David Donald, "Toward a Reconsideration of the Abolitionists," in *Lincoln Reconsidered* (New York: Vintage, 1956), 19–36.

69. Dix to Mrs. Torrey, 27 January 1831 and n.d. [1831], HL.

70. Dix to Mrs. Torrey, n.d. [1831] and 15 April [1831], HL.

71. Channing to Lucy Aiken, 27 August 1831, in *Correspondence of Channing and Aiken*, 83–84; *Works of William Ellery Channing*, 6 vols. (Boston: American Unitarian Association, 1846), VI:381; Channing to Andrews Norton, 1 April 1831, Andrews Norton Papers, HL; Gannett is quoted in Mendelsohn, *Channing: The Reluctant Radical*, 239; *Harriet Martineau's Autobiography*, ed. Maria Chapman, 2 vols. (Boston: J. R. Osgood, 1877), II:273.

72. Quoted in Daniel Walker Howe, *The Unitarian Conscience: Harvard Moral Philosophy, 1805–1861* (Cambridge, Mass.: Harvard University Press, 1970), 288.

73. Channing, *Works*, II:128; "Emancipation," *Works*, VI:61; Howe. *The Unitarian Conscience*, 270–294 provides an insightful treatment of the slavery question as it was confronted and avoided by leading Unitarian intellectuals. See also Douglas C. Stange, *Patterns of Antislavery among American Unitarians, 1831–1860* (Rutherford: Farleigh Dickinson University Press, 1977).

74. Dix to M. T. Torrey, 15 October 1831, HL; Boyer, *America's Virgin Islands*, 51, n. 44.

75. Dix to Torrey, 15 April 1831, HL.

76. Dix to Mrs. Torrey, February [1831], April [1831] and 5 May 1831, HL.

77. Florence Lewisohn, *St. Croix under Seven Flags* (Hollywood, Fla.: Dukane Press, 1970), 228.

78. Dix to Mrs. Torrey, 26 March [1831], HL.

79. Dix to Mrs. Torrey, 25 February [1831], HL.

80. Elizabeth Peabody, *Reminiscences of Rev. Wm. Ellery Channing*, 84–85; [Dix], green leather notebook, 1827–1830, MS no. 1274, HL.

81. Channing to Dix, 31 December 1827, HL.

82. On Channing's charisma and its appeal for his young disciples, see Arthur W. Brown, *Always Young for Liberty: A Biography of William Ellery Channing* (Syracuse: Syracuse University Press, 1956), chap. 15; and Peabody, *Reminiscences*, 84–85.

83. L. J. Bigelow, "Miss Dix, And What She Has Done," *Galaxy*, 15 March 1867, 669.

84. Quoted in Robert Coles, *Dorothy Day: A Radical Devotion* (Reading, Mass.: Addison-Wesley, 1987), 160.

Chapter 3: The English Malady

1. Josephine Waters to Dix, 4 July 1829, HL. Peabody to Dix, 8 July 1827, HL. Dix to Heath, n.d. [c. 1824] and 23 June 1829, HL.

2. Catharine Beecher, *Suggestions Respecting Improvements in Education, Presented to the Trustees* (Hartford, Conn.: Packard & Butler, 1829), 46.

3. Mary Eustis Channing to Dix, n.d., quoted in Francis Tiffany, *Life of Dorothea Lynde Dix* (Cambridge, Mass.: Houghton Mifflin, 1890), p. 34. A. C. Brown to Dix, 23 April 1835, HL.

4. Lucy E. Abbot to Dix, 22 October 1836 and 9 December 1838, HL. Anne G. Cunningham to Dix, 23 October 1836, HL. Fanny Aspinwall to Dix, 24 June 1836, HL. Tiffany, *Life*, 39–40.

5. Dix to Heath, n.d. [c. 1824], HL.

6. Helen Marshall, *Dorothea Dix: Forgotten Samaritan* (Chapel Hill: University of North Carolina Press, 1937), 18, 29–30; Roe, *Dorothea Lynde Dix*, A Paper Read before the Worcester Society of Antiquity, November 20th, 1888 (Worcester: Franklin P. Rice, 1889), 11. The sentimental notion of a broken engagement permanently wounding a young girl's heart has continued to hold dramatic appeal and has been embroidered with novel touches in each retelling. See, for example, Charles Schlaifer and Lucy Freeman, *Heart's Work: Civil War Heroine and Champion of the Mentally Ill, Dorothea Lynde Dix* (New York: Paragon, 1991), 20.

7. Dix to Heath, 26 June 1824 and n.d. [August 1824], HL. Nancy Cott, "Young Women and the Second Great Awakening in New England," *Feminist Studies* 3 (1975) has written about the not uncommon "marriage trauma" that afflicted Victorian women who "sincerely envisioned beaux ideals and neither found them in reality nor would settle for less, and thus refused to marry" (*Bonds of Womanhood*, 80).

8. Andrews Norton to Dix, [1830], HL.

9. Upon closer examination, the choice not to marry appears to have been both more common and more acceptable within Jacksonian society than was traditionally assumed, and women who were vigorous and self-motivated increasingly avoided the bonds of matrimony. See Lee Chambers-Schiller, *Liberty, A Better Husband: Single Women in America: The Generation of 1780–1840* (New Haven: Yale University Press, 1984).

10. Francis Tiffany, *Charles Francis Bernard, His Life and Work* (Boston: Houghton Mifflin, 1895), 21–22, 46–47. Daniel T. McColgan, *Joseph Tuckerman: Pioneer in American Social Work* (Washington, D.C.: Catholic University of America Press, 1940), 199–202.

11. *The Garland of Flora* (Boston: S. G. Goodrich and Co. and Carter and Hendee, 1829), 30–31.

12. Dix to John Torrey, 16 March 1832, Miscellaneous Collection, PHS; Torrey to Dix, 29 February 1832 and 16 April 1832, HL.

13. Dix to Heath, 2 April 1832 and n.d. [1832?], HL; *The Writings of Henry David Thoreau*, ed., Bradford Torrey, 13 vols. (Boston: Houghton Mifflin, 1906), II:317.

14. Emerson to Dix, 16 November 1835, HL.

15. George Bancroft to R[obert] C. Waterston, 18 May 1882, quoted in Robert C. Waterston, *Memoir of George Barrell Emerson, LL.D.* (Cambridge, Mass.: John Wilson and Son, 1884), 6. Dorothea found his high opinion of female intellect especially congenial. "Intellect is equally distributed [and nothing] is to prevent the females from being highly educated," he had said in his *Lecture on the Education of Females* (Boston: Hillard, Gray, Little and Wilkins, 1831). His sketchy autobiography covers Emerson's work with the Massachusetts Board of Education, *Reminiscences of an Old Teacher* (Boston: Alfred Mudge and Son, 1878).

16. George Barrell Emerson to Dix, 16 November 1835, HL.

17. Dix to Emerson, n.d. [February 1836], Chamberlain MSS, BPL.

18. Dix to Emerson, 3 March 1836, Chamberlain MSS, BPL.

19. Dix to George Barrell Emerson, n.d. [February 1836], Chamberlain MSS, Boston Public Library.

20. Dix to Emerson, 7 March 1836, Chamberlain MSS, BPL.

21. Heath to Dix, 14 April 1836; Dix to Heath, 16 April [1836], HL.

22. Dix to Dorothy Lynde Dix (grandmother), 2 June 1836, HL (hereafter cited as Madam Dix). William Lawrence to Dix, 8 June 1836 and 11 June 1836, HL. Edward Fesser to Dix, 29 June 1836, HL. Fesser had placed two children in Dorothea's school, and had volunteered to handle her finances during the first months of her illness in Liverpool.

23. William Ellery Channing to Joanna Baillie, 21 April 1836, HL. Channing's letter to Rathbone has not survived, but this letter contains the formula he doubtless used.

24. "Reminiscences of W. Rathbone Family," HL. William Rathbone IV to John W. Ward, 29 March 1886, HL.

25. Eleanor F. Rathbone, William Rathbone: A Memoir (London: Macmillan, 1905), 38.

26. Charles Wickstead, An Address Delivered in Hope-Street Church, Liverpool, February 16th, 1868 (London: Whitfield, 1868), 44; The Picture of Liverpool, or Stranger's Guide (Liverpool: Thomas Taylor, 1834). William Rathbone's antislavery activities are described in Ramsay Muir, A History of Liverpool (London: Williams and Northgate, 1907), 205–25. William III's political career is chronicled in J. A. Picton, Memorials of Liverpool Historical and Topographical, 2 vols. (London: Green and Co., 1875), I:421–80.

27. Dix to Madam Dix, 28 September 1836, HL. Rathbone, William Rathbone, 13–15, 48–52.

28. Dix to Madam Dix, 28 September 1836; Dix to William Rathbone IV, 29 April 1868, HL; Liverpool Advertiser 15 October 1789; "William Rathbone," Liverpool Mercury, 6 February 1868.

29. Beard, William Rathbone, 46.

30. Hannah Mary Rathbone to Elizabeth Fry, 30 May 1836; Dix to Madam Dix, 28 September 1836 and 29 September 1836, HL.

31. Dix to Elizabeth Rathbone, September 1836; Dix to Madam Dix, 8 January 1837, HL.

32. Dix to Madam Dix, 8 January 1837 and March 1837, HL. Dix to Heath, 27 November 1836, HL.

33. Dix to Madam Dix, 2 June 1836; William Rathbone IV to John W. Ward, 29 March 1886, HL; Dix to Torrey, 1 October 1836; Dix to Heath, 12 November 1836, HL.

34. Heath to Dix, 14 October 1836, HL.

35. Dix to Madam Dix, 5 October 1836, HL. The fact that Dorothea did not save her grandmother's letters to England suggests the bitterness of her feelings toward Madam Dix. Dix to Torrey, 1 October 1836, HL.

36. Rathbone, William Rathbone, 37; Hannah Mary Rathbone to Elizabeth Fry, 30 September 1836, HL.

37. Heath to Dix, 14 October 1836; Dix to Heath, 12 November 1836; Dix to Madam Dix, 13 November 1836, HL.

38. Helen Loring to Dix, August 1837; Dix to Torrey, 2 June 1837, HL. The contrast between Dorothea's measured response to Madam Dix's death and her emotional lamentation on the death of Anne Heath's mother five years earlier is striking. See Dix to Heath, 2 April 1832, HL.

39. H. S. Hayward to Dix, quoted in Tiffany, Life, 48. In his published biography, Tiffany set the date of the letter at 28 September 1836. But in his "Notes for a Biography of

Dorothea Dix," HL, he noted it merely as May 28. The letter is not(t part of the Dix archive in Houghton Library, and there is no way to date it. Yet in light of the facts that Dorothea, in March 1837, was still urging her brother Joseph to write to Fitzwilliam, her mother's home, and that she returned to Boston in late September 1837, Mary Bigelow Dix must have died in May 1837, with Mrs. Hayward's note having been written May 28 of that year.

40. Dix MS Diary Am 1838 (942), HL.

41. Dix MS Diary Am 1838 (942) [1836–1837].

42. Ibid.

43. Ibid.

44. James Cowles Prichard, *A Treatise on Insanity and Other Disorders Affecting the Mind* (London: Sherwoods, Gilbert, and Piper, 1835), 4–5.

45. W. Falconer, *A Dissertation on the Influence of the Passions Upon the Disorders of the Body* (London: Dill, 1788), 77, quoted in Andrew Scull, *The Most Solitary of Afflictions: Madness and Society in Britain, 1700–1900* (New Haven and London: Yale University Press, 1993), 72.

46. The English mad-doctors defined the symptoms of insanity, including melancholia, quite broadly. See John Conolly, *An Inquiry Concerning the Indications of Insanity* (London, 1830); William B. Neville, *On Insanity: Its Nature, Causes and Cure* (London, 1836); and W. A. F. Browne, *What Asylums Were, Are, and Ought to Be* (Edinburgh, 1837). On melancholy and other popular conceptions of madness, see Michael MacDonald, *Mystical Bedlam: Madness, Anxiety and Healing in Seventeenth-Century England* (Cambridge: Cambridge University Press1981), 1–12; and David B. Morris, *The Culture of Pain* (Berkeley: 1991), 94–96. Dorothea Lynde Dix diaries [1836–37], HL, The connection among "religious gloom," melancholia, and insanity was taken for granted in Victorian England and America throughout the nineteenth century. See Norman Dain, *Concepts of Insanity in the United States, 1789–1865* (New Brunswick: R utgers University Press 1964), 183–93; and the patient profile of Eliza Butler in Tomes, *A Generous Confidence*: Thomas Story, *Kirkbridge and the Art of Asylum Keeping* (Cambride University Press, 1984). 226–34.

47. The character and dimensions of this revolution have become the subject of a rich historical literature. The classic Whig interpretation is Kathleen Jones, *Lunacy, Law and Conscience, 1744–1845: The Social History of the Care of the Insane* (London: Routledge and Kegan Paul, 1955), which is counterbalanced by Andrew Scull's scathing critique of incarceration, *Museums of Madness The Social Organization of Insanity in Nineteenth-Century England.* (New York: St Martin's Press, 1979). See also William F. Bynum, "Rationales for Therapy in British Psychiatry, 1780–1835," *Medical History* 18 (1974): 317–34.

48. Donald Fleming, *William H. Welch and the Rise of Modern Medicine* (Boston: Little, 1954), 10–11. Charles E. Rosenberg, *The Cholera Years* (Chicago: University of Chicago Press, 1962), 72–73.

49. Charles E. Rosenberg, "The Bitter Fruit: Heredity, Disease, and Social Thought in 19th-Century America," *Perspectives in American History* 8 (1974): 189–235.

50. Dix to Heath, 23 June 1829 and 3 March 1838, HL.

51. Charles Wesley Dix to Dix, 5 February 1837; Dix to Mrs. Torrey, 23 April 1837 and 20 May 1837, HL.

52. See A. Hulme, *Condition of Liverpool, Religious and Social; Including Notices of the State of Education, Morals, Pauperism, and Crime* (Liverpool: T. Brakell, 1858). On the Liverpool school wars, see Picton, *Memorials of Liverpool*, 470ff. 53. On the contemporary meaning of the New Poor Law, see Gertrude Himmelfarb, *The Idea of Poverty: England in the Early Industrial Age* (New York: Knopf, 1983), 147–90; David Roberts, "Dealing with the Poor in Victorian England," *Rice University Studies* 67 (Spring 1981): 57–74; John Clive, *Macaulay: The Shaping of the Historian* (New York: Knopf, 1973), 142–76. Much work remains to be done on the crosscurrents between British and American social reform in the 1830s and 1840s.

54. On the methods of the New Poor Law reformers, see David Roberts, *Victorian Origins of the British Welfare State* (New Haven: Yale University Press, 1960); Derek Fraser, *The Evolution of the British Welfare State* (New York: Macmillan, 1973); and Norman Gash, *Aristocracy and People: Britain 1815–1865* (Cambridge, Mass: Harvard Iniversity Press, 1979), esp. 187–219.

55. Dix to unnamed correspondent [probably Mrs. Torrey], 13 June 1837, HL. Although she frequently used the phrase, Dix never mentioned Bentham, and she certainly never assumed, as many of Bentham's readers did assume, that the greatest happiness principle meant that the poor were obliged to suffer for the general good of society. What was most Benthamite in Dix's thinking was simply her belief that the state should take a strong and responsible role in the funding and administration of social welfare. See Mary P. Mack, *Jeremy Bentham, An Odyssey of Ideas, 1748–1792*, 2 vols. (London: Heinemann, 1962), vol. 1.

56. Samuel Tuke, *Review of the Early History of the Retreat* (York: Thomas Wilson and Sons, 1846), 10.

57. H. Reynolds to Dix, 22 September 1837, HL.

58. J. G. Kohl, *Travels in England and Wales*, quoted in Anne Digby, *Madness, Morality and Medicine: A Study of the York Retreat, 1796–1914* (Cambridge: Cambridge University Press, 1985), 33; Samuel Tuke, *Description of the Retreat: An Institution near York for Insane Persons of the Society of Friends* (York: Thomas Wilson, 1813), 150.

59. John Rein, *Essays on Hypochondriasis and Other Nervous Affections* (1816), quoted in Scull, *The Most Solitary of Afflictions*, 115; Digby, *Madness, Morality and Medicine*, 34, 49–56.

60. Summarizing the early history of lunacy reform, Dix remarked, "the Retreat at York, distinguished for its humane influences, was founded by the Society of Friends, who, rich in good works, have always been prompt to sustain humane institutions, and advance enterprises for ameliorating the sufferings which beset humanity" ([Dorothea Lynde Dix], *Memorial Soliciting a State Hospital for the Insane, Submitted to the Legislature of New Jersey, January 23, 1845* [Trenton, 1845], 32); Digby, *Madness, Morality and Medicine*, 87.

61. Dix to [Mrs. Torrey?], 13 June 1837, HL.

62. John Hamilton Thon to Dix, n.d. [September 1837], HL.

Chapter 4: The Discovery of "Suffering Humanity"

1. Dix to Mrs. Torrey, 29 May 1837 and 2 June 1837, HL. On the Panic of 1837, see Edward Pessen, *Jacksonian America: Society, Personality, and Politics*, rev. ed. (Homewood, Ill.: Dorsey, 1978), 145–48; and Glyndon G. Van Deusen, *The Jacksonian Era: 1828–1848* (New York: Harper and Row, 1959), 116–19.

2. Mary Harris to Dix, 6 April [no year], HL.

3. Helen Marshall, *Dorothea Dix: Forgotten Samaritan* (Chapel Hill: University of North Carolina Press, 1937), 55, 254.

4. "Financial Records of the Estate of Madam Dix," MS Am 1838 (962), HL; "Will of Mrs. Dorothy Dix," Case No. 31557, Suffolk County Records, Boston, Massachusetts.

5. Dix to Heath, 22 January 1838, HL.

6. Dix to Heath, 24 February 1838, HL.

7. Heath to Dix, 6 January 1838, HL.

8. Dix to Heath, n.d. [winter 1838], HL.

9. Marianna Cutter to Dix, 25 April 1837 and 28 April 1837, HL.

10. Marianna [Cutter] Trott to Francis Tiffany, 19 February 1890, HL.

11. Dix to Benjamin Silliman, 11 December 1858, Miscellaneous MS Collection, PHS.

12. Dix to Heath, 14 October 1839, HL.

13. Dix to Heath, 24 February 1838, HL.

14. Ibid.

15. Dix to Heath, 3 March 1838, HL. Dix remarked on having visited the public institutions of the capital a decade later. See *Memorial of D. L. Dix Praying A grant of land for the relief and support of the indigent curable and incurable insane in the United States*, 30th Congress, 1st Session: Senate Miscellaneous Document No. 150 (27 June 1848), 21.

16. Dix to Heath, 3 March 1838 and 30 March 1838, HL.

17. Dix to Heath, 20 April 1838; Heath to Dix, 1 October 1838, HL.

18. Dix to Heath, 9 July 1838, HL.

19. George Washington Burnap to Dix, 21 November 1838, HL; Dix to Elizabeth Burnap, 10 March [n.d.], Williams Family MSS, Maryland Historical Society; Samuel A. Eliot, *Heralds of a Liberal Faith*, 3 vols. (Boston: American Unitarian Association, 1910), III:50–54; Stange, *Patterns of Antislavery*, 226.

20. On Sheppard's life see John E. Semmes, *John B. Latrobe and His Times, 1803–1891* (Baltimore: Norman, Remington Co., 1917), 285–87. Nothing came of Sheppard's scheme until fifteen years later when he made a bequest of $560,000 for an asylum on which construction began in 1857, the year after his death. Just returned from Europe, Dorothea Dix helped the trustees of the Sheppard asylum purchase Mt. Airy Farm outside Baltimore and contract with architects to design the institution. A sketch of the founding of The Sheppard & Enoch Pratt Hospital may be found in J. Thomas Scharf, *History of Baltimore City and County* (Philadelphia: n.p., 1881), 892–93; see also Bliss Forbush, *The Sheppard & Enoch Pratt Hospital, 1853–1970: A History* (Philadelphia: Lippincott, 1971), 15–26.

21. Hitchcock to Dix, 16 January 1839 and 24 April 1840, HL.

22. Ibid.

23. Hitchcock to Dix, 24 May and 22 June 1841, HL.

24. Hitchcock to Dix, 11 June 1841 and 17 July 1841, HL.

25. Hitchcock to Dix, 17 July 1841, HL.

26. Hitchcock to Dix, 18 April 1842, HL.

27. The source for this account was a conversation in the winter of 1851–52 between Dix and Alexander Randall, a Maryland lawyer and politician. Intrigued by her reputation, Randall confided to his diary that shortly after he met Dix he asked her "if she would

be kind enough to let me know what caused her to take so lively interest in this class of the afflicted." See Alexander Randall Diaries MS [1851–52], Maryland Historical Society.

28. Ibid.

29. This remark appears in a letter, Dix to Alexander Randall, n.d. [c. 1876], HL; L. J. Bigelow, "Miss Dix, And What She Has Done," *Galaxy* 3 (March 15, 1867): 669.

30. John T. G. Nichols to James Freeman Clarke, n.d. [c. 1887], quoted in James Freeman Clarke, *Dorothea L. Dix* (Boston: George H. Ellis, 1887), 5. See also the letter from Nichols to Francis Tiffany in Francis Tiffany, *Charles Francis Bernard, His Life and Work* (Boston: Houghton Mifflin, 1895), 73–74.

31. Charlotte M. Harris to Horatio Appleton Lamb, 17 November 1887, HL.

32. Dix to Madam Dix, 5 October 1836, HL.

33. *Memorial of D. L. Dix Praying A grant of land . . .* (1848), 28.

34. Charles Dickens, *American Notes and Pictures from Italy* (London: Oxford University Press, 1957 [first published 1842]), 45–47.

35. George Hayward to Woodward, 26 June 1841, and Walter Channing to Woodward, 27 June 1841, Woodward Family Papers, MS. Channing told Woodward that Dix wanted to discuss "a case of great interest" to her that probably involved one of the prisoners in the East Cambridge jail. Hayward, who was Dix's personal physician, had long expressed an interest in mental disorder, and had written a treatise, *Some Observations on Dr. Rush's Work, on "The Diseases of the Mind." With Remarks on the Nature and Treatment of Insanity* (Boston: n.p., 1818).

36. A regular visitor to the Boston Athenaeum, Dix would undoubtedly have read review articles like Amariah Brigham's "Insanity and Insane Hospitals," *North American Review* 44 (January 1837): 91–121, and [Samuel Gridley Howe's?], "Lunatic Hospital at Worcester," *Christian Examiner* 26 (May 1839): 257–59.

37. The most useful sketch of Woodward and his career is found in Gerald N. Grob, *The State and the Mentally Ill: A History of Worcester State Hospital in Massachusetts, 1830–1920* (Chapel Hill: University of North Carolina Press, 1966), chap. 2; see also George Chandler, "Life of Dr. Woodward," *American Journal of Insanity* 8 (October 1851): 119–35.

38. Cyrus Pierce to Horace Mann, 14 September 1841, Mann MSS, MHS.

39. Cyrus Pierce to Horace Mann, 13 September 1843, Mann MSS, MHS; Jonathan Messerli, *Horace Mann: A Biography* (New York: Knopf, 1972), 323–24, 366–69.

40. William O. Moseley to Dix, 30 October 1841, HL; Joseph Henry Allen to his father, 13 December 1841, Miscellaneous MSS, Pennsylvania Historical Society.

41. For an example of Dix's initial survey, see Dix to Frank Gourgas, 14 September, and Frank Gourgas to Dix, 27 September 1841, HL.

42. [Dorothea Lynde Dix], *Memorial to the Legislature of Massachusetts* (Boston: Monroe and Francis, 1843), 6.

43. See Godfrey Higgins, *The Evidence Taken Before a Committee of the House of Commons Respecting the Asylum at York; with Observations and Notes, and a Letter to the Committee* (Doncaster, England: Sheardown, 1816); and John Conolly, *An Inquiry Concerning the Indications of Insanity with Suggestions for the Better Protection and Care of the Insane* (London: Taylor, 1830).

44. See M. A. DeWolfe Howe, *The Humane Society of the Commonwealth of Massachusetts: An*

Historical Review 1785–1916 (Boston: Humane Society at the Riverside Press, 1918), 199.

45. *Second Annual Report of the Board of Managers of the Boston Prison Discipline Society, June 1, 1827* (Boston: n.p., 1827), 11, 19ff. Ironically even in using Dwight as a model, Dix was indirectly using British sources. Dwight drew heavily on the methods of English reformers, including the parliamentary investigations into English prisons. Dix also had access to the first American edition of the *Memoirs of John Howard, Compiled from His Diary, His Confidential Letters, and Other Authentic Documents*, ed. James Baldwin Browne (Boston: Lincoln and Edwards, 1831).

46. *Massachusetts House Documents, 1830–1831, No. 39*, "Report," 1–4.

47. Mann's productive career as a lunacy reformer is well documented in Messerli, *Horace Mann*, 122–37.

48. Horace Mann to Lydia Mann, 18 March 1833, Mann MSS, MHS.

49. *Daily Advertiser and Patriot*, 8, 16, 27, and 30 September 1842; *Massachusetts House Document No. 47* (September 10, 1842); *Chapter C, Act of September 16, 1842*. The bill passed the lower house but was never signed into law. On Howe's role, see Harold Schwartz, *Samuel Gridley Howe: Social Reformer, 1801–1876* (Cambridge, Mass.: Harvard University Press, 1956), 99–101.

Chapter 5: "I plead, I implore, I demand . . ."

1. "The Insane of Massachusetts," *North American Review* 56 (January 1843): 171–91. Dix was more than glad to share her research with anyone who would publicize it. See also Robert C. Waterston, "The Insane of Massachusetts," *Christian Examiner* 33 (January 1843): 338–52.

2. [Dorothea Lynde Dix], *Memorial to the Legislature of Massachusetts* (Boston: Monroe and Francis, 1843), 3.

3. Ibid., 4.

4. Ibid., 5ff.

5. Ibid., 4, 24–25.

6. *Report from the Select Committee* . . . (15 July 1807), 6.

7. House of Commons, *Report from the Select Committee Appointed to Enquire into the State of Lunatics* (British Parliamentary Papers, 15 July 1807), 6. Modern scholars have challenged such claims by asylum keepers as self-serving. See Anne Digby, *Madness Morality and Medicine: A Study of the York Retreat, 1796–1914* (Cambridge:Cambridge University Press 1986), and Scull, *Museums of Madness The Social Organization of Insanity in Nineteenth-Century England* (New York, St. Martin's Press, 1979). 76–124.

8. Ibid., 15, 20.

9. Dix, Massachusetts *Memorial*, 29–30. After the Massachusetts *Memorial* became public, Anson Hooker, the jail's attending physician, professed his shock and dismay about the way Dix had twisted his words. See Hooker to Dix, 12 and 24 January, and 3 February 1843, Dix MSS, Houghton Library, Harvard University.

10. On the 1815–16 parliamentary inquiry, see Scull, *Museums of Madness*, 76–82.

11. Ibid., 3–4; House of Commons, *Third Report from the Committee on Madhouses in England, &c. with an Appendix*, 11 June 1816, 4.

12. Dix, Massachusetts *Memorial*, 3.

13. House of Commons, "Appendix to Report from the Committee," *Third Report from the Committee . . .* , 11 June 1816, 14.

14. Dix, Massachusetts *Memorial*, 9–10.

15. Ibid., 8–9.

16. House of Commons, *First Report: Minutes of Evidence Taken before the Select Committee appointed to consider of Provision being made for the better Regulation of Madhouses, in England* (British Parliamentary Papers, 25 May 1815), 1.

17. One prominent student of gothicism has written that "horror fiction gives the reader the tools to 'read' experiences that would otherwise, like nightmares, be incommunicable. . . . the inexpressible and private becomes understandable and communal, shared and safe." See Martin Tropp, *Images of Fear: How Horror Stories Helped Shape Modern Culture (1818–1918)* (Jefferson, N.C.: McFarland, 1990), 4–5. Gothicism usually placed protagonists "in a world created by the circle of their own fears and desires, in a state of enthrallment, both thrilling and destructive." Students of gothic literature have observed that the hallmarks of the convention—fear, terror, and, above all, dread—were related to deep-seated cultural and social anxieties that reflected "the essential insecurities of nineteenth-century readers." In particular, these anxieties seem to have centered on the family unit, the changing roles of men and women, and threats to traditional relations between the sexes. Indeed, it has been argued that the ruined and empty house, perhaps the central metaphor in gothic fiction, stands for the triumph of unreason over domestic order. See William Patrick Day, *In the Circles of Fear and Desire: A Study of Gothic Fantasy* (Chicago: University of Chicago Press, 1985), 4–5; Victor Sage, *Horror Fiction in the Protestant Tradition* (London: Macmillan, 1988), 1–25. Sage imaginatively connects the gothic anxiety about the family to the weakening of traditional religious institutions in the mid-nineteenth century.

18. Dix, Massachusetts *Memorial*, 15, 9.

19. Ibid., 24. Dix's omissions and silences—she never used words like "urine" or "excrement," nor did she refer, except euphemistically, to masturbation or rape—represented a departure from the British tradition of social criticism. Throughout the Victorian period, British reformers wrote in a Swiftian vein, using blunt, descriptive language to shock their audiences. Dix, Howe, Mann, and the dozens of municipal and state commissions that investigated jails and almshouses during the antebellum era left it to their readers' imaginations to supply the squalid details of their pictures.

20. Ibid., 16–17.

21. Ibid., 11.

22. Ibid., 11–12.

23. Ibid., 21.

24. Ibid., 26–27.

25. Dix to Massachusetts General Court Committee for Charitable Appropriations, n.d. [January 1843], HL.

26. *Boston Daily Advertiser and Patriot*, 27 February 1843.

27. John Gorham Palfrey to Dix, 25 February 1843, HL; *Massachusetts House Documents, 1843, No. 38*, 12–13; *Massachusetts Acts and Resolves, 1843*, Chapter 73 (March 24, 1843), 83–84. Howe's role in presenting the Massachusetts *Memorial* and guiding the subsequent legislation is summarized in Harold Schwartz, *Samuel Gridley Howe: Social Reformer, 1801–1876* (Cambridge, Mass.: Harvard University Press, 1956), 98–102.

28. Howe to Dix, 19 January 1843, quoted in Francis Tiffany, *Charles Francis Bernard, His Life and Work* (Boston: Houghton Mifflin, 1895), 89.

29. Horace Mann to Dix, 27 January 1843, HL.

30. Dix to Horace Mann, 1 February 1843, HL.

31. Heath to Dix, 23 [February?] 1843, HL.

32. *Boston Daily Advertiser and Patriot*, 27 February 1843.

33. *Newburyport Herald*, 6 and 9 February 1843. Because the image of the madwoman in Newburyport was so vivid, it elicited many strong responses. One newspaper editor wrote Dix to tell her that he had gone to the almshouse expecting to find the woman in "a common cellar, dark, damp & cold," and had been astonished to find it "nearly as light as the room in which I write," dry, white-washed and well-ventilated (Thomas Bayley Fox to Dix, 17 February 1843, HL).

34. John Waters Proctor to Dix, 10 and 14 February 1843; Dix to Proctor, 13 February 1843, HL. "It must be that she formed her opinion respecting the treatment of Mr. Bull from hearsay," the local Shelburne newspaper reported, "and gave the statement as her imagination had received the impression from her informer" (*Shelburne Democrat*, February 1843).

35. *A Memorial to the Legislature of Massachusetts* (Salem: n.p., 1843), 5–6 and passim.

36. Lucius Manlius Sargent assured Dix that she should not worry about "a morbid sensibility abroad, which may question the propriety of such an investigation, by one of your sex. . . . Woman was last at the cross and first at the tomb, and she is never more in her appropriate station than when placed precisely as you are at this moment" (Sargent to Dix, 22 January 1843, HL).

37. Anson Hooker to Dix, 12 and 24 January 1843, HL.

38. The Boston *Mercantile Journal* voiced what was certainly the received wisdom about Dix: "such a person is not likely to be led astray by her feelings or her prejudices, to view things through a false medium, or to present truths in a disguised or distorted form. . . . For she is not a person whose feelings would be likely to get the better of her judgment" (21 February 1843; see also 11 February 1843).

39. Anson Hooker to Dix, 3 February 1843, HL.

40. Anson Hooker to Dix, 12 January 1843; Nathaniel Watson to Dix, 13 January 1843, HL.

41. William Bentley Fowle to Dix, 9 February 1843, HL.

42. Dix to the Massachusetts General Court Committee for Charitable Appropriations, 14 February 1843, HL.

43. *Boston Courier*, 22 and 25 February 1843.

44. Dix to [Joseph Henry Allen, Sr.], 9 March [1843], HL.

Chapter 6: Voice for the Mad

1. Dorothea Dix, *Memorial. To the Honorable the Legislature of the State of New-York*, New York *Assembly Document No. 20* (January 12, 1844), 6.

2. Thomas Eddy, *Hints for Introducing an Improved Mode of Treating the Insane in Asylums* (New York: Samuel Wood, 1815). Just how heavily Tuke's English model influenced these early developments in New York is shown by Andrew Scull, "The Discovery of the Asylum Revisited: Lunacy Reform in the New American Republic," in Scull, *Social*

Order/Mental Disorder: Anglo-American Psychiatry in Historical Perspective (Berkeley: University of California Press, 1989). 97–101.

3. William Seward, "Annual Message" (1839), quoted in Ellen Dwyer, *Homes for the Mad: Life inside Two Nineteenth-Century Asylums* (New Brunswick: Rutgers University Press, 1987), 36.

4. Luther Bell to Dix, 1 March 1843, HL.

5. Luther Bell to Dix, 4 February 1843, HL.

6. William Wilson to Dix, 11 February 1843, HL.

7. Theodore Romeyn Beck to Dix, n.d. [1843], HL.

8. Dix to George Barrell Emerson, 13 November 1843, Chamberlain MSS, BPL.

9. George Barrell Emerson to Dix, September [n.d.] and 8 October 1843, HL; Dix to Emerson, n.d. [1843], Chamberlain MSS, BPL.

10. *Memorial. To the Honorable the Legislature of the State of New-York*, Assembly Doc. 21 (New York: n.p., 12 January 1844), 3. The broader context for the emergence of state responsibility for public health, of which mental health was but one prominent aspect, in the antebellum period is provided by Barbara Gutman Rosenkrantz, *Public Health and the State: Changing Views in Massachusetts, 1842–1936* (Cambridge, Mass.: Harvard University Press, 1972), 4ff. The culmination of the first period of interest in state-sponsored public health policy was the landmark survey published by the Massachusetts Sanitary Commission, Lemuel Shattuck et al., *Report of the Sanitary Commission of Massachusetts 1850*, facsimile ed. (Cambridge, Mass.: Harvard University Press, 1948). Impressed by her success in lunacy reform, early proponents of public health called for some reformer of Dix's caliber to take up their cause. See, for example, G[ouverneur] E[merson], "Review," *American Journal of the Medical Sciences* 9 (1845): 396–401.

11. Dix, New York *Memorial*, 38, 42.

12. Ibid., 23–24, 48. Almshouses in New York and elsewhere tended to reflect the values and society of their surrounding communities. By the turn of the nineteenth century, cities like Boston and New York had highly developed almshouses that functioned as municipal hospitals. These large institutions usually contained special wards or out-buildings to separate indigent idiots and lunatics from orphans, delinquents, the handicapped, and the aged. Rural communities, on the other hand, tended to care for different classes of inmates in simpler one- or two-room structures. On the development of the almshouse into a full-fledged medical facility, see Charles E. Rosenberg, "From Almshouse to Hospital: The Shaping of Philadelphia General Hospital," *Milbank Memorial Fund Quarterly* 60 (1982): 108–54.

13. Grob, *Mental Institutions in America: Social Policy to 1875* (New York: Free Press, 1993). 325–26, and Pliny Earle, "Gheel," *American Journal of Insanity* 7 (July 1851): 67–78.

14. Ibid., 55–56. The issue of separating curable and incurable inmates—whatever criteria might be used to make the distinction—led Dix more deeply into the areas of treatment and asylum architecture. She had heard from Isaac Ray, who was superintendent of the Maine Insane Hospital at the time, that curative institutions had to be small enough to foster "close communication and fellowship between the chief [sic] and each individual patient." Establishments for the incurable, on the other hand, should be concerned more with the patients' physical well-being, for they were beyond moral treatment (Isaac Ray to Dix, 20 February 1843, HL).

15. Ibid., 6–9. Returning to the Albany almshouse the next year, in December 1843, Dix was pleased to find a new overseer and a much more orderly institution (ibid., 9).

16. Ibid., 20.

17. Ibid., 33–34.

18. Here as elsewhere Dix followed the approach of the British lunacy reformers but showed a squeamishness and reticence to describe the details of abuse, which made her narrative more, not less, provocative. On the parliamentary inquiries see Scull, Andrew Scull, *The Most Solitary of Afflictions: Madness and Society in Britain,* 1700–1900 (New Haven: Yale University Press, 1993), 114-132..

19. Ibid., 48–49.

20. Ibid., 18.

21. Ibid., 57–59.

22. Ibid., 9.

23. Ibid., 21.

24. Ibid., 54.

25. Dwyer, *Homes for the Mad,* 31–32.

26. The New York State legislature printed Dix's petition as an official government document and used it as part of a subsequent committee report that provided incremental funding for the Utica hospital. See Stanley B. Klein, "A Study of Social Legislation Affecting Prisons and Institutions for the Mentally Ill in New York State, 1822–1846," (Ph.D. diss., New York University, 1956), 286ff.

27. E. K. Hunt, *Biographical Sketch of Amariah Brigham, M.D., Late Superintendent of the New York State Lunatic Asylum, Utica, New York* (Utica: McClure, 1858); Dwyer, *Homes for the Mad,* 56–65.

28. Amariah Brigham to Dix, 14 January 1844, HL.

29. Brigham to Kirkbride, 3 March 1845, Kirkbride Papers, IPH.

30. Dix to George Barrell Emerson, September 1843, HL.

31. Dix left only traces of her activities in Vermont, although she later claimed that the cases of abuse chronicled in the Vermont asylum for the Insane's eighth *Annual Report* (1844) were the "repetition in fact, if not almost literal expression of my own notes" (*Memorial of D. L. Dix Praying A grant of land for the relief and support of the indigent curable and incurable insane in the United States,* 30th Congress, 1st Session, Senate Document No. 150 (June 27, 1848). The Maine legislature allocated $20,000 for an insane asylum on the condition that a like sum was to be raised through private philanthropy. See Henry M. Hurd, ed., *The Institutional Care of the Insane in the United States and Canada,* 4 vols. (Baltimore: Johns Hopkins University Press, 1916–17), II:484ff. The Vermont asylum was a hybrid institution, its governance and funding each partly public and partly private. See *The Vermont Asylum for the Insane. Its Annals for Fifty Years* (Brattleboro, 1887); Vermont Asylum for the Insane, *Annual Report,* I–IV (1837–40).

32. Thomas G. Hazard to Dix, 5 August 1843, HL. An active humanitarian, Hazard maintained an active ongoing interest in lunacy reform in Rhode Island through the 1850s.

33. Dix to Emerson, [n.d.] September 1843, Chamberlain MSS, BPL.

34. William Giles Goddard to Dix, 17 October 1843, HL.

35. *Providence Journal,* 10 April 1844.

36. Quoted in [Dorothea L. Dix] *Memorial Soliciting a State hospital for the Insane, Submitted to the Legislature of new Jersey, January 23, 1845,* 2d ed. (Trenton, n.p. 1845), 30–31.

Though the precise chronology is impossible to recreate, Dix undoubtedly had read the original French document well before she wrote about Abram Simmons. Her interest in Pinel was widely shared. His liberation of the insane "had an immediate and obvious appeal to men in the new republic," David Rothman suggests. "They too had just emerged from bondage and intended to bring freedom to others;" see: *Discovery of the Asylum: Social Order and Disorder in the New Republic* Rev. Ed. Boston, Little Brown, 1990. 109–10.

37. Quoted in Francis Tiffany, *Charles Francis Bernard, His Life and Work* (Boston: Houghton Mifflin, 1895), 98–100.

38. Dix to George Barrell Emerson, 11 May 1844, Chamberlain MSS, BPL. Dix apparently entertained the notion of sending Simmons to the McLean Hospital; see Dix to Luther Bell, 24 April 1844, HL.

39. The traditional account appears in Tiffany, *Life*, 101. Inaccurate accounts of the episode continued to bother Dix for years. She told her friend Harriet Hare that she had visited Cyrus Butler "at his own house conducted by Rev[eren]d Hall of Providence[.] Returning thence I met Professor Goddard near [Butler's] residence, went in by his request and had a long conversation respecting the business" (Dix to Harriet Hare, 15 February 1850, HL).

40. Dix to Harriet Hare, 15 February 1850, HL. See *Memoirs of Pliny Earle, M.D.*, ed. Franklin B. Sanborn (Boston: Samuel S. and William Wood, 1898), 367.

41. After Dix left the state, Butler's heirs circulated the story that Nicolas Brown, "before his death, urged the duty upon Mr. Butler." Yet even if Dix did not win over Cyrus Butler in a single decisive meeting, she nonetheless deserves credit for raising public awareness of the lunacy problem in Rhode Island in 1844–45, thereby creating the context for the magnate's uncharacteristic benevolence. In 1849 Edward Brooks Hall told her that he had "always believed . . . that your visit here, in state & city, were among the positive agencies, which brought about the result." See Hall to Dix, 28 April 1849, HL.

42. Hurd, *Institutional Care of the Insane*, III:557.

43. Thomas R. Hazard, "Report on the poor and insane in Rhode Island made to the General Assembly at its January session, 1851," in Hurd, *Institutional Care of the Insane*, III:572.

Chapter 7: The Perils of Politics

1. C. W. H. Dall, "A Lesson for Woman from History," *Monthly Religious Magazine* 6 (March 1849): 108–16.

2. Dix to George Barrell Emerson, 6 November 1844, BPL.

3. Dix to George Barrell Emerson, 1 July 1844, Chamberlain MSS, BPL.

4. Dix to George Barrell Emerson, 1 July 1844, BPL.

5. Henry M. Hurd, ed., *The Institutional Care of the Insane in the United States and Canada*, 4 vols. (Baltimore: Johns Hopkins University Press, 1916–17), III:51–52; *Report of the Commissioners Appointed by the Governor of New Jersey, to Ascertain the Number of Lunatics and Idiots in the State* (Newark: M.S. Harrison, 1840), 9 and passim.

6. Charlotte N. Freedland to Dix, 13 October 1844, HL.

7. Dix, New Jersey *Memorial*, 3.

8. Ibid., 4–5.

9. On the effects of immigration on New Jersey's political climate, see Stuart Galishoff, *Newark: The Nation's Unhealthiest City, 1832–1895* (New Brunswick: Rutgers University Press, 1988), 11–62.

10. Dix, New Jersey *Memorial*, 12

11. Ibid., 3, 5.

12. Ibid., 4.

13. Ibid., 7–8.

14. Ibid., 23–24.

15. Ibid.

16. Ibid., 28–29.

17. Ibid., 31–32.

18. Ibid., 28–29.

19. Ibid., 32–33. Andrew Scull observes that "corporate" or private institutions like the Hartford Retreat and Frankford, not public institutions, were the main channels for Pinel's and Tuke's moral therapies in America. "For the earliest state hospitals, the corporate asylums provided not only a model to be copied, but a source of professional staff and advice once they opened;" see "The Discovery of the Asylum Revisited: Lunacy Reform in the New American Republic," in Scull, *Social Order/Mental Disorder*: Anglo-American Psychiatry in Historical Perspectives (Berkeley: University of California Press, 1989). 116–17.

20. Dix, New Jersey *Memorial*, 33, 37.

21. Ibid., 35–37.

22. Ibid., 43.

23. Ibid., 46.

24. Dix had been hearing the economic argument for asylums for years. Amariah Brigham had predicted that sheer self–interest would eventually move states to build mental hospitals "if feelings of benevolence do not; for it requires but slight observation to see, that the expense of supporting the insane poor will be much lessened by providing them with a good Asylum" (*North American Review* 44 [1837]: 114).

25. Dix to Harriet Hare, 3 February [1845], HL.

26. Dix to Harriet Hare, 3 February [1845], HL.

27. Dix, New Jersey *Memorial*, 5–7.

28. Dix to George Barrell Emerson, 4 April 1845, Chamberlain MSS, BPL.

29. Dix to George Barrell Emerson, 6 July 1845, Chamberlain MSS, BPL.

30. Ibid.

31. Emerson to Dix, 16 September 1844, HL.

32. Dix to Emerson, 16 October 1844, Chamberlain MSS, BPL.

33. Emerson to Dix, 23 October 1844 and 2 January 1845, HL. In the January letter, Emerson chided Dix that he always enjoyed an advantage over her because he was capable of seeing some good in all his fellow creatures.

34. Dix to Emerson, 6 November 1844, 15 December 1844, and n.d. [1844], HL.

35. Dix to Emerson, 2 October 1844, Chamberlain MSS, BPL.

36. Dix to Heath, 22 December 1844, HL.

37. Dix to Harriet Hare, 22 October 1844, HL.

38. Roughly three million immigrants entered the United States during the decade after 1844, the largest surge as a percentage of the total population in American history. See Peter D. McClelland and Richard J. Zeckhauser, *Demographic Dimensions of the New Republic* (Cambridge, Mass.: Harvard University Press, 1982). On the Philadelphia riots, see Michael Feldberg, *The Turbulent Era: Riot and Disorder in Jacksonian America* (New York: Oxford University Press, 1980), 9–32.

39. Dix to Harriet Hare, 22 October 1844, HL.

40. Dix to Nathaniel Ewing, 18 August 1844, HL.

41. The Washington County almshouse keeper, Walter Craig, waited to respond until after Dix's accusations were published in her Pennsylvania *Memorial*. Then he gathered testimony from witnesses that contradicted her description point–by–point, and mailed it to Dix. One of these affidavits was from the almshouse physician, who claimed that over the past three years the almshouse had a perfect record of relieving insanity. He said he was sorry that "unjust or unholy measures should be resorted to by any person to further a good cause." See R. P. Lane to Walter Craig, 3 March 1845, and Joseph Vaneman to Craig, 30 March 1845, HL.

42. Dix undoubtedly read about the Society of Friends' Frankford Retreat in *An Account of the Rise and Progress of the Asylum, Proposed to Be Established near Philadelphia for the Relief of Persons Deprived of the Use of Their Reason* (Philadelphia: Kimber and Konrad, 1814).

43. Hurd, *Institutional Care of the Insane*, III:383–84.

44. *Report in Relation to an Asylum for the Insane Poor . . . March 11, 1839* (Philadelphia: Boas and Coplan, 1839), 22–24; *A Second Appeal to the People of Pennsylvania on the Subject of an Asylum for the Insane Poor of the Commonwealth* (Philadelphia: Brown, Bicking and Guilbert, 1840).

45. D[orothea] L[ynde] Dix, *Memorial Soliciting A State Hospital For The Insane, Submitted To The Legislature Of Pennsylvania, February 3, 1845* (Harrisburg: J.M.G. Lescure, 1845), 14–15, 19, 26.

46. Ibid., 50. Invented by Benjamin Rush at the turn of the nineteenth century, the tranquilizing chair had affixed to its frame straps for securing the seated patient's limbs and torso, and was topped with a viselike box for immobilizing the head. In Dix's day, the device had come to symbolize the unintentional cruelty that resulted from treating the insane with outmoded techniques.

47. Ibid., 5, 53.

48. Ibid., 9–10.

49. *Philadelphia Merchant: The Diary of Thomas P. Cope, 1800–1851*, ed. Eliza Cope Harrison (South Bend, Ind.: Gateway, n.d.), 461.

50. Dix to [illegible], 9 March [1845], Miscellaneous MSS, PHS.

51. Dix to Elizabeth R. Fisher, 17 October 1845, Historical Society of Pennsylvania archives. The citizens of Dauphin County took seriously their responsibility to raise money for the new asylum, dividing each of the county's boroughs into regions supervised by their own fund directors. See Nathaniel B. Eldred to Dix, 9 July 1845, HL.

52. James Lesley to Dix, 17 April 1845, HL; *Diary of Thomas P. Cope*, 28 May and 31 May 1845, 465–66.

53. Dix to the citizens of Muskingum County, 18 August 1844, HL.

54. Dix to George Barrell Emerson, 1 July 1844, Chamberlain MSS, BPL.

55. Dix to George Barrell Emerson, 24 July 1844, HL.

56. Howe subsequently published his views under the title *An Essay on Separate and Congregate Systems of Prison Discipline; Being a Report Made to the Boston Prison Discipline Society* (Boston: William D. Ticknor, 1846). This document was originally tendered to the Boston Prison Discipline Society as a minority report of a subcommittee, which included Howe, Mann, and Sumner, in favor of the Pennsylvania system of imprisonment. See Harold Schwartz, *Samuel Gridley Howe: Social Reformer, 1801–1876* (Cambridge, Mass.: Harvard University Press, 1956), 147–49.

57. On Sumner's role as an agitator, see David Donald, *Charles Sumner and the Coming of the Civil War* (New York: Knopf, 1960), 120–28. Donald contends that Howe and Sumner, among other reasons, wanted to unseat Dwight to give the post to their friend Francis Lieber (pp. 121–22). Rothman provides a useful overview of the competing systems and the often acrimonious debates among their advocates (*Discovery of the Asylum: Social Order and Disorder in the New Republic,* rev. ed. (Boston: Little Brown, 1990). 79–108). An attempt to sort out the economics of the two paradigms may be found in Christopher R. Adamson, "Hard Labor: The Form and Function of Imprisonment in Nineteenth–Century America" (Ph.D. diss., Princeton University, 1982), 100–107. A detailed picture of the Eastern Penitentiary is found in Negley K. Teeters and John D. Shearer, *The Prison at Philadelphia in Cherry Hill: The Separate System of Prison Discipline, 1829–1913* (New York: Columbia University Press, 1957), 201–23.

58. For an example of Dwight's elaborate reports, see *Eighteenth Annual Report of the Board of Managers of the Boston Prison Discipline Society* (Boston: Damrell and Moore, 1843); Emerson to Dix, 8 July 1844, HL.

59. Dix to George Barrell Emerson, 28 October 1845, Chamberlain MSS, BPL.

60. D[orothea] [Lynde] Dix, *Remarks on Prisons and Prison Discipline in the United States*, 2d ed. (Philadelphia: Joseph Kite, 1845), 67; "Prisons and Prison Discipline," *North American Review,* 55 (January, 1846): 124.

61. Dix, *Remarks on Prisons and Prison Discipline,* 65, 76. Christopher R. Adamson finds a distinct expression of Quaker principles in the Pennsylvania system's combination of solitary confinement and hard labor. "Faith in solitary confinement remained strong in the Quaker state, because the reformers viewed the offender as an individual who needed, as it were, to do penitence—to experience remorse and regret" ("Hard Labor," 107).

62. Charles Dickens, *American Notes and Pictures from Italy* (London: Oxford University Press, 1957 [*American Notes* first published 1842]), 109, 99.

63. Dix, *Remarks on Prisons and Prison Discipline,* 76.

64. Ibid., 67, 69.

65. Dix to George Barrell Emerson, 24 July 1844, Chamberlain MSS, BPL.

66. Dix, *Remarks on Prisons and Prison Discipline,* 14–15.

67. Dix, *On Prisons and Prison Discipline,* 23–25.

68. Ibid., 64.

69. Ibid., 55. The inspectors of the Eastern State Penitentiary of Pennsylvania, which Dix visited extensively and described as a model facility, wrote that "the mass of criminals is composed of persons whose childhood and youth were spent in the uncontrolled exercise of various instincts" (*Seventeenth Annual Report* [Philadelphia, 1846], 58, quot-

ed in Rothman, *Discovery of the Asylum*, 72). In Dix's eyes, they must have seemed hauntingly reminiscent of the wayward youths she had described in *American Moral Tales* seventeen years earlier.

70. Ibid., 68.
71. [Dorothea Dix], *An Address by a Recent Female Visiter to the Prisoners in the Eastern Penitentiary of Pennsylvania* (Philadelphia: Joseph and William Kite, 1844), 3, 5.
72. Ibid, 7–10.
73. Ibid., 11.
74. Alexis de Tocqueville and Gustave de Beaumont, *On the Penitentiary System in the United States and Its Application and France* (1835), quoted in Michael Ignatieff, *A Just Measure of Pain: The Penitentiary in the Industrial Revolution* (New York: Pantheon, 1978), 212.
75. James Dunlop to Dix, 24 October 1845, HL; Dix, *Remarks on Prisons and Prison Discipline*, 64.
76. Ibid., 81–89.

Chapter 8: "The Brethren"

1. [Amariah Brigham], "Notices of Books," *American Journal of Insanity* 1 (April 1845): 381–82.
2. Dix, *Tennessee Memorial*, 21–22; Constance M. McGovern, *Masters of Madness: Social Origins of the American Psychiatric Profession* (Hanover: University Press of New England, 1985).
3. A broader organization for medical professionals, the American Medical Association, was established in 1847.
4. Charles H. Nichols to Dix, 18 August 1858, HL.
5. On the early professional development of the American psychiatric profession, see Grob, *Mental Institutions in America*, 132–73; also see John A. Pitts, "The Association of Medical Superintendents of American Institutions for the Insane, 1844–1892: A Case Study of Specialism in American Medicine" (Ph.D. diss., University of Pennsylvania, 1979). The social context of professionalism is discussed in Barbara Gutman Rosenkrantz, "The Search for Professional Order in Nineteenth–Century American Medicine," *Proceedings of the Fourteenth International Congress of the History of Science*, no. 4 (Tokyo and Kyoto, 1974): 113–24.
6. From its origins in eighteenth–century England, moral therapy was delivered by laymen. The disease model of insanity that crystallized in England and America a generation before Dix wrote the Massachusetts *Memorial* accompanied a broad movement by physicians to gain control over madness and its treatment; see Andrew Scull, "Mad–Doctors and Magistrates: English Psychiatry's Struggle for Professional Autonomy in the Nineteenth Century," *European Journal of Sociology* 17 (1976): 279–305. Scull demonstrates that as the doctors became better organized, they came to see moral treatment by laymen as a professional threat; see Andrew Scull, *The Most Solitary of Afflictions: Madness and Society in Britain, 1700-1900* (New Haven: Yale University Press, 1993, 244–266. 132–48.
7. The professionalization of psychiatry and its basis in asylum management are summarized in Rothman, *Discovery of the Asylum: Social Order and Disorder in the New Republic*,

rev. ed. (Boston: Little Brown, 1990). chap. 6, and Grob, *Mental Institutions in America*, chap. 4. "Moral architecture" is Rothman's phrase.

8. Dix to Kirkbride, 15 February 1845, Kirkbride Papers, IPH.

9. Dix to Kirkbride, 22 and 29 July 1845, Kirkbride Papers, IPH; Kirkbride to Dix 27 July 1845; also see Grob, *Mental Institutions in America*, 354. Nancy Tomes notes without explanation that Kirkbride "played no part in the initial legislative campaign to establish a public asylum," but later joined the building committee and board of trustees once the new institution was approved (*A Generous Confidenc: Thomas Story Kirkbride and the Art of Asylum Keeping* (Cambridge: Cambridge University Press, *1975*). 294–96).

10. David Rothman asserted that the asylum doctors' passion for architectural and organizational order within the asylum stemmed from their desire to control broader social disorder (*Discovery of the Asylum*, 133–34). More recently, however, scholars have argued that the first generation of superintendents should be thought of as "moral entrepreneurs" striving to convince other medical professionals and, indeed, everyone else in their communities, of the value of their work. To establish their own legitimacy, the argument goes, much of the superintendents' efforts naturally went toward securing a solid institutional basis for the practice of psychiatry. See "A Generous Confidence: Thomas Story Kirkbride's Philosophy of Asylum Construction and Management," in Andrew Scull, ed., *Madhouses, Mad–Doctors, and Madmen: The Social History of Psychiatry in the Victorian Era* (Philadelphia: University of Pennsylvania Press, 1981), 121–43, and Andrew Scull, "From Madness to Mental Illness: Medical Men as Moral Entrepreneurs," *European Journal of Sociology* 15 (1974): 219–61. Even so, an obsession with the details of monumental structures built at public expense hardly originated with asylum superintendents.

11. Dix to William E. Hacker, 10 May 1848, Hacker MSS, New York Public Library.

12. *American Journal of the Medical Sciences* 13 (1847): 40–56. Kirkbride's most recent biographer claims that when it came to hospital construction and management, Kirkbride wrote the party platform. His twenty–six "propositions" on these subjects were adopted between 1851 and 1853 by the Association of Superintendents as official standards for moral treatment. Kirkbride's main principles held "that hospitals have no more than 250 patients; that the hospital building be carefully planned and constructed; that the institution be organized and administered so as to accommodate a mixed clientele, that is, curable and chronic, paying and charity patients together in the same hospital; and that the medical superintendent have complete control over every facet of the hospital's management" (Tomes, *A Generous Confidence*, 265). Dix generally went along with these ideas and wholeheartedly embraced Kirkbride's architectural philosophy. See Kirkbride to Dix, 23 February 1848, Kirkbride Papers, IPH.

13. Kirkbride to Dix, 9 April 1848, Kirkbride Papers, IPH.

14. Kirkbride to Dix, 30 May 1849; Dix to Kirkbride, 11 June 1849, HL.

15. To keep a lid on capital expenditures, the legislature pressed the asylum commission to spend no more than $10,000 in any one year, and to put off hiring a superintendent until construction was completed. H. Campbell to Dix, 23 November 1847 and 18 May 1848, HL.

16. Dix arranged for Patterson to visit hospitals around the country and helped him build relationships with other medical superintendents. At the end of the Civil War, he told

Dix he was stepping down from his position at the Iowa Hospital because his wife could no longer tolerate living in an asylum. See Patterson to Dix, 21 October 1847, 29 June 1849, 29 March 1850, and 30 September 1865, HL. Alonzo Potter to Dix, 27 September 1849, HL.

17. John H. Nichols to Dix, n.d [1855], HL.

18. Ernest Morrison, *The City on a Hill: A History of the Harrisburg State Hospital* (Harrisburg, Pa.: n.p., 1992), 78–98.

19. John Curwen to Kirkbride, 3 November 1851, Kirkbride MSS, IPH; Curwen to Dix, 14 May, 6 July 1852 and 7 March 1853; Dix to William E. Hacker, 29 April [1852], HL.

20. Curwen to Dix, 2 January 1854, HL.

21. Curwen to Dix, 26 January and 28 February 1852, HL; Charles H. Nichols to Dix, 19 December 1852, HL.

22. Curwen to Dix, 4 May 1857, HL.

23. Curwen to Dix, 10 February 1849, 19 June 1850, and 26 January 1852, HL. For a discussion of Curwen's struggles, which owed in part to Dix's unrealistic notion that a mental hospital could be self–financing, see Tomes, *A Generous Confidence*, 294–99.

24. Dix to Kirkbride, n.d. [summer 1851], Kirkbride MSS, IPH.

25. Charles H. Nichols to Dix, 7 May 1850; Dix to David S. Kennedy, 6 October 1851, HL; Pliny Earle to Thomas Kirkbride, 18 August 1858, quoted in Tomes, *A Generous Confidence*, 84–85; Dix to Augustus Fleming, 13 October 1851, HL.

26. Pliny Earle to Dix, 22 November 1851, HL. An intellectual and theorist who was working on his survey, *Institutions for the Insane in Prussia, Austria and Germany* (1853), Earle never warmed to Dix's political style. In old age he acknowledged the importance of her "campaigning for the neglected insane from State to State and from country to country," but lamented that the institutions she started quickly turned into "centres [*sic*] of intellectual indolence or of semi-political intrigue" (*Memoirs of Pliny Earle, M.D.*, ed. Franklin Benjamin Sanborn [Boston: Damrell & Upham, 1898], 306).

27. Dix, "Memorial to the Governors of the New York City Hospital," [1851], Miscellaneous MS, HL; "Report of the Governors of the New York City Hospital," [1851], Miscellaneous MS, HL.

28. D. S. Kennedy to Dix, 15 December 1851; James Donaldson to Dix, 26 December 1851; Stephen Allen to Dix, 5 November 1851; Allen to the New York Board of Governors of the New York State Hospital, n.d. [December 1851]; James G. King to Dix, 26 December 1851, HL.

29. Nichols to Kirkbride, 11 November 1851, Kirkbride MS, IPH; Nichols to Dix, 27 November 1851; Lydia H. Prime to Dix, 29 October 1851; Dix to George T. Trimble, 2 December [1851]; Nichols to Dix 7 and 23 February 1852, HL. Nichols agreed to stay on at Bloomingdale for six months, until his successor was in place.

30. Buttolph to Kirkbride, 3 October 1853, Kirkbride MSS, IPH.

31. Robert Hare to Dix, 28 August [1853?], HL.

32. Luther Bell to Dix, 29 December 1848, HL. Bell's remarks appear to have been aimed at the Massachusetts abolitionist movement.

33. "I trust you will be entirely successful in your efforts, Kirkbride wrote when he sent her a packet of asylum reports. "*Three million* [acres] for such objects would do something

to redeem the Country from the lasting disgrace which our last *hundred* of millions must indelibly fix upon us" (Kirkbride to Dix, 22 June 1848, Kirkbride MSS, IPH).

34. Luther Bell to G. Peters [Newfoundland], 18 August 1849, HL.

Chapter 9: Conquest of the South

1. Dix to Harriet Hare, 22 December 1845, HL.

2. Ibid., 3.

3. Kentucky Eastern Lunatic Asylum, *Annual Report* (1844), 19–21, quoted in Grob: *Social Policy to 1875* (New York: Free Press, 1975). *Mental Institutions in America*, 344. The substandard conditions in eastern Kentucky were well known. See, for example, [Edward Jarvis], "Insanity in Kentucky," *Boston Medical and Surgical Journal* 24 (21 April 1841): 166–68.

4. D[orothea] L[ynde] Dix, *Memorial Soliciting an Appropriation for the State Hospital for the Insane at Lexington; and also Urging the Necessity for Establishing a New Hospital in the Green River Country* (Frankfort, Ky.: A. G. Hodges, 1846), 5–7.

5. Ibid., 6–15.

6. Ibid., 5, 22–23.

7. Dix to Harriet Hare, 22 December 1845, HL.

8. *Louisville Journal*, 24 December 1845 and 12 January 1846.

9. George Howe, the warden of the Frankfort prison, continued to press Dix to return to Kentucky and convince the legislature to pay for improving his facility. But he had scant success, and on the eve of the Civil War little had changed. See Howe to Dix, 2 October and 28 November 1846, HL; also see William C. Sneed, *A Report on the History and Mode of Management of the Kentucky Penitentiary* (Frankfort, Ky.: A. G. Hodges, 1860).

10. Dix to Charles Nichols, 8 March 1859 [typescript]; Dix to [unknown], 8 April 1846, HL; Lieber to Dix, 24 April and 27 May 1851, Lieber MSS, Huntington Library; Frank Freidel, *Francis Lieber: Nineteenth–Century Liberal* (Baton Rouge: Louisiana State University Press, 1947), 259–61. Dix's favorable impression of the South Carolina State Hospital was not shared by others in the state. See Daniel H. Trezevant, *Letters to His Excellency Governor Manning on the Lunatic Hospital* (Columbia, S.C.: R. W. Gibbes, 1854).

11. Dix to Harriet Hare, 14 March 1846, HL.

12. Dix to George Walker Crawford, 27 March [1846], HL.

13. Kenneth Stampp, *The Peculiar Institution: Slavery in the Antebellum South* (New York: Knopf, 1956), 240; Mark T. Carleton, *Politics and Punishment: The History of the Louisiana State Penal System* (Baton Rouge: Louisiana State University Press, 1971), 5.

14. Eugene D. Genovese, *The Political Economy of Slavery* (New York: Vintage, 1967), 3ff; Christopher R. Adamson, "Hard Labor: The Form and Function of Imprisonment in Nineteenth–Century America" (Ph.D. diss., Princeton University, 1982), 148–54. An illuminating discussion of the larger political framework for Southern institutions is J. Mills Thorton III, *Politics and Power in a Slave Society: Alabama, 1800–1860* (Baton Rouge: Louisiana State University Press, 1978).

15. On the forming of the Tennessee Hospital and the battle for its improvement, see E.

Bruce Thompson, "Reforms in the Care of the Insane in Tennessee, 1830–1850," *Tennessee Historical Quarterly* 3 (December 1944): 319–34.

16. Dix, Tennessee *Memorial*, 6–10.

17. Ibid., 29–32.

18. Ibid., 32.

19. Miscellaneous MS Am. 1838 (960), HL.

20. Dix to Harriet Hare, 1 December 1847, HL.

21. Harriet Campbell to Dix, 26 January 1848; Dix to Mrs. Wheat, 29 January 1848, HL.

22. "Resolution of Thanks from the Tennessee State Legislature," 9 February 1848, HL; Miscellaneous MS Am 1838 (960), HL.

23. Dix to Sarah Joseph Hale, 1 and 17 January 1851, HL.

24. Dix to Heath, 21 January [1851], HL. Hale has traditionally been pictured as a conservative proponent of woman's sphere. The most recent student of *Woman's Record* argues, however, that in reporting the achievements of women, Hale "inadvertently" demolished "the very boundaries between the male political and material sphere and the female spiritual and moral sphere on which her argument has depended," and that, as a result, "Hale cannot ultimately avoid becoming conventionally political" (Nina Baym, "Onward Christian Women: Sarah J. Hale's History of the World," *New England Quarterly* 63 [June 1990]: 261–62).

25. Thomas Jefferson Lee to Nathaniel Ingersoll Bowditch, March 1851; Dix to Lee, March [1851]; Dix to Marcus Morton, 22 May [1851], HL.

26. Dix to Harriet Hare, 27 November 1848, HL.

27. [Dorothea Lynde Dix], *Memorial Soliciting a State Hospital for the Protection and Cure of the Insane, Submitted to the General Assembly of North Carolina. November, 1848* (Raleigh: Seaton Gales, 1848), 3.

28. Ibid., 7–8.

29. Ibid., 11, 30.

30. Ibid., 31.

31. Ibid., 45–47. Responding to the document's powerful rhetoric, Luther Bell suggested that it was Dix's finest work. See Bell to Dix, 29 December 1848, HL.

32. Dix to Harriet Hare, 27 November 1848, HL; *Greensboro Patriot*, 2 December 1848.

33. Dix to Joseph Dix [brother], 15 December [1848]; William Alexander Graham to Dix, 12 December 1848, HL. That Dix was misidentified as from New York City, a place she never lived, suggests that she was at pains to deny any association with Massachusetts, the bastion of antislavery. The political context of the asylum debate is explored in Margaret C. McCulloch, "Founding the North Carolina Asylum for the Insane," *North Carolina Historical Review* 13 (July 1936): 185–201; "A Bill to Provide for Establishment of a Hospital for Insane in North Carolina" (Raleigh: North Carolina Department of History, 1848).

34. The source of this story was a letter from the superintendent of the North Carolina asylum in Raleigh written many years after the events it purported to describe. See Eugene Grissom to Francis Tiffany, [n.d.], quoted in Francis Tiffany, *Charles Francis Bernard, His Life and Work* (Boston: Houghton Mifflin, 1895), 108–9. The high point of Dobbin's career as a public speaker was the 1852 Democratic convention, in which

his fiery speech on behalf of North Carolina "started a snowball effect for Pierce" on the forty–ninth ballot (Larry Gara, *The Presidency of Franklin Pierce* [Lawrence: University Press of Kansas, 1991], 34).

35. In light of the political and economic circumstances in North Carolina, Dix considered the bill an important victory. See Dix to William Alexander Randall, 30 December 1848, HL, and Clark R. Cahow, "The History of the North Carolina Mental Hospitals, 1848–1960" (Ph.D. diss., Duke University, 1967). But the legislature continued to squabble over selecting a site after she left the state. See S. F. Patterson to Dix, 13 and 20 January 1849, HL.

36. Dix to William A. Graham, 30 December 1848, Legislative Papers, North Carolina State Archives, Raleigh, North Carolina.

37. Dix to Harriet Hare, December 1848; Dix to Elizabeth Rathbone, 1 June 1850, HL.

38. Dix to Millard Fillmore, 8 April 1851, *Dix-Fillmore Letters*, in Charles M. Snyder, ed., *The Lady and the President: The Letters of Dorothea Dix and Millard Fillmore* (Lexington: University, of Kentucky Press, 1975). 112.

39. For an illuminating description of the vicissitudes of travel in the antebellum South, see William W. Freehling, *The Road to Disunion: Volume I: Secessionists at Bay, 1776–1854* (New York: Oxford University Press, 1990), 25–38, esp. 26; Dix to Harriet Hare, 15 November 1849 and 22 December 1845, HL.

40. Dix to Kirkbride, 6 March 1848, Kirkbride Papers, IPH; Dix to Richard Lee Fearn, March 1848, in *Mobile Register and Journal*, n.d. [March 1848]; Grob, *Mental Institutions in America*, 364–65; Elizabeth Wisner, *Public Welfare Administration in Louisiana* (Chicago: University of Chicago Press, 1930), 80ff. The inadequacies of the Jackson asylum drove the New Orleans City Council to build a receptacle for the indigent insane on the city jail grounds. Although this hastily built structure was little more than "a lock–up, calaboose or man–kennel," according to one critic, Dix chose to overlook it, perhaps sensing that to criticize it would jeopardize her support in Washington from the Louisiana congressional delegation (Stanford Chaillé, *A Memoir of the Insane Asylum of the State of Louisiana, at Jackson* [New Orleans: n.p., 1858], 11–12, quoted in Grob, *Mental Institutions in America*, 365).

41. *Mobile Register and Journal*, n.d. [March 1848].

42. [Dorothea Lynde Dix], *Memorial Soliciting a State Hospital for the Insane, Submitted to the Legislature of Alabama, November 15, 1849* (Montgomery: Advertiser and State Gazette, 1849); "Benefits of Mild and Remedial Care for the Insane," *Montgomery Advertiser and State Gazette*, October, 1849; Dix to Harriet Hare, 15 November 1849; Dix to Horace Mann, 22 November [1848], HL.

43. Montgomery *Alabama Journal*, 14 December 1849.

44. Dix to Heath, 15 January 1850; Dix to Harriet Hare, 17 January 1850, HL.

45. Dix to Kirkbride, 26 March [1850], Kirkbride Papers, IPH.

46. A. Lopez to Edward Jarvis, 19 September 1859, Jarvis MSS, Countway Medical Library, Harvard Medical School; *An Appeal to the Legislature of Alabama, for the Establishment of a State Hospital for Lunatics and Idiots, Prepared by Order of the Alabama State Medical Association: Mobile, November, 1851* (Mobile: Dade, Thompson, 1851). See also James S. Tarwater, *The Alabama State Hospitals and the Parlow State School and Hospital: A Brief History* (New York: Newcomen Society, 1964).

47. Dix to Heath, 25 November [1849], HL.

48. *Jacksonville Daily Journal*, 8 May 1886.

49. *Memorial Soliciting Adequate Appropriations for the Construction of a State Hospital for the Insane in the State of Mississippi. February, 1850* (Jackson: Fall & Marshall, 1850), 5. The state lunacy commissioners, who had been selected to oversee the project, immediately recognized the value Dix brought to their underfunded task. See *Report of the Commissioners of the Lunatic Asylum, to His Excellency Joseph W. Matthews, January 1, 1850* (Jackson, 1850).

50. Dix to Heath, 25 November [1849], HL.

51. Ibid., 6–13, 20–21.

52. Dix to Harriet Hare, 15 March 1850; Dix to Heath, 16 March 1850 and n.d. [1850], HL.

53. *Memorial on the Use of Tobacco*, n.p. (January 7, 1850), 1. Dix's theories about tobacco were widely shared within the medical community. See, for example, Joel Shew, *Tobacco: Its History, Nature, and Effects on the Body and Mind . . .* (New York: Fowler and Well, [1849]).

54. Dix, *Memorial on the Use of Tobacco*, 6.

55. Dix to Kirkbride, 19 March [1851], Kirkbride MSS, IPH; Dix to R. S. Stewart, 24 November 1851, HL; Dix to Mann, 12 March [1851], Mann MSS, MH.

56. Ibid., 10, 19.

57. *Memorial Of Miss D. L. Dix, To The Honorable The General Assembly In Behalf Of The Insane Of Maryland*, Maryland Senate Document C (25 February 1852), 4–5, 8–9. Prominently as immigration figured in Dix's perception of social disorder, Maryland's experience was typical. Five years later, at Dix's request, John Curwen, superintendent of the new Pennsylvania asylum at Harrisburg, tallied his patients and found that out of 247 inmates, only 37 were foreigners. And these immigrants, he added, were predominantly "Irish, German, Welsh & English" (Curwen to Dix, 4 May 1857, HL).

58. Ibid., 14–17.

59. Thomas Wyse to R. S. Stewart, 19 February 1852, HL; Dix, Maryland *Memorial*, 18.

60. Dix to William E. Hacker, 27 May [1852]; R. S. Stewart to Dix, 22 June and 6 July 1852, HL. Stewart, the politically naive leader of the asylum project, felt that Dix had put him in a bind by asking for $100,000 when she must have known that it would ultimately cost twice that much. By the spring of 1853, however, under Dix's guidance, he was discovering that he could probably milk $200,000 from the state as long as he did not ask for too much at any one time. See R. S. Stewart to Dix, 4 October and 2 December 1852, 28 January and 3 March 1853, HL. Two years after the initial bill had passed, Dix was still being called on to lobby the governor and the legislature. See Thomas Donaldson to Dix, 8 and 24 January 1854, HL. Seesaw changes in political support for the asylum continued long after the Civil War according to the official *Report on the Public Charities, Reformatories, Prisons and Almshouses, of the State of Maryland, by C. W. Chancellor, M. D., Secretary of the State Board of Health, Made to His Excellency, John Lee Carroll, Governor, July, 1877* (Frederick, Md.: Baughman, 1877).

Chapter 10: Slavery and the Limits of a Moral Vision

1. Dix to Emerson, 14 March 1846, Chamberlain MSS, BPL; Dix to Heath, 31 March 1845 and Dix to Harriet Hare, 14 March 1846, HL. An interesting commentary of

the attitudes of Northern intellectuals with respect to Southern culture is Howard R. Floan, *The South in Northern Eyes, 1831 to 1861* (Austin: University of Texas Press, 1958). Northern "men of letters, for the most part, did not know the South," Floan wrote. As a consequence, "their attitudes toward the South were in reality attitudes toward slavery. . . . Since benevolent slavery seemed to these writers a contradiction in terms, their eyes could see only the abuses of slavery, and the totality of these extreme instances in turn was, for them, the South" (185).

2. This, of course, is the main theme of David Rothman, *Discovery of the Asylum* David Rothman, *The Discovery of the Asylum: Social order and Disorder in the New Republic,* rev. ed. (Boston: Little, Brown, 1990).

3. Dix to Heath, 8 December 1859, HL.

4. Jackson *Weekly Southron*, 15 March 1850.

5. The broadening of the franchise in the South during the Age of Jackson had surprisingly little impact on the traditional structure of politics and society. See Fletcher M. Green, "Democracy in the Old South," *Journal of Southern History* 12 (February 1946): 3–23, and Michael Wayne, "An Old South Morality Play: Reconsidering the Social Underpinnings of the Proslavery Ideology," *Journal of American History* 77 (December 1990): 838–63.

6. An 1833 statue barred the importation of slaves into Kentucky "except for emigrants by their own use," a law that served gradually to decrease the state's black population. See William W. Freehling, *The Road to Disunion*, vol. 1, *Secessionists at Bay, 1776–1854* (New York: Oxford University Press, 1990), 462–69.

7. D[orothea] L[ynde] Dix, *A Review of the Present Condition of the State Penitentiary of Kentucky . . .* (Frankfort, Ky.: A. G. Hodges, 1846), 5. From the perspective of Northern reform, Dix's vague gradualism—what David Brion Davis has called "the sense of reliance on indirect and slow–working means to achieve a desired social objective"—was closer to the spirit of the British abolitionists of the 1820s than to the increasing immediatism of American antislavery in the 1840s. See Davis, "The Emergence of Immediatism in British and American Antislavery Thought," *Mississippi Valley Historical Review* 49 (September 1962): 209–30. From the perspective of the Kentucky legislature, however, her views were quite reasonable and familiar. "The unerring wisdom of the Eternal Legislator," wrote Kentucky's George W. Johnson, would eventually phase out slavery "without danger, crime, or disturbance of society, by the easy, gradual, and unseen, but imperative action of the law of nature" (*Frankfort Yeoman*, 30 November 1848, quoted in Freehling, *Road to Disunion*, 469).

8. Dix to Heath, 18 February 1850 and 2 April [1847], HL. The apparent self–righteousness and self–promotion of the abolitionists—epitomized in Garrison's cry, "I will be heard"—irked Dix, for whom arrogance was the cardinal sin.

9. Dix to Fillmore, 23 March and 8 April [1851], *Dix-Fillmore Letters*, Charles M. Snyder, *The Lady and the President: The Letters of Dorothea Dix and Millard Fillmore* (Lexington: University of Kentucky Press, 1975) 104–8.

10. Dix to William E. Hacker, 26 April 1851, Hacker MSS, New York Public Library. Dix shared her hosts' fear of potential slave insurrections—an apprehension that had been growing steadily in the South since the Nat Turner rebellion in 1831. Panics like the one she described were usually unfounded, though hardly uncommon. See Ken-

neth Stampp, *The Peculiar Institution: Slavery in the Antebellum South* (New York: Knopf, 1956), 136–38.

11. Francis Parkman to Charles Eliot Norton, 10 November 1850, quoted in George M. Fredrickson, *The Inner Civil War: Northern Intellectuals and the Crisis of the Union* (New York: Harper and Row, 1965), 34. Lincoln's remark is quoted in James M. McPherson, *The Battle Cry of Freedom: The Civil War Era* (New York: Oxford University Press, 1988), 55. On the moral balancing acts of Northern politicians during the antebellum period, see David M. Potter, *The Impending Crisis, 1848–1861*, ed. Don E. Fehrenbacher (New York: Harper and Row, 1976), esp. 44–50, and Peter F. Walker, *Moral Choices: Memory, Desire, and Imagination in Nineteenth-Century American Abolition* (Baton Rouge: Louisiana State University Press, 1978).

12. Dix to Millard Fillmore, 11 March [1857] and 9 February 1859, *Dix-Fillmore Letters*, 279, 313.

13. Dix to Emerson, 14 March 1846, Chamberlain MSS, BPL; Jackson *Weekly Southron*, 15 March 1850; Francis Lieber to Dix, 17 June and 5 November 1846, HL.

14. Harold Schwartz, *Samuel Gridley Howe: Social Reformer, 1801–1876* (Cambridge, Mass.: Harvard University Press, 1956), 177.

15. Mann's rhetoric recalled the fervid style of his writings on lunacy reform. Black slaves, he declared, were confined in "horrid and black receptacles where human beings are penned like cattle" ("Speech Delivered in the House of Representatives of the United States, February 23, 1849," quoted in Jonathan Messerli, *Horace Mann: A Biography* [New York: Knopf, 1972], 497). Mann and many of his fellow Whigs felt freer to speak their minds after the elections of 1846 and 1847, in which their party won control of the House. Still, Whiggery was a political ideology of moderation. As James M. McPherson wrote, "While the Democratic notion of progress envisioned the spread of existing institutions over *space*, the Whig idea envisaged the improvement of those institutions over *time*" (*Battle Cry of Freedom*, 49). Also see Daniel Walker Howe, *The Political Culture of the American Whigs* (Chicago: University of Chicago Press, 1979).

16. Dix, Pennsylvania *Memorial*, 5; Kentucky *Memorial*, 13; Pennsylvania *Memorial*, 3.

17. Dix to Millard Fillmore, 26 December 1854, *Dix-Fillmore Letters*, 228.

18. Dix to Joseph Dix [brother], 21 September 1848, HL; Dix to Fillmore, 15 February [1854], *Dix-Fillmore Letters*, 180.

19. D[orothea] L[ynde] Dix, *Memorial Soliciting Enlarged and Improved Accommodations for the Insane of the State of Tennessee, by the Establishment of a New Hospital* (Nashville: B. R. McKennie, 1847), 5. Dix continued to promulgate the view that insanity was far more widespread in the North than in the South, provoking Millard Fillmore to tell her that he doubted her statistics (Fillmore to Dix, 20 October 1850, *Dix-Fillmore Letters*, 95). The theory that mental illness was a by-product of higher civilization was widely shared on both sides of the Atlantic. Antebellum Southern asylum superintendents had nonetheless to contend with significant numbers of black lunatics—slave and free—whom they generally accommodated in segregated facilities. See Gerald Grob, *Mental Institutions in America: Social Policy to 1875* (New York: Free Press, 1973). *Mental Institutions in America*, 243–55, and Norman Dain, *Disordered Minds: The First Century of Eastern State Hospital in Williamsburg, Virginia, 1766–1866* (Williamsburg, Va.: Colonial Williamsburg Foundation, 1971), 105–27.

20. With evident approval, Dix sent David Tilden Brown, a Pennsylvania physician who later headed the Bloomingdale asylum, a copy of a stinging indictment of the failure of West Indian emancipation written by her friend Tennessee Senator John Bell. See D[avid] T[ilden] Brown to Dix, 27 November 1850, HL. This point of view was far from uncommon. According to David Brion Davis, "by the early 1840s [many] political and religious leaders had reached [the conclusion that] Britain had acted too hastily; black emancipation, though inevitable in the long run, required more time" (*Slavery and Human Progress* [New York: Oxford University Press, 1984], 224–26).

21. Dix to Thomas Story Kirkbride, 26 March [1848], Kirkbride Papers, IPH.

22. Dix duly noted blacks when she found them in prisons and almshouses, but she did not go as far as the Pennsylvania Prison Society, which inaccurately claimed that while blacks made up just 4 percent of the state population, they represented 40 percent of its prisoners. The whole spectrum of Southern racial assumptions and social justifications for slavery are well summarized in Drew Gilpin Faust, ed., *The Ideology of Slavery: Proslavery Thought in the Antebellum South, 1830–1860* (Baton Rouge: Louisiana State University Press, 1981). These arguments and images are placed in broader historical perspective in George M. Fredrickson, *The Black Image in the White Mind: The Debate on Afro–American Character and Destiny, 1817–1914* (New York: Oxford University Press, 1971). Larry E. Tise convincingly argues that racial assumptions like Dix's were commonplace in all regions of Jacksonian America, creating the basis for both Southern proslavery ideology and Northern resistance to abolitionism. See his *Proslavery: A History of the Defense of Slavery in America, 1701–1840* (Athens: University of Georgia Press, 1978).

23. Quoted in Andrew Delbanco, "Sentimental Education," *The New Republic* (18 April 1994): 42.

Chapter 11: "I bask in court favor"

1. Dix to Harriet Hare, 23 May 1847, HL.

2. Federal *Memorial* (1848), 32. For a discussion of social legislation in antebellum America, see Theda Skocpol, *Protecting Soldiers and Mothers: The Political Origins of Social Policy in the United States* (Cambridge, Mass.: Harvard University Press, 1992), 67–101.

3. On the gradual shift in early-Victorian Britain from a system of private madhouses to a "a network of publicly financed and state–run asylums," see Andrew Scull, *The Most Solitary of Afflictions: Madness and Society in Britain, 1700–1900* (New Haven: Yale University Press, 1993).and William Ll. Parry–Jones, *The Trade in Lunacy: A Study of Private Madhouses in England in the Eighteenth and Nineteenth Centuries* (London: Routledge & Kegan Paul, 1972), 29–127.

4. Dix to Harriet Hare, 27 May 1847, HL; Margaret Bayard Smith, *The First Forty Years of Washington Society* (New York: 1906), 310.

5. Dix to Harriet Hare, 23 May 1847, HL.

6. Dix to Mrs. Smith, 10 August 1847, Pennsylvania Historical Society Manuscript Collections.

7. Dix to Heath, 24 July 1847; Heath to Dix, 13 August 1847.

8. Laura Dewey Bridgman to Dix, 16 July 1847, HL; Dix to Mrs. Smith, 10 August

1847, Pennsylvania Historical Society Manuscript Collections; Dix to Mann, 1 July [1848], HL. Bridgman, who from childhood lived within the confines of the Perkins Institution, seemed to prove that a class of people long thought to be imbeciles "needed only an education to be brought within the circle of society" (Harold Schwartz, *Samuel Gridley Howe: Social Reformer, 1801–1876* [Cambridge, Mass.: Harvard University Press, 1956], 71).

9. Dix to Harriet Hare, 5 June 1847; Dix to Joseph Dix, 5 June 1848, HL. The incident or rumor about Clay to which Dix referred is not known. Although Clay was seventy–one years old at the time, age seemed not to slow his tendency to flirt with young women. Two years later, in 1850, he carried on a well–publicized flirtation with "Grace Greenwood, a vivacious and attractive young abolitionist" (Clement Eaton, *Henry Clay and the Art of American Politics* [Boston: Little, Brown, 1957], 158–60).

10. Dix to Heath, 7 January 1848, HL.

11. Dix to Kirkbride, 3 and 21 June 1848, Kirkbride MSS, IPH.

12. Luther Bell to Dix, 5 June 1848, HL. Bell's disgust with the 1840 census was widely shared by Northerners, who suspected that its finding of rampant lunacy among free blacks was nothing more than a thinly veiled argument for slavery. In July, Dix was trying to locate a copy of Edward Jarvis's "pamphlet upon the inaccuracies of the census of 1840" (see Dix to Horace Mann, 1 July [1848], and Samuel Gridley Howe to Dix, 10 July [1848], HL). The debate about the census is detailed in Gerald N. Grob, *Insanity and Idiocy in Massachusetts: Report of the Commission on Lunacy, 1855 by Edward Jarvis* (Cambridge, Mass.: Harvard University Press, 1971), 44ff., and Albert Deutsch, "The First U.S. Census of the Insane (1840) and Its Use as Pro–Slavery Propaganda," *Bulletin of the History of Medicine* 15 (May 1944): 469–82. Dix, Congressional *Memorial* (1848), 5. By August, Dix had realized her error and arranged to reprint the *Memorial* at her own expense. See Dix to Horace Mann, 12 August 1848, HL.

13. Dix to Harriet Hare, 5 May 1848, HL.

14. Dix's phrase "toiling millions" has in this context a distinct English inflection. Congressional *Memorial*, 1–3. An effort to place Dix's ideas about the causes of insanity in the broader context of contemporary asylum physicians' theories is to be found in Norman Dain, *Concepts of Insanity in the United States, 1789–1865* (New Brunswick: Rutgers University Press, 1964), 165–82.

15. Sir Andrew Halliday, *A Letter to Lord Robert Seymour: with a Report on the Number of Lunatics and Idiots in England and Wales* (London: Underwood, 1829); Dix, Federal *Memorial* (1848), 27. For an account of Britain's "rising numbers of madmen," see Scull, *Museums of Madness*, 222–33. Scull argues that the explanation for insanity increasing faster than the population throughout-nineteenth century Britain lay in the "social production" of insanity, which was aggressively fostered by the professional aspirations of the "entrepreneurial" psychiatric profession. "The general relationship between the construction of asylums and the increase in insanity," he writes, "again suggests that on the whole it was the existence and expansion of the asylum system which created the increased demand for its own services, rather than the other way around" (p. 245). The medical diagnosis of insanity, according to this theory, was progressively enlarged to keep pace with the increasing capacity of the British asylum system.

16. Dix, Federal *Memorial* (1848), 8, 9, 15, 27.

17. Ibid, 31–32.

18. Ben Perley Poore, *Reminiscences of Sixty Years in the National Metropolis*, 2 vols. (Philadelphia:Hubbard Bros., 1886), I:369; United States Senate Commission on Art, *The Senate Chamber, 1810–1859* (Washington, D.C.: U.S. Government Printing Office, 1990), 6–11.

19. As the sponsor of the Log Cabin bill—a measure that in 1841 instituted a policy of preemption of farms of 160 acres of government land at a minimum price of $1.25 an acre—Benton was a logical choice to lead the fight for Dix's land grant bill. The moment he weighed the proposed bill's implication of expanded federal powers, however, Benton probably decided that openly supporting it could become a political liability with his Missouri constituents.

20. Dix to Harriet Hare, 5 May 1848, HL.

21. United States Senate, "A Bill Making a grant of public lands to the several States of the Union for certain purposes," Senate S. 328, 21 July 1848; Dix to Harriet Hare, 21 July 1848, HL.

22. Dix to Harriet Hare, 21 July 1848, HL.

23. Allan Nevins, *Ordeal of the Union*, 2 vols. (New York: Scribner's, 1947), I:402; Dix to Harriet Hare, 31 July 1848, HL.

24. Horace Mann to Mary Peabody Mann, 21 February 1849, Mann MSS, MHS. Dix to Heath, 24 January 1849, HL.

25. Dix to Mrs. L. A. Smith, 5 July 1848, Miscellaneous MSS, Pennsylvania Historical Society.

26. C. P. Sengstack to Dix, 16 January 1849; H. Campbell to Dix, 15 January 1849, HL. As usual, Dix scoffed at "those who will vote negatively" against the bill "on constitutional grounds, imaginarily involving the federal integrity" (Dix to Joseph Dix [brother], 30 January 1849, HL).

27. Dix to Joseph Dix [brother], n.d. [February 1849] and 23 February 1849, HL.

28. Dix to Mann, 27 March 1849, Mann MSS, MHS.

29. Heath to Dix, 15 January 1849; Dix to Joseph Dix, 17 June 1849, HL.

30. Charles Sumner to Dix, 6 July 1848, HL. Sumner's words must have had special resonance for Dix, not least because he was so like her in his relentless drive to force politics to conform to moral principle. Sumner's law partner and friend, George Hillard, observed that "his mind and character require the stimulus of something outward and exoteric [sic], some strong pressure, to take him out of himself and prevent him from a morbid habit of inactive brooding. He is a man of moral enthusiasm; made to identify himself with some great Cause and accept and surrender himself to it unconditionally" (Hillard to Francis Lieber, 28 March 1849, quoted in David Donald, *Charles Sumner and the Coming of the Civil War* [New York: Knopf, 1960], 176).

31. Howe to Dix, 15 June 1849, HL.

32. John Adams Dix to Dix, 1 May 1849, HL.

33. John Adams Dix to Dix, 6 July 1849 and 16 July 1851, HL.

34. Dix to Mann, 22 November [1849], HL; Horace Mann to Dix, 18 and 15 December 1849, and Dix to Mann, 24 December 1849, Mann MSS, MHS. In 1850 Mann broke with Webster over antislavery and was ousted from the Whig party.

35. Mann to Dix, 28 January and 14 May 1850, HL.

36. Dix to Heath, 25 May 1850, HL; Dix to Mann, n.d. [May 1850], Mann MSS, MHS.

37. Dix to Mann, n.d. [1850], Mann MSS, HL.

38. United States House of Representative, "A Bill Making a grant of public lands to the several States of the Union for the relief and support of indigent insane persons," HR 383, 8 August 1850; Dix to Mann, 3 letters, n.d. [1850], Mann MSS, HL. Dix's alternative measure, which is no longer extant, probably scaled down the total acreage set forth in the bill from ten million acres to some lower figure.

39. Horace Mann to Mary Peabody Mann, 16 August 1850, Mann MSS, MHS.

40. Mann to Mary Peabody Mann, 21 May 1850, Mann MSS, MHS.

41. Mann to Mary Peabody Mann, 16 September 1850, Mann MSS, MHS. Ordinarily Mann did not succumb to such empty rhetoric. A few days earlier he had written a good one—sentence summary of Dix's practical work: "Only to think of her going around first to establish Hospitals, then to take care of them, and to fill them and then to enrich them with libraries and apparatus and beautify them with embellishments" (Mann to Mary Peabody Mann, 12 September 1850, Mann MSS, MHS).

42. Dix to [Elizabeth] Rathbone, 9 June 1850, HL.

43. Dix had kept up her long-standing interest in botany, taking advantage of her travels to collect and preserve examples of American flora that she sent to her far-flung scientific correspondents. Her friendship with Henry began in 1848, while he was still a professor at Princeton, when she sent him a box of specimens. See Joseph Henry to Dix, 19 October 1848, 10 May and 15 November 1850, HL; Dix to William E. Hacker, 24 May 1850, Hacker MSS, New York Public Library. Later Henry tended to treat Dix as an equal, especially when he spoke of the politics of the Smithsonian, a topic he assumed she would appreciate. See, for example, Henry to Dix, 6 August 1858, HL.

44. Dix to Mann, n.d. [May 1850], Mann MSS, MHS.

45. Dix to Heath, 16 July 1850, HL.

46. Dix to Mann, 4 June, n.d. [June?], 28 July and 5 July 1850, Mann MSS, MHS. Overcoming some embarrassment for breaking a promise to Howe, Dix decided not to submit a separate "Memorial for the Blind and the Deaf and Dumb." Rather than approach Congress twice, she told Mann, she could combine their needs with those of the insane. In the end, though, pressure from the House of Representatives forced her to add 2,225,000 acres for the deaf, dumb, and blind to her 10,000,000 acre measure.

47. [Amariah Brigham], "Memorial of D. L. Dix . . . ," *American Journal of Insanity* 5 (January 1849): 286–87.

48. Dix to Kirkbride, 7 June 1850 and 19 March [1851]; Kirkbride to Dix, 8 July 1850, Kirkbride MSS, IPH; Dix to Horace Mann, n.d. [1850], Mann MSS, MHS. Most of the superintendents continued to support Dix from the sidelines. Kirkbride typically expressed "full confidence your bill will pass, and nothing but the supreme selfishness of politicians . . . keeps Congress from doing some good acts which would tend to redeem them in the estimation of the people" (Kirkbride to Dix, 30 July 1850, Kirkbride MSS, IPH).

49. Dix to Mann, [September] 1850, Mann MSS, MHS.

50. Dix to Heath, 27 October [1850], HL; Dix to Mann, 30 November 1850, Mann MSS, MHS.

51. Dix to Fillmore, [30] and [31] August 1850, *Dix-Fillmore Letters*, 85–86.

52. "I hold myself subject to a close rule of never receiving gifts. You will own the propriety of this I am sure" (Dix to Mann, n.d. [June? 1850], Mann MSS, MHS). "I am gratified to perceive that you cherish so highly the little paper folder," Fillmore wrote, apologizing for neglecting to send the bouquet he had meant to give her when she visited the White House (Fillmore to Dix, 20 October 1850, *Dix-Fillmore Letters*, 95). See also Dix to Fillmore, 14 September 1850; Fillmore to Dix, 22 September 1850, ibid., 88–90.

53. Fillmore to Fish, 9 September 1850, quoted in Elbert B. Smith, *The Presidencies of Zachary Taylor & Millard Fillmore* (Lawrence: University Press of Kansas, 1988), 195.

54. Fillmore to Dix, 27 September 1850, *Dix-Fillmore Letters*, 91–92.

55. Fillmore to Dix, 7 October, 29 and 31 December 1850, *Dix-Fillmore Letters*, 93–94.

56. Dix knew Peale from her early visits to Philadelphia. See Dix to Fillmore, [6 March 1850?], *Dix-Fillmore Letters*, 100; Dix to Heath, 21 January [1851], HL; Smith, *Zachary Taylor & Millard Fillmore*, 198.

57. Dix to Heath, 21 January [1851], HL.

58. Dix to Heath, 5 and 29 August [1850], HL.

59. Dix to Fillmore, n.d. [January? 1851), *Dix-Fillmore Letters*, 97. The land bill passed by a vote of thirty–six to sixteen. See Cong. Globe, 31 Cong., I Sess., 1290; Dix to Heath, 11 February 1851.

60. Dix to Harriet Hare, 26 February [1851]; Dix to Heath, 6 and 9 March [1851], HL; Dix to Fillmore, [7 March 1851], *Dix-Fillmore Letter*, 101–2.

Chapter 12: "The poor weak president has . . . lacerated my life"

1. [Dorothea L. Dix], "Memorial to the Honorable the Legislative Assembly of the Province of Nova Scotia and Its Dependencies," Appendix of Journals of House of Assembly, No. 18 (1850).

2. Ibid., 4, 16.

3. Dix to Harriet Hare, 15 November 1849; Dix to Horace Mann, 8 December [1849], Mann MSS, MHS; Henry Bell to Dix, 19 February, 3 April, 4 July 1850; [Dorothea Lynde Dix], "Memorial to the Honorable the Legislative Assembly of the Province of Nova Scotia and Its Dependencies. Appendix of Journals of House of Assembly, No. 18 (Nova Scotia, 1850), in Henry M. Hurd, ed., *The Institutional Care of the Insane in the United States and Canada*, 4 vols. (Baltimore: Johns Hopkins University Press, 1916), I:482–97.

4. Dix to Elizabeth Rathbone, 21 July 1853, HL.

5. Dix to Miss Greene, 17 June [1853]; Bell to Dix, 5 July and 13 April 1853, HL.

6. Henry H. Stabb to Dix, 4 July 1853, HL. Stabb waited to hold off distributing the books to his patients until he could look through them, he explained, as he had "various creeds professed amongst the Patients and [found] it necessary to be very careful to avoid offence being unwittingly offered to their relatives or clergymen."

7. Dix to Elizabeth Rathbone, 21 July 1853, HL.

8. Dix to *New York Journal of Commerce*, 14 February 1854, HL. Dix apparently wrote this letter to put to rest more fanciful accounts of the incident. In one version, the ship was abandoned by everyone but its captain, who had been transformed into a "raving

maniac" and refused to enter the lifeboat. Dix "rode to the Beach on horse-back," beseeched the sailors to return to the ship, tie up their crazed captain, and bring him to safety. When he was brought to the beach, "bound hand and foot," Dix supposedly "loosened the cords and took him by the arm, and led him to a Boat House built for the ship-wrecked and by kind words calmed his mind and persuaded him to thank the sailors for saving his life" (E. Merriam to [unknown], 10 October 1853, HL).

9. Ibid.; John Adams Dix to Dix, 29 August 1853, HL.

10. Dix to Bell, 4 August 1853 and n.d. [1853], HL. After several mishaps, including the sinking of the brig on which they were originally shipped to Halifax, the Sable Island lifeboats were installed in October 1854. In December, they were credited with saving 180 lives when a passenger ship ran aground. See Bell to Dix, 16 January, 26 October, and 7 December 1854; Bell to Joseph Francis, 12 May and 2 December 1854, HL; *Halifax Advertiser*, 19 December 1854.

11. Hurd, *Institutional Care of the Insane*, IV:113–14.

12. Nichols to Dix, 23 February, 18 March, and 4 May 1852, HL. Meanwhile, in Nichols's view, the Bloomingdale trustees compounded the error of firing him by appointing Benjamin McCready, a man with no asylum management experience, to head the hospital.

13. Nichols to Dix, 11 September 1852, HL.

14. Nichols to Dix, 18 September 1852, HL.

15. Dix to Nichols, 2 October 1852; Nichols to Dix, 20 October 1852, HL. Even though she had already told Nichols of his appointment, Dix solicited opinions about his qualifications from other superintendents. See, for example, Kirkbride to Dix, 26 October 1852, Kirkbride MSS, IPH, in which Kirkbride heartily endorsed Nichols.

16. Newspaper fragment, Washington, D. C., 7 November 1852, in Dix MSS, HL.

17. Nichols to Dix, 20 October, 13 November, 5, 6, 8, and 18 December 1852, HL. Dix apparently used all her powers of persuasion to convince Thomas Blagden, the owner of the proposed site, to part with his "beloved farm" for the $25,000 Congress had allotted instead of his asking price of $40,000. After she met with him, Blagden wrote that he regarded Dix as an "instrument in the hands of God," and feared "that the Almighty's blessing will not rest on nor abide with, those who may place obstacles in your way" (Blagden to Dix, 13 November 1852, HL).

18. Nichols to Dix, 28 March 1853, HL.

19. Nichols to Dix, 2 letters, n.d. [1853], HL.

20. *Report of the Secretary of the Interior made in Compliance with a resolution of the Senate in relation to the United States Insane Asylum in the District of Columbia*, 33d Congress, 1st Session: Senate Document No. 35 (21 February 1854).

21. Government Hospital for the Insane, *Annual Report* (1856) I:7–8.

22. *Report of the Superintendent of the Government Hospital for the Insane* (Washington, D.C.: n.p., 1855), 4–10.

23. Dix to Nichols, 13 May 1858, in Raymond L. Hogan, "Some Newly Found Letters of Dorothea Lynde Dix," unpublished ms., St. Elizabeth's Hospital, Washington, D.C., 6.

24. Dix to Nichols, 12 March 1861 [typescript], HL. Through the 1870s in his regular correspondence with Dix, Nichols complained of unjust assaults on his management practices and personality. Formal presentations of the evidence against him in two major investigations are "Hearings Before the Committee of Investigations Concern-

ing Charges Against Supt. C. H. Nichols, 1869" and "Papers Relative to Charges vs. C. H. Nichols, 1876," National Archives, Record Group 4.18.

25. Quoted in David Donald, *Charles Sumner and the Coming of the Civil War* (New York: Knopf, 1960), 249.

26. Iowa Senator Augustus C. Dodge, for example, tried to amend the land bill for the relief of the indigent insane to include the homestead act, "and let the two measures for the benefit of the sane and the insane go *pari passu*" (*Congressional Globe*, 33d Congress, 1st Session, 1093). His attempt was blocked by Southern senators who believed that granting land to settlers would eventually squeeze the rights of slaveholders. Pierce, on constitutional grounds, threatened to veto any homestead legislation. This became a moot point, however, because the homestead bill that was passed by the House was subsequently watered down by a substitute measure that lowered the price of some government lands. See Gerald W. Wolff, *The Kansas-Nebraska Bill: Party, Section, and the Coming of the Civil War* (New York: Revisionist Press, 1977), 183ff.

27. *Congressional Globe*, 11 February 1851, 507–8.

28. Stribling to Kirkbride, 21 August 1852, quoted in Robert E. Jones, "Correspondence of the A.P.A. Founder," *American Journal of Psychiatry* 119 (June 1963): 1131.

29. The fullest biographical treatment of Pierce remains Roy Nichols, *Franklin Pierce: Young Hickory of the Granite Hills* (Philadelphia: University of Pennsylvania Press, 1931).

30. Dix to Fillmore, 8 December 1853, *Dix-Fillmore Letters*, 162.

31. Fillmore to Dix, 20 December 1853, *Dix-illmore Letters*, 165. The conciseness of Fillmore's analysis leads one to suspect that he may have entertained the same reservations about the constitutionality of Dix's bill that he attributed to Pierce. This would explain his failure to stand up for the bill in 1851 and 1852, and may even suggest that, while in office, he quietly encouraged congressional delay.

32. Federal *Memorial* (1848), 7.

33. A. B. Hutton to Dix, 10 July 1850, HL. A state commission in New Jersey that assembled to advocate Dix's bill noted that "Congress has already given away one hundred and thirty-four millions of acres of the public domain, most of it the most valuable because connected with the privilege of selection. . . . When it is seen that our own state will be endowed with about one million of dollars by [Dix's] success, can it be doubted what is the duty of our Senators and representatives on this great question" (*Report of the Committee on Joint Resolution for Donating Public Lands for the Support of the Indigent Insane* [Trenton: n.p., 1854]). *National Intelligencer*, 11 March 1854.

34. *Connecticut Courant*, 26 March 1852; *Philadelphia North American*, 25 August 1852; *Friends' Review*, fragmentary clipping, [1852]: 474, HL.

35. Dix to Fillmore, *Dix-Fillmore Letters*, 172.

36. William E. Gienapp, *The Origins of the Republican Party, 1852–1856* (New York: Oxford University Press, 1987), provides a lucid discussion of Congress and its relationship to the Pierce administration. The Kansas-Nebraska debates and the political climate of Congress in 1854 are well described in Allan Nevins, *Ordeal of the Union*, 2 vols. (New York: Scribner's, 1947), II:78–159. Dix to Fillmore, 11 February [1854], *Dix-Fillmore Letters*, 175.

37. *Speech of Hon. Richard Yates, of Illinois, on the Land Policy of the United States, and in Defense of the West, delivered in the House of Representatives, April 23, 1852* (Washington, D.C.: n.p., 1852).

38. *Congressional Globe*, 33d Congress, 1st Session, 1094.

39. Dix to Heath, 9 March and 28 April [1854], HL. Dix's conviction that she had Pierce's support is evident from a marginal note she wrote on her copy of the *National Intelligencer*, 11 May 1854, in which she added that "Senator John Bell and others were fully informed on this subject."

40. Kirkbride to Dix, 20 April 1854, HL.

41. Pierce's most recent biographer describes him as a weak president whose "strongest actions were presenting the third annual message before the House was organized, his vetoes, and his recall of Congress to enact an army bill." Even the Kansas-Nebraska Act was entirely the creation of Congress, and gained the president's reluctant support only after it passed (Lawrence Gara, *The Presidency of Franklin Pierce* [Lawrence: University of Kansas Press, 1991], 182–83).

42. *Special Message of President Pierce to the Senate of the United States; May 3, 1854* (Washington, D.C.: Government [sic] printer, 1854), 4–6.

43. Ibid.

44. Ibid, 14–16.

45. For an account of the veto as the courageous act of a tragic president, see Nichols, *Franklin Pierce*, 348–50. "Speech of Mr. Badger, of N. Carolina, delivered in the Senate of the United States, May 11, 1854 on the President's Veto Message," n.p., 13, HL; *National Intelligencer*, 13 and 20 May 1854; *Speech of Albert G. Brown of Mississippi, the President's Veto Message, and in Defence of the Bill Making a Grant to the Several States for the Benefit of the Indigent Insane*. Delivered in the Senate of the United States, May 17, 1854 (Washington, D.C.: John T. and Lem. Towers, 1854).

46. *Speech of Hon. John M. Clayton, of Delaware, on the Veto Message of the President, on the Bill for the Benefit of the Indigent Insane*. Delivered in the Senate 15 June 1854 (Washington, D.C.: Congressional Globe, 1854).

47. *National Intelligencer*, 11 and 13 May 1854; *Boston Daily Advertiser*, 6 and 9 May 1854; *Atlas*, 6 May 1854.

48. *Speech of Hon. D. T. Disney, of Ohio, delivered in the House of Representatives, April 27 and June 7, 1854, on The Disposition of the Public Domain* (Washington, D.C.: n.p., 1854); *Congressional Globe*, 33d. Cong., 4 May 1854; *Washington Daily Union*, 27 May 1854. *President's Veto Message. Speech of Mr. C. C. Clay, Jr., of Alabama, on the President's Veto Message, Rejecting the Indigent Insane Bill, and against Giving Away the Public Lands*. Delivered in the Senate of the United States, June 20, 1854 (Washington: John and Lem. Towers, 1854).

49. James G. King to Dix, 2 February, 1 and 7 March 1853, HL.

50. Heath to Dix, 22 April and 22 May 1854, HL.

51. Dix to Fillmore, 20 May [1854], *Dix-Fillmore Letters*, 196; Nichols, *Franklin Pierce*, 248; *New York Herald*, 6 May 1854; *Congressional Globe*, 11 February 1851, 507–8.

52. Dix to Heath, 18 May [1854], HL; Dix to Fillmore, 13 July [1854], *Dix-Fillmore Letters*, 199; Dix to Heath, 31 May [1854], HL. Before the Civil War congressional overrides of vetoes were rare, and only Pierce and John Tyler suffered the humiliation of seeing legislation they had vetoed overridden by Congress (Richard A. Watson, "Origins and Early Development of the Veto Power," *Presidential Studies Quarterly* 17 [1987]: 409).

53. Dix to Heath, 29 July [1854], HL; Dix to Fillmore, 11 March [1857], *Dix-Fillmore Letters*, 279.

54. The phrase "economics of compassion" appears in Ellen Dwyer, *Homes for the Mad: Life Inside Two Nineteenth-Century Asylums* (New Brunswick, N.J.: Rutgers University Press, 1987).

Chapter 13: The American Missionary to the Mad

1. Dix to Heath, 25 February [1854]; Dix to [Elizabeth Rathbone], 29 August 1854, HL.
2. New York *Daily Tribune*, 11 September 1854.
3. Dix to Fillmore, 2 September [1855], *Dix–Fillmore Letters*, 219; Dix to Heath, 11 September 1854, HL.
4. John Connolly to Dix, 20 April 1855, HL.
5. Dix to William Rathbone IV, 29 April 1868, HL.
6. Dix to Heath, 22 September 1854, HL.
7. F. M. L. Thompson, *The Rise of Respectable Society: A Social History of Victorian Britain, 1830–1900* (Cambridge, Mass.: Harvard University Press, 1988).
8. Mayhew's career is chronicled in Anne Humphreys, *Travels into the Poor Man's Country: The Work of Henry Mayhew* (Athens: University of Georgia Press, 1977). The quotation on his method is from Henry Mayhew, *Country Chronicle*, 6 November 1849, quoted in Gertrude Himmelfarb, *The Idea of Poverty: England in the Early Industrial Age* (New York: Knopf, 1983), 320.
9. Dix to Heath, 26 February 1855, HL.
10. Dix to Fillmore, 26 December 1854, *Dix–Fillmore Letters*, 225, 228.
11. Dix to Heath, 18 April 1855, HL; Dix to Fillmore, 26 December 1854, *Dix–Fillmore Letters*, 229.
12. Ursula R. Q. Henriques, *Before the Welfare State: Social Administration in Early Victorian England* (New York: Longman, 1979), 259–66.
13. Nationwide criteria for medical licensure were part of the Medical Qualifications Act of 1858, a milestone in organizing the professional class of physicians. See M. J. Peterson, *The Medical Profession in Mid–Victorian London* (Berkeley: University of California Press, 1978). At every stage, British asylum physicians enjoyed far better standing with Parliament than American superintendents did with state legislatures Andrew Scull, *The Most Solitary of Afflictions: Madness and Society in Britain, 1700-1900* (New Haven: Yale University Press, 1993), 259–266.
14. Anthony Ashley Cooper (1801–85), Lord Ashley (after 1851 the seventh earl of Shaftesbury), speech in the House of Commons, 23 July 1844, quoted in Kathleen Jones, *A History of the Mental Health Services* (London: Routledge & Kegan Paul, 1972), 144.
15. Dix to Fillmore, 26 December 1854, *Dix–Fillmore Letters*, 226–27.
16. Dix to Heath, 2 October [1854], HL.
17. Dix to Elizabeth Rathbone, n.d. [October 1854] and 25 October 1854.
18. Dix to Heath, 8 December 1854; John Curwen to Dix, 4 May 1857, HL; George Barrell Emerson, "Asylums for the Insane," *Boston Daily Advertiser*, 28 December 1869.
19. Dix to Elizabeth Rathbone, n.d. [November 1854], HL; Harriet Martineau, *Letters from Ireland* (London: John Murray, 1855), 170; Joseph Workman, "Notes of a Visit to

Lunatic Asylums in Great Britain and Ireland," *American Journal of Insanity* 16 (January 1860): 288; *The Biographical Edition of the Works of William Makepeace Thackery*, vol. 5, *The Irish Sketchbook* (London: Smith, Elder, 1898), 571. For a discussion of the political circumstances that fueled this ambitious lunacy reform agenda, see Mark Finnane, *Insanity and the Insane in Post–Famine Ireland* (London: Croom Helm, 1981), 18–52.

20. Dix to Heath, 26 February 1855, HL.

21. W. A. F. Browne, *What Asylums Were, Are, and Ought to Be: Being the Substance of Five Lectures Delivered before the Managers of the Montrose Royal Lunatic Asylum* (Edinburgh: Adam and Charles Black, 1837). On Browne's career see Andrew Scull, ed., *The Asylum as Utopia: W.A.F. Browne and the Mid–Nineteenth Century Consolidation of Psychiatry* (New York: Tavistock/Routledge, 1991), vii–lxxvii.

22. R. A. Cage, *The Scottish Poor Law, 1745–1845* (Edinburgh: Scottish University Press, 1981).

23. *London Times*, 30 May 1857; *New Jerusalem Messenger*, n.d., fragmentary, [May 1859?], HL. The Scottish Lunacy Commission determined that of 2,732 nonpoor lunatics, 652 were in royal asylums, 1,453 were with relatives, 231 were in licensed madhouses, and the rest were in a variety of other circumstances. Among paupers, 1,511 were in royal asylums, 1,217 with relatives, 426 in licensed houses, 667 in poorhouses, and the rest scattered in various other institutions, including 141 listed at large.

24. Dix to Elizabeth Rathbone, n.d. [February 1855]; Dix to Mrs. Torrey, 8 March 1855, HL.

25. Duncan McLaren, letter to the editor, *Edinburgh Daily Express*, 9 June 1857; Dix to Mrs. Torrey, 8 March 1855, HL.

26. *Report by her Majesty's Commissioners appointed to inquire into the condition of Lunatic Asylums in Scotland* (1857), quoted in "Condition of the Insane in Scotland," *American Journal of Insanity* 15 (January 1859): 293.

27. Dix to Mrs. Torrey, 8 March 1855, HL. The home secretary was Sir George Grey.

28. George Douglas Campbell to Dix, 1 and 2 March 1855; Dix to Mrs. Torrey, 8 March 1855, HL.

29. Dix to Heath, 18 April and 12 May 1855, HL.

30. N. Hervey, "A Slavish Bowing Down: The Lunacy Commission and the Psychiatric Profession, 1845–60," in W. F. Bynum, Roy Porter, and Michael Shepherd, eds , *The Anatomy of Madness: Essays in the History of Psychiatry*, vol. 2, *Institutions and Society* (London: Tavistock, 1985), 98–131.

31. M. B. Stark to Elizabeth Rathbone, 16 June [1855?], HL.

32. Dix to Mrs. Torrey, 8 March 1855; George Douglas Campbell to Dix, 12 April 1855, HL.

33. George Douglas Campbell to Dix, 12 April 1855; Dix to Mrs. Torrey, 8 March 1855, HL.

34. Dix to Elizabeth Rathbone, 27 and 28 February 1855; Dix to Anthony Ashley Cooper, the seventh earl of Shaftesbury, n.d. [March 1855], HL.

35. Dix to Heath, 18 April 1855, HL.

36. James Coxe to Dix, 11 April 1855; Samuel Gaskell to Dix, [April 1855], HL.

37. W. A. F. Browne to Dix, 10 April and 12 July 1855, HL.

38. James Coxe to Dix, 16 and 24 April 1855; Campbell to Dix, 16 June 1855, HL.

39. James Coxe to Dix, 14 May and 2 August 1855; Dix to Heath, 12 May 1855, HL.

40. [John Charles Bucknill], "Reports of the Irish, Scotch, and American Asylums, 1855," *Asylum Journal of Mental Science* 2 (1855): 124. Emphasis added.

41. Mrs. E. H. Walsh to unknown, 3 June 1855, quoted in Francis Tiffany, *Life of Dorothea Lynde Dix*, (Boston: Houghton Mifflin, 1891), 275; William Rathbone to Dix, 6 May and 8 July 1855, HL.

42. Dix to Heath, 12 May 1855, HL.

43. Daniel Hack Tuke to Francis Tiffany, August 1888, quoted in Tiffany, *Life of Dorothea L. Dix*, 241.

44. Dix to Horace A. Buttolph, 16 May 1855, HL.

45. Quoted in Tiffany, *Life of Dorothea L. Dix*, 263–64.

46. D. H. Van Leuven to Daniel Hack Tuke, 8 May 1855, HL.

47. Ibid.

48. Dix to Heath, 1 June 1855, HL.

49. Dix to Fillmore, 22 June [1855], *Dix–Fillmore Letters*, 234; Dix to Horace A. Buttolph, 15 July 1855, HL.

50. Dix to Horace A. Buttolph, 15 July 1855, HL.

51. Dix to Horace A. Buttolph, 18 July 1855; Dix to Elizabeth Rathbone, July 1855, HL.

52. Dix to Horace A. Buttolph, 18 July 1855, HL.

53. James Coxe to Dix, 4 June 1857, HL.

54. *Report by her Majesty's Commissioners appointed to inquire into the state of lunatic asylums in Scotland; and the existing law in reference to lunatics and lunatic asylums in that part of the United Kingdom* (London, 1859 [first published 1857]); *Glasgow Herald*, 3 June 1857; *London Times* 30 May 1857.

55. *Edinburgh Daily Scotsman*, 1 June 1857; *Edinburgh Daily Express*, 6 June 1857.

56. Dix to Elizabeth Rathbone, 5 July 1857, HL; *Edinburgh Daily Express*, 12 June 1857.

57. James Coxe to Dix, 20 June 1857, HL.

58. W. A. F. Browne to Dix, 23 September 1857, HL.

59. *Edinburgh Daily Express*, 15 June 1857; *Edinburgh Daily Scotsman*, 22 June 1857.

60. Dix to Horace A. Buttolph, 12 April 1855, HL.

61. Dix to Horace Buttolph, 25 July [1855]; Dix to Elizabeth Rathbone, 5 July 1857, HL.

62. Dix to Elizabeth Rathbone, 3 March 1860; Dix to William Rathbone, 18 March [1860], HL.

63. *Commissioners in Lunacy Annual Report, 1856*, quoted in Scull, *Museums of Madness*, 248; "Ninth Report of the Commissioners in Lunacy, to the Lord Chancellor," *American Journal of Insanity* 12 (January 1856): 250.

64. *Crichton Royal Asylum, 17th Annual Report* (1856), 24–26, quoted in Andrew Scull, ed., *The Asylum as Utopia: W.A.F. Browne and the Mid–Nineteenth Century Consolidation of Psychiatry* (New York: Tavistock/Routledge, 1991), xlix.

65. "Condition of the Insane in Scotland," *American Journal of Insanity* 15 (January 1859): 283.

66. Dix to Elizabeth Rathbone, September 1855; Dix to William Rathbone, n.d. [September 1855], HL.

67. Dix to Horace A. Buttolph, 3 December 1855, HL.

68. Dix to Horace A. Buttolph, 28 February 1856, HL.

69. Fillmore to S. G. Haven, 22 January 1856, quoted in Robert J. Rayback, "Millard Fill-

more: Biography of a President," *Publications of the Buffalo Historical Society* (Buffalo: Stuart, 1959), 400; Tiffany, *Life of Dorothea Lynde Dix,*, (Boston: Houghton Mifflin, 1891) 299.

70. E. E. Y. Hales, *Pio Nono: A Study in European Politics and Religion in the Nineteenth Century* (Garden City, N.Y.: Doubleday, 1962); Joseph Jay Deiss, *The Roman Years of Margaret Fuller* (New York: Crowell, 1969), 51

71. Frank J. Coppa, *Pope Pius IX: Crusader in a Secular Age* (Boston: Twayne, 1979), 19–42.

72. Dix to Heath, 1 May 1856, HL.

73. J. P. Bancroft to Dix, 7 February 1876, HL.

74. Dix to Elizabeth Rathbone, 2 April 1856; Dix to Heath, 9 May 1856; Dix to Elizabeth Rathbone, 16 March 1856, HL.

75. Quoted in Tiffany, *Life of Dorothea L. Dix*, 306; Dix to Elizabeth Rathbone, 5 August 1856, HL.

76. Dix to William Rathbone, 3 September 1856; Dix to Heath, 30 January 1857, HL.

Chapter 14: Into the Tempest

1. Dix to Elizabeth Rathbone, 27 September 1856; Dix to Heath, 27 September 1856, HL.

2. D. T. Brown to Dix, 2 October 1856; Dix to Heath, 30 December 1856, HL.

3. *Washington Star*, 15 February 1854; Dix to Fillmore, 20 February [1854], *Dix-Fillmore Letters*, 183–86.

4. Dix to Fillmore, 25 December [1856], *Dix-Fillmore Letters*, 273; Ellen Dwyer, *Homes for the Mad: Life inside Two Nineteenth–Century Asylums* (New Brunswick: Rutgers University Press, 1987), 67–71; John P. Gray, "Homicide in Insanity," *American Journal of Insanity* 14 (October 1857), 144–45.

5. Dwyer, *Homes for the Mad*, 38–41; Dix to Fillmore, 4 and 19 January [1857], *Dix-Fillmore Letters*, 274–75.

6. William Whitney Godding to Dix, May 1870, 13 September 1870, and 7 May 1877; George Barrell Emerson to Dix, 13 October 1868, HL.

7. "It is only by *increasing the size of institutions and their diminishing cost per head of superintendence, that you can keep the chronic insane out—more houses, mad–house dens*, because that is the *only way* in which a scientific and benevolent care can be made to cost less than it now does" (Charles H. Nichols to Dix, 31 October 1866, HL). For the counterpoint to this argument see Kirkbride to Dix, 3 February 1867 and 7 January 1870; Curwen to Dix, 25 December 1869; Buttolph to Dix, 5 January 1870, HL.

8. R. L. Parsons to Dix, 6 June 1870; William Whitney Godding to Dix, 7 May 1877, HL.

9. Dix to Fillmore, 27 April [1857], *Dix-Fillmore Letters*, 285; John Chapin, "Insanity in the State of New York," *American Journal of Insanity* 13 (January 1856): 39–52; Dwyer, *Homes for the Mad*, 38–49.

10. Dix to Fillmore, 3 June 1857, *Dix-Fillmore Letters*, 289; John Harper to Dix, 25 July 1857 and 4 December 1860, HL.

11. Mary Peabody Mann to Dix, 5 March and 22 April 1859, HL.

12. Dix to Charles Nichols, 8 March 1859, "Some Newly Found Letters of Dorothea Lynde Dix," unpublished MS, St. Elizabeth's Hospital, Washington, D.C., 11.

13. Datebook for 1857, Am 1838 (943 HL); Dix to Heath 11 April 1859; Dix to Mrs. Torrey, 13 April 1859, HL.

14. Dix to Heath, 8 December 1859, HL.

15. Dix to Mrs. Torrey, 7 April 1859; Dix to Harriet Hare, 28 March 1859, HL.

16. M. W. Phillips to Dix, 27 September 1859, HL; Henry M. Hurd, ed., *The Institutional Care of the Insane in the United States and Canada* 4 vols.(Baltimore: Johns Hopkins University Press, 1916), II:873–74.

17. Ottilia Assing, "The Insurrection at Harper's Ferry," *Morgenblatt fuer gebildete Staende*, quoted in William McFeely, *Frederick Douglass*, (New York: Norton, 1991) 201.

18. Dix to Fillmore, 21 November [1859], *Dix-Fillmore Letters*, 323–24; Dix to Elizabeth Rathbone, n.d. [January 1860], HL.

19. Dix to Nichols, 4 November 1860 [typescript], HL.

20. Dix to Heath, 23 December 1860, HL.

21. Dix to Elizabeth Rathbone, 19 December 1860, HL; Frank Freidel, *Francis Lieber: Nineteenth–Century Liberal* (Baton Rouge: Louisiana State University Press, 1947), 223–316.

22. Ibid.

23. Walt Whitman, *Memoranda During the War [&] Death of Abraham Lincoln*, facsimile ed. (Bloomington: Indiana University Press, 1962), 65, quoted in Justin Kaplan, *Walt Whitman: A Life* (New York: Simon and Schuster, 1980), 300; Dix to Heath, 24 April 1863, HL.

24. Dix to Charles H. Nichols, 11 January 1861 [typescript]; Dix to Heath, 12 January 1861, HL.

25. Charles H. Nichols to Dix, 22 February 1861; Dix to Heath, 12 and 26 January 1861, HL.

26. Dix to Fillmore, 12 January 1861, *Dix-Fillmore Letters*, 341–42.

27. Dix to Heath, 12 and 26 January 1861, HL; Dix to Fillmore, 10 April [1860], *Dix-Fillmore Letters*, 327–28.

28. Hurd, *Institutional Care of the Insane*, II:186–91.

29. Dix to Heath, 21 February 1861, HL.

30. Ibid.

31. Dix to Heath, 18 June 1860, HL; Freidel, *Francis Lieber*, 288–89; Allan Nevins, *The War for the Union: Volume I: The Improvised War, 1861–1862* (New York: Charles Scribner's Sons, 1959), 1–6.

32. Samuel M. Felton to Francis Tiffany, 8 May 1888, quoted in Tiffany, *Life of Dorothea Lynde Dix*, (Boston: Houghton Mifflin, 1891) 332–33.

33. Felton to Tiffany, 8 May 1888, quoted in Tiffany, *Life of Dorothea L. Dix*, 334; Norma B. Cuthbert, ed., *Lincoln and the Baltimore Plot* (San Marino, Calif.: Huntington Library, 1971; Nevins, *War for the Union*, I:80.

34. Felton to Tiffany, 8 May 1888, quoted in Tiffany, *Life of Dorothea L. Dix*, 333.

Chapter 15: "Our Florence Nightingale"

1. Henry S. Commager, ed., *Blue and Gray*, (New York: Avon, 1961), I, 47; and Philip S. Foner, *Business and Slavery: The New York Merchants and the Irrepressible Conflict* (Chapel Hill: University of North Carolina Press, 1941), 207, quoted in James M. McPherson,

The Battle Cry of Freedom: The Civil War Era (New York: Oxford University Press, 1988), 274.

2. Tiffany, *Life of Dorothea Lynde Dix*, 339.

3. Dix to Heath, 20 April [1861], HL.

4. Dix to Heath, 20 April [1861], HL.

5. Dix to Heath, 20 April [1861], HL.

6. Ibid.

7. Quoted in Elspeth Huxley, *Florence Nightingale* (New York: Putnam, 1975), 138. See also the photograph of Nightingale taken on her return from the Crimea on p. 140.

8. Sue M. Goldie, *"I Have Done My Duty": Florence Nightingale in the Crimean War, 1854–56* (Manchester: Manchester University Press, 1987); Martha Vicinus and Bea Nergaard, eds., *Ever Yours, Florence Nightingale: Selected Letters* (Cambridge, Mass.: Harvard University Press, 1990).

9. Charles E. Rosenberg, "Florence Nightingale on Contagion: The Hospital as Moral Universe," in *Healing and History: Essays for George Rosen*, ed. Charles E. Rosenberg (New York: Science History Publications and Dawson, 1979), 116–36.

10. C. W. Bracebridge to Dix, 22 August [1856], 10 and 16 October 1856, HL.

11. William Rathbone, *The Organization of Nursing in Liverpool* (London: Longman, Green, Render and Dyer, 1865); Herbert Rathbone, *A Short History and Description of District Nursing in Liverpool* (Liverpool: D. Marples, 1899); Gwen Hardy, *William Rathbone and the Early History of District Nursing* (Ormskirk: Hesketh, 1978); Eleanor Rathbone, *William Rathbone: A Memoir* (London: Macmillan, 1905).

12. Fillmore to Dix, 13 February 1856, *Dix-Fillmore Letters*, 246; Dix to Elizabeth Rathbone, 3 March 1860, HL.

13. Dix to William Rathbone IV, 23 April [1863], HL; L. J. Bigelow, "Miss Dix, And What She Has Done," *Galaxy*, 15 March 1867, 671.

14. Charles J. Stillé, *History of the United States Sanitary Commission* (Philadelphia: Lippincott, 1866), 118–19.

15. *The War of the Rebellion: A Compilation of the Official Records of the Union and Confederate Armies* (Washington: U.S. Government Printing Office, 1880–1901) Series III, Part 1, 107. Elizabeth Blackwell and her sister Emily had hoped to head the army nurses, but they encountered deeply entrenched opposition from leaders of the New York medical establishment. See Emily Blackwell to Barbara Smith Bodichon, 1 June 1861, Blackwell MSS, Rare Book and Manuscript Collections, Columbia University.

16. R.C. Wood to Dix, 23 April 1861, quoted in Helen Marshall, *Dorothea Dix: Forgotten Samaritan* (Chapel Hill: University of North Carolina Press, 1937), 204.

17. Quoted in Mary A. Livermore, *My Story of the War: A Woman's Narrative of Four Years' Personal Experience as a Nurse in the Union Army . . .* (Hartford, Conn.: A.D. Worthington, 1889), 127; Dix to Louisa Lee Schuyler, 29 April 1861, Schuyler MSS, New York Historical Society.

18. "Hospital Supplies," *Pennsylvania Daily Telegraph*, 1 May 1861.

19. *Boston Transcript*, 4 May 1861; Henry W. Bellows to C. J. Stillé, 15 November 1865, quoted in William Q.Maxwell, *Lincoln's Fifth Wheel*, (New York: Longmans Green, 1956), 6; George Hayward to Edward Jarvis, 30 August 1862, Jarvis MSS, Countway Library, Harvard Medical School.

20. Maxwell, *Lincoln's Fifth Wheel*, 79.

21. Dix to Charles Nichols, 9 May 1861, HL; *The Diary of George Templeton Strong*, 4 vols., eds. Allan Nevins and Milton Halsey Thomas, vol. 3, *The Civil War: 1860–1865* (New York: Macmillan, 1952), 173–74.

22. Dix to William Rathbone, 28 November [1862], HL; L. J. Bigelow, "Miss Dix, And What She Has Done," *Galaxy*, 15 March 1867, 676.

23. *Diary of George Templeton Strong*, III, 182; Maxwell, *Lincoln's Fifth Wheel*, 100–106; John C. Frémont to Dix, 21 August 1861, and Frémont to Jessie Frémont, n.d. [1861], HL.

24. Quoted in George Worthington Adams, *Doctors in Blue* (New York: Henry Schuman, 1952), 177–78; Walter Lowenfels, *Walt Whitman's Civil War* (New York: Knopf, 1960), 116.

25. Joseph K. Barnes et al., *The Medical and Surgical History of the War of the Rebellion, 1861–1865* (Washington: U.S. Government Printing Office, 1875), I:262; *Boston Transcript*, 6 June 1861.

26. Sophronia E. Bucklin, *In Hospital and Camp* (Philadelphia: Lippincott, 1869), n.p., quoted in Sylvia G. L. Dannett, ed., *Noble Women of the North* (New York: Thomas Yoseloff, 1959), 65–66.

27. James Phinney Munroe, *Adventures of an Army Nurse in Two Wars: Edited from the Diary and Correspondence of Mary Phinney, Baroness von Olnhausen* (Boston: [n.p.], 1904), n.p., in Dannett, *Nobel Women of the North*, 92–95.

28. Ellen Wright to Laura Stratton, 31 January 1863, quoted in *Bonnet Brigades*, 47; *A Woman Doctor's Civil War: Esther Hall Hawks' Diary*, ed. Gerald Schwartz (Columbia: University of South Carolina Press, 1984), 15; *South after Gettysburg: Letters of Cornelia Hancock, 1863–1868*, ed., Henrietta Stratton Jaquette (New York: Crowell, 1956), 6, 131.

29. L. M. Alcott, *Hospital Sketches* (Boston: James Redpath, 1863), 69.

30. Dix to Horace A. Buttolph, 3 December 1855, Hl; Dix to Fillmore, 22 October [1856], *Dix-Fillmore Letters*, 255; Dix to Elizabeth Rathbone, 27 August 1860, HL.

31. Mary Livermore, *My Story of the War* (Hartford, Conn.: A.D. Worthington, 1887), 218.

32. Mary Denis Maher, *To Bind Up the Wounds: Catholic Sister Nurses in the U.S. Civil War* (New York: Greenwood Press, 1989).

33. Jane Stuart Woolsey, *Hospital Days* (Boston, [n.p.] 1870), n.p., quoted in Dannett, *Nobel Women of the North*, 88.

34. Samuel Gridley Howe, "Sanitary Conditions and New England Troops," Boston *Evening Transcript*, 30 May 1861; Georgeanna M. Woolsey, "Three Weeks at Gettysburg," (1863), quoted in Dennett, *Noble Women of the North*, 159; *Diary of George Templeton Strong*, III, 182.

35. Dix to Winfield Scott, 17 June 1861, HL; Roe, *Dorothea Lynde Dix*, A Paper Read before the Worcester Society of Antiquity, November 20th, 1888 (Worcester: Franklin P. Rice, 1889), 41. Fears of powerlessness troubled physicians throughout the century. Accordingly, "the inability to command deference was the root of the profession's trouble," writes Paul Starr (*The Social Transformation of American Medicine* [New York: Basic Books, 1982], 88).

36. *U.S. Sanitary Commission Bulletin* 1, no. 10 (15 March 1864): 295.

37. *Diary of George Templeton Strong*, III, 181; Olmsted to John Murray Forbes, 15 December 1861, quoted in McPherson, *Battle Cry of Freedom*, 482.

38. *Diary of George Templeton Strong*, 218–20; Maxwell, *Lincoln's Fifth Wheel*, 137–39; Charles Stille, *History of the U.S. Sanitary Commission* (Philadelphia: Lippincott, 1866).

39. Surgeon General's Office, Circular No. 7, 14 July 1862.

40. Maher, *To Bind Up the Wounds*, 76–77.

41. Simon Cameron to William Alexander Hammond, n.d. [1862]; Lincoln to Dix, 4 May 1862; Lincoln to Medical Director of the Military Hospital at Winchester, Virginia, 30 March 1863, HL.

42. *Reports on the Extent and Nature of the Materials Available for the Preparation of a Medical and Surgical History of the Rebellion*, Circular No. 6, 1 November 1865 (Philadelphia: Lippincott, 1865); Joseph K. Barnes et al., *Medical and Surgical History of the War of the Rebellion, 1861–65*, 6 vols., 2d ed. (Washington: U.S. Government Printing Office, 1875–88). Hammond noted on a copy of General Order 351, which was sent to the Holy Cross Sisters, that all Sisters of Charity were exempt from its provisions (Maher, *To Bind Up the Wounds*, 128).

43. Dix to Heath, 16 March 1863, HL.

44. Dennett, *Noble Women of the North*, 304–5.

45. Elizabeth Brown Pryor, *Clara Barton: Professional Angel* (Philadelphia: University of Pennsylvania Press, 1987).

46. Dix to Heath, 15 September 1863, HL.

47. Anne T. Wittenmeyer, *Under the Guns: A Woman's Reminiscences of the Civil War* (Boston: [n.p.], 1895), n.p., quoted in Dennett, *Noble Women of the North*, 340–42.

48. Pliny Earle to Dix, 31 July 1865; Dix to Heath, 11 September [1866], HL; C.H. Crane to Dix, 11 September 1866, Surgeon General's letterbook, reprinted in Marshall, *Forgotten Samaritan*, 230.

49. Dix to Elizabeth Rathbone, 5 May and 18 August 1866; Dix to Mrs. Torrey, 11 December 1867; Edwin M. Stanton to Dix, 3 December 1866 and 12 May 1866, HL.

Chapter 16: A Buried Life

1. William L. Peck to Charles H. Nichols, 27 May 1870, HL.

2. Dix to Heath, 27 February 1871, HL.

3. James R. Bickerdyke to Dix, 15 March, 4 May, and 29 June 1874; Anne Gilkison to Dix, 11 April 1874, HL.

4. Benjamin Silliman to Dix, 6 May 1868, HL.

5. Harriet C. Kerlin to Francis Tiffany, n.d., quoted in Tiffany, *Life of Dorothea L. Dix*, 358.

6. Emerson to Dix, 7 July 1870, HL.

7. Clara Knapp to Dix, 28 June 1875; Frances Willard to Dix, 27 February 1886, HL.

8. Maria Mitchell to Dix, 20 October 1871, HL.

9. Whittier to Dix, 18 August 1879, HL.

10. Henry Snell to Dix, 20 July 1878; Jonathan Ware to Dix, 3 and 11 April 1880, HL.

11. MS Journal beginning 2 June 1869; G. A. Shurtless to Dix, 13 December 1869; Alpheus Packard to Dix, 14 July 1871 and 16 April 1873, HL.

12. Alfred Hunger to Dix, 31 January 1870; John H. Callender to Dix, 3 and 19 March 1870, HL.

13. Quoted in David Donald, "The Limits of Innovation, 1865–1869," in Bernard Bailyn et al., *The Great Republic* (Boston: Little, Brown, 1977), 742.

14. Eugene Grissom to Dix, 22 August 1870, HL.

15. *Raleigh Daily Standard*, 18 January 1870; *Tennessee Republican Banner*, 12 February 1870.

16. Dix to Heath, 20 December [1870]; John Curwen to Dix, 9 April 1872, HL.

17. John Harper to Dix, 13 April 1867, HL.

18. Samuel McClintock Hamill to Dix, 8 November 1871, HL.

19. William L. Peck to Dix, 22 March 1869; Richard Gundon to Dix, 19 March 1869, HL.

20. Daniel Roberts Brower to Dix, 13 July 1871; 14 February, 6 May, and 26 June 1872; 25 January 1876, HL.

21. B. D. Eastman to Dix, 18 October 1876, HL.

22. Isaac Ray, "Doubtful Recoveries," *American Journal of Insanity* 20 (July 1863): 26–44; Pliny Earle, *The Curability of Insanity: A Series of Studies* (Philadelphia: Lippincott, 1887).

23. Conference of Charities and Corrections, *Proceedings*, IV (1877), 7.

24. Massachusetts Board of State Charities, *Fourth Annual Report* (1867), xl, quoted in Gerald N. Grob, *The State and the Mentally Ill: A History of the Worcester State Hospital in Massachusetts, 1830–1920* (Chapel Hill: University of North Carolina Press, 1966), 193.

25. H. M. Harlow to Dix, 30 July 1879 and 27 February 1881; J. P. Brown to Dix, 17 February 1880, HL.

26. *Annual Report of the Northampton State Hospital* (1877).

27. William Whitney Godding to Dix, 13 September 1870, HL.

28. R. L. Parsons to Dix, 6 June 1870, HL.

29. Thomas Kirkbride to Dix, 7 January 1870; Buttolph to Dix, 5 January 1870, HL.

30. John Curwen to Dix, 25 December 1869; Charles Nichols to Dix, 31 October 1866, HL.

31. J. P. Bancroft to Dix, 15 November 1869 and 7 June 1870, HL.

32. H. M. Quinby to Dix, 22 November 1879, HL.

33. Isaac Ray to Judge Charles Does, 20 September 1870, quoted in Grob, *Mental Institutions in America: Social Policy to 1875* (New York: Free Press, 1973), 296.

34. See, for example, Isaac H. Hunt, *Three Years in a Mad–House! By a Victim* (n.p., 1852); E. P. W. Packard, *Modern Persecution, or Insane Asylums Unveiled, as Demonstrated by the Report of the Investigating Committee of the Legislature of Illinois*, 2 vols. (Hartford, Conn.: Case, Lockwood & Brainard, 1873).

35. The phrase is taken from Andrew Scull's *Museums of Madness: The Social Organization of Insanity in Nineteenth Century England* (London: Allen Lane, 1979).

36. Whittier to Dix, 14 August 1883; John Adams Dix to Dorothea Dix, 8 February 1869 and 19 June 1878, HL; Dorothea Dix to Alexander Randall, 23 August 1878, HL. Shortly before her death, Anne Heath, Dix's closest female friend, also urged her to give "the voracious world" a true account of her career so "that they may get the Truth, & not say you were born in Halifax and taught needle work in Virginia &c" (Heath to Dix, 22 December 1873, HL).

37. Emerson to Dix, 7 January 1870, HL.

38. Dorothea Dix to Alexander Randall, 10 May 1880, HL.

39. Dix proposed to the Harvard Unitarian James Freeman Clarke that he write her biography. But Clarke, who deeply admired her as "a great example of what a woman can

do when she devotes herself to a good & great reform," demurred, lamenting that the task was too great. See James Freeman Clarke to Dix, 18 December 1881, HL; *James Freeman Clarke: Autobiography, Diary and Correspondence*, ed. Edward Everett Hale (Boston: Houghton, Mifflin, 1899), 383–84.

40. George F. Jelly to Francis Tiffany, n.d., quoted in Tiffany, *Life of Dorothea L. Dix*, 363.
41. Dix to unknown, 28 August 1871; Dix to Horatio Appleton Lamb, 22 February 1884; Will of Dorothea Dix, 1881, Am 1838 (954), HL.
42. *New York Home Journal*, 11 September 1889.
43. Quoted in Tiffany, *Life of Dorothea L. Dix*, 375.
44. State Senator Murphy's speech on the floor of the Pennsylvania legislature, as reported in *The Sentinel*, 13 January 1872.
45. "Dorothea L. Dix," *Christian Life*, 1 November 1887.
46. Charles W. Birtwell to Horatio Appleton Lamb, 19 February 1888, HL.
47. For an overview of the social control debate, see David Rothman, "Social Control: The Uses and Abuses of the Concept in the History of Incarceration," *Rice University Studies* 67 (Winter 1981): 9–20; John A. Mayer, "Notes towards a Working Definition of Social Control in Historical Analysis," in *Social Control and the State*, ed. Stanley Cohen and Andrew Scull (Oxford: Oxford University Press, 1983); Andrew Scull, "The Discovery of the Asylum Revisited: Lunacy Reform in the New American Republic," in Scull, ed., *Social Order/Mental Disorder: Anglo–American Psychiatry in Historical Perspective* (Berkeley: University of California Press, 1989).

BIBLIOGRAPHY

I. PRIMARY SOURCES

A. MANUSCRIPTS

Bangs Family MSS, American Antiquarian Society, Worcester, Massachusetts.

Butler Hospital MSS Collection, Butler Hospital, Providence, Rhode Island.

Butler Hospital MSS, John Carter Brown Library, Brown University, Providence, Rhode Island.

Simon Cameron MSS, Dauphin County Historical Society, Harrisburg, Pennsylvania.

George Barrell Emerson MSS, Chamberlain Autograph Collection, Boston Public Library, Boston, Massachusetts.

Dorothea Lynde Dix MSS, Houghton Library, Harvard University, Cambridge, Massachusetts.

Dorothea Lynde Dix MSS, Library of Congress, Washington, D.C.

William E, Hacker MSS, New York Public Library, New York, New York.

John L. Harper MSS, Western Pennsylvania Historical Association, Pittsburgh, Pennsylvania.

Samuel Gridley Howe MSS, Houghton Library, Harvard University, Cambridge, Massachusetts.

Thomas Story Kirkbride MSS, Institute of the Pennsylvania Hospital, Philadelphia, Pennsylvania.

Edward Jarvis MSS, Countway Library, Harvard Medical School, Boston, Massachusetts.

Francis Lieber MSS, Huntington Library, San Marino, California.

Horace Mann MSS, Massachusetts Historical Society, Boston, Massachusetts.

Massachusetts State Archives MSS, State House, Boston, Massachusetts.

Miscellaneous MSS, Pennsylvania Historical Society, Philadelphia, Pennsylvania.

Alexander Randall MS Diaries, Maryland Historical Society, Baltimore, Maryland.

Williams Family MSS, Maryland Historical Society, Baltimore, Maryland.

Samuel B. Woodward and Woodward Family MSS, American Antiquarian Society, Worcester, Massachusetts.

B. PUBLISHED WORKS BY DOROTHEA LYNDE DIX

American Moral Tales, For Young Persons. Boston: Leonard C. Bowles and B. H. Green, 1832.

Conversations on Common Things: or, Guide to Knowledge: With Questions. Boston: Munroe & Francis, 1824.

Meditations for Private Hours. Boston: Munroe & Francis, 1828.

Memorial of D. L. Dix, Praying A grant of land for the relief and support of the indigent curable and incurable insane in the United States. 30th Congress, 1st Session: Senate Misc. Document No. 150, June 27, 1848.

Memorial of D. L. Dix, Praying an appropriation of land for the relief of the insane. 31st Congress, 1st Session: Senate Misc. Document No. 118, 25 June 1850.

"Memorial of Miss Dix, the Honorable the Senate and House of Representatives of the State of Illinois," in *Reports of the Illinois State Hospital for the Insane, 1847–1862*. Chicago: F. Fulton & Co., 1863, 9–31.

Memorial. To the Honorable the Legislature of the State of New York, Assembly Document No. 20. New York: n.p., 12 January 1844.

Memorial. To the Legislature of Massachusetts. Boston: Munroe & Francis, 1843.

Memorial of Miss D. L. Dix, to the Honorable the General Assembly in Behalf of the Insane of Maryland. [Maryland] Senate Document C: 25 February 1852.

Memorial Soliciting Adequate Appropriations for the Construction of a State Hospital for the Insane in the State of Mississippi. February, 1850. Jackson: Fall & Marshall, 1850.

Memorial Soliciting an Appropriation for the State Hospital for the Insane at Lexington; and also Urging the Necessity for Establishing a New Hospital in the Green River Country. Frankfort: A.G. Hodges, 1846.

Memorial Soliciting Enlarged and Improved Accommodations for the Insane of the State of Tennessee, by the Establishment of a New Hospital. Nashville: B.R. M'Kennie, 1847.

Memorial Soliciting a State Hospital for the Insane, Submitted to the Legislature of New Jersey, January 23, 1845. Trenton, n.p., 1845.

Memorial Soliciting a State Hospital for the Insane, Submitted to the Legislature of Pennsylvania, February 3, 1845. Harrisburg: J.M.G. Lescure, 1845.

Memorial Soliciting a State Hospital for the Protection and Cure of the Insane, Submitted to the General Assembly of North Carolina. House of Commons Document, No. 2. Raleigh: Seaton Gales, 1848.

Remarks on Prisons and Prison Discipline in the United States. Boston: Munroe & Francis, 1845.

A Review of the Present Condition of the State Penitentiary of Kentucky, with Brief Notices and Remarks upon the Jails and Poor-Houses in some of the Most Populous Counties. Frankfort: A.G. Hodges, 1946.

Selected Hymns for the Use of Children in Families, and Sunday Schools. Boston: Munroe & Francis, 1833.

Sequel to Marion Wilder, by the Author of "John Williams," "George Miles," &c. Boston: Bowles & Dearborn, 1828.

C. NEWSPAPERS

Boston Courier 1843.

Boston Daily Advertiser and Patriot 1843, 1854.

Boston Mercantile Journal 1843.

Connecticut Courant 1854.

Greensboro Patriot (North Carolina) 1848, 1852.

Halifax Advertiser 1853.

Liverpool Mercury 1868.

Montgomery Advertiser and Star Gazette (Alabama) 1849.

National Intelligencer 1848–1854.

Newburyport Herald 1843.

New York Herald 1854.

New York Journal of Commerce 1854.

Philadelphia Friends' Review 1854.

Philadelphia North American 1853–1854.

Providence Journal 1844.

Shelburne Democrat (Massachusetts) 1843.

Washington Daily Union 1854.

D. BOOKS AND PAMPHLETS

An Account of the Rise and Progress of the Frankford Asylum, Proposed to Be Established near Philadelphia for the Relief of Persons Deprived of the Use of Their Reason. Philadelphia: Kimber and Conrad, 1814.

[Alabama State Medical Association]. *An Appeal to the Legislature of Alabama for the Establishment of a State Hospital for Lunatics and Idiots, Prepared by Order of the Alabama State Medical Association: Mobile, November, 1851*. Mobile: Dade, Thompson, 1851.

An Appeal to the People of Pennsylvania on the Subject of an Asylum for the Insane Poor of the Commonwealth. Philadelphia: Printed for the Committee, 1838.

An Appeal to the Citizens of New Hampshire in Behalf of the Suffering Insane. Portsmouth: C.W. Brewster, 1838.

Allen, Matthew. *Essay on the Classification of the Insane*. London: Taylor, 1837.

Beecher, Catharine. *Suggestions Respecting Improvements in Education, Presented to the Trustees*. Hartford: Packard & Butler, 1829.

Blakewell, Samuel Glover. *An Essay on Insanity*. Edinburgh: Neill, 1833.

Blakewell, Thomas. *A Letter to the Chairman of the Select Committee on the State of Madhouses, to Which Is Subjoined Remarks on the Nature, Causes, and Cure of Mental Derangement*. Stafford, England: Chester, 1815.

Bowditch, Nathaniel I. *A History of the Massachusetts General Hospital*. Boston: [Privately printed], 1851.

Brigham, Amariah. *An Inquiry Concerning the Diseases and Functions of the Brain, the Spinal Cord, and the Nerves*. New York: George Adlard, 1840.

————. *Remarks on the Influence of Mental Cultivation and Mental Excitement upon Health*. Philadelphia: Lea & Blanchard, 1845.

Browne, James Baldwin. *Memoirs of John Howard, Compiled from His Diary, His Confidential Letter, and Other Authentic Documents*. Boston: Lincoln and Edwards, 1831.

Browne, W[illiam] A[lexander] F[rancis]. *What Asylums Were, Are, and Ought to Be: Being the Substance of Five Lectures Delivered Before the Managers of the Montrose Royal Lunatic Asylum*. Edinburgh: Black, 1837.

Channing, William Ellery. *The Correspondence of William Ellery Channing and Lucy Aiken, From 1826 to 1842*. Boston: Roberts Brothers, 1874.

————. *Works of William Ellery Channing*. 6 vols. Boston: American Unitarian Association, 1846.

Chase, Lucien Bonaparte. *History of the Polk Administration*. New York: Putnam, 1850.

Clarke, James Freeman. *Dorothea L. Dix*. Boston: George H. Ellis, 1887.

————. *James Freeman Clarke: Autobiography, Diary and Correspondence*, ed. Edward Everett Hale. Boston: Houghton, Mifflin, 1899.

Conolly, John. *An Inquiry Concerning the Indications of Insanity with Suggestions for the Better Protection and Care of the Insane*. London: Taylor, 1830.

————. *The Construction and Government of Lunatic Asylums and Hospitals for the Insane*. London: Churchill, 1847.

Dix, Morgan. *Memoirs of John Adams Dix; Compiled by His Son, Morgan Dix*. New York: Harper & Brothers, 1883.

Earle, Pliny. *The Curability of Insanity: A Series of Studies*. Philadelphia: Lippincott, 1887.

Eddy, Thomas. *Hints for Introducing an Improved Mode of Treating the Insane in Asylums*. New York: Samuel Wood, 1815.

————. *Memoirs of Pliny Earle, M. D., With Extracts from his Diary and Letters (1830–1892) and Selections from His Professional Writings (1839–1891)*. Edited by F. B. Sanborn. Boston: Damrell & Upham, 1898.

Ellis, William Charles. *A Letter to Thomas Thompson, Esq., M.P., Containing Considerations on the Necessity of Proper Places Being Provided by the Legislature for the Reception of All Insane Persons and on Some of the Abuses Which Have Been Found to Exist in Madhouses, with a Plan to Remedy Them*. Hull, England: Topping and Dawson, 1815

————. *A Treatise on the Nature, Symptoms, Causes, and Treatment of Insanity, with Practical Observations on Lunatic Asylums, and a Description of the Pauper Lunatic Asylum for the County of Middlesex at Hanwell, with a Detailed Account of Its Management*. London: Holdsworth, 1838.

Emerson, George Barrell. *Lecture on the Education of Females*. Boston: Hillard, Gray, Little and Wilkins, 1831.

————. *Reminiscences of an Old Teacher*. Boston: Alfred Mudge and Son, 1878.

Evans, Charles. *An Account of the Asylum for the Relief of Persons Deprived of Their Reason near Frankford, Pennsylvania*. Philadelphia: Rakestraw, 1846.

Fowler, Orson S. *Hereditary Descent: Its Laws and Facts, Illustrated and Applied to the Improvement of Mankind . . .* New York: Fowler, 1843.

[Friends' Asylum for the Insane]. *Rules for the Manage of the Asylum. Adopted by the Board of Managers, Ninth Month 8th, 1828*. Philadelphia: Conrad, 1828.

Hall, Nathaniel. *An Address Delivered in the First Church, Dorchester, Thursday, April 7, 1842, At the Funeral of Rev. Thaddeus Mason Harris, D.D.* Boston: B. H. Green, 1842.

Halliday, Sir Andrew. *A Letter to Lord Robert Seymour: with a Report on the Number of Lunatics and Idiots in England and Wales*. London: Underwood, 1829.

Hayward, George. *Some Observations on Dr. Rush's Work, on "The Diseases of the Mind." With Remarks on the Nature and Treatment of Insanity.* Boston: n.p., 1818.

[Hazzard, Thomas G.]. *Report on the Poor and Insane in Rhode Island. Made to the General Assembly, 1851.* Providence: n.p., 1851.

Higgins, Godfrey. *The Evidence Taken Before a Committee of the House of Commons Respecting the Asylum at York; with Observations and Notes, and a Letter to the Committee.* Doncaster, England: Sheardown, 1816.

Howe, Samuel Gridley. *An Essay on Separate and Congregate Systems of Prison Discipline; Being a Report Made to the Boston Prison Discipline Society.* Boston: William Ticknor, 1846.

Hulme, A. *Condition of Liverpool, Religious and Social; Including Notices of the State of Education, Morals, Pauperism, and Crime.* Liverpool: T. Brakell, 1858.

[Kennard, Caroline A.]. *Miss Dorothea L. Dix and her Life-Work.* Brookline, Mass.: privately printed, 1887.

Kirkbride, Thomas Story. *On the Construction, Organization, and General Arrangements of Hospitals for the Insane.* Philadelphia: Lindsay and Blakiston, 1854.

Lieber, Francis. *A Popular Essay on Subjects of Penal Law, and on Uninterrupted Solitary Confinement at Labor, as Contradistinguished to Solitary Confinement at Night and Joint Labor by Day, in a Letter to John Bacon, Esquire, President of the Philadelphia Society for Alleviating the Miseries of Public Prisons.* Philadelphia: n.p., 1838.

Lincoln, Levi and Isaac Davis. *Reminiscences of the Original Associates and Past Members of the Worcester Fire Society.* Worcester: Charles Hamilton, 1870.

Lincoln, William. *History of Worcester, Massachusetts, From Its Earliest Settlement to September, 1836.* Worcester: Charles Hersey, 1862.

Lists of Temporary Students at Harvard College. Cambridge, Mass.: Charles Wilson and Sons, 1914.

Mayo, Thomas. *An Essay on the Relation of the Theory of Morals to Insanity.* London: Fellowes, 1834.

Millingen, J. G. *Aphorisms on the Treatment and Management of the Insane, with Considerations on Public and Private Lunatic Asylums, Pointing out the Errors in the Present System.* London: Churchill, 1840.

Monro, Henry. *Remarks on Insanity: Its Nature and Treatment.* London: Churchill, 1850.

Neville, William B. *On Insanity, Its Nature, Causes, and Cure.* London: Longman, 1836.

Nicell, S. W. *An Enquiry into the Present State of Visitation in Asylums for the Reception of the Insane.* London: Harvey and Darnton, 1828.

Peabody, Elizabeth. *The Letters of Elizabeth Palmer Peabody, American Renaissance Woman*, ed. Bruce A. Ronda. Middletown, Conn.: Wesleyan University Press, 1984.

Picton, J. A. *Memorials of Liverpool Historical and Topographical.* 2 vols. London: Green, 1875.

The Picture of Liverpool, or Stranger's Guide. Liverpool, Thomas Taylor, 1834.

Pilsbury, William H. *History of Methodism in Maine, 1793–1886.* Augusta: Charles E. Nash, 1887.

Pinel, Philippe. *A Treatise on Insanity . . .* Trans. D. D. Davis. London: Cadell and Davis, 1806.

Prichard, James Cowles. *A Treatise on Insanity and Other Disorders Affecting the Mind.* London: Sherwood, Gilbert and Piper, 1835.

Reports and Other Documents Relating to the State Hospital at Worcester, Mass. Boston: Dutton and Wentworth, 1837.

Robinson, Alex C. *Report of the Lunatic Department of the Baltimore Alms-House; Presented to the*

Board of Trustees, December, 1840. To Which is Added an Appendix, Containing an Appeal in Behalf of the insane Poor of Maryland. Baltimore: S. Robinson, 1841.

Roe, Alfred S. *Dorothea Lynde Dix, A Paper Read before the Worcester Society of Antiquity, November 20th, 1888.* Worcester: Franklin P. Rice, 1889.

Rush, Benjamin. *Medical Inquiries and Observations upon the Diseases of the Mind.* Philadelphia: Kimber and Richardson, 1830.

Sharf, J. Thomas. *History of Baltimore City and County.* Philadelphia: n.p., 1891.

Shew, Joel. *Tobacco: Its History, Nature, and Effects on the Body and Mind . . .* New York: Fowler and Well, [1849].

Sneed, William C. *A Report on the History and Mode of Management of the Kentucky Penitentiary.* Frankfort: A.G. Hodges, 1860.

Snyder, Charles M. *The Lady and the President: The Letters of Dorothea Dix and Millard Fillmore.* Lexington: University Press of Kentucky, 1976.

Sprague, William B. *Annals of the American Unitarian Pulpit.* New York: Robert Carter, 1865.

Tiffany, Francis. *Charles Francis Bernard, His Life and Work.* Boston: Houghton, Mifflin, 1895.

Thomas, Isaiah. "The Diary of Isaiah Thomas, 1805–1808," ed. Benjamin Thomas Hill, in *Transactions and Collections*, vol. 9. Worcester: American Antiquarian Society, 1909.

Trezevant, Daniel H. *Letters to His Excellency Governor Manning on the Lunatic Hospital.* Columbia, S.C.: R. W. Gibbes, 1854.

Tuke, Daniel Hack. *The Moral Management of the Insane.* London: Churchill, 1854.

————. *Reform in the Treatment of the Insane.* London: Churchill, 1854.

Tuke, Samuel. *Description of the Retreat: An Institution near York for Insane Persons of the Society of Friends.* York: Thomas Wilson and Sons, 1813.

————. *A Letter to Thomas Eddy of New York on Pauper Lunatic Asylums.* New York: Samuel Wood, 1815.

Wall, Caleb A. *Reminiscences of Worcester from the Earliest Period, Historical and Genealogical.* Worcester: Tyler and Seagrave, 1877.

Waterston, Robert C. *The Condition of the Insane in Massachusetts.* Boston: James Munroe, 1843.

————. *Memorial of George Barrell Emerson, LL.D.* Cambridge, Mass.: John Wilson and Son, 1884.

Wyman, Rufus. *A Discourse on Mental Philosophy as Connected with Mental Disease, Delivered Before the Massachusetts Medical Society.* Boston: Office of the Daily Advertiser, 1830.

E. ARTICLES

Beck, Theodoric Romeyn. "An Account of Some of the Lunatic Asylums in the united States," *New-York Medical and Physical Journal* 7 (April-June 1828): 186–206.

Bigelow, L. J. "Miss Dix, And What She Has Done," *Galaxy* 3 (15 March 1867): 669.

"Blackwell's Island Lunatic Asylum," *Harper's New Monthly Magazine* 32 (February 1866): 273–94.

[Brigham, Amariah]. "Definition of Insanity—Nature of the Disease," *American Journal of Insanity* 1 (October 1844): 97–116.

————. "Insanity and Insane Hospitals," *North American Review* 46 (January 1837): 91–121.

————. "Institutions for the Insane in the United States," *American journal of Insanity* 5 (July 1848): 53–62.

————. "Number of the Insane and Idiotic, with Brief Notices of the Lunatic Asylums in the United States," *American Journal of Insanity* 1 (July 1844): 78–81.

Chaillé, Stanford. "Insane Asylum of the State of Louisiana, at Jackson," *New Orleans Medical and Surgical Journal* 15 (January 1858): 103–24.

Chandler, George. "Life of Dr. Woodward," *American Journal of Insanity* 8 (October 1851): 119–35.

Child, Lydia Maria. "The Missionary of Prisons," *The Present* 1 (5 December 1843): 209–12.

Earle, Pliny. "On the Curability of Insanity," *American Journal of the Medical Sciences* 5 (April 1843): 344–63.

————. "Gheel," *American Journal of Insanity* 7 (July 1851): 67–78.

Hayden, C. B. "On the Distribution of Insanity," *Southern Literary Messenger* 10 (March 1844): 178–81.

[Howe, Samuel Gridley]. "Insanity in Massachusetts," *North American Review* 56 (January 1843): 171–91.

————. "Lunatic Hospital at Worcester," *Christian Examiner* 26 (May 1839): 257–59.

Jarvis, Edward. "Insanity among the Colored Population of the Free States," *American Journal of Insanity* 8 (January 1852): 268–82.

————. "On the Supposed Increase of Insanity," *American Journal of Insanity* 8 (January 1852): 333–64.

————. "Statistics of Insanity in the United States," *Boston Medical and Surgical Journal* 27 (21 September and 30 November 1842): 116–21, 282–82.

Kirkbride, Thomas Story. "Remarks on the Construction and Arrangements of Hospitals for the Insane," *American Journal of the Medical Sciences* 13 (1847): 40–56.

Ray, Isaac. "Observations on the Principal Hospitals for the Insane, in Great Britain, France and Germany," *American Journal of Insanity* 2 (April 1846): 289–390.

"Startling Facts from the Census (from the *New-York Observer*)," *American Journal of Insanity* 8 (October 1851): 153–55.

Waterston, Robert C. "The Insane of Massachusetts," *Christian Examiner* 33 (January 1843): 338–52.

[Woodward, Samuel]. "Insane Hospitals in the United States, in Operation in May, 1838," *Boston Medical and Surgical Journal* 18 (June 22, 1838): 309–13.

F. OFFICIAL DOCUMENTS

Brown, Albert G. *Speech of Albert G. Brown of Mississippi, the President's Veto Message, and in Defence of the Bill Making a Grant to the Several States for the Benefit of the Indigent Insane. Delivered in the Senate of the United States, May 17, 1854.* (Washington: John T. and Lem. Towers, 1854).

Chadwick, Edwin. *Report on the Sanitary Conditions of the Labouring Population of Great Britain.* London: Clowes, 1842.

Checkland S. G. and E. O. A. Checkland, eds. *The Poor Law of 1834.* London: Penguin, 1974.

Chancellor, C. W. *Report on the Public Charities, Reformatories, Prisons and Almshouses, of the State of Maryland* . . . Frederick, Md.: Baughman, 1877.

Clay, C. C., Jr. *President's Veto Message. Speech of Mr. C. C. Clay, Jr., of Alabama, on the President's Veto Message, Rejecting the Indigent Insane Bill, and against Giving Away the Public Lands. Delivered in the Senate of the United States, June 20, 1854.* Washington: John and Lem. Towers, 1854.

Clayton, John M. *Speech of Hon. John M. Clayton, of Delaware, on the Veto Message of the President, on the Bill for the Benefit of the Indigent Insane.* Delivered in the Senate 15 June 1854. Washington: Congressional Globe, 1854.

Collins, Stephen. *Report on Pauper Insanity; Presented to the City Council of Baltimore, on March 28th, 1845, by Dr. Stephen Collins, Chairman of the Committee.* Baltimore: James Lucas, 1845.

Commissioners in Lunacy. *Further Report Relative to the Haydock Lodge Lunatic Asylum.* London: Spottiswoode and Shaw, 1847.

Connecticut Assembly. *Report of the Committee for Locating a Site for a Hospital for the Insane Poor.* New Haven: Babcock and Wildman, 1840.

History of the Town of Shrewsbury, Massachusetts, From Its Settlement in 1717 to 1828 . . . Boston: n.p., 1847.

House of Commons. *Report of the Select Committee on Criminal and Pauper Lunatics.* London, 1807.

————. *First Report: Minutes of Evidence Taken before the Select Committee appointed to consider of Provision being made for the better Regulation of Madhouses, In England.* London, 23 May 1815.

————. *Report from the Committee on Madhouses in England.* London, 11 July 1815.

————. *Second Report: Minutes of Evidence Taken before the Select Committee.* . . . London, 2 June 1815.

————. *Third Report from the Committee on Madhouses in England, &c. with an Appendix.* London, 11 June 1816.

————. *Report from Select Committee on Pauper Lunatics in the County of Middlesex, and on Lunatic Asylums.* London, 29 June 1827.

————. *Report from Select Committee on Hereford Lunatic Asylum; with the Minutes of Evidence, Appendix, and Index.* London, 27 June 1839.

————. *Report of the Select Committee on the Care and Treatment of Lunatics.* London, 1859–1860.

————. *Poor Law Report of 1834*, ed. S. G. Checkland and E. O. A. Checkland (London: Penguin, 1974).

House of Lords. *Minutes of Evidence Taken Before the Select Committee of the House of Lords on the Bills Relating to Lunatics and Lunatic Asylums.* London, 1828.

Irish University Press. *British Parliamentary Papers: Reports from Select Committees on Criminal and Pauper Lunatics and on the Better Regulation of Madhouses in England with Minutes of Evidence and Appendices: Mental Health,* vols. 1–2. Shannon: Irish University Press, 1968.

Jarvis, Edward. *Report on Insanity and Idiocy in Massachusetts, by the Commission on Lunacy, Under Resolve of the Legislature of 1854.* Boston: William White, 1855.

Memorial of the Board of Directors for Public Institutions in Relation to the Condition of the Lunatic Hospital. 1863. City Document No. 11. (Boston: n.p., 1863).

New York Board of Aldermen. *Report of the Commissioners of the Alms House, Bridewell and Penitentiary, Document No. 32* (September 11, 1837).

Pierce, Franklin. *Special Message of President Pierce to the Senate of the United States; May 3, 1854.* Washington, D.C.: Government printer, 1854.

Report of the Commissioners Appointed by the Governor of New Jersey, to Ascertain the Number of Lunatics and Idiots in the State. Newark: M.S. Harrison, 1840.

Report of the Commissioners of the Lunatic Asylum, to His Excellency Joseph W. Matthews, January 1, 1850. Jackson: n.p., 1850.

Report of the Committee Appointed by the Board of Guardians of the Poor of the City and Districts of Philadelphia, to visit the Cities of Baltimore, New-York, Providence, Boston and Salem. Philadelphia: Samuel Parker, 1827.

A Second Appeal to the People of Pennsylvania on the Subject of an Asylum for the Insane Poor of the Commonwealth. Philadelphia: Brown, Bicking and Guilbert, 1840.

Shattuck, Lemuel et al. *Report of the Sanitary Commission of Massachusetts 1850.* Facsimile ed., Cambridge, Mass.: Harvard University Press, 1948.

Vital Records of Shrewsbury, Massachusetts, To the end of the Year 1849 . . . Worcester: n.p., 1904.

II. SECONDARY SOURCES

A. BOOKS

Aron, Cindy Sondik. *Ladies and Gentlemen of the Civil Service: Middle-Class Workers in Victorian America.* New York: Oxford University Press, 1987.

Alexander, Franz and S. Selesnick. *The History of Psychiatry: An Evaluation of Psychiatric Thought and Practice from Prehistoric Times to the Present.* New York: Harper and Row, 1966.

Arieno, Marlene A. *Victorian Lunatics: A Social Epidemiology of Mental Illness in Mid-Nineteenth-Century England.* London: Associated University Presses, 1989.

Bachrach, Leona. *Deinstitutionalization: An Analytical Review and Sociological Perspective.* Rockville, Md.: National Institute of Mental Health, 1976.

Baker, George Claude, Jr. *An Introduction to the History of Early New England Methodism.* 3 vols. Nashville, Tenn.: Abington Press, 1964.

Barker-Benfield, G. J. *The Horrors of the Half-Known Life: Male Attitudes toward Women and Sexuality in Nineteenth-Century America.* New York: Harper and Row, 1976.

Belknap, Ivan. *Human Problems of a State Mental Hospital.* New York: McGraw-Hill, 1956.

Berg, Barbara J. *The Remembered Gate: Origins of American Feminism: The Woman and the City, 1800–1860.* New York: Oxford University Press, 1978.

Bergeron, Paul H. *The Presidency of James K. Polk.* Lawrence: University of Kansas Press, 1987.

Bledstein, B. J. *The Culture of Professionalism: The Middle Class and the Development of Higher Education in America.* New York: Norton, 1976.

Bockoven, J. Sanborne. *Moral Treatment in American Psychiatry.* New York: Springer, 1963.

Bond, Earle D. *Dr. Kirkbride and His Mental Hospital.* Philadelphia: Lippincott, 1947.

Boyer, Paul. *Urban Masses and Moral Order in America, 1820–1920*. Cambridge, Mass.: Harvard University Press, 1978.

Braginsky, B., D. Braginsky, and K. Ring. *Methods of Madness: The Mental Hospital as a Last Resort*. New York: Holt, Rinehart, and Winston, 1969.

Branca, Patricia. *Silent Sisterhood: Middle Class Women in the Victorian Home*. London: Croon Helm, 1975.

Bremner, Robert H. *American Philanthropy*. Chicago: University of Chicago Press, 1960.

Brenzel, Barbara M. *Daughters of the State: A Social Portrait of the First Reform School for Girls in North America, 1856–1905*. Cambridge, Mass.: Harvard University Press, 1983.

Brown, Arthur W. *Always Young for Liberty: A Biography of William Ellery Channing*. Syracuse, N.Y.: Syracuse University Press, 1956.

Brown, Richard D. *Modernization: The Transformation of American Life*. New York: Hill and Wang, 1976.

Burdett, Henry C. *Hospitals and Asylums of the World: Their Origin, History, Construction, Administration, Management, and Legislation*. 4 vols. London: J. & A. Churchill, 1891.

Bynum, W. F., Roy Porter, and Michael Shepherd, eds. *The Anatomy of Madness: Essays in the History of Psychiatry*. vol. 1, *People and Ideas*; vol. 2, *Institutions and Society*. London: Tavistock, 1985.

Carleton, Mark T. *Politics and Punishment: The History of the Louisiana State Penal System*. Baton Rouge: Louisiana State University Press, 1971.

Cassedy, James H. *American Medicine and Statistical Thinking, 1800–1860*. Cambridge, Mass.: Harvard University Press, 1984.

Castel, Robert. *The Regulation of Madness: The Origins of Incarceration in France*. Berkeley: University of California Press, 1988.

Chadbourne, Ava Harriet. *Maine Place Names and the Peopling of Its Towns*. Portland: B. Wheelwright, 1955.

Chadwick, John White. *William Ellery Channing: Minister of Religion*. Boston: Houghton, Mifflin, 1903.

Chambers-Schiller, Lee. *Liberty, A Better Husband. Single Women in America: The Generations of 1780–1840*. New Haven: Yale University Press, 1984.

Cohen, Stanley and Andrew Scull. *Social Control and the State: Historical and Comparative Essays*. Oxford: Martin Robertson, 1983.

Conrad, Susan P. *Perish the Thought: Intellectual Women in Romantic America, 1830–1860*. Secaucus, N.J.: Citadel, 1976.

Cott, Nancy F. *The Bonds of Womanhood: "Woman's Sphere" in New England, 1780–1835*. New Haven: Yale University Press, 1977.

Cross, Whitney. *The Burned-over District: The Social and Intellectual History of Enthusiastic Religion in Western New York, 1800–1850*. Ithaca, N.Y.: Cornell University Press, 1950.

Dain, Norman. *Concepts of Insanity in the United States, 1789–1865*. Pittsburgh: University of Pittsburgh Press, 1964.

————. *Disordered Minds: The First Century of Eastern State Hospital in Williamsburg, Virginia, 1766–1866*. Williamsburg: Colonial Williamsburg Foundation, 1971.

Davies, John D. *Phrenology: Fad and Science: A 19-th Century American Crusade*. New Haven: Yale University Press, 1955.

Davis, David Brion. *The Problem of Slavery in the Age of the Revolution*. Ithaca, N.Y.: Cornell University Press, 1975.

————. *The Problem of Slavery in Western Culture*. Ithaca, N.Y.: Cornell University Press, 1967.

————. *Slavery and Human Progress*. New York: Oxford University Press, 1984.

Davis, David Brion, ed. *Antebellum Reform*. New York: Harper and Row, 1967.

Day, William Patrick. *In the Circles of Fear and Desire: A Study of Gothic Fantasy*. Chicago: University of Chicago Press, 1985.

De Giustino, David A. *The Conquest of Mind: Phrenology and Victorian Social Thought*. London: Croon Helm, 1975.

Delbanco, Andrew. *William Ellery Channing: An Essay on the Liberal Spirit in America*. Cambridge, Mass.: Harvard University Press, 1981.

Deutsch, Albert. *The Mentally Ill in America: A History of Their Care and Treatment from Colonial Times*. 2d ed. New York: Columbia University Press, 1949.

Digby, Anne. *Madness, Morality and Medicine: A Study of the York Retreat, 1796–1914*. Cambridge: Cambridge University Press, 1985.

Doerner, Klaus. *Madmen and the Bourgeoisie*. Oxford: Basil Blackwell, 1981.

Donald, David Herbert. *Charles Sumner and the Coming of the Civil War*. New York: Knopf, 1960.

————. *Charles Sumner and the Rights of Man*. New York: Knopf, 1970.

————. *Lincoln Reconsidered*. New York: Vintage, 1956.

Douglas, Ann. *The Feminization of American Culture*. New York: Knopf, 1977.

Dwyer, Ellen. *Homes for the Mad: Life Inside Two Nineteenth-Century Asylums*. New Brunswick, N.J.: Rutgers University Press, 1987.

Eaton, Clement. *Henry Clay and the Art of American Politics*. Boston: Little, Brown, 1957.

Eckhardt, Celia Morris. *Fanny Wright: Rebel in America*. Cambridge, Mass.: Harvard University Press, 1984.

Eliot, Samuel A. *Heralds of a Liberal Faith*. 3 vols. Boston: American Unitarian Association, 1910.

Epstein, Barbara. *The Politics of Domesticity: Women, Evangelism, and Temperance in Nineteenth-Century America*. Middletown, Conn.: Wesleyan University Press, 1981.

Evans, Robin. *The Fabrication of Virtue: English Prison Architecture, 1750–1842*. Cambridge: Cambridge University Press, 1982.

Faust, Drew Gilpin, ed. *The Ideology of Slavery: Proslavery Thought in the Antebellum South, 1830–1860*. Baton Rouge: Louisiana State University Press, 1981.

Feldberg, Michael. *The Turbulent Era: Riot and Disorder in Jacksonian America*. New York: Oxford University Press, 1980.

Fleming, Donald. *William H. Welch and the Rise of Modern Medicine*. Boston: Little, Brown, 1954.

Foner, Eric. *Free Soil, Free Labor, Free Men: The Ideology of the Republican Party before the Civil War*. New York: Oxford University Press, 1970.

Forbush, Bliss. *The Sheppard & Enoch Pratt Hospital, 1853–1970: A History*. Philadelphia: Lippincott, 1971.

Foucault, Michel. *Folie et déraison, Histoire de la folie l'âge classique*. Paris: Plon, 1961.

————. *Discipline and Punish: The Birth of the Prison*. New York: Pantheon, 1977.

————. *Madness and Civilization: A History of Insanity in the Age of Reason*. Translated by Richard Howard. New York: Pantheon, 1965.

Fox, Richard. *So Far Disordered in Mind*. Berkeley: University of California Press, 1978.

Fredrickson, George M. *The Black Image in the White Mind: The Debate on Afro-American Character and Destiny, 1817–1914*. New York: Harper and Row, 1971.

———. *The Inner Civil War: Northern Intellectuals and the Crisis of the Union*. New York: Harper and Row, 1965.

Fraser, Derek. *The Evolution of the British Welfare State*. New York: Macmillan, 1973.

Freehling, William W. *The Road to Disunion: Volume I: Secessionists at Bay, 1776–1854*. New York and Oxford: Oxford University Press, 1990.

Freidson, Eliot. *Profession of Medicine*. New York: Dodd, Mead, 1970.

———. *Professional Powers. A Study of the Institutionalization of Formal Knowledge*. Chicago: University of Chicago Press, 1986.

Frye, Northrup. *The Secular Scripture*. Cambridge, Mass.: Harvard University Press, 1976.

Gara, Larry. *The Presidency of Franklin Pierce*. Lawrence: University Press of Kansas, 1991.

Geffen, Elizabeth M. *Philadelphia Unitarianism, 1796–1861*. Philadelphia: University of Pennsylvania Press, 1961.

Gienapp, William E. *The Origins of the Republican Party, 1852–1856*. New York: Oxford University Press, 1987.

Genovese, Eugene D. *The Political Economy of Slavery*. New York: Vintage, 1967.

Gibbs, George. *The Gibbs Family of Rhode Island and Some Related Families*. New York: privately printed, 1933.

Galishoff, Stuart. *Newark: The Nations's Unhealthiest City, 1832–1895*. New Brunswick, N.J.: Rutgers University Press, 1988.

Gilbert, Sandra M. and Susan Gubar. *The Madwoman in the Attic: The Woman Writer and the Nineteenth-Century Literary Imagination*. New Haven, Conn.: Yale University Press, 1979.

Ginzberg, Lori D. *Women and the Work of Benevolence: Morality, Politics, and Class in the Nineteenth-Century United States*. New Haven: Yale University Press, 1990.

Goffman, Erving. *Asylums: Essays on the Social Situation of Mental Patients*. Garden City, N.Y.: Doubleday, 1961.

Goldstein, Jan. *Console and Classify: The French Psychiatric Profession in the Nineteenth Century*. Cambridge: Cambridge University Press, 1987.

Griffin, Clifford S. *Their Brothers' Keepers: Moral Stewardship in the United States, 1800–1865*. New Brunswick, N.J.: Rutgers University Press, 1960.

Grob, Gerald. *Edward Jarvis and the Medical World of Nineteenth-Century America*. Knoxville: University of Tennessee Press, 1978.

———. *From Asylum to Community: Mental Health Policy in Modern America*. Princeton, N.J.: Princeton University Press, 1991.

———. *Mental Institutions in America: Social Policy to 1875*. New York: Free Press, 1973.

———. *The State and the Mentally Ill: A History of the Worcester State Hospital in Massachusetts, 1830–1920*. Chapel Hill: University of North Carolina Press, 1966.

Gusfield, Joseph. *Symbolic Crusade: Status Politics and the American Temperance Movement*. Urbana: University of Illinois Press, 1966.

Gutman, Herbert G. *Work, Culture, and Society in Industrializing America: Essays in American Working-class and Social History*. New York: Vintage, 1976.

Hall, J. K., ed. *One Hundred Years of American Psychiatry, 1844–1944*. New York: Columbia University Press, 1944.

Hardesty, Nancy A. *Women Called to Witness: Evangelical Feminism in the 19th Century*. Nashville, Tenn.: Abingdon Press, 1984.

Hartman, Mary S. and Lois Banner, eds. *Clio's Consciousness Raised: New Perspectives on the History of Women*. New York: Harper and Row, 1974.

Hatch, Louis Clinton, ed. *Maine: A History*. Somersworth: New Hampshire Publishing Co., 1974.

Henretta, James A. *The Evolution of American Society, 1700–1815: An Interdisciplinary Analysis*. Lexington, Mass.: Heath, 1973.

Henriques, Ursula R. Q. *Before the Welfare State: Social Administration in Early Victorian England*. London: Longman, 1979.

Hewitt, Nancy A. *Women's Activism and Social Change: Rochester, New York, 1822–1872*. Ithaca, N.Y.: Cornell University Press, 1984.

Himmelfarb, Gertrude. *Lord Acton: A Study in Conscience in Politics*. London: Routledge and Keagan Paul, 1952.

———. *The Idea of Poverty: England in the Early Industrial Age*. New York: Knopf, 1984.

———. *Poverty and Compassion: The Moral Imagination of the Late Victorians*. New York: Knopf, 1991.

Howe, Daniel Walker. *The Political Culture of the American Whigs*. Chicago: University of Chicago Press, 1979.

———. *The Unitarian Conscience: Harvard Moral Philosophy, 1805–1861*. Cambridge, Mass.: Harvard University Press, 1970.

Howe, M. A. DeWolfe. *The Humane Society of the Commonwealth of Massachusetts: An Historical Review 1785–1916*. Boston: Humane Society at the Riverside Press, 1918.

Hurd, Henry M., ed. *The Institutional Care of the Insane in the United States and Canada*. 4 vols. Baltimore: Johns Hopkins University Press, 1916.

Hutchison, William R. *The Modernist Impulse in American Protestantism*. Cambridge, Mass.: Harvard University Press, 1976.

———. *The Transcendentalist Ministers: Church Reform in the New England Renaissance*. New Haven: Yale University Press, 1959.

Huxley, Elspeth Joscelin Grant. *Florence Nightingale*. New York: Putnam, 1975.

Ignatieff, Michael. *A Just Measure of Pain: The Penitentiary in the Industrial Revolution, 1750–1850*. New York: Pantheon, 1978.

James, Edward T., Janet Wilson James, and Paul S. Boyer, eds. *Notable American Women, 1607–1950: A Biographical Dictionary*. Cambridge, Mass.: Harvard University Press, 1971.

Jones, Kathleen. *A History of the Mental Health Services*. London: Routledge and Kegan Paul, 1972.

———. *Lunacy, Law and Conscience, 1744–1845: The Social History of the Care of the Insane*. London: Routledge and Kegan Paul, 1955.

———. *The Making of Social Policy in Britain 1830–1990*. London: Athlone, 1991.

Katz, Michael B. *In the Shadow of the Poorhouse: A Social History of Welfare in America*. New York: Basic Books, 1986.

———. *The Irony of Early School Reform: Education and Innovation in Mid-Nineteenth Century Massachusetts*. Boston: Beacon Press, 1968.

———. *Poverty and Policy in American History*. New York: Academic Press, 1983.

Kelley, Mary. *Private Women, Public Stage: Literary Domesticity in Nineteenth-Century America*, New York: Oxford University Press, 1984.

Kett, Joseph F. *The Formation of the American Medical Profession*. New Haven, Conn.: Yale University Press, 1968.

—————. *Rites of Passage: Adolescence in America 1790 to Present*. New York: Basic Books, 1977.

Knights, Peter R. *The Plain People of Boston, 1830–1860: A Study in City Growth*. New York: Oxford University Press, 1971.

Kraditor, Aileen. *Means and Ends in American Abolitionism*. New York: Pantheon, 1969.

—————, ed. *Up from the Pedestal: Selected Writings in the History of American Feminism*. Chicago: University of Chicago Press, 1968.

Kuhn, Anne L. *The Mother's Role in Childhood Education: New England Concepts, 1830–1860*. New Haven: Yale University Press, 1947.

Lerner, Gerda. *The Grimké Sisters from South Carolina: Rebels against Slavery*. Boston: Houghton, Mifflin, 1967.

Levine, Daniel. *Poverty and Society: The Growth of the American Welfare State in International Comparison*. New Brunswick, N.J.: Rutgers University Press, 1988.

Lévy, Maurice. *Le Roman "Gothique" Anglais, 1764–1824*. Toulouse: Association des publications des Facultés des lettres et sciences humaines de Toulouse, 1968.

Lewis, Gordon K. *The Virgin Island: A Caribbean Lilliput*. Evanston, Ill.: Northwestern University Press, 1972.

Little, Nina F. *Early Years of the McLean Asylum*. Boston: Countway Library of Medicine, 1972.

Loveland, Anne C. *Southern Evangelicals and the Social Order, 1800–1860*. Baton Rouge: Louisiana State University Press, 1980.

Lubove, Roy. *The Professional Altruist: The Emergence of Social Work as a Career 1880–1930*. Cambridge, Mass.: Harvard University Press, 1965.

Ludlum, David M. *Social Ferment in Vermont, 1791–1850*. New York: Columbia University Press, 1939.

Lumpkin, Katherine Du Pre. *The Emancipation of Angelina Grimké*. Chapel Hill: University of North Carolina Press, 1974.

McClelland, Peter D. and Richard J. Zeckhauser. *Demographic Dimensions of the New Republic*. Cambridge, Mass.: Harvard University Press, 1982.

McColgan, Daniel T. *Joseph Tuckerman: Pioneer in American Social Work*. Washington, D.C.: Catholic University of America Press, 1940.

MacDonald, Michael. *Mystical Bedlam: Madness, Anxiety, and Healing in Seventeenth-Century England*. Cambridge: Cambridge University Press, 1981.

McFeely, William S. *Frederick Douglass*. New York: Norton, 1991.

Mack, Mary P. *Jeremy Bentham, An Odyssey of Ideas, 1748–1792*. 2 vols. London: Heinemann, 1962.

McGovern, Constance. *Masters of Madness: Social Origins of the American Psychiatric Profession*. Hanover, N.H.: University Press of New England, 1985.

McPherson, James M. *The Battle Cry of Freedom: The Civil War Era*. New York: Oxford University Press, 1988.

Marini, Stephen A. *Radical Sects of Revolutionary New England*. Cambridge, Mass.: Harvard University Press, 1982.

Marshall, Helen E. *Dorothea Dix: Forgotten Samaritan*. Chapel Hill: University of North Carolina Press, 1937.

Martin, George T., Jr., and Mayer N. Zald, eds. *Social Welfare in Society*. New York: Columbia University Press, 1981.

Matthews, Donald. *Religion in the Old South*. Chicago: University of Chicago Press, 1977.

Messerli, Jonathan. *Horace Mann: A Biography*. New York Knopf, 1972.

Mohl, Raymond A. *Poverty in New York, 1783–1825*. New York: Oxford University Press, 1971.

Moore, John Hebron. *The Emergence of the Cotton Kingdom in the Old Southwest: Mississippi, 1770–1860*. Baton Rouge: Louisiana State University Press, 1988.

Morison, Samuel Eliot. *The Oxford History of the American People*. New York: Oxford University Press, 1965.

Morrison, Ernest. *The City on the Hill: A History of the Harrisburg State Hospital*. Harrisburg, Pa.: n.p., 1992.

Nevins, Allan. *Ordeal of the Union*. 2 vols. New York: Scribner's, 1947.

Nichols, Roy. *Franklin Pierce: Young Hickory of the Granite Hills*. Philadelphia: University of Pennsylvania Press, 1931.

Nye, Robert. *Crime, Madness, and Politics in Modern France*. Princeton, N.J.: Princeton University Press, 1984.

Oates, Stephen B. *A Woman of Valor: Clara Barton and the Civil War*. New York: Free Press, 1994.

O'Donoghue, E. D. *The Story of Bethlehem Hospital*. London: Fisher and Unwin, 1913.

Owen, David. *English Philanthropy, 1660–1960*. Cambridge, Mass.: Harvard University Press, 1964.

Parks, Joseph Howard. *John Bell of Tennessee*. Baton Rouge: Louisiana State University Press, 1950.

Parry-Jones, William L. *The Trade in Lunacy: A Study of Private Madhouses in England in the Eighteenth and Nineteenth Centuries*. London: Routledge and Kegan Paul/University of Toronto Press, 1972.

Pessen, Edward. *Jacksonian America: Society, Personality, and Politics*. rev. ed. Homewood, Ill.: Dorsey, 1978.

Peterson, M. J. *The Medical Profession in Mid-Victorian London*. Berkeley: University of California Press, 1978.

Porter, Roy. *Mind-Forg'd Manacles: A History of Madness in England from the Restoration to the Regency*. London: Athlone, 1987.

Porter, Roy, and Dorothy Porter. *In Sickness and in Health: The British Experience, 1650–1850*. London: Fourth Estate, 1988.

Potter, David M. *The Impending Crisis, 1848–1861*. Compiled and edited by Don E. Fehrenbacher. New York: Harper and Row, 1976.

Ringe, Donald A. *American Gothic: Imagination and Reason in Nineteenth-Century Fiction*. Lexington: University Press of Kentucky, 1982.

Roberts, David. *Victorian Origins of the British Welfare State*. New Haven: Yale University Press, 1960.

Rosen, George. *Madness in Society: Chapters in the Historical Sociology of Mental Illness*. Chicago: University of Chicago Press, 1968.

Rosenberg, Charles. *The Care of Strangers: The Rise of America's Hospital System*. New York: Basic Books, 1987.

———. *The Cholera Years*. Chicago: University of Chicago Press, 1962.

———. *The Trial of the Assassin Guiteau*. Chicago: University of Chicago Press, 1968.

Rosenberg, Rosalind. *Beyond Separate Spheres: Intellectual Roots of Modern Feminism*. New Haven: Yale University Press, 1982.

Rosenkrantz, Barbara Gutman. *Public Health and the State: Changing Views in Massachusetts, 1842–1936*. Cambridge, Mass.: Harvard University Press, 1972.

Roth, Randolph A. *The Democratic Dilemma: Religion, Reform, and the Social Order in the Connecticut River Valley of Vermont, 1791–1850*. Cambridge, England: Cambridge University Press, 1987.

Rothman, David J. *Conscience and Convenience: The Asylum and Its Alternatives in Progressive America*. Boston: Little, Brown, 1980.

————. *The Discovery of the Asylum: Social Order and Disorder in the New Republic*. rev. ed. Boston: Little, Brown, 1990.

Russell, William L. *The New York Hospital: A History of the Psychiatric Service, 1771–1936*. New York: Columbia University Press, 1945.

Ryan, Mary P. *Womanhood in America: From Colonial Times to the Present*. New York: Franklin Watts, 1975.

Sage, Victor. *Horror Fiction in the Protestant Tradition*. London: Macmillan, 1988.

Scheff, Thomas. *Being Mentally Ill: A Sociological Theory*. Chicago: University of Chicago Press, 1966.

Schiebinger, Londa. *The Mind Has No Sex?* Cambridge, Mass.: Harvard University Press, 1990.

Schwartz, Harold. *Samuel Gridley Howe: Social Reformer, 1801–1876*. Cambridge, Mass.: Harvard University Press, 1956.

Scott, Joan Wallach. *Gender and the Politics of History*. New York: Columbia University Press, 1989.

Scull, Andrew. *Decarceration: Community Treatment and the Deviant—A Radical View*. 2d ed. New Brunswick, N.J.: Rutgers University Press, 1984.

————. *The Most Solitary of Afflictions: Madness and Society in Britain, 1700–1900*. New Haven: Yale University Press, 1993.

————. *Museums of Madness: The Social Organization of Insanity in Nineteenth Century England*. New York: St. Martin's Press, 1979.

————. *Social Order/Mental Disorder: Anglo-American Psychiatry in Historical Perspective*. Berkeley: University of California Press, 1989.

Scull, Andrew, ed. *The Asylum as Utopia: W. A. F. Browne and the Mid-Nineteenth Century Consolidation of Psychiatry*. London: Tavistock/Routledge, 1991.

————. *Madhouses, Mad-doctors, and Madmen: The Social History of Psychiatry in the Victorian Era*. Philadelphia: University of Pennsylvania Press, 1981.

Semmes, John E. *John B. Latrobe and His Times, 1803–1891*. Baltimore: Norman, Remington, 1917.

Showalter, Elaine. *The Female Malady: Women, Madness, and English Culture, 1830–1980*. New York: Pantheon, 1985.

Shyrock, Richard H. *The Development of Modern Medicine*. Philadelphia: University of Pennsylvania Press, 1936.

Sklar, Kathryn Kish. *Catharine Beecher: A Study in American Domesticity*. New Haven: Yale University Press, 1973.

Smith, Elbert B. *The Presidencies of Zachary & Millard Fillmore*. Lawrence: University of Kansas Press, 1988.

Smith, Timothy L. *Revivalism and Social Reform: American Protestantism on the Eve of the Civil War*. Nashville, Tenn.: Abingdon Press, 1957.

Smith-Rosenberg, Carroll. *Disorderly Conduct: Visions of Gender in Victorian America*. New York: Knopf, 1985.

————. *Religion and the Rise of the American City: The New York Mission Movement, 1812–1870*. Ithaca, N.Y.: Cornell University Press, 1971.

Stampp, Kenneth. *The Peculiar Institution: Slavery in the Antebellum South*. New York: Knopf, 1956.

Stange, Douglas C. *Patterns of Antislavery among American Unitarians, 1831–1860*. Rutherford, N.J.: Fairleigh Dickinson University Press, 1977.

Stansell, Christine. *City of Women: Sex and Class in New York, 1789–1860*. New York: Knopf, 1986.

Starr, Paul. *The Social Transformation of American Medicine*. New York: Basic Books, 1982.

Stewart, James Brewer. *Holy Warriors: The Abolitionists and American Slavery*. New York: Hill and Wang, 1978.

Still, Arthur and Irving Velody, eds. *Rewriting the History of Madness*. London: Routledge, 1991.

Szasz, Thomas. *The Manufacture of Madness*. New York: Dell, 1970.

————. *The Myth of Mental Illness: Foundation of a Theory of Personal Conduct*. New York: Harper and Row, 1961.

Tarwater, James S. *The Alabama State Hospitals and the Parlow State School and Hospital: A Brief History*. New York: Newcomen Society, 1964.

Teeters, Negley K. and John D. Shearer. *The Prison at Philadelphia in Cherry Hill: The Separate System of Prison Discipline, 1829–1913*. New York: Columbia University Press, 1957.

Thompson, E. P. *The Making of the English Working Class*. New York: Vintage, 1963.

Thompson, G. R., ed. *The Gothic Imagination: Essays in Dark Romanticism*. Pullman, Wash.: Washington State University Press, 1974.

Thompson, J. D. and G. Goldin. *The Hospital: A Social and Architectural History*. New Haven: Yale University Press, 1975.

Thompson, F. M. L., ed. *The Cambridge Social History of Britain*. vol 3. *Social Agencies and Institutions*. Cambridge: Cambridge University Press, 1990.

Thorton, J. Mills III. *Politics and Power in a Slave Society: Alabama, 1800–1860*. Baton Rouge: Louisiana State University Press, 1978.

Tiffany, Francis. *Life of Dorothea Lynde Dix*. Boston: Houghton, Mifflin, 1891.

Tise, Larry E. *Proslavery: A History of the Defense of Slavery in America, 1701–1840*. Athens: University of Georgia Press, 1978.

Tomes, Nancy. *A Generous Confidence: Thomas Story Kirkbride and the Art of Asylum-Keeping*. New York: Cambridge University Press, 1984.

Trattner, Walter I., ed. *Biographical Dictionary of Social Welfare in America*. New York: Greenwood, 1986.

Tropp, Martin. *Images of Fear: How Horror Stories Helped Shape Modern Culture (1818–1918)*. London: McFarland, 1990.

Tuke, Samuel. *Description of the Retreat*. York, England: Thomas Wilson and Sons, 1813.

Tyler, Alice Felt. *Freedom's Ferment: Phases of American Social History from the Colonial Period to the Outbreak of the Civil War*. Minneapolis: University of Minnesota Press, 1944.

Van Deusen, Glyndon G. *The Jacksonian Era: 1828–1848*. New York: Harper and Row, 1959.

Vicinus, Martha. *Independent Women: Work and Community for Single Women, 1850–1920*. Chicago: University of Chicago Press, 1985.

Walker, Peter F. *Moral Choices: Memory, Desire, and Imagination in Nineteenth-Century American Abolition*. Baton Rouge: Louisiana State University Press, 1978.

Walsh, Mary Roth. *"Doctors Wanted: No Women Need Apply": Sexual Barriers in the Medical Profession, 1835–1975*. New Haven: Yale University Press, 1977.

Walters, Ronald G. *American Reformers: 1815–1860*. New York: Hill and Wang, 1978.

Ward, David. *Poverty, Ethnicity, and the American City, 1840–1925: Changing Conceptions of the Slum and the Ghetto*. Cambridge, England: Cambridge University Press, 1989.

Warner, John Harley. *The Therapeutic Perspective: Medical Practice, Knowledge, and Identity in America, 1820–1885*. Cambridge, Mass.: Harvard University Press, 1986.

Westergaard, Waldeman. *The Danish West Indies under Company Rule (1671–1754) with a Supplementary Chapter, 1755–1917*. New York: Macmillan, 1917.

Wilentz, Sean. *Chants Democratic: New York City and the Rise of the American Working Class, 1788–1850*. New York: Oxford University Press, 1984.

Wilson, Dorothy Clarke. *Stranger and Traveler: The Story of Dorothea Dix, American Reformer*. Boston: Little, Brown, 1975.

Wisner, Elizabeth. *Public Welfare Administration in Louisiana*. Chicago: University of Chicago Press, 1930.

Wolff, Gerald W. *The Kansas-Nebraska Bill: Party, Section, and the Coming of the civil War*. New York: Revisionist Press, 1977.

Wright, C. Conrad. *The Beginnings of Unitarianism in America*. Boston: Starr King Press, 1955.

————. *The Liberal Christians: Essays on American Unitarian History*. Boston: Beacon Press, 1970.

————. *A Stream of Light: A Sesquicentennial History of American Unitarianism*. Boston: Unitarian Universalist Association, 1975.

B. ARTICLES

Alexander, Ruth M. "'We Are Engaged as a Band of Sisters': Class and Domesticity in the Washingtonian Temperance Movement, 1840–1850," *Journal of American History* 75 (December 1988): 763–85.

Baker, Paula. "The Domestication of Politics: Women and American Political Society, 1780–1920," *American Historical Review* 89 (June 1984): 620–47.

Banner, Lois W. "Religious Benevolence as Social Control: A Critique of an Interpretation," *Journal of American History* 60 (June 1973): 23–41.

Basch, Norma. "Equity vs. Equality: Emerging Concepts of Women's Political Status in the Age of Jackson," *Journal of the Early Republic* 3 (Fall 1983): 297–318.

Baym, Nina. "Onward Christian Women: Sarah J. Hale's History of the World," *New England Quarterly* 63 (June 1990): 249–70.

Benson, Susan Porter. "Business Heads and Sympathizing Hearts: The Women of the Providence Employment Society, 1837–1858," *Journal of Social History* 12 (Winter 1978): 302–12.

Berthoff, Rowland. "Conventional Mentality: Free Blacks, Women, and Business Corporations as Unequal Persons, 1820–1870," *Journal of American History* 76 (December 1989): 753–84.

Boylan, Anne M. "Timid Girls, Venerable Widows and Dignified Matrons: Life Cycle Patterns among Organized Women in New York and Boston, 1797–1840," *American Quarterly* 38 (Winter 1986): 779–97.

―――――. "Women in Groups: An Analysis of Women's Benevolent Organizations in New York and Boston, 1797–1840," *Journal of American History* 71 (December 1984): 497–523.

Brown, Richard D. "Modernization and Modern Personality in Early America, 1600–1865: A Sketch of a Synthesis," *Journal of Interdisciplinary History* 2 (1972): 201–28.

Carlson, Eric T. and Norman Dain. "The Psychotherapy That Was Moral Treatment," *American Journal of Psychiatry* 117 (December 1960): 1034–37.

Chambers, Clarke A. "Toward a Redefinition of Welfare History," *Journal of American History* 73 (June 1986): 407–33.

Clark, Alexander L. and Jack P. Gibbs. "Social Control: A Reformulation," *Social Problems* 12 (Spring 1965): 398–415.

Cott, Nancy F. "Passionlessness: An Interpretation of Victorian Sexual Ideology, 1790–1850," *SIGNS* 4 (Winter 1978): 219–36.

―――――. "Young Women in the Second Great Awakening in New England," *Feminist Studies* 3 (1975): 15–29.

Curti, Merle. "The History of American Philanthropy as a Field of Research," *American Historical Review* 62 (January 1957): 352–63.

Dain, Norman, and Eric T. Carlson. "Milieu Therapy in the Nineteenth Century: Patient Care at the Friends' Asylum, Frankford, Pennsylvania, 1817–1861," *Journal of Nervous and Mental Disease* 131 (October 1960): 277–90.

Davis, David Brion. "British Emancipation as a New Moral Dispensation," *Rice University Studies* 67 (Winter 1981): 43–55.

Degler, Carl N. "What Ought to Be and What Was: Women's Sexuality in the Nineteenth Century," *American Historical Review* 79 (December 1974): 1467–90.

Deutsch, Albert. "The First U.S. Census of the Insane (1840) and Its Use as Pro-Slavery Propaganda," *Bulletin of the History of Medicine*, 15 (May 1944): 469–82.

Engerman, Stanley L. and Robert E. Gallman. "United States Economic Growth, 1783–1860," *Research in Economic History* 8 (1983): 1–46.

Fox, Richard. "Beyond 'Social Control': Institutions and Disorder in Bourgeois Society," *History of Education Quarterly* 16 (1976): 203–7.

Freedman, Estelle. "Separatism as Strategy: Female Institution Building and American Feminism, 1870–1930," *Feminist Studies* 5 (Fall 1979): 512–29.

Ginzberg, Lori D. "'Moral Suasion Is Moral Balderdash': Women, Politics, and Social Activism in the 1850s," *Journal of American History* 73 (December 1986): 601–22.

Gollaher, David L. "Dorothea Dix and the English Origins of the American Asylum Movement," *Canadian Review of American Studies* 23 (Spring 1993): 149–75.

Gordon, Mary McDougall. "Patriots and Christians: A Reassessment of Nineteenth-Century School Reformers," *Journal of Social History* 11 (Summer 1978): 554–73.

Green, Fletcher M. "Democracy in the Old South," *Journal of Southern History* 12 (February 1946): 3–23.

Griffin, Clifford S. "Religious Benevolence as Social Control," *Mississippi Valley Historical Review* 44 (December 1957): 423–44.

Grob, Gerald N. "Mental Illness, Indigency, and Welfare: The Mental Hospital in Nine-teenth-Century America," in *Anonymous Americans: Explorations in Nineteenth-Century Social Policy to 1875*, ed. Tamara K. Hareven, 250–279. Englewood Cliffs, N.J.: Pren-tice-Hall, 1971.

——. "Public Policymaking and Social Policy," unpbl. paper delivered at the Confer-ence on the History of Public Policy, Cambridge, Massachusetts, 3 November 1978.

——. "Rediscovering Asylums: The Unhistorical History of the Mental Hospital," *Hastings Center Report* (August 1977): 33–41.

——. "Reflections on the History of Social Policy in America," *Reviews in American His-tory* 7 (September 1979): 293–306.

——. "Samuel B. Woodward and the Practice of Psychiatry in Early Nineteenth-Centu-ry America," *Bulletin of the History of Medicine* 36 (1962): 420–43.

——. "The Social History of Medicine and Disease in America: Problems and Possibili-ties," *Journal of Social History* 10 (Summer 1977): 391–409.

——. "Welfare and Poverty in American History," *Reviews in American History* 1 (1973): 43–52.

Gutman, Herbert S. "Work, Culture and Society in Industrializing America, 1815–1919," *American Historical Review* 78 (June 1973): 531–88.

Hathaway, Marion. "Dorothea Dix and Social Reform in Western Pennsylvania, 1845–1875," *Western Pennsylvania Historical Magazine*, 17 (December 1943): 247–57.

Hewitt, Nancy A. "Beyond the Search for Sisterhood: American Women's History in the 1980s," *Social History* 10 (October 1985): 299–321.

Himelhoch, Myra, and Arthur Shaffer. "Elizabeth Packard: Nineteenth-Century Crusader for the Rights of Mental Patients," *Journal of American Studies* 13 (December 1979): 343–75.

Hollingshead, A. B. "The Concept of Social Control," *American Sociological Review* 6 (April 1941): 217–24.

Ignatieff, Michael. "State, Civil Society and Total Institutions: A Critique of Recent Social Histories of Punishment," in *Social Control and the State*, ed. Stanley Cohen and Andrew Scull, 75–105. Oxford: Michael Robertson, 1983.

Ingleby, David. "Mental Health and Social Order," in *Social Control and the State*, ed. Stanley Cohen and Andrew Scull, 141–88. Oxford: Michael Robertson, 1983.

Jones, Robert E. "Correspondence of the A.P.A. Founders," *American Journal of Psychiatry* 119 (June 1963): 1121–34.

Kelly, Mary. "A Woman Alone: Catharine Maria Sedgwick's Spinsterhood in Nineteenth-Century America," *New England Quarterly* 51 (June 1978): 209–25.

Kerber, Linda K. "Separate Spheres, Female Worlds, Woman's Place: The Rhetoric of Women's History," *Journal of American History* 75 (June 1988): 9–39.

Kirk, Jeffrey. "Marriage, Career, and Feminine Ideology in Nineteenth-Century America: Reconstructing the Marital Experience of Lydia Maria Child, 1828–1874," *Feminist Studies* 2 (1975): 113–30.

Kohlstedt, Sally Gregory. "In from the Periphery: American Women in Science, 1830–1880," *SIGNS* 4 (Autumn 1978): 81–96.

Lasser, Carol S. "A 'Pleasingly Oppressive' Burden: The Transformation of Domestic Ser-vice and Female Charity in Salem, 1800–1840," *Essex Institute Historical Collections* 116 (July 1980): 156–75.

Leavitt, Judith Walzer. "Medicine in Context: A Review Essay of the History of American Medicine," *American Historical Review* 95 (December 1990): 1471–84.

Lerner, Gerda. "The Lady and the Mill Girl: Changes in the Status of Women in the Age of Jackson," *Midcontinent American Studies Journal* 10 (Spring 1969): 5–15.

Lockridge, Kenneth. "Land, Population and the Evolution of New England Society," *Past and Present* 39 (April 1968): 62–80.

Luchins, Abraham S. "The Rise and Decline of the American Asylum Movement," *Journal of Psychology* 122 (September 1988): 471–486.

McArthur, Judith N. "Demon Rum on the Boards: Temperance Melodrama and the Tradition of Antebellum Reform," *Journal of the Early Republic* 9 (Winter 1989): 517–40.

McCall, Laura. "'The Reign of Brute Force Is Now Over': A Content Analysis of *Godey's Lady's Book*, 1830–1860," *Journal of the Early Republic* 9 (Fall 1989): 217–36.

McCandless, Peter. "Dangerous to Themselves and Others: The Victorian Debate over the Prevention of Wrongful Confinement," *Journal of British Studies* 23 (Fall 1983): 84–104.

McCulloch, Margaret C. "Founding the North Carolina Asylum for the Insane," *North Carolina Historical Review*, 13 (July 1936): 185–201.

McGaw, Judith A. "No Passive Victims, No Separate Spheres: A Feminist Perspective on Technology's History," in *Context: History and the History of Technology—Essays in Honor of Mel Kranzberg*, ed. Stephen Cutliffe and Robert W. Post. Bethlehem: Pennsylavania State University Press, 1988.

McGerr, Michael. "Political Style and Women's Power, 1830–1930," *Journal of American History* 77 (December 1990): 864–85.

McGovern, Constance M. "The Insane, the Asylum, and the State in Nineteenth-Century Vermont," *Vermont History* 52 (Fall 1984): 205–24.

McGowen, Randall. "A Powerful Sympathy: Terror, the Prison, and Humanitarian Reform in Early Nineteenth-Century Britain," *Journal of British Studies* 25 (July, 1986): 312–34.

Manning, Seaton W. "The Tragedy of the Ten-Million-Acre Bill," *Social History Review* 36 (March 1962): 44–50.

Mayer, John A. "Notes towards a Working Definition of Social Control in Historical Analysis," in *Social Control and the State*, ed. Stanley Cohen and Andrew Scull, 17–38. Oxford: Martin Robertson, 1983.

Mohl, Raymond A. "Mainstream Social Welfare History and Its Problems," *Reviews in American History* 7 (December 1979): 469–76.

Muraskin, William A. "The Social Control Theory in American History: A Critique," *Journal of Social History* 9 (Summer 1976): 559–69.

Numbers, Ronald L. "The History of American Medicine: A Field in Ferment," *Reviews in American History* 10 (December 1982): 245–63.

Porter, Roy. "Shutting People Up," *Social Studies of Science* 12 (1982): 467–76.

Roberts, David. "Dealing with the Poor in Victorian England," *Rice University Studies* 67 (Winter 1981): 57–73.

Rochefort, David A. "Progressive and Social Control Perspectives on Social Welfare," *Social Service Review* 55 (December 1981): 568–92.

Rosenberg, Charles E. "And Heal the Sick: The Hospital and the Patient in Nineteenth Century America," *Journal of Social History* 10 (June 1977): 428–47.

———. "The Bitter Fruit: Heredity, Disease, and Social Thought in Nineteenth Century America," *Perspectives in American History* 8 (1974): 189–235.

————. "Disease and the Social Order in America: Perceptions and Expectations," *Millbank Quarterly* 64, suppl. 1 (1986): 34–55.

————. "Disease in History: Frames and Framers," *Millbank Quarterly* 67, suppl. 1 (1989): 1–15.

————. "From Almshouse to Hospital: The Shaping of Philadelphia General Hospital," *Millbank Quarterly* 60, suppl. 1 (1982): 108–54

————. "The Practice of Medicine in New York a Century Ago," *Bulletin of the History of Medicine* 41 (Summer 1967): 223–53.

————. "Sexuality, Class and Role in Nineteenth-Century America," *American Quarterly* 25 (May 1973): 131–54.

————. "The Therapeutic Revolution: Medicine, Meaning, and Social Change in Nineteenth Century America," in Morris J. Vogel and Charles E. Rosenberg, eds., *The Therapeutic Revolution: Essays in the Social History of American Medicine* (Philadelphia: University of Pennsylvania Press, 1979), 3–25.

Rosenkrantz, Barbara Gutman. "The Search for Professional Order in Nineteenth-Century American Medicine," *Proceedings of the Fourteenth International Congress of the History of Science*, no. 4, 113–24. Tokyo and Kyoto, 1974.

Rothman, David J. "Social Control: The Uses and Abuses of the Concept in the History of Incarceration," *Rice University Studies* 67 (Winter 1981): 9–20.

Ryan, Mary P. "A Woman's Awakening: Evangelical Religion and the Families of Utica, New York, 1800–1840," *American Quarterly* 30 (Winter 1978): 602–23.

Scott, Anne Firor. "Almira Lincoln Phelps: The Self-Made Woman in the Nineteenth Century," *Maryland Historical Magazine* 75 (Summer 1980): 203–16.

————. "On Seeing and Not Seeing: A Case of Historical Invisibility," *Journal of American History* 71 (June 1984): 7–21.

Scott, Joan W. "Gender: A Useful Category of Historical Analysis," *American Historical Review* 91 (December 1986): 1053–75.

Scull, Andrew. "A Brilliant Career? John Conolly and Victorian Psychiatry," *Victorian Studies* 27 (Winter 1984): 203–35.

————. "Desperate remedies: a Gothic tale of madness and modern medicine," *Psychological Medicine* 17 (1987): 561–77.

————. "From Madness to Mental Illness: Medical Men as Moral Entrepreneurs," *European Journal of Sociology* 15 (1974): 219–61.

————. "Humanitarianism or Control: Observations on the Historiography of Anglo-American Psychiatry," *Rice University Studies* 67 (1981): 21–41.

————. "Madness and Segregative Control: The Rise of the Insane Asylum," *Social Problems* 24 (1977): 338–51.

Scull, Andrew and Diane Favreau. "'A Chance to Cut Is a Chance to Cure': Sexual Surgery for Psychosis in Three Nineteenth Century Societies," *Research in Law, Deviance and Social Control*, 8 (1986): 3–39.

Sklar, Kathryn Kish. "A Call for Comparisons," *American Historical Review* 95 (October 1990): 1109–14.

————. "Organized Womanhood: Archival Sources on Women and Progressive Reform," *Journal of American History*, 75 (June 1988): 176–83.

Smith-Rosenberg, Carroll. "Beauty, the Beast, and the Militant Woman: A Case Study of

Sex Roles and Social Stress in Jacksonian America," *American Quarterly* 23 (October 1971): 562–84.

————. "The Female World of Love and Ritual: Relations between Women in Nineteenth-Century America," *SIGNS* 1 (Autumn 1975): 1–29.

————. "Misprisoning Pamela: Representations of Gender and Class in Nineteenth-Century America," *Michigan Quarterly Review* 26 (Winter 1987): 9–28.

————. "The New Woman and the Psychohistorian: A Modest Proposal," *Group for the Use of Psychology in History Newsletter* 4 (December 1975): 4–11.

————. "Politics and Culture in Women's History: A Symposium," *Feminist Studies* 6 (Spring 1980): 54–64.

Smith-Rosenberg, Carroll, and Charles Rosenberg. "The Female Animal: Medical and Biological Views of Woman and Her Role in Nineteenth-Century America," *Journal of American History* 60 (1973): 332–56.

Stansell, Christine. "Revisiting the Angel in the House: Revisions of Victorian Womanhood," *New England Quarterly* 60 (September, 1987): 466–83.

Summers, Anne. "The Mysterious Demise of Sarah Gamp: The Domiciliary Nurse and Her Detractors, c. 1830–1860," *Victorian Studies* 32 (Spring, 1989): 365–86.

Thomas, John L. "Romantic Reform in America, 1815–1865," *American Quarterly* 17 (Winter, 1965): 656–81.

Thompson, E. Bruce. "Reforms in the Care of the Insane in Tennessee, 1830–1850," *Tennessee Historical Quarterly* 3 (December 1944): 319–34.

Tomes, Nancy. "The Anatomy of Madness: New Directions in the History of Psychiatry," *Social Studies of Science* 17 (May 1987): 358–71.

Tyor, Peter L. and Jamil S. Zainaldin. "Asylum and Society: An Approach to Institutional Change," *Journal of Social History* 13 (Fall 1979): 23–48.

Watson, Harry L. "Conflict and Collaboration: Yeomen, Slaveholders, and Politics in the Antebellum South," *Social History* 10 (October 1985): 273–98.

Wayne, Michael. "An Old South Morality Play: Reconsidering the Social Underpinnings of the Proslavery Ideology," *Journal of American History* 77 (December 1990): 838–63.

Welter, Barbara. "Cult of True Womanhood, 1820–1860," *American Quarterly* 18 (Summer, 1966): 151–74.

Wellman, Judith. "Crossing over Cross: Whitney Cross's Burned-over District as Social History," *Reviews in American History* 17 (March, 1989): 159–74.

C. UNPUBLISHED THESES AND DISSERTATIONS

Adamson, Christopher R. "Hard Labor: The Form and Function of Imprisonment in Nineteenth-Century America." Ph.D. diss., Princeton University, 1982.

Baker, Paula. "The Moral Framework of Public Life: Gender and Politics in Rural New York, 1870–1930." Ph.D. diss., Rutgers University, 1987.

Barabee, Paul. "A Study of the Mental Hospital: The Effect of Its Social Structure on Its Functions." Ph.D. diss., Harvard University, 1951.

Cahow, Clark R. "The History of the North Carolina Mental Hospitals, 1848–1960." Ph.D. diss, Duke University, 1967.

Eaton, Barbara Leslie. "Women, Religion and the Family: Revivalism as an Indicator of

Social Change in Early New England." Ph.D. diss., University of California, Berkeley, 1974.

Klein, Stanley B. "A Study of Social Legislation Affecting Prisons and Institutions for the Mentally Ill in New York State, 1822–1846." Ph.D. diss., New York University, 1956.

McCandless, Peter. "Insanity and Society: A Study of the English Lunacy Reform Movement, 1815–70." Ph.D. diss., University of Wisconsin, 1974.

McGovern, Constance M. "The Early Career of Pliny Earle: A Founder of American Psychiatry." M.A. thesis, University of Massachusetts, 1971.

Pitts, John A. "The Association of Medical Superintendents of American Institutions for the Insane, 1844–1892: A Case Study of Specialism in American Medicine." Ph.D. diss., University of Pennsylvania, 1979.

Ryan, Mary P. "American Society and the Cult of Domesticity, 1830–1860." Ph.D. diss., University of California, Santa Barbara, 1971.

Spalding, Margaret Joy. "Dorothea Dix and the Care of the Insane from 1841 to the Pierce Veto of 1854." Ph.D. diss., Bryn Mawr College, Graduate School of Social Research, 1976.

INDEX

Abolitionists, 75, 236, 269, 281, 290, 458n 68

Acland, Sir Henry Wentworth, 105

Adams, Henry, 120, 392, 428

Aiken, Lucy, 80

Alcott, Bronson, 85

Alcott, Louisa May, 413

Alienists. *See* Asylum physicians

Allen, Joseph Henry, 133

Allston, Washington, 67

Almshouses, 167, 469n 12. *See* also names of city and county almshouses

American Journal of Insanity, 173–174, 217, 218, 244, 279, 283, 299, 344, 379, 382, 434

American Unitarian Association, 57

Andersonville prison, 424

Andrew, John, 396

Anthony, Susan B., 443

Antonelli, Cardinal Giacomo, 371, 414

Association of Medical Superintendents of American Institutions for the Insane, 173, 217–234, 266, 475n 5

  attitude toward prison reform, 217–218

  comitment to therapeutic asylums, 436–437

  opposition to Dix's federal land bill, 299–300

Atherton, Charles G., 301, 304–305

Asylum

  debates about separate institutions for incurable patients, 167–168, 437–439, 469n 14

  debates about size, 164–165, 435–441

  economic arguments for, 192–193, 228, 472n 19

  economic problems, 252–253, 263, 438–439

  post-Civil War transformation, 434–441

  rates of cure, 317, 434–435, 437

  operational routine, 226–227

Asylum physicians, 476n 10

  ambivalence toward Dix, 218–219, 221

  in Britain, 492n 13

  political ineptitude, 228, 300

  professional status undermined by Dix, 234

  provincialism, 220–221

Awl, William, 192